DIFFERENTIAL EQUATIONS

A Blaisdell Book in Pure and Applied Mathematics

GEORGE SPRINGER, *Indiana University*
CONSULTING EDITOR

DIFFERENTIAL EQUATIONS

Shepley L. Ross

University of New Hampshire

BLAISDELL PUBLISHING COMPANY

A Division of Ginn and Company

WALTHAM, MASSACHUSETTS · TORONTO · LONDON

PREFACE

This book is an introduction to the basic methods, theory, and applications of differential equations. It presupposes a knowledge of elementary calculus.

The presentation of the material is quite detailed. Important concepts are introduced by means of carefully worded definitions; significant results are stated precisely as theorems, and methods of solution are described with considerable explanation. Definitions, theorems, and methods are amply illustrated with very detailed examples. In fact, the most useful and fundamental techniques are illuminated by several thoroughly worked-out examples. Detailed and careful proofs of most of the basic theorems are included. Indeed, the wealth of detail in proofs and illustrative examples is one of the unusual features of the presentation.

The book is divided into two main parts. The first part (Chapters 1 through 7) deals with the most basic concepts, theorems, methods, and applications of the subject. The second part introduces the reader to certain specialized and more advanced methods and provides a systematic introduction to the fundamental theory.

Chapter 1 introduces and illustrates the most fundamental concepts of differential equations, with emphasis on the meaning of a solution and on problems involving supplementary conditions. Chapter 2 presents the traditional methods of solving the most familiar types of first-order equations. It is arranged so that the less important types may be treated briefly, or even omitted, without difficulty. Chapter 3 introduces the reader to certain basic applications of first order equations. In Chapter 4 the important higher order linear equations first make their appearance. The basic concepts and theorems are first introduced and illustrated in detail, but most of the proofs are reserved for a later chapter (Chapter 11). The greater part of the chapter is concerned with methods of solving linear equations with constant coefficients. Chapter 5 applies the methods of Chapter 4 to problems in vibrations and electric circuits. Series solutions are the topic of Chapter 6, which includes a brief introduction to Bessel's Equation and Bessel Functions. Linear systems are introduced and applied in Chapter 7.

Proceeding to the second part of the book, Chapter 8 introduces certain approximate methods for solving first order equations, with emphasis on numerical methods. In Chapter 9 the basic concepts and results concerning the Laplace Transform are developed and applied to linear differential equations with constant coefficients. The fundamental theory of ordinary differential equations is introduced in Chapters 10 and 11. Chapter 10 is concerned primarily with the statement and proof of the basic existence theorem for a first order initial value problem. Proceeding from this, Chapter 11 presents complete statements and proofs of the principal theorems on linear equations of higher order. Important topics included here are the Wronskian Theory, the adjoint equation, and the classical Sturm theory. Following this, Chapter 12 opens with an introduction to Sturm-Liouville boundary value problems and proceeds to a study of trigonometric Fourier series. Chapter 13 is concerned with nonlinear differential equations, a subject of ever-increasing interest and importance. Among the topics introduced are critical points, limit cycles, and the method of Kryloff and Bogoliuboff. The final chapter (Chapter 14) is an introduction to certain methods and concepts of partial differential equations. The method of separation of variables is treated formally but in considerable detail; and such concepts as canonical forms, initial value problems, and characteristics are introduced.

The book can be used as a text in several different types of courses. One such course is the more-or-less traditional one-semester introductory course. Such a course could be based on Chapters 1 through 7 if elementary applications are to be included. Alternatively, it could be based on Chapters 1, 2, 4, 6, 7, 8, and 9 if applications are to be omitted in favor of such special topics as numerical methods and Laplace Transforms. An introductory course designed to lead to the methods of partial differential equations as rapidly as possible could follow Chapters 1, 2 (in part), 4, 6, 12, and 14 (in part). Another possible variation could be based on Chapters 1, 4, and 6, and parts of Chapters 2, 3, 5, 7, 8, and 9.

The book can also be used as a text in various intermediate courses for Juniors and Seniors who have already had a one-semester introduction to the subject. An intermediate course emphasizing further methods could be based on Chapters 8, 9, 12, 13, and 14. An intermediate course designed as an introduction to fundamental theory could be based on Chapters 10, 11, 12, 13, and 14.

There is enough material for a leisurely-paced full year introductory course. In such a course one could very easily follow the book "from cover to cover," placing emphasis on whatever topics were most desired.

It is a pleasure to record my thanks to a number of people who have aided me in one way or another in the preparation of this book. First, I would like to acknowledge my debt to Professor Francis Scheid of Boston University, whose excellent lectures on differential equations did so much to increase my interest in and understanding of this subject. Next, it is indeed a special pleasure to express my thanks to my colleagues, Professors David M. Burton, Robert O. Kimball, and M. Evans Munroe of the University of New Hampshire, for helpful suggestions, kindly advice, and constant encouragement. I am also grateful to Miss Constance Foley for her thoughtful advice.

Further, I wish to thank Professor George Springer of the University of Kansas and Professor Gerald Freilich of City College, New York. Both Professor Springer and Professor Freilich read the manuscript and made a number of valuable comments which resulted in various improvements. I also express my thanks to Professor Fritz John of New York University for his reading of and comments on Chapter 13.

Thanks go to Mr. Mitchell Billis, Mr. Ronald Cote, and Miss Jeanne LaDuke for aid in preparing the answers for the exercises. I am very grateful to Mrs. Gwen Chesbro for her outstanding work in typing the greater part of the manuscript. I am also grateful to Miss Marguerite Bourassa, Miss Susan Hoyt, and Mrs. Doris MacKinnon for additional typing.

I am pleased to record my appreciation to the staff of the Blaisdell Publishing Company for their encouragement, patience, suggestions, and cooperation.

Finally, it is with the greatest of pleasure that I record my sincere gratitude to three people who have done more for me than I can ever hope to repay: my mother, my father, and my wife. As a small indication of this gratitude, I happily dedicate this book to them.

December, 1962   SHEPLEY L. ROSS

CONTENTS

PART II. Further Methods, Fundamental Theory, and Special Topics

PART I

Fundamental Methods and Applications

1

DIFFERENTIAL EQUATIONS
AND THEIR SOLUTIONS

The subject of differential equations constitutes a large and very important branch of modern mathematics. From the early days of the calculus the subject has been an area of great theoretical research and practical applications, and it continues to be so in our day. This much stated, several questions naturally arise. Just what is a differential equation and what does it signify? Where and how do differential equations originate and of what use are they? Confronted with a differential equation, what does one do with it, how does one do it, and what are the results of such activity? These questions indicate three major aspects of the subject: theory, method, and application. The purpose of this chapter is to introduce the reader to the basic aspects of the subject and at the same time give a brief survey of the three aspects just mentioned. In the course of the chapter, we shall find answers to the general questions raised above, answers which will become more and more meaningful as we proceed with the study of differential equations in the following chapters.

1.1 Classification of Differential Equations; Their Origin and Application

A. Differential Equations and Their Classification

DEFINITION. An equation involving derivatives or differentials of one or more dependent variables with respect to one or more independent variables is called a *differential equation.**

---

*In connection with this basic definition, we do *not* include in the class of differential equations those equations which are actually differential identities. For example, we exclude such expressions as

$$\frac{d}{dx}(e^{ax}) = ae^{ax}, \quad \frac{d}{dx}(uv) = u\frac{dv}{dx} + v\frac{du}{dx}, \text{ and so forth.}$$

Example 1.1. For examples of differential equations we list the following.

$$(1.1) \qquad \frac{d^2y}{dx^2} + xy\left(\frac{dy}{dx}\right)^2 = 0$$

$$(1.2) \qquad \frac{d^4x}{dt^4} + 5\frac{d^2x}{dt^2} + 3x = \sin t$$

$$(1.3) \qquad \frac{\partial v}{\partial s} + \frac{\partial v}{\partial t} = v$$

$$(1.4) \qquad \frac{\partial^2 u}{\partial x^2} + \frac{\partial^2 u}{\partial y^2} + \frac{\partial^2 u}{\partial z^2} = 0.$$

From the brief list of differential equations in Example 1.1 it is clear that the various variables and derivatives involved in a differential equation can occur in a variety of ways. Clearly some kind of classification must be made. To begin with, we classify differential equations according to whether there is one or more than one independent variable involved.

DEFINITION. A differential equation involving ordinary derivatives of one or more dependent variables with respect to a single independent variable is called an *ordinary differential equation*.

Example 1.2. Equations (1.1) and (1.2) are ordinary differential equations. In equation (1.1) the variable x is the single independent variable, and y is a dependent variable. In equation (1.2) the independent variable is t, whereas x is dependent.

DEFINITION. A differential equation involving partial derivatives of one or more dependent variables with respect to one or more independent variables is called a *partial differential equation*.

Example 1.3. Equations (1.3) and (1.4) are partial differential equations. In equation (1.3) the variables s and t are independent variables and v is a dependent variable. In equation (1.4) there are three independent variables, x, y, and z; in this equation u is dependent.

We further classify differential equations, both ordinary and partial, according to the order of the highest derivative appearing in the equation. For this purpose we give the following definition.

DEFINITION. The order of the highest ordered derivative involved in a differential equation is called the *order* of the differential equation.

Example 1.4. The ordinary differential equation (1.1) is of the second order, since the highest derivative involved is a second derivative. Equation (1.2) is an ordinary differential equation of the fourth order. The partial differential equations (1.3) and (1.4) are of the first and second orders, respectively.

As a means of classifying both ordinary and partial differential equations still further, we introduce the following concept.

DEFINITION.   A differential equation is called *linear* if (a) every dependent variable and every derivative involved occurs to the first degree only, and (b) no products of dependent variables and/or derivatives occur.   A differential equation which is not linear is called a *nonlinear differential equation.*

Example 1.5.   The following ordinary differential equations are both linear.   In each case y is the dependent variable.   Observe that y and its various derivatives occur to the first degree only and that no products of y and/or any of its derivatives are present.

(1.5)
$$\frac{d^2y}{dx^2} + 5\frac{dy}{dx} + 6y = 0$$

(1.6)
$$\frac{d^4y}{dx^4} + x^2\frac{d^3y}{dx^3} + x^3\frac{dy}{dx} = xe^x.$$

Example 1.6.   The following ordinary differential equations are all nonlinear.

(1.7)
$$\frac{d^2y}{dx^2} + 5\frac{dy}{dx} + 6y^2 = 0$$

(1.8)
$$\frac{d^2y}{dx^2} + 5\left(\frac{dy}{dx}\right)^3 + 6y = 0$$

(1.9)
$$\frac{d^2y}{dx^2} + 5y\frac{dy}{dx} + 6y = 0.$$

Equation (1.7) is nonlinear because the dependent variable y appears to the second degree in the term $6y^2$.   Equation (1.8) owes its nonlinearity to the presence of the term $5\left(\frac{dy}{dx}\right)^3$ which involves the third power of the first derivative.   Finally, equation (1.9) is nonlinear because of the term $5y\frac{dy}{dx}$ which involves the product of the dependent variable and its first derivative.

Example 1.7.   The partial differential equation
$$\frac{\partial y}{\partial t} = \frac{\partial^2 y}{\partial x^2}$$
is linear, but the differential equation
$$\left(\frac{\partial y}{\partial t}\right)^2 = \frac{\partial^2 y}{\partial x^2}$$
is not.

Linear differential equations are further classified according to the nature of the coefficients of the dependent variables and their derivatives.   For example, equation (1.5) is said to be linear with *constant coefficients*, while equation (1.6) is linear with *variable coefficients.*

B. Origin and Application of Differential Equations

Having classified differential equations in various ways, let us now consider briefly where, and how, such equations actually originate.   In this way we shall obtain some indication of the great variety of subjects to which the theory and methods of differential equations may be applied.

Differential equations occur in connection with numerous problems which are encountered in the various branches of science and engineering. We indicate a few such problems in the following list, which could easily be extended to fill many pages.

(1) The problem of determining the motion of a projectile, rocket, satellite, or planet.
(2) The problem of determining the charge or current in an electric circuit.
(3) The problem of the conduction of heat in a rod or in a slab.
(4) The problem of determining the vibrations of a wire or a membrane.
(5) The study of the rate of decomposition of a radioactive substance or the rate of growth of a population.
(6) The study of the reactions of chemicals.
(7) The problem of the determination of curves which have certain geometrical properties.

The mathematical formulation of such problems gives rise to differential equations. But just how does this occur? In the situations under consideration in each of the above problems the objects involved obey certain scientific laws. These laws involve various rates of change of one or more quantities with respect to other quantities. Let us recall that such rates of change are expressed mathematically by derivatives. In the mathematical formulation of each of the above situations, the various rates of change are thus expressed by various derivatives and the scientific laws themselves become mathematical equations involving derivatives, that is, differential equations.

In this process of mathematical formulation certain simplifying assumptions generally have to be made in order that the resulting differential equations be tractable. For example, if the actual situation in a certain aspect of the problem is of a relatively complicated nature, we are often forced to modify this by assuming instead an approximate situation which is of a comparatively simple nature. Indeed, certain relatively unimportant aspects of the problem must often be entirely eliminated. The result of such changes from the actual nature of things means that the resulting differential equation is actually that of an idealized situation. Nonetheless, the information obtained from such an equation is of the greatest value to the scientist.

A natural question now is the following: How does one obtain useful information from a differential equation? The answer is essentially that if it is possible to do so, one solves the differential equation to obtain a solution; if this is not possible, one uses the theory of differential equations to obtain information *about* the solution. To understand the meaning of this answer, we must discuss what is meant by a solution of a differential equation; this is done in the next section.

Exercises

Classify each of the following differential equations as ordinary or partial differential equations; state the order of each equation; and determine whether the equation under consideration is linear or nonlinear.

1. $\dfrac{dy}{dx} + x^2 y = x e^x$.   O - 1 - L

2. $\dfrac{d^3y}{dx^3} + 4\dfrac{d^2y}{dx^2} - 5\dfrac{dy}{dx} + 3y = \sin x.$ O - 3 - L

3. $\dfrac{\partial^2 u}{\partial x^2} + \dfrac{\partial^2 u}{\partial y^2} = 0.$ P - 2 - L

4. $x^2 dy + y^2 dx = 0.$ O - 1 - N

5. $\dfrac{d^4y}{dx^4} + 3\left(\dfrac{d^2y}{dx^2}\right)^5 + 5y = 0.$ O - 4 - N   Deg 5

6. $\dfrac{\partial^4 u}{\partial x^2 \partial y^2} + \dfrac{\partial^2 u}{\partial x^2} + \dfrac{\partial^2 u}{\partial y^2} + u = 0.$ P - 4 - L

7. $\dfrac{d^2y}{dx^2} + y\sin x = 0.$ O - 2 - L

8. $\dfrac{d^2y}{dx^2} + x\sin y = 0.$ O - 2 - N

9. $\dfrac{d^6x}{dt^6} + \left(\dfrac{d^4x}{dt^4}\right)\left(\dfrac{d^3x}{dt^3}\right) + x = t.$ O - 6 - N · D 2

10. $\left(\dfrac{dr}{ds}\right)^3 = \sqrt{\dfrac{d^2r}{ds^2} + 1}.$ O - 2 - N

1.2 Solutions

A. *Nature of Solutions*

We now consider the concept of a solution of the nth-order ordinary differential equation.

DEFINITION.   Consider the nth-order ordinary differential equation

(1.10) $$F\left[x,y,\frac{dy}{dx}, \cdots, \frac{d^n y}{dx^n}\right] = 0,$$

where F is a real function of its $(n + 2)$ arguments $x,y,\dfrac{dy}{dx}, \cdots, \dfrac{d^n y}{dx^n}.$

(1). Let f be a real function defined for all x in a real interval I and having an nth derivative (and hence also all lower ordered derivatives) for all $x \in I$. The function f is called an *explicit solution* of the differential equation (1.10) on I if it fulfills the following two requirements:

(A) $$F[x, f(x), f'(x), \ldots, f^{(n)}(x)]$$

is defined for all $x \in I$, and

(B) $$F[x, f(x), f'(x), \ldots, f^{(n)}(x)] = 0$$

for all $x \in I$. That is, the substitution of $f(x)$ and its various derivatives for y and its corresponding derivatives, respectively, in (1.10) reduces (1.10) to an identity on I.

(2). A relation $g(x,y) = 0$ is called an *implicit solution* of (1.10) if this relation defines at least one real function f of the variable x on an interval I such that this function is an explicit solution of (1.10) on this interval.

(3). Both explicit solutions and implicit solutions will usually be called simply *solutions*.

Roughly speaking, then, we may say that a solution of the differential equation (1.10) is a relation, explicit or implicit, between x and y, not containing derivatives, which identically satisfies (1.10).

Example 1.8.   The function f defined for all real x by

(1.11) $$f(x) = 2\sin x + 3\cos x$$

is an explicit solution of the differential equation

(1.12) $$\frac{d^2y}{dx^2} + y = 0$$

for all real x.   First note that f is defined and has a second derivative for all real x.   Next observe that

$$f'(x) = 2\cos x - 3\sin x,$$
$$f''(x) = -2\sin x - 3\cos x.$$

Upon substituting $f''(x)$ for $\frac{d^2y}{dx^2}$ and $f(x)$ for y in the differential equation (1.12), it reduces to the identity

$$(-2\sin x - 3\cos x) + (2\sin x + 3\cos x) = 0,$$

which holds for all real x.   Thus the function f defined by (1.11) is an explicit solution of the differential equation (1.12) for all real x.

Example 1.9.   The relation

(1.13) $$x^2 + y^2 = 25$$

is an implicit solution of the differential equation

(1.14) $$x + y\frac{dy}{dx} = 0$$

on the interval I defined by $-5 < x < 5$.   For the relation (1.13) defines the two real functions f_1 and f_2 given by

$$f_1(x) = \sqrt{25 - x^2}$$

and

$$f_2(x) = -\sqrt{25 - x^2},$$

respectively, for all real $x \in I$, and both of these functions are explicit solutions of the differential equations (1.14) on I.

Let us illustrate this for the function f_1.   Since

$$f_1(x) = \sqrt{25 - x^2},$$

we see that

$$f_1'(x) = \frac{-x}{\sqrt{25 - x^2}}$$

for all real $x \in I$.

Substituting $f_1(x)$ for y and $f_1'(x)$ for $\frac{dy}{dx}$ in (1.14), we obtain the identity

$$x + [\sqrt{25 - x^2}]\left[\frac{-x}{\sqrt{25 - x^2}}\right] = 0 \quad \text{or} \quad x - x = 0,$$

which holds for all real $x \in I$. Thus the function f_1 is an explicit solution of (1.14) on the interval I.

Now consider the relation

(1.15) $$x^2 + y^2 = -25.$$

Is this also an implicit solution of Equation (1.14)? Let us differentiate the relation (1.15) implicitly with respect to x. We obtain

$$2x + 2y\frac{dy}{dx} = 0 \quad \text{or} \quad \frac{dy}{dx} = -\frac{x}{y}.$$

Substituting this into the differential equation (1.14), we obtain the *formal* identity

$$x + y\left(-\frac{x}{y}\right) = 0.$$

Thus the relation (1.15) *formally* satisfies the differential equation (1.14). Can we conclude from this alone that (1.15) is an implicit solution of (1.14)? The answer to this question is "no"; for we have no assurance from this that the relation (1.15) defines any function which is an explicit solution of (1.14) on any real interval I. All that we have shown is that (1.15) is a relation between x and y which, upon implicit differentiation and substitution, *formally* reduces the differential equation (1.14) to a *formal* identity. It is called a *formal* solution; it has the *appearance* of a solution; but that is all that we know about it at this stage of our investigation.

Let us investigate a little further. Solving (1.15) for y, we find that

$$y = \pm\sqrt{-25 - x^2}.$$

Since this expression yields nonreal values of y for all real values of x, we conclude that the relation (1.15) does not define any real function on any interval. Thus the relation (1.15) is not truly an implicit solution but merely a *formal solution* of the differential equation (1.14).

In applying the methods of the following chapters we shall often obtain relations which we can readily verify are at least formal solutions. Our main objective will be to gain familiarity with the methods themselves and we shall often be content to refer to the relations so obtained as "solutions," although we have no assurance that these relations are actually true implicit solutions. If a critical examination of the situation is required, one must undertake to determine whether or not these formal solutions so obtained are actually true implicit solutions which define explicit solutions.

Let us now consider the first order differential equation

(1.16) $$\frac{dy}{dx} = 2x.$$

The function f_0 defined for all real x by $f_0(x) = x^2$ is a solution of equation (1.16). So also are the functions $f_1, f_2,$ and f_3, defined for all real x by $f_1(x) = x^2 + 1, f_2(x) = x^2 + 2,$ and $f_3(x) = x^2 + 3$, respectively. In fact, the function f defined for all real x by

$$(1.17) \qquad\qquad f(x) = x^2 + c$$

is a solution of equation (1.16) for *any* real constant c. We therefore refer to the constant c in (1.17) as an *arbitrary constant*, and we may say that the *first-order* differential equation (1.16) has a solution which involves *one arbitrary constant*. This solution f is called a _general solution_ of Equation (1.16), and any solution obtained from it by giving the arbitrary constant a particular value is called a _particular solution_ of (1.16).

We proceed to the second-order differential equation

$$(1.18) \qquad\qquad \frac{d^2y}{dx^2} + y = 0$$

and consider the function f defined for all real x by

$$(1.19) \qquad\qquad f(x) = c_1 \sin x + c_2 \cos x.$$

We can easily verify that this function f is a solution of equation (1.18) for *any* real values of the constants c_1 and c_2. We therefore refer to these constants c_1 and c_2 in (1.19) as *arbitrary constants* and say that the *second-order* differential equation (1.18) has a solution which involves *two arbitrary constants*. Further the constants c_1 and c_2 in (1.19) are *essential* in the sense that we can not replace the two constants in (1.19) by *one* single constant and still maintain the same degree of generality. The solution (1.19) is called the *general solution* of (1.18), and any solution obtained from it by giving particular values to either or both of the arbitrary constants c_1 and c_2 is called a *particular solution* of (1.18). For example, the function g defined for all real x by

$$g(x) = 5 \sin x - 6 \cos x$$

is a particular solution of (1.18).

In view of these illustrations it seems reasonable to call a solution of an nth order ordinary differential equation a general solution if it contains n essentially arbitrary constants. This is actually what we shall do. However, we might first consider this concept of *essential* constants a little more carefully. We shall say that a set of arbitrary constants involved in a relation are *essentially arbitrary constants* if this set of arbitrary constants can *not* be replaced by a *smaller* number of arbitrary constants which will still maintain the same degree of generality. We shall not attempt to go into a general discussion of precisely what is meant by maintaining the same degree of generality. Instead we shall proceed to consider two simple illustrations which should make the concept clear enough for our purposes. Let us first consider the arbitrary constants c_1 and c_2 in the relation

$$y = c_1 e^x + c_2 e^{2x}.$$

These constants are essentially arbitrary. We can not replace them by one single arbitrary constant without loss in generality. On the other hand, consider the arbitrary constants c_1 and c_2 in the relation

$$(1.20) \qquad\qquad y = (c_1 + c_2) e^x.$$

We may replace c_1 and c_2 by the single arbitrary constant c_3 and write

(1.21)
$$y = c_3 e^x,$$

and still the solution (1.21) is just as general as (1.20). Giving certain values to c_1 and c_2 amounts to the same thing as giving one certain value to c_3. Thus the two constants c_1 and c_2 in (1.20) are *not* essential; for these two constants can be replaced by the one constant c_3 and the same degree of generality is still maintained. With the concept of essentially arbitrary constants in mind, let us now return to our main objective: the definition of general solution.

DEFINITION. Let

(1.22)
$$F\left(x,y,\frac{dy}{dx}, \cdots, \frac{d^n y}{dx^n}\right) = 0$$

be an nth order ordinary differential equation.

(1) A solution of (1.22) containing n essentially arbitrary constants will be called a *general solution* of (1.22).

(2) A solution of (1.22) obtained from a general solution of (1.22) by giving particular values to one or more of the n essentially arbitrary constants will be called a *particular solution* of (1.22).

(3) A solution of (1.22) which can *not* be obtained from any general solution of (1.22) by any choice of the n essentially arbitrary constants will be called a *singular solution* of (1.22).

Example 1.10. Consider the second-order differential equation

(1.23)
$$\frac{d^2 y}{dx^2} - 3\frac{dy}{dx} + 2y = 0$$

and the function f defined for all real x by

(1.24)
$$f(x) = c_1 e^x + c_2 e^{2x}.$$

The student may readily verify that (1.24) is a solution of (1.23) for *any* choice of the constants c_1 and c_2. Thus (1.24) is a solution of the *second*-order differential equation (1.23) containing the *two* arbitrary constants c_1 and c_2, and, as we have noted above, these two constants are *essentially* arbitrary constants. Thus (1.24) is a *general solution* of (1.23).

Particular solutions of (1.23) are, for example, the functions defined by

$$f_1(x) = 5e^x + 6e^{2x},$$
$$f_2(x) = \tfrac{1}{2}e^x - 3e^{2x},$$

and
$$f_3(x) = a_0 e^x + w_0 e^{2x},$$

where a_0 is *your* age in years and w_0 is *your* weight in pounds. It can be shown that the differential equation (1.23) has no singular solutions.

Example 1.11. One can verify that the function f defined for all real x by

(1.25)
$$f(x) = c_1 e^x + c_2 e^{-x} + c_3 \sin x + c_4 \cos x$$

is a solution of the fourth-order differential equation

(1.26) $$\frac{d^4y}{dx^4} - y = 0$$

for any choices of the four constants c_1, c_2, c_3, and c_4. These four constants can not be replaced by any smaller number and still maintain the same degree of generality. Thus (1.25) is a solution of the *fourth*-order differential equation (1.26) containing *four* essentially arbitrary constants and so is a *general solution* of (1.26). Some *particular solutions* are the functions defined by

$$f_1(x) = e^x + 2e^{-x} + 5\sin x - 3\cos x,$$
$$f_2(x) = -e^x + \tfrac{1}{2}e^{-x} + 4\sin x + \pi\cos x,$$
$$f_3(x) = \sin x.$$

The differential equation (1.26) is another one having no singular solutions.

Example 1.12. The function f defined for all real x by

(1.27) $$f(x) = (x + c)^2$$

is a solution of the differential equation

(1.28) $$\left(\frac{dy}{dx}\right)^2 - 4y = 0,$$

as the reader may verify. Since (1.28) is a *first*-order differential equation and the solution (1.27) contains *one* arbitrary constant, we may say that (1.27) is a *general solution* of (1.28). Some *particular solutions* are the functions defined by

$$f_1(x) = x^2,$$
$$f_2(x) = (x + 5)^2,$$
$$f_3(x) = (x - \tfrac{1}{3})^2.$$

Of course these particular solutions are all obtained from (1.27) by giving particular values to the arbitrary constant c (namely, the values 0, 5, and $-\tfrac{1}{3}$, respectively). Now observe that the function g defined for all real x by

(1.29) $$g(x) = 0$$

is also a solution of equation (1.28). No choice of the constant c in (1.27) can possibly yield (1.29). Thus the function g defined by (1.29) is a *singular solution* of the differential equation (1.28).

B. Analytical and Geometrical Interpretations of Differential Equations and Solutions

What does a differential equation actually say, analytically speaking? To answer this let us consider what sort of expressions could be used to indicate a real function of a real variable. For example, consider the familiar "sine function." We usually express the functional values of the so-called sine function by the closed form notation $f(x) = \sin x$. But we could express the same values by the infinite series representation

$$f(x) = x - \frac{x^3}{3!} + \frac{x^5}{5!} - \cdots = \sum_{n=1}^{\infty} \frac{(-1)^{n+1}x^{2n-1}}{(2n-1)!}$$

or by the integral representation

$$f(x) = \int_0^x \cos t \, dt.$$

Now let us return to differential equations and consider the simple differential equation

$$\frac{dy}{dx} = \cos x.$$

The general solution of this is the function f defined for all real x by $f(x) = \sin x + c$, where c is an arbitrary constant. A particular solution which satisfies the condition that $y = 0$ at $x = 0$ is that given by $y = f_1(x)$, where $f_1(x) = \sin x$. We shall see later that this particular solution is the only solution satisfying this condition. Thus we may say that the differential equation

$$\frac{dy}{dx} = \cos x$$

plus the condition that $y = 0$ at $x = 0$ also defines the function f_1 with values $f_1(x) = \sin x$. Further, the differential equation $\frac{dy}{dx} = \cos x$ is a means of defining the *family* of functions f_c with values $f_c(x) = \sin x + c$.

This simple example enables us to answer the question which we asked at the beginning of this section. Extending the observations made, we may say that a differential equation is merely an expression which may serve as a means of defining certain functions, its "solutions." Indeed, many of the now familiar functions originally appeared in the form of differential equations which defined them.

Now what does a differential equation actually say, geometrically speaking, and what is the geometric significance of its solutions? Let us first recall that a real function F may be represented geometrically by a curve $y = F(x)$ in the xy plane and that the value of the derivative of F at x, $F'(x)$, may be interpreted as the slope of the curve $y = F(x)$ at x. Thus the general first-order differential equation

$$(1.30) \qquad \frac{dy}{dx} = f(x,y),$$

where f is a real function, may be interpreted geometrically as defining a slope $f(x,y)$ at every point (x,y) at which the function f is defined. Now let us assume that the general solution of the differential equation (1.30) can be written in the form

$$(1.31) \qquad y = F(x,c),$$

where c is an arbitrary constant. Equation (1.31) defines a family of functions which is represented geometrically by a so-called one-parameter family of curves in the xy plane, the slopes of which at each point are given by the differential equation (1.30). These curves, the "graphs" of the solutions of the differential equation (1.30), are called the *integral curves* of the differential equation (1.30).

If an integral curve is required to pass through a particular point (x_0, y_0), then (x_0, y_0) must satisfy equation (1.31), giving $y_0 = F(x_0, c)$. This determines the arbitrary constant c as a definite constant c_0 and leads to the particular integral curve having the equation

$y = F(x, c_0)$. The function F thus determined is simply a particular solution of the differential equation (1.30), one whose graph passes through the point (x_0, y_0).

As a simple example, we again consider the differential equation $\dfrac{dy}{dx} = \cos x$ discussed previously. The general solution may be written in the form $y = \sin x + c$ and represents a one-parameter family of curves in the xy plane which is such that the slope of any particular curve of the family at a given point (x, y) is given by $\cos x$. These "sine curves," the graphs of the functions whose values are given by $y = \sin x + c$, are the integral curves of the differential equation $\dfrac{dy}{dx} = \cos x$.

Extending this discussion, we may interpret an nth order differential equation as defining a so-called n-parameter family of curves in the xy plane.

C. Methods of Solution

When we say that we shall solve a differential equation we mean that we shall find one or more of its solutions. How is this done and what does it really mean? The greater part of this text is concerned with various methods of solving differential equations. The method to be employed depends upon the type of differential equation under consideration, and we shall not enter into the details of specific methods here.

But suppose we solve a differential equation, using one or another of the various methods. Does this necessarily mean that we have found an explicit solution f expressed in the so-called closed form of a finite sum of known elementary functions? That is, roughly speaking, when we have solved a differential equation, does this necessarily mean that we have found a "formula" for the solution? The answer is "no." Comparatively few differential equations have solutions so expressible; in fact, a closed-form solution is really a luxury in differential equations. In Chapters 2 and 4 we shall consider certain types of differential equations which do have such closed form solutions and study the exact methods available for finding these desirable solutions. But, as we have just noted, such equations are actually in the minority and we must consider what it means to "solve" equations for which exact methods are unavailable. Such equations are solved approximately by various methods, some of which are considered in Chapters 6, 8, and 13. Among such methods are series methods, numerical methods, and graphical methods. What do such approximate methods actually yield? The answer to this depends upon the method under consideration.

Series methods yield solutions in the form of infinite series; numerical methods give approximate values of the solution functions corresponding to selected values of the independent variables; and graphical methods produce approximately the graphs of solutions (the integral curves). These methods are not so desirable as exact methods because of the amount of work involved in them and because the results obtained from them are only approximate; but if exact methods are not applicable, one has no choice but to turn to approximate methods. Modern science and engineering problems continue to give rise to differential equations to which exact methods do not apply, and approximate methods are becoming increasingly more important.

Exercises

1. Show that each of the functions defined in column I below is a solution of the corresponding differential equation in column II on every interval $a < x < b$ of the x axis.

| I | II |

(a) $f(x) = x + 3e^{-x}$ $\dfrac{dy}{dx} + y = x + 1.$

(b) $f(x) = 2e^{3x} - 5e^{4x}$ $\dfrac{d^2y}{dx^2} - 7\dfrac{dy}{dx} + 12y = 0.$

(c) $f(x) = e^x + 2x^2 + 6x + 7$ $\dfrac{d^2y}{dx^2} - 3\dfrac{dy}{dx} + 2y = 4x^2.$

(d) $f(x) = \dfrac{1}{1 + x^2}$ $(1 + x^2)\dfrac{d^2y}{dx^2} + 4x\dfrac{dy}{dx} + 2y = 0.$

2. (a) Show that $x^3 + 3xy^2 = 1$ is an implicit solution of the differential equation $2xy\dfrac{dy}{dx} + x^2 + y^2 = 0$ on the interval $0 < x < 1$.

   (b) Show that $5x^2y^2 - 2x^3y^2 = 1$ is an implicit solution of the differential equation $x\dfrac{dy}{dx} + y = x^3y^3$ on the interval $0 < x < 5/2$.

3. (a) Show that the function f defined by $f(x) = c_1e^{4x} + c_2e^{-2x}$, where c_1 and c_2 are arbitrary constants, is a general solution of the differential equation

$$\frac{d^2y}{dx^2} - 2\frac{dy}{dx} - 8y = 0.$$

   (b) Show that the function g defined by $g(x) = c_1e^{2x} + c_2xe^{2x} + c_3e^{-2x}$, where c_1, c_2, and c_3 are arbitrary constants, is a general solution of the differential equation

$$\frac{d^3y}{dx^3} - 2\frac{d^2y}{dx^2} - 4\frac{dy}{dx} + 8y = 0.$$

4. (a) For certain values of the constant m the function f defined by $f(x) = e^{mx}$ is a solution of the differential equation

$$\frac{d^3y}{dx^3} - 3\frac{d^2y}{dx^2} - 4\frac{dy}{dx} + 12y = 0.$$

Determine all such values of m.

   (b) For certain values of the constant n the function g defined by $g(x) = x^n$ is a solution of the differential equation

$$x^3\frac{d^3y}{dx^3} + 2x^2\frac{d^2y}{dx^2} - 10x\frac{dy}{dx} - 8y = 0.$$

Determine all such values of n.

5. Show that the function f defined by $f(x) = 3e^{2x} - 2xe^{2x} - \cos 2x$ satisfies the differential equation

$$\frac{d^2y}{dx^2} - 4\frac{dy}{dx} + 4y = -8\sin 2x$$

and also the conditions that $f(0) = 2$ and $f'(0) = 4$.

1.3   Initial Value Problems, Boundary-Value Problems, and Existence of Solutions

A. Initial Value Problems and Boundary-Value Problems

We shall begin this section by considering a rather simple problem.

Problem. Find a solution f of the differential equation

$$(1.32) \qquad \frac{dy}{dx} = 2x$$

such that at $x = 1$ this solution f has the value 4.

Solution. First let us be certain that we thoroughly understand this problem. We seek a real function f which fulfills the two following requirements:

  (1) The function f must satisfy the differential equation (1.32). That is, the function f must be such that $f'(x) = 2x$ for all real x in an interval I.

  (2) The function f must have the value 4 at $x = 1$. That is, the function f must be such that $f(1) = 4$.

We have observed (page 8) that the general solution of the differential equation (1.32) is given by

$$(1.33) \qquad f(x) = x^2 + c,$$

where c is an arbitrary constant. Let us attempt to determine the constant c so that (1.33) satisfies requirement (2). We must have $4 = 1 + c$, and hence $c = 3$. Thus the particular solution f defined by

$$f(x) = x^2 + 3$$

is a solution of the differential equation (1.32) which has the value 4 at $x = 1$. In other words, the function f defined by $f(x) = x^2 + 3$ satisfies both of the requirements set forth in the problem.

An abbreviated notation for this type of problem and its solution. This entire problem [the differential equation (1.32) plus the requirement that the solution have the value 4 at $x = 1$] may be written in the following somewhat abbreviated form:

$$\begin{cases} \dfrac{dy}{dx} = 2x \\ y(1) = 4. \end{cases}$$

The notation $y(1) = 4$ stands for the supplementary condition that the solution have the value 4 at $x = 1$. Further, the solution of the problem, the function f defined by $f(x) = x^2 + 3$, may be written in the notation

$$y = x^2 + 3.$$

The notations $y(1) = 4$ and $y = x^2 + 3$ are in some ways undesirable, but they have the advantages of being both customary and convenient. For these reasons a similar abbreviated notation will be generally employed on the following pages.

In the application of differential equations the problems most frequently encountered are similar to the above introductory problem in that they involve *both* a differential equation *and* one or more supplementary conditions (or "side conditions") which the solution of the given differential equation must satisfy. If all of the associated supplementary conditions relate to one x value, the problem is called an *initial-value problem* (or one-point boundary-value problem). If the conditions relate to two different x values, the problem is called a *two-point boundary value problem* (or simply a boundary-value problem). We shall illustrate these concepts with examples and then consider one such type of problem in detail.

Example 1.13.

$$\begin{cases} \dfrac{d^2y}{dx^2} + y = 0 \\ \quad y(1) = 3 \\ \quad y'(1) = -4. \end{cases}$$

This problem consists in finding a solution of the differential equation

$$\frac{d^2y}{dx^2} + y = 0$$

which assumes the value 3 at $x = 1$ and whose first derivative assumes the value -4 at $x = 1$. Both of these conditions relate to one x value, namely, $x = 1$. Thus this is an initial-value problem. We shall see later that this problem has a unique solution.

Example 1.14.

$$\begin{cases} \dfrac{d^2y}{dx^2} + y = 0 \\ \quad y(0) = 1 \\ \quad y\left(\dfrac{\pi}{2}\right) = 5. \end{cases}$$

In this problem we again seek a solution of the same differential equation, but this time the solution must assume the value 1 at $x = 0$ and the value 5 at $x = \pi/2$. That is, the conditions relate to the *two* different x values, 0 and $\pi/2$. This is a (two-point) boundary-value problem. This problem also has a unique solution; but the boundary-value problem

$$\begin{cases} \dfrac{d^2y}{dx^2} + y = 0 \\ \quad y(0) = 1 \\ \quad y(\pi) = 5, \end{cases}$$

has no solution at all! This simple fact may lead one to the correct conclusion that boundary-value problems are not to be taken lightly!

We now turn to a more detailed consideration of the initial-value problem for a first-order differential equation.

DEFINITION.   Consider the first-order differential equation

(1.34)
$$\frac{dy}{dx} = f(x, y),$$

where f is a continuous function of x and y in some domain* D of the xy plane; and let (x_0, y_0) be a point of D. The *initial-value problem* associated with (1.34) is to find a solution ϕ of (1.34), defined on some interval containing x_0, and satisfying the *initial condition*

$$\phi(x_0) = y_0.$$

In the customary abbreviated notation, this initial-value problem may be written

$$\begin{cases} \dfrac{dy}{dx} = f(x,y) \\ y(x_0) = y_0. \end{cases}$$

To solve this problem we must find a function ϕ which not only satisfies the differential equation (1.34) but which also has the value y_0 when x has the value x_0. Geometrically speaking, we seek an integral curve of (1.34) which passes through the point (x_0, y_0). In order to obtain a solution one first determines the general solution

$$(1.35) \qquad\qquad\qquad g(x,y,c) = 0$$

of the differential equation. Since (x_0, y_0) must satisfy this, we obtain

$$g(x_0, y_0, c) = 0.$$

Solving this for c we obtain a particular value c_0. We now replace the arbitrary constant c by the particular constant c_0 in equation (1.35), thus obtaining the particular solution $g(x,y,c_0) = 0$. From this the explicit solution satisfying the conditions of the problem is then obtained.

Example 1.15. Solve the initial-value problem

$$(1.36) \qquad\qquad\qquad \frac{dy}{dx} = -\frac{x}{y},$$

$$(1.37) \qquad\qquad\qquad y(3) = 4,$$

given that the general solution of the differential equation (1.36) may be written

$$(1.38) \qquad\qquad\qquad x^2 + y^2 = c^2.$$

The condition (1.37) means that we seek the solution of (1.36) such that $y = 4$ at $x = 3$. Thus the pair of values (3,4) must satisfy the relation (1.38). Substituting $x = 3$ and $y = 4$ into (1.38), we find

$$9 + 16 = c^2 \qquad \text{or} \qquad c^2 = 25.$$

Now substituting this value of c^2 into (1.38), we have

$$x^2 + y^2 = 25.$$

Solving this for y, we obtain

$$y = \pm\sqrt{25 - x^2}.$$

---

*A *domain* is an open, connected set. For those unfamiliar with such concepts, D may be regarded as the interior of some simple closed curve in the plane.

Obviously the positive sign must be chosen to give y the value $+4$ at $x = 3$. Thus the function f defined by

$$f(x) = \sqrt{25 - x^2}, \quad -5 < x < 5,$$

is the solution of the problem. In the abbreviated notation introduced, we write this solution as $y = \sqrt{25 - x^2}$.

B. Existence of Solutions

In Example 1.15 we were able to find a solution of the initial-value problem under consideration. But do all initial-value and boundary-value problems have solutions? We have already answered this question in the negative, for we have pointed out that the boundary-value problem

$$\begin{cases} \dfrac{d^2 y}{dx^2} + y = 0, \\ y(0) = 1, \\ y(\pi) = 5, \end{cases}$$

mentioned at the end of Example 1.14, has no solution! Thus arises the question of *existence* of solutions: given an initial-value or boundary-value problem, does it actually have a solution? We shall attempt to give answers to this question as we encounter various problems of these types in later chapters. For the present let us consider the question for the initial-value problem defined on page 15. Here we can give a definite answer. Every initial value problem that satisfies the definition on page 15 has *at least one* solution.

But now another question is suggested, the question of *uniqueness*. Does such a problem ever have *more than one* solution? Let us consider the initial-value problem

$$\begin{cases} \dfrac{dy}{dx} = y^{1/3}, \\ y(0) = 0. \end{cases}$$

One may verify that the functions f_1 and f_2 defined, respectively,

by $\qquad\qquad\qquad f_1(x) = 0$ for all real x;

and $\qquad\qquad\qquad f_2(x) = (\tfrac{2}{3}x)^{3/2}, \quad x \geq 0; \quad f_2(x) = 0, \quad x \leq 0;$

are *both* solutions of this initial-value problem! In fact, this problem has infinitely many solutions! The answer to the uniqueness question is clear: the initial-value problem, as stated, need not have a *unique* solution. In order to ensure uniqueness, some additional requirement must certainly be imposed. We shall see what this is in Theorem 1.1, which we shall now state.

THEOREM 1.1.   Basic Existence and Uniqueness Theorem.

Hypothesis.   Consider the differential equation

(1.34)
$$\frac{dy}{dx} = f(x,y),$$

where

(a) The function f is a (single-valued) continuous function of x and y in some domain D of the xy plane, and

(b) The partial derivative $\dfrac{\partial f}{\partial y}$ is also a (single-valued) continuous function of x and y in D; and let (x_0, y_0) be a point in D.

Conclusion. There exists a unique solution ϕ of the differential equation (1.34), defined on some interval $|x - x_0| \leq h$, where h is sufficiently small, which satisfies the condition

$$(1.39) \qquad\qquad \phi(x_0) = y_0.$$

Explanatory Remarks. This basic theorem is the first theorem from the theory of differential equations which we have encountered. We shall therefore attempt to explain its meaning in detail.

(a) It is an *Existence and Uniqueness Theorem.* This means that it is a theorem which tells us that under certain conditions (stated in the hypothesis) something *exists* (the solution described in the conclusion) and is *unique* (there is *only one* such solution). It gives no hint whatsoever concerning *how* to find this solution but merely tells us that the problem *has* a solution.

(b) The *hypothesis* tells us what conditions are required of the quantities involved. It deals with two objects: the differential equation (1.34) and the point (x_0, y_0). As far as the differential equation (1.34) is concerned, the hypothesis requires that *both* the function f *and* the function $\dfrac{\partial f}{\partial y}$ (obtained by differentiating $f(x,y)$ partially with respect to y) must be continuous in some domain D of the xy plane. As far as the point (x_0, y_0) is concerned, it must be a point in this same domain D, where f and $\dfrac{\partial f}{\partial y}$ are so well-behaved (that is, continuous).

(c) The *conclusion* tells us of what we can be assured when the stated hypothesis are satisfied. It tells us that we are assured that there exists one and only one solution ϕ of the differential equation, which is defined on some interval $|x - x_0| \leq h$ centered about x_0 and which assumes the value y_0 when x takes on the value x_0. That is, it tells us that, under the given hypothesis on $f(x,y)$, the *initial-value problem*

$$\begin{cases} \dfrac{dy}{dx} = f(x,y) \\ y(x_0) = y_0 \end{cases}$$

has a *unique solution* which is valid in some interval about the initial point x_0.

(d) The *proof* of this theorem will not be given here. We shall prove it under somewhat less restrictive hypotheses in Chapter 10. We point out at this time that the conditions of the hypothesis are sufficient but not necessary. That is, they assure us of the conclusion stated; but a unique solution might exist without all the conditions of the hypothesis being satisfied. We shall consider this in greater detail in Chapter 10. Another matter which we shall reserve until then is a more precise discussion of the "*h*" of the conclusion. For the moment let us say that it is merely a number which is "small enough."

(e) The *value* of an existence theorem may be worth a bit of attention. What good is it, one might ask, if it does not tell us how to obtain the solution? The answer to this question is quite simple: an existence theorem will assure us that there *is* a solution to look for! It would be rather pointless to spend time, energy, and even money in trying to find a solution when there was actually no solution to be found! As for the value of the uniqueness, it would be equally pointless to waste time and energy finding one particular solution only to learn later that there were others and that the one found was not the one wanted!

We have included this rather lengthy discussion in the hope that the student, who has probably never before encountered a theorem of this type, will obtain a clearer idea of what this important theorem really means. We further hope that this discussion will help him to analyze theorems which he will encounter in the future, both in this book and elsewhere. We now consider two simple examples which illustrate Theorem 1.1.

Example 1.16.   Consider the initial-value problem

$$\begin{cases} \dfrac{dy}{dx} = x^2 + y^2 \\ y(1) = 3. \end{cases}$$

Let us apply Theorem 1.1. We first check the *hypothesis*. Here $f(x,y) = x^2 + y^2$ and $\dfrac{\partial f(x,y)}{\partial y} = 2y$. Both of the functions f and $\dfrac{\partial f}{\partial y}$ are continuous in every domain D of the xy plane. The initial condition $y(1) = 3$ means that $x_0 = 1$ and $y_0 = 3$, and the point $(1, 3)$ certainly lies in some such domain D. Thus all hypotheses are satisfied and the conclusion holds. That is, there is a unique solution ϕ of the differential equation $\dfrac{dy}{dx} = x^2 + y^2$, defined on some interval $|x - 1| \leq h$ about $x_0 = 1$, which satisfies the initial condition, that is, which is such that $\phi(1) = 3$.

Example 1.17.   Consider the two problems

$$\text{(A)} \quad \begin{cases} \dfrac{dy}{dx} = \dfrac{y}{\sqrt{x}} \\ y(1) = 2 \end{cases} \quad \text{and} \quad \text{(B)} \quad \begin{cases} \dfrac{dy}{dx} = \dfrac{y}{\sqrt{x}} \\ y(0) = 2. \end{cases}$$

Here

$$f(x,y) = \dfrac{y}{x^{1/2}} \quad \text{and} \quad \dfrac{\partial f(x,y)}{\partial y} = \dfrac{1}{x^{1/2}}.$$

These functions are both continuous *except* for $x = 0$ (that is, along the y axis). In Problem (A), $x_0 = 1$, $y_0 = 2$. The square of side 1 centered about $(1, 2)$ does *not* contain the y axis, and so both f and $\dfrac{\partial f}{\partial y}$ satisfy the required hypotheses in this square. Its interior may thus be taken to be the domain D of Theorem 1.1; and $(1, 2)$ certainly lies within it. Thus the conclusion of Theorem 1.1 applies to Problem (A) and we know the problem has a unique solution defined in some sufficiently small interval about $x_0 = 1$.

Now let us turn to Problem (B). Here $x_0 = 0$, $y_0 = 2$. At this point neither f nor $\dfrac{\partial f}{\partial y}$ are continuous. In other words, the point $(0, 2)$ can not be included in a domain D where the required hypotheses are satisfied. Thus we can *not* conclude from Theorem

1.1 that Problem (B) has a solution. We are *not* saying that it does *not* have one. Theorem 1.1 simply gives no information one way or the other.

Exercises

1. Show that $y = 4e^{2x} + 2e^{-3x}$ is a solution of the initial-value problem

$$\begin{cases} \dfrac{d^2y}{dx^2} + \dfrac{dy}{dx} - 6y = 0 \\[2mm] y(0) = 6 \\[2mm] y'(0) = 2. \end{cases}$$

Is $y = 2e^{2x} + 4e^{-3x}$ also a solution of this problem? Explain why or why not.

2. Given that the general solution of $\dfrac{dy}{dx} + y = 2xe^{-x}$ may be written $y = (x^2 + c)e^{-x}$, solve the following initial-value problems:

(A) $\begin{cases} \dfrac{dy}{dx} + y = 2xe^{-x} \\[2mm] y(0) = 2 \end{cases}$ (B) $\begin{cases} \dfrac{dy}{dx} + y = 2xe^{-x} \\[2mm] y(-1) = e + 3. \end{cases}$

3. Given that the general solution of $\dfrac{d^2y}{dx^2} - \dfrac{dy}{dx} - 12y = 0$ may be written $y = c_1e^{4x} + c_2e^{-3x}$, solve the following initial-value problems:

(A) $\begin{cases} \dfrac{d^2y}{dx^2} - \dfrac{dy}{dx} - 12y = 0 \\[2mm] y(0) = 5 \\[2mm] y'(0) = 6. \end{cases}$ (B) $\begin{cases} \dfrac{d^2y}{dx^2} - \dfrac{dy}{dx} - 12y = 0 \\[2mm] y(0) = -2 \\[2mm] y'(0) = 6. \end{cases}$

4. The general solution of the differential equation $\dfrac{d^2y}{dx^2} + y = 0$ may be written in the form $y = c_1\sin x + c_2\cos x$. Using this information, show that boundary problems (A) and (B) below possess solutions but that Problem (C) does not.

(A) $\begin{cases} \dfrac{d^2y}{dx^2} + y = 0 \\[2mm] y(0) = 0 \\[2mm] y(\pi/2) = 1. \end{cases}$ (B) $\begin{cases} \dfrac{d^2y}{dx^2} + y = 0 \\[2mm] y(0) = 1 \\[2mm] y'(\pi/2) = -1. \end{cases}$ (C) $\begin{cases} \dfrac{d^2y}{dx^2} + y = 0 \\[2mm] y(0) = 0 \\[2mm] y(\pi) = 1. \end{cases}$

5. Given that the general solution of

$$x^3\frac{d^3y}{dx^3} - 3x^2\frac{d^2y}{dx^2} + 6x\frac{dy}{dx} - 6y = 0$$

may be written $y = c_1x + c_2x^2 + c_3x^3$, solve the initial-value problem consisting of the above differential equation plus the three conditions

$$y(2) = 0, \quad y'(2) = 2, \quad y''(2) = 6.$$

6. Apply Theorem 1.1 to show that each of the following initial-value problems has a unique solution defined on some sufficiently small interval $|x - 1| \leq h$ about $x_0 = 1$.

(A) $\begin{cases} \dfrac{dy}{dx} = x^2 \sin y \\ y(1) = -2. \end{cases}$ (B) $\begin{cases} \dfrac{dy}{dx} = \dfrac{y^2}{x-2} \\ y(1) = 0. \end{cases}$

7. Consider the initial-value problem

$$\begin{cases} \dfrac{dy}{dx} = P(x)y^2 + Q(x)y \\ y(2) = 5, \end{cases}$$

where $P(x)$ and $Q(x)$ are both third degree polynomials in x. Has this problem a unique solution on some interval $|x - 2| \le h$ about $x_0 = 2$? Explain why or why not.

SUGGESTED READING

Agnew (1)   Ford (17)
Coddington (12)   Kaplan (30)
            Leighton (36)

2

FIRST-ORDER EQUATIONS FOR WHICH
EXACT SOLUTIONS ARE OBTAINABLE

In this chapter we consider certain basic types of first-order equations for which exact solutions may be obtained by definite procedures. The purpose of this chapter is to gain ability to recognize these various types and to apply the corresponding methods of solutions. Of the types considered here, the so-called exact equations considered in Section 2.1 are in a sense the most basic, while the separable equations of Section 2.2 are in a sense the "easiest." The most important, from the point of view of applications, are the separable equations of Section 2.2 and the linear equations of Section 2.3. The remaining types are of various very special forms, and the corresponding methods of solution involve various devices. In short, we might describe this chapter as a collection of special "methods," "devices," "tricks," or "recipes," in descending order of kindness!

2.1 Exact Differential Equations and Integrating Factors

A. Standard Forms of First-Order Differential Equations

The first-order differential equations to be studied in this chapter may be expressed in either the form

(2.1)
$$\frac{dy}{dx} = f(x,y)$$

or the form

(2.2)
$$M(x,y)dx + N(x,y)dy = 0.$$

An equation in one of these forms may readily be written in the other form. For example, the equation

$$\frac{dy}{dx} = \frac{x^2 + y^2}{x - y}$$

is of the form (2.1). It may be written

$$(x^2 + y^2)dx + (y - x)dy = 0,$$

which is of the form (2.2). The equation

$$(\sin x + y)dx + (x + 3y)dy = 0,$$

which is of the form (2.2), may be written in the form (2.1) as

$$\frac{dy}{dx} = -\frac{\sin x + y}{x + 3y}.$$

B. Exact Differential Equations

DEFINITION. Suppose $u = F(x,y)$, where F has continuous first partial derivatives. The *total differential du* is defined by the formula

$$du = \frac{\partial u}{\partial x}dx + \frac{\partial u}{\partial y}dy.$$

Example 2.1.   Let u be given in terms of x and y by

$$u = xy^2 + 2x^3y$$

for all real (x,y). Then

$$\frac{\partial u}{\partial x} = y^2 + 6x^2y, \qquad \frac{\partial u}{\partial y} = 2xy + 2x^3,$$

and the total differential du is defined by

$$du = (y^2 + 6x^2y)dx + (2xy + 2x^3)dy.$$

DEFINITION. The expression

(2.3) $$Mdx + Ndy$$

is called an *exact differential* if there exists some u for which this expression is the total differential du. In other words, the expression (2.3) is an exact differential if there exists some u such that

$$\frac{\partial u}{\partial x} = M \qquad \text{and} \qquad \frac{\partial u}{\partial y} = N.$$

If $Mdx + Ndy$ is an exact differential, then the differential equation

$$Mdx + Ndy = 0$$

is called an *exact differential equation.*

Example 2.2.   The differential equation

(2.4) $$y^2dx + 2xydy = 0$$

is an exact differential equation, for the expression $y^2dx + 2xydy$ is an exact differential. Indeed, it is the total differential of u, where $u = xy^2$, since the coefficient of dx is $\frac{\partial u}{\partial x} = y^2$ and that of dy is $\frac{\partial u}{\partial y} = 2xy$. On the other hand, the more simple appearing equation

(2.5) $$ydx + 2xdy = 0,$$

obtained from (2.4) by dividing through by y, is *not* exact.

   In Example 2.2 we stated without hesitation that the differential equation (2.4) is exact but the differential equation (2.5) is not. In the case of the equation (2.4) we verified our assertion by actually exhibiting the function u of which the expression $y^2dx + 2xydy$ is the total differential. But in the case of equation (2.5), we did not back up our statement by showing that there is *no u* such that $ydx + 2xdy$ is its total differential. It is clear that we need a simple test to determine whether or not a given differential equation is exact. This is given by the following theorem.

   THEOREM 2.1.   Consider the differential equation

(2.6) $$Mdx + Ndy = 0,$$

where M and N have continuous first partial derivatives.

(1) *If* the differential equation (2.6) is exact,
then

(2.7) $$\frac{\partial M}{\partial y} = \frac{\partial N}{\partial x}.$$

(2) *Conversely*, *if*

$$\frac{\partial M}{\partial y} = \frac{\partial N}{\partial x},$$

then the differential equation (2.6) is exact.

   Proof.   Part 1.   If the differential equation (2.6) is exact, then $Mdx + Ndy$ is an exact differential. By definition of an exact differential, there exists a u such that

$$\frac{\partial u}{\partial x} = M \quad \text{and} \quad \frac{\partial u}{\partial y} = N.$$

Then

$$\frac{\partial^2 u}{\partial y \partial x} = \frac{\partial M}{\partial y} \quad \text{and} \quad \frac{\partial^2 u}{\partial x \partial y} = \frac{\partial N}{\partial x}.$$

But, using the continuity of the first partial derivatives of M and N, we have

$$\frac{\partial^2 u}{\partial y \partial x} = \frac{\partial^2 u}{\partial x \partial y}$$

and therefore

$$\frac{\partial M}{\partial y} = \frac{\partial N}{\partial x}.$$

Part 2.   This being the converse of Part 1, we start with the hypothesis that

$$\frac{\partial M}{\partial y} = \frac{\partial N}{\partial x}$$

and set out to show that $Mdx + Ndy = 0$ is exact. This means that we must prove that there exists a u such that

(2.8)
$$\frac{\partial u}{\partial x} = M$$

and

(2.9)
$$\frac{\partial u}{\partial y} = N.$$

We can certainly find some u satisfying *either* (2.8) or (2.9), but what about *both?* Let us assume that u satisfies (2.8) and proceed.
Then

(2.10)
$$u = \int M\partial x + \phi(y),$$

where $\int M\partial x$ indicates a "partial integration" with respect to x, holding y constant, and ϕ is an arbitrary function of y only (this corresponds to a "constant of integration"). Differentiating (2.10) partially with respect to y, we obtain

$$\frac{\partial u}{\partial y} = \frac{\partial}{\partial y}\int M\partial x + \frac{d\phi}{dy}.$$

Now if (2.9) is to be satisfied, we must have

(2.11)
$$N = \frac{\partial}{\partial y}\int M\partial x + \frac{d\phi}{dy}$$

and hence

$$\frac{d\phi}{dy} = N - \frac{\partial}{\partial y}\int M\partial x.$$

Since ϕ is a function of y only, the derivative $\dfrac{d\phi}{dy}$ must also be independent of x. That is, in order for (2.11) to hold,

(2.12)
$$N - \frac{\partial}{\partial y}\int M\partial x$$

must be independent of x. Since

$$\frac{\partial}{\partial x}\left[N - \frac{\partial}{\partial y}\int M\partial x\right] = \frac{\partial N}{\partial x} - \frac{\partial^2}{\partial x\partial y}\int M\partial x = \frac{\partial N}{\partial x} - \frac{\partial^2}{\partial y\partial x}\int M\partial x = \frac{\partial N}{\partial x} - \frac{\partial M}{\partial y} = 0$$

(since $\dfrac{\partial M}{\partial y} = \dfrac{\partial N}{\partial x}$ *by hypothesis*), we thus see that (2.12) *is* independent of x.

Thus we may write

$$\phi(y) = \int\left[N - \int\frac{\partial M}{\partial y}\partial x\right]dy.$$

Substituting this into Equation (2.10), we have

(2.13) $$u = \int M \partial x + \int \left[N - \int \frac{\partial M}{\partial y} \partial x \right] dy.$$

This u thus satisfies both (2.8) and (2.9), and so $Mdx + Ndy = 0$ *is* exact.   *Q.E.D.*

Students well-versed in the terminology of higher mathematics will recognize that Theorem 2.1 may be stated in the following words: "A necessary and sufficient condition that equation (2.6) be exact is that condition (2.7) hold." For students not so well-versed, let us simply emphasize that condition (2.7), $\dfrac{\partial M}{\partial y} = \dfrac{\partial N}{\partial x}$, is the criterion for exactness. If (2.7) holds, then (2.6) is exact: if (2.7) does *not* hold, then (2.6) is *not* exact.

Example 2.3.   We apply the exactness criterion (2.7) to the Equations (2.4) and (2.5) introduced in Example 2.2. For the equation

(2.4) $$y^2 dx + 2xy \, dy = 0$$

we have $M = y^2$, $N = 2xy$, and $\dfrac{\partial M}{\partial y} = 2y = \dfrac{\partial N}{\partial x}$. Thus the Equation (2.4) is exact. On the other hand, for the equation

(2.5) $$ydx + 2xdy = 0,$$

we have $M = y$, $N = 2x$, and $\dfrac{\partial M}{\partial y} = 1 \neq 2 = \dfrac{\partial N}{\partial x}$. Thus the Equation (2.5) is *not* exact.

Example 2.4.   Consider the differential equation

$$(2x\sin y + y^3 e^x)dx + (x^2 \cos y + 3y^2 e^x)dy = 0.$$

Here

$$M = 2x\sin y + y^3 e^x,$$
$$N = x^2 \cos y + 3y^2 e^x,$$
$$\frac{\partial M}{\partial y} = 2x\cos y + 3y^2 e^x = \frac{\partial N}{\partial x}.$$

Thus this differential equation is exact.

C. *The Solution of Exact Differential Equations*

Now that we have a test with which to determine exactness, let us proceed to solve exact differential equations. If the equation $Mdx + Ndy = 0$ is exact, then there exists some u such that $\dfrac{\partial u}{\partial x} = M$ and $\dfrac{\partial u}{\partial y} = N$. Then the equation may be written

$$\frac{\partial u}{\partial x}dx + \frac{\partial u}{\partial y}dy = 0 \qquad \text{or simply} \qquad du = 0.$$

The relation $u = c$ is obviously a solution of this, where c is an arbitrary constant. We summarize this observation in the following theorem.

THEOREM 2.2. The general solution of the exact differential equation $Mdx + Ndy = 0$ is given by $u = c$, where u is such that $\frac{\partial u}{\partial x} = M$ and $\frac{\partial u}{\partial y} = N$, and c is an arbitrary constant.

Referring to Theorem 2.1, we observe that u is given by formula (2.13). However, in solving exact differential equations it is neither necessary nor desirable to use this formula. Instead one obtains u either by proceeding as in the proof of Theorem 2.1, Part 2, or by the so-called "method of grouping," which will be explained in the following examples.

Example 2.5. $(3x^2 + 4xy)dx + (2x^2 + 2y)dy = 0$.

Our first duty is to determine whether or not the equation is exact. Here $M = 3x^2 + 4xy$ and $N = 2x^2 + 2y$, $\frac{\partial M}{\partial y} = 4x$ and $\frac{\partial N}{\partial x} = 4x$, and so the equation is exact. Thus we must find u such that $\frac{\partial u}{\partial x} = M = 3x^2 + 4xy$ and $\frac{\partial u}{\partial y} = N = 2x^2 + 2y$. From the first of these,

$$u = \int M\partial x + \phi(y) = \int (3x^2 + 4xy)\partial x + \phi(y) = x^3 + 2x^2y + \phi(y).$$

Then

$$\frac{\partial u}{\partial y} = 2x^2 + \frac{d\phi}{dy}.$$

But we must have $\frac{\partial u}{\partial y} = N = 2x^2 + 2y$.

Thus

$$2x^2 + 2y = 2x^2 + \frac{d\phi}{dy}$$

or

$$\frac{d\phi}{dy} = 2y.$$

Thus $\phi(y) = y^2 + c_0$, where c_0 is an arbitrary constant, and so

$$u = x^3 + 2x^2y + y^2 + c_0.$$

The general solution is $u = c_1$ or

$$x^3 + 2x^2y + y^2 + c_0 = c_1.$$

Absorbing together the nonessential constants c_0 and c_1 we may write our solution as

$$x^3 + 2x^2y + y^2 = c,$$

where $c = c_1 - c_0$ is an arbitrary constant.

The student will observe that there is no loss in generality by taking $c_0 = 0$ and writing $\phi(y) = y^2$. We now consider an alternate procedure.

Method of Grouping. We shall now solve the differential equation of this example by grouping the terms in such a way that its left member appears as the sum of certain exact differentials. We write the differential equation

$$(3x^2 + 4xy)dx + (2x^2 + 2y)dy = 0$$

in the form

$$3x^2dx + (4xydx + 2x^2dy) + 2ydy = 0.$$

We now recognize this as

$$d(x^3) + d(2x^2y) + d(y^2) = d(c),$$

where c is an arbitrary constant, or

$$d(x^3 + 2x^2y + y^2) = d(c).$$

From this we have at once

$$x^3 + 2x^2y + y^2 = c.$$

Clearly this procedure is much quicker, but it requires a good "working knowledge" of differentials and a certain amount of ingenuity to determine just how the terms should be grouped. The standard method may require more "work" and take longer, but it is perfectly straightforward. It is recommended for those who like to follow a pattern and for those who have a tendency to jump at conclusions.

Just to make certain that we have both procedures well in hand, we shall consider an initial-value problem involving an exact differential equation.

Example 2.6. Solve the initial-value problem

$$(2x\cos y + 3x^2y)dx + (x^3 - x^2\sin y - y)dy = 0,$$

$$y(0) = 2.$$

We first observe that the equation is exact:

$$\frac{\partial M}{\partial y} = -2x\sin y + 3x^2 = \frac{\partial N}{\partial x}.$$

"Standard" Method. We must find u such that

$$\frac{\partial u}{\partial x} = M = 2x\cos y + 3x^2y$$

and

$$\frac{\partial u}{\partial y} = N = x^3 - x^2\sin y - y.$$

Then

$$u = \int M\partial x + \phi(y)$$

$$= \int (2x\cos y + 3x^2y)\partial x + \phi(y)$$

$$= x^2\cos y + x^3y + \phi(y),$$

$$\frac{\partial u}{\partial y} = -x^2\sin y + x^3 + \frac{d\phi}{dy}.$$

But also

$$\frac{\partial u}{\partial y} = N = x^3 - x^2 \sin y - y$$

and so

$$\frac{d\phi}{dy} = -y$$

and hence

$$\phi(y) = -\frac{y^2}{2} + c_0.$$

Thus

$$u = x^2 \cos y + x^3 y - \frac{y^2}{2} + c_0,$$

and the general solution $u = c_1$ may be written

$$x^2 \cos y + x^3 y - \frac{y^2}{2} = c.$$

Applying the initial condition $y = 2$ when $x = 0$, we find $c = -2$. Thus the solution of the given initial-value problem is

$$x^2 \cos y + x^3 y - \frac{y^2}{2} = -2.$$

"*Method of Grouping.*" We group the terms as follows:

$$(2x\cos y\,dx - x^2\sin y\,dy) + (3x^2 y\,dx + x^3\,dy) - y\,dy = 0.$$

Thus we have

$$d(x^2 \cos y) + d(x^3 y) - d\left(\frac{y^2}{2}\right) = d(c);$$

and so

$$x^2 \cos y + x^3 y - \frac{y^2}{2} = c$$

is the general solution of the differential equation. Of course the initial condition $y(0) = 2$ again yields the particular solution already obtained.

D. Integrating Factors

Given the differential equation

$$Mdx + Ndy = 0,$$

if $\frac{\partial M}{\partial y} = \frac{\partial N}{\partial x}$, then the equation is exact and we can obtain its solution by one of the procedures explained above. But if $\frac{\partial M}{\partial y} \neq \frac{\partial N}{\partial x}$, then the equation is *not* exact and the above procedures do not apply. What shall we do in such a case? Perhaps we can multiply the nonexact equation by some expression which will transform it into an equivalent exact equation. If so, we can proceed to solve the resulting exact equation by one of the above procedures. Let us consider again the equation

(2.5) $ydx + 2xdy = 0$

which was introduced in Example 2.2. In that example we observed that this equation is *not* exact. However, if we multiply it by y it is transformed into the equivalent equation

(2.4) $y^2dx + 2xydy = 0$,

which, as we observed in Example 2.2, *is* exact. Since the resulting equation (2.4) (being exact) is integrable, we call y an *integrating factor* of the equation (2.5). In general, we have the following definition:

DEFINITION. Suppose that the differential equation

(2.14) $Mdx + Ndy = 0$

is *not* exact but that the differential equation

(2.15) $\mu Mdx + \mu Ndy = 0$

is exact, where $\mu = F(x,y)$ for a suitably chosen function F. Then μ is called an *integrating factor* of the differential equation (2.14).

Example 2.7.   Consider the differential equation

(2.16) $(3y + 4xy^2)dx + (2x + 3x^2y)dy = 0$.

This equation is of the form (2.14), where $M = 3y + 4xy^2$,

$$N = 2x + 3x^2y, \quad \frac{\partial M}{\partial y} = 3 + 8xy, \quad \text{and} \quad \frac{\partial N}{\partial x} = 2 + 6xy.$$

Since $\dfrac{\partial M}{\partial y} \neq \dfrac{\partial N}{\partial x}$, Equation (2.16) is *not* exact.

Let $\mu = x^2y$. Then the corresponding differential equation of the form (2.15) is

$$(3x^2y^2 + 4x^3y^3)dx + (2x^3y + 3x^4y^2)dy = 0.$$

This equation *is* exact, since

$$\frac{\partial(\mu M)}{\partial y} = 6x^2y + 12x^3y^2 = \frac{\partial(\mu N)}{\partial x}.$$

Hence $\mu = x^2y$ is an integrating factor of Equation (2.16).

The question now arises: How is an integrating factor found? We shall not attempt to answer this question at this time. Instead we shall proceed to a study of the important classes of separable equations in Section 2.2 and linear equations in Section 2.3. We shall see that the former type always possess integrating factors which are perfectly obvious, while the latter always has integrating factors of a certain special form. We shall return to the question raised above in Section 2.4. Our object here has been merely to introduce the concept of an integrating factor.

Exercises

In Exercises 1 through 10 determine whether or not each of the given equations is exact; solve those which are exact.

1. $(3x + 2y)dx + (2x + y)dy = 0$.

2. $(y^2 + 3)dx + (2xy - 4)dy = 0$.

3. $(2xy + 1)dx + (x^2 + 4y)dy = 0$.

4. $(3x^2y + 2)dx - (x^3 + y)dy = 0$.

5. $(6xy + 2y^2 - 5)dx + (3x^2 + 4xy - 6)dy = 0$.

6. $(\theta^2 + 1)\cos r dr + 2\theta \sin r d\theta = 0$.

7. $(y\sec^2 x + \sec x \tan x)dx + (\tan x + 2y)dy = 0$.

8. $\left(\dfrac{x}{y^2} + x\right)dx + \left(\dfrac{x^2}{y^3} + y\right)dy = 0$.

9. $\left(\dfrac{2s - 1}{t}\right)ds + \left(\dfrac{s - s^2}{t^2}\right)dt = 0$.

10. $\dfrac{2y^{3/2} + 1}{x^{1/2}}dx + (3x^{1/2}y^{1/2} - 1)dy = 0$.

Solve the initial-value problems in Exercises 11 through 14.

11. $\begin{cases} (2xy - 3)dx + (x^2 + 4y)dy = 0, \\ y(1) = 2. \end{cases}$

12. $\begin{cases} (2y\sin x\cos x + y^2\sin x)dx + (\sin^2 x - 2y\cos x)dy = 0, \\ y(0) = 3. \end{cases}$

13. $\begin{cases} \left(\dfrac{3 - y}{x^2}\right)dx + \left(\dfrac{y^2 - 2x}{xy^2}\right)dy = 0, \\ y(-1) = 2. \end{cases}$

14. $\begin{cases} \dfrac{1}{x^{2/3}y^{1/3}}dx + \dfrac{2x^{4/3}y^{2/3} - x^{1/3}}{y^{4/3}}dy = 0, \\ y(1) = 8. \end{cases}$

15. In each of the following equations determine the constant A such that the equation is exact, and solve the resulting exact equation.

    (a) $(x^2 + 3xy)dx + (Ax^2 + 4y)dy = 0$.

    (b) $\left(\dfrac{1}{x^2} + \dfrac{1}{y^2}\right)dx + \left(\dfrac{Ax + 1}{y^3}\right)dy = 0$.

16. In each of the following equations determine the most general function $N(x,y)$ such that the equation is exact.

    (a) $(x^3 + xy^2)dx + N(x,y)dy = 0$.

(b) $(x^{-2}y^{-2} + xy^{-3})dx + N(x,y)dy = 0.$

17. Consider the differential equation

$$(4x + 3y^2)dx + 2xydy = 0.$$

(a) Show that this equation is not exact.
(b) Find an integrating factor of the form x^n, where n is a positive integer.
(c) Multiply the given equation through by the integrating factor found in (b) and solve the resulting exact equation.

18. Consider a differential equation of the form

$$[y + xf(x^2 + y^2)]dx + [yf(x^2 + y^2) - x]dy = 0.$$

(a) Show that an equation of this form is not exact.
(b) Show that $1/(x^2 + y^2)$ is an integrating factor of an equation of this form.

19. Use the result of Exercise 18(b) to solve the equation

$$[y + x(x^2 + y^2)^2]dx + [y(x^2 + y^2)^2 - x]dy = 0.$$

2.2 Separable Equations and Equations Reducible to This Form

A. Separable Equations

DEFINITION. An equation of the form

(2.17)
$$F(x)\ G(y)dx + f(x)g(y)dy = 0$$

is called an *equation with variables separable* or simply a *separable equation*.

For example, the equation $(x^3 + x^2)ydx + x^2(y^3 + 2y)dy = 0$ is a separable equation.
In general the separable equation (2.17) is not exact, but it possesses an obvious integrating factor, namely $1/f(x)G(y)$. For if we multiply Equation (2.17) by this expression, we separate the variables, reducing (2.17) to the equivalent equation

(2.18)
$$\frac{F(x)}{f(x)}dx + \frac{g(y)}{G(y)}dy = 0.$$

This equation is exact, since

$$\frac{\partial}{\partial y}\left[\frac{F(x)}{f(x)}\right] = 0 = \frac{\partial}{\partial x}\left[\frac{g(y)}{G(y)}\right].$$

Denoting $F(x)/f(x)$ by $M(x)$ and $g(y)/G(y)$ by $N(y)$, Equation (2.18) takes the form $M(x)dx + N(y)dy = 0$. Since M is a function of x only and N is a function of y only, we see at once that the solution is

(2.19)
$$\int M(x)dx + \int N(y)dy = c,$$

where c is an arbitrary constant. Thus the problem of solving the separable equation (2.17) has reduced to that of performing the integrations indicated in Equation (2.19). It is in this sense that separable equations are the simplest first-order differential equations.

Example 2.8. $(x^3 + x^2)ydx + x^2(y^3 + 2y)dy = 0$.   Separating the variables by dividing by x^2y we obtain

$$\frac{x^3 + x^2}{x^2}dx + \frac{y^3 + 2y}{y}dy = 0$$

or

$$(x + 1)dx + (y^2 + 2)dy = 0.$$

From this we have

$$\int (x + 1)dx + \int (y^2 + 2)dy = c$$

or

$$\frac{x^2}{2} + x + \frac{y^3}{3} + 2y = c.$$

Observe that in separating the variables we divided by x^2y. We did this under the tacit assumption that neither x nor y is zero. Since our purpose here is to gain facility in solving separable equations, we shall always make the assumption that any factors by which we divide are not zero.

Example 2.9.   Solve the initial-value problem which consists of the differential equation

(2.20) $$x\sin y\,dx + (x^2 + 1)\cos y\,dy = 0$$

and the initial condition

(2.21) $$y(1) = \frac{\pi}{2}.$$

We first obtain the general solution of the differential equation (2.20). Separating the variables by dividing by $(x^2 + 1)\sin y$, we obtain

$$\frac{x}{x^2 + 1}dx + \frac{\cos y}{\sin y}dy = 0.$$

Thus

$$\int \frac{xdx}{x^2 + 1} + \int \frac{\cos y}{\sin y}dy = c_0,$$

where c_0 is an arbitrary constant.
Carrying out the integrations, we find

(2.22) $$\tfrac{1}{2}\ln (x^2 + 1) + \ln |\sin y| = c_0.$$

We could leave the general solution in this form, but we can put it in a neater form in the following way. Since each term of the left member of this equation involves the logarithm of a function, it would seem reasonable that something might be accomplished by writing the arbitrary constant c_0 in the form $\ln |c_1|$. This we do, obtaining

$$\tfrac{1}{2}\ln (x^2 + 1) + \ln |\sin y| = \ln |c_1|.$$

Multiplying by 2, we have

$$\ln (x^2 + 1) + 2 \ln |\sin y| = 2 \ln |c_1|.$$

Since

$$2 \ln |\sin y| = \ln (\sin y)^2,$$

and

$$2 \ln |c_1| = \ln c_1^2 = \ln |c|,$$

where

$$|c| = c_1^2,$$

we now have

$$\ln (x^2 + 1) + \ln \sin^2 y = \ln |c|.$$

Since $\ln A + \ln B = \ln AB$, this equation may be written

$$\ln (x^2 + 1) \sin^2 y = \ln |c|.$$

From this we have at once

(2.23) $(x^2 + 1) \sin^2 y = c.$

Clearly (2.23) is of a neater form than (2.22).

We now apply the initial condition (2.21) to the general solution (2.23). We have

$$(1^2 + 1) \sin^2 \frac{\pi}{2} = c$$

and so $c = 2$. Therefore the solution of the initial-value problem under consideration is

$$(x^2 + 1) \sin^2 y = 2.$$

B. Homogeneous Equations

We now consider a class of differential equations which can be reduced to separable equations by a change of variables.

DEFINITION.   The first-order differential equation $Mdx + Ndy = 0$ is said to be *homogeneous* if, when written in the form $\dfrac{dy}{dx} = f(x,y)$, there exists g such that $f(x,y)$ can be expressed in the form $g\left(\dfrac{y}{x}\right)$.

Example 2.10.   The differential equation $(x^2 - 3y^2)dx + 2xydy = 0$ is homogeneous. To see this, we first write this equation in the form

$$\frac{dy}{dx} = \frac{3y^2 - x^2}{2xy}.$$

Now observing that

$$\frac{3y^2 - x^2}{2xy} = \frac{3y}{2x} - \frac{x}{2y} = \frac{3}{2}\left(\frac{y}{x}\right) - \frac{1}{2}\left[\frac{1}{(y/x)}\right],$$

we see that the differential equation under consideration may be written as

$$\frac{dy}{dx} = \frac{3}{2}\left(\frac{y}{x}\right) - \frac{1}{2}\left[\frac{1}{(y/x)}\right],$$

in which the right member is of the form $g\left(\dfrac{y}{x}\right)$ for a certain g.

   Example 2.11.   The equation

$$(y + \sqrt{x^2 + y^2})dx - xdy = 0$$

is homogeneous. When written in the form

$$\frac{dy}{dx} = \frac{y + \sqrt{x^2 + y^2}}{x},$$

the right member may be expressed as

$$\frac{y}{x} \pm \frac{\sqrt{x^2 + y^2}}{\sqrt{x^2}}$$

or $\dfrac{y}{x} \pm \sqrt{1 + \left(\dfrac{y}{x}\right)^2}$, depending on the sign of x. This is obviously of the form $g\left(\dfrac{y}{x}\right)$.

   Before proceeding to the actual solution of homogeneous equations we shall consider a slightly different procedure for recognizing such equations. A function F is called *homogeneous of degree n* if $F(tx,ty) = t^n F(x,y)$. This means that if tx and ty are substituted for x and y, respectively, in $F(x,y)$, and if t^n is then factored out, the other factor which remains is the original expression $F(x,y)$ itself. For example, the function F given by $F(x,y) = x^2 + y^2$ is homogeneous of degree 2, since $F(tx,ty) = (tx)^2 + (ty)^2 = t^2(x^2 + y^2) = t^2 F(x,y)$.

   Now suppose the functions M and N in the differential equation $Mdx + Ndy = 0$ are both homogeneous of the *same* degree n. Then since $M(tx,ty) = t^n M(x,y)$, we have $M\left(1,\dfrac{y}{x}\right) = M\left(\dfrac{1}{x}\cdot x, \dfrac{1}{x}\cdot y\right) = \left(\dfrac{1}{x}\right)^n M(x,y)$; and, in like manner, $N\left(1,\dfrac{y}{x}\right) = \left(\dfrac{1}{x}\right)^n N(x,y)$.

   Now writing the differential equation $Mdx + Ndy = 0$ in the form

$$\frac{dy}{dx} = -\frac{M(x,y)}{N(x,y)},$$

we find

$$\frac{dy}{dx} = -\frac{\left(\dfrac{1}{x}\right)^{-n} M\left(1,\dfrac{y}{x}\right)}{\left(\dfrac{1}{x}\right)^{-n} N\left(1,\dfrac{y}{x}\right)} = -\frac{M\left(1,\dfrac{y}{x}\right)}{N\left(1,\dfrac{y}{x}\right)}.$$

Clearly the expression on the right is of the form $g(y/x)$, and so the equation $Mdx + Ndy = 0$ is homogeneous in the sense of the original definition of homogeneity. Thus we conclude that if M and N in $Mdx + Ndy = 0$ are both homogeneous functions of the same degree n, then the differential equation is a homogeneous differential equation.

   Let us now look back at Examples 2.10 and 2.11 in this light. In Example 2.10, $M = x^2 - 3y^2$ and $N = 2xy$. Both M and N are homogeneous of degree 2. Thus we know at once that the equation $(x^2 - 3y^2)dx + 2xydy = 0$ is a homogeneous equation. In Example 2.11, $M = y + \sqrt{x^2 + y^2}$ and $N = -x$. Clearly N is homogeneous of degree 1.

Since

$$M(tx,ty) = ty + \sqrt{(tx)^2 + (ty)^2} = t(y + \sqrt{x^2 + y^2}) = t^1 M(x,y),$$

we see that M is also homogeneous of degree 1. Thus we conclude that the equation

$$(y + \sqrt{x^2 + y^2})dx - xdy = 0$$

is indeed homogeneous.

We now show that every homogeneous equation can be reduced to a separable equation by proving the following theorem.

THEOREM 2.3.   If

(2.24) $$Mdx + Ndy = 0$$

is a homogeneous equation, then the change of variables $y = vx$ transforms (2.24) into a separable equation in the variables v and x.

Proof. Since $Mdx + Ndy = 0$ is homogeneous, it may be written in the form

$$\frac{dy}{dx} = g\left(\frac{y}{x}\right).$$

Let $y = vx$. Then

$$\frac{dy}{dx} = v + x\frac{dv}{dx}$$

and (2.24) becomes

$$v + x\frac{dv}{dx} = g(v)$$

or

$$[v - g(v)]dx + xdv = 0.$$

This equation is separable. Separating the variables we obtain

(2.25) $$\frac{dv}{v - g(v)} + \frac{dx}{x} = 0.$$

Q.E.D.

Thus to solve a homogeneous differential equation of the form (2.24), we let $y = vx$ and transform the homogeneous equation into a separable equation of the form (2.25). From this, we have

$$\int\frac{dv}{v - g(v)} + \int\frac{dx}{x} = c,$$

where c is an arbitrary constant. Letting $F(v)$ denote $\int\dfrac{dv}{v - g(v)}$ and returning to the original dependent variable y, the solution takes the form

$$F\left(\frac{y}{x}\right) + \ln |x| = c.$$

Example 2.12. Solve the equation

$$(x^2 - 3y^2)dx + 2xydy = 0.$$

We have already observed that this equation is homogeneous. Writing it in the form

$$\frac{dy}{dx} = -\frac{x}{2y} + \frac{3y}{2x}$$

and letting $y = vx$, we obtain

$$v + x\frac{dv}{dx} = -\frac{1}{2v} + \frac{3v}{2},$$

or

$$x\frac{dv}{dx} = -\frac{1}{2v} + \frac{v}{2},$$

or, finally,

$$x\frac{dv}{dx} = \frac{v^2 - 1}{2v}.$$

This equation is separable. Separating the variables, we obtain

$$\frac{2vdv}{v^2 - 1} = \frac{dx}{x}.$$

Integrating, we find

$$\ln|v^2 - 1| = \ln|x| + \ln|c|,$$

and hence

$$v^2 - 1 = cx.$$

Now, replacing v by $\frac{y}{x}$ we obtain the solution in the form

$$\frac{y^2}{x^2} - 1 = cx$$

or

$$y^2 - x^2 = cx^3.$$

Example 2.13. Solve the initial-value problem

$$\left(y + \sqrt{x^2 + y^2}\right)dx - xdy = 0,$$
$$y(1) = 0.$$

We have seen that the differential equation is homogeneous. As before, we write it in the form

$$\frac{dy}{dx} = \frac{y + \sqrt{x^2 + y^2}}{x}.$$

Since the initial x value is 1, we take $x = \sqrt{x^2}$ and obtain

$$\frac{dy}{dx} = \frac{y}{x} + \sqrt{1 + (y/x)^2}.$$

We let $y = vx$ and obtain

$$v + x\frac{dv}{dx} = v + \sqrt{1 + v^2}$$

or

$$x\frac{dv}{dx} = \sqrt{1 + v^2}.$$

Separating variables, we find

$$\frac{dv}{\sqrt{v^2 + 1}} = \frac{dx}{x}.$$

Using tables, we perform the required integrations to obtain

$$\ln|v + \sqrt{v^2 + 1}| = \ln|x| + \ln|c|,$$

or

$$v + \sqrt{v^2 + 1} = cx.$$

Now replacing v by $\frac{y}{x}$, we obtain the general solution of the differential equation in the form

$$\frac{y}{x} + \sqrt{\frac{y^2}{x^2} + 1} = cx$$

or

$$y + \sqrt{x^2 + y^2} = cx^2.$$

The initial condition requires that $y = 0$ when $x = 1$. This gives $c = 1$ and hence

$$y + \sqrt{x^2 + y^2} = x^2,$$

from which it follows that

$$y = \tfrac{1}{2}(x^2 - 1).$$

Exercises

Solve each of the differential equations in Exercises 1 through 14.

1. $4xy\,dx + (x^2 + 1)dy = 0.$

2. $(xy + 2x + y + 2)dx + (x^2 + 2x)dy = 0.$

3. $2r(s^2 + 1)dr + (r^4 + 1)ds = 0.$ *Int factor* $\dfrac{1}{(s^2+1)(r^4+1)}$

4. $\csc y\,dx + \sec x\,dy = 0.$

5. $\tan\theta\,dr + 2r\,d\theta = 0.$

6. $(e^v + 1)\cos u\,du + e^v(\sin u + 1)dv = 0.$

7. $(x + 4)(y^2 + 1)dx + y(x^2 + 3x + 2)dy = 0.$

8. $(x + y)dx - x\,dy = 0.$

9. $(2xy + 3y^2)dx - (2xy + x^2)dy = 0.$

10. $v^3\,du + (u^3 - uv^2)dv = 0.$

11. $\left(x\tan\dfrac{y}{x} + y\right)dx - x\,dy = 0.$

12. $(2s^2 + 2st + t^2)ds + (s^2 + 2st - t^2)dt = 0.$

13. $(x^3 + y^2 \sqrt{x^2 + y^2})dx - xy \sqrt{x^2 + y^2}dy = 0.$

14. $\left(\sqrt{x + y} + \sqrt{x - y}\right)dx + \left(\sqrt{x - y} - \sqrt{x + y}\right)dy = 0.$

Solve the initial-value problems in Exercises 15 through 20.

15. $(y + 2)dx + y(x + 4)dy = 0$

$y(-3) = -1.$

16. $8\cos^2 y\, dx + \csc^2 x\, dy = 0$

$y\left(\dfrac{\pi}{12}\right) = \dfrac{\pi}{4}.$

17. $(3x + 8)(y^2 + 4)dx - 4y(x^2 + 5x + 6)dy = 0$

$y(1) = 2.$

18. $(x^2 + 3y^2)dx - 2xy\, dy = 0$

$y(2) = 6.$

19. $(2x - 5y)dx + (4x - y)dy = 0$

$y(1) = 4.$

20. $(3x^2 + 9xy + 5y^2)dx - (6x^2 + 4xy)dy = 0$

$y(2) = -6.$

21. Show that the homogeneous equation

$$(Ax^2 + By^2)dx + (Cxy + Dy^2)dy = 0$$

is exact if and only if $2B = C$.

22. Solve by two methods:

$$(x^2 + 2y^2)dx + (4xy - y^2)dy = 0.$$

23. (a) Prove that if $Mdx + Ndy = 0$ is a homogeneous equation, then the change of variables $x = uy$ transforms this equation into a separable equation in the variables u and x.
   (b) Use the result of (a) to solve the equation of Example 2.12 of the text.
   (c) Use the result of (a) to solve the equation of Example 2.13 of the text.

24. Suppose the equation $Mdx + Ndy = 0$ is homogeneous. Show that the transformation $x = r\cos\theta,\ y = r\sin\theta$ reduces this equation to a separable equation in the variables r and θ.

25. Suppose the equation

(A)
$$Mdx + Ndy = 0$$

is homogeneous.

(a) Show that equation (A) is invariant under the transformation

$$x = k\xi$$

(B)
$$y = k\eta,$$

where k is a constant.

(b) Show that the general solution of equation (A) can be written in the form

(C)
$$x = c\phi\left(\frac{y}{x}\right),$$

where c is an arbitrary constant.

(c) Use the result of (b) to show that the general solution (C) is also invariant under the transformation (B).

(d) Interpret geometrically the results proved in (a) and (c).

2.3   Linear Equations and Bernoulli Equations

A. Linear Equations

In Chapter I we gave a definition of linear as applied to differential equations in general; we now consider the linear ordinary differential equation of the first order.

DEFINITION. A first-order ordinary differential equation is called *linear* if it can be written in the form

(2.26)
$$\frac{dy}{dx} + P(x)y = Q(x).$$

For example, the equation

$$x\frac{dy}{dx} + (x + 1)y = x^3$$

is a first-order linear differential equation, for it can be written as

$$\frac{dy}{dx} + \left(1 + \frac{1}{x}\right)y = x^2,$$

which is of the form (2.26) with $P(x) = 1 + \dfrac{1}{x}$ and $Q(x) = x^2$.

Let us write the equation (2.26) in the form

(2.27)
$$[P(x)y - Q(x)]dx + dy = 0.$$

Equation (2.27) is of the form

$$Mdx + Ndy = 0,$$

where
$$M = P(x)y - Q(x) \quad \text{and} \quad N = 1.$$

Since
$$\frac{\partial M}{\partial y} = P(x) \quad \text{and} \quad \frac{\partial N}{\partial x} = 0,$$

the equation (2.27) is *not* exact unless $P(x) = 0$, in which case Equation (2.26) degenerates into a simple separable equation. However, the equation (2.27) possesses an integrating factor which depends on x only and may easily be found. Let us proceed to find it. Let us multiply equation (2.27) by $\mu(x)$, obtaining

(2.28) $$[\mu(x)P(x)y - \mu(x)Q(x)]dx + \mu(x)dy = 0.$$

By definition, $\mu(x)$ is an integrating factor of Equation (2.28) if and only if Equation (2.28) is exact; that is, if and only if

$$\frac{\partial}{\partial y}[\mu(x)P(x)y - \mu(x)Q(x)] = \frac{\partial}{\partial x}[\mu(x)].$$

This condition reduces to

$$\mu(x)P(x) = \frac{d}{dx}[\mu(x)]$$

or simply

(2.29) $$\mu P = \frac{d\mu}{dx}.$$

Equation (2.29) is a separable equation in the dependent variable μ and the independent variable x, where P is a known function of x. Separating the variables, we have

$$\frac{d\mu}{\mu} = Pdx.$$

Integrating, we obtain the particular solution

$$\ln|\mu| = \int Pdx$$

or

(2.30) $$\mu = e^{\int Pdx}.$$

Thus the linear equation (2.26) possesses an integrating factor of the form (2.30). Multiplying (2.26) by (2.30) gives

$$e^{\int Pdx}\frac{dy}{dx} + e^{\int Pdx}Py = Qe^{\int Pdx}, \qquad \text{This is an exact.}$$

which is precisely

$$\frac{d}{dx}[e^{\int Pdx}y] = Qe^{\int Pdx}.$$

Integrating this we obtain the solution of Equation (2.26) in the form

$$e^{\int Pdx}y = \int e^{\int Pdx}Qdx + c,$$

where c is an arbitrary constant.

Summarizing this discussion, we have the following theorem:

THEOREM 2.4.   The linear differential equation

$$\frac{dy}{dx} + P(x)y = Q(x)$$

has an integrating factor of the form

$$e^{\int Pdx}. \qquad \text{(OVER)}$$

The general solution of this equation is

$$y = e^{-\int P dx}\left[\int e^{\int P dx} Q\, dx + c\right].$$

We consider several examples.

Example 2.14.

(2.31)
$$\frac{dy}{dx} + \left(\frac{2x+1}{x}\right)y = e^{-2x}.$$

Here

$$P(x) = \frac{2x+1}{x}$$

and hence an integrating factor is

$$e^{\int P(x)dx} = e^{\int\left(\frac{2x+1}{x}\right)dx} = e^{2x+\ln|x|} = e^{2x}e^{\ln|x|} = xe^{2x}.$$

Multiplying Equation (2.31) through by this integrating factor, we obtain

$$xe^{2x}\frac{dy}{dx} + e^{2x}(2x+1)y = x$$

or

$$\frac{d}{dx}[xe^{2x}y] = x.$$

Integrating, we obtain the solution

$$xe^{2x}y = \frac{x^2}{2} + c$$

or

$$y = \frac{1}{2}xe^{-2x} + \frac{c}{x}e^{-2x},$$

where c is an arbitrary constant.

Example 2.15. Solve the initial-value problem which consists of the differential equation

(2.32)
$$(x^2 + 1)\frac{dy}{dx} + 4xy = x$$

and the initial condition

(2.33)
$$y(2) = 1.$$

The differential equation (2.32) is not in the form (2.26). We therefore divide by $x^2 + 1$ to obtain

(2.34)
$$\frac{dy}{dx} + \frac{4x}{x^2+1}y = \frac{x}{x^2+1}.$$

Equation (2.34) is in the standard form (2.26), where $P(x) = \dfrac{4x}{x^2 + 1}$. An integrating factor is

$$e^{\int P\,dx} = e^{\int \frac{4x\,dx}{x^2+1}} = e^{\ln(x^2+1)^2} = (x^2 + 1)^2.$$

Multiplying equation (2.34) through by this integrating factor, we have

$$(x^2 + 1)^2\frac{dy}{dx} + 4x(x^2 + 1)y = x(x^2 + 1)$$

or

$$\frac{d}{dx}[(x^2 + 1)^2 y] = x^3 + x.$$

We now integrate to obtain the general solution of equation (2.32) in the form

$$(x^2 + 1)^2 y = \frac{x^4}{4} + \frac{x^2}{2} + c.$$

Applying the initial condition (2.33), we have

$$25 = 6 + c.$$

Thus $c = 19$ and the solution of the initial-value problem under consideration is

$$(x^2 + 1)^2 y = \frac{x^4}{4} + \frac{x^2}{2} + 19.$$

Example 2.16.   Consider the differential equation

(2.35) $$y^2\,dx + (3xy - 1)\,dy = 0.$$

Solving for $\dfrac{dy}{dx}$, this becomes

$$\frac{dy}{dx} = \frac{y^2}{1 - 3xy},$$

which is clearly *not* linear in y. Also, equation (2.35) is *not* exact, separable, or homogeneous. It appears to be of a type which we have not yet encountered; but let us look a little closer. Observe that in a first-order differential equation the roles of dx and dy are interchangeable. Looking at equation (2.35) with this in mind, we write it as

$$\frac{dx}{dy} = \frac{1 - 3xy}{y^2}$$

or

(2.36) $$\frac{dx}{dy} + \frac{3}{y}x = \frac{1}{y^2}.$$

Now observe that equation (2.36) is of the form

$$\frac{dx}{dy} + P(y)x = Q(y)$$

and so is *linear in x*. Thus the theory developed in this section may be applied to the equation (2.36) merely by interchanging the roles played by x and y. Thus an integrating factor is

$$e^{\int P\,dy} = e^{\int \frac{3}{y}\,dy} = e^{\ln y^3} = y^3.$$

Multiplying (2.36) by y^3 we obtain

$$y^3 \frac{dx}{dy} + 3y^2 x = y$$

or

$$\frac{d}{dy}[y^3 x] = y.$$

Integrating, we find the solution in the form

$$y^3 x = \frac{y^2}{2} + c$$

or

$$x = \frac{1}{2y} + \frac{c}{y^3},$$

where c is an arbitrary constant.

B. Bernoulli Equations

We now consider a rather special type of equation which can be reduced to a linear equation by an appropriate transformation. This is the so-called Bernoulli equation.

DEFINITION.   An equation of the form

(2.37)
$$\frac{dy}{dx} + P(x)y = Q(x)y^n$$

is called a *Bernoulli Differential Equation.*

We observe that if $n = 1$, the Bernoulli equation (2.37) reduces to the separable linear equation

$$\frac{dy}{dx} + [P(x) - Q(x)]y = 0.$$

Therefore in this special case the equation (2.37) is readily solvable as either a separable equation or a linear equation. However, in the general case in which $n \neq 1$ this simple situation does not hold and we must proceed in a different manner. We now state and prove Theorem 2.5, which gives a method of solution in the general case.

THEOREM 2.5.   Suppose $n \neq 1$.   Then the transformation $v = y^{1-n}$ reduces the Bernoulli equation

(2.37)
$$\frac{dy}{dx} + P(x)y = Q(x)y^n$$

to a linear equation in v.

Proof.   We first multiply Equation (2.37) by y^{-n}, thereby expressing it in the equivalent form

(2.38)
$$y^{-n}\frac{dy}{dx} + P(x)y^{1-n} = Q(x).$$

If we let $v = y^{1-n}$, then $\dfrac{dv}{dx} = (1-n)y^{-n}\dfrac{dy}{dx}$ and Equation (2.38) transforms into

$$\frac{1}{1-n}\frac{dv}{dx} + P(x)v = Q(x)$$

or, equivalently,

$$\frac{dv}{dx} + (1-n)P(x)v = (1-n)Q(x).$$

Letting

$$P_1(x) = (1-n)P(x)$$

and

$$Q_1(x) = (1-n)Q(x),$$

this may be written

$$\frac{dv}{dx} + P_1(x)v = Q_1(x),$$

which is linear in v.   *Q.E.D.*

Example 2.17.

(2.39)
$$\frac{dy}{dx} + y = xy^3.$$

This is a Bernoulli differential equation, where $n = 3$. We first multiply the equation through by y^{-3}, thereby expressing it in the equivalent form

(2.40)
$$y^{-3}\frac{dy}{dx} + y^{-2} = x.$$

If we let $v = y^{1-n} = y^{-2}$, then $\dfrac{dv}{dx} = -2y^{-3}\dfrac{dy}{dx}$ and Equation (2.40) transforms into the linear equation

$$-\frac{1}{2}\frac{dv}{dx} + v = x.$$

Writing this linear equation in the standard form

(2.41)
$$\frac{dv}{dx} - 2v = -2x,$$

we see that an integrating factor for this equation is

$$e^{\int P\,dx} = e^{-\int 2\,dx} = e^{-2x}.$$

Multiplying (2.41) by e^{-2x}, we find

$$e^{-2x}\frac{dv}{dx} - 2e^{-2x}v = -2xe^{-2x}$$

or

$$\frac{d}{dx}[e^{-2x}v] = -2xe^{-2x}.$$

Integrating, we find

$$e^{-2x}v = \frac{1}{2}e^{-2x}(2x+1) + c$$

or

$$v = x + \frac{1}{2} + ce^{2x}.$$

But

$$v = \frac{1}{y^2}.$$

Thus we obtain the solution of (2.39) in the form

$$\frac{1}{y^2} = x + \frac{1}{2} + ce^{2x}.$$

Exercises

Solve the given differential equations in Exercises 1 through 15.

1. $\dfrac{dy}{dx} + \dfrac{3y}{x} = 6x^2$.

2. $x^4\dfrac{dy}{dx} + 2x^3y = 1$.

3. $\dfrac{dx}{dt} + \dfrac{x}{t^2} = \dfrac{1}{t^2}$.

4. $(u^2 + 1)\dfrac{dv}{du} + 4uv = 3u$.

5. $x\dfrac{dy}{dx} + \dfrac{2x+1}{x+1}y = x - 1$.

6. $(x^2 + x - 2)\dfrac{dy}{dx} + 3(x+1)y = x - 1$.

7. $x\,dy + (xy + y - 1)dx = 0$.

8. $y\,dx + (xy^2 + x - y)dy = 0$.

9. $\dfrac{dr}{d\theta} + r\tan\theta = \cos\theta$.

10. $\cos\theta dr + (r\sin\theta - \cos^4\theta)d\theta = 0.$

11. $(\cos^2 x - y\cos x)dx - (1 + \sin x)dy = 0.$

12. $\dfrac{dy}{dx} - \dfrac{y}{x} = -\dfrac{y^2}{x}.$

13. $x\dfrac{dy}{dx} + y = -2x^6 y^4.$

14. $dy + (4y - 8y^{-3})x\,dx = 0.$

15. $\dfrac{dx}{dt} + \dfrac{t+1}{2t}x = \dfrac{t+1}{xt}.$

Solve the initial-value problems in Exercises 16 though 22.

16. $\begin{cases} x\dfrac{dy}{dx} - 2y = 2x^4 \\[2mm] y(2) = 8. \end{cases}$

17. $\begin{cases} \dfrac{dy}{dx} + 3x^2 y = x^2 \\[2mm] y(0) = 2. \end{cases}$

18. $\begin{cases} 2x\,(y+1)dx - (x^2 + 1)dy = 0 \\[2mm] y(1) = -5. \end{cases}$

19. $\begin{cases} \dfrac{dr}{d\theta} + r\tan\theta = \cos^2\theta \\[2mm] r\left(\dfrac{\pi}{4}\right) = 1. \end{cases}$

20. $\begin{cases} \dfrac{dx}{dt} - x = \sin 2t \\[2mm] x(0) = 0. \end{cases}$

21. $\begin{cases} \dfrac{dy}{dx} + \dfrac{y}{2x} = \dfrac{x}{y^3} \\[2mm] y(1) = 2. \end{cases}$

22. $\begin{cases} x\dfrac{dy}{dx} + y = (xy)^{3/2} \\[2mm] y(1) = 4. \end{cases}$

23. Consider the equation $a\dfrac{dy}{dx} + by = ke^{-\lambda x}$, where a, b, and k are positive constants and λ is a nonnegative constant.

   (a) Solve this equation.

   (b) Show that if $\lambda = 0$ every solution approaches k/b as $x \to \infty$ but if $\lambda > 0$ every solution approaches 0 as $x \to \infty$.

24. Solve the initial-value problem

$$\begin{cases} \dfrac{dy}{dx} + y = f(x), & \text{where } f(x) = \begin{cases} 2, 0 \le x < 1, \\ 0, x \ge 1, \end{cases} \\ y(0) = 0. \end{cases}$$

25. Solve the initial-value problem

$$\begin{cases} \dfrac{dy}{dx} + y = f(x), & \text{where } f(x) = \begin{cases} 5, 0 \le x < 10, \\ 1, x \ge 10, \end{cases} \\ y(0) = 6. \end{cases}$$

26. Consider the differential equation $\dfrac{dy}{dx} + P(x)y = 0.$

    (a) Show that if f and g are two solutions of this equation and c_1 and c_2 are arbitrary constants, then $c_1 f + c_2 g$ is also a solution of this equation.

    (b) Extending the result of (a), show that if $f_1, f_2, \cdots, f_n$ are n solutions of this equation and $c_1, c_2, \cdots, c_n$ are n arbitrary constants, then

$$\sum_{k=1}^{n} c_k f_k$$

is also a solution of this equation.

27. Consider the differential equation

(A) $$\frac{dy}{dx} + P(x)y = 0,$$

where P is continuous on a real interval I.

    (a) Show that the function f such that $f(x) = 0$ for all $x \in I$ is a solution of this equation.

    (b) Show that if f is a solution of (A) such that $f(x_0) = 0$ for some $x_0 \in I$, then $f(x) = 0$ for all $x \in I$.

    (c) Show that if f and g are two solutions of (A) such that $f(x_0) = g(x_0)$ for some $x_0 \in I$, then $f(x) = g(x)$ for all $x \in I$.

28. (a) Prove that if f and g are two different solutions of

(A) $$\frac{dy}{dx} + P(x)y = Q(x),$$

then $f - g$ is a solution of the equation

$$\frac{dy}{dx} + P(x)y = 0.$$

    (b) Thus show that if f and g are two different solutions of Equation (A) and c is an arbitrary constant, then

$$c(f - g) + f$$

is a general solution of (A).

29. (a) Let f_1 be a solution of

$$\frac{dy}{dx} + P(x)y = Q_1(x)$$

and f_2 be a solution of

$$\frac{dy}{dx} + P(x)y = Q_2(x),$$

where P, Q_1, and Q_2 are all defined on the same real interval I. Prove that $f_1 + f_2$ is a solution of

$$\frac{dy}{dx} + P(x)y = Q_1(x) + Q_2(x)$$

on I.

    (b) Use the result of (a) to solve the equation

$$\frac{dy}{dx} + y = 2\sin x + 5\sin 2x.$$

30. (a) Extend the result of Exercise 29(a) to cover the case of the equation

$$\frac{dy}{dx} + P(x)y = \sum_{k=1}^{n} Q_k(x),$$

where P, $Q_k(k = 1,2, \cdots, n)$ are all defined on the same real interval I.

    (b) Use the result obtained in (a) to solve the equation

$$\frac{dy}{dx} + y = \sum_{k=1}^{5} \sin kx.$$

31. (a) Show that the transformation $v = f(y)$ reduces the equation

$$\frac{df(y)}{dy}\frac{dy}{dx} + P(x)f(y) = Q(x)$$

to a linear equation in v.

    (b) Use the result of (a) to solve the equation

$$(y + 1)\frac{dy}{dx} + x(y^2 + 2y) = x.$$

32. The equation

(A) $$\frac{dy}{dx} = A(x)y^2 + B(x)y + C(x)$$

is called Riccati's Equation.

    (a) Show that if $A(x) = 0$ for all x, then Equation (A) is a linear equation, whereas if $C(x) = 0$ for all x, then equation (A) is a Bernoulli equation.

    (b) Show that if f is any solution of the equation (A), then the transformation

$$y = f + \frac{1}{v}$$

reduces (A) to a linear equation in v.

    (c) Consider the Riccati equation

(B) $$\frac{dy}{dx} = (1 - x)y^2 + (2x - 1)y - x.$$

and observe that the function f defined by $f(x) = 1$ is a solution. Use this fact and the result of (b) to find a solution of (B) which contains an arbitrary constant.

2.4 Special Integrating Factors and Transformations

We have thus far encountered five distinct types of first-order equations for which solutions may be obtained by exact methods, namely, <u>Exact, Separable, Homogeneous, Linear, and Bernoulli equations</u>. In the case of exact equations, we follow a definite procedure to directly obtain the general solution. For the other four types definite procedures for solution are also available, but in these cases the procedures are actually not quite so direct. In the cases of both separable and linear equations we actually multiply by appropriate integrating factors which reduce the given equations to equations which are of the more basic exact type. For both homogeneous and Bernoulli equations we make appropriate transformations which reduce such equations to equations which are of the more basic separable and linear types, respectively.

This suggests two general plans of attack to be used in solving a differential equation which is *not* of one of the five types mentioned. Either (1) we might multiply the given equation by an appropriate integrating factor and directly reduce it to an exact equation, or (2) we might make an appropriate transformation which will reduce the given equation to an equation of some more basic type (say, one of the five types already studied). Unfortunately no general directions can be given for finding an appropriate integrating factor or transformation in all cases. However, there is a variety of special types of equations which either possess special types of integrating factors or to which special transformations may be applied. We shall consider a few of these in this section. Since these types are relatively unimportant, in most cases we shall simply state the relevant theorem and leave the proof to the exercises.

A. Finding Integrating Factors

The so-called separable equations considered in Section 2.2 of this chapter always possess integrating factors which may be determined by immediate inspection. While it is true that some nonseparable equations also possess integrating factors which may be determined "by inspection," such equations are rarely encountered except in differential equations texts on pages devoted to an exposition of this dubious "method." Even then a considerable amount of knowledge and skill are often required.

Let us attempt to attack the problem more systematically. Suppose the equation

$$(2.42) \qquad\qquad M\,dx + N\,dy = 0$$

is *not* exact and that μ is an integrating factor of it. Then the equation

$$(2.43) \qquad\qquad \mu M\,dx + \mu N\,dy = 0$$

is exact. Now using the criterion (2.7) for exactness, Equation (2.43) is exact if and only if

$$\frac{\partial}{\partial y}(\mu M) = \frac{\partial}{\partial x}(\mu N).$$

This equation reduces to

$$(2.44) \qquad\qquad N\frac{\partial \mu}{\partial x} - M\frac{\partial \mu}{\partial y} = \left(\frac{\partial M}{\partial y} - \frac{\partial N}{\partial x}\right)\mu,$$

and thus μ is an integrating factor of the differential equation (2.42) if and only if it is a solution of the differential equation (2.44). Equation (2.44) is a partial differential equation for the general integrating factor μ, and we are in no position to attempt to solve such an equation. Let us instead attempt to determine integrating factors of certain special types. But what special types might we consider? Let us recall that the linear differential equation

$$\frac{dy}{dx} + Py = Q$$

always possesses the integrating factor $e^{\int P dx}$, which depends only upon x. Perhaps other equations also have integrating factors which depend only upon x. We therefore multiply Equation (2.42) by μ, where μ depends upon x alone. We obtain

$$\mu M dx + \mu N dy = 0.$$

This is exact if and only if

$$\frac{\partial}{\partial y}(\mu M) = \frac{\partial}{\partial x}(\mu N).$$

Now M and N are known functions of both x and y, but here the integrating factor μ depends only upon x. Thus the above condition reduces to

$$\mu \frac{\partial M}{\partial y} = \mu \frac{\partial N}{\partial x} + N \frac{d\mu}{dx}$$

or

(2.45)
$$\frac{d\mu}{\mu} = \frac{1}{N}\left(\frac{\partial M}{\partial y} - \frac{\partial N}{\partial x}\right)dx.$$

If

$$\frac{1}{N}\left(\frac{\partial M}{\partial y} - \frac{\partial N}{\partial x}\right)$$

involves the variable y, this equation then involves two dependent variables and we again have difficulties. However, if

$$\frac{1}{N}\left(\frac{\partial M}{\partial y} - \frac{\partial N}{\partial x}\right)$$

depends upon x only, Equation (2.45) is a "separated" equation in x and the single dependent variable μ. In this case we may integrate to obtain the integrating factor

$$\mu = e^{\int \frac{1}{N}\left(\frac{\partial M}{\partial y} - \frac{\partial N}{\partial x}\right)dx}.$$

In like manner, if

$$\frac{1}{M}\left(\frac{\partial N}{\partial x} - \frac{\partial M}{\partial y}\right)$$

depends upon y only, then we may obtain an integrating factor which depends only on y. We summarize these observations in the following theorem.

THEOREM 2.6. Consider the differential equation

(2.42) $Mdx + Ndy = 0.$

If

(2.46) $$\frac{1}{N}\left(\frac{\partial M}{\partial y} - \frac{\partial N}{\partial x}\right)$$

depends upon x only, then

(2.47) $$e^{\int \frac{1}{N}\left(\frac{\partial M}{\partial y} - \frac{\partial N}{\partial x}\right)dx}$$

is an integrating factor of the equation (2.42).

If

(2.48) $$\frac{1}{M}\left(\frac{\partial N}{\partial x} - \frac{\partial M}{\partial y}\right)$$

depends upon y only, then

(2.49) $$e^{\int \frac{1}{M}\left(\frac{\partial N}{\partial x} - \frac{\partial M}{\partial y}\right)dy}$$

is an integrating factor of the equation (2.42).

We emphasize that given a differential equation, we have no assurance in general that either of these procedures will apply. It may well turn out that (2.46) involves y and (2.48) involves x for the differential equation under consideration. Then we must seek other procedures. However, since the calculation of the expressions (2.46) and (2.48) is generally quite simple, it is often worthwhile to calculate them before trying something more complicated.

Example 2.18.

(2.50) $(2x^2 + y)dx + (x^2y - x)dy = 0.$

Let us first observe that this equation is *not* exact, separable, homogeneous, linear, or Bernoulli. Let us then see if Theorem 2.6 applies. Here $M = 2x^2 + y$, and $N = x^2y - x$, and the expression (2.46) becomes

$$\frac{1}{x^2y - x}[1 - (2xy - 1)] = \frac{2(1 - xy)}{x(xy - 1)} = -\frac{2}{x}.$$

This depends upon x only, and so

$$e^{-\int \frac{2}{x}dx} = e^{-2\ln|x|} = \frac{1}{x^2}$$

is an integrating factor of Equation (2.50). Multiplying (2.50) by this integrating factor, we obtain the equation

(2.51) $$\left(2 + \frac{y}{x^2}\right)dx + \left(y - \frac{1}{x}\right)dy = 0.$$

The student may readily verify that equation (2.51) is indeed exact and that the solution is

$$2x + \frac{y^2}{2} - \frac{y}{x} = c.$$

More and more specialized results concerning particular types of integrating factors corresponding to particular types of equations are known. However, instead of going into such special cases we shall now proceed to investigate certain useful transformations.

B. A Special Transformation

We have already made use of transformations in reducing both homogeneous and Bernoulli equations to more tractable types. Another type of equation which can be reduced to a more basic type by means of a suitable transformation is an equation of the form

$$(a_1x + b_1y + c_1)dx + (a_2x + b_2y + c_2)dy = 0.$$

We state the following theorem concerning this equation.

THEOREM 2.7.   Consider the equation

(2.52) $$\qquad (a_1x + b_1y + c_1)dx + (a_2x + b_2y + c_2)dy = 0,$$

where a_1, b_1, c_1, a_2, b_2, and c_2 are constants.

Case 1.   If $\dfrac{a_2}{a_1} \neq \dfrac{b_2}{b_1}$, then the transformation

$$x = X + h,$$
$$y = Y + k,$$

where (h,k) is the solution of the system

$$a_1h + b_1k + c_1 = 0$$
$$a_2h + b_2k + c_2 = 0,$$

reduces the equation (2.52) to the homogeneous equation

$$(a_1X + b_1Y)dX + (a_2X + b_2Y)dY = 0$$

in the variables X and Y.

Case 2.   If $\dfrac{a_2}{a_1} = \dfrac{b_2}{b_1} = k$, then the transformation $z = a_1x + b_1y$ reduces the equation (2.52) to a separable equation in the variables x and z.

Examples 2.19 and 2.20 illustrate the two cases of this theorem.

Example 2.19.

(2.53) $$\qquad (x - 2y + 1)dx + (4x - 3y - 6)dy = 0.$$

Here $a_1 = 1$, $b_1 = -2$, $a_2 = 4$, $b_2 = -3$, and so $\dfrac{a_2}{a_1} = 4$ but $\dfrac{b_2}{b_1} = \dfrac{3}{2} \neq \dfrac{a_2}{a_1}$.

Therefore this is Case 1 of Theorem 2.7. We make the transformation

$$x = X + h$$
$$y = Y + k,$$

where (h,k) is the solution of the system

$$h - 2k + 1 = 0$$
$$4h - 3k - 6 = 0.$$

The solution of this system is $h = 3$, $k = 2$, and so the transformation is

$$x = X + 3$$
$$y = Y + 2.$$

This reduces equation (2.53) to the homogeneous equation

(2.54) $$(X - 2Y)dX + (4X - 3Y)dY = 0.$$

Now following the procedure in Section 2.2 we first put this homogeneous equation in the form

$$\frac{dY}{dX} = \frac{1 - 2\left(\frac{Y}{X}\right)}{3\left(\frac{Y}{X}\right) - 4}$$

and let $Y = vX$ to obtain

$$v + X\frac{dv}{dX} = \frac{1 - 2v}{3v - 4}.$$

This reduces to

(2.55) $$\frac{(3v - 4)dv}{3v^2 - 2v - 1} = -\frac{dX}{X}.$$

Integrating (we recommend the use of tables here), we obtain

$$\frac{1}{2}\ln|3v^2 - 2v - 1| - \frac{3}{4}\ln\left|\frac{3v - 3}{3v + 1}\right| = -\ln|X| + \ln|c_1|,$$

or

$$\ln(3v^2 - 2v - 1)^2 - \ln\left|\frac{3v - 3}{3v + 1}\right|^3 = \ln\left|\frac{c_2}{X^4}\right|,$$

or

$$\ln\left|\frac{(3v + 1)^5}{v - 1}\right| = \ln\left|\frac{c_3}{X^4}\right|,$$

or, finally, $X^4(3v + 1)^5 = c(v - 1)$.

This is the general solution of the separable equation (2.55). Now replacing v by Y/X we obtain the general solution of the homogeneous equation (2.54) in the form

$$(3Y + X)^5 = c(Y - X).$$

Finally, replacing X by $x - 3$ and Y by $y - 2$ from the original transformation, we obtain the general solution of the differential equation (2.53) in the form

$$[3(y - 2) + (x - 3)]^5 = c(y - 2 - x + 3)$$

or

$$(x + 3y - 9)^5 = c(y - x + 1).$$

Example 2.20.

(2.56) $$(x + 2y + 3)dx + (2x + 4y - 1)dy = 0.$$

Here $a_1 = 1$, $b_1 = 2$, $a_2 = 2$, $b_2 = 4$, and $\dfrac{a_2}{a_1} = \dfrac{b_2}{b_1} = 2$. Therefore this is Case 2 of Theorem 2.7. We therefore let

$$z = x + 2y,$$

and equation (2.56) transforms into

$$(z + 3)dx + (2z - 1)\left(\frac{dz - dx}{2}\right) = 0$$

or

$$7dx + (2z - 1)dz = 0,$$

which is separable. Integrating, we have

$$7x + z^2 - z = c.$$

Replacing z by $x + 2y$ we obtain the solution of equation (2.56) in the form

$$7x + (x + 2y)^2 - (x + 2y) = c$$

or

$$x^2 + 4xy + 4y^2 + 6x - 2y = c.$$

C. Other Special Types and Methods; An Important Reference

Many other special types of first-order equations exist for which corresponding special methods of solution are known. We shall not go into such highly specialized types in this book. Instead we refer the reader to the book *Differentialgleichungen: Losungs-methoden und Losungen* by E. Kamke (Chelsea: New York, 1948). This remarkable volume contains discussions of a large number of special types of equations and their solutions. We strongly suggest that the reader consult this book whenever he encounters an unfamiliar type of equation. Of course one may encounter an equation for which no exact method of solution is known. In such a case one must resort to various methods of approximation. We shall consider some of these general methods in Chapter 8.

Exercises

Solve each differential equation in Exercises 1 through 4 by first finding an integrating factor.

1. $(5xy + 4y^2 + 1)dx + (x^2 + 2xy)dy = 0$.

2. $(2x + \tan y)dx + (x - x^2\tan y)dy = 0$.

3. $[y^2(x + 1) + y]dx + (2xy + 1)dy = 0.$

4. $(4xy^2 + 6y)dx + (5x^2y + 8x)dy = 0.$

[*Hint.* This differential equation has an integrating factor of the form $x^p y^q.$]

Solve each differential equation in Exercises 5 through 7 by making a suitable transformation.

5. $(5x + 2y + 1)dx + (2x + y + 1)dy = 0.$

6. $(3x - y + 1)dx - (6x - 2y - 3)dy = 0,$

7. $(x - 2y - 3)dx + (2x + y - 1)dy = 0.$

Solve the initial-value problems in Exercises 8 through 10.

8. $\begin{cases} (6x + 4y + 1)dx + (4x + 2y + 2)dy = 0 \\ y(\frac{1}{2}) = 3. \end{cases}$

9. $\begin{cases} (3x - y - 6)dx + (x + y + 2)dy = 0 \\ y(2) = -2. \end{cases}$

10. $\begin{cases} (2x + 3y + 1)dx + (4x + 6y + 1)dy = 0 \\ y(-2) = 2. \end{cases}$

11. Prove Theorem 2.6.

12. Prove Theorem 2.7.

13. Show that if μ and ν are integrating factors of

(A) $$Mdx + Ndy = 0$$

such that μ/ν is not constant, then

$$\mu = c\nu$$

is a solution of Equation (A) for every constant c.

14. Show that if the equation

(A) $$Mdx + Ndy = 0$$

is homogeneous and $Mx + Ny \neq 0$, then $1/(Mx + Ny)$ is an integrating factor of (A).

15. Show that if the equation $Mdx + Ndy = 0$ is both homogeneous and exact and if $Mx + Ny$ is not a constant, then the solution of this equation is $Mx + Ny = c$, where c is an arbitrary constant.

SUGGESTED READING

I. Basic Methods:

    Agnew (1)
    Ford (17)
    Kaplan (30)
    Martin and Reissner (38)
    Rainville (45)

II. Further Methods:

    Ince (26)
    Kamke (28)

3

APPLICATIONS OF FIRST-ORDER EQUATIONS

In Chapter 1 we pointed out that differential equations originate from the mathematical formulation of a great variety of problems in science and engineering. In this chapter we consider problems that give rise to some of the types of first-order ordinary differential equations studied in Chapter 2. First, we formulate the problem mathematically, thereby obtaining a differential equation. Then we solve the equation and attempt to interpret the solution in terms of the quantities involved in the original problem.

3.1. Orthogonal and Oblique Trajectories

A. Orthogonal Trajectories

DEFINITION. Let

$$(3.1) \qquad\qquad F(x,y,c) = 0$$

be a given one-parameter family of curves in the xy plane. A curve which intersects the curves of the family (3.1) at right angles is called an *orthogonal trajectory* of the given family.

Example 3.1. Consider the family of circles

$$(3.2) \qquad\qquad x^2 + y^2 = c^2$$

with center at the origin and radius c. Each straight line through the origin,

$$(3.3) \qquad\qquad y = kx$$

is an orthogonal trajectory of the family of circles (3.2). Conversely, each circle of the family (3.2) is an orthogonal trajectory of the family of straight lines (3.3). The families (3.2) and (3.3) are orthogonal trajectories of each other. In Figure 3.1 several members

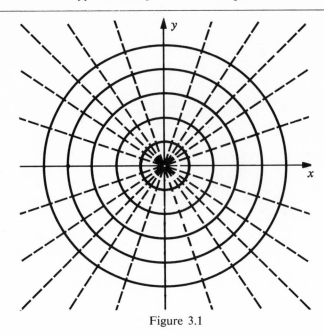

Figure 3.1

of the family of circles (3.2), drawn solidly, and several members of the family of straight lines (3.3), drawn with dashes, are shown.

The problem of finding the orthogonal trajectories of a given family of curves arises in many physical situations. For example, in a two-dimensional electric field the lines of force (flux lines) and the equipotential curves are orthogonal trajectories of each other.

We now proceed to find the orthogonal trajectories of a family of curves

(3.1) $F(x,y,c) = 0.$

We obtain the differential equation of the family (3.1) by first differentiating the equation (3.1) implicitly with respect to x and then eliminating the parameter c between the derived equation so obtained and the given equation (3.1) itself. We assume that the resulting differential equation of the family (3.1) can be expressed in the form

(3.4) $\dfrac{dy}{dx} = f(x,y).$

Thus the curve C of the given family (3.1) which passes through the point (x,y) has the slope $f(x,y)$ there. Since an orthogonal trajectory of the given family intersects each curve of the family at right angles, the slope of the orthogonal trajectory to C at (x,y) is

$$-\frac{1}{f(x,y)}.$$

Thus the differential equation of the family of orthogonal trajectories is

(3.5) $\dfrac{dy}{dx} = -\dfrac{1}{f(x,y)}.$

The general solution

$$G(x,y,c) = 0$$

of the differential equation (3.5) represents the family of orthogonal trajectories of the original family (3.1).

We summarize this procedure as follows:

Procedure for finding the orthogonal trajectories of a given family of curves.

Step (1). From the equation

(3.1) $$F(x,y,c) = 0$$

of the given family find the differential equation

(3.4) $$\frac{dy}{dx} = f(x,y)$$

of this family.

Step (2). In the differential equation $\frac{dy}{dx} = f(x,y)$ so found in step (1), replace $f(x,y)$ by its

negative reciprocal $-\dfrac{1}{f(x,y)}$. This gives the differential equation

(3.5) $$\frac{dy}{dx} = -\frac{1}{f(x,y)}$$

of the orthogonal trajectories.

Step (3). Obtain the general solution

$$G(x,y,c) = 0$$

of the differential equation (3.5), thus obtaining the desired family of orthogonal trajectories.

Caution. In Step (1), in finding the differential equation (3.4) of the given family be sure to eliminate the parameter c during the process.

Example 3.2.   In Example 3.1 we stated that the orthogonal trajectories of the family of circles

(3.2) $$x^2 + y^2 = c^2$$

are the family of straight lines

(3.3) $$y = kx.$$

Let us verify this using the procedure outlined above.

Step (1).   Differentiating the equation

(3.2) $$x^2 + y^2 = c^2$$

of the given family, we obtain

$$x + y\frac{dy}{dx} = 0.$$

From this we obtain the differential equation

(3.6) $$\frac{dy}{dx} = -\frac{x}{y}$$

of the given family (3.2). (Note that the parameter c was automatically eliminated in this case.)

Step (2).   We replace $-\dfrac{x}{y}$ by its negative reciprocal $\dfrac{y}{x}$ in the differential equation (3.6) to obtain the differential equation

$$(3.7) \qquad\qquad \frac{dy}{dx} = \frac{y}{x}$$

of the orthogonal trajectories.

Step (3).   We now solve the differential equation (3.7).
Separating variables, we have

$$\frac{dy}{y} = \frac{dx}{x};$$

and integrating, we obtain

$$(3.3) \qquad\qquad y = kx.$$

This is the general solution of the differential equation (3.7) and thus represents the family of orthogonal trajectories of the given family of circles (3.2) (except for the single line $x = 0$).

Example 3.3.   Find the orthogonal trajectories of the family of parabolas $y = cx^2$.

Step (1).   We first find the differential equation of the given family

$$(3.8) \qquad\qquad y = cx^2.$$

Differentiating, we obtain

$$(3.9) \qquad\qquad \frac{dy}{dx} = 2cx.$$

Eliminating the parameter c between Equations (3.8) and (3.9), we obtain the differential equation of the family (3.8) in the form

$$(3.10) \qquad\qquad \frac{dy}{dx} = \frac{2y}{x}.$$

Step (2).   We now find the differential equation of the orthogonal trajectories by replacing $\dfrac{2y}{x}$ in (3.10) by its negative reciprocal, obtaining

$$(3.11) \qquad\qquad \frac{dy}{dx} = -\frac{x}{2y}.$$

Step (3).   We now solve the differential equation (3.11).   Separating variables, we have

$$2y\,dy = -x\,dx.$$

Integrating, we obtain the general solution of (3.11) in the form

$$x^2 + 2y^2 = k^2,$$

where k is an arbitrary constant.   This is the family of orthogonal trajectories of (3.8);

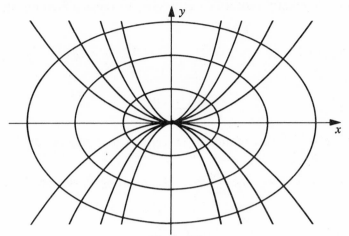

Figure 3.2

it is clearly a family of ellipses with centers at the origin and major axes along the x axis. Some members of the original family of parabolas and some of the orthogonal trajectories (the ellipses) are shown in Figure 3.2.

B. Oblique Trajectories

DEFINITION.   Let

(3.12) $F(x,y,c) = 0$

be a one-parameter family of curves. A curve which intersects the curves of the family (3.12) at a constant angle $\alpha \neq 90°$ is called an *oblique trajectory* of the given family.

Suppose the differential equation of a family is

(3.13) $\dfrac{dy}{dx} = f(x,y).$

Then the curve of the family (3.13) through the point (x,y) has slope $f(x,y)$ at (x,y) and hence its tangent line has angle of inclination $\tan^{-1}[f(x,y)]$ there. The tangent line of an oblique trajectory which intersects this curve at the angle α will thus have angle of inclination

$$\phi = \tan^{-1}[f(x,y)] + \alpha$$

at the point (x,y). Hence the slope of this oblique trajectory is given by

$$\tan[\tan^{-1}f(x,y) + \alpha] = \frac{f(x,y) + \tan \alpha}{1 - f(x,y)\tan \alpha}.$$

Thus the differential equation of such a family of oblique trajectories is given by

$$\frac{dy}{dx} = \frac{f(x,y) + \tan \alpha}{1 - f(x,y)\tan \alpha}.$$

Thus to obtain a family of oblique trajectories intersecting a given family of curves at the constant angle $\alpha \neq 90°$, we may follow the three steps in the above procedure (page 59) for finding the orthogonal trajectories, except that we replace Step (2) by the following step:

Step (2′).   In the differential equation $\dfrac{dy}{dx} = f(x,y)$ of the given family, replace $f(x,y)$ by the expression

(3.14) $$\frac{f(x,y) + \tan \alpha}{1 - f(x,y) \tan \alpha}.$$

Example 3.4.   Find a family of oblique trajectories that intersect the family of straight lines $y = cx$ at angle $45°$.

Step (1).   From $y = cx$, we find $\dfrac{dy}{dx} = c$. Eliminating c, we obtain the differential equation

(3.15) $$\frac{dy}{dx} = \frac{y}{x}$$

of the given family of straight lines.

Step (2′).   We replace $f(x,y) = \dfrac{y}{x}$ in Equation (3.15) by

$$\frac{f(x,y) + \tan \alpha}{1 - f(x,y) \tan \alpha} = \frac{\dfrac{y}{x} + 1}{1 - \dfrac{y}{x}} = \frac{x + y}{x - y}$$

($\tan \alpha = \tan 45° = 1$ here.)
Thus the differential equation of the desired oblique trajectories is

(3.16) $$\frac{dy}{dx} = \frac{x + y}{x - y}.$$

Step (3).   We now solve the differential equation (3.16). Observing that it is a homogeneous differential equation, we let $y = vx$ to obtain

$$v + x\frac{dv}{dx} = \frac{1 + v}{1 - v}.$$

After simplifications this becomes

$$\frac{(v - 1)dv}{v^2 + 1} = -\frac{dx}{x}.$$

Integrating we obtain

$$\frac{1}{2} \ln (v^2 + 1) - \arctan v = -\ln |x| - \ln |c|$$

or

$$\ln c^2 x^2 (v^2 + 1) - 2 \arctan v = 0.$$

Replacing v by $\dfrac{y}{x}$, we obtain the family of oblique trajectories in the form

$$\ln c^2(x^2 + y^2) - 2 \arctan \frac{y}{x} = 0.$$

Exercises

In Exercises 1–9 find the orthogonal trajectories of each given family of curves. In each case sketch several members of the family and several of the orthogonal trajectories on the same set of axes.

1. $y = cx^3$.

2. $y^2 = cx$.

3. $cx^2 + y^2 = 1$.

4. $y = e^{cx}$.

5. $y = x - 1 + ce^{-x}$.

6. $x - y = cx^2$.

7. $x^2 + y^2 = cx^3$.

8. $x^2 = 2y - 1 + ce^{-2y}$.

9. $x = \dfrac{y^2}{4} + \dfrac{c}{y^2}$.

10. Find the orthogonal trajectories of the family of ellipses having center at the origin, a focus at the point $(c, 0)$ and semi-major axis of length $2c$.

11. Find the orthogonal trajectories of the family of circles which are tangent to the y axis at the origin.

12. Find the value of K such that the parabolas $y = c_1x^2 + K$ are the orthogonal trajectories of the family of ellipses $x^2 + 2y^2 - y = c_2$.

13. Find the value of n such that the curves $x^n + y^n = c_1$ are the orthogonal trajectories of the family $y = \dfrac{x}{1 - c_2x}$.

14. A given family of curves is said to be *self-orthogonal* if its family of orthogonal trajectories is the same as the given family. Show that the family of parabolas $y^2 = 2cx + c^2$ is self-orthogonal.

3.2 Problems in Mechanics

A. Introduction

Before we apply our knowledge of differential equations to certain problems in mechanics, let us briefly recall certain principles of that subject. The *momentum* of a body is defined to be the product mv of its mass m and its velocity v. The velocity v and hence the momentum are vector quantities. We now state the following basic law of mechanics:

Newton's Second Law

The time rate of change of momentum of a body is proportional to the resultant force acting on the body and is in the direction of this resultant force.

In mathematical language, this law states that

$$\frac{d}{dt}(mv) = KF,$$

where m is the mass of the body, v is its velocity, F is the resultant force acting upon it, and K is a constant of proportionality. If the mass m is considered constant, this reduces to

$$m\frac{dv}{dt} = KF,$$

or

(3.17)
$$a = K\frac{F}{m},$$

or

(3.18)
$$F = kma,$$

where $k = \frac{1}{K}$, and $a = \frac{dv}{dt}$ is the acceleration of the body. The form (3.17) is a direct mathematical statement of the manner in which Newton's Second Law is usually expressed in words, the mass being considered constant. However, we shall make use of the equivalent form (3.18). The magnitude of the constant of proportionality k depends upon the units employed for force, mass, and acceleration. Obviously the simplest systems of units are those for which $k = 1$. When such a system is used (3.18) reduces to

(3.19)
$$F = ma.$$

It is in this form that we shall use Newton's Second Law. Observe that equation (3.19) is a vector equation.

Several systems of units for which $k = 1$ are in use. In this text we shall use only two: the centimeter-gram-second system (cgs) and the English gravitational system (English). We summarize the various units of these two systems in the following table.

Table 3.1

	English system	cgs system
force	pound	dyne
mass	slug	gram
distance	foot	centimeter
time	second	second
acceleration	ft/sec^2	cm/sec^2

Recall that the force of gravitational attraction which the earth exerts on a body is called the weight of the body. The weight, being a force, is expressed in force units. Thus in the English system the weight is measured in pounds, and in the cgs system in dynes.

Let us now apply Newton's Second Law to a freely falling body (a body falling toward the earth in the absence of air resistance). Let the mass of the body be m and let w denote its weight. The only force acting on the body is its weight and so this is the resultant force. The acceleration is that due to gravity, denoted by g, which is approximately 32 ft/sec² in the English system or 980 cm/sec² in the cgs system (for points near the earth's surface). Newton's Second Law $F = ma$ thus reduces to $w = mg$. Thus

$$(3.20) \qquad m = \frac{w}{g},$$

a relation which we shall frequently employ.

Let us now consider a body B in rectilinear motion, that is, in motion along a straight line L. On L we choose a fixed reference point as origin O, a fixed direction as positive, and a unit of distance. Then the coordinate x of the position of B from the origin O tells us the distance or displacement of B. (See Figure 3.3.)

The *instantaneous velocity* of B is the time rate of change of x:

$$v = \frac{dx}{dt};$$

and the *instantaneous acceleration* of B is the time rate of change of v:

$$a = \frac{dv}{dt} = \frac{d^2x}{dt^2}.$$

Note that x, v, and a are vector quantities. All forces, displacements, velocities, and accelerations in the positive direction on L are positive quantities; while those in the negative direction are negative quantities.

If we now apply Newton's Second Law $F = ma$ to the motion of B along L, noting that

$$\frac{dv}{dt} = \frac{dv}{dx}\frac{dx}{dt} = v\frac{dv}{dx},$$

we may express the law in any of the following three forms:

$$(3.21) \qquad m\frac{dv}{dt} = F$$

$$(3.22) \qquad m\frac{d^2x}{dt^2} = F$$

$$(3.23) \qquad mv\frac{dv}{dx} = F,$$

where F is the resultant force acting on the body. The form to use depends upon the

Figure 3.3

way in which F is expressed. For example, if F is a function of time t only and we desire to obtain the velocity v as a function of t, we would use (3.21); whereas if F is expressed as a function of the displacement x and we wish to find v as a function of x, we would employ (3.23).

B. Falling Body Problems

We shall now consider some examples of a body falling through air toward the earth. In such a circumstance the body encounters air resistance as it falls. The amount of air resistance depends upon the velocity of the body, but no general law exactly expressing this dependence is known. In some instances the law $R = kv$ appears to be quite satisfactory, while in others $R = kv^2$ appears to be more exact. In any case, the constant of proportionality k in turn depends on several circumstances. In the examples which follow we shall assume certain reasonable resistance laws in each case. Thus we shall actually be dealing with idealized problems in which the true resistance law is approximated and in which certain comparatively negligible factors are disregarded.

Example 3.5. A body weighing 8 lb falls from rest toward the earth from a great height. As it falls, air resistance acts upon it, and we shall assume that this resistance (in lb) is numerically equal to $2v$, where v is the velocity (in ft/sec). Find the velocity and distance fallen at time t seconds.

Formulation. We choose the positive x axis vertically downward along the path of the body B and the origin at the point from which the body fell. The forces acting on the body are:

(1) F_1, its weight, 8 lb, which acts downward and hence is positive.
(2) F_2, the air resistance, numerically equal to $2v$, which acts upward and hence is the negative quantity $-2v$.

See Figure 3.4 where these forces are indicated.

Newton's Second Law $F = ma$ becomes

$$m\frac{dv}{dt} = F_1 + F_2$$

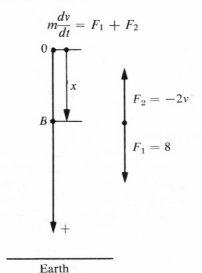

Figure 3.4

or, taking $g = 32$ and using $m = \dfrac{w}{g} = \dfrac{8}{32} = \dfrac{1}{4}$,

(3.24) $$\frac{1}{4}\frac{dv}{dt} = 8 - 2v.$$

Since the body was initially at rest, we have the initial condition

(3.25) $$v(0) = 0.$$

Solution. The equation (3.24) is separable. Separating variables, we have

$$\frac{dv}{8 - 2v} = 4dt.$$

Integrating we find

$$-\frac{1}{2}\ln|8 - 2v| = 4t + c_0,$$

which reduces to

$$8 - 2v = c_1 e^{-8t}.$$

Applying the condition (3.25) we find $c_1 = 8$. Thus the velocity at time t is given by

(3.26) $$v = 4(1 - e^{-8t}).$$

Now to determine the distance fallen at time t, we write (3.26) in the form

$$\frac{dx}{dt} = 4(1 - e^{-8t})$$

and note that $x(0) = 0$. Integrating the above equation, we obtain

$$x = 4\left(t + \frac{1}{8}e^{-8t}\right) + c_2.$$

Since $x = 0$ when $t = 0$, we find $c_2 = -\frac{1}{2}$ and hence the distance fallen is given by

(3.27) $$x = 4\left(t + \frac{1}{8}e^{-8t} - \frac{1}{8}\right).$$

Interpretation of Results. Equation (3.26) shows us that as $t \to \infty$, the velocity v approaches the *limiting velocity* 4 (ft/sec). We also observe that this limiting velocity is approximately attained in a very short time. Equation (3.27) states that as $t \to \infty$, x also $\to \infty$. Does this imply that the body will plow through the earth and continue forever? Of course not; for when the body reaches the earth's surface its motion will certainly cease. How then do we reconcile this obvious end to the motion with the statement of Equation (3.27)? It is simple; when the body reaches the earth's surface, the differential equation (3.24) and hence the equation (3.27) no longer apply!

Example 3.6. A paratrooper equipped with parachute and other essential equipment falls from rest toward the earth. The total weight of the man plus the equipment is w lb. Before the parachute opens, the air resistance R (in pounds) is numerically equal to kv^2, where k is a constant of proportionality and v is the velocity (in ft/sec). After the parachute opens the air resistance is considerably greater. Let us assume that it is then given by Kv^2, where the new proportionality constant K is considerably greater than k: $K \gg k$. If the parachute opens t_1 seconds after the fall begins, what is the velocity at any time $t_2 > t_1$?

Formulation.   We again choose the positive x axis vertically downward with the origin at the point where the fall began.   Let us break the problem into two parts:(1) *before* the parachute opens; (2) *after* it opens.

We first consider problem (1).   *Before* the parachute opens the forces acting upon the paratrooper are:

   (1) F_1, the weight, w lb, which acts downward and hence is positive.

   (2) F_2, the air resistance, numerically equal to kv^2, which acts upward and hence is the negative quantity $-kv^2$.

Newton's Second Law $F = ma$, where $F = F_1 + F_2$ gives

$$m\frac{dv}{dt} = w - kv^2.$$

Since the paratrooper was initially at rest, $v = 0$ when $t = 0$.   Thus, problem (1), concerned with the time *before* the parachute opens, is formulated as follows:

(3.28)

(3.29)

$$(1) \quad \begin{cases} m\dfrac{dv}{dt} = w - kv^2 \\[2mm] v(0) = 0. \end{cases}$$

We now turn to the formulation of problem (2).   Reasoning as before, we see that *after* the parachute opens, the forces acting upon the paratrooper are:

   (1) $F_1 = w$, exactly as before;

   (2) $F_2 = -Kv^2$ (instead of $-kv^2$).

Thus, proceeding as above, we have the following formulation of problem (2), dealing with the time *after* the parachute opens:

(3.30)

(3.31)

$$(2) \quad \begin{cases} m\dfrac{dv}{dt} = w - Kv^2 \\[2mm] v(t_1) = v_1, \end{cases}$$

where v_1 is the velocity which had already been attained when the parachute opened at time t_1.

Solution.   We shall first consider problem (1).   Letting $m = \dfrac{w}{g}$, Equation (3.28) becomes

$$\frac{w}{g}\frac{dv}{dt} = w - kv^2.$$

Separating variables, we obtain

$$\frac{dv}{w - kv^2} = \frac{g}{w}dt.$$

Integration yields

$$\ln \left| \frac{\sqrt{\frac{w}{k}} + v}{\sqrt{\frac{w}{k}} - v} \right| = 2g\sqrt{\frac{k}{w}}t + c_0.$$

Letting $\sqrt{\frac{w}{k}} = \gamma$, we have

$$\frac{\gamma + v}{\gamma - v} = c_1 e^{\frac{2g}{\gamma}t}.$$

From this we find

(3.32)
$$v = \gamma \left[\frac{c_1 e^{\frac{2g}{\gamma}t} - 1}{c_1 e^{\frac{2g}{\gamma}t} + 1} \right].$$

Applying the initial condition (3.29) that $v = 0$ at $t = 0$, we find that $c_1 = 1$. Hence the solution to problem (1) becomes

(3.33)
$$v = \sqrt{\frac{w}{k}} \left[\frac{e^{2g\sqrt{\frac{k}{w}}t} - 1}{e^{2g\sqrt{\frac{k}{w}}t} + 1} \right],$$

which is valid for $0 < t < t_1$.
Recalling that

$$\tanh y = \frac{e^y - e^{-y}}{e^y + e^{-y}} = \frac{e^{2y} - 1}{e^{2y} + 1},$$

we may put this in the neater (but perhaps more mysterious) form

$$v = \sqrt{\frac{w}{k}} \tanh \left(g\sqrt{\frac{k}{w}}t \right).$$

Now let us consider problem (2). Since Equation (3.30) is essentially the same as equation (3.28) with K in place of k, using (3.32) we have at once its general solution in the form

(3.34)
$$v = \sqrt{\frac{w}{K}} \left[\frac{c_2 e^{2g\sqrt{\frac{K}{w}}t} - 1}{c_2 e^{2g\sqrt{\frac{K}{w}}t} + 1} \right].$$

The initial condition now is $v = v_1$ when $t = t_1$, where the value v_1 is that given by (3.33) when $t = t_1$:

$$v_1 = \sqrt{\frac{w}{k}} \left[\frac{e^{2g\sqrt{\frac{k}{w}}t_1} - 1}{e^{2g\sqrt{\frac{k}{w}}t_1} + 1} \right].$$

Thus applying $v(t_1) = v_1$ to Equation (3.34) we have

$$\frac{e^{2g\sqrt{\frac{k}{w}}t_1} - 1}{e^{2g\sqrt{\frac{k}{w}}t_1} + 1} = \frac{c_2 e^{2g\sqrt{\frac{K}{w}}t_1} - 1}{c_2 e^{2g\sqrt{\frac{K}{w}}t_1} + 1}.$$

Solving for c_2, we obtain

$$c_2 = e^{\frac{2g}{\sqrt{w}}\left[\sqrt{k}-\sqrt{K}\right]t_1}.$$

Thus, at last, the solution of problem (2) is

(3.35)
$$v = \sqrt{\frac{w}{K}} \left\{ \frac{e^{\frac{2g}{\sqrt{w}}\left[\sqrt{K}(t-t_1)+\sqrt{k}t_1\right]} - 1}{e^{\frac{2g}{\sqrt{w}}\left[\sqrt{K}(t-t_1)+\sqrt{k}t_1\right]} + 1} \right\},$$

which is valid for $t > t_1$.

As before, if we desire, we may write this as

$$v = \sqrt{\frac{w}{K}} \tanh \left[\frac{g}{\sqrt{w}}\sqrt{K}(t - t_1) + \sqrt{k}t_1 \right].$$

Interpretation of Results. Let us first consider the solution of problem (1), given by Equation (3.33). According to this, as $t \to \infty$, v approaches the limiting velocity $\sqrt{\frac{w}{k}}$. Thus if the parachute never opened, the velocity would have been approximately $\sqrt{\frac{w}{k}}$ at the time when the unfortunate paratrooper would have struck the earth! But, according to the statement of the problem, the parachute *does* open at time t_1 (we tacitly and thoughtfully assume $t_1 \ll T$, where T is the time when the earth *is* reached!). Then, referring to the solution of problem (2), equation (3.35), we see that as $t \to \infty$, v approaches the limiting velocity $\sqrt{\frac{w}{K}}$. Thus, assuming that the parachute opens at a considerable distance above the earth, the velocity is approximately $\sqrt{\frac{w}{K}}$ when the earth is finally reached. Let us sum up these observations as follows:

1. If the parachute did not open, the paratrooper would strike the earth with velocity approximately equal to $\sqrt{\frac{w}{k}}$.

2. If the parachute did open at a considerable distance above the earth, he would strike the earth with velocity approximately equal to $\sqrt{\frac{w}{K}}$.

Let us consider how these two values compare. Before the parachute opens, the air resistance has magnitude kv^2; while after it opens, the resistance is Kv^2, where K is considerably larger than k.

Hence,

$$\sqrt{\frac{w}{K}} < \sqrt{\frac{w}{k}}.$$

We thus obtain the well-known fact that the velocity of impact with the open parachute is a small fraction of the impact velocity which would have occurred if the
parachute had not opened. For example, if we assume that $w = 200$, $k = \frac{1}{150}$, and
$K = \frac{4}{5}$, we have

$$\sqrt{\frac{w}{k}} = \sqrt{(200)(150)} \approx 173 (\text{ft/sec}),$$

while

$$\sqrt{\frac{w}{K}} = \sqrt{250} \qquad \approx 16 (\text{ft/sec}).$$

The calculations in this problem are somewhat complicated; but the moral is clear:
Make certain that the parachute opens!

C. Frictional Forces

If a body moves on a rough surface, it will encounter not only air resistance but also
another resistance force due to the roughness of the surface. This additional force is
called *friction*. It is shown in physics that the friction is given by μN, where
1. μ is a constant of proportionality called the *coefficient of friction*, which depends
    upon the roughness of the given surface; and
2. N is the normal (that is, perpendicular) force which the surface exerts on the body.
We now apply Newton's Second Law to a problem in which friction is involved.

Example 3.7.   An object weighing 48 lb is released from rest at the top of a plane
metal slide which is inclined 30° to the horizontal. Air resistance (in pounds) is numerically
equal to one-half the velocity (in ft/sec), and the coefficient of friction is $\frac{1}{4}$.
(a) What is the velocity of the object 2 seconds after it is released?
(b) If the slide is 24 feet long, what is the velocity when the object reaches the bottom?

Formulation.   The line of motion is along the slide. We choose the origin at the top
and the positive x direction down the slide. If we temporarily neglect the friction and
air resistance, the forces acting upon the object A are:
(1) its weight, 48 lb, which acts vertically downward; and
(2) the normal force, N, exerted by the slide which acts in an upward direction per-
     pendicular to the slide. (See Figure 3.5.)

Figure 3.5

The components of the weight parallel and perpendicular to the slide have magnitude

$$48 \sin 30° = 24$$

and

$$48 \cos 30° = 24\sqrt{3},$$

respectively. The components perpendicular to the slide are in equilibrium and hence the normal force N has magnitude $24\sqrt{3}$.

Now, taking into consideration the friction and air resistance, we see that the forces acting on the object as it moves along the slide are the following:

(1) F_1, the component of the weight parallel to the plane, having numerical value 24. Since this force acts in the positive (downward) direction along the slide, we have

$$F_1 = 24.$$

(2) F_2, the frictional force, having numerical value $\mu N = \frac{1}{4}(24\sqrt{3})$. Since this acts in the negative (upward) direction along the slide, we have

$$F_2 = -6\sqrt{3}.$$

(3) F_3, the air resistance, having numerical value $\frac{1}{2}v$. Since $v > 0$ and this also acts in the negative direction, we have

$$F_2 = -\frac{1}{2}v.$$

We apply Newton's Second Law $F = ma$. Here $F = F_1 + F_2 + F_3 = 24 - 6\sqrt{3} - \frac{1}{2}v$ and $m = \dfrac{w}{g} = \dfrac{48}{32} = \dfrac{3}{2}$. Thus we have the differential equation

(3.36) $$\frac{3}{2}\frac{dv}{dt} = 24 - 6\sqrt{3} - \frac{1}{2}v.$$

Since the object is released from rest, the initial condition is

(3.37) $$v(0) = 0.$$

Solution. Equation (3.36) is separable; separating variables we have

$$\frac{dv}{48 - 12\sqrt{3} - v} = \frac{dt}{3}.$$

Integrating and simplifying, we find

$$v = 48 - 12\sqrt{3} - c_1 e^{-t/3}.$$

The condition (3.37) gives $c_1 = 48 - 12\sqrt{3}$.
Thus we obtain

(3.38) $$v = (48 - 12\sqrt{3})(1 - e^{-t/3}).$$

Question (a) is thus answered by letting $t = 2$ in Equation (3.38). We find

$$v(2) = (48 - 12\sqrt{3})(1 - e^{-2/3}) \approx 10.2 \text{ (ft/sec).}$$

In order to answer question (b), we integrate (3.38) to obtain

$$x = (48 - 12\sqrt{3})(t + 3e^{-t/3}) + c_2.$$

Since $x(0) = 0$, $c_2 = -(48 - 12\sqrt{3})(3)$. Thus the distance covered at time t is given by

(3.39) $$x = (48 - 12\sqrt{3})(t + 3e^{-t/3} - 3).$$

Since the slide is 24 feet long, the object reaches the bottom at the time T determined from the transcendental equation

$$24 = (48 - 12\sqrt{3})(T + 3e^{-T/3} - 3),$$

which may be written as

$$3e^{-T/3} = \frac{47 + 2\sqrt{3}}{13} - T.$$

The value of T which satisfies this equation is approximately 2.6. Thus from equation (3.38) the velocity of the object when it reaches the bottom is given approximately by

$$(48 - 12\sqrt{3})(1 - e^{-0.9}) \approx 12.3 \text{ (ft/sec)}.$$

Exercises

1. A stone weighing 4 lb falls from rest toward the earth from a great height. As it falls it is acted upon by air resistance which is numerically equal to $\frac{1}{2} v$ (in pounds), where v is the velocity (in ft/sec).
   (a) Find the velocity and distance fallen at time t seconds.
   (b) Find the velocity and distance fallen at the end of 5 seconds.

2. A ball weighing 6 lb is thrown vertically downward toward the earth from a height of 1,000 feet with an initial velocity of 6 feet per second. As it falls it is acted upon by air resistance which is numerically equal to $\frac{2}{3} v$ (in lb.), where v is the velocity (in ft/sec).
   (a) What is the velocity and distance fallen at the end of one minute?
   (b) With what velocity does the ball strike the earth?

3. A ball weighing $\frac{3}{4}$ lb is thrown vertically upward from a point 6 feet above the surface of the earth with an initial velocity of 20 feet per second. As it rises it is acted upon by air resistance which is numerically equal to $\frac{1}{64} v$ (in pounds), where v is the velocity (in ft/sec). How high will the ball rise?

4. A ship which weighs 32,000 tons starts from rest under the force of a constant propeller thrust of 100,000 lb. The resistance in lbs. is numerically equal to 8,000 v, where v is in ft/sec.
   (a) Find the velocity of the ship as a function of the time.
   (b) Find the limiting velocity (that is, the limit of v as $t \to +\infty$).
   (c) Find how long it takes the ship to attain a velocity of 80 % of the limiting velocity.

5. Two men are riding in a motorboat and the combined weight of men, motor, boat, and equipment is 640 lb. The motor exerts a constant force of 20 lb on the boat in the direction of motion, while the resistance (in pounds) is numerically equal to one and one-half times the velocity (in ft/sec). If the boat started from rest, find the velocity of the boat after (a) 20 seconds, (b) 1 minute.

6. A boat weighing 150 lb with a single rider weighing 170 lb is being towed in a certain direction at the rate of 20 miles per hour. At time $t = 0$ the tow rope is suddenly cast off and the rider begins to row in the same direction, exerting a force equivalent to a constant force of 12 lb in this direction. The resistance (in pounds) is numerically equal to twice the velocity (in ft/sec).

(a) Find the velocity of the boat 15 seconds after the tow rope was cast off.

(b) How many seconds after the tow rope is cast off will the velocity be one-half that at which the boat was being towed?

7. A bullet weighing 2 ounces is fired vertically downward from a stationary helicopter with a muzzle velocity of 1200 feet per second. The air resistance (in pounds) is numerically equal to $10^{-5}v^2$, where v is the velocity (in ft/sec). Find the velocity of the bullet as a function of the time.

8. A shell weighing 1 lb is fired vertically upward from the earth's surface with a muzzle velocity of 1000 feet per second. The air resistance (in pounds) is numerically equal to $10^{-4}v^2$, where v is the velocity (in ft/sec).

(a) Find the velocity of the rising shell as a function of the time.

(b) How long will the shell rise?

9. An object weighing 16 lb is dropped from rest on the surface of a calm lake and thereafter starts to sink. While its weight tends to force it downward, the buoyancy of the object tends to force it back upward. If this buoyancy force is one of 6 lb and the resistance of the water (in pounds) is numerically equal to twice the square of the velocity (in feet per second), find the formula for the velocity of the sinking object as a function of the time.

10. An object weighing 12 lb is placed beneath the surface of a calm lake. The buoyancy of the object is 30 lb; because of this the object begins to rise. If the resistance of the water (in pounds) is numerically equal to the square of the velocity (in feet per second) and the object surfaces in 5 seconds, find the velocity of the object at the instant when it reaches the surface.

11. A man is pushing a loaded sled across a level field of ice at the constant speed of 10 feet per second. When the man is half-way across the ice field, he stops pushing and lets the loaded sled continue on. The combined weight of the sled and its load is 80 lb; the air resistance (in pounds) is numerically equal to $\frac{3}{4}v$, where v is the velocity of the sled (in ft/sec); and the coefficient of friction of the runners on the ice is 0.04. How far will the sled continue to move after the man stops pushing?

12. A boy on his sled has just slid down a hill onto a level field of ice and is starting to slow down. At the instant when their speed is 5 feet per second, the boy's father runs up and begins to push the sled forward, exerting a constant force of 15 lb in the direction of motion. The combined weight of the boy and the sled is 96 lb, the air resistance (in pounds) is numerically equal to one-half the velocity (in ft/sec), and the coefficient of friction of the runners on the ice is 0.05. How fast is the sled moving 10 seconds after the father begins pushing?

 13. A case of canned milk weighing 24 lb is released from rest at the top of a plane metal slide which is 30 feet long and inclined 45° to the horizontal. Air resistance (in pounds) is numerically equal to one-third the velocity (in ft/sec) and the coefficient of friction is 0.4.

(a) What is the velocity of the moving case 1 second after it is released?

(b) What is the velocity when the case reaches the bottom of the slide?

14. A boy goes sledding down a long 30° slope. The combined weight of the boy and his sled is 72 lb and the air resistance (in pounds) is numerically equal to twice their velocity (in ft/sec). If they started from rest and their velocity at the end of 5 seconds is 10 feet per second, what is the coefficient of friction of the sled runners on the snow?

15. An object weighing 32 lb is released from rest 50 feet above the surface of a calm lake. Before the object reaches the surface of the lake, the air resistance (in pounds) is given by $2v$, where v is the velocity (in ft/sec). After the object passes beneath the surface, the water resistance (in pounds) is given by $6v$. Further, the object is then buoyed up by a buoyancy force of 8 lb. Find the velocity of the object 2 seconds after it passes beneath the surface of the lake.

3.3 Rate Problems

In certain problems the rate at which a quantity changes is a known function of the amount present and/or the time, and it is desired to find the quantity itself. If x denotes the amount of the quantity present at time t, then $\dfrac{dx}{dt}$ denotes the rate at which the quantity changes and we are at once led to a differential equation. In this section we consider certain problems of this type.

A. Rate of Growth and Decay

Example 3.8. The rate at which radioactive nuclei decay is proportional to the number of such nuclei that are present in a given sample. Half of the original number of radioactive nuclei have undergone disintegration in a period of 1500 years.

(a) What percentage of the original radioactive nuclei will remain after 4500 years?

(b) In how many years will only one tenth of the original number remain?

Mathematical Formulation. Let x be the amount of radioactive nuclei present after t years. Then $\dfrac{dx}{dt}$ represents the rate at which the nuclei decay. Since the nuclei decay at a rate proportional to the amount present, we have

$$(3.40) \qquad\qquad \frac{dx}{dt} = Kx,$$

where K is a constant of proportionality. The amount x is clearly positive; further, since x is decreasing, $\dfrac{dx}{dt} < 0$. Thus, from Equation (3.40), we must have $K < 0$. In order to emphasize that x is decreasing, we prefer to replace K by a positive constant preceded by a minus sign. Thus we let $k = -K > 0$ and write the differential equation (3.40) in the form

$$(3.41) \qquad\qquad \frac{dx}{dt} = -kx.$$

Letting x_0 denote the amount initially present, we also have the initial condition

$$(3.42) \qquad\qquad x(0) = x_0.$$

We know that we shall need such a condition in order to determine the arbitrary constant which will appear in the general solution of the differential equation (3.41). However, we shall apparently need something else, for the equation (3.41) contains an unknown constant of proportionality k. This "something else" appears in the statement of the problem, for we are told that half of the original number disintegrate in 1500 years. Thus half also remain at that time, and this at once gives the condition

$$(3.43) \qquad\qquad x(1500) = \frac{1}{2}x_0.$$

Solution. The differential equation (3.41) is clearly separable; separating variables, integrating, and simplifying, we have at once

$$x = ce^{-kt}.$$

Applying the initial condition (3.42), $x = x_0$ when $t = 0$, we find that $c = x_0$ and hence we obtain

(3.44) $$x = x_0 e^{-kt}.$$

We have not yet determined k. Thus we now apply condition (3.43), $x = \frac{1}{2}x_0$ when $t = 1500$, to the equation (3.44). We find

$$\frac{1}{2}x_0 = x_0 e^{-1500k},$$

or

$$(e^{-k})^{1500} = \frac{1}{2},$$

or finally

(3.45) $$e^{-k} = \left(\frac{1}{2}\right)^{\frac{1}{1500}}.$$

From this equation we could determine k explicitly and substitute the result into equation (3.44). However, we see from Equation (3.44) that we actually do not need k itself but rather only e^{-k}, which we have just obtained in Equation (3.45). Thus we substitute e^{-k} from (3.45) into (3.44) to obtain

$$x = x_0(e^{-k})^t = x_0\left[\left(\frac{1}{2}\right)^{\frac{1}{1500}}\right]^t$$

or

(3.46) $$x = x_0\left(\frac{1}{2}\right)^{\frac{t}{1500}}.$$

Equation (3.46) gives the number x of radioactive nuclei which are present at time t. Question (a) asks us what percentage of the original number will remain after 4500 years. We thus let $t = 4500$ in Equation (3.46) and find

$$x = x_0\left(\frac{1}{2}\right)^3 = \frac{x_0}{8}.$$

Thus, one eighth or 12.5 per cent of the original number remain after 4500 years. Question (b) asks us when only one tenth will remain. Thus we let $x = \frac{1}{10}x_0$ in Equation (3.46) and solve for t. We have

$$\frac{1}{10} = \left(\frac{1}{2}\right)^{\frac{t}{1500}}$$

and so

$$\frac{t}{1500} = \frac{\ln\dfrac{1}{10}}{\ln\dfrac{1}{2}}$$

or

$$t = \frac{1500 \ln 10}{\ln 2} \approx 4985 \text{ (years)}.$$

B. Mixture Problems

We now consider rate problems involving mixtures. A substance S is allowed to flow into a certain mixture in a container at a certain rate, and the mixture is kept uniform by stirring or some other process. Further, in one such situation, this uniform mixture simultaneously flows out of the container at another (generally different) rate; while in another situation this may not be the case. In either case we seek to determine the quantity of the substance S present in the mixture at time t.

Letting x denote the amount of S present at time t, the derivative $\frac{dx}{dt}$ denotes the rate of change of x with respect to t. If "IN" denotes the rate at which S enters the mixture and "OUT" the rate at which it leaves, we have at once the basic equation

(3.47)
$$\frac{dx}{dt} = \text{IN} - \text{OUT}$$

from which to determine the amount x of S at time t. We now consider examples.

Example 3.9. A tank initially contains 50 gallons of pure water. Starting at time $t = 0$ a brine containing 2 lb of dissolved salt per gallon flows into the tank at the rate of 3 gallons per minute. The mixture is kept uniform by stirring and the well-stirred mixture simultaneously flows out of the tank at the same rate.
(a) How much salt is in the tank at any time $t > 0$?
(b) How much salt is present at the end of 25 min?
(c) How much salt is present after a long time?

Mathematical Formulation. Let x denote the amount of salt at time t. We apply the basic equation (3.47),

$$\frac{dx}{dt} = \text{IN} - \text{OUT}.$$

The brine flows in at the rate of 3 gallons per minute, and each gallon contains 2 lb of salt. Thus

$$\text{IN} = (2 \text{ lb/gal})(3 \text{ gal/min}) = 6 \text{ lb/min}.$$

Since the rate of outflow equals the rate of inflow, the tank contains 50 gallons of the mixture at any time t. This 50 gal contains x lb of salt at time t, and so the concentration of salt at time t is $\frac{x}{50}$ lb/gal. Thus, since the mixture flows out at the rate of 3 gal/min, we have

$$\text{OUT} = \left(\frac{x}{50} \text{ lb/gal} \right)(3 \text{ gal/min}) = \frac{3x}{50} \text{ lb/min}.$$

Thus the differential equation for x as a function of t is

(3.48)
$$\frac{dx}{dt} = 6 - \frac{3x}{50}.$$

Since initially there was no salt in the tank, we also have the initial condition

(3.49) $x(0) = 0.$

Solution.   The equation (3.48) is both linear and separable. Separating variables, we have

$$\frac{dx}{100 - x} = \frac{3}{50}dt.$$

Integrating and simplifying, we obtain

$$x = 100 + ce^{-\frac{3}{50}t}.$$

Applying the condition (3.49), $x = 0$ at $t = 0$, we find that $c = -100$. Thus we have:

(3.50) $x = 100(1 - e^{-\frac{3}{50}t}).$

This is the answer to question (a). As for question (b), at the end of 25 minutes, $t = 25$, and equation (3.50) gives

$$x(25) = 100(1 - e^{-1.5}) \approx 78(\text{lb}).$$

Question (c) essentially asks us how much salt is present as $t \rightarrow \infty$. To answer this we let $t \rightarrow \infty$ in Equation (3.50) and observe that $x \rightarrow 100$.

Example 3.10.   A large tank initially contains 50 gallons of brine in which there is dissolved 10 lb of salt. Brine containing 2 lb of dissolved salt per gallon flows into the tank at the rate of 5 gallons per minute. The mixture is kept uniform by stirring and the stirred mixture simultaneously flows out at the slower rate of 3 gallons per minute. How much salt is in the tank at any time $t > 0$?

Mathematical Formulation.   Let $x = $ the amount of salt at time t. Again we shall use equation (3.47):

$$\frac{dx}{dt} = \text{IN} - \text{OUT}.$$

Proceeding as in Example 3.9,

$$\text{IN} = (2 \text{ lb/gal})(5 \text{ gal/min}) = 10 \text{ lb/min};$$

also, once again

$$\text{OUT} = (C \text{ lb/gal})(3 \text{ gal/min}),$$

where C lb/gal denotes the concentration. But here, since the rate of outflow is different from that of inflow, the concentration is not quite so simple. At time $t = 0$, the tank contains 50 gallons of brine. Since brine flows in at the rate of 5 gallons per minute but flows out at the slower rate of 3 gallons per minute, there is a net gain of $5 - 3 = 2$ gallons per minute of brine in the tank. Thus at the end of t minutes the amount of brine in the tank is

$$50 + 2t \text{ gal.}$$

Hence the concentration at time t minutes is

$$\frac{x}{50 + 2t} \text{ lb/gal,}$$

and so

$$\text{OUT} = \frac{3x}{50 + 2t} \text{ lb/min.}$$

Thus the differential equation becomes

(3.51) $$\frac{dx}{dt} = 10 - \frac{3x}{50 + 2t}.$$

Since there was initially 10 lb of salt in the tank, we have the initial condition

(3.52) $$x(0) = 10.$$

Solution. The differential equation (3.51) is *not* separable but it *is* linear. Putting it in standard form,

$$\frac{dx}{dt} + \frac{3}{2t + 50}x = 10,$$

we find the integrating factor

$$e^{\int \frac{3}{2t+50}dt} = (2t + 50)^{3/2}.$$

Multiplying through by this, we have

$$(2t + 50)^{3/2}\frac{dx}{dt} + 3(2t + 50)^{1/2}x = 10(2t + 50)^{3/2}$$

or

$$\frac{d}{dt}[(2t + 50)^{3/2}x] = 10(2t + 50)^{3/2}.$$

Thus

$$(2t + 50)^{3/2}x = 2(2t + 50)^{5/2} + c$$

or

$$x = 4(t + 25) + \frac{c}{(2t + 50)^{3/2}}.$$

Applying condition (3.52), $x = 10$ at $t = 0$, we find

$$10 = 100 + \frac{c}{(50)^{3/2}}$$

or

$$c = -(90)(50)^{3/2} = -22500\sqrt{2}.$$

Thus the amount of salt at any time $t > 0$ is given by

$$x = 4t + 100 - \frac{22500\sqrt{2}}{(2t + 50)^{3/2}}.$$

Exercises

1. Assume that the rate at which radioactive nuclei decay is proportional to the number of such nuclei that are present in a given sample. In a certain sample ten per cent of the original number of radioactive nuclei have undergone disintegration in a period of 200 years.

   (a) What percentage of the original radioactive nuclei will remain after 1,000 years?

   (b) In how many years will only one-fourth of the original number remain?

2. A certain chemical is converted into another chemical by a chemical reaction. The rate at which the first chemical is converted is proportional to the amount of this chemical present at any instant. Ten per cent of the original amount of the first chemical has been converted in five minutes.

   (a) What per cent of the first chemical will have been converted in twenty minutes?

   (b) In how many minutes will sixty per cent of the first chemical have been converted?

3. A chemical reaction converts a certain chemical into another chemical, and the rate at which the first chemical is converted is proportional to the amount of this chemical present at any time. At the end of one hour, 50 grams of the first chemical remain; while at the end of three hours, only 25 grams remain.

   (a) How many grams of the first chemical were present initially?

   (b) How many grams of the first chemical will remain at the end of five hours?

   (c) In how many hours will only 2 grams of the first chemical remain?

4. Assume that the population of a certain city increases at a rate proportional to the number of inhabitants at any time. If the population doubles in 40 years, in how many years will it triple?

5. The population of the city of Bingville increases at a rate proportional to the number of its inhabitants present at any time t. If the population of Bingville was 30,000 in 1950 and 35,000 in 1960, what will be the population of Bingville in 1970?

6. In a certain bacteria culture the rate of increase in the number of bacteria is proportional to the number present.

   (a) If the number triples in 5 hours, how many will be present in 10 hours?

   (b) When will the number present be ten times the number initially present?

7. A tank initially contains 100 gallons of brine in which there is dissolved 20 lb of salt. Starting at time $t = 0$, brine containing 3 lb of dissolved salt per gallon flows into the tank at the rate of 4 gallons per minute. The mixture is kept uniform by stirring and the well-stirred mixture simultaneously flows out of the tank at the same rate.

   (a) How much salt is in the tank at the end of 10 minutes?

   (b) When is there 160 lb of salt in the tank?

8. A large tank initially contains 100 gallons of brine in which 10 lb of salt is dissolved. Starting at $t = 0$, pure water flows into the tank at the rate of 5 gallons per minute. The mixture is kept uniform by stirring and the well-stirred mixture simultaneously flows out at the slower rate of 2 gallons per minute.

   (a) How much salt is in the tank at the end of 15 minutes and what is the concentration at that time?

   (b) If the capacity of the tank is 250 gallons, what is the concentration at the instant the tank overflows?

9. A tank initially contains 100 gallons of pure water. Starting at $t = 0$, a brine containing 4 lb of salt per gallon flows into the tank at the rate of 5 gallons per minute. The mixture is kept uniform by stirring and the well-stirred mixture flows out at the slower rate of 3 gallons per minute.
   (a) How much salt is in the tank at the end of 20 minutes?
   (b) When is there 50 lb of salt in the tank?

10. A large tank initially contains 200 gallons of brine in which 15 lb of salt is dissolved. Starting at $t = 0$, brine containing 4 lb of salt per gallon flows into the tank at the rate of 3.5 gallons per minute. The mixture is kept uniform by stirring and the well-stirred mixture leaves the tank at the rate of 4 gallons per minute.
   (a) How much salt is in the tank at the end of one hour?
   (b) How much salt is in the tank when the tank contains only 50 gallons of brine?

11. The air in a room whose volume is 10,000 cubic feet tests 0.15 per cent carbon dioxide. Starting at $t = 0$, outside air testing 0.05 per cent carbon dioxide is admitted at the rate of 5,000 cubic feet per minute.
   (a) What is the percentage of carbon dioxide in the air in the room after 3 minutes?
   (b) When does the air in the room test 0.1 per cent carbon dioxide?

12. The air in a room 50 feet by 20 feet by 8 feet tests 0.2 per cent carbon dioxide. Starting at $t = 0$, outside air testing 0.05 per cent carbon dioxide is admitted to the room. How many cubic feet of this outside air must be admitted per minute in order that the air in the room test 0.1 per cent at the end of 30 minutes?

13. Newton's Law of cooling states that the rate at which a body cools is proportional to the difference between the temperature of the body and that of the medium in which it is situated. A body of temperature 80° F is placed at time $t = 0$ in a medium the temperature of which is maintained at 50° F. At the end of 5 minutes, the body has cooled to a temperature of 70° F.
   (a) What is the temperature of the body at the end of 10 minutes?
   (b) When will the temperature of the body be 60° F?

14. A body cools from 60° C to 50° C in 15 minutes in air which is maintained at 30° C. How long will it take this body to cool from 100° C to 80° C in air which is maintained at 50° C? Assume Newton's Law of cooling (Exercise 13).

15. The rate at which a certain substance dissolves in water is proportional to the product of the amount undissolved and the difference $c_1 - c_2$, where c_1 is the concentration in the saturated solution and c_2 is the concentration in the actual solution. If saturated, 50 grams of water would dissolve 20 grams of the substance. If 10 grams of the substance is placed in 50 grams of water and half of the substance is then dissolved in 90 minutes, how much will be dissolved in 3 hours?

16. Under natural circumstances the population of mice on a certain island would increase at a rate proportional to the number of mice present at any time, provided the island had no cats. There were no cats on the island from the beginning of 1950 to the beginning of 1960, and during this time the mouse population doubled, reaching an all time high of 100,000 at the beginning of 1960. At this time the people of the island, alarmed by the increasing number of mice, imported a number of cats to kill the mice. If the above natural rate of increase of mice was thereafter offset by the work of the cats, who killed 1,000 mice a month, how many mice remained at the beginning of 1961?

SUGGESTED READING

Agnew (1)   Rainville (45)
Kaplan (30)   Spiegel (50)

4

EXPLICIT METHODS OF SOLVING HIGHER ORDER LINEAR DIFFERENTIAL EQUATIONS

The subject of ordinary linear differential equations is one of great theoretical and practical importance. Theoretically, the subject is one of simplicity and elegance. Practically, linear differential equations originate in a variety of applications to science and engineering. Fortunately many of the linear differential equations which thus occur are of a special type, linear with constant coefficients, for which explicit methods of solution are available. The main purpose of this chapter is to study certain of these methods. First, however, we need to consider certain basic theorems which will be used throughout the chapter. We begin by stating and illustrating these important theorems, reserving proofs for Chapter 11.

4.1 Basic Theory of Linear Differential Equations

A. Definition and Basic Existence Theorem

DEFINITION. A *linear differential equation of order n* is an equation of the form

(4.1)
$$a_0(x)\frac{d^n y}{dx^n} + a_1(x)\frac{d^{n-1} y}{dx^{n-1}} + \cdots + a_{n-1}(x)\frac{dy}{dx} + a_n(x)y = b(x),$$

where a_0 is not identically zero. We shall assume that $a_0, a_1, \ldots, a_n$, and b are continuous real functions on a real interval $a \leq x \leq b$ and that $a_0(x) \neq 0$ for any x on $a \leq x \leq b$. The right hand member is called the *nonhomogeneous term*. If b is identically zero the equation reduces to

$$a_0(x)\frac{d^n y}{dx^n} + a_1(x)\frac{d^{n-1} y}{dx^{n-1}} + \cdots + a_{n-1}(x)\frac{dy}{dx} + a_n(x)y = 0$$

and is then called *homogeneous*.

Example 4.1. $\dfrac{d^2y}{dx^2} + 3x\dfrac{dy}{dx} + x^3y = e^x$ is a linear differential equation of the second order.

Example 4.2. $\dfrac{d^3y}{dx^3} + x\dfrac{d^2y}{dx^2} + 3x^2\dfrac{dy}{dx} - 5y = \sin x$ is a linear differential equation of the third order.

We now state the basic existence theorem for initial-value problems associated with an nth order linear differential equation:

THEOREM 4.1.

Hypothesis 1.   Consider

(4.1) $a_0(x)\dfrac{d^ny}{dx^n} + a_1(x)\dfrac{d^{n-1}y}{dx^{n-1}} + \cdots + a_{n-1}(x)\dfrac{dy}{dx} + a_n(x)y = b(x),$

where $a_0, a_1, \ldots, a_n$, and b are continuous real functions on a real interval $a \leq x \leq b$ and $a_0(x) \neq 0$ for any x on $a \leq x \leq b$.

2.   Let x_0 be any point of the interval $a \leq x \leq b$, and let $c_0, c_1, \ldots, c_{n-1}$ be n arbitrary real constants.

Conclusion.   There exists a unique solution f of (4.1) such that $f(x_0) = c_0, f'(x_0) = c_1,$ $\ldots, f^{(n-1)}(x_0) = c_{n-1}$, and this solution is defined over the entire interval $a \leq x \leq b$.

Suppose we are considering an nth order linear differential equation (4.1), the co-efficients and nonhomogeneous term of which all possess the continuity requirements set forth in hypothesis 1 of Theorem 4.1 on a certain interval of the x axis. Then, given *any* point x_0 of this interval and *any* n real numbers $c_0, c_1, \ldots, c_{n-1}$, the theorem assures us that there is *precisely one* solution of the differential equation which assumes the value c_0 at $x = x_0$ and whose kth derivative assumes the value c_k for each $k = 1, 2, \ldots, n-1$ at $x = x_0$. Further, the theorem tells us that this unique solution is defined for *all* x in the above-mentioned interval.

Example 4.3.   Consider the initial-value problem

$$\begin{cases} \dfrac{d^2y}{dx^2} + 3x\dfrac{dy}{dx} + x^3y = e^x \\[2mm] y(1) = 2 \\[2mm] y'(1) = -5. \end{cases}$$

The coefficients 1, $3x$, and x^3, as well as the nonhomogeneous term e^x, in this second-order differential equation are all continuous for all values of x, $-\infty < x < \infty$. The point x_0 here is the point 1, which certainly belongs to this interval; and the real numbers c_0 and c_1 are 2 and -5, respectively. Thus Theorem 4.1 tells us that a solution of the given problem exists, is unique, and is defined for all x, $-\infty < x < \infty$.

Example 4.4. Consider the initial-value problem

$$\begin{cases} 2\dfrac{d^3y}{dx^3} + x\dfrac{d^2y}{dx^2} + 3x^2\dfrac{dy}{dx} - 5y = \sin x \\[2mm] y(4) = 3 \\[2mm] y'(4) = 5 \\[2mm] y''(4) = -\dfrac{7}{2}. \end{cases}$$

Here we have a third-order problem. The coefficients 2, x, $3x^2$, and -5, as well as the nonhomogeneous term $\sin x$, are all continuous for all x, $-\infty < x < \infty$. The point $x_0 = 4$ certainly belongs to this interval; the real numbers c_0, c_1, and c_2 in this problem are 3, 5, and $-\frac{7}{2}$, respectively. Theorem 4.1 tells us that this problem also has a unique solution which is defined for all x, $-\infty < x < \infty$.

A useful corollary to Theorem 4.1 is the following:

Corollary: Hypothesis: Let f be a solution of the *homogeneous* equation

$$(4.2) \qquad a_0(x)\frac{d^ny}{dx^n} + a_1(x)\frac{d^{n-1}y}{dx^{n-1}} + \cdots + a_{n-1}(x)\frac{dy}{dx} + a_n(x)y = 0$$

such that $f(x_0) = 0, f'(x_0) = 0, \ldots, f^{(n-1)}(x_0) = 0$, where x_0 is a point of the interval $a \leq x \leq b$ in which the coefficients $a_0, a_1, \ldots, a_n$ are all continuous and $a_0(x) \neq 0$. *Conclusion.* $f(x) = 0$ for all x on $a \leq x \leq b$.

Let us suppose that we are considering a homogeneous equation of the form (4.2), all the coefficients of which are continuous on a certain interval of the x axis. Suppose further that we have a solution f of this equation which is such that f and its first $n-1$ derivatives all equal zero at a point x_0 of this interval. Then this corollary tells us that this solution is the "trivial" solution f such that $f(x) = 0$ for *all* x on the above-mentioned interval.

Example 4.5. The solution f of the third-order homogeneous equation

$$\frac{d^3y}{dx^3} + 2\frac{d^2y}{dx^2} + 4x\frac{dy}{dx} + x^2y = 0$$

which is such that

$$f(2) = f'(2) = f''(2) = 0$$

is the trivial solution f such that $f(x) = 0$ for *all* x.

B. The Homogeneous Equation

We now consider the fundamental results concerning the homogeneous equation (4.2). We first state the following basic theorem:

THEOREM 4.2. Basic Theorem on Linear Homogeneous Differential Equations.

Hypothesis. Let $f_1, f_2, \ldots, f_m$ be any m solutions of the homogeneous linear differential equation (4.2).

Conclusion.   Then $c_1f_1 + c_2f_2 + \cdots + c_mf_m$ is also a solution of (4.2), where c_1, $c_2, \ldots, c_m$ are m arbitrary constants.

Theorem 4.2 tells us that if m known solutions of (4.2) are each multiplied by an arbitrary constant and the resulting products are then added together, the resulting sum is also a solution of (4.2). We may put this theorem in a very simple form by means of the concept of linear combination, which we now introduce.

DEFINITION.   If $f_1, f_2, \ldots, f_m$ are m given functions, and $c_1, \ldots, c_m$ are m constants, then the expression

$$c_1f_1 + c_2f_2 + \cdots + c_mf_m$$

is called a *linear combination* of $f_1, f_2, \ldots, f_m$.

In terms of this concept, Theorem 4.2 may be stated as follows:

THEOREM 4.2.   (restated) Any linear combination of solutions of the homogeneous linear differential equation (4.2) is also a solution of (4.2).

Example 4.6.   The student will readily verify that $\sin x$ and $\cos x$ are solutions of

$$\frac{d^2y}{dx^2} + y = 0.$$

Theorem 4.2 states that $c_1 \sin x + c_2 \cos x$ is also a solution for any constants c_1 and c_2. For example,

$$5 \sin x + 6 \cos x$$

is a solution.

Example 4.7.   The student may verify that e^x, e^{-x}, and e^{2x} are solutions of

$$\frac{d^3y}{dx^3} - 2\frac{d^2y}{dx^2} - \frac{dy}{dx} + 2y = 0.$$

Theorem 4.2 states that $c_1e^x + c_2e^{-x} + c_3e^{2x}$ is also a solution for any constants c_1, c_2, and c_3. For example,

$$2e^x - 3e^{-x} + \frac{2}{3}e^{2x}$$

is a solution.

We now consider what constitutes the general solution of (4.2). To understand this we first introduce the concepts of *linear dependence* and *linear independence*.

DEFINITION. The n functions $f_1, f_2, \ldots, f_n$ are called *linearly dependent* on $a \leq x \leq b$ if there exist constants $c_1, c_2, \ldots, c_n$, *not all zero*, such that

$$c_1 f_1(x) + c_2 f_2(x) + \cdots + c_n f_n(x) = 0$$

for all x such that $a \leq x \leq b$.

In particular, two functions f_1 and f_2 are *linearly dependent* on $a \leq x \leq b$ if there exist constants c_1, c_2, *not both zero*, such that

$$c_1 f_1(x) + c_2 f_2(x) = 0$$

for all x such that $a \leq x \leq b$.

Example 4.8. We observe that x and $2x$ are linearly dependent on the interval $0 \leq x \leq 1$. For there exist constants c_1 and c_2 *not both zero* such that

$$c_1 x + c_2(2x) = 0$$

for all x on the interval $0 \leq x \leq 1$. For example, let $c_1 = 2, c_2 = -1$.

Example 4.9. We observe that $\sin x$, $3\sin x$, and $-\sin x$ are linearly dependent on the interval $-1 \leq x \leq 2$. For there exist constants c_1, c_2, c_3, *not all zero*, such that

$$c_1 \sin x + c_2(3 \sin x) + c_3(-\sin x) = 0$$

for all x on the interval $-1 \leq x \leq 2$. For example, let $c_1 = 1, c_2 = 1, c_3 = 4$.

DEFINITION. The n functions $f_1, f_2, \ldots, f_n$ are called *linearly independent* on the interval $a \leq x \leq b$ if they are *not* linearly dependent there. That is, the functions $f_1, f_2, \ldots, f_n$ are *linearly independent* on $a \leq x \leq b$ if the relation

$$c_1 f_1(x) + c_2 f_2(x) + \cdots + c_n f_n(x) = 0$$

for all x such that $a \leq x \leq b$ implies that

$$c_1 = c_2 = \cdots = c_n = 0.$$

(In other words, the only identically vanishing linear combination of $f_1, f_2, \ldots f_n$ is the "trivial" linear combination

$$0 \cdot f_1 + 0 \cdot f_2 + \cdots + 0 \cdot f_n).$$

Example 4.10. We observe that x and x^2 are linearly independent on $0 \leq x \leq 1$, since $c_1 x + c_2 x^2 = 0$ for all x on $0 \leq x \leq 1$ implies that both $c_1 = 0$ and $c_2 = 0$.

Our next theorem is concerned with the existence of sets of linearly independent solutions of an nth order homogeneous linear differential equation and with the significance of such linearly independent sets.

THEOREM 4.3. *The nth order homogeneous linear differential equation (4.2) always possesses n solutions which are linearly independent. Further if $f_1, f_2, \ldots, f_n$ are n linearly independent solutions of (4.2), then every solution f of (4.2) can be expressed as a linear combination*

$$c_1 f_1 + c_2 f_2 + \cdots + c_n f_n$$

of these n linearly independent solutions by proper choice of the constants $c_1, c_2, \ldots, c_n$.

Given an nth order homogeneous linear differential equation, this theorem assures us first that a set of n linearly independent solutions actually exists. The existence of such a linearly independent set assured, the theorem goes on to tell us that *any solution whatsoever* of (4.2) can be written as a linear combination of such a linearly independent set of n solutions by suitable choice of the constants $c_1, c_2, \ldots c_n$.

Now let $f_1, f_2, \ldots, f_n$ be a set of n linearly independent solutions of (4.2). Then by Theorem 4.2 we know that the linear combination

$$(4.3) \qquad\qquad c_1 f_1 + c_2 f_2 + \cdots + c_n f_n,$$

where $c_1, c_2, \ldots, c_n$ are n *arbitrary* constants, is also a solution of (4.2). Further, by Theorem 4.3 we know that if f is *any* solution of (4.2), then it can be expressed in the form (4.3) by a suitable choice of the constants $c_1, c_2, \ldots, c_n$. Thus the solution (4.3), which is a linear combination of n linearly independent solutions of (4.2), appears to be a "general" solution of (4.2). Since the n constituent solutions $f_1, f_2, \ldots, f_n$ in (4.3) are linearly independent, the solution (4.3) is indeed a solution of the nth order differential equation (4.2) which contains n *essentially arbitrary* constants. Thus we may formulate the definition of general solution of an nth order homogeneous linear differential equation as follows:

DEFINITION.   If $f_1, f_2, \ldots, f_n$ are n linearly independent solutions of the nth order homogeneous linear differential equation (4.2) on $a \leq x \leq b$, then the function f defined by

$$f(x) = c_1 f_1(x) + c_2 f_2(x) + \cdots + c_n f_n(x), \quad a \leq x \leq b,$$

where $c_1, c_2, \ldots, c_n$ are arbitrary constants, is called a *general solution* of (4.2) on $a \leq x \leq b$.

Therefore, if we can find n linearly independent solutions of (4.2), we can at once write the general solution of (4.2) as a linear combination of these n solutions.

Example 4.11.   We have observed that $\sin x$ and $\cos x$ are solutions of $\dfrac{d^2 y}{dx^2} + y = 0$ for all x, $-\infty < x < \infty$ Further, one can show that these two solutions are linearly independent. Thus, the general solution may be expressed as the linear combination

$$c_1 \sin x + c_2 \cos x,$$

where c_1 and c_2 are arbitrary constants. We write this as $y = c_1 \sin x + c_2 \cos x$.

Example 4.12.   The solutions e^x, e^{-x}, and e^{2x} of

$$\frac{d^3 y}{dx^3} - 2\frac{d^2 y}{dx^2} - \frac{dy}{dx} + 2y = 0$$

may be shown to be linearly independent for all x, $-\infty < x < \infty$. Thus the general solution may be expressed as the linear combination

$$c_1 e^x + c_2 e^{-x} + c_3 e^{2x},$$

where c_1, c_2, and c_3 are arbitrary constants. We write this as

$$y = c_1 e^x + c_2 e^{-x} + c_3 e^{2x}.$$

The next theorem gives a simple criterion for determining whether or not n solutions of (4.2) are linearly independent. We first introduce another concept.

DEFINITION. Let $f_1, f_2, \ldots, f_n$ be n real functions each of which has an $(n-1)$st derivative on a real interval $a \le x \le b$. The determinant

$$W(f_1, f_2, \ldots f_n) = \begin{vmatrix} f_1 & f_2 & \cdots & f_n \\ f_1' & f_2' & \cdots & f_n' \\ \cdots & \cdots & \cdots & \cdots \\ f_1^{(n-1)} & f_2^{(n-1)} & \cdots & f_n^{(n-1)} \end{vmatrix},$$

in which primes denote derivatives, is called the *Wronskian* of these n functions. We observe that $W(f_1, f_2, \ldots, f_n)$ is itself a real function defined on $a \le x \le b$. Its value at x is denoted by $W(f_1, f_2, \ldots, f_n)(x)$.

THEOREM 4.4. The n solutions $f_1, f_2, \ldots, f_n$ of the nth order homogeneous linear differential equation (4.2) are linearly independent on $a \le x \le b$ if and only if the Wronskian of $f_1, f_2, \ldots, f_n$ is different from zero for some x on the interval $a \le x \le b$.

We have further:

THEOREM 4.5. The Wronskian of n solutions $f_1, f_2, \ldots, f_n$ of (4.2) is either identically zero on $a \le x \le b$ or else is never zero on $a \le x \le b$.

Thus if we can find n solutions of (4.2), we can apply the Theorems 4.4 and 4.5 to determine whether or not they are linearly independent. If they are linearly independent, then we can form the general solution as a linear combination of these n linearly independent solutions.

In the case of the general *second*-order homogeneous linear differential equation

$$a_0(x)\frac{d^2y}{dx^2} + a_1(x)\frac{dy}{dx} + a_2(x)y = 0,$$

the Wronskian of two solutions f_1 and f_2 is the second-order determinant

$$\begin{vmatrix} f_1 & f_2 \\ f_1' & f_2' \end{vmatrix} = f_1 f_2' - f_1' f_2.$$

Example 4.13. We apply Theorem 4.4 to show that the solutions $\sin x$ and $\cos x$ of

$$\frac{d^2y}{dx^2} + y = 0$$

are linearly independent.

$$W(\sin x, \cos x) = \begin{vmatrix} \sin x & \cos x \\ \cos x & -\sin x \end{vmatrix} = -\sin^2 x - \cos^2 x = -1 \ne 0.$$

Thus, since $W(\sin x, \cos x) \neq 0$, we conclude that $\sin x$ and $\cos x$ are indeed linearly independent.

Example 4.14.   The solutions e^x, e^{-x}, and e^{2x} of

$$\frac{d^3y}{dx^3} - 2\frac{d^2y}{dx^2} - \frac{dy}{dx} + 2y = 0$$

are linearly independent, for

$$W(e^x, e^{-x}, e^{2x}) = \begin{vmatrix} e^x & e^{-x} & e^{2x} \\ e^x & -e^{-x} & 2e^{2x} \\ e^x & e^{-x} & 4e^{2x} \end{vmatrix} = e^{2x} \begin{vmatrix} 1 & 1 & 1 \\ 1 & -1 & 2 \\ 1 & 1 & 4 \end{vmatrix} = -6e^{2x} \neq 0.$$

C. Reduction of Order

In Section 4.2 we shall begin to study methods for obtaining explicit solutions of higher order linear differential equations. There and in later sections we shall find that the following theorem on reduction of order is often quite useful.

THEOREM 4.6.

Hypothesis. Let f be a nontrivial solution of the nth order homogeneous linear differential equation

$$(4.2) \qquad a_0(x)\frac{d^ny}{dx^n} + a_1(x)\frac{d^{n-1}y}{dx^{n-1}} + \cdots + a_{n-1}(x)\frac{dy}{dx} + a_n(x)y = 0.$$

Conclusion. The transformation $y = fu$ reduces Equation (4.2) to an $(n-1)$st order homogeneous linear differential equation in the dependent variable $w = \dfrac{du}{dx}$.

This theorem tells us that if one nonzero solution of the nth order homogeneous linear differential equation (4.2) is known, then by making the appropriate transformation we may reduce the given equation to another homogeneous linear equation which is one order lower than the original. Since this theorem will be most useful for us in connection with second order homogeneous linear equations (the case where $n = 2$), we shall now investigate the second order case in detail. Suppose f is a known nontrivial solution of the second-order homogeneous linear equation

$$(4.4) \qquad a_0(x)\frac{d^2y}{dx^2} + a_1(x)\frac{dy}{dx} + a_2(x)y = 0.$$

Let us make the transformation

$$(4.5) \qquad y = fu,$$

where f is the known solution of (4.4) and u is a function of x which will be determined. Then, differentiating, we obtain

$$(4.6) \qquad \frac{dy}{dx} = f\frac{du}{dx} + u\frac{df}{dx},$$

(4.7)
$$\frac{d^2y}{dx^2} = f\frac{d^2u}{dx^2} + 2\frac{df}{dx}\frac{du}{dx} + \frac{d^2f}{dx^2}u.$$

Substituting (4.5), (4.6), and (4.7) into (4.4), we obtain

$$a_0\left[f\frac{d^2u}{dx^2} + 2\frac{df}{dx}\frac{du}{dx} + \frac{d^2f}{dx^2}u\right] + a_1\left[f\frac{du}{dx} + u\frac{df}{dx}\right] + a_2fu = 0$$

or

$$a_0f\frac{d^2u}{dx^2} + \left[2a_0\frac{df}{dx} + a_1f\right]\frac{du}{dx} + \left[a_0\frac{d^2f}{dx^2} + a_1\frac{df}{dx} + a_2f\right]u = 0.$$

Since f is a solution of (4.4), the coefficient of u is zero, and so the last equation reduces to

$$a_0f\frac{d^2u}{dx^2} + \left[2a_0\frac{df}{dx} + a_1f\right]\frac{du}{dx} = 0.$$

Letting $w = \dfrac{du}{dx}$, this becomes

(4.8)
$$a_0f\frac{dw}{dx} + \left[2a_0\frac{df}{dx} + a_1f\right]w = 0.$$

This is a *first*-order homogeneous linear differential equation in the dependent variable w. The equation is separable; thus assuming $f \neq 0$ and $a_0 \neq 0$, we may write

$$\frac{dw}{w} = -\left[2\frac{f'}{f} + \frac{a_1}{a_0}\right]dx,$$

where f' denotes df/dx.
Thus integrating, we obtain

$$\ln|w| = -\ln f^2 - \int\frac{a_1}{a_0}dx + \ln|c|$$

or

$$w = \frac{ce^{-\int\frac{a_1}{a_0}dx}}{f^2}.$$

This is the general solution of Equation (4.8); choosing the particular solution for which $c = 1$, recalling that $\dfrac{du}{dx} = w$, and integrating again, we now obtain

$$u = \int\frac{e^{-\int\frac{a_1}{a_0}dx}}{f^2}dx.$$

Finally, from (4.5), we obtain

(4.9)
$$y = f\int\frac{e^{-\int\frac{a_1}{a_0}dx}}{f^2}dx.$$

The function in the right member of (4.9), which we shall henceforth denote by g, is actually a solution of the original second-order equation (4.4). Furthermore, this "new" solution g and the original known solution f are linearly independent, since

$$W(f, g) = \begin{vmatrix} f & g \\ f' & g' \end{vmatrix} = \begin{vmatrix} f & fu \\ f' & fu' + f'u \end{vmatrix}$$

$$= f^2 u' = e^{-\int \frac{a_1}{a_0} dx} \neq 0.$$

Thus the linear combination

$$c_1 f + c_2 g$$

is the general solution of Equation (4.4). We now summarize this discussion in the following theorem.

THEOREM 4.7.

Hypothesis. Let f be a nontrivial solution of the second-order homogeneous linear differential equation

$$a_0(x)\frac{d^2 y}{dx^2} + a_1(x)\frac{dy}{dx} + a_2(x)y = 0.$$

Conclusion 1. The transformation $y = fu$ reduces Equation (4.4) to the *first*-order homogeneous linear differential equation

$$a_0 f \frac{dw}{dx} + \left[2a_0 \frac{df}{dx} + a_1 f \right] w = 0$$

in the dependent variable w, where $w = \dfrac{du}{dx}$.

Conclusion 2. The particular solution

$$w = \frac{e^{-\int \frac{a_1}{a_0} dx}}{f^2}$$

of Equation (4.8) gives rise to the function u, where

$$u = \int \frac{e^{-\int \frac{a_1}{a_0} dx}}{f^2} dx$$

The function g, where $g = fu$, is then a solution of the second-order equation (4.4).

Conclusion 3. The original known solution f and the "new" solution g are linearly independent solutions of (4.4), and hence the general solution of (4.4) may be expressed as the linear combination

$$c_1 f + c_2 g.$$

Let us emphasize the utility of this theorem and at the same time clearly recognize its limitations. Certainly its utility is by now obvious. It tells us that if one solution of the second-order equation (4.4) is known, then we can reduce the order to obtain a linearly independent solution and thereby obtain the general solution of (4.4). But the limitations of the theorem are equally obvious. One solution of Equation (4.4) must already be known to us in order to apply the theorem. How does one "already know" a solution? In general one does not. In some cases the form of the equation itself or related physical considerations suggest that there may be a solution of a certain special form, for example, an exponential solution or a linear solution. However, such cases are not too common and if no solution at all can be so ascertained, then the theorem will not aid us.

Example 4.15.   Given that $y = x$ is a solution of

(4.10)
$$(x^2 + 1)\frac{d^2y}{dx^2} - 2x\frac{dy}{dx} + 2y = 0,$$

find a linearly independent solution by reducing the order.

Solution.   First observe that $y = x$ *does* satisfy Equation (4.10). Then let

$$y = xu.$$

Then

$$\frac{dy}{dx} = x\frac{du}{dx} + u \quad \text{and} \quad \frac{d^2y}{dx^2} = x\frac{d^2u}{dx^2} + 2\frac{du}{dx}.$$

Substituting the expressions for y, $\frac{dy}{dx}$, and $\frac{d^2y}{dx^2}$ into Equation (4.10), we obtain

$$(x^2 + 1)\left(x\frac{d^2u}{dx^2} + 2\frac{du}{dx}\right) - 2x\left(x\frac{du}{dx} + u\right) + 2xu = 0$$

or

$$x(x^2 + 1)\frac{d^2u}{dx^2} + 2\frac{du}{dx} = 0.$$

Letting $w = \frac{du}{dx}$ we obtain the *first*-order homogeneous linear equation

$$x(x^2 + 1)\frac{dw}{dx} + 2w = 0.$$

Treating this as a separable equation, we obtain

$$\frac{dw}{w} = -\frac{2dx}{x(x^2 + 1)}$$

or

$$\frac{dw}{w} = \left[-\frac{2}{x} + \frac{2x}{x^2 + 1}\right]dx.$$

Integrating, we obtain the general solution

$$w = \frac{c(x^2 + 1)}{x^2}.$$

Choosing $c = 1$, we recall that $\dfrac{du}{dx} = w$ and integrate to obtain

$$u = x - \frac{1}{x}.$$

Now forming $g = fu$, where f denotes the known solution x, we obtain the function g defined by

$$g(x) = x\left(x - \frac{1}{x}\right) = x^2 - 1.$$

By Theorem 4.7 we know that this is the desired linearly independent solution. The general solution of Equation (4.10) may thus be expressed as the linear combination $c_1 x + c_2(x^2 - 1)$ of the linearly independent solutions f and g. We thus write the general solution of Equation (4.10) as

$$y = c_1 x + c_2(x^2 - 1).$$

D. The Nonhomogeneous Equation

We now return briefly to the nonhomogeneous equation

$$(4.1) \qquad a_0(x)\frac{d^n y}{dx^n} + a_1(x)\frac{d^{n-1} y}{dx^{n-1}} + \cdots + a_{n-1}(x)\frac{dy}{dx} + a_n(x)y = b(x).$$

The basic theorem dealing with this equation is the following.

THEOREM 4.8.

Hypothesis. (i) Let v be any solution of the given (nonhomogeneous) nth-order linear differential equation (4.1). (ii) Let u be any solution of the corresponding homogeneous equation

$$(4.2) \qquad a_0(x)\frac{d^n y}{dx^n} + a_1(x)\frac{d^{n-1} y}{dx^{n-1}} + \cdots + a_{n-1}(x)\frac{dy}{dx} + a_n(x)y = 0.$$

Conclusion. Then $u + v$ is also a solution of the given (nonhomogeneous) equation (4.1).

Example 4.16. Observe that $y = x$ is a solution of the nonhomogeneous equation

$$\frac{d^2 y}{dx^2} + y = x.$$

and that $y = \sin x$ is a solution of the corresponding homogeneous equation

$$\frac{d^2 y}{dx^2} + y = 0.$$

Then by Theorem 4.8 the sum

$$\sin x + x$$

is also a solution of the given nonhomogeneous equation

$$\frac{d^2y}{dx^2} + y = x.$$

The student should check that this is indeed true.

Now suppose u is the *general solution* of the homogeneous equation (4.2); that is, it is a general linear combination of n linearly independent solutions of (4.2). Let v be any particular solution of the nonhomogeneous equation (4.1), where v contains no arbitrary constants. Then applying Theorem 4.8, we see that $u + v$ is a solution of the nth order nonhomogeneous equation and that this solution involves n arbitrary constants. We call such a solution a *general solution* of Equation (4.1). We summarize this in the following definition:

DEFINITION.   Consider the nth-order (nonhomogeneous) linear differential equation

$$(4.1) \qquad a_0(x)\frac{d^ny}{dx^n} + a_1(x)\frac{d^{n-1}y}{dx^{n-1}} + \cdots + a_{n-1}(x)\frac{dy}{dx} + a_n(x)y = b(x)$$

and the corresponding homogeneous equation

$$(4.2) \qquad a_0(x)\frac{d^ny}{dx^n} + a_1(x)\frac{d^{n-1}y}{dx^{n-1}} + \cdots + a_{n-1}(x)\frac{dy}{dx} + a_n(x)y = 0.$$

(I)   The general solution of (4.2) is called the *complementary function* of Equation (4.1). We shall denote this by y_c.

(II)   Any particular solution of (4.1) involving no arbitrary constants is called a *particular integral* of (4.1). We shall denote this by y_p.

(III)   The solution $y_c + y_p$ of (4.1), where y_c is the complementary function and y_p is a particular integral of (4.1), is called the *general solution* of (4.1).

Thus to find the general solution of (4.1), we need merely find:

(a) *The complementary function*, that is, a general linear combination of n linearly independent solutions of the corresponding homogeneous equation (4.2); and

(b) a *particular integral*, that is, any particular solution of (4.1) involving no arbitrary constants.

Example 4.17.   Consider the differential equation

$$\frac{d^2y}{dx^2} + y = x.$$

The complementary function is the general solution

$$y_c = c_1 \sin x + c_2 \cos x$$

of the corresponding homogeneous equation

$$\frac{d^2y}{dx^2} + y = 0.$$

A particular integral is given by

$$y_p = x.$$

Thus the general solution of the given equation may be written

$$y = y_c + y_p = c_1 \sin x + c_2 \cos x + x.$$

In the remaining sections of this chapter we shall proceed to study methods of obtaining the two constituent parts of the general solution.

Exercises

1. Theorem 4.1 applies to one of the following problems but not to the other. Determine to which of the problems the theorem applies and state precisely the conclusion which can be drawn in this case. Explain why the theorem does not apply to the remaining problem.

(a)
$$\begin{cases} \dfrac{d^2y}{dx^2} + 5\dfrac{dy}{dx} + 6y = e^x \\ y(0) = 5 \\ y'(0) = 7. \end{cases}$$

(b)
$$\begin{cases} \dfrac{d^2y}{dx^2} + 5\dfrac{dy}{dx} + 6y = e^x \\ y(0) = 5 \\ y'(1) = 7. \end{cases}$$

2. Answer orally: What is the solution of the following initial-value problem? Why?

$$\begin{cases} \dfrac{d^2y}{dx^2} + x\dfrac{dy}{dx} + x^2y = 0 \\ y(1) = 0 \\ y'(1) = 0. \end{cases}$$

3. Prove Theorem 4.2 for the case $m = n = 2$. That is, prove that if $f_1(x)$ and $f_2(x)$ are two solutions of

$$a_0(x)\frac{d^2y}{dx^2} + a_1(x)\frac{dy}{dx} + a_2(x)y = 0,$$

then $c_1f_1(x) + c_2f_2(x)$ is also a solution of this equation, where c_1 and c_2 are arbitrary constants.

4. Consider the differential equation

$$\frac{d^2y}{dx^2} - 5\frac{dy}{dx} + 6y = 0.$$

(a) Show that e^{2x} and e^{3x} are linearly independent solutions of this equation on the interval $-\infty < x < \infty$.

(b) Write the general solution of the given equation.

(c) Find the solution which satisfies the conditions $y(0) = 2$, $y'(0) = 3$. Explain why this solution is unique.

5. Consider the differential equation

$$x^2\frac{d^2y}{dx^2} + x\frac{dy}{dx} - 4y = 0.$$

(a) Show that x^2 and $\dfrac{1}{x^2}$ are linearly independent solutions of this equation on the interval $0 < x < \infty$.

(b) Write the general solution of the given equation.

(c) Find the solution which satisfies the conditions $y(2) = 3$, $y'(2) = -1$. Over what interval is this solution defined?

6. The functions e^x and e^{4x} are both solutions of the differential equation

$$\frac{d^2y}{dx^2} - 5\frac{dy}{dx} + 4y = 0.$$

(a) Show that these solutions are linearly independent on the interval $-\infty < x < \infty$.

(b) What theorem enables us to conclude at once that $2e^x - 3e^{4x}$ is also a solution of the given differential equation?

(c) Show that the solution of part (b) and the solution e^x are also linearly independent on $-\infty < x < \infty$.

7. Given that e^{-x}, e^{3x}, and e^{4x} are all solutions of

$$\frac{d^3y}{dx^3} - 6\frac{d^2y}{dx^2} + 5\frac{dy}{dx} + 12y = 0,$$

show that they are linearly independent on the interval $-\infty < x < \infty$ and write the general solution.

8. Verify the truth of Theorem 4.6 for the equation

$$(x^2 - 1)\frac{d^2y}{dx^2} - 2x\frac{dy}{dx} + 2y = 0,$$

given that $f(x) = x$ is a solution.

9. Given that $y = e^{2x}$ is a solution of

$$(2x + 1)\frac{d^2y}{dx^2} - 4(x + 1)\frac{dy}{dx} + 4y = 0,$$

find a linearly independent solution by reducing the order. Write the general solution.

10. Given that $y = x^2$ is a solution of

$$(x^3 - x^2)\frac{d^2y}{dx^2} - (x^3 + 2x^2 - 2x)\frac{dy}{dx} + (2x^2 + 2x - 2)y = 0,$$

find a linearly independent solution by reducing the order. Write the general solution.

11. Prove Theorem 4.8 for the case $n = 2$. That is, prove that if u is any solution of

$$a_0(x)\frac{d^2y}{dx^2} + a_1(x)\frac{dy}{dx} + a_2(x)y = 0$$

and v is any solution of

$$a_0(x)\frac{d^2y}{dx^2} + a_1(x)\frac{dy}{dx} + a_2(x)y = b(x),$$

then $u + v$ is also a solution of this latter nonhomogeneous equation.

12. Consider the nonhomogeneous differential equation

$$\frac{d^2y}{dx^2} - 3\frac{dy}{dx} + 2y = 4x^2.$$

(a) Show that e^x and e^{2x} are linearly independent solutions of the corresponding homogeneous equation

$$\frac{d^2y}{dx^2} - 3\frac{dy}{dx} + 2y = 0.$$

(b) What is the complementary function of the given nonhomogeneous equation?
(c) Show that $2x^2 + 6x + 7$ is a particular integral of the given equation.
(d) What is the general solution of the given equation?

4.2 The Homogeneous Linear Equation With Constant Coefficients

A. Introduction

In this section we consider the special case of the nth order homogeneous linear differential equation in which all of the coefficients are real constants. That is, we shall be concerned with the equation

(4.11) $$a_0\frac{d^ny}{dx^n} + a_1\frac{d^{n-1}y}{dx^{n-1}} + \cdots + a_{n-1}\frac{dy}{dx} + a_ny = 0$$

where $a_0, a_1, \ldots, a_{n-1} \ a_n$ are real constants. We shall show that the general solution of this equation can be found explicitly.

In an attempt to find solutions of a differential equation we would naturally inquire whether or not any familiar type of function might possibly have the properties which would enable it to be a solution. The differential equation (4.11) requires a function f having the property such that if it and its various derivatives are each multiplied by certain constants, the a_i, and the resulting products, $a_i\frac{d^{n-i}f}{dx^{n-i}}$, are then added, the result will equal zero. For this to be the case we would need a function such that its derivatives were constant multiples of itself. Do we know of functions f having this property that $\frac{d^k}{dx^k}[f(x)] = cf(x)$ for all x? The answer is "Yes," for the exponential function f such that $f(x) = e^{mx}$, where m is a constant, is such that

$$\frac{d^k}{dx^k}[e^{mx}] = m^ke^{mx}.$$

Thus we shall seek solutions of (4.11) of the form $y = e^{mx}$, where the constant m will be chosen such that e^{mx} *does* satisfy the equation. Assuming then that $y = e^{mx}$ is a solution for certain m, we have:

$$\frac{dy}{dx} = me^{mx}$$

$$\frac{d^2y}{dx^2} = m^2e^{mx}$$

$$\cdot$$
$$\cdot$$
$$\cdot$$

$$\frac{d^ny}{dx^n} = m^ne^{mx}.$$

Substituting in (4.11), we obtain

$$a_0 m^n e^{mx} + a_1 m^{n-1} e^{mx} + \cdots + a_{n-1} m e^{mx} + a_n e^{mx} = 0$$

or

$$e^{mx}(a_0 m^n + a_1 m^{n-1} \cdots + a_{n-1} m + a_n) = 0.$$

Since $e^{mx} \neq 0$, we obtain the polynomial equation in the unknown m:

(4.12) $$a_0 m^n + a_1 m^{n-1} + \cdots + a_{n-1} m + a_n = 0.$$

This equation is called the *auxiliary equation* or the *characteristic equation* of the given differential equation (4.11). If $y = e^{mx}$ is a solution of (4.11) then we see that the constant m must satisfy (4.12). Hence, to solve (4.11), we write the auxiliary equation (4.12) and solve it for m. Observe that (4.12) is formally obtained from (4.11) by merely replacing the kth derivative in (4.11) by m^k. ($k = 0, 1, 2, \ldots, n$.) Three cases arise, according as the roots of (4.12) are real and distinct, real and repeated, or complex.

B. Case 1. Distinct Real Roots

Suppose the roots of (4.12) are the n distinct real numbers

$$m_1, m_2, \ldots, m_n.$$

Then

$$e^{m_1 x}, e^{m_2 x}, \ldots, e^{m_n x}$$

are n distinct solutions of (4.11). Further, using the Wronskian determinant one may show that these n solutions are linearly independent. Thus we have the following result.

THEOREM 4.9. Consider the nth-order homogeneous linear differential equation (4.11) with constant coefficients. If the auxiliary equation (4.12) has the n distinct real roots $m_1, m_2, \ldots, m_n$, then the general solution of (4.11) is

$$y = c_1 e^{m_1 x} + c_2 e^{m_2 x} + \cdots + c_n e^{m_n x},$$

where $c_1, c_2, \ldots, c_n$ are arbitrary constants.

Example 4.18. $\dfrac{d^2 y}{dx^2} - 3\dfrac{dy}{dx} + 2y = 0.$

The auxiliary equation is

$$m^2 - 3m + 2 = 0.$$

Hence

$$(m - 1)(m - 2) = 0, \quad m_1 = 1, m_2 = 2.$$

The roots are real and distinct. Thus e^x and e^{2x} are solutions and the general solution may be written

$$y = c_1 e^x + c_2 e^{2x}.$$

We verify that e^x and e^{2x} are indeed linearly independent.

Their Wronskian is $W(e^x, e^{2x}) = \begin{vmatrix} e^x & e^{2x} \\ e^x & 2e^{2x} \end{vmatrix} = e^{3x} \neq 0.$

Thus by Theorem 4.4 we are assured of their linear independence.

Example 4.19. $\dfrac{d^3y}{dx^3} - 4\dfrac{d^2y}{dx^2} + \dfrac{dy}{dx} + 6y = 0.$

The auxiliary equation is

$$m^3 - 4m^2 + m + 6 = 0.$$

We observe that $m = -1$ is a root of this equation. By synthetic division we obtain the factorization

$$(m + 1)(m^2 - 5m + 6) = 0$$

or

$$(m + 1)(m - 2)(m - 3) = 0.$$

Thus the roots are the distinct real numbers

$$m_1 = -1, m_2 = 2, m_3 = 3,$$

and the general solution is

$$y = c_1 e^{-x} + c_2 e^{2x} + c_3 e^{3x}.$$

C. Case II.   Repeated Real Roots

We shall begin our study of this case by considering a simple example.

Example 4.20: Introductory Example.   Consider the differential equation

(4.13) $\dfrac{d^2y}{dx^2} - 6\dfrac{dy}{dx} + 9y = 0.$

The auxiliary equation is

$$m^2 - 6m + 9 = 0$$

or

$$(m - 3)^2 = 0.$$

The roots of this equation are

$$m_1 = 3, m_2 = 3$$

(real but *not* distinct).

Corresponding to the root m_1 we have the solution e^{3x}, and corresponding to m_2 we have the *same* solution e^{3x}. The linear combination $c_1 e^{3x} + c_2 e^{3x}$ of these "two" solutions is clearly *not* the general solution of the differential equation (4.13), for it is *not* a linear combination of two *linearly independent* solutions. Indeed we may write the combination $c_1 e^{3x} + c_2 e^{3x}$ as simply $c_0 e^{3x}$, where $c_0 = c_1 + c_2$; and clearly $y = c_0 e^{3x}$, involving *one* arbitrary constant, is not the general solution of the given *second*-order equation.

We must find a linearly independent solution; but how shall we proceed to do so? Since we already know the one solution e^{3x}, we may apply Theorem 4.7 and reduce the order. We let

$$y = e^{3x}u,$$

where u is to be determined.

Then
$$\frac{dy}{dx} = e^{3x}\frac{du}{dx} + 3e^{3x}u,$$

$$\frac{d^2y}{dx^2} = e^{3x}\frac{d^2u}{dx^2} + 6e^{3x}\frac{du}{dx} + 9e^{3x}u.$$

Substituting into equation (4.13) we have

$$\left(e^{3x}\frac{d^2u}{dx^2} + 6e^{3x}\frac{du}{dx} + 9e^{3x}u\right) - 6\left(e^{3x}\frac{du}{dx} + 3e^{3x}u\right) + 9e^{3x}u = 0$$

or

$$e^{3x}\frac{d^2u}{dx^2} = 0.$$

Letting $w = \dfrac{du}{dx}$, we have the first-order equation

$$e^{3x}\frac{dw}{dx} = 0$$

or simply

$$\frac{dw}{dx} = 0.$$

The general solution of this first-order equation is simply $w = c$, where c is an arbitrary constant. Choosing the particular solution $w = 1$ and recalling that $\dfrac{du}{dx} = w$, we find

$$u = x + c_0,$$

where c_0 is an arbitrary constant. By Theorem 4.7 we know that for any choice of the constant c_0, $ue^{3x} = (x + c_0)e^{3x}$ is a solution of the given second order equation (4.13). Further, by Theorem 4.7, we know that this solution and the previously known solution e^{3x} are linearly independent. Choosing $c_0 = 0$ we obtain the solution

$$y = xe^{3x},$$

and thus corresponding to the *double* root 3 we find the linearly independent solutions

$$e^{3x} \quad \text{and} \quad xe^{3x}$$

of equation (4.13).

Thus the general solution of Equation (4.13) may be written

(4.14) $$y = c_1e^{3x} + c_2xe^{3x}$$

or

(4.15) $$y = (c_1 + c_2x)e^{3x}.$$

With this example as a guide, let us return to the general nth-order equation (4.11). If the auxiliary equation (4.12) has the *double* real root m, we would surely expect that e^{mx} and xe^{mx} would be the corresponding linearly independent solutions. This is indeed the case. Specifically, suppose the roots of (4.12) are the double real root m and the $(n-2)$ distinct real roots

$$m_1, m_2, \ldots, m_{n-2}.$$

Then linearly independent solutions of (4.11) are

$$e^{mx}, xe^{mx}, e^{m_1x}, e^{m_2x}, \ldots, e^{m_{n-2}x},$$

and the general solution may be written

$$y = c_1e^{mx} + c_2xe^{mx} + c_3e^{m_1x} + c_4e^{m_2x} + \cdots + c_ne^{m_{n-2}x}$$

or

$$y = (c_1 + c_2x)e^{mx} + c_3e^{m_1x} + c_4e^{m_2x} + \cdots + c_ne^{m_{n-2}x}.$$

In like manner, if the auxiliary equation (4.12) has the triple real root m, corresponding linearly independent solutions are

$$e^{mx}, xe^{mx}, \quad \text{and} \quad x^2e^{mx}.$$

The corresponding part of the general solution may be written

$$(c_1 + c_2x + c_3x^2)e^{mx}.$$

Proceeding further in like manner, we summarize case II in the following theorem:

repeated real roots

THEOREM 4.10.   (i) Consider the nth order homogeneous linear differential equation (4.11) with constant coefficients. If the auxiliary equation (4.12) has the real root m occurring k times, then the part of the general solution of (4.11) corresponding to this k-fold repeated root is

$$(c_1 + c_2x + c_3x^2 + \cdots + c_kx^{k-1})e^{mx}.$$

(ii) If, further, the remaining roots of the auxiliary equation (4.12) are the distinct real numbers $m_{k+1}, \ldots m_n$, then the general solution of (4.11) is

$$y = (c_1 + c_2x + c_3x^2 + \cdots + c_kx^{k-1})e^{mx} + c_{k+1}e^{m_{k+1}x} + \cdots + c_ne^{m_nx}.$$

(iii) If, however, any of the remaining roots are also repeated, then the parts of the general solution of (4.11) corresponding to each of these other repeated roots are expressions similar to that corresponding to m in part (i).

We now consider several examples.

Example 4.21.   Find the general solution of

$$\frac{d^3y}{dx^3} - 4\frac{d^2y}{dx^2} - 3\frac{dy}{dx} + 18y = 0.$$

The auxiliary equation

$$m^3 - 4m^2 - 3m + 18 = 0$$

has the roots 3, 3, -2. The general solution is

$$y = c_1e^{3x} + c_2xe^{3x} + c_3e^{-2x}$$

or

$$y = (c_1 + c_2x)e^{3x} + c_3e^{-2x}.$$

Example 4.22. Find the general solution of

$$\frac{d^4y}{dx^4} - 5\frac{d^3y}{dx^3} + 6\frac{d^2y}{dx^2} + 4\frac{dy}{dx} - 8y = 0.$$

The auxiliary equation is

$$m^4 - 5m^3 + 6m^2 + 4m - 8 = 0,$$

with roots $2,2,2,-1$. The part of the general solution corresponding to the threefold root 2 is

$$y = (c_1 + c_2x + c_3x^2)e^{2x}$$

and that corresponding to the simple root -1 is simply

$$y = c_4e^{-x}.$$

Thus the general solution is

$$y = (c_1 + c_2x + c_3x^2)e^{2x} + c_4e^{-x}.$$

D. Case III. *Conjugate Complex Roots*

Now suppose that the auxiliary equation has the complex number $a + bi$ (a, b real, $i^2 = -1$, $b \neq 0$) as a nonrepeated root. Then, since the coefficients are real, the conjugate complex number $a - bi$ is also a nonrepeated root. The corresponding part of the general solution is

$$k_1e^{(a+bi)x} + k_2e^{(a-bi)x},$$

where k_1 and k_2 are arbitrary constants. The solutions defined by $e^{(a+bi)x}$ and $e^{(a-bi)x}$ are complex functions of the real variable x. It is desirable to replace these by two *real* linearly independent solutions. This can be accomplished by using Euler's Formula,

$$e^{i\theta} = \cos\theta + i\sin\theta,*$$

which holds for all real θ.

Using this we have:

$$k_1e^{(a+bi)x} + k_2e^{(a-bi)x}$$

$$= k_1e^{ax}e^{bix} + k_2e^{ax}e^{-bix}$$

$$= e^{ax}[k_1e^{ibx} + k_2e^{-ibx}]$$

$$= e^{ax}[k_1(\cos bx + i\sin bx) + k_2(\cos bx - i\sin bx)]$$

$$= e^{ax}[(k_1 + k_2)\cos bx + i(k_1 - k_2)\sin bx]$$

$$= e^{ax}[c_1\sin bx + c_2\cos bx],$$

---

*We borrow this basic identity from complex variable theory, as well as the fact that $e^{ax+bix} = e^{ax}e^{ibx}$ holds for complex exponents.

where $c_1 = i(k_1 - k_2)$, $c_2 = k_1 + k_2$ are two new arbitrary constants. Thus the part of the general solution corresponding to the nonrepeated conjugate complex roots $a + bi$ is

$$e^{ax}[c_1 \sin bx + c_2 \cos bx].$$

Combining this with the results of case II, we have the following theorem covering case III.

THEOREM 4.11. (i) Consider the nth-order homogeneous linear differential equation (4.11) with constant coefficients. If the auxiliary equation (4.12) has the conjugate complex roots $a + bi$ and $a - bi$, neither repeated, then the corresponding part of the general solution of (4.11) may be written

$$y = e^{ax}(c_1 \sin bx + c_2 \cos bx).$$

(ii) If, however, $a + bi$ and $a - bi$ are each k-fold roots of the auxiliary equation (4.12), then the corresponding part of the general solution of (4.11) may be written

$$y = e^{ax}[(c_1 + c_2 x + c_3 x^2 + \cdots + c_k x^{k-1}) \sin bx \\ + (c_{k+1} + c_{k+2}x + c_{k+3}x^2 + \cdots + c_{2k}x^{k-1}) \cos bx].$$

We now give several examples.

Example 4.23.   Find the general solution of

$$\frac{d^2y}{dx^2} + y = 0.$$

We have already used this equation to illustrate the theorems of Section 4.1. Let us now obtain its solution using Theorem 4.11. The auxiliary equation $m^2 + 1 = 0$ has the roots $m = \pm i$. These are the pure imaginary complex numbers $a \pm bi$, where $a = 0$, $b = 1$. The general solution is thus

$$y = e^{0x}(c_1 \sin 1 \cdot x + c_2 \cos 1 \cdot x),$$

which is simply

$$y = c_1 \sin x + c_2 \cos x.$$

Example 4.24.   Find the general solution of

$$\frac{d^2y}{dx^2} - 6\frac{dy}{dx} + 25y = 0.$$

The auxiliary equation is $m^2 - 6m + 25 = 0$.
Solving it, we find

$$m = \frac{6 \pm \sqrt{36 - 100}}{2} = \frac{6 \pm 8i}{2} = 3 \pm 4i.$$

Here the roots are the conjugate complex numbers $a \pm bi$, where $a = 3$, $b = 4$. The general solution may be written

$$y = e^{3x}(c_1 \sin 4x + c_2 \cos 4x).$$

Example 4.25.   Find the general solution of

$$\frac{d^4y}{dx^4} - 4\frac{d^3y}{dx^3} + 14\frac{d^2y}{dx^2} - 20\frac{dy}{dx} + 25y = 0.$$

The auxiliary equation is

$$m^4 - 4m^3 + 14m^2 - 20m + 25 = 0.$$

The solution of this equation presents some ingenuity and labor. Since our purpose in this example is not to display our mastery of the solution of algebraic equations but rather to illustrate the above principles of determining the general solution of differential equations, we unblushingly list the roots without further apologies.
They are

$$1 + 2i, 1 - 2i, 1 + 2i, 1 - 2i.$$

Since each pair of conjugate complex roots is double, the general solution is

$$y = e^x[(c_1 + c_2x)\sin 2x + (c_3 + c_4x)\cos 2x]$$

or

$$y = c_1e^x\sin 2x + c_2xe^x\sin 2x + c_3e^x\cos 2x + c_4xe^x\cos 2x.$$

E. An Initial-Value Problem

We now apply the results concerning the general solution of a homogeneous linear equation with constant coefficients to an initial-value problem involving such an equation.

Example 4.26.   Solve the initial-value problem

$$(4.16) \qquad\qquad\qquad \frac{d^2y}{dx^2} - 6\frac{dy}{dx} + 25y = 0$$

$$(4.17) \qquad\qquad\qquad y(0) = -3$$

$$(4.18) \qquad\qquad\qquad y'(0) = -1.$$

First let us note that by Theorem 4.1 this problem has a unique solution defined for all $x, -\infty < x < \infty$. We now proceed to find this solution; that is, we seek the particular solution of the differential equation (4.16) which satisfies the two initial conditions (4.17) and (4.18). We have already found the general solution of the differential equation (4.16) in Example 4.24.
It is

$$(4.19) \qquad\qquad\qquad y = e^{3x}(c_1\sin 4x + c_2\cos 4x).$$

From this, we find

$$(4.20) \qquad\qquad \frac{dy}{dx} = e^{3x}[(3c_1 - 4c_2)\sin 4x + (4c_1 + 3c_2)\cos 4x].$$

We now apply the initial conditions. Applying condition (4.17), $y(0) = -3$, to Equation (4.19), we find

$$-3 = e^0(c_1\sin 0 + c_2\cos 0)$$

which reduces at once to

(4.21) $c_2 = -3.$

Applying condition (4.18), $y'(0) = -1$, to Equation (4.20), we obtain

$$-1 = e^0[(3c_1 - 4c_2)\sin 0 + (4c_1 + 3c_2)\cos 0]$$

which reduces to

(4.22) $4c_1 + 3c_2 = -1.$

Solving Equations (4.21) and (4.22) for the unknowns c_1 and c_2, we find

$$\begin{cases} c_1 = 2 \\ c_2 = -3. \end{cases}$$

Replacing c_1 and c_2 in Equation (4.19) by these values, we obtain the unique solution of the given initial-value problem in the form

$$y = e^{3x}(2\sin 4x - 3\cos 4x).$$

We may write this in an alternate form by first multiplying and dividing by $\sqrt{(2^2) + (-3)^2} = \sqrt{13}$ to obtain

$$y = \sqrt{13}e^{3x}\left[\frac{2}{\sqrt{13}}\sin 4x - \frac{3}{\sqrt{13}}\cos 4x\right].$$

From this we may express the solution in the alternate form

$$y = \sqrt{13}e^{3x}\sin(4x + \phi),$$

where the angle ϕ is defined by the equations

$$\begin{cases} \sin \phi = -\dfrac{3}{\sqrt{13}} \\ \cos \phi = \dfrac{2}{\sqrt{13}}. \end{cases}$$

Exercises

Find the general solution of each of the differential equations in Exercises 1 through 24.

1. $\dfrac{d^2y}{dx^2} - 5\dfrac{dy}{dx} + 6y = 0.$

2. $\dfrac{d^2y}{dx^2} - 2\dfrac{dy}{dx} - 3y = 0.$

3. $4\dfrac{d^2y}{dx^2} - 12\dfrac{dy}{dx} + 5y = 0.$

4. $3\dfrac{d^2y}{dx^2} - 14\dfrac{dy}{dx} - 5y = 0.$

5. $\dfrac{d^3y}{dx^3} - 3\dfrac{d^2y}{dx^2} - \dfrac{dy}{dx} + 3y = 0.$

6. $\dfrac{d^3y}{dx^3} - 6\dfrac{d^2y}{dx^2} + 5\dfrac{dy}{dx} + 12y = 0.$

7. $\dfrac{d^2y}{dx^2} - 8\dfrac{dy}{dx} + 16y = 0.$

8. $4\dfrac{d^2y}{dx^2} + 4\dfrac{dy}{dx} + y = 0.$

9. $\dfrac{d^2y}{dx^2} - 4\dfrac{dy}{dx} + 13y = 0.$

10. $\dfrac{d^2y}{dx^2} + 6\dfrac{dy}{dx} + 25y = 0.$

11. $\dfrac{d^2y}{dx^2} + 9y = 0.$

12. $4\dfrac{d^2y}{dx^2} + y = 0.$

13. $\dfrac{d^3y}{dx^3} - 5\dfrac{d^2y}{dx^2} + 7\dfrac{dy}{dx} - 3y = 0.$

14. $4\dfrac{d^3y}{dx^3} + 4\dfrac{d^2y}{dx^2} - 7\dfrac{dy}{dx} + 2y = 0.$

15. $\dfrac{d^3y}{dx^3} - 6\dfrac{d^2y}{dx^2} + 12\dfrac{dy}{dx} - 8y = 0.$

16. $\dfrac{d^3y}{dx^3} + 4\dfrac{d^2y}{dx^2} + 5\dfrac{dy}{dx} + 6y = 0.$

17. $\dfrac{d^3y}{dx^3} - \dfrac{d^2y}{dx^2} + \dfrac{dy}{dx} - y = 0.$

18. $\dfrac{d^4y}{dx^4} + 8\dfrac{d^2y}{dx^2} + 16y = 0.$

19. $\dfrac{d^5y}{dx^5} - 2\dfrac{d^4y}{dx^4} + \dfrac{d^3y}{dx^3} = 0.$

20. $\dfrac{d^4y}{dx^4} - \dfrac{d^3y}{dx^3} - 3\dfrac{d^2y}{dx^2} + \dfrac{dy}{dx} + 2y = 0.$

21. $\dfrac{d^4y}{dx^4} - 3\dfrac{d^3y}{dx^3} - 2\dfrac{d^2y}{dx^2} + 2\dfrac{dy}{dx} + 12y = 0.$

22. $\dfrac{d^4y}{dx^4} + 6\dfrac{d^3y}{dx^3} + 15\dfrac{d^2y}{dx^2} + 20\dfrac{dy}{dx} + 12y = 0.$

23. $\dfrac{d^4y}{dx^4} + y = 0.$

24. $\dfrac{d^5y}{dx^5} = 0.$

Solve the initial-value problems in Exercises 25 through 30.

25. $\begin{cases} \dfrac{d^2y}{dx^2} - \dfrac{dy}{dx} - 12y = 0 \\ y(0) = 3 \\ y'(0) = 5. \end{cases}$

26. $\begin{cases} 9\dfrac{d^2y}{dx^2} - 6\dfrac{dy}{dx} + y = 0 \\ y(0) = 3 \\ y'(0) = -1. \end{cases}$

27. $\begin{cases} \dfrac{d^2y}{dx^2} - 4\dfrac{dy}{dx} + 29y = 0 \\ y(0) = 0 \\ y'(0) = 5. \end{cases}$

28. $\begin{cases} 4\dfrac{d^2y}{dx^2} + 4\dfrac{dy}{dx} + 37y = 0 \\ y(0) = 2 \\ y'(0) = -4. \end{cases}$

29. $\begin{cases} \dfrac{d^3y}{dx^3} - 6\dfrac{d^2y}{dx^2} + 11\dfrac{dy}{dx} - 6y = 0 \\ y(0) = 0 \\ y'(0) = 0 \\ y''(0) = 2. \end{cases}$

30. $\begin{cases} \dfrac{d^3y}{dx^3} - 2\dfrac{d^2y}{dx^2} + 4\dfrac{dy}{dx} - 8y = 0 \\ y(0) = 2 \\ y'(0) = 0 \\ y''(0) = 0. \end{cases}$

31. The roots of the auxiliary equation, corresponding to a certain 10th-order homogeneous linear differential equation with constant coefficients, are

$$4, 4, 4, 4, 2 + 3i, 2 - 3i, 2 + 3i, 2 - 3i, 2 + 3i, 2 - 3i.$$

Write the general solution.

32. Given that $\sin x$ is a solution of

$$\frac{d^4y}{dx^4} + 2\frac{d^3y}{dx^3} + 6\frac{d^2y}{dx^2} + 2\frac{dy}{dx} + 5y = 0,$$

find the general solution.

4.3   The Method of Undetermined Coefficients

A. The Method.

We now consider the (nonhomogeneous) differential equation

(4.23)
$$a_0\frac{d^ny}{dx^n} + a_1\frac{d^{n-1}y}{dx^{n-1}} + \cdots + a_{n-1}\frac{dy}{dx} + a_ny = b(x),$$

where the coefficients $a_0, a_1, \ldots, a_n$ are constants but where the nonhomogeneous term b is (in general) a nonconstant function of x. Recall that the general solution of (4.23) may be written

$$y = y_c + y_p,$$

where y_c is the *complementary function*, that is, the general solution of the corresponding homogeneous equation ([Equation (4.23)] with b replaced by 0), and y_p is a *particular integral*, that is, any solution of (4.23) containing no arbitrary constants. In Section 4.2 we learned how to find the complementary function; now we consider methods of determining a particular integral.

We consider first the method of *undetermined coefficients*. Mathematically speaking, the class of functions b to which this method applies is actually quite restricted; but this mathematically narrow class includes functions of frequent occurrence and considerable importance in various physical applications. And this method has one distinct advantage — when it *does apply*, it is relatively simple!

We first introduce certain preliminary definitions

DEFINITION.   We shall call a function a *UC function* if it is *either* (1) a function defined by one of the following:

(i) x^n, where n is a positive integer or zero.

(ii) e^{ax}, where a is a constant $\neq 0$.

(iii) $\sin (bx + c)$, where b and c are constants, $b \neq 0$.

(iv) $\cos (bx + c)$, where b and c are constants, $b \neq 0$.

or (2) a function defined as a finite product of two or more functions of these four types.

The method of undetermined coefficients applies when the nonhomogeneous function b in the differential equation is a finite linear combination of UC functions. Observe that given a UC function f, each successive derivative of f is either itself a constant multiple of a UC function or else a linear combination of UC functions.

DEFINITION.   Consider a UC function f. The set of functions consisting of f itself and all linearly independent UC functions of which the successive derivatives of f are either constant multiples or linear combinations will be called the *UC set* of f.

Example 4.27.   The function f defined for all real x by $f(x) = x^3$ is a UC function. Computing derivatives of f, we find

$$f'(x) = 3x^2, \quad f''(x) = 6x, \quad f'''(x) = 6 = 6 \cdot 1,$$

$$f^{(n)}(x) = 0 \quad \text{for} \quad n > 3.$$

The linearly independent *UC* functions of which the successive derivatives of f are either constant multiples or linear combinations are those given by

$$x^2, \qquad x, \qquad 1.$$

Thus the *UC set* of x^3 is the set $S = \{x^3, x^2, x, 1\}$.

Example 4.28. The function f defined for all real x by $f(x) = \sin 2x$ is a U C function. Computing derivatives of f, we find

$$f'(x) = 2\cos 2x, \qquad f''(x) = -4\sin 2x, \ldots.$$

The only linearly independent U C function of which the successive derivatives of f are constant multiples or linear combinations is that given by $\cos 2x$. Thus the *UC set* of $\sin 2x$ is the set $S = \{\sin 2x, \cos 2x\}$.

Example 4.29. The function f defined for all real x by $f(x) = x^2\sin x$ is the product of the two U C functions defined by x^2 and $\sin x$. Hence f is itself a U C function. Computing derivatives of f, we find

$$f'(x) = 2x\sin x + x^2\cos x,$$
$$f''(x) = 2\sin x + 4x\cos x - x^2\sin x,$$
$$f'''(x) = 6\cos x - 6x\sin x - x^2\cos x,$$
$$\cdots \cdots \cdots$$

No "new" types of functions will occur from further differentiation. Each derivative of f is a linear combination of certain of the six UC functions given by $x^2\sin x$, $x^2\cos x$, $x\sin x$, $x\cos x$, $\sin x$, and $\cos x$. Thus the set

$$S = \{x^2\sin x, \qquad x^2\cos x, \qquad x\sin x, \qquad x\cos x, \qquad \sin x, \qquad \cos x\}$$

is the *UC set* of $x^2\sin x$.

We now outline the method of undetermined coefficients for finding a particular integral y_p of

$$a_0\frac{d^n y}{dx^n} + a_1\frac{d^{n-1}y}{dx^{n-1}} + \cdots + a_{n-1}\frac{dy}{dx} + a_n y = b(x),$$

where b is a finite linear combination

$$b = A_1 u_1 + A_2 u_2 + \cdots + A_m u_m$$

of U C functions $u_1, u_2, \ldots, u_m$, the A_i being known constants. Assuming the complementary function y_c has already been obtained, we proceed as follows:

(1) For *each* of the U C functions

$$u_1, \ldots, u_m$$

of which b is a linear combination, form the corresponding UC set, thus obtaining the respective sets

$$S_1, S_2, \cdots, S_m.$$

(2) Suppose that one of the U C sets so formed, say S_j, is identical with or completely included in another, say S_k. In this case, we omit the (identical or smaller) set S_j from further consideration (retaining the set S_k).

(3) We now consider in turn each of the U C sets which still remain after step (2). Suppose now that one of these U C sets, say S_l, includes one or more members which are solutions of the corresponding homogeneous differential equation. If this is the case, we multiply *each* member of S_l by the lowest integral power of x so that the resulting revised set will contain no members which are solutions of the corresponding homogeneous differential equation. We now replace S_l by this revised set, so obtained. Note that here we consider one U C set at a time and perform the indicated multiplication, if needed, only upon the members of the one U C set under consideration at the moment.

(4) In general there now remains:

    (i) certain of the original U C sets, which were neither omitted in step (2) nor needed revision in step (3), and

    (ii) certain revised sets resulting from the needed revision in step (3).

Now form a linear combination of *all* of the elements of *all* of the sets of these two categories, with unknown constant coefficients (*undetermined coefficients*).

(5) Determine these unknown coefficients by substituting the linear combination formed in step (4) into the differential equation and demanding that it identically satisfy the differential equation (that is, that it be a particular solution).

We frankly admit that this outline of procedure may seem unnecessarily complicated. Once it is understood, however, it frees one from the need of considering separately all of the special cases which it covers.

B. Examples

A few illustrative examples, with reference to the above outline, should make the procedure clear. Our first example will be a simple one in which the situations of steps (2) and (3) do not occur.

Example 4.30.

$$\frac{d^2y}{dx^2} - 2\frac{dy}{dx} - 3y = 2e^x - 10\sin x.$$

The corresponding homogeneous equation is

$$\frac{d^2y}{dx^2} - 2\frac{dy}{dx} - 3y = 0$$

and the complementary function is

$$y_c = c_1 e^{3x} + c_2 e^{-x}.$$

The nonhomogeneous term is the linear combination $2e^x - 10\sin x$ of the two U C functions given by e^x and $\sin x$.

(1) Form the U C set for each of these two functions. We find

$$S_1 = \{e^x\},$$
$$S_2 = \{\sin x, \cos x\}.$$

(2) Note that neither of these sets is identical with nor included in the other; hence both are retained.

(3) Furthermore, by examining the complementary function, we see that none of the functions e^x, $\sin x$, $\cos x$ in either of these sets is a solution of the corresponding homogeneous equation. Hence neither set needs to be revised.

(4) Thus the original sets S_1 and S_2 remain intact in this problem, and we form the linear combination

$$A e^x + B\sin x + C\cos x$$

of the three elements e^x, $\sin x$, $\cos x$ of S_1 and S_2, with the undetermined coefficients A, B, C.

(5) We determine these unknown coefficients by substituting the linear combination formed in step (4) into the differential equation and demanding that it satisfy the differential equation identically. That is, we take

$$y_p = A e^x + B\sin x + C\cos x$$

as a particular solution. Then

$$y_p' = A e^x + B\cos x - C\sin x,$$
$$y_p'' = A e^x - B\sin x - C\cos x.$$

Actually substituting, we find

$$[A e^x - B\sin x - C\cos x] - 2[A e^x + B\cos x - C\sin x] - 3[A e^x + B\sin x + C\cos x]$$
$$= 2e^x - 10\sin x$$

or

$$-4A e^x + (-4B + 2C)\sin x + (-4C - 2B)\cos x = 2e^x - 10\sin x.$$

Equating coefficients of like terms, we obtain the equations

$$\begin{cases} -4A = 2 \\ -4B + 2C = -10 \\ -4C - 2B = 0. \end{cases}$$

From these equations, we find that

$$\begin{cases} A = -\dfrac{1}{2} \\ B = 2 \\ C = -1, \end{cases}$$

and hence we obtain the particular integral

$$y_p = -\frac{1}{2}e^x + 2\sin x - \cos x.$$

Thus the general solution of the differential equation under consideration is

$$y = y_c + y_p = c_1 e^{3x} + c_2 e^{-x} - \frac{1}{2}e^x + 2\sin x - \cos x.$$

Example 4.31.

$$\frac{d^2y}{dx^2} - 3\frac{dy}{dx} + 2y = 2x^2 + e^x + 2xe^x + 4e^{3x}.$$

The corresponding homogeneous equation is

$$\frac{d^2y}{dx^2} - 3\frac{dy}{dx} + 2y = 0$$

and the complementary function is

$$y_c = c_1e^x + c_2e^{2x}.$$

The nonhomogeneous term is the linear combination

$$2x^2 + e^x + 2xe^x + 4e^{3x}$$

of the four UC functions given by x^2, e^x, xe^x, and e^{3x}.

(1) Form the UC set for each of these functions. We have

$$S_1 = \{x^2, x, 1\},$$
$$S_2 = \{e^x\},$$
$$S_3 = \{xe^x, e^x\},$$
$$S_4 = \{e^{3x}\}.$$

(2) We note that S_2 is completely included in S_3, so S_2 is omitted from further consideration, leaving the 3 sets

$$S_1 = \{x^2, x, 1\}, \quad S_3 = \{xe^x, e^x\}, \quad S_4 = \{e^{3x}\}.$$

(3) We now observe that $S_3 = \{xe^x, e^x\}$ includes e^x, which is included in the complementary function and so is a solution of the corresponding homogeneous differential equation. Thus we multiply *each* member of S_3 by x to obtain the revised family

$$S_3' = \{x^2e^x, xe^x\},$$

which contains no members which are solutions of the corresponding homogeneous equation.

(4) Thus there remain the original UC sets

$$S_1 = \{x^2, x, 1\}$$

and

$$S_4 = \{e^{3x}\}$$

and the revised set

$$S_3' = \{x^2e^x, xe^x\}.$$

These contain the six elements

$$x^2, \quad x, \quad 1, \quad e^{3x}, \quad x^2e^x, \quad xe^x.$$

We form the linear combination

$$Ax^2 + Bx + C + De^{3x} + Ex^2e^x + Fxe^x$$

of these six elements.

(5) Thus we take as our particular solution,

$$y_p = Ax^2 + Bx + C + De^{3x} + Ex^2e^x + Fxe^x.$$

From this, we have:

$$y_p' = 2Ax + B + 3De^{3x} + Ex^2e^x + 2Exe^x + Fxe^x + Fe^x,$$
$$y_p'' = 2A + 9De^{3x} + Ex^2e^x + 4Exe^x + 2Ee^x + Fxe^x + 2Fe^x.$$

We substitute y_p, y_p', y_p'' into the differential equation for $y, \dfrac{dy}{dx}, \dfrac{d^2y}{dx^2}$, respectively, to obtain:

$$2A + 9De^{3x} + Ex^2e^x + (4E + F)xe^x + (2E + 2F)e^x$$
$$- 3[2Ax + B + 3De^{3x} + Ex^2e^x + (2E + F)xe^x + Fe^x]$$
$$+ 2[Ax^2 + Bx + C + De^{3x} + Ex^2e^x + Fxe^x]$$
$$= 2x^2 + e^x + 2xe^x + 4e^{3x}$$

(or $2A - 3B + 2C) + (2B - 6A)x + 2Ax^2 + 2De^{3x} + (-2E)xe^x + (2E - F)e^x$

$$= 2x^2 + e^x + 2xe^x + 4e^{3x}.$$

Equating coefficients of like terms, we have:

$$\begin{cases} 2A - 3B + 2C = 0 \\ 2B - 6A = 0 \\ 2A = 2 \\ 2D = 4 \\ -2E = 2 \\ 2E - F = 1. \end{cases}$$

From this $A = 1$, $B = 3$, $C = \frac{7}{2}$, $D = 2$, $E = -1$, $F = -3$, and so the particular integral is

$$y_p = x^2 + 3x + \frac{7}{2} + 2e^{3x} - x^2e^x - 3xe^x.$$

The general solution is therefore

$$y = y_c + y_p = c_1e^x + c_2e^{2x} + x^2 + 3x + \frac{7}{2} + 2e^{3x} - x^2e^x - 3xe^x.$$

Example 4.32.

$$\frac{d^4y}{dx^4} + \frac{d^2y}{dx^2} = 3x^2 + 4\sin x - 2\cos x.$$

The corresponding homogeneous equation is $\dfrac{d^4y}{dx^4} + \dfrac{d^2y}{dx^2} = 0$, and the complementary function is

$$y_c = c_1 + c_2x + c_3\sin x + c_4\cos x.$$

The nonhomogeneous term is the linear combination

$$3x^2 + 4\sin x - 2\cos x$$

of the three UC functions given by

$$x^2, \sin x, \quad \text{and} \quad \cos x.$$

(1) Form the UC set for each of these three functions. These sets are, respectively,

$$S_1 = \{x^2, x, 1\},$$
$$S_2 = \{\sin x, \cos x\},$$
$$S_3 = \{\cos x, \sin x\}.$$

(2) Observe that S_2 and S_3 are identical and so we retain only one of them, leaving the two sets

$$S_1 = \{x^2, x, 1\}, \quad S_2 = \{\sin x, \cos x\}.$$

(3) Now observe that $S_1 = \{x^2, x, 1\}$ includes 1 and x, which, as the complementary function shows, are both solutions of the corresponding homogeneous differential equation. Thus we multiply each member of the set S_1 by x^2 to obtain the revised set

$$S_1' = \{x^4, x^3, x^2\},$$

none of whose members are solutions of the homogeneous differential equation. We observe that multiplication by x instead of x^2 would not be sufficient, since the resulting set would be $\{x^3, x^2, x\}$, which still includes the homogeneous solution x. Turning to the set S_2, observe that both of its members, $\sin x$ and $\cos x$, are also solutions of the homogeneous differential equation. Hence we replace S_2 by the revised set

$$S_2' = \{x\sin x, x\cos x\}.$$

(4) None of the original UC sets remain here. They have been replaced by the revised sets S_1' and S_2' containing the five elements

$$x^4, x^3, x^2, x\sin x, x\cos x.$$

We form a linear combination of these,

$$Ax^4 + Bx^3 + Cx^2 + Dx\sin x + Ex\cos x,$$

with undetermined coefficients A, B, C, D, E.

(5) We now take this as our particular solution

$$y_p = Ax^4 + Bx^3 + Cx^2 + Dx\sin x + Ex\cos x.$$

Then

$$y_p' = 4Ax^3 + 3Bx^2 + 2Cx + Dx\cos x + D\sin x - Ex\sin x + E\cos x,$$
$$y_p'' = 12Ax^2 + 6Bx + 2C - Dx\sin x + 2D\cos x - Ex\cos x - 2E\sin x,$$
$$y_p''' = 24Ax + 6B - Dx\cos x - 3D\sin x + Ex\sin x - 3E\cos x,$$
$$y_p^{iv} = 24A + Dx\sin x - 4D\cos x + Ex\cos x + 4E\sin x.$$

Substituting into the differential equation, we obtain

$$24A + Dx\sin x - 4D\cos x + Ex\cos x + 4E\sin x + 12Ax^2 + 6Bx + 2C - Dx\sin x$$
$$+ 2D\cos x - Ex\cos x - 2E\sin x$$
$$= 3x^2 + 4\sin x - 2\cos x.$$

Equating coefficients, we find

$$\begin{cases} 24A + 2C = 0 \\ 6B = 0 \\ 12A = 3 \\ -2D = -2 \\ 2E = 4. \end{cases}$$

Hence $A = \frac{1}{4}$, $B = 0$, $C = -3$, $D = 1$, $E = 2$, and the particular integral is

$$y_p = \frac{1}{4}x^4 - 3x^2 + x\sin x + 2x\cos x.$$

The general solution is

$$y = y_c + y_p = c_1 + c_2 x + c_3\sin x + c_4\cos x + \frac{1}{4}x^4 - 3x^2 + x\sin x + 2x\cos x.$$

Example 4.33. An Initial-Value Problem. We close this section by applying our results to the solution of the initial-value problem

$$(4.24) \qquad \begin{cases} \dfrac{d^2y}{dx^2} - 2\dfrac{dy}{dx} - 3y = 2e^x - 10\sin x, \\[2mm] y(0) = 2 \\[2mm] y'(0) = 4. \end{cases}$$

(4.25)

(4.26)

By Theorem 4.1, this problem has a unique solution, defined for all x, $-\infty < x < \infty$; let us proceed to find it. In Example 4.30 we found that the general solution of the differential equation (4.24) is

$$(4.27) \qquad y = c_1 e^{3x} + c_2 e^{-x} - \frac{1}{2}e^x + 2\sin x - \cos x.$$

From this, we have

$$(4.28) \qquad \frac{dy}{dx} = 3c_1 e^{3x} - c_2 e^{-x} - \tfrac{1}{2}e^x + 2\cos x + \sin x.$$

Applying the initial conditions (4.25) and (4.26) to Equations (4.27) and (4.28), respectively, we have

$$\begin{cases} 2 = c_1 e^0 + c_2 e^0 - \dfrac{1}{2}e^0 + 2\sin 0 - \cos 0. \\[3mm] 4 = 3c_1 e^0 - c_2 e^0 - \dfrac{1}{2}e^0 + 2\cos 0 + \sin 0. \end{cases}$$

These equations simplify at once to the following:

$$\begin{cases} c_1 + c_2 = \dfrac{7}{2} \\[2mm] 3c_1 - c_2 = \dfrac{5}{2}. \end{cases}$$

From these two equations we obtain

$$\begin{cases} c_1 = \dfrac{3}{2} \\[2mm] c_2 = 2. \end{cases}$$

Substituting these values for c_1 and c_2 into Equation (4.27) we obtain the unique solution of the given initial-value problem in the form

$$y = \frac{3}{2}e^{3x} + 2e^{-x} - \frac{1}{2}e^x + 2\sin x - \cos x.$$

Exercises

Find the general solution of each of the differential equations in Exercises 1 through 17.

1. $\dfrac{d^2y}{dx^2} - 3\dfrac{dy}{dx} + 2y = 4x^2.$

2. $\dfrac{d^2y}{dx^2} - 2\dfrac{dy}{dx} - 8y = 4e^{2x} - 21e^{-3x}.$

3. $\dfrac{d^2y}{dx^2} + 2\dfrac{dy}{dx} + 5y = 6\sin 2x + 7\cos 2x.$

4. $\dfrac{d^2y}{dx^2} + 2\dfrac{dy}{dx} + 2y = 10\sin 4x.$

5. $\dfrac{d^2y}{dx^2} + 2\dfrac{dy}{dx} + 4y = \cos 4x.$

6. $\dfrac{d^3y}{dx^3} + 2\dfrac{d^2y}{dx^2} - 3\dfrac{dy}{dx} - 10y = 8xe^{-2x}.$

7. $\dfrac{d^3y}{dx^3} + \dfrac{d^2y}{dx^2} + 3\dfrac{dy}{dx} - 5y = 5\sin 2x + 10x^2 - 3x + 7.$

8. $4\dfrac{d^3y}{dx^3} - 4\dfrac{d^2y}{dx^2} - 5\dfrac{dy}{dx} + 3y = 3x^3 - 8x.$

9. $\dfrac{d^2y}{dx^2} + \dfrac{dy}{dx} - 6y = 10e^{2x} - 18e^{3x} - 6x - 11.$

10. $\dfrac{d^3y}{dx^3} - 3\dfrac{d^2y}{dx^2} + 4y = 4e^x - 18e^{-x}.$

11. $\dfrac{d^3y}{dx^3} + \dfrac{dy}{dx} = 2x^2 + 4\sin x.$

12. $\dfrac{d^4y}{dx^4} - 3\dfrac{d^3y}{dx^3} + 2\dfrac{d^2y}{dx^2} = 3e^{-x} + 6e^{2x} - 6x.$

13. $\dfrac{d^3y}{dx^3} - 6\dfrac{d^2y}{dx^2} + 11\dfrac{dy}{dx} - 6y = xe^x - 4e^{2x} + 6e^{4x}.$

14. $\dfrac{d^2y}{dx^2} + y = x\sin x.$

15. $\dfrac{d^2y}{dx^2} + 4y = 12x^2 - 16x\cos 2x.$

16. $\dfrac{d^4y}{dx^4} - 5\dfrac{d^3y}{dx^3} + 7\dfrac{d^2y}{dx^2} - 5\dfrac{dy}{dx} + 6y = 5\sin x - 12\sin 2x.$

17. $\dfrac{d^4y}{dx^4} + 2\dfrac{d^3y}{dx^3} - 3\dfrac{d^2y}{dx^2} = 18x^2 + 16xe^x + 4e^{3x} - 9.$

Solve the initial-value problems in Exercises 18 through 21.

18. $\begin{cases} \dfrac{d^2y}{dx^2} - 4\dfrac{dy}{dx} + 3y = 9x^2 + 4. \\[2mm] y(0) = 6 \\[1mm] y'(0) = 8. \end{cases}$

19. $\begin{cases} \dfrac{d^2y}{dx^2} + 4\dfrac{dy}{dx} + 13y = 5\sin 2x \\[2mm] y(0) = 1 \\[1mm] y'(0) = -2. \end{cases}$

20. $\begin{cases} \dfrac{d^2y}{dx^2} + y = 3x^2 - 4\sin x \\[2mm] y(0) = 0 \\[1mm] y'(0) = 1. \end{cases}$

21. $\begin{cases} \dfrac{d^3y}{dx^3} - 4\dfrac{d^2y}{dx^2} + \dfrac{dy}{dx} + 6y = 3xe^x + 2e^x - \sin x \\[2mm] y(0) = \dfrac{33}{40} \\[2mm] y'(0) = 0 \\[1mm] y''(0) = 0. \end{cases}$

For each of the differential equations in Exercises 22 through 30 *set up* the correct linear combination of functions with undetermined literal coefficients to use in finding a particular integral by the method of undetermined coefficients. (Do not actually find the particular integrals.)

22. $\dfrac{d^2y}{dx^2} - 6\dfrac{dy}{dx} + 8y = x^3 + x + e^{-2x}.$

23. $\dfrac{d^2y}{dx^2} + 9y = e^{3x} + e^{-3x} + e^{3x}\sin 3x.$

24. $\dfrac{d^3y}{dx^3} - 3\dfrac{d^2y}{dx^2} + 2\dfrac{dy}{dx} = x^2e^x + 3xe^{2x} + 5x^2.$

25. $\dfrac{d^3y}{dx^3} - 6\dfrac{d^2y}{dx^2} + 12\dfrac{dy}{dx} - 8y = xe^{2x} + x^2e^{3x}.$

26. $\dfrac{d^4y}{dx^4} + 3\dfrac{d^3y}{dx^3} + 4\dfrac{d^2y}{dx^2} + 3\dfrac{dy}{dx} + y = x^2e^{-x} + 3e^{-1/2x}\cos\dfrac{\sqrt{3}}{2}x.$

27. $\dfrac{d^4y}{dx^4} - 16y = x^2\sin 2x + x^4e^{2x}.$

28. $\dfrac{d^6y}{dx^6} + 2\dfrac{d^5y}{dx^5} + 5\dfrac{d^4y}{dx^4} = x^3 + x^2e^{-x} + e^{-x}\sin 2x.$

29. $\dfrac{d^4y}{dx^4} + 3\dfrac{d^2y}{dx^2} - 4y = \cos^2 x - \cosh x.$

30. $\dfrac{d^4y}{dx^4} + 10\dfrac{d^2y}{dx^2} + 9y = \sin x\sin 2x.$

4.4 Variation of Parameters

A. The Method

   While the process of carrying out the method of undetermined coefficients is actually quite straightforward (involving only techniques of college algebra and differentiation), the method applies in general to a rather small class of problems. For example, it would not apply to the apparently simple equation

$$\frac{d^2y}{dx^2} + y = \tan x.$$

We thus seek a method of finding a particular integral which applies in all cases (including variable coefficients) in which the complementary function is known. Such a method is the method of *variation of parameters*, which we now consider.

   We shall develop this method in connection with the general second order linear differential equation with variable coefficients

$$(4.29) \qquad a_0(x)\frac{d^2y}{dx^2} + a_1(x)\frac{dy}{dx} + a_2(x)y = b(x).$$

Suppose that y_1 and y_2 are linearly independent solutions of the corresponding homogeneous equation

$$(4.30) \qquad a_0(x)\frac{d^2y}{dx^2} + a_1(x)\frac{dy}{dx} + a_2(x)y = 0.$$

Then the complementary function of equation (4.29) is

$$c_1y_1 + c_2y_2,$$

where c_1 and c_2 are arbitrary constants. The procedure in the method of variation of parameters is to replace the arbitrary constants c_1 and c_2 in the complementary function by respective *functions* v_1 and v_2 which will be determined so that the resulting function

$$(4.31) \qquad\qquad v_1 y_1 + v_2 y_2$$

will be a particular integral of equation (4.29) (hence the name, *variation* of parameters).

We have at our disposal the *two functions* v_1 and v_2 with which to satisfy the *one condition* that (4.31) be a solution of (4.29). Since we have *two* functions but only *one* condition on them, we are thus free to impose a second condition, provided this second condition does not violate the first one. We shall see when and how to impose this additional condition as we proceed.

We thus assume a solution of the form (4.31) and write

$$(4.32) \qquad\qquad y_p = v_1 y_1 + v_2 y_2.$$

Differentiating (4.32), we have

$$(4.33) \qquad\qquad y_p' = v_1 y_1' + v_2 y_2' + v_1' y_1 + v_2' y_2,$$

where we use primes to denote differentiations. At this point we impose the aforementioned second condition; we simplify y_p' by demanding that

$$(4.34) \qquad\qquad v_1' y_1 + v_2' y_2 = 0.$$

With this condition imposed, (4.33) reduces to

$$(4.35) \qquad\qquad y_p' = v_1 y_1' + v_2 y_2'.$$

Now differentiating (4.35), we obtain

$$(4.36) \qquad\qquad y_p'' = v_1 y_1'' + v_2 y_2'' + v_1' y_1' + v_2' y_2'.$$

We now impose the basic condition that (4.32) be a solution of Equation (4.29). Thus we substitute (4.32), (4.35), and (4.36) for y, $\dfrac{dy}{dx}$, and $\dfrac{d^2 y}{dx^2}$, respectively, in Equation (4.29) and obtain the identity

$$a_0[v_1 y_1'' + v_2 y_2'' + v_1' y_1' + v_2' y_2'] + a_1[v_1 y_1' + v_2 y_2'] + a_2[v_1 y_1 + v_2 y_2] = b.$$

This can be written as

$$(4.37) \quad v_1[a_0 y_1'' + a_1 y_1' + a_2 y_1] + v_2[a_0 y_2'' + a_1 y_2' + a_2 y_2] + a_0[v_1' y_1' + v_2' y_2'] = b.$$

Since y_1 and y_2 are solutions of the corresponding homogeneous differential equation (4.30), the expressions in the first two brackets in (4.37) are identically zero. This leaves merely

$$(4.38) \qquad\qquad v_1' y_1' + v_2' y_2' = \frac{b}{a_0}.$$

This is actually what the basic condition demands. Thus the two imposed conditions require that the functions v_1 and v_2 be chosen such that the system of equations

$$(4.39) \qquad\qquad \begin{cases} y_1 v_1' + y_2 v_2' = 0 \\[2mm] y_1' v_1' + y_2' v_2' = \dfrac{b}{a_0} \end{cases}$$

is satisfied. The determinant of coefficients of this system is precisely

$$W(y_1, y_2) = \begin{vmatrix} y_1 & y_2 \\ y_1' & y_2' \end{vmatrix}.$$

Since y_1 and y_2 are linearly independent solutions of the corresponding homogeneous differential equation (4.30), we know that $W(y_1, y_2) \neq 0$. Hence the system (4.39) has a unique solution. Actually solving this system we obtain

$$v_1' = \frac{\begin{vmatrix} 0 & y_2 \\ \dfrac{b}{a_0} & y_2' \end{vmatrix}}{\begin{vmatrix} y_1 & y_2 \\ y_1' & y_2' \end{vmatrix}} = -\frac{by_2}{a_0 W(y_1, y_2)}$$

$$v_2' = \frac{\begin{vmatrix} y_1 & 0 \\ y_1' & \dfrac{b}{a_0} \end{vmatrix}}{\begin{vmatrix} y_1 & y_2 \\ y_1' & y_2' \end{vmatrix}} = \frac{by_1}{a_0 W(y_1, y_2)}.$$

Thus we obtain the functions v_1 and v_2 given by

$$v_1(x) = -\int^x \frac{b(t)y_2(t)dt}{a_0(t) W[y_1(t), y_2(t)]}$$

(4.40)

$$v_2(x) = \int^x \frac{b(t)y_1(t)dt}{a_0(t) W[y_1(t), y_2(t)]}.$$

Therefore a particular integral of equation (4.29) is

$$y_p = v_1 y_1 + v_2 y_2,$$

where v_1 and v_2 are defined by (4.40).

B. Examples

Example 4.34.

(4.41)
$$\frac{d^2y}{dx^2} + y = \tan x.$$

The complementary function is

$$y_c = c_1 \sin x + c_2 \cos x.$$

We assume

(4.42)
$$y_p = v_1 \sin x + v_2 \cos x,$$

where the functions v_1 and v_2 will be determined such that this is a particular integral of the differential equation (4.41). Then

$$y_p' = v_1 \cos x - v_2 \sin x + v_1' \sin x + v_2' \cos x.$$

We impose the condition

(4.43) $$v_1'\sin x + v_2'\cos x = 0,$$

leaving

$$y_p' = v_1\cos x - v_2\sin x.$$

From this

(4.44) $$y_p'' = -v_1\sin x - v_2\cos x + v_1'\cos x - v_2'\sin x.$$

Substituting (4.42) and (4.44) into (4.41) we obtain

(4.45) $$v_1'\cos x - v_2'\sin x = \tan x.$$

Thus we have the two equations (4.43) and (4.45) from which to determine v_1', v_2':

$$\begin{cases} v_1'\sin x + v_2'\cos x = 0 \\ v_1'\cos x - v_2'\sin x = \tan x. \end{cases}$$

Solving we find:

$$v_1' = \frac{\begin{vmatrix} 0 & \cos x \\ \tan x & -\sin x \end{vmatrix}}{\begin{vmatrix} \sin x & \cos x \\ \cos x & -\sin x \end{vmatrix}} = \frac{-\cos x \tan x}{-1} = \sin x,$$

$$v_2' = \frac{\begin{vmatrix} \sin x & 0 \\ \cos x & \tan x \end{vmatrix}}{\begin{vmatrix} \sin x & \cos x \\ \cos x & -\sin x \end{vmatrix}} = \frac{\sin x \tan x}{-1} = \frac{-\sin^2 x}{\cos x}$$

$$= \frac{\cos^2 x - 1}{\cos x} = \cos x - \sec x.$$

Integrating we find:

(4.46) $$\begin{cases} v_1 = -\cos x + c_3, \\ v_2 = \sin x - \ln|\sec x + \tan x| + c_4. \end{cases}$$

Substituting (4.46) into (4.42) we have

$$y_p = [-\cos x + c_3]\sin x + [\sin x - \ln|\sec x + \tan x| + c_4]\cos x$$

$$= -\sin x \cos x + c_3\sin x + \sin x \cos x$$
$$\quad - \ln|\sec x + \tan x|(\cos x) + c_4\cos x$$

$$= c_3\sin x + c_4\cos x - (\cos x)[\ln|\sec x + \tan x|].$$

Since a particular integral is a solution free of arbitrary constants, we may assign any particular values A and B to c_3 and c_4, respectively, and the result will be the particular integral

$$A\sin x + B\cos x - (\cos x)[\ln|\sec x + \tan x|].$$

Thus $y = y_c + y_p$ becomes:

$$y = c_1\sin x + c_2\cos x + A\sin x + B\cos x - (\cos x)\ln|\sec x + \tan x|$$

which we may write as

$$y = C_1\sin x + C_2\cos x - (\cos x) \ln |\sec x + \tan x|,$$

where $C_1 = c_1 + A$, $C_2 = c_2 + B$.

Thus we see that we might as well have chosen the constants c_3 and c_4 both equal to 0 in (4.46), for essentially the same result, $y = c_1 \sin x + c_2 \cos x - (\cos x) \ln |\sec x + \tan x|$, would have been obtained. This is the general solution of the differential equation (4.41).

The method of variation of parameters extends to higher order linear equations. The proof of the validity of this method for the general nth-order equation will be given in Chapter 11. We now illustrate the extension to a third-order equation in Example 4.35, although we hasten to point out that the equation of this example can be solved more readily by the method of undetermined coefficients.

Example 4.35.

(4.47)
$$\frac{d^3y}{dx^3} - 6\frac{d^2y}{dx^2} + 11\frac{dy}{dx} - 6y = e^x.$$

The complementary function is

$$y_c = c_1e^x + c_2e^{2x} + c_3e^{3x}.$$

We assume as a particular integral

(4.48)
$$y_p = v_1e^x + v_2e^{2x} + v_3e^{3x}.$$

Since we have *three* functions v_1, v_2, v_3 at our disposal in this case, we can apply three conditions. We have:

$$y_p' = v_1e^x + 2v_2e^{2x} + 3v_3e^{3x} + v_1'e^x + v_2'e^{2x} + v_3'e^{3x}.$$

Proceeding in a manner analogous to that of the second-order case, we impose the condition

(4.49)
$$v_1'e^x + v_2'e^{2x} + v_3'e^{3x} = 0,$$

leaving

(4.50)
$$y_p' = v_1e^x + 2v_2e^{2x} + 3v_3e^{3x}.$$

Then

$$y_p'' = v_1e^x + 4v_2e^{2x} + 9v_3e^{3x} + v_1'e^x + 2v_2'e^{2x} + 3v_3'e^{3x}.$$

We now impose the condition

(4.51)
$$v_1'e^x + 2v_2'e^{2x} + 3v_3'e^{3x} = 0,$$

leaving

(4.52)
$$y_p'' = v_1e^x + 4v_2e^{2x} + 9v_3e^{3x}.$$

From this,

(4.53)
$$y_p''' = v_1e^x + 8v_2e^{2x} + 27v_3e^{3x} + v_1'e^x + 4v_2'e^{2x} + 9v_3'e^{3x}.$$

We substitute (4.48), (4.50), (4.52), and (4.53) into the differential equation (4.47), obtaining:

$$v_1 e^x + 8v_2 e^{2x} + 27v_3 e^{3x} + v_1' e^x + 4v_2' e^{2x} + 9v_3' e^{3x}$$
$$- 6v_1 e^x - 24v_2 e^{2x} - 54v_3 e^{3x}$$
$$+ 11v_1 e^x + 22v_2 e^{2x} + 33v_3 e^{3x}$$
$$- 6v_1 e^x - 6v_2 e^{2x} - 6v_3 e^{3x} = e^x$$

or

(4.54) $$v' e^x + 4v_2' e^{2x} + 9v_3' e^{3x} = e^x.$$

Thus we have the three equations (4.49), (4.51), (4.54) from which to determine v_1', v_2', v_3':

$$\begin{cases} v_1' e^x + v_2' e^{2x} + v_3' e^{3x} = 0 \\ v_1' e^x + 2v_2' e^{2x} + 3v_3' e^{3x} = 0 \\ v_1' e^x + 4v_2' e^{2x} + 9v_3' e^{3x} = e^x. \end{cases}$$

Solving, we find:

$$v_1' = \frac{\begin{vmatrix} 0 & e^{2x} & e^{3x} \\ 0 & 2e^{2x} & 3e^{3x} \\ e^x & 4e^{2x} & 9e^{3x} \end{vmatrix}}{\begin{vmatrix} e^x & e^{2x} & e^{3x} \\ e^x & 2e^{2x} & 3e^{3x} \\ e^x & 4e^{2x} & 9e^{3x} \end{vmatrix}} = \frac{e^{6x}\begin{vmatrix} 1 & 1 \\ 2 & 3 \end{vmatrix}}{e^{6x}\begin{vmatrix} 1 & 1 & 1 \\ 1 & 2 & 3 \\ 1 & 4 & 9 \end{vmatrix}} = \frac{1}{2},$$

$$v_2' = \frac{\begin{vmatrix} e^x & 0 & e^{3x} \\ e^x & 0 & 3e^{3x} \\ e^x & e^x & 9e^{3x} \end{vmatrix}}{\begin{vmatrix} e^x & e^{2x} & e^{3x} \\ e^x & 2e^{2x} & 3e^{3x} \\ e^x & 4e^{2x} & 9e^{3x} \end{vmatrix}} = \frac{-e^{5x}\begin{vmatrix} 1 & 1 \\ 1 & 3 \end{vmatrix}}{2e^{6x}} = -e^{-x},$$

$$v_3' = \frac{\begin{vmatrix} e^x & e^{2x} & 0 \\ e^x & 2e^{2x} & 0 \\ e^x & 4e^{2x} & e^x \end{vmatrix}}{\begin{vmatrix} e^x & e^{2x} & e^{3x} \\ e^x & 2e^{2x} & 3e^{3x} \\ e^x & 4e^{2x} & 9e^{3x} \end{vmatrix}} = \frac{e^{4x}\begin{vmatrix} 1 & 1 \\ 1 & 2 \end{vmatrix}}{2e^{6x}} = \frac{1}{2}e^{-2x}.$$

We now integrate, choosing all the constants of integration to be zero (as the previous example showed was possible). We find:

$$v_1 = \frac{1}{2}x, \quad v_2 = e^{-x}, \quad v_3 = -\frac{1}{4}e^{-2x}.$$

Thus

$$y_p = \frac{1}{2}xe^x + e^{-x}e^{2x} - \frac{1}{4}e^{-2x}e^{3x} = \frac{1}{2}xe^x + \frac{3}{4}e^x,$$

and so

$$y = y_c + y_p = c_1 e^x + c_2 e^{2x} + c_3 e^{3x} + \frac{1}{2}xe^x + \frac{3}{4}e^x$$

$$= c_1'e^x + c_2e^{2x} + c_3e^{3x} + \frac{1}{2}xe^x,$$

where $c_1' = c_1 + \frac{3}{4}$.

In Examples 4.34 and 4.35 the coefficients in the differential equation were constants. The general discussion at the beginning of this section shows that the method applies equally well to linear differential equations with variable coefficients, once the complementary function y_c is known. We now illustrate its application to such an equation in Example 4.36.

Example 4.36.

(4.55) $$(x^2 + 1)\frac{d^2y}{dx^2} - 2x\frac{dy}{dx} + 2y = 6(x^2 + 1)^2.$$

In Example 4.15 we solved the corresponding homogeneous equation

$$(x^2 + 1)\frac{d^2y}{dx^2} - 2x\frac{dy}{dx} + 2y = 0.$$

From the results of that example, we see that the complementary function of equation (4.55) is

$$y_c = c_1x + c_2(x^2 - 1).$$

To find a particular integral of equation (4.55), we therefore let

(4.56) $$y_p = v_1x + v_2(x^2 - 1),$$

where v_1 and v_2 are functions of x. Then

$$y_p' = v_1 \cdot 1 + v_2 \cdot 2x + v_1'x + v_2'(x^2 - 1).$$

We impose the condition

(4.57) $$v_1'x + v_2'(x^2 - 1) = 0,$$

leaving

(4.58) $$y_p' = v_1 \cdot 1 + v_2 \cdot 2x.$$

From this, we find

(4.59) $$y_p'' = v_1' + 2v_2 + v_2' \cdot 2x.$$

Substituting (4.56), (4.58), and (4.59) into (4.55) we obtain

$$(x^2 + 1)(v_1' + 2v_2 + 2xv_2') - 2x(v_1 + 2xv_2) + 2[v_1x + v_2(x^2 - 1)] = 6(x^2 + 1)^2$$

or

(4.60) $$(x^2 + 1)(v_1' + 2xv_2') = 6(x^2 + 1)^2.$$

Thus we have the two equations (4.57) and (4.60) from which to determine v_1' and v_2'; that is, v_1' and v_2' satisfy the system

$$\begin{cases} v_1'x + v_2'(x^2 - 1) = 0, \\ v_1' + v_2'(2x) = 6(x^2 + 1). \end{cases}$$

Solving this system, we find

$$v_1' = \frac{\begin{vmatrix} 0 & x^2 - 1 \\ 6(x^2 + 1) & 2x \end{vmatrix}}{\begin{vmatrix} x & x^2 - 1 \\ 1 & 2x \end{vmatrix}} = \frac{-6(x^2 + 1)(x^2 - 1)}{x^2 + 1} = -6(x^2 - 1)$$

$$v_2' = \frac{\begin{vmatrix} x & 0 \\ 1 & 6(x^2 + 1) \end{vmatrix}}{\begin{vmatrix} x & x^2 - 1 \\ 1 & 2x \end{vmatrix}} = \frac{6x(x^2 + 1)}{x^2 + 1} = 6x.$$

Integrating, we obtain

(4.61)
$$\begin{cases} v_1 = -2x^3 + 6x, \\ v_2 = 3x^2, \end{cases}$$

where we have chosen both constants of integration to be zero. Substituting (4.61) into (4.56), we have

$$\begin{aligned} y_p &= (-2x^3 + 6x)x + 3x^2(x^2 - 1) \\ &= x^4 + 3x^2. \end{aligned}$$

Therefore the general solution of equation (4.55) may be expressed in the form

$$\begin{aligned} y &= y_c + y_p \\ &= c_1 x + c_2(x^2 - 1) + x^4 + 3x^2. \end{aligned}$$

C. *The Superposition Principle for Particular Integrals*

If the nonhomogeneous member of a linear differential equation is expressed as a linear combination of two or more functions, the following theorem may often be used to advantage in finding a particular integral.

THEOREM 4.12.

Hypothesis.

(1) Let f be a particular integral of

(4.62) $$a_0(x)\frac{d^n y}{dx^n} + a_1(x)\frac{d^{n-1}y}{dx^{n-1}} + \cdots + a_{n-1}(x)\frac{dy}{dx} + a_n(x)y = F(x).$$

(2) Let g be a particular integral of

(4.63) $$a_0(x)\frac{d^n y}{dx^n} + a_1(x)\frac{d^{n-1}y}{dx^{n-1}} + \cdots + a_{n-1}(x)\frac{dy}{dx} + a_n(x)y = G(x).$$

Conclusion.   Then $k_1 f + k_2 g$ is a particular integral of

(4.64) $$a_0(x)\frac{d^n y}{dx^n} + a_1(x)\frac{d^{n-1}y}{dx^{n-1}} + \cdots + a_{n-1}(x)\frac{dy}{dx} + a_n(x)y = k_1 F(x) + k_2 G(x),$$

where k_1 and k_2 are constants.

Let us apply this theorem to an equation of the form (4.64), where the coefficients $a_0, \ldots, a_n$ are constants. Suppose that F is a simple U C function but that G is not. Then we could *not* apply the method of undetermined coefficients to find a particular integral of Equation (4.64). However, we could find a particular integral of equation (4.62) by the method of undetermined coefficients, and then use variation of parameters to find a particular integral of Equation (4.63). Then applying Theorem 4.12, the appropriate linear combination of these two particular integrals, found by different methods, is a particular integral of Equation (4.64).

Example 4.37. Find a particular integral of

$$(4.65) \qquad \frac{d^2y}{dx^2} + y = 3e^x + 5\tan x.$$

We consider the two equations

$$(4.66) \qquad \frac{d^2y}{dx^2} + y = e^x$$

and

$$(4.67) \qquad \frac{d^2y}{dx^2} + y = \tan x.$$

Since the function defined by e^x is a U C function, a particular integral of Equation (4.66) may be found by the method of undetermined coefficients. Letting $y_p = Ae^x$, we find at once that $A = \frac{1}{2}$; hence a particular integral of (4.66) is

$$y_p = \frac{1}{2}e^x.$$

Since the function defined by $\tan x$ is *not* a U C function, we turn to variation of parameters to find a particular integral of Equation (4.67). We have already solved this problem in Example 4.34; we found there that a particular integral of (4.67) is

$$y_p = -(\cos x)\ln |\sec x + \tan x|.$$

Thus, applying Theorem 4.12, a particular integral of Equation (4.65) is

$$y_p = \frac{3}{2}e^x - 5(\cos x)\ln |\sec x + \tan x|.$$

Exercises

Find the general solution of each of the differential equations in Exercises 1 through 13.

1. $\dfrac{d^2y}{dx^2} + y = \cot x.$

2. $\dfrac{d^2y}{dx^2} + y = \tan^2 x.$

3. $\dfrac{d^2y}{dx^2} + y = \sec x.$

4. $\dfrac{d^2y}{dx^2} + y = \sec^3 x.$

5. $\dfrac{d^2y}{dx^2} + 4y = \sec^2 2x.$

6. $\dfrac{d^2y}{dx^2} - 2\dfrac{dy}{dx} + y = x\ln x, \quad (x > 0).$

7. $\dfrac{d^2y}{dx^2} - 2\dfrac{dy}{dx} + y = xe^x\ln x, \quad (x > 0).$

8. $\dfrac{d^2y}{dx^2} - 2\dfrac{dy}{dx} + y = (\ln x)^2, \quad (x > 0).$

9. $\dfrac{d^2y}{dx^2} - 2\dfrac{dy}{dx} + y = e^x\sin^{-1}x.$

10. $\dfrac{d^2y}{dx^2} + 3\dfrac{dy}{dx} + 2y = \dfrac{e^{-x}}{x}.$

11. $\dfrac{d^2y}{dx^2} + 3\dfrac{dy}{dx} + 2y = \dfrac{1}{1 + e^x}.$

12. $\dfrac{d^2y}{dx^2} + 3\dfrac{dy}{dx} + 2y = \dfrac{1}{1 + e^{2x}}.$

13. $\dfrac{d^2y}{dx^2} + y = \dfrac{1}{1 + \sin x}.$

14. Find the general solution by two methods:

$$\frac{d^3y}{dx^3} - 3\frac{d^2y}{dx^2} - \frac{dy}{dx} + 3y = x^2e^x.$$

15. Given that $y = x$ and $y = \dfrac{1}{x + 1}$ are linearly independent solutions of

$$(2x + 1)(x + 1)\frac{d^2y}{dx^2} + 2x\frac{dy}{dx} - 2y = 0,$$

find the general solution of

$$(2x + 1)(x + 1)\frac{d^2y}{dx^2} + 2x\frac{dy}{dx} - 2y = (2x + 1)^2.$$

16. Given that $y = \sin x$ and $y = x\sin x$ are linearly independent solutions of

$$(\sin^2 x)\frac{d^2y}{dx^2} - 2\sin x\cos x\frac{dy}{dx} + (\cos^2 x + 1)y = 0,$$

find the general solution of

$$(\sin^2 x)\frac{d^2y}{dx^2} - 2\sin x\cos x\frac{dy}{dx} + (\cos^2 x + 1)y = \sin^3 x.$$

4.5 The Cauchy-Euler Equation

A. The Equation and the Method of Solution

In the preceding sections we have seen how to obtain the general solution of the *n*th order linear differential equation with *constant* coefficients. We have seen that in such cases the form of the complementary function may be readily determined. The general *n*th order linear equation with *variable* coefficients is quite a different matter, however, and only in certain special cases can the complementary function be obtained explicitly in closed form. One special case of considerable practical importance for which it is fortunate that this can be done is the so-called *Cauchy-Euler Equation* (or *equidimensional equation*). This is an equation of the form

$$(4.68) \qquad a_0 x^n \frac{d^n y}{dx^n} + a_1 x^{n-1} \frac{d^{n-1} y}{dx^{n-1}} + \cdots + a_{n-1} x \frac{dy}{dx} + a_n y = b(x),$$

where $a_0, a_1, \ldots, a_{n-1}, a_n$ are constants. Note the characteristic feature of this equation: each term in the left member is a constant multiple of an expression of the form

$$x^k \frac{d^k y}{dx^k}.$$

How should one proceed to solve such an equation? About the only hopeful thought that comes to mind at this stage of our study is to attempt a transformation. But what transformation should we attempt and where will it lead us? While it is certainly worthwhile to stop for a moment and consider what sort of transformation we might use in solving a "new" type of equation when we first encounter it, it is certainly not worthwhile to spend a great deal of time looking for clever devices which mathematicians have known about for many years. Let us thus control our adventurous spirit and read the facts stated in the following theorem.

THEOREM 4.13. The transformation $x = e^t$ reduces the equation

$$(4.68) \qquad a_0 x^n \frac{d^n y}{dx^n} + a_1 x^{n-1} \frac{d^{n-1} y}{dx^{n-1}} + \cdots + a_{n-1} x \frac{dy}{dx} + a_n y = b(x)$$

to a linear differential equation with constant coefficients.

This is what we need! Following our custom, we shall prove the theorem for the case of the second-order Cauchy-Euler differential equation

$$(4.69) \qquad a_0 x^2 \frac{d^2 y}{dx^2} + a_1 x \frac{dy}{dx} + a_2 y = b(x).$$

The proof in the general *n*th order case proceeds in a similar fashion. Letting $x = e^t$, assuming $x > 0$, we have $t = \ln x$. Then

$$\frac{dy}{dx} = \frac{dy}{dt} \frac{dt}{dx} = \frac{1}{x} \frac{dy}{dt}$$

and

$$\frac{d^2y}{dx^2} = \frac{1}{x}\frac{d}{dx}\left(\frac{dy}{dt}\right) + \frac{dy}{dt}\frac{d}{dx}\left(\frac{1}{x}\right) = \frac{1}{x}\left[\frac{d^2y}{dt^2}\frac{dt}{dx}\right] - \frac{1}{x^2}\frac{dy}{dt}$$

$$= \frac{1}{x}\left(\frac{d^2y}{dt^2}\frac{1}{x}\right) - \frac{1}{x^2}\frac{dy}{dt} = \frac{1}{x^2}\left(\frac{d^2y}{dt^2} - \frac{dy}{dt}\right).$$

Thus

$$x\frac{dy}{dx} = \frac{dy}{dt} \quad\text{and}\quad x^2\frac{d^2y}{dx^2} = \frac{d^2y}{dt^2} - \frac{dy}{dt}.$$

Substituting into equation (4.69) we obtain

$$a_0\left(\frac{d^2y}{dt^2} - \frac{dy}{dt}\right) + a_1\frac{dy}{dt} + a_2y = b(e^t)$$

or

(4.70)
$$A_0\frac{d^2y}{dt^2} + A_1\frac{dy}{dt} + A_2y = B(t),$$

where

$$A_0 = a_0, \quad A_1 = a_1 - a_0, \quad A_2 = a_2, \quad B(t) = b(e^t).$$

This is a second-order linear differential equation with *constant* coefficients, which was what we wished to show.

Remarks. 1. Note that the leading coefficient a_0x^n in Equation (4.68) is zero for $x = 0$. Thus the basic interval $a \le x \le b$, referred to in the general theorems of Section 4.1, does *not* include $x = 0$.

2. Observe that in the above proof we assumed that $x > 0$. If $x < 0$, the substitution $x = -e^t$ is actually the correct one. Unless the contrary is explicitly stated, we shall assume $x > 0$ when finding the general solution of a Cauchy-Euler differential equation.

B. Examples

Example 4.38.

(4.71)
$$x^2\frac{d^2y}{dx^2} - 2x\frac{dy}{dx} + 2y = x^3.$$

Let $x = e^t$. Then, assuming $x > 0$, we have $t = \ln x$, and

$$\frac{dy}{dx} = \frac{dy}{dt}\frac{dt}{dx} = \frac{1}{x}\frac{dy}{dt},$$

$$\frac{d^2y}{dx^2} = \frac{1}{x}\left(\frac{d^2y}{dt^2}\frac{dt}{dx}\right) - \frac{1}{x^2}\frac{dy}{dt} = \frac{1}{x^2}\left(\frac{d^2y}{dt^2} - \frac{dy}{dt}\right).$$

Thus the equation (4.71) becomes

$$\frac{d^2y}{dt^2} - \frac{dy}{dt} - 2\frac{dy}{dt} + 2y = e^{3t}$$

or

$$(4.72) \qquad \frac{d^2y}{dt^2} - 3\frac{dy}{dt} + 2y = e^{3t}.$$

The complementary function of this equation is $y_c = c_1e^t + c_2e^{2t}$. We find a particular integral by the method of undetermined coefficients. We assume $y_p = Ae^{3t}$.
Then $y_p' = 3Ae^{3t}$, $y_p'' = 9Ae^{3t}$, and substituting into Equation (4.72), we obtain

$$2Ae^{3t} = e^{3t}.$$

Thus $A = \frac{1}{2}$ and we have $y_p = \frac{1}{2}e^{3t}$. The general solution of Equation (4.72) is then

$$y = c_1e^t + c_2e^{2t} + \frac{1}{2}e^{3t}.$$

But we are not yet finished! We must return to the original independent variable x. Since $e^t = x$, we find

$$y = c_1x + c_2x^2 + \frac{1}{2}x^3.$$

This is the general solution of Equation (4.71).

Remarks. 1. Note carefully that under the transformation $x = e^t$ the right member of (4.71), x^3, transforms into e^{3t}. The student should be careful to transform *both* sides of the equation if he intends to obtain a particular integral of the given equation by finding a particular integral of the transformed equation, as we have done here.
2. We hasten to point out that the following alternate procedure may be used. After finding the complementary function of the transformed equation one can immediately write the complementary function of the original given equation and then proceed to obtain a particular integral of the original equation by variation of parameters. In Example 4.38, upon finding the complementary function $c_1e^t + c_2e^{2t}$ of Equation (4.72), one can immediately write the complementary function $c_1x + c_2x^2$ of Equation (4.71), then assume the particular integral $y_p = v_1x + v_2x^2$, and from here proceed by the method of variation of parameters. However, when the nonhomogeneous function b transforms into a linear combination of UC functions, as it does in this example, the procedure illustrated is generally simpler.

Example 4.39.

$$(4.73) \qquad x^3\frac{d^3y}{dx^3} - 4x^2\frac{d^2y}{dx^2} + 8x\frac{dy}{dx} - 8y = 4\ln x.$$

Assuming $x > 0$, we let $x = e^t$. Then $t = \ln x$, and

$$\frac{dy}{dx} = \frac{1}{x}\frac{dy}{dt},$$

$$\frac{d^2y}{dx^2} = \frac{1}{x^2}\left(\frac{d^2y}{dt^2} - \frac{dy}{dt}\right).$$

Now we must consider $\dfrac{d^3y}{dx^3}$.

$$\begin{aligned}
\frac{d^3y}{dx^3} &= \frac{1}{x^2}\frac{d}{dx}\left(\frac{d^2y}{dt^2} - \frac{dy}{dt}\right) - \frac{2}{x^3}\left(\frac{d^2y}{dt^2} - \frac{dy}{dt}\right)\\
&= \frac{1}{x^2}\left[\frac{d^3y}{dt^3}\frac{dt}{dx} - \frac{d^2y}{dt^2}\frac{dt}{dx}\right] - \frac{2}{x^3}\left(\frac{d^2y}{dt^2} - \frac{dy}{dt}\right)\\
&= \frac{1}{x^3}\left(\frac{d^3y}{dt^3} - \frac{d^2y}{dt^2}\right) - \frac{2}{x^3}\left(\frac{d^2y}{dt^2} - \frac{dy}{dt}\right)\\
&= \frac{1}{x^3}\left(\frac{d^3y}{dt^3} - 3\frac{d^2y}{dt^2} + 2\frac{dy}{dt}\right).
\end{aligned}$$

Thus, substituting into equation (4.73), we obtain

$$\left(\frac{d^3y}{dt^3} - 3\frac{d^2y}{dt^2} + 2\frac{dy}{dt}\right) - 4\left(\frac{d^2y}{dt^2} - \frac{dy}{dt}\right) + 8\left(\frac{dy}{dt}\right) - 8y = 4t$$

or

(4.74)
$$\frac{d^3y}{dt^3} - 7\frac{d^2y}{dt^2} + 14\frac{dy}{dt} - 8y = 4t.$$

The complementary function of the transformed equation (4.74) is

$$y_c = c_1e^t + c_2e^{2t} + c_3e^{4t}.$$

We proceed to obtain a particular integral of equation (4.74) by the method of undetermined coefficients.   We assume $y_p = At + B$.   Then $y_p' = A$, $y_p'' = y_p''' = 0$.   Substituting into Equation (4.74), we find

$$14A - 8At - 8B = 4t.$$

Thus

$$\begin{cases} -8A = 4\\ 14A - 8B = 0, \end{cases}$$

and so $A = -\frac{1}{2}$, $B = -\frac{7}{8}$.

Thus the general solution of Equation (4.74) is

$$y = c_1e^t + c_2e^{2t} + c_3e^{4t} - \frac{1}{2}t - \frac{7}{8},$$

and so the general solution of Equation (4.73) is

$$y = c_1x + c_2x^2 + c_3x^4 - \frac{1}{2}\ln x - \frac{7}{8}.$$

Exercises

Find the general solution of each of the differential equations in Exercises 1 through 15.

1. $x^2\dfrac{d^2y}{dx^2} - 3x\dfrac{dy}{dx} + 3y = 0.$

2. $x^2\dfrac{d^2y}{dx^2} + x\dfrac{dy}{dx} - 4y = 0.$

3. $4x^2\dfrac{d^2y}{dx^2} - 4x\dfrac{dy}{dx} + 3y = 0.$

4. $x^2\dfrac{d^2y}{dx^2} - 3x\dfrac{dy}{dx} + 4y = 0.$

5. $x^2\dfrac{d^2y}{dx^2} + x\dfrac{dy}{dx} + 4y = 0.$

6. $x^2\dfrac{d^2y}{dx^2} - 3x\dfrac{dy}{dx} + 13y = 0.$

7. $x^3\dfrac{d^3y}{dx^3} - 3x^2\dfrac{d^2y}{dx^2} + 6x\dfrac{dy}{dx} - 6y = 0.$

8. $x^3\dfrac{d^3y}{dx^3} + 2x^2\dfrac{d^2y}{dx^2} - 10x\dfrac{dy}{dx} - 8y = 0.$

9. $x^3\dfrac{d^3y}{dx^3} - x^2\dfrac{d^2y}{dx^2} - 6x\dfrac{dy}{dx} + 18y = 0.$

10. $x^2\dfrac{d^2y}{dx^2} - 4x\dfrac{dy}{dx} + 6y = 4x - 6.$

11. $x^2\dfrac{d^2y}{dx^2} - 5x\dfrac{dy}{dx} + 8y = 2x^3.$

12. $x^2\dfrac{d^2y}{dx^2} + 4x\dfrac{dy}{dx} + 2y = 4\ln x, \quad (x > 0).$

13. $x^2\dfrac{d^2y}{dx^2} + x\dfrac{dy}{dx} + 4y = 2x\ln x, \quad (x > 0).$

14. $x^2\dfrac{d^2y}{dx^2} + x\dfrac{dy}{dx} + y = \dfrac{1}{1 + x}.$

15. $x^3\dfrac{d^3y}{dx^3} - x^2\dfrac{d^2y}{dx^2} + 2x\dfrac{dy}{dx} - 2y = x^3.$

Solve the initial value problems in Exercises 16 through 20.

16. $\begin{cases} x^2\dfrac{d^2y}{dx^2} - 2x\dfrac{dy}{dx} - 10y = 0 \\ y(1) = 5 \\ y'(1) = 4. \end{cases}$

17. $\begin{cases} x^2\dfrac{d^2y}{dx^2} - 4x\dfrac{dy}{dx} + 6y = 0 \\ y(2) = 0 \\ y'(2) = 4. \end{cases}$

18. $\begin{cases} x^2\dfrac{d^2y}{dx^2} - 5x\dfrac{dy}{dx} + 8y = 2x^3 \\ y(-2) = 1 \\ y'(-2) = 7. \end{cases}$

19. $\begin{cases} x^2\dfrac{d^2y}{dx^2} - 6y = \ln x, \quad (x > 0) \\ y(1) = \frac{1}{6} \\ y'(1) = -\frac{1}{6}. \end{cases}$

20. Solve:

$$(x + 2)^2\frac{d^2y}{dx^2} - (x + 2)\frac{dy}{dx} - 3y = 0.$$

21. Solve:

$$(2x - 3)^2\frac{d^2y}{dx^2} - 6(2x - 3)\frac{dy}{dx} + 12y = 0.$$

SUGGESTED READING

Agnew (1)

Coddington (12)

Ford (17)

Greenspan (20)

Kaplan (30)

Leighton (36)

Martin and Reissner (38)

Rainville (45)

5

APPLICATIONS OF SECOND-ORDER
LINEAR DIFFERENTIAL EQUATIONS WITH
CONSTANT COEFFICIENTS

Higher order linear differential equations, which were introduced in the previous chapter, are equations having a great variety of important applications. In particular, second-order linear differential equations with constant coefficients have numerous applications in physics and in electrical and mechanical engineering. Two of these applications will be considered in the present chapter. In Sections 5.1 through 5.5 we shall discuss the motion of a mass vibrating up and down at the end of a spring, while in Section 5.6 we shall consider problems in electric circuit theory.

5.1 The Differential Equation of the Vibrations of a Mass on a Spring

The Basic Problem. A coil spring is suspended vertically from a fixed point on a ceiling, beam, or other similar object. A mass is attached to its lower end and allowed to come to rest in an equilibrium position. The system is then set in motion either (1) by pulling the mass down a distance below its equilibrium position (or pushing it up a distance above it) and subsequently releasing it with an initial velocity (zero or nonzero, downward or upward) at $t = 0$; or (2) by forcing the mass out of its equilibrium position by giving it a nonzero initial velocity (downward or upward) at $t = 0$. Our problem is to determine the resulting motion of the mass on the spring. In order to do so we must also consider certain other phenomena which may be present. For one thing, assuming the system is located in some sort of medium (say "ordinary" air or perhaps water), this medium produces a resistance force which tends to retard the motion. Also, certain external forces may be present. For example, a magnetic force from outside the system may be acting upon the mass. Let us then attempt to determine the motion of the mass on the spring, taking into account both the resistance of the medium and possible external forces. We shall do this by first obtaining and then solving the differential equation for the motion.

In order to set up the differential equation for this problem we shall need two laws of physics: Newton's Second Law and Hooke's Law. Newton's Second Law was encountered in Chapter 3, and we shall not go into a further discussion of it here. Let us then recall the other law which we shall need.

Hooke's Law. The magnitude of the force needed to produce a certain elongation of a spring is directly proportional to the amount of this elongation, provided this elongation is not too great. In mathematical form,

$$|F| = ks,$$

where F is the magnitude of the force, s is the amount of elongation, and k is a constant of proportionality which we shall call the *spring constant*.

The spring constant k depends upon the spring under consideration and is a measure of its stiffness. For example, if a 30 lb. weight stretches a spring 2 feet, then Hooke's Law gives $30 = (k)(2)$; thus for this spring $k = 15$ lb/ft.

When a mass is hung upon a spring of spring constant k and thus produces an elongation of amount s, the force F of the mass upon the spring therefore has magnitude ks. The spring at the same time exerts a force upon the mass called the *restoring force* of the spring. This force is equal in magnitude but opposite in sign to F and hence has magnitude $-ks$.

Let us formulate the problem systematically. Let the coil spring have natural (unstretched) length L. The mass m is attached to its lower end and comes to rest in its equilibrium position, thereby stretching the spring an amount l so that its stretched length is $L + l$. We choose the axis along the line of the spring, with the origin O at the equilibrium position and the positive direction downward. Thus letting x denote the displacement of the mass from O along this line, we see that x is positive, zero, or negative according to whether the mass is below, at, or above its equilibrium position. (See Figure 5.1.)

Forces Acting Upon the Mass.

We now enumerate the various forces which act upon the mass. Forces tending to pull the mass downward are positive, while those tending to pull it upward are negative. The forces are:

1. F_1, the *force of gravity*, of magnitude mg, where g is the acceleration due to gravity. Since this acts in the downward direction, it is positive, and so

(5.1) $$F_1 = mg.$$

2. F_2, the *restoring force* of the spring. Since $x + l$ is the total amount of elongation, by Hooke's Law the magnitude of this force is $k(x + l)$. When the mass is *below* the end of the unstretched spring, this force acts in the *upward* direction and so is *negative*. Also, for the mass in such a position, $x + l$ is *positive*. Thus, when the mass is *below* the end of the unstretched spring, the restoring force is given by

(5.2) $$F_2 = -k(x + l).$$

(a) natural length L

(b) mass in equilibrium position; spring has stretched length $L + l$

(c) mass distance x below equilibrium position; spring stretched to length $L + l + x$

Figure 5.1

This also gives the restoring force when the mass is *above* the end of the unstretched spring, as one can see by replacing each italicized word in the three preceding sentences by its opposite. When the mass is at rest in its equilibrium position the restoring force F_2 is equal in magnitude but opposite in direction to the force of gravity and so is given by $-mg$. Since in this position $x = 0$, Equation (5.2) gives

$$-mg = -k(0 + l)$$

or

$$mg = kl.$$

Replacing kl by mg in Equation (5.2) we see that the restoring force can thus be written as

(5.3) $$F_2 = -kx - mg.$$

3. F_3, the *resisting force* of the medium, called the *damping force*. Although the magnitude of this force is not known *exactly*, it is known that for small velocities it is *approximately* proportional to the magnitude of the velocity:

(5.4) $$|F_3| = a\left|\frac{dx}{dt}\right|,$$

where $a > 0$ is called the *damping constant*. When the mass is moving *downward*, F_3 acts in the *upward* direction (opposite to that of the motion) and so $F_3 < 0$. Also, since m is moving *downward*, x is *increasing* and $\frac{dx}{dt}$ is *positive*. Thus, assuming Equation (5.4) to hold, when the mass is moving *downward*, the damping force is given by

(5.5) $$F_3 = -a\frac{dx}{dt}, \quad (a > 0).$$

This also gives the damping force when the mass is moving *upward*, as one may see by replacing each italicized word in the three preceding sentences by its opposite.

4. F_4, any *external impressed forces* which act upon the mass. Let us denote the resultant of all such external forces at time t simply by $F(t)$ and write

(5.6) $$F_4 = F(t).$$

We now apply Newton's Second Law, $F = ma$, where $F = F_1 + F_2 + F_3 + F_4$. Using (5.1), (5.3), (5.5), and (5.6), we find

$$m\frac{d^2x}{dt^2} = mg - kx - mg - a\frac{dx}{dt} + F(t)$$

or

(5.7) $$m\frac{d^2x}{dt^2} + a\frac{dx}{dt} + kx = F(t).$$

This we take as the differential equation for the motion of the mass on the spring. Observe that it is a nonhomogeneous second-order linear differential equation with constant coefficients. If $a = 0$ the motion is called *undamped;* otherwise it is called *damped.* If there are no external impressed forces, $F(t) = 0$ for all t and the motion is called *free;* otherwise it is called *forced.* In the following sections we consider the solution of (5.7) in each of these cases.

5.2 Free, Undamped Motion

We now consider the special case of *free, undamped motion,* that is, the case in which both $a = 0$ and $F(t) = 0$ for all t. The differential equation (5.7) then reduces to

(5.8) $$m\frac{d^2x}{dt^2} + kx = 0,$$

where $m \; (> 0)$ is the mass and $k \; (> 0)$ is the spring constant. Dividing through by m and letting $\dfrac{k}{m} = \lambda^2$, we write (5.8) in the form

(5.9) $$\frac{d^2x}{dt^2} + \lambda^2 x = 0.$$

The auxiliary equation

$$r^2 + \lambda^2 = 0$$

has roots $r = \pm\lambda i$ and hence the general solution of (5.8) can be written

(5.10) $$x = c_1\sin\lambda t + c_2\cos\lambda t,$$

where c_1 and c_2 are arbitrary constants.

Let us now assume that the mass was initially displaced a distance x_0 from its equilibrium position and released from that point with initial velocity v_0. Then, in addition to the differential equation (5.8) [or (5.9)], we have the initial conditions

(5.11)
(5.12) $$\begin{cases} x(0) = x_0 \\ x'(0) = v_0. \end{cases}$$

Differentiating (5.10) with respect to t, we have

(5.13)
$$\frac{dx}{dt} = c_1\lambda\cos\lambda t - c_2\lambda\sin\lambda t.$$

Applying conditions (5.11) and (5.12) to Equations (5.10) and (5.13), respectively, we see at once that

$$\begin{cases} c_2 = x_0 \\ c_1\lambda = v_0. \end{cases}$$

Substituting the values of c_1 and c_2 so determined into Equation (5.10) gives the particular solution of the differential equation (5.8) satisfying the conditions (5.11) and (5.12) in the form

$$x = \frac{v_0}{\lambda}\sin\lambda t + x_0\cos\lambda t.$$

We put this in an alternative form by first writing it as

(5.14)
$$x = c\left[\frac{\left(\frac{v_0}{\lambda}\right)}{c}\sin\lambda t + \frac{x_0}{c}\cos\lambda t\right],$$

where

(5.15)
$$c = \sqrt{\left(\frac{v_0}{\lambda}\right)^2 + x_0^2} > 0.$$

Then, letting

(5.16)
$$\begin{cases} \dfrac{\left(\dfrac{v_0}{\lambda}\right)}{c} = -\sin\phi \\[2ex] \dfrac{x_0}{c} = \cos\phi, \end{cases}$$

Equation (5.14) reduces at once to

(5.17)
$$x = c\cos(\lambda t + \phi),$$

where c is given by Equation (5.15) and ϕ is determined by Equations (5.16). Since $\lambda = \sqrt{\frac{k}{m}}$, we now write the solution (5.17) in the form

(5.18)
$$x = c\cos\left(\sqrt{\frac{k}{m}}t + \phi\right).$$

This, then, gives the displacement x of the mass from the equilibrium position O as a function of the time t $(t > 0)$. We see at once that the free, undamped motion of the mass is a *simple harmonic motion*. The constant c is called the *amplitude* of the motion and gives the maximum (positive) displacement of the mass from its equilibrium position. The motion is a *periodic* motion, and the mass oscillates back and forth between $x = c$

and $x = -c$. We have $x = c$ if and only if

$$\sqrt{\frac{k}{m}}t + \phi = \pm 2n\pi,$$

$n = 0, 1, 2, 3, \ldots ; t > 0$. Thus the maximum (positive) displacement occurs if and only if

$$(5.19) \qquad\qquad t = \sqrt{\frac{m}{k}}(\pm 2n\pi - \phi) > 0,$$

where $n = 0, 1, 2, 3, \ldots$.
The time interval between two successive maxima is called the *period* of the motion. Using (5.19), we see that it is given by

$$(5.20) \qquad\qquad \frac{2\pi}{\sqrt{\dfrac{k}{m}}} = \frac{2\pi}{\lambda}.$$

The reciprocal of the period, which gives the number of oscillations per second, is called the *natural frequency* (or simply *frequency*) of the motion. The number ϕ is called the *phase constant* (or *phase angle*). The graph of this motion is shown in Figure 5.2.

Example 5.1.   An 8 lb weight is placed upon the lower end of a coil spring suspended from the ceiling. The weight comes to rest in its equilibrium position, thereby stretching the spring 6 inches. The weight is then pulled down 3 inches below its equilibrium position and released at $t = 0$ with an initial velocity of 1 ft/sec, directed downward. Neglecting the resistance of the medium and assuming that no external forces are present, determine the amplitude, period, and frequency of the resulting motion.

Formulation.   This is clearly an example of free, undamped motion and hence equation (5.8) applies. Since the 8 lb weight stretches the spring 6 inches = 1/2 foot, Hooke's

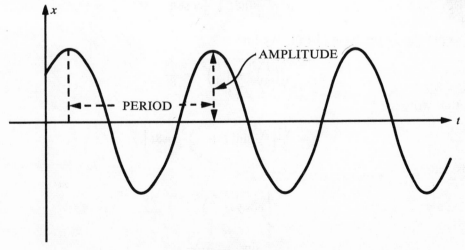

Figure 5.2

Law $F = ks$ gives $8 = k(\frac{1}{2})$ and so $k = 16$ lb/ft. Also, $m = \dfrac{w}{g} = \dfrac{8}{32}$ (slugs), and so equation (5.8) gives

$$\frac{8}{32}\frac{d^2x}{dt^2} + 16x = 0$$

or

$$(5.21) \qquad \frac{d^2x}{dt^2} + 64x = 0.$$

Since the weight was released with a downward initial velocity of 1 ft/sec from a point 3 inches ($= 1/4$ foot) below its equilibrium position, we also have the initial conditions

$$(5.22) \qquad \begin{cases} x(0) = \dfrac{1}{4} \\[2mm] x'(0) = 1. \end{cases}$$

Solution. The auxiliary equation corresponding to Equation (5.21) is $r^2 + 64 = 0$, and hence $r = \pm 8i$. Thus the general solution of the differential equation (5.21) may be written

$$(5.23) \qquad x = c_1\sin 8t + c_2\cos 8t,$$

where c_1 and c_2 are arbitrary constants.

Applying the first of conditions (5.22) to this, we find $c_2 = \frac{1}{4}$. Differentiating (5.23), we have

$$\frac{dx}{dt} = 8c_1\cos 8t - 8c_2\sin 8t.$$

Applying the second of conditions (5.22) to this, we have $8c_1 = 1$ and hence $c_1 = \frac{1}{8}$. Thus the solution of the differential equation (5.21) satisfying the conditions (5.22) is

$$(5.24) \qquad x = \frac{1}{8}\sin 8t + \frac{1}{4}\cos 8t.$$

Let us put this in the form (5.18). We find

$$\sqrt{\left(\frac{1}{8}\right)^2 + \left(\frac{1}{4}\right)^2} = \frac{\sqrt{5}}{8}$$

and thus write

$$x = \frac{\sqrt{5}}{8}\left[\frac{\sqrt{5}}{5}\sin 8t + \frac{2\sqrt{5}}{5}\cos 8t\right].$$

Thus, letting

$$(5.25) \qquad \begin{cases} \cos\phi = \dfrac{2\sqrt{5}}{5} \\[3mm] \sin\phi = -\dfrac{\sqrt{5}}{5} \end{cases}$$

we write the solution (5.24) in the form

$$(5.26) \qquad\qquad x = \frac{\sqrt{5}}{8}\cos(8t + \phi),$$

where ϕ is determined by equations (5.25). From these equations we find that $\phi \approx -0.46$ radians. Taking $\sqrt{5} \approx 2.236$, the solution (5.26) is thus given approximately by

$$x = 0.280\cos(8t - 0.46).$$

The amplitude of the motion is $\frac{\sqrt{5}}{8} \approx 0.280$ (ft). By formula (5.20), the period is $\frac{2\pi}{8} = \frac{\pi}{4}$ (sec), and the frequency is $4/\pi$ oscillations/sec. The graph is shown in Figure 5.3.

Before leaving this problem, let us be certain that we can set up initial conditions correctly. Let us replace the third sentence in the statement of the problem by the following: "The weight is then *pushed up* 4 inches *above* its equilibrium position and released at $t = 0$, with an initial velocity of 2 ft/sec, directed *upward*." The initial conditions (5.22) would then have been replaced by

$$\begin{cases} x(0) = -\dfrac{1}{3} \\[2mm] x'(0) = -2. \end{cases}$$

The minus sign appears before the $\frac{1}{3}$ because the initial position is 4 inches $= \frac{1}{3}$ foot *above* the equilibrium position and hence is *negative*. The minus sign before the 2 is due to the fact that the initial velocity is directed *upward*, that is, in the *negative* direction.

Exercises

Note: In Exercises 1–7 neglect the resistance of the medium and assume that no external forces are present.

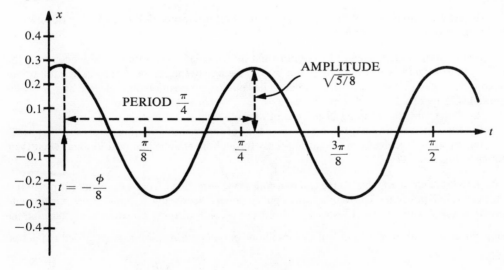

Figure 5.3

1. A 12 lb weight is placed upon the lower end of a coil spring suspended from the ceiling. The weight comes to rest in its equilibrium position, thereby stretching the spring 1.5 inches. The weight is then pulled down 2 inches below its equilibrium position and released from rest at $t = 0$. Find the displacement of the weight as a function of the time; determine the amplitude, period, and frequency of the resulting motion; and graph the displacement as a function of the time.

2. A 16 lb weight is placed upon the lower end of a coil spring suspended vertically from a fixed support. The weight comes to rest in its equilibrium position, thereby stretching the spring 6 inches. Determine the resulting displacement as a function of time in each of the following cases:
   (a) if the weight is then pulled down 4 inches below its equilibrium position and released at $t = 0$ with an initial velocity of 2 feet per second, directed downward.
   (b) if the weight is then pulled down 4 inches below its equilibrium position and released at $t = 0$ with an initial velocity of 2 feet per second, directed upward.
   (c) if the weight is then pushed up 4 inches above its equilibrium position and released at $t = 0$ with an initial velocity of 2 feet per second, directed downward.

3. A 4 lb weight is attached to the lower end of a coil spring suspended from the ceiling. The weight comes to rest in its equilibrium position, thereby stretching the spring 6 inches. At time $t = 0$ the weight is then struck so as to set it into motion with an initial velocity of 2 ft/sec, directed downward.
   (a) Determine the resulting displacement and velocity of the weight as functions of the time.
   (b) Find the amplitude, period, and frequency of the motion.
   (c) Determine the times at which the weight is 1.5 in. below its equilibrium position and moving downward.
   (d) Determine the times at which it is 1.5 in. below its equilibrium position and moving upward.

4. A 64 lb weight is placed upon the lower end of a coil spring suspended from a rigid beam. The weight comes to rest in its equilibrium position, thereby stretching the spring 2 ft. The weight is then pulled down 1 ft below its equilibrium position and released from rest at $t = 0$.
   (a) What is the position of the weight at $t = \dfrac{5\pi}{12}$? How fast and which way is it moving at the time?
   (b) At what time is the weight 6 in. above its equilibrium position and moving downward? What is its velocity at such time?

5. A coil spring is such that a 25 lb weight would stretch it 6 in. The spring is suspended from the ceiling, a 16 lb weight is attached to the end of it, and the weight then comes to rest in its equilibrium position. It is then pulled down 4 inches below its equilibrium position and released at $t = 0$ with an initial velocity of 2 ft/sec, directed upward.
   (a) Determine the resulting displacement of the weight as a function of the time.
   (b) Find the amplitude, period, and frequency of the resulting motion.
   (c) At what time does the weight first pass through its equilibrium position and what is its velocity at this instant?

6. An 8 lb weight is attached to the end of a coil spring suspended from a beam and comes to rest in its equilibrium position. The weight is then pulled down A feet below its equilibrium position and released at $t = 0$ with an initial velocity of 3 feet per second, directed downward. Determine the spring constant k and the constant A if the amplitude of the resulting motion is $\sqrt{\dfrac{10}{2}}$ and the period is $\dfrac{\pi}{2}$.

7. An 8 lb weight is placed at the end of coil spring suspended from the ceiling. After coming to rest in its equilibrium position, the weight is set into vertical motion and the period of the resulting motion is 4 sec. After a time this motion is stopped, and the 8 lb weight is replaced by another weight. After this other weight has come to rest in its equilibrium position, it is set into vertical motion. If the period of this new motion is 6 sec, how heavy is the second weight?

8. A simple pendulum is composed of a mass m (the bob) at the end of a straight wire of negligible mass and length l. It is suspended from a fixed point S (its point of support) and is free to vibrate in a vertical plane (see Figure 5.4). Let SP denote the straight wire; and let θ denote the angle which SP makes with the vertical SP_0 at time t, positive when measured counterclockwise. We neglect air resistance and assume that only two forces act on the mass m: F_1, the tension in the wire; and F_2, the force due to gravity, which acts vertically downward and is of magnitude mg. We write $F_2 = F_T + T_N$, where F_T is the component of F_2 along the tangent to the path of m and F_N is the component of F_2 normal to F_T. Then $F_N = -F_1$ and $F_T = -mg\sin\theta$, and so the net force acting on m is $F_1 + F_2 = F_1 + F_T + F_N = -mg\sin\theta$, along the arc P_0P. Letting s denote the length of the arc P_0P, the acceleration along this arc is $\dfrac{d^2s}{dt^2}$. Hence applying Newton's Second Law, we have $m\dfrac{d^2s}{dt^2} = -mg\sin\theta$. But since $s = l\theta$, this reduces to the differential equation

$$ml\frac{d^2\theta}{dt^2} = -mg\sin\theta \quad \text{or} \quad \frac{d^2\theta}{dt^2} + \frac{g}{l}\sin\theta = 0.$$

(a) The equation $\dfrac{d^2\theta}{dt^2} + \dfrac{g}{l}\sin\theta = 0$ is a *nonlinear* second-order differential equation. Now recall that

$$\sin\theta = \theta - \frac{\theta^3}{3!} + \frac{\theta^5}{5!} - \cdots .$$

Hence if θ is sufficiently small, we may replace $\sin\theta$ by θ and consider the *approximate linear* equation

$$\frac{d^2\theta}{dt^2} + \frac{g}{l}\theta = 0.$$

Assume that $\theta = \theta_0$ and $\dfrac{d\theta}{dt} = 0$ when $t = 0$. Obtain the solution of this approximate equation which satisfies these initial conditions and find the amplitude and period of the resulting solution. Observe that this period is independent of the initial displacement.

Figure 5.4

(b) Now return to the nonlinear equation

$$\frac{d^2\theta}{dt^2} + \frac{g}{l}\sin\theta = 0.$$

Multiply through by $2\frac{d\theta}{dt}$, integrate, and apply the initial condition $\theta = \theta_0$, $\frac{d\theta}{dt} = 0$. Then separate variables in the resulting equation to obtain

$$\frac{d\theta}{\sqrt{\cos\theta - \cos\theta_0}} = \pm\sqrt{\frac{2g}{l}}dt.$$

From this equation we can determine the angular velocity $\frac{d\theta}{dt}$ as a function of θ. However, the left member can not be integrated in terms of elementary functions to obtain the exact solution $\theta(t)$ of the nonlinear differential equation.

5.3 Free, Damped Motion

We now consider the effect of the resistance of the medium upon the mass on the spring. Still assuming that no external forces are present, this is then the case of *free, damped motion*. Hence with the damping coefficient $a > 0$ and $F(t) = 0$ for all t, the basic differential equation (5.7) reduces to

$$(5.27) \qquad\qquad m\frac{d^2x}{dt^2} + a\frac{dx}{dt} + kx = 0.$$

Dividing through by m and putting $\frac{k}{m} = \lambda^2$ and $\frac{a}{m} = 2b$ (for convenience) we have the differential equation (5.27) in the form

$$\frac{d^2x}{dt^2} + 2b\frac{dx}{dt} + \lambda^2 x = 0.$$

Observe that since a is positive, b is also positive. The auxiliary equation is

$$(5.29) \qquad\qquad r^2 + 2br + \lambda^2 = 0.$$

Using the quadratic formula we find that the roots of (5.29) are

$$(5.30) \qquad\qquad \frac{-2b \pm \sqrt{4b^2 - 4\lambda^2}}{2} = -b \pm \sqrt{b^2 - \lambda^2}.$$

Three distinct cases occur, depending upon the nature of these roots, which in turn depends upon the sign of $b^2 - \lambda^2$.

Case (i) Damped, Oscillatory Motion. Here we consider the case in which $b < \lambda$, which implies that $b^2 - \lambda^2 < 0$. Then the roots (5.30) are the conjugate complex numbers $-b \pm \sqrt{\lambda^2 - b^2}\,i$ and the general solution of Equation (5.28) is thus

$$(5.31) \qquad\qquad x = e^{-bt}(c_1\sin\sqrt{\lambda^2 - b^2}\,t + c_2\cos\sqrt{\lambda^2 - b^2}\,t),$$

where c_1 and c_2 are arbitrary constants.
We may write this in the alternate form

$$(5.32) \qquad\qquad x = ce^{-bt}\cos(\sqrt{\lambda^2 - b^2}\,t + \phi),$$

where $c = \sqrt{c_1^2 + c_2^2} > 0$ and ϕ is determined by the equations

$$
\begin{cases}
\dfrac{c_1}{\sqrt{c_1^2 + c_2^2}} = -\sin\phi \\[3mm]
\dfrac{c_2}{\sqrt{c_1^2 + c_2^2}} = \cos\phi.
\end{cases}
$$

The right member of Equation (5.32) consists of two factors, ce^{-bt} and $\cos(\sqrt{\lambda^2 - b^2}\, t + \phi)$. The factor ce^{-bt} is called the *damping factor* or *time-varying amplitude*. Since $c > 0$, it is positive; and since $b > 0$, it tends to zero monotonically as $t \to \infty$. In other words, as time goes on this positive factor becomes smaller and smaller and eventually becomes negligible. The remaining factor, $\cos(\sqrt{\lambda^2 - b^2}\, t + \phi)$ is, of course, of a periodic, oscillatory character; indeed it represents a simple harmonic motion. The product of these two factors, which is precisely the right member of Equation (5.32), therefore represents an oscillatory motion in which the oscillations become successively smaller and smaller. The oscillations are said to be "damped out," and the motion is described as *damped, oscillatory motion*. Of course, the motion is no longer periodic, but the time interval between two successive (positive) maximum displacements is still referred to as the *period*. This is given by

$$
\frac{2\pi}{\sqrt{\lambda^2 - b^2}}.
$$

The graph of such a motion is shown in Figure 5.5, in which the damping factor ce^{-bt} and its negative are indicated by dashed curves.

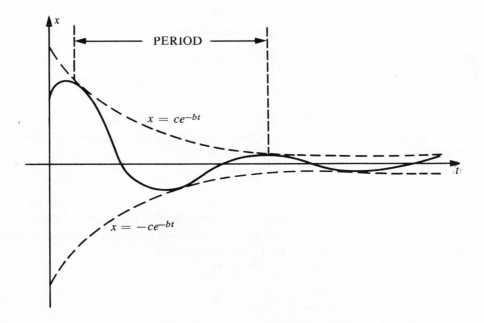

Figure 5.5

The ratio of the amplitude at any time T to that at time $T - \dfrac{2\pi}{\sqrt{\lambda^2 - b^2}}$ one period before T is the constant

$$e^{-\frac{2\pi b}{\sqrt{\lambda^2-b^2}}}$$

Thus the quantity $\dfrac{2\pi b}{\sqrt{\lambda^2 - b^2}}$ is the decrease in the logarithm of the amplitude ce^{-bt} over a time interval of one period. It is called the *logarithmic decrement*.

If we now return to the original notation of the differential equation (5.27), we see from equation (5.32) that in terms of the original constants m, a, and k, the general solution of (5.27) is

(5.33)
$$x = ce^{-\frac{a}{2m}t} \cos\left(\sqrt{\frac{k}{m} - \frac{a^2}{4m^2}}\, t + \phi\right).$$

Since $b < \lambda$ is equivalent to $\dfrac{a}{2m} < \sqrt{\dfrac{k}{m}}$, we can say that the general solution of (5.27) is given by (5.33) and that damped, oscillatory motion occurs when $a < 2\sqrt{km}$. The frequency of the oscillations

(5.34)
$$\cos\left(\sqrt{\frac{k}{m} - \frac{a^2}{4m^2}}\, t + \phi\right)$$

is

$$\frac{1}{2\pi}\sqrt{\frac{k}{m} - \frac{a^2}{4m^2}}.$$

If damping were not present, a would equal zero and the natural frequency of undamped system would be $\dfrac{1}{2\pi}\sqrt{\dfrac{k}{m}}$. Thus the frequency of the oscillations (5.34) in the damped oscillatory motion (5.33) is less than the natural frequency of the corresponding undamped system.

Case (ii): *Critical Damping*. This is the case in which $b = \lambda$, which implies that $b^2 - \lambda^2 = 0$. The roots (5.30) are thus both equal to the real negative number $-b$, and the general solution of Equation (5.28) is thus

(5.35)
$$x = (c_1 + c_2 t)e^{-bt}.$$

The motion is no longer oscillatory; the damping is just great enough to prevent oscillations. Any slight decrease in the amount of damping, however, will change the situation back to that of case (i) and damped oscillatory motion will then occur. Case (ii) then is a borderline case; the motion is said to be *critically damped*.

From equation (5.35) we see that

$$\lim_{t\to\infty} x = \lim_{t\to\infty} \frac{c_1 + c_2 t}{e^{bt}} = 0.$$

Hence the mass tends to its equilibrium position as $t \to \infty$. Depending upon the initial conditions present, the following possibilities can occur in this motion:

a. The mass neither passes through its equilibrium position nor attains an extremum (maximum or minimum) displacement from equilibrium for $t > 0$. It simply approaches its equilibrium position monotonically as $t \to \infty$. (See Figure 5.6(a).)
b. The mass does not pass through its equilibrium position for $t > 0$, but its displacement from equilibrium attains a single extremum for $t = T_1 > 0$. After this extreme displacement occurs, the mass tends to its equilibrium position monotonically as $t \to \infty$. (See Figure 5.6(b).)
c. The mass passes through its equilibrium position once at $t = T_2 > 0$ and then attains an extreme displacement at $t = T_3 > T_2$, following which it tends to its equilibrium position monotonically as $t \to \infty$. (See Figure 5.6(c).)

Case (iii) Over-Critical Damping. Finally, we consider here the case in which $b > \lambda$, which implies that $b^2 - \lambda^2 > 0$. Here the roots (5.30) are the distinct, real negative numbers

$$r_1 = -b + \sqrt{b^2 - \lambda^2}$$

and

$$r_2 = -b - \sqrt{b^2 - \lambda^2}.$$

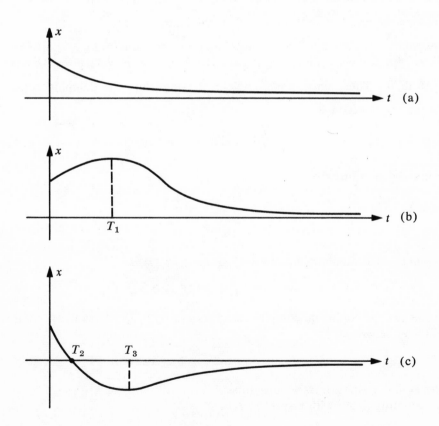

Figure 5.6

The general solution of (5.28) in this case is

(5.36) $$x = c_1 e^{r_1 t} + c_2 e^{r_2 t}.$$

The damping is now so great that no oscillations can occur. Further, we can no longer say that *every* decrease in the amount of damping will result in oscillations, as we could in case (*ii*). The motion here is said to be *over-critically damped* (or simply *overdamped*).

Equation (5.36) shows us at once that the displacement x approaches zero as $t \to \infty$. As in case (*ii*) this approach to zero is monotonic for t sufficiently large. Indeed, the three possible motions in cases (*ii*) and (*iii*.) are qualitatively the same. Thus the three motions illustrated in Figure 5.6 can also serve to illustrate the three types of motion possible in case (*iii*).

Example 5.2. A 32 lb weight is attached to the lower end of a coil spring suspended from the ceiling. The weight comes to rest in its equilibrium position, thereby stretching the spring 2 feet. The weight is then pulled down 6 inches below its equilibrium position and released at $t = 0$. No external forces are present; but the resistance of the medium in lbs. is numerically equal to $4\frac{dx}{dt}$, where $\frac{dx}{dt}$ is the instantaneous velocity in ft/sec. Determine the resulting motion of the weight on the spring.

Formulation. This is a free, damped motion and Equation (5.27) applies. Since the 32 lb weight stretches the spring 2 feet, Hooke's Law $F = ks$ gives $32 = k(2)$ and so $k = 16$ lb/ft. Thus, since $m = \frac{w}{g} = \frac{32}{32} = 1$ (slug), and the damping constant $a = 4$, Equation (5.27) becomes

(5.37) $$\frac{d^2x}{dt^2} + 4\frac{dx}{dt} + 16x = 0.$$

The initial conditions are

(5.38) $$\begin{cases} x(0) = \dfrac{1}{2} \\ x'(0) = 0. \end{cases}$$

Solution. The auxiliary equation of equation (5.37) is

$$r^2 + 4r + 16 = 0.$$

Its roots are the conjugate complex numbers $-2 \pm 2\sqrt{3}i$. Thus the general solution of (5.37) may be written

(5.39) $$x = e^{-2t}(c_1 \sin 2\sqrt{3}t + c_2 \cos 2\sqrt{3}t),$$

where c_1 and c_2 are arbitrary constants.
Differentiating (5.39) with respect to t we obtain

(5.40) $$\frac{dx}{dt} = e^{-2t}[(-2c_1 - 2\sqrt{3}c_2)\sin 2\sqrt{3}t + (2\sqrt{3}c_1 - 2c_2)\cos 2\sqrt{3}t].$$

Applying the initial conditions (5.38) to Equations (5.39) and (5.40), we obtain

$$\begin{cases} c_2 = \dfrac{1}{2} \\ 2\sqrt{3}c_1 - 2c_2 = 0. \end{cases}$$

Thus $c_1 = \dfrac{\sqrt{3}}{6}$, $c_2 = \dfrac{1}{2}$ and the solution is

(5.41)
$$x = e^{-2t}\left(\frac{\sqrt{3}}{6}\sin 2\sqrt{3}t + \frac{1}{2}\cos 2\sqrt{3}t \right).$$

Let us put this in the alternative form (5.32). We have

$$\frac{\sqrt{3}}{6}\sin 2\sqrt{3}t + \frac{1}{2}\cos 2\sqrt{3}t = \frac{\sqrt{3}}{3}\left[\frac{1}{2}\sin 2\sqrt{3}t + \frac{\sqrt{3}}{2}\cos 2\sqrt{3}t \right] = \frac{\sqrt{3}}{3}\cos\left(2\sqrt{3}t - \frac{\pi}{6} \right).$$

Thus the solution (5.41) may be written

(5.42)
$$x = \frac{\sqrt{3}}{3}e^{-2t}\cos\left(2\sqrt{3}t - \frac{\pi}{6} \right).$$

Interpretation. This is a *damped oscillatory motion* [case (*i*)]. The damping factor is $\dfrac{\sqrt{3}}{3}e^{-2t}$, the "period" is $\dfrac{2\pi}{2\sqrt{3}} = \dfrac{\sqrt{3}\pi}{3}$, and the logarithmic decrement is $\dfrac{2\sqrt{3}\pi}{3}$. The graph of the solution (5.42) is shown in Figure 5.7 where the curves $x = \pm\dfrac{\sqrt{3}}{3}e^{-2t}$ are drawn dashed.

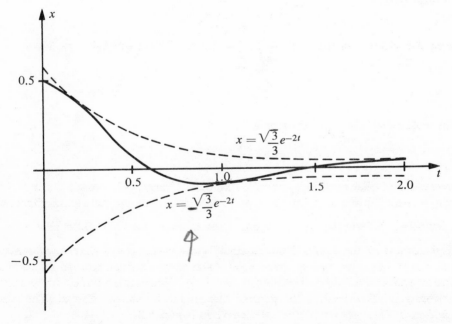

Figure 5.7

Example 5.3. Determine the motion of the weight on the spring described in Example 5.2 if the resistance of the medium in lbs. is numerically equal to $8\dfrac{dx}{dt}$ instead of $4\dfrac{dx}{dt}$ (as stated there), all other circumstances being the same as stated in Example 5.2.

Formulation. Once again equation 5.27 applies, and exactly as in Example 5.2 we find that $m = 1$ (slug) and $k = 16$ lb/ft. But now the damping has increased, and we have $a = 8$. Thus Equation (5.27) now becomes

(5.43) $$\frac{d^2x}{dt^2} + 8\frac{dx}{dt} + 16x = 0.$$

The initial conditions

(5.44) $$\begin{cases} x(0) = \dfrac{1}{2} \\ x'(0) = 0, \end{cases}$$

are, of course, unchanged from Example 5.2.

Solution. The auxiliary equation is now

$$r^2 + 8r + 16 = 0$$

and has the equal roots $r = -4, -4$. The general solution of Equation (5.43) is thus

(5.45) $$x = (c_1 + c_2 t)e^{-4t},$$

where c_1 and c_2 are arbitrary constants.
Differentiating (5.45) with respect to t, we have

(5.46) $$\frac{dx}{dt} = (c_2 - 4c_1 - 4c_2 t)e^{-4t}$$

Applying the initial conditions (5.44) to Equations (5.45) and (5.46) we obtain

$$\begin{cases} c_1 = \dfrac{1}{2} \\ c_2 - 4c_1 = 0. \end{cases}$$

Thus $c_1 = \frac{1}{2}$, $c_2 = 2$ and the solution is

(5.47) $$x = \left(\frac{1}{2} + 2t\right)e^{-4t}.$$

Interpretation. The motion is critically damped. Using (5.47), we see that $x = 0$ if and only if $t = -\frac{1}{4}$. Thus $x \neq 0$ for $t > 0$ and the weight does not pass through its equilibrium position. Differentiating (5.47) one finds at once that $\dfrac{dx}{dt} < 0$ for all $t > 0$. Thus the displacement of the weight from its equilibrium position is a decreasing function of t for all $t > 0$. In other words, the weight starts to move back toward its equilibrium position at once and $x \to 0$ monotonically as $t \to \infty$. The motion is therefore an example of possibility (a) described in the general discussion of case (*ii*) above. The graph of the solution (5.47) is shown as the solid curve in Figure 5.8.

Example 5.4. Determine the motion of the weight on the spring described in Example

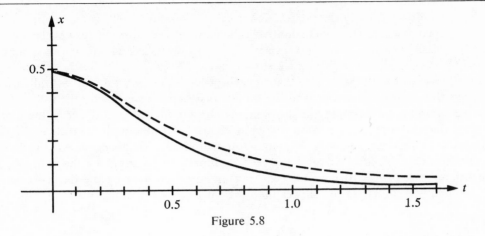

Figure 5.8

5.2 if the resistance of the medium in pounds is numerically equal to $10\dfrac{dx}{dt}$ instead of $4\dfrac{dx}{dt}$ (as stated there), all other circumstances being the same as stated in Example 5.2.

Formulation. The only difference between this and the two previous examples is in the damping constant. In Example 5.2, $a = 4$; in Example 5.3, $a = 8$; and now we have even greater damping, for here $a = 10$. As before $m = 1$ (slug) and $k = 16$ lb/ft. The differential equation (5.27) thus becomes

$$(5.48) \qquad \frac{d^2x}{dt^2} + 10\frac{dx}{dt} + 16x = 0.$$

The initial conditions (5.44) or (5.38) still hold.

Solution. The auxiliary equation is now

$$r^2 + 10r + 16 = 0$$

and its roots are $r = -2, -8$. Thus the general solution of Equation (5.48) is

$$x = c_1 e^{-2t} + c_2 e^{-8t},$$

where c_1 and c_2 are arbitrary constants.
Differentiating this with respect to t to obtain

$$\frac{dx}{dt} = -2c_1 e^{-2t} - 8c_2 e^{-8t}$$

and applying the initial conditions (5.44), we find the following equations for the determination of c_1 and c_2:

$$\begin{cases} c_1 + c_2 = \dfrac{1}{2} \\ -2c_1 - 8c_2 = 0. \end{cases}$$

The solution of this system is $c_1 = \frac{2}{3}$, $c_2 = -\frac{1}{6}$; thus the solution of the problem is

$$(5.49) \qquad x = \frac{2}{3}e^{-2t} - \frac{1}{6}e^{-8t}.$$

Interpretation. Clearly the motion described by Equation (5.49) is an example of the over-damped case [case (*iii*)]. Qualitatively the motion is the same as that of the solution (5.47) of Example 5.3. Here, however, due to the increased damping, the weight returns to its equilibrium position at a slower rate. The graph of (5.49) is shown as the dashed curve in Figure 5.8. Note that in each of Examples 5.2, 5.3, and 5.4, all circumstances (the weight, the spring, and the initial conditions) were exactly the same, *except* for the damping. In Example 5.2, the damping constant $a = 4$, and the resulting motion was the damped oscillatory motion shown in Figure 5.7. In Example 5.3 the damping was increased to such an extent ($a = 8$) that oscillations no longer occurred, the motion being shown by the solid curve of Figure 5.8. Finally in Example 5.4 the damping was further increased ($a = 10$) and the resulting motion, indicated by the dashed curve of Figure 5.8, was similar to but slower than that of Example 5.3.

Exercises

1. An 8 lb weight is attached to the lower end of a coil spring suspended from the ceiling and comes to rest in its equilibrium position, thereby stretching the spring 0.4 feet. The weight is then pulled down 6 inches below its equilibrium position and released at $t = 0$. The resistance of the medium in pounds is numerically equal to $2\dfrac{dx}{dt}$, where $\dfrac{dx}{dt}$ is the instantaneous velocity in feet per second.

   (a) Set up the differential equation for the motion and list the initial conditions.
   (b) Solve the initial-value problem set up in part (a) to determine the displacement of the weight as a function of the time.
   (c) Express the solution found in step (b) in the alternate form (5.32) of the text.
   (d) What is the so-called "period" of the motion?
   (e) Graph the displacement as a function of the time.

2. A 16 lb weight is placed upon the lower end of a coil spring suspended from the ceiling and comes to rest in its equilibrium position, thereby stretching the spring 8 inches. At time $t = 0$ the weight is then struck so as to set it into motion with an initial velocity of 2 feet per second, directed downward. The medium offers a resistance in pounds numerically equal to $6\dfrac{dx}{dt}$, where $\dfrac{dx}{dt}$ is the instantaneous velocity in feet per second. Determine the resulting displacement of the weight as a function of time and graph this displacement.

3. An 8 lb weight is attached to the lower end of a coil spring suspended from a fixed support. The weight comes to rest in its equilibrium position, thereby stretching the spring 6 inches. The weight is then pulled down 9 inches below its equilibrium position and released at $t = 0$. The medium offers a resistance in pounds numerically equal to $4\dfrac{dx}{dt}$, where $\dfrac{dx}{dt}$ is the instantaneous velocity in feet per second. Determine the displacement of the weight as a function of the time and graph this displacement.

4. A 16 lb weight is attached to the lower end of a coil spring suspended from a fixed support. The weight comes to rest in its equilibrium position, thereby stretching the spring 6 inches. The weight is then pulled down 3 inches below its equilibrium position and released at $t = 0$. The medium offers a resistance in pounds numerically equal to $10\dfrac{dx}{dt}$, where $\dfrac{dx}{dt}$ is the instantaneous

velocity in feet per second. Determine the displacement of the weight as a function of the time and graph this displacement.

5. A spring is such that a force of 20 lb would stretch it 6 inches. The spring hangs vertically and a 4 lb weight is attached to the end of it. After this 4 lb weight comes to rest in its equilibrium position it is pulled down 8 inches below this position and then released at $t = 0$. The medium offers a resistance in pounds numerically equal to $2\dfrac{dx}{dt}$, where $\dfrac{dx}{dt}$ is the instantaneous velocity in feet per second.

    (a) Determine the displacement of the weight as a function of the time and express this displacement in the alternate form (5.32) of the text.

    (b) Find the so-called "period" and determine the logarithmic decrement.

    (c) At what time does the weight first pass through its equilibrium position?

6. A 4 lb weight is hung upon the lower end of a coil spring hanging vertically from a fixed support. The weight comes to rest in its equilibrium position, thereby stretching the spring 8 inches. The weight is then pulled down a certain distance below this equilibrium position and released at $t = 0$. The medium offers a resistance in pounds numerically equal to $a\dfrac{dx}{dt}$, where $a > 0$ and $\dfrac{dx}{dt}$ is the instantaneous velocity in feet per second. Show that the motion is oscillatory if $a < \sqrt{3}$, critically damped if $a = \sqrt{3}$, and overdamped if $a > \sqrt{3}$.

7. A 4 lb weight is attached to the lower end of a coil spring which hangs vertically from a fixed support. The weight comes to rest in its equilibrium position, thereby stretching the spring 6 inches. The weight is then pulled down 3 inches below this equilibrium position and released at $t = 0$. The medium offers a resistance in pounds numerically equal to $a\dfrac{dx}{dt}$, where $a > 0$ and $\dfrac{dx}{dt}$ is the instantaneous velocity in feet per second.

    (a) Determine the value of a such that the resulting motion would be critically damped and determine the displacement for this critical value of a.

    (b) Determine the displacement if a is equal to one-half the critical value found in step (a).

    (c) Determine the displacement if a is equal to twice the critical value found in step (a).

8. A 10 lb weight is attached to the lower end of a coil spring suspended from the ceiling, the spring constant being 20 lb per foot. The weight comes to rest in its equilibrium position. It is then pulled down 6 inches below this position and released at $t = 0$ with an initial velocity of 1 foot per second, directed downward. The resistance of the medium in pounds is numerically equal to $a\dfrac{dx}{dt}$, where $a > 0$ and $\dfrac{dx}{dt}$ is the instantaneous velocity in feet per second.

    (a) Determine the smallest value of the damping coefficient a for which the motion is not oscillatory.

    (b) Using the value of a found in part (a) find the displacement of the weight as a function of the time.

    (c) Show that the weight attains a single extreme displacement from its equilibrium position at time $t = \frac{1}{40}$, determine this extreme displacement, and show that the weight then tends monotonically to its equilibrium position as $t \to \infty$.

    (d) Graph the displacement found in step (b).

9. A 32 lb weight is attached to the lower end of a coil spring suspended from the ceiling. After the weight comes to rest in its equilibrium position, it is then pulled down a certain distance below this position and released at $t = 0$. If the medium offered no resistance, the natural frequency of the resulting undamped motion would be $\dfrac{4}{\pi}$ cycles per second. However, the medium does offer a re-

sistance in pounds numerically equal to $a\dfrac{dx}{dt}$, where $a > 0$ and $\dfrac{dx}{dt}$ is the instantaneous velocity in feet per second; and the frequency of the resulting damped oscillatory motion is only half as great as the natural frequency.

(a) Determine the spring constant k.

(b) Find the value of the damping coefficient a.

10. The differential equation for the vertical motion of a mass m on a coil spring of spring constant k in a medium in which the damping is proportional to the instantaneous velocity is given by equation (5.27). In the case of damped oscillatory motion the solution of this equation is given by (5.33). Show that the displacement x so defined attains an extremum (maximum or minimum) at the times t_n ($n = 0, 1, 2, \ldots$) given by

$$t_n = \frac{1}{\omega_1}\left[\arctan\left(-\frac{a}{2m\omega_1}\right) + n\pi - \phi\right],$$

where

$$\omega_1 = \sqrt{\frac{k}{m} - \frac{a^2}{4m^2}}.$$

11. The differential equation for the vertical motion of a unit mass on a certain coil spring in a certain medium is

$$\frac{d^2x}{dt^2} + 2b\frac{dx}{dt} + b^2x = 0,$$

where $b > 0$. The initial displacement of the mass is A feet and its initial velocity is B feet per second.

(a) Show that the motion is critically damped and that the displacement is given by

$$x = (A + Bt + Abt)e^{-bt}.$$

(b) If A and B are such that

$$-\frac{A}{B + Ab} \quad \text{and} \quad \frac{B}{b(B + Ab)}$$

are both negative, show that the mass approaches its equilibrium position monotonically as $t \to \infty$ without either passing through this equilibrium position or attaining an extreme displacement from it for $t > 0$.

(c) If A and B are such that $-\dfrac{A}{B + Ab}$ is negative but $\dfrac{B}{b(B + Ab)}$ is positive, show that the mass does not pass through its equilibrium position for $t > 0$, that its displacement from this position attains a single extremum at $t = \dfrac{B}{b(B + Ab)}$, and that thereafter the mass tends to its equilibrium position monotonically as $t \to \infty$.

(d) If A and B are such that $-\dfrac{A}{B + Ab}$ is positive, show that the mass passes through its equilibrium position at $t = -\dfrac{A}{B + Ab}$, attains an extreme displacement at $t = \dfrac{B}{b(B + Ab)}$, and thereafter tends to its equilibrium position monotonically as $t \to \infty$.

5.4   Forced Motion

We now consider an important special case of *forced motion*. That is, we not only consider the effect of damping upon the mass on the spring but also the effect upon it of a periodic external impressed force F defined by $F(t) = F_1 \cos \omega t$ for all $t \geq 0$, where F_1 and ω are constants. Then the basic differential equation (5.7) becomes

$$(5.50) \qquad m\frac{d^2x}{dt^2} + a\frac{dx}{dt} + kx = F_1 \cos\omega t.$$

Dividing through by m and letting

$$\frac{a}{m} = 2b, \quad \frac{k}{m} = \lambda^2, \quad \text{and} \quad \frac{F_1}{m} = E_1,$$

this takes the more convenient form

$$(5.51) \qquad \frac{d^2x}{dt^2} + 2b\frac{dx}{dt} + \lambda^2x = E_1 \cos\omega t.$$

We shall assume that the positive damping constant a is small enough so that the damping is less than critical. In other words we assume that $b < \lambda$. Hence by Equation (5.32) the complementary function of Equation (5.51) can be written

$$(5.52) \qquad x_c = ce^{-bt}\cos(\sqrt{\lambda^2 - b^2}\,t + \phi).$$

We shall now find a particular integral of (5.51) by the method of undetermined coefficients. We let

$$(5.53) \qquad x_p = A\cos\omega t + B\sin\omega t.$$

Then

$$\frac{dx_p}{dt} = -\omega A\sin\omega t + \omega B\cos\omega t,$$

$$\frac{d^2x_p}{dt^2} = -\omega^2 A\cos\omega t - \omega^2 B\sin\omega t.$$

Substituting into Equation (5.51), we have

$$[-2b\omega A + (\lambda^2 - \omega^2)B]\sin\omega t + [(\lambda^2 - \omega^2)A + 2b\omega B]\cos\omega t = E_1\cos\omega t.$$

Thus, we have the following two equations from which to determine A and B:

$$\begin{cases} -2b\omega A + (\lambda^2 - \omega^2)B = 0 \\ (\lambda^2 - \omega^2)A + 2b\omega B = E_1. \end{cases}$$

Solving these, we obtain

$$(5.54) \qquad \begin{cases} A = \dfrac{E_1(\lambda^2 - \omega^2)}{(\lambda^2 - \omega^2)^2 + 4b^2\omega^2} \\[3mm] B = \dfrac{2b\omega E_1}{(\lambda^2 - \omega^2)^2 + 4b^2\omega^2}. \end{cases}$$

Substituting these values into Equation (5.53), we obtain a particular integral in the form

$$x_p = \frac{E_1}{(\lambda^2 - \omega^2)^2 + 4b^2\omega^2}[(\lambda^2 - \omega^2)\cos\omega t + 2b\omega\sin\omega t].$$

We now put this in the alternate "phase angle" form; we write

$(\lambda^2 - \omega^2)\cos\omega t + 2b\omega\sin\omega t$

$$= \sqrt{(\lambda^2 - \omega^2)^2 + 4b^2\omega^2}\left[\frac{\lambda^2 - \omega^2}{\sqrt{(\lambda^2 - \omega^2)^2 + 4b^2\omega^2}}\cos\omega t + \frac{2b\omega}{\sqrt{(\lambda^2 - \omega^2)^2 + 4b^2\omega^2}}\sin\omega t\right]$$

$$= \sqrt{(\lambda^2 - \omega^2)^2 + 4b^2\omega^2}[\cos\omega t\cos\theta + \sin\omega t\sin\theta]$$

$$= \sqrt{(\lambda^2 - \omega^2)^2 + 4b^2\omega^2}\cos(\omega t - \theta),$$

where

(5.55)
$$\begin{cases} \cos\theta = \dfrac{\lambda^2 - \omega^2}{\sqrt{(\lambda^2 - \omega^2)^2 + 4b^2\omega^2}} \\[4mm] \sin\theta = \dfrac{2b\omega}{\sqrt{(\lambda^2 - \omega^2)^2 + 4b^2\omega^2}}. \end{cases}$$

Thus the particular integral appears in the form

(5.56)
$$x_p = \frac{E_1}{\sqrt{(\lambda^2 - \omega^2)^2 + 4b^2\omega^2}}\cos(\omega t - \theta),$$

where θ is determined from Equations (5.55). Thus, using (5.52) and (5.56) the general solution of Equation (5.51) is

(5.57) $$x = x_c + x_p = ce^{-bt}\cos(\sqrt{\lambda^2 - b^2}\,t + \phi) + \frac{E_1}{\sqrt{(\lambda^2 - \omega^2)^2 + 4b^2\omega^2}}\cos(\omega t - \theta).$$

Observe that this solution is the sum of two terms. The first term, $ce^{-bt}\cos(\sqrt{\lambda^2 - b^2}\,t + \phi)$, represents the damped oscillation which would be the entire motion of the system if the external force $F_1\cos\omega t$ were not present. The second term,

$$\frac{E_1}{\sqrt{(\lambda^2 - \omega^2)^2 + 4b^2\omega^2}}\cos(\omega t - \theta),$$

which results from the presence of the external force, represents a simple harmonic motion of period $\dfrac{2\pi}{\omega}$. Because of the damping factor ce^{-bt} the contribution of the first term will become smaller and smaller as time goes on and will eventually become negligible. The first term is thus called the *transient* term. The second term, however, being a cosine term of constant amplitude, continues to contribute to the motion in a periodic, oscillatory manner. Eventually, the transient term having become relatively small, the entire motion will consist essentially of that given by this second term. This second term is thus called the *steady-state* term.

Example 5.5. A 16 lb weight is attached to the lower end of a coil spring suspended from the ceiling, the spring constant of the spring being 10 lb/ft. The weight comes to rest in its equilibrium position. Beginning at $t = 0$ an external force given by $F(t) = 5\cos 2t$

is applied to the system. Determine the resulting motion if the damping force in pounds is numerically equal to $2\dfrac{dx}{dt}$, where $\dfrac{dx}{dt}$ is the instantaneous velocity in ft/sec.

Formulation.   The basic differential equation for the motion is

(5.58) $$m\frac{d^2x}{dt^2} + a\frac{dx}{dt} + kx = F(t).$$

Here $m = \dfrac{w}{g} = \dfrac{16}{32} = \dfrac{1}{2}$ (slug), $a = 2$, $k = 10$, and $F(t) = 5\cos 2t$. Thus equation (5.58) becomes

$$\frac{1}{2}\frac{d^2x}{dt^2} + 2\frac{dx}{dt} + 10x = 5\cos 2t$$

or

(5.59) $$\frac{d^2x}{dt^2} + 4\frac{dx}{dt} + 20x = 10\cos 2t.$$

The initial conditions are

(5.60) $$\begin{cases} x(0) = 0 \\ x'(0) = 0. \end{cases}$$

Solution.   The auxiliary equation of the homogeneous equation corresponding to (5.59) is $r^2 + 4r + 20 = 0$; its roots are $-2 \pm 4i$. Thus the complementary function of equation (5.59) is

$$x_c = e^{-2t}(c_1\sin 4t + c_2\cos 4t),$$

where c_1 and c_2 are arbitrary constants. Using the method of undetermined coefficients to obtain a particular integral, we let

$$x_p = A\cos 2t + B\sin 2t.$$

Upon differentiating and substituting into (5.59), we find the following equations for the determination of A and B.

$$\begin{cases} -8A + 16B = 0 \\ 16A + 8B = 10. \end{cases}$$

Solving these, we find

$$A = \frac{1}{2}, \quad B = \frac{1}{4}.$$

Thus a particular integral is

$$x_p = \frac{1}{2}\cos 2t + \frac{1}{4}\sin 2t$$

and the general solution of (5.59) is

(5.61) $$x = x_c + x_p = e^{-2t}(c_1\sin 4t + c_2\cos 4t) + \frac{1}{2}\cos 2t + \frac{1}{4}\sin 2t.$$

Differentiating (5.61) with respect to t, we obtain

(5.62) $\dfrac{dx}{dt} = e^{-2t}[(-2c_1 - 4c_2)\sin 4t + (-2c_2 + 4c_1)\cos 4t] - \sin 2t + \dfrac{1}{2}\cos 2t.$

Applying the initial conditions (5.60) to Equations (5.61) and (5.62), we see that

$$\begin{cases} c_2 + \dfrac{1}{2} = 0 \\[2mm] 4c_1 - 2c_2 + \dfrac{1}{2} = 0. \end{cases}$$

From these equations we find that

$$c_1 = -\frac{3}{8}, \quad c_2 = -\frac{1}{2}.$$

Hence the solution is

(5.63) $x = e^{-2t}\left(-\dfrac{3}{8}\sin 4t - \dfrac{1}{2}\cos 4t\right) + \dfrac{1}{2}\cos 2t + \dfrac{1}{4}\sin 2t.$

Let us write this in the "phase angle" form. We have first

$$3\sin 4t + 4\cos 4t = 5\left(\frac{3}{5}\sin 4t + \frac{4}{5}\cos 4t\right) = 5\cos(4t - \phi),$$

where

(5.64) $\cos\phi = \dfrac{4}{5}, \quad \sin\phi = \dfrac{3}{5}.$

Also, we have

$$2\cos 2t + \sin 2t = \sqrt{5}\left(\frac{2}{\sqrt{5}}\cos 2t + \frac{1}{\sqrt{5}}\sin 2t\right) = \sqrt{5}\cos(2t - \theta),$$

where

(5.65) $\cos\theta = \dfrac{2}{\sqrt{5}}, \quad \sin\theta = \dfrac{1}{\sqrt{5}}.$

Thus we may write the solution (5.63) as

(5.66) $x = -\dfrac{5e^{-2t}}{8}\cos(4t - \phi) + \dfrac{\sqrt{5}}{4}\cos(2t - \theta),$

where ϕ and θ are determined by Equations (5.64) and (5.65), respectively. We find that $\phi \approx 0.64$ (rad) and $\theta \approx 0.46$ (rad). Thus the solution (5.66) is given approximately by

$$x = -0.63e^{-2t}\cos(4t - 0.64) + 0.56\cos(2t - 0.46).$$

Interpretation. The term

$$-\frac{5e^{-2t}}{8}\cos(4t - \phi) \approx -0.63e^{-2t}\cos(4t - 0.64)$$

is the *transient* term, representing a damped oscillatory motion. It becomes negligible in a short time; for example, for $t > 3$, its numerical value is less than 0.002. Its graph is shown in Figure 5.9(a). The term

$$\frac{\sqrt{5}}{4}\cos(2t - \theta) \approx 0.56\cos(2t - 0.46)$$

is the *steady-state* term, representing a simple harmonic motion of amplitude

$$\frac{\sqrt{5}}{4} \approx 0.56$$

and period π. Its graph appears in Figure 5.9(b). The graph in Figure 5.9(c) is that of the complete solution (5.66). It is clear from this that the effect of the transient term soon becomes negligible, and that after a short time the contribution of the steady-state term is essentially all that remains.

Exercises

1. A 6 lb weight is attached to the lower end of a coil spring suspended from the ceiling, the spring constant of the spring being 27 lb per foot. The weight comes to rest in its equilibrium position, and beginning at $t = 0$ an external force given by $F(t) = 12\cos20t$ is applied to the system. Determine the resulting displacement as a function of the time, assuming damping is negligible.

2. A 16 lb weight is attached to the lower end of a coil spring suspended from the ceiling. The weight comes to rest in its equilibrium position thereby stretching the spring 0.4 ft. Then beginning at $t = 0$ an external force given by $F(t) = 40\cos16t$ is applied to the system. The medium offers a resistance in pounds numerically equal to $4\dfrac{dx}{dt}$, where $\dfrac{dx}{dt}$ is the instantaneous velocity in feet per second.

   (a) Find the displacement of the weight as a function of the time.
   (b) Graph separately the transient and steady-state terms of the motion found in step (a) and then use the curves so obtained to graph the entire displacement itself.

3. A 10 lb weight is hung on the lower end of a coil spring suspended from the ceiling, the spring constant of the spring being 20 lb per foot. The weight comes to rest in its equilibrium position, and beginning at $t = 0$ an external force given by $F(t) = 10\cos8t$ is applied to the system. The medium offers a resistance in pounds numerically equal to $5\dfrac{dx}{dt}$, where $\dfrac{dx}{dt}$ is the instantaneous velocity in feet per second. Find the displacement of the weight as a function of the time.

4. A 4 lb weight is hung on the lower end of a coil spring suspended from a beam. The weight comes to rest in its equilibrium position, thereby stretching the spring 3 inches. The weight is then pulled down 6 inches below this position and released at $t = 0$. At this instant an external force given by $F(t) = 13\sin4t$ is applied to the system. The resistance of the medium in pounds is numerically equal to twice the instantaneous velocity, measured in feet per second.

   (a) Find the displacement of the weight as a function of the time.
   (b) Observe that the displacement is the sum of a transient term and a steady state term, and find the amplitude of the steady state term.

5. A 6 lb weight is hung on the lower end of a coil spring suspended from the ceiling. The weight comes to rest in its equilibrium position, thereby stretching the spring 4 inches. Then beginning at $t = 0$ an external force given by $F(t) = 27\sin4t - 3\cos4t$ is applied to the system. If the

Figure 5.9

medium offers a resistance in pounds numerically equal to three times the instantaneous velocity, measured in feet per second, find the displacement as a function of the time.

6. A certain coil spring having spring constant 10 lb per foot is suspended from the ceiling. A 32 lb weight is attached to the lower end of the spring and comes to rest in its equilibrium position. Beginning at $t = 0$ an external force given by $F(t) = \sin t + \frac{1}{4}\sin 2t + \frac{1}{9}\sin 3t$ is applied to the system. The medium offers a resistance in pounds numerically equal to twice the instantaneous velocity, measured in feet per second. Find the displacement of the weight as a function of the time, using the superposition principle (Chapter 4, Theorem 4.12) to obtain the steady-state term.

7. A coil spring having spring constant 20 lb per foot is suspended from the ceiling. A 32 lb weight is attached to the lower end of the spring and comes to rest in its equilibrium position. Beginning at $t = 0$ an external force given by $F(t) = 40\cos 2t$ is applied to the system. This force then remains in effect until $t = \pi$, at which instant it ceases to be applied. For $t > \pi$, no external forces are present. The medium offers a resistance in pounds numerically equal to $4\dfrac{dx}{dt}$, where $\dfrac{dx}{dt}$ is the instantaneous velocity in feet per second. Find the displacement of the weight as a function of the time for all $t \geq 0$.

8. Consider the basic differential equation (5.7) for the motion of a mass m vibrating up and down on a coil spring suspended vertically from a fixed support; and suppose the external impressed force F is the periodic function defined by $F(t) = F_2 \sin \omega t$ for all $t \geq 0$, where F_2 and ω are constants. Show that in this case the steady state term in the solution of equation (5.7) may be written

$$x_p = \frac{E_2}{\sqrt{(\lambda^2 - \omega^2)^2 + 4b^2\omega^2}}\sin(\omega t - \theta),$$

where $b = \dfrac{a}{2m}$, $\lambda^2 = \dfrac{k}{m}$, $E_2 = \dfrac{F_2}{m}$, and θ is determined from equations (5.55).

9. A 32 lb weight is attached to the lower end of a coil spring suspended vertically from a fixed support and comes to rest in its equilibrium position, thereby stretching the spring 6 inches. Beginning at $t = 0$ an external force given by $F(t) = 15\cos 7t$ is applied to the system. Assume that the damping is negligible.

    (a) Find the displacement of the weight as a function of the time.

    (b) Show that this displacement may be expressed in the form $x = A(t)\sin\dfrac{15t}{2}$, where $A(t) = 2\sin\frac{1}{2}t$. The function $A(t)$ may be regarded as the "slowly-varying" amplitude of the more rapid oscillation $\sin\dfrac{15t}{2}$. When a phenomenon involving such fluctuations in maximum amplitude takes place in acoustical applications, *beats* are said to occur.

    (c) Carefully graph the slowly-varying amplitude $A(t) = 2\sin\dfrac{t}{2}$ and its negative $-A(t)$ and then use these "bounding curves" to graph the displacement $x = A(t)\sin\dfrac{15t}{2}$.

10. A 16 lb weight is attached to the lower end of a coil spring which is suspended vertically from a support and for which the spring constant k is 10 lb foot. The weight comes to rest in its equilibrium position and is then pulled down 6 inches below this position and released at $t = 0$. At this instant the support of the spring begins a vertical oscillation such that its distance from its initial position is given by $\frac{1}{2}\sin 2t$ for $t \geq 0$. The resistance of the medium in pounds is numerically equal to $2\dfrac{dx}{dt}$, where $\dfrac{dx}{dt}$ is the instantaneous velocity of the moving weight in feet per second.

(a) Show that the differential equation for the displacement of the weight from its equilibrium position is

$$\frac{1}{2}\frac{d^2x}{dt^2} = -10(x - y) - 2\frac{dx}{dt}, \quad \text{where } y = \frac{1}{2}\sin 2t,$$

and hence that this differential equation may be written

$$\frac{d^2x}{dt^2} + 4\frac{dx}{dt} + 20x = 10\sin 2t.$$

(b) Solve the differential equation obtained in step (a), apply the relevant initial conditions, and thus obtain the displacement x as a function of time.

5.5 Resonance Phenomena

We now consider the amplitude of the steady-state vibration which results from the periodic external force defined for all t by $F(t) = F_1 \cos \omega t$, where we assume that $F_1 > 0$. For fixed b, λ, and E_1 we see from Equation (5.56) that this is the function f of ω defined by

$$(5.67) \qquad\qquad f(\omega) = \frac{E_1}{\sqrt{(\lambda^2 - \omega^2)^2 + 4b^2\omega^2}}.$$

If $\omega = 0$, the force $F(t)$ is the constant F_1 and the amplitude $f(\omega)$ has the value $\frac{E_1}{\lambda^2} > 0$. Also, as $\omega \to \infty$, we see from (5.67) that $f(\omega) \to 0$. Let us consider the function f for $0 < \omega < \infty$. Calculating the derivative $f'(\omega)$ we find that this derivative equals zero only if

$$4\omega[2b^2 - (\lambda^2 - \omega^2)] = 0$$

and hence only if $\omega = 0$ or $\omega = \sqrt{\lambda^2 - 2b^2}$. If $\lambda^2 < 2b^2$, $\sqrt{\lambda^2 - 2b^2}$ is a complex number. Hence in this case f has no extremum for $0 < \omega < \infty$, but rather f decreases monotonically for $0 < \omega < \infty$ from the value $\frac{E_1}{\lambda^2}$ at $\omega = 0$ and approaches zero as $\omega \to \infty$. Let us assume that $\lambda^2 > 2b^2$. Then the function f has a relative maximum at $\omega_1 = \sqrt{\lambda^2 - 2b^2}$, and this maximum value is given by

$$f(\omega_1) = \frac{E_1}{\sqrt{(2b^2)^2 + 4b^2(\lambda^2 - 2b^2)}} = \frac{E_1}{2b\sqrt{\lambda^2 - b^2}}.$$

When the frequency of the forcing function $F_1 \cos \omega t$ is such that $\omega = \omega_1$, then the forcing function is said to be in *resonance* with the system. In other words, the forcing function defined by $F_1 \cos \omega t$ is in resonance with the system when ω assumes the value ω_1 at which $f(\omega)$ is a maximum. The value $\frac{\omega_1}{2\pi}$ is called the *resonance frequency* of the system. Note carefully that resonance can occur only if $\lambda^2 > 2b^2$. Since then $\lambda^2 > b^2$, the damping must be less than critical in such a case.

We now return to the original notation of Equation (5.50). In terms of the quantities m, a, k, and F_1 of that equation, the function f is given by

(5.68)
$$f(\omega) = \frac{\dfrac{F_1}{m}}{\sqrt{\left(\dfrac{k}{m} - \omega^2\right)^2 + \left(\dfrac{a}{m}\right)^2 \omega^2}}.$$

In this original notation the resonance frequency is

(5.69)
$$\frac{1}{2\pi}\sqrt{\frac{k}{m} - \frac{a^2}{2m^2}}.$$

Since the frequency of the corresponding free, damped oscillation is

$$\frac{1}{2\pi}\sqrt{\frac{k}{m} - \frac{a^2}{4m^2}},$$

we see that the resonance frequency is less than that of the corresponding free, damped oscillation.

The graph of $f(\omega)$ is called the *resonance curve* of the system. For a given system with fixed m, k, and F_1, there is a resonance curve corresponding to each value of the damping coefficient $a \geq 0$. Let us choose $m = k = F_1 = 1$, for example, and graph the resonance curves corresponding to certain selected values of a. In this case we have

$$f(\omega) = \frac{1}{\sqrt{(1 - \omega^2)^2 + a^2\omega^2}}$$

and the resonance frequency is given by $\dfrac{1}{2\pi}\sqrt{1 - \dfrac{a^2}{2}}$. The graphs appear in Figure 5.10.

Observe that resonance occurs in this case only if $a < \sqrt{2}$. As a decreases from $\sqrt{2}$ to 0, the value ω_1 at which resonance occurs increases from 0 to 1 and the corresponding maximum value of $f(\omega)$ becomes larger and larger. In the limiting case $a = 0$, the maximum has disappeared and an infinite discontinuity occurs at $\omega = 1$. In this case our solution actually breaks down, for then

$$f(\omega) = \frac{1}{\sqrt{(1 - \omega^2)^2}} = \frac{1}{1 - \omega^2}$$

and $f(1)$ is undefined. This limiting case is an example of *undamped resonance*, a phenomenon which we shall now investigate.

Undamped resonance occurs when there is no damping and the frequency of the impressed force is equal to the natural frequency of the system. Since in this case $a = 0$ and the frequency $\dfrac{\omega}{2\pi}$ equals the natural frequency $\dfrac{1}{2\pi}\sqrt{\dfrac{k}{m}}$, the differential equation (5.50) reduces to

$$m\frac{d^2x}{dt^2} + kx = F_1\cos\sqrt{\frac{k}{m}}t$$

or

(5.70)
$$\frac{d^2x}{dt^2} + \frac{k}{m}x = E_1\cos\sqrt{\frac{k}{m}}t,$$

Figure 5.10

where $E_1 = \dfrac{F_1}{m}$. Since the complementary function of equation (5.70) is

(5.71) $$x_c = c_1 \sin\sqrt{\frac{k}{m}}t + c_2\cos\sqrt{\frac{k}{m}}t,$$

we can not assume a particular integral of the form

$$A\sin\sqrt{\frac{k}{m}}t + B\cos\sqrt{\frac{k}{m}}t.$$

Rather we must assume

$$x_p = At\sin\sqrt{\frac{k}{m}}t + Bt\cos\sqrt{\frac{k}{m}}t.$$

Differentiating this twice and substituting into equation (5.70), we find that

$$A = \frac{E_1}{2}\sqrt{\frac{m}{k}} \quad \text{and} \quad B = 0.$$

Thus the particular integral of equation (5.70) resulting from the forcing function

$E_1 \cos\sqrt{\dfrac{k}{m}}t$ is given by

$$x_p = \frac{E_1}{2}\sqrt{\frac{m}{k}}t\sin\sqrt{\frac{k}{m}}t.$$

Expressing the complementary function (5.71) in the equivalent "phase-angle" form, we see that the general solution of Equation (5.70) is given by

(5.72) $$x = c\cos\left(\sqrt{\frac{k}{m}}t + \phi\right) + \frac{E_1}{2}\sqrt{\frac{m}{k}}t\sin\sqrt{\frac{k}{m}}t.$$

The motion defined by (5.72) is thus the sum of a periodic term and an oscillatory term whose amplitude $\dfrac{E_1}{2}\sqrt{\dfrac{m}{k}}t$ increases with t. The graph of the function defined by this latter term,

$$\frac{E_1}{2}\sqrt{\frac{m}{k}}t\sin\sqrt{\frac{k}{m}}t,$$

appears in Figure 5.11. As t increases, this term clearly dominates the entire motion. One might argue that Equation (5.72) informs us that as $t \to \infty$ the oscillations will become infinite. However, common sense intervenes and convinces us that before this exciting phenomenon can occur the system will break down and then Equation (5.72) will no longer apply!

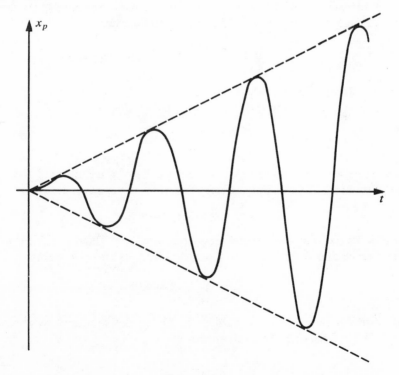

Figure 5.11

Example 5.6. A 64 lb weight is attached to the lower end of a coil spring suspended from the ceiling, the spring constant being 18 lb/ft. The weight comes to rest in its equilibrium position. It is then pulled down 6 inches below its equilibrium position and released at $t = 0$. At this instant an external force given by $F(t) = 3\cos\omega t$ is applied to the system.

   (a) Assuming the damping force in pounds is numerically equal to $4\dfrac{dx}{dt}$, where $\dfrac{dx}{dt}$ is the instantaneous velocity in ft/sec, determine the resonance frequency of the resulting motion.
   (b) Assuming there is no damping, determine the value of ω which gives rise to undamped resonance.

Solution. Since $m = \dfrac{w}{g} = \dfrac{64}{32} = 2$ (slugs), $k = 18$, and $F(t) = 3\cos\omega t$, the differential equation is

$$2\frac{d^2x}{dt^2} + a\frac{dx}{dt} + 18x = 3\cos\omega t,$$

where a is the damping coefficient. In part (a), $a = 4$ and so in this case the differential equation reduces to

$$2\frac{d^2x}{dt^2} + 4\frac{dx}{dt} + 18x = 3\cos\omega t.$$

Here we are not asked to solve the differential equation but merely to determine the resonance frequency. Using formula (5.69) we find that this is

$$\frac{1}{2\pi}\sqrt{\frac{18}{2} - \frac{1}{2}\left(\frac{16}{4}\right)} = \frac{1}{2\pi}\sqrt{7} \approx 0.42 (\text{cycles/sec}).$$

Thus resonance occurs when $\omega = \sqrt{7} \approx 2.65$.
   In part (b), $a = 0$ and so the differential equation reduces to

(5.73) $$\frac{d^2x}{dt^2} + 9x = \frac{3}{2}\cos\omega t.$$

Undamped resonance occurs when the frequency $\omega/2\pi$ of the impressed force is equal to the natural frequency. The complementary function of Equation (5.73) is

$$x_c = c_1\sin3t + c_2\cos3t,$$

and from this we see that the natural frequency is $3/2\pi$. Thus $\omega = 3$ gives rise to undamped resonance and the differential equation (5.73) in this case becomes

(5.74) $$\frac{d^2x}{dt^2} + 9x = \frac{3}{2}\cos3t.$$

The initial conditions are $x(0) = \frac{1}{2}$, $x'(0) = 0$. The reader should show that the solution of Equation (5.74) satisfying these conditions is

$$x = \frac{1}{2}\cos3t + \frac{1}{4}t\sin3t.$$

Exercises

1. A 12 lb weight is attached to the lower end of a coil spring suspended from the ceiling. The weight comes to rest in its equilibrium position thereby stretching the spring 6 inches. Beginning at $t = 0$ an external force given by $F(t) = 2\cos\omega t$ is applied to the system.

(a) If the damping force in pounds is numerically equal to $3\dfrac{dx}{dt}$, where $\dfrac{dx}{dt}$ is the instantaneous velocity in feet per second, determine the resonance frequency of the resulting motion and find the displacement as a function of the time when the forcing function is in resonance with the system.

(b) Assuming there is no damping, determine the value of ω which gives rise to undamped resonance and find the displacement as a function of the time in this case.

2. A 20 lb weight is attached to the lower end of a coil spring suspended from the ceiling. The weight comes to rest in its equilibrium position, thereby stretching the spring 6 inches. Various external forces of the form $F(t) = \cos\omega t$ are applied to the system and it is found that the resonance frequency is 0.5 cycles per second. Assuming that the resistance of the medium in pounds is numerically equal to $a\dfrac{dx}{dt}$, where $\dfrac{dx}{dt}$ is the instantaneous velocity in feet per second, determine the damping coefficient a.

3. The differential equation for the motion of a unit mass on a certain coil spring under the action of an external force of the form $F(t) = 30\cos\omega t$ is

$$\frac{d^2x}{dt^2} + a\frac{dx}{dt} + 24x = 30\cos\omega t,$$

where $a \geq 0$ is the damping coefficient.

(a) Graph the resonance curves of the system for $a = 0, 2, 4, 6$, and $4\sqrt{3}$.

(b) If $a = 4$, find the resonance frequency and determine the amplitude of the steady-state vibration when the forcing function is in resonance with the system.

(c) Proceed as in part (b) if $a = 2$.

5.6   Electric Circuit Problems

In this section we consider the application of differential equations to series circuits containing (1) an electromotive force, and (2) resistors, inductors, and capacitors. We assume that the reader is somewhat familiar with these items and so we shall avoid an extensive discussion. Let us simply recall that the electromotive force (for example, a battery or generator) produces a flow of current in a closed circuit and that this current produces a so-called *voltage drop* across each resistor, inductor, and capacitor. Further, the following three laws concerning the voltage drops across these various elements are known to hold:

(1) The voltage drop across a resistor is given by

(5.75) $$E_R = Ri,$$

where R is a constant of proportionality called the *resistance*, and i is the current.

(2) The voltage drop across an inductor is given by

(5.76) $$E_L = L\frac{di}{dt},$$

where L is a constant of proportionality called the *inductance*, and i again denotes the current.

(3) The voltage drop across a capacitor is given by

(5.77)
$$E_c = \frac{1}{c}q,$$

where c is a constant of proportionality called the *capacitance* and q is the instantaneous charge. Since $i = \dfrac{dq}{dt}$, this is often written as $E_c = \dfrac{1}{c}\displaystyle\int i\,dt$.

The units in common use are listed in the following table:

Table 5.1

quantity and symbol	unit
emf or voltage, E	volt (V)
current, i	ampere
charge, q	coulomb
resistance, R	ohm (Ω)
inductance, L	henry (h)
capacitance, c	farad

The fundamental law in the study of electric circuits is the following:

Kirchhoff's Voltage Law (Form 1). The algebraic sum of the instantaneous voltage drops around a closed circuit in a specific direction is zero.

Since voltage drops across resistors, inductors, and capacitors have the opposite sign from voltages arising from electromotive forces, we may state this law in the following alternative form:

Kirchhoff's Voltage Law (Form 2). The sum of the voltage drops across resistors, inductors, and capacitors is equal to the total electromotive force in a closed circuit. We now consider the circuit shown in Figure 5.12.

Figure 5.12

Here and in later diagrams the following conventional symbols are employed:

—◯— E Electromotive force (battery or generator)

—WWW— R Resistor

—◌◌◌◌◌— L Inductor

—┤├— c Capacitor.

Let us apply Kirchhoff's Law to the circuit of Figure 5.12. Letting E denote the electromotive force, and using the laws (1), (2), and (3) for voltage drops which were given above, we are led at once to the equation

$$(5.78) \qquad L\frac{di}{dt} + Ri + \frac{1}{c}q = E.$$

This equation contains *two* dependent variables i and q. However, we recall that these two variables are related to each other by the equation

$$(5.79) \qquad i = \frac{dq}{dt}.$$

Using this we may eliminate i from equation (5.78) and write it in the form

$$(5.80) \qquad L\frac{d^2q}{dt^2} + R\frac{dq}{dt} + \frac{1}{c}q = E.$$

Equation (5.80) is a second-order linear differential equation in the single dependent variable q. On the other hand, if we differentiate equation (5.78) with respect to t and make use of (5.79), we may eliminate q from equation (5.78) and write

$$(5.81) \qquad L\frac{d^2i}{dt^2} + R\frac{di}{dt} + \frac{1}{c}i = \frac{dE}{dt}.$$

This is a second-order linear differential equation in the single independent variable i.

Thus we have the two second order linear differential equations (5.80) and (5.81) for the charge q and current i, respectively. Further observe that in two very simple cases the problem reduces to a *first*-order linear differential equation. If the circuit contains no capacitor, equation (5.78) itself reduces directly to

$$L\frac{di}{dt} + Ri = E;$$

while if no inductor is present, equation (5.80) reduces to

$$R\frac{dq}{dt} + \frac{1}{c}q = E.$$

Before considering examples, we observe an interesting and useful analogy. The differential equation (5.80) for the charge is exactly the same as the differential equation (5.7) of section 5.1 for the vibrations of a mass on a coil spring, except for the notations used. That is, the electrical system described by equation (5.80) is analogous to the mechanical system described by equation (5.7) of Section 5.1. This analogy is brought out by the following table:

Table 5.2

Mechanical System	Electrical System
mass m	inductance L
damping constant a	resistance R
spring constant k	reciprocal of capacitance $\dfrac{1}{c}$
impressed force $F(t)$	impressed voltage or emf E
displacement x	charge q
velocity $v = \dfrac{dx}{dt}$	current $i = \dfrac{dq}{dt}$

Example 5.7. A circuit has in series an electromotive force given by $E = 100\sin 40t$ V, a resistor of 10 Ω and an inductor of 0.5 h. If the initial current is 0, find the current at time $t > 0$.

Formulation. The circuit diagram is shown in Figure 5.13.

Let i denote the current in amperes at time t. The total electromotive force is $100\sin 40t$ V. Using the laws (1) and (2), we find that the voltage drops are as follows:

(1) across the resistor: $E_R = Ri = 10i$.

(2) across the inductor: $E_L = L\dfrac{di}{dt} = \dfrac{1}{2}\dfrac{di}{dt}$.

Applying Kirchhoff's Law, we have the differential equation

$$\frac{1}{2}\frac{di}{dt} + 10i = 100\sin 40t$$

or

(5.82) $$\frac{di}{dt} + 20i = 200\sin 40t.$$

Since the initial current is 0, the initial condition is

(5.83) $$i(0) = 0.$$

Solution. Equation (5.82) is a first-order linear equation. An integrating factor is

$$e^{\int 20\,dt} = e^{20t}.$$

$$R$$

$$E$$

$$L$$

Figure 5.13

Multiplying (5.82) by this, we obtain

$$e^{20t}\frac{di}{dt} + 20e^{20t}i = 200e^{20t}\sin 40t$$

or

$$\frac{d}{dt}[e^{20t}i] = 200e^{20t}\sin 40t.$$

Integrating and simplifying, we find

$$i = 2(\sin 40t - 2\cos 40t) + ce^{-20t}.$$

Applying the condition (5.83), $i = 0$ when $t = 0$, we find $c = 4$. Thus the solution is

$$i = 2(\sin 40t - 2\cos 40t) + 4e^{-20t}.$$

Expressing the trigonometric terms in a "phase-angle" form, we have

$$i = 2\sqrt{5}\left[\frac{1}{\sqrt{5}}\sin 40t - \frac{2}{\sqrt{5}}\cos 40t\right] + 4e^{-20t}$$

or

(5.84) $$i = 2\sqrt{5}\sin(40t + \phi) + 4e^{-20t},$$

where ϕ is determined by the equation

$$\phi = \arccos\frac{1}{\sqrt{5}} = \arcsin\left(-\frac{2}{\sqrt{5}}\right).$$

We find $\phi \approx -1.11$ rad, and hence the current is given approximately by

$$i = 4.47\sin(40t - 1.11) + 4e^{-20t}.$$

Interpretation.   The current is clearly expressed as the sum of a sinusoidal term and an exponential. The exponential becomes so very small in a short time that its effect is soon practically negligible; it is the *transient* term. Thus, after a short time, essentially all that remains is the sinusoidal term; it is the *steady-state current*. Observe that its *period* $\frac{\pi}{20}$ is the same as that of the electromotive force. However, the *phase angle* $\phi \approx -1.11$ indicates that the electromotive force leads the steady-state current by approximately $\frac{1}{40}$ (1.11). The graph of the current as a function of time appears in Figure 5.14.

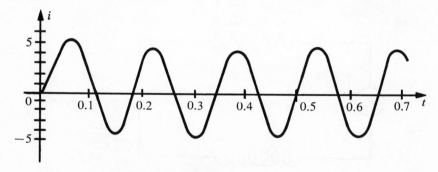

Figure 5.14

Example 5.8. A circuit has in series an electromotive force given by $E = 100\sin 60t$ V, a resistor of 2 Ω, an inductor of 0.1 h, and a capacitor of $\frac{1}{260}$ farads. (See Figure 5.15.) If the initial current and the initial charge on the capacitor are both zero, find the charge on the capacitor at any time $t > 0$.

Formulation (1), by directly applying Kirchhoff's Law: Let i denote the current and q the charge on the capacitor at time t. The total electromotive force is $100\sin 60t$ (volts). Using the voltage drop laws (1), (2), and (3) we find that the voltage drops are as follows:

1. across the resistor: $E_R = Ri = 2i$.

2. across the inductor: $E_L = L\dfrac{di}{dt} = \dfrac{1}{10}\dfrac{di}{dt}$.

3. across the capacitor: $E_c = \dfrac{1}{c}q = 260q$.

Now applying Kirchhoff's Law we have at once:

$$\frac{1}{10}\frac{di}{dt} + 2i + 260q = 100\sin 60t.$$

Since $i = \dfrac{dq}{dt}$, this reduces to

(5.85) $$\frac{1}{10}\frac{d^2q}{dt^2} + 2\frac{dq}{dt} + 260q = 100\sin 60t.$$

Formulation (2), applying Equation (5.80) for the charge: We have $L = \dfrac{1}{10}$, $R = 2$, $c = \dfrac{1}{260}$, $E = 100\sin 60t$. Substituting these values directly into Equation (5.80) we again obtain Equation (5.85) at once.

Multiplying Equation (5.85) through by 10, we consider our differential equation in the form

(5.86) $$\frac{d^2q}{dt^2} + 20\frac{dq}{dt} + 2600q = 1000\sin 60t.$$

Since the charge q is initially zero, we have as a first initial condition

(5.87) $$q(0) = 0$$

Figure 5.15

Since the current i is also initially zero and $i = \dfrac{dq}{dt}$, we take the second initial condition in the form

(5.88) $$q'(0) = 0$$

Solution. The homogeneous equation corresponding to (5.86) has the auxiliary equation

$$r^2 + 20r + 2600 = 0.$$

The roots of this equation are $-10 \pm 50i$ and so the complementary function of equation (5.86) is

$$q_c = e^{-10t}(c_1\sin 50t + c_2\cos 50t).$$

Employing the method of undetermined coefficients to find a particular integral of (5.86), we write

$$q_p = A\sin 60t + B\cos 60t.$$

Differentiating twice and substituting into Equation (5.86) we find that

$$A = -\frac{25}{61} \quad \text{and} \quad B = -\frac{30}{61},$$

and so the general solution of Equation (5.86) is

(5.89) $$q = e^{-10t}(c_1\sin 50t + c_2\cos 50t) - \frac{25}{61}\sin 60t - \frac{30}{61}\cos 60t.$$

Differentiating (5.89), we obtain

(5.90) $$\frac{dq}{dt} = e^{-10t}[(-10c_1 - 50c_2)\sin 50t + (50c_1 - 10c_2)\cos 60t]$$
$$- \frac{1500}{61}\cos 60t + \frac{1800}{61}\sin 60t.$$

Applying condition (5.87) to Equation (5.89) and condition (5.88) to Equation (5.90), we have

$$c_2 - \frac{30}{61} = 0 \quad \text{and} \quad 50c_1 - 10c_2 - \frac{1500}{61} = 0.$$

From these equations, we find that

$$c_1 = \frac{36}{61} \quad \text{and} \quad c_2 = \frac{30}{61}.$$

Thus the solution of the problem is

$$q = \frac{6e^{-10t}}{61}[6\sin 50t + 5\cos 50t] - \frac{5}{61}[5\sin 60t + 6\cos 60t]$$

or

$$q = \frac{6\sqrt{61}}{61}e^{-10t}\cos(50t - \phi) - \frac{5\sqrt{61}}{61}\cos(60t - \theta),$$

where $\cos\phi = \dfrac{5}{\sqrt{61}}$, $\sin\phi = \dfrac{6}{\sqrt{61}}$ and $\cos\theta = \dfrac{6}{\sqrt{61}}$, $\sin\theta = \dfrac{5}{\sqrt{61}}$.

From these equations we determine $\phi \approx 0.88$ (radians) and $\theta \approx 0.69$ (radians). Thus our solution is given approximately by

$$q = 0.77e^{-10t}\cos(50t - 0.88) - 0.64\cos(60t - 0.69).$$

Interpretation. The first term in the above solution clearly becomes negligible after a relatively short time; it is the *transient* term. After a sufficient time essentially all that remains is the periodic second term; this is the *steady-state term*. The graphs of these two components and that of their sum (the complete solution) are shown in Figure 5.16.

Exercises

1. A circuit has in series a constant electromotive force of 40 V, a resistor of $10\,\Omega$ and an induction of 0.2 h. If the initial current is 0, find the current at time $t > 0$.

2. Solve problem 1 if the electromotive force is given by $E(t) = 150\cos 200t$ V instead of the constant electromotive force given in that problem.

3. A circuit has in series a constant electromotive force of 100 V, a resistor of $10\,\Omega$, and a capacitor of $2 \cdot 10^{-4}$ farads. The switch is closed at time $t = 0$, and the charge on the capacitor at this instant is zero. Find the charge and the current at time $t > 0$.

4. A circuit has in series an electromotive force given by $E(t) = 5\sin 100t$ V, a resistor of $10\,\Omega$, an inductor of 0.05 h, and a capacitor of $2 \cdot 10^{-4}$ farads. If the initial current and the initial charge on the capacitor are both zero, find the charge on the capacitor at any time $t > 0$.

5. A circuit has in series an electromotive force given by $E(t) = 100\sin 200t$ V, a resistor of $40\,\Omega$, an inductor of 0.25 h, and a capacitor of $4 \cdot 10^{-4}$ farads. If the initial current is zero, and the initial charge on the capacitor is 0.01 coulombs, find the current at any time $t > 0$.

6. A circuit has in series an electromotive force given by $E(t) = 200e^{-100t}$ V, a resistor of $80\,\Omega$, an inductor of 0.2 h, and a capacitor of $5 \cdot 10^{-6}$ farads. If the initial current and the initial charge on the capacitor are zero, find the current at any time $t > 0$.

7. A circuit has in series a resistor of $R\,\Omega$, an inductor of L h, and a capacitor of C farads. The initial current is zero and the initial charge on the capacitor is Q_0 coulombs.
    (a) Show that the charge and the current are damped oscillatory functions of time if and only if $R < 2\sqrt{\dfrac{L}{C}}$, and find the expressions for the charge and the current in this case.

    (b) If $R \geq 2\sqrt{\dfrac{L}{C}}$, discuss the nature of the charge and the current as functions of time.

8. A circuit has in series an electromotive force given by $E(t) = E_0\sin\omega t$ V, a resistance of $R\,\Omega$, an inductor of L h, and a capacitor of C farads.
    (a) Show that the steady-state current is

$$i = \frac{E_0}{Z}\left[\frac{R}{Z}\sin\omega t - \frac{X}{Z}\cos\omega t\right]$$

where $X = L\omega - \dfrac{1}{C\omega}$ and $Z = \sqrt{X^2 + R^2}$. The quantity x is called the *reactance* of the circuit and Z is called the *impedance*.

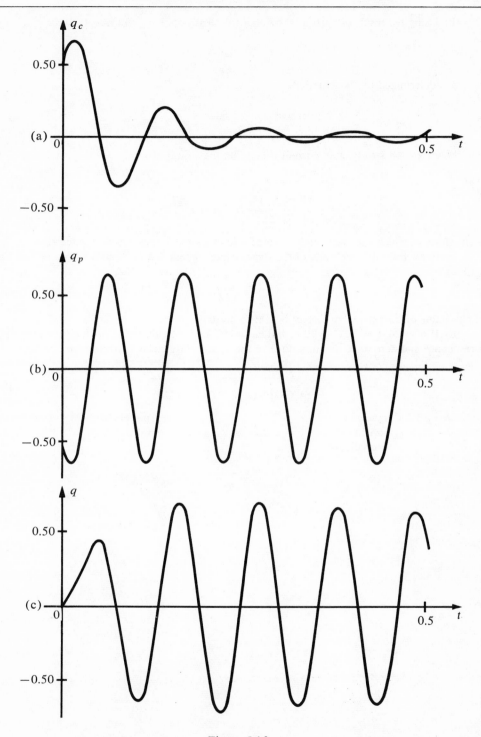

Figure 5.16

(b) Using the result of part (a) show that the steady-state current may be written

$$i = \frac{E_0}{Z}\sin(\omega t - \phi),$$

where ϕ is determined by the equations

$$\cos\phi = \frac{R}{Z}, \quad \sin\phi = \frac{X}{Z}.$$

Thus show that the steady-state current attains its maximum absolute value $\frac{E_0}{Z}$ at times $t_n + \frac{\phi}{\omega}$, where

$$t_n = \frac{1}{\omega}\left[\frac{(2n-1)\pi}{2}\right], \quad (n = 1, 2, 3, \ldots),$$

are the times at which the electromotive force attains its maximum absolute value E_0.

(c) Show that the amplitude of the steady-state current is a maximum when

$$\omega = \frac{1}{\sqrt{LC}}.$$

For this value of ω *electrical resonance* is said to occur.

(d) If $R = 20$, $L = \frac{1}{4}$, $C = 10^{-4}$, and $E_0 = 100$, find the value of ω which gives rise to electrical resonance and determine the amplitude of the steady-state current in this case.

SUGGESTED READING

Agnew (1)
Kaplan (30)
Rainville (45)

Spiegel (50)
Wylie (57)

6

SERIES SOLUTIONS OF
LINEAR DIFFERENTIAL EQUATIONS

In Chapter 4 we learned that certain types of higher order linear differential equations (for example, those with constant coefficients) have solutions which can be expressed as finite linear combinations of known elementary functions. In general, however, higher order linear equations have no solutions which can be expressed in such a simple manner. Thus we must seek other means of expression for the solutions of these equations. One such means of expression is furnished by infinite series representations, and the present chapter is devoted to methods of obtaining solutions in infinite series form.

6.1 Power Series Solutions About an Ordinary Point

A. Basic Concepts and Results.

Consider the second-order homogeneous linear differential equation

$$(6.1) \qquad a_0(x)\frac{d^2y}{dx^2} + a_1(x)\frac{dy}{dx} + a_2(x)y = 0,$$

and suppose that this equation has no solution which is expressible as a finite linear combination of known elementary functions. Let us assume, however, that it does have a solution which can be expressed in the form of an infinite series. Specifically, we assume that it has a solution expressible in the form

$$(6.2) \qquad c_0 + c_1(x - x_0) + c_2(x - x_0)^2 + \cdots = \sum_{n=0}^{\infty} c_n(x - x_0)^n,$$

where $c_0, c_1, c_2, \ldots$ are constants. An expression of the form (6.2) is called a *power series* in $x - x_0$. We have thus assumed that the differential equation (6.1) has a so-called *power series solution* of the form (6.2). This assumption being valid, we can proceed to determine the coefficients $c_0, c_1, c_2, \ldots$ in (6.2) in such a manner that the expression (6.2) does indeed satisfy the equation (6.1).

But under what conditions is this assumption actually valid? That is, under what conditions can we be certain that the differential equation (6.1) actually *does* have a solution of the form (6.2)? This is a question of considerable importance; for it would be quite absurd to actually try to find a "solution" of the form (6.2) if there were really no such solution to be found! In order to answer this important question concerning the existence of a solution of the form (6.2), we shall first introduce certain basic definitions. For this purpose let us write the differential equation (6.1) in the equivalent normalized form

$$(6.3) \qquad \frac{d^2y}{dx^2} + P_1(x)\frac{dy}{dx} + P_2(x)y = 0,$$

where

$$P_1(x) = \frac{a_1(x)}{a_0(x)} \quad \text{and} \quad P_2(x) = \frac{a_2(x)}{a_0(x)}.$$

DEFINITION. A function f is said to be *analytic* at x_0 if its Taylor Series about x_0,

$$\sum_{n=0}^{\infty} \frac{f^{(n)}(x_0)}{n!}(x - x_0)^n,$$

exists and converges to $f(x)$ for all x in some open interval including x_0.

We note that all polynomial functions are analytic everywhere; so also are the functions with values e^x, $\sin x$, and $\cos x$. A rational function is analytic except at those values of x at which its denominator is zero. For example, the rational function defined by $\frac{1}{x^2 - 3x + 2}$ is analytic except at $x = 1$ and $x = 2$.

DEFINITION. The point x_0 is called an *ordinary point* of the differential equation (6.1) if *both* of the functions P_1 and P_2 in the equivalent normalized equation (6.3) are analytic at x_0. If either (or both) of these functions is *not* analytic at x_0, then x_0 is called a *singular point* of the differential equation (6.1).

Example 6.1. Consider the differential equation

$$(6.4) \qquad \frac{d^2y}{dx^2} + x\frac{dy}{dx} + (x^2 + 2)y = 0.$$

Here $P_1(x) = x$ and $P_2(x) = x^2 + 2$. Both of the functions P_1 and P_2 are polynomial functions and so they are analytic everywhere. Thus all points are ordinary points of this differential equation.

Example 6.2.   Consider the differential equation

(6.5)
$$(x - 1)\frac{d^2y}{dx^2} + x\frac{dy}{dx} + \frac{1}{x}y = 0.$$

Equation (6.5) has not been written in the normalized form (6.3). We must first express (6.5) in the normalized form, thereby obtaining

$$\frac{d^2y}{dx^2} + \frac{x}{x - 1}\frac{dy}{dx} + \frac{1}{x(x - 1)}y = 0.$$

Here

$$P_1(x) = \frac{x}{x - 1} \quad \text{and} \quad P_2(x) = \frac{1}{x(x - 1)}.$$

The function P_1 is analytic, except at $x = 1$, and P_2 is analytic except at $x = 0$ and $x = 1$. Thus $x = 0$ and $x = 1$ are singular points of the differential equation under consideration. All other points are ordinary points. Note clearly that $x = 0$ is a singular point, even though P_1 *is* analytic at $x = 0$. We mention this fact to emphasize that *both* P_1 and P_2 must be analytic at x_0 in order for x_0 to be an ordinary point.

We are now in a position to state a theorem concerning the existence of power series solutions of the form (6.2).

THEOREM 6.1.

Hypothesis.   The point x_0 is an ordinary point of the differential equation (6.1).

Conclusion.   The differential equation (6.1) has two nontrivial linearly independent power series solutions of the form

(6.2)
$$\sum_{n=0}^{\infty} c_n(x - x_0)^n,$$

and these power series converge in some interval $|x - x_0| < R$ (where $R > 0$) about x_0.

This theorem gives us a sufficient condition for the existence of power series solutions of the differential equation (6.1). It states that if x_0 is an ordinary point of equation (6.1), then this equation has *two* power series solutions in powers of $x - x_0$ and that these two power series solutions are *linearly independent*. Thus if x_0 is an ordinary point of (6.1), we may obtain the *general solution* of (6.1) as a linear combination of these two linearly independent power series. We shall omit the proof of this important theorem.

Example 6.3.   In Example 6.1 we noted that all points are ordinary points of the differential equation (6.4). Thus this differential equation has two linearly independent solutions of the form (6.2) about *any* point x_0.

Example 6.4. In Example 6.2 we observed that $x = 0$ and $x = 1$ are the only singular points of the differential equation (6.5). Thus this differential equation has two linearly independent solutions of the form (6.2) about any point $x_0 \neq 0$ or 1. For example, the equation has two linearly independent solutions of the form

$$\sum_{n=0}^{\infty} c_n(x - 2)^n$$

about the ordinary point 2. However, we are *not* assured that there exists any solution of the form

$$\sum_{n=0}^{\infty} c_n x^n$$

about the singular point 0 or any solution of the form

$$\sum_{n=0}^{\infty} c_n(x - 1)^n$$

about the singular point 1.

B. The Method of Solution.

Now that we are assured that under appropriate hypotheses the equation (6.1) actually does have power series solutions of the form (6.2), how do we proceed to find these solutions? In other words, how do we determine the coefficients c_0, c_1, c_2, ... in the expression

$$(6.2) \qquad \sum_{n=0}^{\infty} c_n(x - x_0)^n$$

so that this expression actually does satisfy the equation (6.1)? We shall first give a brief outline of the procedure for finding these coefficients and shall then illustrate the procedure in detail by considering specific examples.

Assuming that x_0 is an ordinary point of the differential equation (6.1), so that solutions in powers of $x - x_0$ actually do exist, we denote such a solution by

$$(6.6) \qquad y = c_0 + c_1(x - x_0) + c_2(x - x_0)^2 + \cdots = \sum_{n=0}^{\infty} c_n(x - x_0)^n.$$

Since the series in (6.6) converges on an interval $|x - x_0| < R$ about x_0, it may be differentiated term by term on this interval twice in succession to obtain

$$(6.7) \qquad \frac{dy}{dx} = c_1 + 2c_2(x - x_0) + 3c_3(x - x_0)^2 + \cdots = \sum_{n=1}^{\infty} nc_n(x - x_0)^{n-1}$$

and

$$(6.8) \qquad \frac{d^2y}{dx^2} = 2c_2 + 6c_3(x - x_0) + 12c_4(x - x_0)^2 + \cdots = \sum_{n=2}^{\infty} n(n - 1)c_n(x - x_0)^{n-2},$$

respectively. We now substitute the series in the right members of (6.6), (6.7), and (6.8) for y and its first two derivatives, respectively, in the differential equation (6.1). We then simplify the resulting expression so that it takes the form

$$(6.9) \qquad K_0 + K_1(x - x_0) + K_2(x - x_0)^2 + \cdots = 0,$$

where the coefficients $K_i (i = 0, 1, 2, \ldots)$ are functions of certain coefficients c_n of the solution (6.6). In order that (6.9) be valid for all x in the interval of convergence $|x - x_0| < R$, we must set

$$K_0 = K_1 = K_2 = \cdots = 0.$$

In other words, we must equate to zero the coefficient of each power of $(x - x_0)$ in the left member of (6.9). This leads to a set of conditions which must be satisfied by the various coefficients c_n in the series (6.6) in order that (6.6) be a solution of the differential equation (6.1). If the c_n are chosen to satisfy the set of conditions which thus occurs, then the resulting series (6.6) is the desired solution of the differential equation (6.1). We shall illustrate this procedure in detail in the two examples which follow.

Example 6.5. Find the power series solution of the differential equation

$$(6.4) \qquad \frac{d^2y}{dx^2} + x\frac{dy}{dx} + (x^2 + 2)y = 0$$

in powers of x (that is, about $x_0 = 0$).

Solution. We have already observed that $x_0 = 0$ is an ordinary point of the differential equation (6.4) and that two linearly independent solutions of the desired type actually exist. Our procedure will yield both of these solutions at once.

We thus assume a solution of the form (6.6) with $x_0 = 0$. That is, we assume

$$(6.10) \qquad y = \sum_{n=0}^{\infty} c_n x^n.$$

Differentiating term by term we obtain

$$(6.11) \qquad \frac{dy}{dx} = \sum_{n=1}^{\infty} n c_n x^{n-1}$$

and

$$(6.12) \qquad \frac{d^2y}{dx^2} = \sum_{n=2}^{\infty} n(n-1) c_n x^{n-2}.$$

Substituting the series (6.10), (6.11), and (6.12) into the differential equation (6.4), we obtain

$$\sum_{n=2}^{\infty} n(n-1)c_n x^{n-2} + x\sum_{n=1}^{\infty} n c_n x^{n-1} + x^2 \sum_{n=0}^{\infty} c_n x^n + 2\sum_{n=0}^{\infty} c_n x^n = 0.$$

Since x is independent of the index of summation n, we may rewrite this as

$$(6.13) \qquad \sum_{n=2}^{\infty} n(n-1)c_n x^{n-2} + \sum_{n=1}^{\infty} n c_n x^n + \sum_{n=0}^{\infty} c_n x^{n+2} + 2\sum_{n=0}^{\infty} c_n x^n = 0.$$

In order to put the left member of equation (6.13) in the form (6.9), we shall rewrite the first and third summations in (6.13) so that x in each of these summations will have the exponent n. Let us consider the first summation

$$(6.14) \qquad \sum_{n=2}^{\infty} n(n-1)c_n x^{n-2}$$

in (6.13). We let $m = n-2$ in (6.14). Then $n = m + 2$, and since $m = 0$ for $n = 2$, the summation (6.14) takes the form

$$(6.15) \qquad \sum_{m=0}^{\infty} (m + 2)(m + 1)c_{m+2}x^m.$$

Now since the variable of summation is merely a "dummy" variable, we may replace m by n in (6.15) to write the first summation in (6.13) as

$$(6.16) \qquad \sum_{n=0}^{\infty} (n + 2)(n + 1)c_{n+2}x^n.$$

In like manner, letting $m = n + 2$, the third summation

$$(6.17) \qquad \sum_{n=0}^{\infty} c_n x^{n+2}$$

in (6.13) first takes the form

$$(6.18) \qquad \sum_{m=2}^{\infty} c_{m-2}x^m.$$

Then replacing m by n in (6.18), the third summation in (6.13) may be written as

$$(6.19) \qquad \sum_{n=2}^{\infty} c_{n-2}x^n.$$

Thus replacing (6.14) by its equivalent (6.16) and (6.17) by its equivalent (6.19), the equation (6.13) may be written

$$(6.20) \qquad \sum_{n=0}^{\infty} (n + 2)(n + 1)c_{n+2}x^n + \sum_{n=1}^{\infty} nc_n x^n + \sum_{n=2}^{\infty} c_{n-2}x^n + 2 \sum_{n=0}^{\infty} c_n x^n = 0.$$

Although x has the same exponent n in each summation in (6.20), the ranges of the various summations are not all the same. In the first and fourth summations n ranges from 0 to ∞, in the second n ranges from 1 to ∞, and in the third the range is from 2 to ∞. The common range is from 2 to ∞. We now write out individually the terms in each summation which do *not* belong to this common range, and we continue to employ the "sigma" notation to denote the remainder of each such summation. For example, in the first summation

$$\sum_{n=0}^{\infty} (n + 2)(n + 1)c_{n+2}x^n$$

of (6.20) we write out individually the terms corresponding to $n = 0$ and $n = 1$ and denote the remainder of this summation by

$$\sum_{n=2}^{\infty} (n + 2)(n + 1)c_{n+2}x^n.$$

We thus rewrite

$$\sum_{n=0}^{\infty} (n + 2)(n + 1)c_{n+2}x^n \text{ in (6.20) as}$$

$$2c_2 + 6c_3x + \sum_{n=2}^{\infty} (n + 2)(n + 1)c_{n+2}x^n.$$

In like manner, we rewrite

$$\sum_{n=1}^{\infty} nc_nx^n \quad \text{in (6.20) as} \quad c_1x + \sum_{n=2}^{\infty} nc_nx^n$$

and

$$2 \sum_{n=0}^{\infty} c_nx^n \quad \text{in (6.20) as} \quad 2c_0 + 2c_1x + 2 \sum_{n=2}^{\infty} c_nx^n.$$

Thus equation (6.20) is now written as

$$2c_2 + 6c_3x + \sum_{n=2}^{\infty} (n + 2)(n + 1)c_{n+2}x^n + c_1x + \sum_{n=2}^{\infty} nc_nx^n$$

$$+ \sum_{n=2}^{\infty} c_{n-2}x^n + 2c_0 + 2c_1x + 2 \sum_{n=2}^{\infty} c_nx^n = 0.$$

We can now combine like powers of x and write this equation as

(6.21) $(2c_0 + 2c_2) + (3c_1 + 6c_3)x + \sum_{n=2}^{\infty} [(n + 2)(n + 1)c_{n+2} + (n + 2)c_n + c_{n-2}]x^n = 0.$

Equation (6.21) is in the desired form (6.9). For (6.21) to be valid for all x in the interval of convergence $|x - x_0| < R$, the coefficient of each power of x in the left member of (6.21) must be equated to zero. This leads immediately to the conditions

(6.22) $2c_0 + 2c_2 = 0,$

(6.23) $3c_1 + 6c_3 = 0,$

and

(6.24) $(n + 2)(n + 1)c_{n+2} + (n + 2)c_n + c_{n-2} = 0, \quad n \geq 2.$

The condition (6.22) enables us to express c_2 in terms of c_0. Doing so, we find that

(6.25) $c_2 = -c_0.$

The condition (6.23) enables us to express c_3 in terms of c_1. This leads to

(6.26) $c_3 = -\frac{1}{2}c_1.$

The condition (6.24) is called a *recurrence formula*. It enables us to express each coefficient c_{n+2} for $n \geq 2$ in terms of the previous coefficients c_n and c_{n-2}, thus giving

(6.27) $c_{n+2} = -\frac{(n + 2)c_n + c_{n-2}}{(n + 1)(n + 2)}, \quad n \geq 2.$

For $n = 2$, formula (6.27) is

$$c_4 = -\frac{4c_2 + c_0}{12}.$$

Now using (6.25), this reduces to

(6.28)
$$c_4 = \frac{1}{4}c_0,$$

which expresses c_4 in terms of c_0. For $n = 3$, formula (6.27) is

$$c_5 = -\frac{5c_3 + c_1}{20}.$$

Now using (6.26), this reduces to

(6.29)
$$c_5 = \frac{3}{40}c_1,$$

which expresses c_5 in terms of c_1. In the same way we may express each even coefficient in terms of c_0 and each odd coefficient in terms of c_1.

Substituting the values of c_2, c_3, c_4, and c_5, given by (6.25), (6.26), (6.28), and (6.29), respectively, into the assumed solution (6.10), we have

$$y = c_0 + c_1 x - c_0 x^2 - \frac{1}{2}c_1 x^3 + \frac{1}{4}c_0 x^4 + \frac{3}{40}c_1 x^5 + \cdots.$$

Collecting terms in c_0 and c_1, we have finally

(6.30) $$y = c_0\left(1 - x^2 + \frac{1}{4}x^4 + \cdots\right) + c_1\left(x - \frac{1}{2}x^3 + \frac{3}{40}x^5 + \cdots\right),$$

which gives the solution of the differential equation (6.4) in powers of x through terms in x^5. The two series in parentheses in (6.30) are the power series expansions of two linearly independent solutions of (6.4), and the constants c_0 and c_1 are arbitrary constants. Thus (6.30) represents the general solution of (6.4) in powers of x (through terms in x^5).

Example 6.6.   Find a power series solution of the initial-value problem

(6.31)
$$\begin{cases} (x^2 - 1)\dfrac{d^2y}{dx^2} + 3x\dfrac{dy}{dx} + xy = 0, \\[2mm] y(0) = 4, \\[1mm] y'(0) = 6. \end{cases}$$

(6.32)

(6.33)

Solution.   We first observe that all points except $x = \pm1$ are ordinary points for the differential equation (6.31). Thus we could assume solutions of the form (6.6) for any $x_0 \neq \pm1$. However, since the initial values of y and its first derivative are prescribed at $x = 0$, we shall choose $x_0 = 0$ and seek solutions in powers of x. Thus we assume

(6.34)
$$y = \sum_{n=0}^{\infty} c_n x^n.$$

Differentiating term by term we obtain

(6.35)
$$\frac{dy}{dx} = \sum_{n=1}^{\infty} n c_n x^{n-1}$$

and

$$(6.36) \qquad \frac{d^2y}{dx^2} = \sum_{n=2}^{\infty} n(n-1)c_n x^{n-2}.$$

Substituting the series (6.34), (6.35), and (6.36) into the differential equation (6.31), we obtain

$$(6.37) \qquad \sum_{n=2}^{\infty} n(n-1)c_n x^n - \sum_{n=2}^{\infty} n(n-1)c_n x^{n-2} + 3 \sum_{n=1}^{\infty} n c_n x^n + \sum_{n=0}^{\infty} c_n x^{n+1} = 0.$$

We now rewrite the second and fourth summations in (6.37) so that x in each of these summations has the exponent n. Doing this, Equation (6.37) takes the form

$$(6.38) \qquad \sum_{n=2}^{\infty} n(n-1)c_n x^n - \sum_{n=0}^{\infty} (n+2)(n+1)c_{n+2} x^n + 3 \sum_{n=1}^{\infty} n c_n x^n + \sum_{n=1}^{\infty} c_{n-1} x^n = 0.$$

The common range of the four summations in (6.38) is from 2 to ∞. We can write out the individual terms in each summation which do *not* belong to this common range and thus express (6.38) in the form

$$\sum_{n=2}^{\infty} n(n-1)c_n x^n - 2c_2 - 6c_3 x - \sum_{n=2}^{\infty} (n+2)(n+1)c_{n+2} x^n$$
$$+ 3c_1 x + 3 \sum_{n=2}^{\infty} n c_n x^n + c_0 x + \sum_{n=2}^{\infty} c_{n-1} x^n = 0.$$

Combining like powers of x, this takes the form

$$(6.39) \quad -2c_2 + (c_0 + 3c_1 - 6c_3)x$$
$$+ \sum_{n=2}^{\infty} [-(n+2)(n+1)c_{n+2} + n(n+2)c_n + c_{n-1}]x^n = 0.$$

For (6.39) to be valid for all x in the interval of convergence $|x - x_0| < R$, the coefficient of each power of x in the left member of (6.39) must be equated to zero. In doing this, we are led to the relations

$$(6.40) \qquad\qquad -2c_2 = 0,$$

$$(6.41) \qquad\qquad c_0 + 3c_1 - 6c_3 = 0,$$

and

$$(6.42) \qquad -(n+2)(n+1)c_{n+2} + n(n+2)c_n + c_{n-1} = 0, \quad n \geq 2.$$

From (6.40), we find that $c_2 = 0$; and from (6.41), $c_3 = \frac{1}{6}c_0 + \frac{1}{2}c_1$. The recurrence formula (6.42) gives

$$c_{n+2} = \frac{n(n+2)c_n + c_{n-1}}{(n+1)(n+2)}, \quad n \geq 2.$$

Using this, we find successively

$$c_4 = \frac{8c_2 + c_1}{12} = \frac{1}{12}c_1,$$

$$c_5 = \frac{15c_3 + c_2}{20} = \frac{1}{8}c_0 + \frac{3}{8}c_1,$$

$$\cdot \ \cdot \ \cdot \ \cdot$$

Substituting these values of c_2, c_3, c_4, c_5, ... into the assumed solution (6.34), we have

$$y = c_0 + c_1 x + \left(\frac{c_0}{6} + \frac{c_1}{2}\right)x^3 + \frac{c_1}{12}x^4 + \left(\frac{c_0}{8} + \frac{3c_1}{8}\right)x^5 + \cdots$$

or

(6.43) $$y = c_0\left(1 + \frac{1}{6}x^3 + \frac{1}{8}x^5 + \cdots\right) + c_1\left(x + \frac{1}{2}x^3 + \frac{1}{12}x^4 + \frac{3}{8}x^5 + \cdots\right).$$

The solution (6.43) is the general solution of the differential equation (6.31) in powers of x (through terms in x^5).

We must now apply the initial conditions (6.32) and (6.33). Applying (6.32) to (6.43), we immediately find that

$$c_0 = 4.$$

Differentiating (6.43), we have

(6.44) $$\frac{dy}{dx} = c_0\left(\frac{1}{2}x^2 + \frac{5}{8}x^4 + \cdots\right) + c_1\left(1 + \frac{3}{2}x^2 + \frac{1}{3}x^3 + \frac{15}{8}x^4 + \cdots\right).$$

Applying (6.33) to (6.44) we find that

$$c_1 = 6.$$

Thus the solution of the given initial-value problem in powers of x (through terms in x^5) is

$$y = 4\left(1 + \frac{1}{6}x^3 + \frac{1}{8}x^5 + \cdots\right) + 6\left(x + \frac{1}{2}x^3 + \frac{1}{12}x^4 + \frac{3}{8}x^5 + \cdots\right)$$

or

$$y = 4 + 6x + \frac{11}{3}x^3 + \frac{1}{2}x^4 + \frac{11}{4}x^5 + \cdots.$$

Remark 1. Suppose the initial values of y and its first derivative in conditions (6.32) and (6.33) of Example 6.6 are prescribed at $x = 2$, instead of $x = 0$. Then we have the initial-value problem

(6.45) $$\begin{cases} (x^2 - 1)\dfrac{d^2y}{dx^2} + 3x\dfrac{dy}{dx} + xy = 0, \\ \quad y(2) = 4, \quad y'(2) = 6. \end{cases}$$

Since the initial values in this problem are prescribed at $x = 2$, we would seek solutions in powers of $x - 2$. That is, in this case we would seek solutions of the form

(6.46) $$y = \sum_{n=0}^{\infty} c_n(x - 2)^n.$$

The simplest procedure for obtaining a solution of the form (6.46) is first to make the substitution $t = x - 2$. This replaces the initial-value problem (6.45) by the equivalent problem

(6.47)
$$\begin{cases} (t^2 + 4t + 3)\dfrac{d^2y}{dt^2} + (3t + 6)\dfrac{dy}{dt} + (t + 2)y = 0, \\ y(0) = 4, \quad y'(0) = 6 \end{cases}$$

in which t is the independent variable and the initial values are prescribed at $t = 0$. One then seeks a solution of the problem (6.47) in powers of t,

(6.48)
$$y = \sum_{n=0}^{\infty} c_n t^n.$$

Differentiating (6.48) and substituting into the differential equation in (6.47), one determines the c_n as in Examples 6.5 and 6.6. The initial conditions in (6.47) are then applied. Replacing t by $x - 2$ in the resulting solution (6.48), one obtains the desired solution (6.46) of the original problem (6.45).

Remark 2.   In Examples 6.5 and 6.6 we obtained power series solutions of the differential equations under consideration but made no attempt to discuss the convergence of these solutions. According to Theorem 6.1, if x_0 is an ordinary point of the differential equation

(6.1)
$$a_0(x)\frac{d^2y}{dx^2} + a_1(x)\frac{dy}{dx} + a_2(x)y = 0,$$

then the power series solutions of the form (6.2) converge in some interval $|x - x_0| < R$ (where $R > 0$) about x_0. Let us again write (6.1) in the normalized form

(6.3)
$$\frac{d^2y}{dx^2} + P_1(x)\frac{dy}{dx} + P_2(x)y = 0,$$

where

$$P_1(x) = \frac{a_1(x)}{a_0(x)} \quad \text{and} \quad P_2(x) = \frac{a_2(x)}{a_0(x)}.$$

If x_0 is an ordinary point of (6.1), the functions P_1 and P_2 have Taylor Series Expansions about x_0 which converge in intervals $|x - x_0| < R_1$ and $|x - x_0| < R_2$, respectively, about x_0. It can be proved that the interval of convergence $|x - x_0| < R$ of a series solution (6.2) of (6.1) is at least as great as the smaller of the intervals $|x - x_0| < R_1$ and $|x - x_0| < R_2$.

In the differential equation (6.4) of Example 6.5, $P_1(x) = x$ and $P_2(x) = x^2 + 2$. Thus in this example the Taylor Series Expansions for P_1 and P_2 about the ordinary point $x_0 = 0$ coverage for all x. Hence the series solutions (6.30) of (6.4) also converge for all x.

In the differential equation (6.31) of Example 6.6,

$$P_1(x) = \frac{3x}{x^2 - 1} \quad \text{and} \quad P_2(x) = \frac{x}{x^2 - 1}.$$

In this example the Taylor Series for P_1 and P_2 about $x_0 = 0$ both converge for $|x| < 1$. Thus the solutions (6.43) of (6.31) converge at least for $|x| < 1$.

Exercises

Find power series solutions in powers of x of each of the differential equations in Exercises 1 through 10.

1. $\dfrac{d^2y}{dx^2} + x\dfrac{dy}{dx} + y = 0.$

2. $\dfrac{d^2y}{dx^2} + 8x\dfrac{dy}{dx} - 4y = 0.$

3. $\dfrac{d^2y}{dx^2} + x\dfrac{dy}{dx} + (2x^2 + 1)y = 0.$

4. $\dfrac{d^2y}{dx^2} + x\dfrac{dy}{dx} + (x^2 - 4)y = 0.$

5. $\dfrac{d^2y}{dx^2} + x\dfrac{dy}{dx} + (3x + 2)y = 0.$

6. $\dfrac{d^2y}{dx^2} - x\dfrac{dy}{dx} + (3x - 2)y = 0.$

7. $(x^2 + 1)\dfrac{d^2y}{dx^2} + x\dfrac{dy}{dx} + xy = 0.$

8. $(x - 1)\dfrac{d^2y}{dx^2} - (3x - 2)\dfrac{dy}{dx} + 2xy = 0.$

9. $(x^3 - 1)\dfrac{d^2y}{dx^2} + x^2\dfrac{dy}{dx} + xy = 0.$

10. $(x + 3)\dfrac{d^2y}{dx^2} + (x + 2)\dfrac{dy}{dx} + y = 0.$

Find the power series solution of each of the initial-value problems in Exercises 11 through 14.

11. $\begin{cases} \dfrac{d^2y}{dx^2} - x\dfrac{dy}{dx} - y = 0, \\[2mm] y(0) = 1, \\ y'(0) = 0. \end{cases}$

12. $\begin{cases} \dfrac{d^2y}{dx^2} + x\dfrac{dy}{dx} - 2y = 0, \\[2mm] y(0) = 0, \\ y'(0) = 1. \end{cases}$

13. $\begin{cases} (x^2 + 1)\dfrac{d^2y}{dx^2} + x\dfrac{dy}{dx} + 2xy = 0 \\[2mm] y(0) = 2, \\ y'(0) = 3. \end{cases}$

14. $\left|\begin{array}{l} (2x^2 - 3)\dfrac{d^2y}{dx^2} - 2x\dfrac{dy}{dx} + y = 0 \\[2mm] y(0) = -1, \\ y'(0) = 5. \end{array}\right.$

Find power series solutions in powers of $(x - 1)$ of each of the differential equations in Exercises 15 and 16.

15. $x^2\dfrac{d^2y}{dx^2} + x\dfrac{dy}{dx} + y = 0.$

16. $x^2\dfrac{d^2y}{dx^2} + 3x\dfrac{dy}{dx} - y = 0.$

17. Find the power series solution in powers of $(x - 1)$ of the initial-value problem

$\left|\begin{array}{l} x\dfrac{d^2y}{dx^2} + \dfrac{dy}{dx} + 2y = 0, \\[2mm] y(1) = 2, \\ y'(1) = 4. \end{array}\right.$

18. The differential equation

$$(1 - x^2)\frac{d^2y}{dx^2} - 2x\frac{dy}{dx} + n(n + 1)y = 0,$$

where n is a constant, is called *Legendre's Differential Equation.*

   (a) Show that $x = 0$ is an ordinary point of this differential equation, and find two linearly independent power series solutions in powers of x.

   (b) Show that if n is a nonnegative integer, then one of the two solutions found in part (a) is a polynomial of degree n.

6.2   Solutions About Singular Points; the Method of Frobenius

A. Regular Singular Points.

We again consider the homogeneous linear differential equation

(6.1) $$a_0(x)\frac{d^2y}{dx^2} + a_1(x)\frac{dy}{dx} + a_2(x)y = 0,$$

and we assume that x_0 is a *singular* point of (6.1). Then Theorem 6.1 does *not* apply at the point x_0, and we are *not* assured of a power series solution

(6.2) $$y = \sum_{n=0}^{\infty} c_n(x - x_0)^n$$

of (6.1) in powers of $x - x_0$. Indeed an equation of the form (6.1) with a singular point at x_0 does *not*, in general, have a solution of the form (6.2). Clearly we must seek a different type of solution in such a case, but what type of solution can we expect? It happens that under certain conditions we are justified in assuming a solution of the form

(6.49) $$y = (x - x_0)^r \sum_{n=0}^{\infty} c_n(x - x_0)^n,$$

where r is a certain (real or complex) constant. Such a solution is clearly a power series in $x - x_0$ multiplied by a certain *power* of $x - x_0$. In order to state conditions under which a solution of this form is assured, we proceed to classify singular points.

We again write the differential equation (6.1) in the equivalent normalized form

$$(6.3) \qquad \frac{d^2y}{dx^2} + P_1(x)\frac{dy}{dx} + P_2(x)y = 0,$$

where

$$P_1(x) = \frac{a_1(x)}{a_0(x)} \quad \text{and} \quad P_2(x) = \frac{a_2(x)}{a_0(x)}.$$

DEFINITION. Consider the differential equation (6.1), and assume that at least one of the functions P_1 and P_2 in the equivalent normalized equation (6.3) is *not* analytic at x_0, so that x_0 is a singular point of (6.1). If the functions defined by the products

$$(6.50) \qquad (x - x_0)P_1(x) \quad \text{and} \quad (x - x_0)^2 P_2(x)$$

are both analytic at x_0, then x_0 is called a *regular singular point* of the differential equation (6.1). If either (or both) of the functions defined by the products (6.50) is not analytic at x_0, then x_0 is called an *irregular singular point* of (6.1).

Example 6.7. Consider the differential equation

$$(6.51) \qquad 2x^2\frac{d^2y}{dx^2} - x\frac{dy}{dx} + (x - 5)y = 0.$$

Writing this in the normalized form (6.3), we have

$$\frac{d^2y}{dx^2} - \frac{1}{2x}\frac{dy}{dx} + \frac{x - 5}{2x^2}y = 0.$$

Here $P_1(x) = -\dfrac{1}{2x}$ and $P_2(x) = \dfrac{x - 5}{2x^2}$. Since both P_1 and P_2 fail to be analytic at $x = 0$, we conclude that $x = 0$ is a singular point of (6.51). We now consider the functions defined by the products

$$xP_1(x) = -\frac{1}{2} \quad \text{and} \quad x^2 P_2(x) = \frac{x - 5}{2}$$

of the form (6.50). Both of these product functions are analytic at $x = 0$, and so $x = 0$ is a *regular* singular point of the differential equation (6.51).

Example 6.8. Consider the differential equation

$$(6.52) \qquad x^2(x - 2)^2\frac{d^2y}{dx^2} + 2(x - 2)\frac{dy}{dx} + (x + 1)y = 0.$$

In the normalized form (6.3), this is

$$\frac{d^2y}{dx^2} + \frac{2}{x^2(x - 2)}\frac{dy}{dx} + \frac{x + 1}{x^2(x - 2)^2}y = 0.$$

Here $P_1(x) = \dfrac{2}{x^2(x-2)}$ and $P_2(x) = \dfrac{x+1}{x^2(x-2)^2}$.

Clearly the singular points of the differential equation (6.52) are $x = 0$ and $x = 2$. We investigate them one at a time.

Consider $x = 0$ first, and form the functions defined by the products

$$xP_1(x) = \frac{2}{x(x-2)} \quad \text{and} \quad x^2P_2(x) = \frac{x+1}{(x-2)^2}$$

of the form (6.50). The product function defined by $x^2P_2(x)$ is analytic at $x = 0$, but that defined by $xP_1(x)$ is *not*. Thus $x = 0$ is an *irregular* singular point of (6.52).

Now consider $x = 2$. Forming the products (6.50) for this point, we have

$$(x-2)P_1(x) = \frac{2}{x^2} \quad \text{and} \quad (x-2)^2P_2(x) = \frac{x+1}{x^2}.$$

Both of the product functions thus defined are analytic at $x = 2$, and hence $x = 2$ is a *regular* singular point of (6.52).

Now that we can distinguish between regular and irregular singular points, we shall state a basic theorem concerning solutions of the form (6.49) about regular singular points. We shall later give a more complete theorem on this topic.

THEOREM 6.2.

Hypothesis. The point x_0 is a regular singular point of the differential equation (6.1).

Conclusion. The differential equation (6.1) has *at least one* nontrivial solution of the form

(6.49)
$$(x - x_0)^r \sum_{n=0}^{\infty} c_n(x - x_0)^n,$$

where r is a definite (real or complex) constant which may be determined, and this solution is valid in some deleted interval $0 < |x - x_0| < R$ (where $R > 0$) about x_0.

Example 6.9. In Example 6.7 we saw that $x = 0$ is a regular singular point of the differential equation

(6.51)
$$2x^2\frac{d^2y}{dx^2} - x\frac{dy}{dx} + (x - 5)y = 0.$$

By Theorem 6.2 we conclude that this equation has at least one nontrivial solution of the form

$$x^r \sum_{n=0}^{\infty} c_nx^n,$$

valid in some deleted interval $0 < |x| < R$ about $x = 0$.

Example 6.10. In Example 6.8 we saw that $x = 2$ is a regular singular point of the differential equation

(6.52) $$x^2(x - 2)^2\frac{d^2y}{dx^2} + 2(x - 2)\frac{dy}{dx} + (x + 1)y = 0.$$

Thus we know that this equation has at least one nontrivial solution of the form

$$(x - 2)^r \sum_{n=0}^{\infty} c_n(x - 2)^n,$$

valid in some deleted interval $0 < |x - 2| < R$ about $x = 2$.

We also observed that $x = 0$ is a singular point of the equation (6.52). However, this singular point is irregular and so Theorem 6.2 does not apply to it. We are *not* assured that the differential equation (6.52) has a solution of the form

$$x^r \sum_{n=0}^{\infty} c_n x^n$$

in any deleted interval about $x = 0$.

B. The Method of Frobenius.

Now that we are assured of at least one solution of the form (6.49) about a regular singular point x_0 of the differential equation (6.1), how do we proceed to determine the coefficients c_n and the number r in this solution? The procedure is similar to that introduced in Section 6.1 and is commonly called the *Method of Frobenius*. We shall briefly outline the method and then illustrate it by applying it to the differential equation (6.51).

Outline of the Method of Frobenius.

(1) Let x_0 be a regular singular point of the differential equation (6.1) and assume a solution

$$y = (x - x_0)^r \sum_{n=0}^{\infty} c_n(x - x_0)^n$$

of the form (6.49), where $c_0 \neq 0$. We write this solution in the form

(6.53) $$y = \sum_{n=0}^{\infty} c_n(x - x_0)^{n+r},$$

where $c_0 \neq 0$.

(2) Assuming term by term differentiation of (6.53) is valid, we obtain

(6.54) $$\frac{dy}{dx} = \sum_{n=0}^{\infty} (n + r)c_n(x - x_0)^{n+r-1}$$

and

(6.55) $$\frac{d^2y}{dx^2} = \sum_{n=0}^{\infty} (n + r)(n + r - 1)c_n(x - x_0)^{n+r-2}.$$

We now substitute the series (6.53), (6.54), and (6.55) for y and its first two derivatives, respectively, into the differential equation (6.1).

(3) We now proceed (essentially as in Section 6.1) to simplify the resulting expression so that it takes the form

(6.56) $K_0(x - x_0)^{r+k} + K_1(x - x_0)^{r+k+1} + K_2(x - x_0)^{r+k+2} + \cdots = 0,$

where k is a certain integer and the coefficients $K_i(i = 0, 1, 2, \ldots)$ are functions of r and certain of the coefficients c_n of the solution (6.53).

(4) In order that (6.56) be valid for all x in the deleted interval $0 < |x - x_0| < R$, we must set

$$K_0 = K_1 = K_2 = \cdots = 0.$$

Upon equating to zero the coefficient K_0 of the *lowest* power $r + k$ of $(x - x_0)$, we obtain a quadratic equation in r, called the *indicial equation* of the differential equation (6.1). The two roots r_1 and r_2 (where $r_1 \geq r_2$) of this quadratic equation are called the *exponents* of the differential equation (6.1) and are the only possible values for the constant r in the assumed solution (6.53). Thus at this stage the "unknown" constant r is determined.

(5) We now equate to zero the remaining coefficients $K_1, K_2, \ldots$ in (6.56). We are thus led to a set of conditions, involving the constant r, which must be satisfied by the various coefficients c_n in the series (6.53).

(6) We now substitute the larger root r_1 for r into the conditions obtained in step (5), and then choose the c_n to satisfy these conditions. If the c_n are so chosen, the resulting series (6.53) with $r = r_1$ is a solution of the desired form.

(7) If $r_2 \neq r_1$, we may repeat the procedure of step (6) using the smaller root r_2 instead of r_1. In this way a second solution of the desired form (6.53) may be obtained. However, this second solution may not be linearly independent of the solution obtained in step (6). We shall discuss this situation after we have considered an example.

Example 6.11.   Use the method of Frobenius to find solutions near $x = 0$ of the differential equation

(6.51) $2x^2\dfrac{d^2y}{dx^2} - x\dfrac{dy}{dx} + (x - 5)y = 0.$

Solution.   Since $x = 0$ is a regular singular point of the differential equation (6.51), we assume

(6.57) $y = \displaystyle\sum_{n=0}^{\infty} c_n x^{n+r},$

where $c_0 \neq 0$. Then

(6.58) $\dfrac{dy}{dx} = \displaystyle\sum_{n=0}^{\infty} (n + r)c_n x^{n+r-1}$

and

(6.59)
$$\frac{d^2y}{dx^2} = \sum_{n=0}^{\infty} (n + r)(n + r - 1)c_n x^{n+r-2}.$$

Substituting the series (6.57), (6.58), and (6.59) into (6.51), we have

$$2\sum_{n=0}^{\infty} (n + r)(n + r - 1)c_n x^{n+r} - \sum_{n=0}^{\infty} (n + r)c_n x^{n+r} + \sum_{n=0}^{\infty} c_n x^{n+r+1} - 5\sum_{n=0}^{\infty} c_n x^{n+r} = 0.$$

Simplifying, as in the examples of section 6.1, we may write this as

$$\sum_{n=0}^{\infty} [2(n + r)(n + r - 1) - (n + r) - 5]c_n x^{n+r} + \sum_{n=1}^{\infty} c_{n-1} x^{n+r} = 0$$

or

(6.60)
$$[2r(r - 1) - r - 5]c_0 x^r$$

$$+ \sum_{n=1}^{\infty} \{[2(n + r)(n + r - 1) - (n + r) - 5]c_n + c_{n-1}\} x^{n+r} = 0.$$

This is of the form (6.56), where $k = 0$.

Equating to zero the coefficient of the lowest power of x (that is, the coefficient of x^r) in (6.60), we are led to the quandratic equation

$$2r(r - 1) - r - 5 = 0$$

(since we have assumed that $c_0 \neq 0$). This is the *indicial* equation of the differential equation (6.51). We write it in the form

$$2r^2 - 3r - 5 = 0$$

and observe that its roots are

$$r_1 = \frac{5}{2} \quad \text{and} \quad r_2 = -1.$$

These are the so-called *exponents* of the differential equation (6.51) and are the only possible values for the previously unknown constant r in the solution (6.57).

Equating to zero the coefficients of the higher powers of x in (6.60), we obtain the *recurrence formula*

(6.61)
$$[2(n + r)(n + r - 1) - (n + r) - 5]c_n + c_{n-1} = 0, \quad n \geq 1.$$

Letting $r = r_1 = \frac{5}{2}$ in (6.61), we obtain the recurrence formula

$$\left[2\left(n + \frac{5}{2}\right)\left(n + \frac{3}{2}\right) - \left(n + \frac{5}{2}\right) - 5\right]c_n + c_{n-1} = 0, \quad n \geq 1,$$

corresponding to the exponent $\frac{5}{2}$. This simplifies to the form

$$n(2n + 7)c_n + c_{n-1} = 0, \quad n \geq 1,$$

or, finally,

(6.62)
$$c_n = -\frac{c_{n-1}}{n(2n + 7)}, \quad n \geq 1.$$

Using (6.62) we find that

$$c_1 = -\frac{c_0}{9}, \quad c_2 = -\frac{c_1}{22} = \frac{c_0}{198}, \quad c_3 = -\frac{c_2}{39} = -\frac{c_0}{7722}, \dots$$

Letting $r = \frac{5}{2}$ in (6.57), and using these values of $c_1, c_2, c_3, \dots$, we obtain the solution

(6.63)
$$y = c_0\left(x^{5/2} - \frac{1}{9}x^{7/2} + \frac{1}{198}x^{9/2} - \frac{1}{7722}x^{11/2} + \cdots\right)$$

$$= c_0 x^{5/2}\left(1 - \frac{1}{9}x + \frac{1}{198}x^2 - \frac{1}{7722}x^3 + \cdots\right),$$

corresponding to the larger exponent $r = 5/2$.
   We now let $r = r_2 = -1$ in (6.61) to obtain the recurrence formula

$$[2(n-1)(n-2) - (n-1) - 5]c_n + c_{n-1} = 0, \quad n \geq 1,$$

corresponding to this smaller exponent. This simplifies to the form

$$n(2n-7)c_n + c_{n-1} = 0, \quad n \geq 1,$$

or, finally

(6.64)
$$c_n = -\frac{c_{n-1}}{n(2n-7)}, \quad n \geq 1.$$

Using (6.64) we find that

$$c_1 = \frac{1}{5}c_0, \quad c_2 = \frac{1}{6}c_1 = \frac{1}{30}c_0, \quad c_3 = \frac{1}{3}c_2 = \frac{1}{90}c_0, \dots$$

Letting $r = -1$ in (6.57), and using these values of $c_1, c_2, c_3, \dots$ we obtain the solution

(6.65)
$$y = c_0\left(x^{-1} + \frac{1}{5} + \frac{1}{30}x + \frac{1}{90}x^2 - \cdots\right)$$

$$= c_0 x^{-1}\left(1 + \frac{1}{5}x + \frac{1}{30}x^2 + \frac{1}{90}x^3 - \cdots\right),$$

corresponding to the smaller exponent $r = -1$.
   The two solutions (6.63) and (6.65) corresponding to the two exponents $5/2$ and -1, respectively, are linearly independent. Thus the general solution of (6.51) may be written

$$y = C_1 x^{5/2}\left(1 - \frac{1}{9}x + \frac{1}{198}x^2 - \frac{1}{7722}x^3 + \cdots\right)$$

$$+ C_2 x^{-1}\left(1 + \frac{1}{5}x + \frac{1}{30}x^2 + \frac{1}{90}x^3 - \cdots\right),$$

where C_1 and C_2 are arbitrary constants.

   Observe that in Example 6.11 *two* linearly independent solutions of the form (6.49) were obtained. However, in the general discussion preceding Example 6.11, we indicated that this is not always the case. Thus we are led to ask the following questions:
   (1) Under what conditions are we assured that the differential equation (6.1) has *two*

linearly independent solutions

$$(x - x_0)^r \sum_{n=0}^{\infty} c_n(x - x_0)^n$$

of the form (6.49) about a regular singular point x_0?

(2) If the differential equation (6.1) does *not* have two linearly independent solutions of the form (6.49) about a regular singular point x_0, then what is the form of a solution which *is* linearly independent of the basic solution of the form (6.49)?

In answer to these questions we state the following theorem.

THEOREM 6.3.

Hypothesis.   The point x_0 is a regular singular point of the differential equation (6.1). Let r_1 and r_2 (where $r_1 \geq r_2$) be the roots of the indicial equation associated with the point x_0.

Conclusions.   (i) If $r_1 - r_2 \neq 0$ or a positive integer N, then the differential equation (6.1) has two nontrivial linearly independent solutions

(6.66) $$y = (x - x_0)^{r_1} \sum_{n=0}^{\infty} c_n(x - x_0)^n$$

and

(6.67) $$y = (x - x_0)^{r_2} \sum_{n=0}^{\infty} c_n^*(x - x_0)^n$$

of the form (6.49), where $c_0 \neq 0$, $c_0^* \neq 0$.

(ii) If $r_1 - r_2 = 0$ or a positive integer N, then the differential equation (6.1) has two nontrivial linearly independent solutions

(6.66) $$y = (x - x_0)^{r_1} \sum_{n=0}^{\infty} c_n(x - x_0)^n,$$

where $c_0 \neq 0$, and

(6.68) $$y = (x - x_0)^{r_2} \sum_{n=0}^{\infty} c_n^*(x - x_0)^n + Cy_1(x) \ln |x - x_0|,$$

where $c_0^* \neq 0$, C is a constant, and $y_1(x)$ denotes the right member of (6.66).

In particular, if $r_1 - r_2 = 0$, then $C \neq 0$; but if $r_1 - r_2 = N$, a positive integer, then C may be zero or it may not.

The solutions in conclusions (i) and (ii) are valid in some deleted interval $0 < |x - x_0| < R$ about x_0.

From conclusions (i) and (ii) of Theorem 6.3 we see that if x_0 is a regular singular point of (6.1), then there is *always* a solution (6.66) of the form (6.49) corresponding to the *larger* root r_1 of the indicial equation associated with x_0. From conclusion (i) we see that if the difference $r_1 - r_2$ between the roots of the indicial equation is *not* zero or a positive integer, then there is also a linearly independent solution (6.67) of the form (6.49) corresponding to the *smaller* root r_1. However, from conclusion (ii) we see that if the difference $r_1 - r_2$ *is* zero or a positive integer, then a solution which is linearly independent of the "basic" solution (6.66) is of the generally more complicated form (6.68). If the difference $r_1 - r_2$ is a positive integer and the constant C in (6.68) is zero, then of course (6.68) reduces to the simpler form (6.67). However, if $r_1 - r_2$ is a positive integer and $C \neq 0$ or if $r_1 - r_2 = 0$, then the "second" solution (6.68) involves the logarithmic term $Cy_1(x) \ln|x - x_0|$ and is not of the simple form (6.49).

We now consider several examples which will give further practice in the method of Frobenius, illustrate the conclusions of Theorem 6.3, and indicate how a solution of the form (6.68) may be found in cases in which it exists.

Example 6.12.   Use the method of Frobenius to find solutions near $x = 0$ of the differential equation

(6.69)
$$2x^2\frac{d^2y}{dx^2} + x\frac{dy}{dx} + (x^2 - 3)y = 0.$$

Solution.   We observe at once that $x = 0$ is a regular singular point of the differential equation (6.69). Hence we assume a solution

(6.70)
$$y = \sum_{n=0}^{\infty} c_n x^{n+r},$$

where $c_0 \neq 0$. Differentiating (6.70), we obtain

$$\frac{dy}{dx} = \sum_{n=0}^{\infty} (n + r)c_n x^{n+r-1} \quad \text{and} \quad \frac{d^2y}{dx^2} = \sum_{n=0}^{\infty} (n + r)(n + r - 1)\tilde{c}_n x^{n+r-2}.$$

Upon substituting (6.70) and these derivatives into (6.69) we find

$$2\sum_{n=0}^{\infty} (n + r)(n + r - 1)c_n x^{n+r} + \sum_{n=0}^{\infty} (n + r)c_n x^{n+r} + \sum_{n=0}^{\infty} c_n x^{n+r+2} - 3\sum_{n=0}^{\infty} c_n x^{n+r} = 0.$$

Simplifying, as in the previous examples, we write this as

$$\sum_{n=0}^{\infty} [2(n + r)(n + r - 1) + (n + r) - 3]c_n x^{n+r} + \sum_{n=2}^{\infty} c_{n-2} x^{n+r} = 0$$

or

(6.71)
$$[2r(r - 1) + r - 3]c_0 x^r + [2(r + 1)r + (r + 1) - 3]c_1 x^{r+1}$$

$$+ \sum_{n=2}^{\infty} \{[2(n + r)(n + r - 1) + (n + r) - 3]c_n + c_{n-2}\} x^{n+r} = 0.$$

This is of the form (6.56), where $k = 0$.

Equating to zero the coefficient of the lowest power of x in (6.71), we obtain the indicial equation

$$2r(r - 1) + r - 3 = 0 \quad \text{or} \quad 2r^2 - r - 3 = 0.$$

The roots of this equation are

$$r_1 = \frac{3}{2} \quad \text{and} \quad r_2 = -1.$$

Since the difference $r_1 - r_2 = \frac{5}{2}$ between these roots is *not* zero or a positive integer, conclusion (i) of Theorem 6.3 tells us that the equation (6.69) has *two* linearly independent solutions of the form (6.70), one corresponding to each of the roots r_1 and r_2.

Equating to zero the coefficients of the higher powers of x in (6.71), we obtain the condition

(6.72) $$[2(r+1)r + (r+1) - 3]c_1 = 0$$

and the recurrence formula

(6.73) $$[2(n+r)(n+r-1) + (n+r) - 3]c_n + c_{n-2} = 0, \quad n \geq 2.$$

Letting $r = r_1 = \frac{3}{2}$ in (6.72), we obtain $7c_1 = 0$ and hence $c_1 = 0$. Letting $r = r_1 = \frac{3}{2}$ in (6.73), we obtain (after slight simplifications) the recurrence formula

$$n(2n+5)c_n + c_{n-2} = 0, \quad n \geq 2,$$

corresponding to the larger exponent $\frac{3}{2}$. Writing this in the form

$$c_n = -\frac{c_{n-2}}{n(2n+5)}, \quad n \geq 2,$$

we obtain

$$c_2 = -\frac{c_0}{18}, \quad c_3 = -\frac{c_1}{33} = 0 \text{ (since } c_1 = 0), \quad c_4 = -\frac{c_2}{52} = \frac{c_0}{936}, \dots$$

Note that *all* odd coefficients are zero, since $c_1 = 0$. Letting $r = \frac{3}{2}$ in (6.70) and using these values of $c_1, c_2, c_3, \dots$, we obtain the solution corresponding to the larger exponent $r_1 = \frac{3}{2}$. This solution is $y = y_1(x)$, where

(6.74) $$y_1(x) = c_0 x^{3/2}\left(1 - \frac{1}{18}x^2 + \frac{1}{936}x^4 - \cdots\right).$$

Now let $r = r_2 = -1$ in (6.72). We obtain $-3c_1 = 0$ and hence $c_1 = 0$. Letting $r = r_2 = -1$ in (6.73), we obtain the recurrence formula

$$n(2n-5)c_n + c_{n-2} = 0, \quad n \geq 2,$$

corresponding to the smaller exponent -1. Writing this in the form

$$c_n = -\frac{c_{n-2}}{n(2n-5)}, \quad n \geq 2,$$

we obtain

$$c_2 = \frac{c_0}{2}, \quad c_3 = -\frac{c_1}{3} = 0 \text{ (since } c_1 = 0),$$

$$c_4 = -\frac{c_2}{12} = -\frac{c_0}{24}, \dots$$

In this case also all odd coefficients are zero. Letting $r = -1$ in (6.70) and using these values of $c_1, c_2, c_3, \dots$, we obtain the solution corresponding to the smaller exponent $r_2 = -1$. This solution is $y = y_2(x)$, where

(6.75) $$y_2(x) = c_0 x^{-1}\left(1 + \frac{1}{2}x^2 - \frac{1}{24}x^4 + \cdots\right).$$

Since the solutions defined by (6.74) and (6.75) are linearly independent, the general solution of (6.69) may be written

$$y = C_1 y_1(x) + C_2 y_2(x),$$

where C_1 and C_2 are arbitrary constants and $y_1(x)$ and $y_2(x)$ are defined by (6.74) and (6.75), respectively.

Example 6.13. Use the method of Frobenius to find solutions near $x = 0$ of the differential equation

(6.76)
$$x^2 \frac{d^2 y}{dx^2} - x \frac{dy}{dx} - \left(x^2 + \frac{5}{4} \right) y = 0.$$

Solution. We observe that $x = 0$ is a regular singular point of this differential equation and so assume a solution

(6.77)
$$y = \sum_{n=0}^{\infty} c_n x^{n+r},$$

where $c_0 \neq 0$. Upon differentiating (6.77) twice and substituting into (6.76), we obtain

$$\sum_{n=0}^{\infty} (n+r)(n+r-1)c_n x^{n+r} - \sum_{n=0}^{\infty} (n+r)c_n x^{n+r} - \sum_{n=0}^{\infty} c_n x^{n+r+2} - \frac{5}{4} \sum_{n=0}^{\infty} c_n x^{n+r} = 0.$$

Simplifying, we write this in the form

$$\sum_{n=0}^{\infty} \left[(n+r)(n+r-1) - (n+r) - \frac{5}{4} \right] c_n x^{n+r} - \sum_{n=2}^{\infty} c_{n-2} x^{n+r} = 0$$

or

(6.78)
$$\left[r(r-1) - r - \frac{5}{4} \right] c_0 x^r + \left[(r+1)r - (r+1) - \frac{5}{4} \right] c_1 x^{r+1}$$

$$+ \sum_{n=2}^{\infty} \left\{ \left[(n+r)(n+r-1) - (n+r) - \frac{5}{4} \right] c_n - c_{n-2} \right\} x^{n+r} = 0.$$

Equating to zero the coefficient of the lowest power of x in (6.78), we obtain the indicial equation

$$r^2 - 2r - \frac{5}{4} = 0.$$

The roots of this equation are

$$r_1 = \frac{5}{2}, \quad r_2 = -\frac{1}{2}.$$

Although these roots themselves are not integers, the difference $r_1 - r_2$ between them is the positive integer 3. By conclusion (ii) of Theorem 6.3 we know that the differential equation (6.76) has a solution of the assumed form (6.77) corresponding to the larger root $r_1 = \frac{5}{2}$. We proceed to obtain this solution.

Equating to zero the coefficients of the higher powers of x in (6.78), we obtain the condition

(6.79)
$$\left[(r+1)r - (r+1) - \frac{5}{4} \right] c_1 = 0$$

and the recurrence formula

(6.80)
$$\left[(n+r)(n+r-1) - (n+r) - \frac{5}{4} \right] c_n - c_{n-2} = 0, \quad n \geq 2.$$

Letting $r = r_1 = \frac{5}{2}$ in (6.79), we obtain

$$4c_1 = 0 \quad \text{and hence} \quad c_1 = 0.$$

Letting $r = r_1 = \frac{5}{2}$ in (6.80), we obtain the recurrence formula

$$n(n+3)c_n - c_{n-2} = 0, \quad n \geq 2,$$

corresponding to the larger exponent $\frac{5}{2}$. Since $n \geq 2$, we may write this in the form

$$c_n = \frac{c_{n-2}}{n(n+3)}, \quad n \geq 2.$$

From this we obtain successively

$$c_2 = \frac{c_0}{2 \cdot 5}, \quad c_3 = \frac{c_1}{3 \cdot 6} = 0 \text{ (since } c_1 = 0), \quad c_4 = \frac{c_2}{4 \cdot 7} = \frac{c_0}{2 \cdot 4 \cdot 5 \cdot 7}, \quad \cdots$$

We note that all odd coefficients are zero. The general even coefficient may be written

$$c_{2n} = \frac{c_0}{[2 \cdot 4 \cdot 6 \cdots (2n)][5 \cdot 7 \cdot 9 \cdots (2n+3)]}, \quad n \geq 1.$$

Letting $r = \frac{5}{2}$ in (6.77) and using these values of c_{2n}, we obtain the solution corresponding to the larger exponent $r_1 = \frac{5}{2}$. This solution is $y = y_1(x)$, where

(6.81)
$$y_1(x) = c_0 x^{5/2} \left[1 + \frac{x^2}{2 \cdot 5} + \frac{x^4}{2 \cdot 4 \cdot 5 \cdot 7} + \cdots \right],$$

$$= c_0 x^{5/2} \left[1 + \sum_{n=1}^{\infty} \frac{x^{2n}}{[2 \cdot 4 \cdot 6 \cdots (2n)][5 \cdot 7 \cdot 9 \cdots (2n+3)]} \right].$$

We now consider the smaller root $r_2 = -\frac{1}{2}$. Theorem 6.3 does *not* assure us that the differential equation (6.76) has a linearly independent solution of the assumed form (6.77) corresponding to this smaller root. Conclusion (ii) of that theorem merely tells us that there is a linearly independent solution of the form

(6.82)
$$\sum_{n=0}^{\infty} c_n^* x^{n+r_2} + C y_1(x) \ln |x|,$$

where C may or may not be zero. Of course if $C = 0$, then the linearly independent solution (6.82) *is* of the assumed form (6.77) and we can let $r = r_2 = -\frac{1}{2}$ in the formula (6.79) and the recurrence formula (6.80) and proceed as in the previous examples. Let us assume (hopefully, but without justification!) that this is indeed the case.

Thus we let $r = r_2 = -\frac{1}{2}$ in (6.79) and (6.80). Letting $r = -\frac{1}{2}$ in (6.79) we obtain

$-2c_1 = 0$ and hence $c_1 = 0$. Letting $r = -\frac{1}{2}$ in (6.80) we obtain the recurrence formula

$$(6.83) \qquad n(n - 3)c_n - c_{n-2} = 0, \quad n \geq 2,$$

corresponding to the smaller exponent $-\frac{1}{2}$. For $n \neq 3$, this may be written

$$(6.84) \qquad c_n = \frac{c_{n-2}}{n(n - 3)}, \quad n \geq 2, n \neq 3.$$

For $n = 2$, formula (6.84) gives $c_2 = -c_0/2$. For $n = 3$, formula (6.84) does not apply and we must use (6.83). For $n = 3$ formula (6.83) is $0 \cdot c_3 - c_1 = 0$ or simply $0 = 0$ (since $c_1 = 0$). Hence, for $n = 3$, the recurrence formula (6.83) is automatically satisfied with *any* choice of c_3. Thus c_3 is independent of the arbitrary constant c_0; it is a second arbitrary constant! For $n > 3$, we can again use (6.84). Proceeding, we have

$$c_4 = \frac{c_2}{4} = -\frac{c_0}{2 \cdot 4}, \quad c_5 = \frac{c_3}{2 \cdot 5},$$

$$c_6 = \frac{c_4}{6 \cdot 3} = -\frac{c_0}{2 \cdot 4 \cdot 6 \cdot 3}, \quad c_7 = \frac{c_5}{4 \cdot 7} = \frac{c_3}{2 \cdot 4 \cdot 5 \cdot 7},$$

$$\cdots .$$

We note that all even coefficients may be expressed in terms of c_0 and that all odd coefficients beyond c_3 may be expressed in terms of c_3. In fact, we may write

$$c_{2n} = -\frac{c_0}{[2 \cdot 4 \cdot 6 \cdots (2n)][3 \cdot 5 \cdot 7 \cdots (2n - 3)]}, \quad n \geq 3$$

(even coefficients c_6 and beyond), and

$$c_{2n+1} = \frac{c_3}{[2 \cdot 4 \cdot 6 \cdots (2n - 2)][5 \cdot 7 \cdot 9 \cdots (2n + 1)]}, \quad n \geq 2$$

(odd coefficients c_5 and beyond). Letting $r = -\frac{1}{2}$ in (6.77) and using the values of c_n in terms of c_0 (for even n) and c_3 (for odd n beyond c_3), we obtain the solution corresponding to the smaller root $r_2 = -\frac{1}{2}$. This solution is $y = y_2(x)$, where

$$(6.85) \quad y_2(x) = c_0 x^{-1/2}\left[1 - \frac{x^2}{2} - \frac{x^4}{2 \cdot 4} - \frac{x^6}{2 \cdot 4 \cdot 6 \cdot 3} - \cdots\right]$$

$$+ c_3 x^{-1/2}\left[x^3 + \frac{x^5}{2 \cdot 5} + \frac{x^7}{2 \cdot 4 \cdot 5 \cdot 7} + \cdots\right]$$

$$= c_0 x^{-1/2}\left[1 - \frac{x^2}{2} - \frac{x^4}{2 \cdot 4} - \sum_{n=3}^{\infty} \frac{x^{2n}}{[2 \cdot 4 \cdot 6 \cdots (2n)][3 \cdot 5 \cdot 7 \cdots (2n - 3)]}\right]$$

$$+ c_3 x^{-1/2}\left[x^3 + \sum_{n=2}^{\infty} \frac{x^{2n+1}}{[2 \cdot 4 \cdot 6 \cdots (2n - 2)][5 \cdot 7 \cdot 9 \cdots (2n + 1)]}\right],$$

and c_0 and c_3 are arbitrary constants.

If we now let $c_0 = 1$ in (6.81) we obtain the particular solution $y = y_{11}(x)$, where

$$y_{11}(x) = x^{5/2}\left[1 + \sum_{n=1}^{\infty} \frac{x^{2n}}{[2 \cdot 4 \cdot 6 \cdots (2n)][5 \cdot 7 \cdot 9 \cdots (2n+3)]}\right]$$

corresponding to the larger exponent $\frac{5}{2}$; and if we let $c_0 = 1$ and $c_3 = 0$ in (6.85) we obtain the particular solution $y = y_{21}(x)$, where

$$y_{21}(x) = x^{-1/2}\left[1 - \frac{x^2}{2} - \frac{x^4}{2 \cdot 4} - \sum_{n=3}^{\infty} \frac{x^{2n}}{[2 \cdot 4 \cdot 6 \cdots (2n)][3 \cdot 5 \cdot 7 \cdots (2n-3)]}\right]$$

corresponding to the smaller exponent $-\frac{1}{2}$. These two particular solutions, which are both of the assumed form (6.77), are linearly independent. Thus the general solution of the differential equation (6.76) may be written

(6.86) $$y = C_1 y_{11}(x) + C_2 y_{21}(x),$$

where C_1 and C_2 are arbitrary constants.

Now let us examine more carefully the solution y_2 defined by (6.85). The expression

$$x^{-1/2}\left[x^3 + \sum_{n=2}^{\infty} \frac{x^{2n+1}}{[2 \cdot 4 \cdot 6 \cdots (2n-2)][5 \cdot 7 \cdot 9 \cdots (2n+1)]}\right]$$

of which c_3 is the coefficient in (6.85) may be written

$$x^{5/2}\left[1 + \sum_{n=2}^{\infty} \frac{x^{2n-2}}{[2 \cdot 4 \cdot 6 \cdots (2n-2)][5 \cdot 7 \cdot 9 \cdots (2n+1)]}\right]$$

$$= x^{5/2}\left[1 + \sum_{n=1}^{\infty} \frac{x^{2n}}{[2 \cdot 4 \cdot 6 \cdots (2n)][5 \cdot 7 \cdot 9 \cdots (2n+3)]}\right]$$

and this is precisely $y_{11}(x)$. Thus we may write

(6.87) $$y_2(x) = c_0 y_{21}(x) + c_3 y_{11}(x),$$

where c_0 and c_3 are arbitrary constants. Now compare (6.86) and (6.87). We see that the solution $y = y_2(x)$ by itself is actually the general solution of the differential equation (6.76), even though $y_2(x)$ was obtained using only the smaller exponent $-\frac{1}{2}$.

We thus observe that if the difference $r_1 - r_2$ between the roots of the indicial equation is a positive integer, it is sometimes possible to obtain the general solution using the smaller root alone, without bothering to find explicitly the solution corresponding to the larger root. Indeed, if the difference $r_1 - r_2$ is a positive integer, it is a worthwhile practice to work with the smaller root first, in the hope that this smaller root by itself may lead directly to the general solution.

Example 6.14. Use the method of Frobenius to find solutions near $x = 0$ of the differential equation

(6.88) $$x^2 \frac{d^2y}{dx^2} + (x^2 - 3x)\frac{dy}{dx} + 3y = 0.$$

Solution.   Observing that $x = 0$ is a regular singular point of (6.88), we assume a solution

(6.89)
$$y = \sum_{n=0}^{\infty} c_n x^{n+r},$$

where $c_0 \neq 0$. Upon differentiating (6.89) twice and substituting into (6.88), we obtain

$$\sum_{n=0}^{\infty} (n+r)(n+r-1)c_n x^{n+r} + \sum_{n=0}^{\infty} (n+r)c_n x^{n+r+1}$$

$$-3\sum_{n=0}^{\infty} (n+r)c_n x^{n+r} + 3\sum_{n=0}^{\infty} c_n x^{n+r} = 0.$$

Simplifying, we write this in the form

$$\sum_{n=0}^{\infty} [(n+r)(n+r-1) - 3(n+r) + 3]c_n x^{n+r} + \sum_{n=1}^{\infty} (n+r-1)c_{n-1} x^{n+r} = 0$$

or

(6.90) $[r(r-1) - 3r + 3]c_0 x^r$

$$+ \sum_{n=1}^{\infty} \{[(n+r)(n+r-1) - 3(n+r) + 3]c_n + (n+r-1)c_{n-1}\} x^{n+r} = 0.$$

Equating to zero the coefficient of the lowest power of x in (6.90) we obtain the indicial equation

$$r^2 - 4r + 3 = 0.$$

The roots of this equation are

$$r_1 = 3, r_2 = 1.$$

The difference $r_1 - r_2$ between these roots is the positive integer 2. We know from Theorem 6.3 that the differential equation (6.88) has a solution of the assumed form (6.89) corresponding to the larger root $r_1 = 3$. We shall find this first, even though the results of Example 6.13 suggest that we should work first with the smaller root $r_2 = 1$ in the hopes of finding the general solution directly from this smaller root.

Equating to zero the coefficients of the higher powers of x in (6.90), we obtain the recurrence formula

(6.91) $[(n+r)(n+r-1) - 3(n+r) + 3]c_n + (n+r-1)c_{n-1} = 0, \quad n \geq 1.$

Letting $r = r_1 = 3$ in (6.91), we obtain the recurrence formula

$$n(n+2)c_n + (n+2)c_{n-1} = 0, \quad n \geq 1,$$

corresponding to the larger exponent 3. Since $n \geq 1$, we may write this in the form

$$c_n = -\frac{c_{n-1}}{n}, \quad n \geq 1.$$

From this we find successively

$$c_1 = -c_0, \quad c_2 = -\frac{c_1}{2} = \frac{c_0}{2!}, \quad c_3 = -\frac{c_2}{3} = -\frac{c_0}{3!}, \quad \cdots, \quad c_n = \frac{(-1)^n c_0}{n!}, \quad \cdots.$$

Letting $r = 3$ in (6.89) and using these values of c_n, we obtain the solution corresponding to the larger exponent $r_1 = 3$. This solution is $y = y_1(x)$, where

$$y_1(x) = c_0 x^3 \left[1 - x + \frac{x^2}{2!} - \frac{x^3}{3!} + \cdots + \frac{(-1)^n x^n}{n!} + \cdots \right].$$

We recognize the series in brackets in this solution as the Maclaurin Expansion for e^{-x}. Thus we may write

(6.92) $$y_1(x) = c_0 x^3 e^{-x}$$

and express the solution corresponding to r_1 in the closed form

$$y = c_0 x^3 e^{-x},$$

where c_0 is an arbitrary constant.

We now consider the smaller root $r_2 = 1$. As in Example 6.13, we have no assurance that the differential equation has a linearly independent solution of the assumed form (6.89) corresponding to this smaller root. However, as in that example, we shall tentatively assume that such a solution actually does exist and let $r = r_2 = 1$ in (6.91) in the hopes of finding "it." Further, we are now aware that this step by itself *might* even provide us with the *general* solution.

Thus we let $r = r_2 = 1$ in (6.91) to obtain the recurrence formula

(6.93) $$n(n - 2)c_n + nc_{n-1} = 0, \quad n \geq 1,$$

corresponding to the smaller exponent 1. For $n \neq 2$, this may be written

(6.94) $$c_n = -\frac{c_{n-1}}{n - 2}, \quad n \geq 1, n \neq 2.$$

For $n = 1$, formula (6.94) gives $c_1 = c_0$. For $n = 2$, formula (6.94) does not apply and we must use (6.93). For $n = 2$ formula (6.93) is $0 \cdot c_2 + 2c_1 = 0$, and hence we must have $c_1 = 0$. But then, since $c_1 = c_0$, we must have $c_0 = 0$. However, $c_0 \neq 0$ in the assumed solution (6.89). This contradiction shows that there is no solution of the form (6.89), with $c_0 \neq 0$, corresponding to the smaller root 1.

Further, we observe that the use of (6.94) for $n \geq 3$ will only lead us to the solution y_1 already obtained. For, from the condition $0 \cdot c_2 + 2c_1 = 0$ we see that c_2 is arbitrary; and using (6.94) for $n \geq 3$, we obtain successively

$$c_3 = -c_2, \quad c_4 = -\frac{c_3}{2} = \frac{c_2}{2!}, \quad c_5 = -\frac{c_4}{3} = -\frac{c_2}{3!}, \quad \cdots, \quad c_{n+2} = \frac{(-1)^n c_2}{n!}, \quad n \geq 1, \cdots.$$

Thus letting $r = 1$ in (6.89) and using these values of c_n, we obtain formally

$$y = c_2 x \left[x^2 - x^3 + \frac{x^4}{2!} - \frac{x^5}{3!} + \cdots + \frac{(-1)^n x^{n+2}}{n!} + \cdots \right],$$

$$= c_2 x^3 \left[1 - x + \frac{x^2}{2!} - \frac{x^3}{3!} + \cdots + \frac{(-1)^n x^n}{n!} + \cdots \right],$$

$$= c_2 x^3 e^{-x}.$$

Comparing this with (6.92), we see that it is essentially the solution $y = y_1(x)$.

We now seek a solution of (6.88) which is linearly independent of the solution y_1.

From Theorem 6.3 we now know that this solution is of the form

$$(6.95) \qquad \sum_{n=0}^{\infty} c_n^* x^{n+1} + Cy_1(x) \ln |x|,$$

where $c_0^* \neq 0$ and $C \neq 0$. Various methods for obtaining such a solution are available; we shall employ the method of Reduction of Order (Section 4.1). We let $y = fu$, where f is a known solution of (6.88). Choosing for f the known solution y_1 defined by (6.92), with $c_0 = 1$, we thus let

$$(6.96) \qquad y = x^3 e^{-x} u.$$

From this we obtain

$$(6.97) \qquad \frac{dy}{dx} = x^3 e^{-x} \frac{du}{dx} + (3x^2 e^{-x} - x^3 e^{-x})u$$

and

$$(6.98) \qquad \frac{d^2 y}{dx^2} = x^3 e^{-x} \frac{d^2 u}{dx^2} + 2(3x^2 e^{-x} - x^3 e^{-x})\frac{du}{dx} + (x^3 e^{-x} - 6x^2 e^{-x} + 6xe^{-x})u.$$

Substituting (6.96), (6.97), and (6.98) for y and its first two derivatives, respectively, in the differential equation (6.88), after some simplifications we obtain

$$(6.99) \qquad x\frac{d^2 u}{dx^2} + (3 - x)\frac{du}{dx} = 0.$$

Letting $v = du/dx$, this reduces at once to the first-order differential equation

$$x\frac{dv}{dx} + (3 - x)v = 0,$$

a particular solution of which is $v = x^{-3}e^x$. Thus a particular solution of (6.99) is given by

$$u = \int x^{-3}e^x dx,$$

and hence $y = y_2(x)$, where

$$(6.100) \qquad y_2(x) = x^3 e^{-x} \int x^{-3} e^x dx$$

is a particular solution of (6.88) which is linearly independent of the solution y_1 defined by (6.92).

We now show that the solution y_2 defined by (6.100) is of the form (6.95). Introducing the MacLaurin Series for e^x in (6.100) we have

$$y_2(x) = x^3 e^{-x} \int x^{-3}\left[1 + x + \frac{x^2}{2} + \frac{x^3}{6} + \frac{x^4}{24} + \cdots\right]dx$$

$$= x^3 e^{-x} \int \left[x^{-3} + x^{-2} + \frac{1}{2}x^{-1} + \frac{1}{6} + \frac{x}{24} + \cdots\right]dx.$$

Integrating term-by-term, we obtain

$$y_2(x) = x^3 e^{-x}\left[-\frac{1}{2x^2} - \frac{1}{x} + \frac{1}{2}\ln|x| + \frac{1}{6}x + \frac{1}{48}x^2 + \cdots\right].$$

Now introducing the MacLaurin Series for e^{-x}, we may write

$$y_2(x) = \left[x^3 - x^4 + \frac{x^5}{2} - \frac{x^6}{6} + \cdots \right]\left[-\frac{1}{2x^2} - \frac{1}{x} + \frac{1}{6}x + \frac{1}{48}x^2 + \cdots \right] + \frac{1}{2}x^3 e^{-x} \ln|x|.$$

Finally, multiplying the two series involved, we have

$$y_2(x) = \left[-\frac{1}{2}x - \frac{1}{2}x^2 + \frac{3}{4}x^3 - \frac{1}{4}x^4 + \cdots \right] + \frac{1}{2}x^3 e^{-x} \ln|x|,$$

which is of the form (6.95), where $y_1(x) = x^3 e^{-x}$. The general solution of the differential equation (6.88) may thus be written

$$y = C_1 y_1(x) + C_2 y_2(x),$$

where C_1 and C_2 are arbitrary constants.

In this example it was fortunate that we were able to express the first solution y_1 in closed form, for this simplified the computations involved in finding the second solution y_2. Of course the method of reduction of order may be applied to find the second solution, even if we can not express the first solution in closed form. In such cases the various steps of the method must be carried out in terms of the series expression for y_1. The computations which result are generally quite complicated.

Examples 6.12, 6.13, and 6.14 illustrate all of the possibilities listed in the conclusions of Theorem 6.3 except the case in which $r_1 - r_2 = 0$ (that is, the case in which the roots of the indicial equation are equal). In this case it is obvious that both roots lead to the *same* solution

$$y_1 = (x - x_0)^r \sum_{n=0}^{\infty} c_n(x - x_0)^n,$$

where r is the common value of r_1 and r_2. Thus, as Conclusion (ii) of Theorem 6.3 states, a linearly independent solution is of the form

$$y_2 = (x - x_0)^r \sum_{n=0}^{\infty} c_n^*(x - x_0)^n + C y_1(x) \ln|x - x_0|,$$

where $C \neq 0$. Once $y_1(x)$ has been found, we may obtain y_2 by the method of Reduction of Order. This procedure has already been illustrated in finding the second solution of the equation in Example 6.14. A further illustration is provided in Section 6.3 by the solution of Bessel's Equation of Order Zero.

Exercises

Locate and classify the singular points of each of the differential equations in Exercises 1 through 4.

1. $(x^2 - 3x)\dfrac{d^2y}{dx^2} + (x + 2)\dfrac{dy}{dx} + y = 0.$

2. $(x^3 + x^2)\dfrac{d^2y}{dx^2} + (x^2 - 2x)\dfrac{dy}{dx} + 4y = 0.$

3. $(x^4 - 2x^3 + x^2)\dfrac{d^2y}{dx^2} + 2(x - 1)\dfrac{dy}{dx} + x^2y = 0.$

4. $(x^5 + x^4 - 6x^3)\dfrac{d^2y}{dx^2} + x^2\dfrac{dy}{dx} + (x - 2)y = 0.$

Use the method of Frobenius to find solutions near $x = 0$ of each of the differential equations in Exercises 5 through 26.

5. $2x^2\dfrac{d^2y}{dx^2} + x\dfrac{dy}{dx} + (x^2 - 1)y = 0.$

6. $2x^2\dfrac{d^2y}{dx^2} + x\dfrac{dy}{dx} + (2x^2 - 3)y = 0.$

7. $x^2\dfrac{d^2y}{dx^2} - x\dfrac{dy}{dx} + \left(x^2 + \dfrac{8}{9}\right)y = 0.$

8. $x^2\dfrac{d^2y}{dx^2} - x\dfrac{dy}{dx} + \left(2x^2 + \dfrac{5}{9}\right)y = 0.$

9. $x^2\dfrac{d^2y}{dx^2} + x\dfrac{dy}{dx} + \left(x^2 - \dfrac{1}{9}\right)y = 0.$

10. $2x\dfrac{d^2y}{dx^2} + \dfrac{dy}{dx} + 2y = 0.$

11. $3x\dfrac{d^2y}{dx^2} - (x - 2)\dfrac{dy}{dx} - 2y = 0.$

12. $x\dfrac{d^2y}{dx^2} + 2\dfrac{dy}{dx} + xy = 0.$

13. $x^2\dfrac{d^2y}{dx^2} + x\dfrac{dy}{dx} + \left(x^2 - \dfrac{1}{4}\right)y = 0.$

14. $x^2\dfrac{d^2y}{dx^2} + (x^4 + x)\dfrac{dy}{dx} - y = 0.$

15. $x\dfrac{d^2y}{dx^2} - (x^2 + 2)\dfrac{dy}{dx} + xy = 0.$

16. $x^2\dfrac{d^2y}{dx^2} + x^2\dfrac{dy}{dx} - 2y = 0.$

17. $(2x^2 - x)\dfrac{d^2y}{dx^2} + (2x - 2)\dfrac{dy}{dx} + (-2x^2 + 3x - 2)y = 0.$

18. $x^2\dfrac{d^2y}{dx^2} - x\dfrac{dy}{dx} + \dfrac{3}{4}y = 0.$

19. $x^2\dfrac{d^2y}{dx^2} - x\dfrac{dy}{dx} + (x - 1)y = 0.$

20. $x^2\dfrac{d^2y}{dx^2} + (x^3 - x)\dfrac{dy}{dx} - 3y = 0.$

21. $x^2\dfrac{d^2y}{dx^2} - x\dfrac{dy}{dx} + 8(x^2 - 1)y = 0.$

22. $x^2\dfrac{d^2y}{dx^2} + x^2\dfrac{dy}{dx} - \dfrac{3}{4}y = 0.$

23. $x\dfrac{d^2y}{dx^2} + \dfrac{dy}{dx} + 2y = 0.$

24. $2x\dfrac{d^2y}{dx^2} + 6\dfrac{dy}{dx} + y = 0.$

25. $x^2\dfrac{d^2y}{dx^2} - x\dfrac{dy}{dx} + (x^2 + 1)y = 0.$

26. $x^2\dfrac{d^2y}{dx^2} - x\dfrac{dy}{dx} + (x^2 - 3)y = 0.$

6.3   Bessel's Equation and Bessel Functions

A. Bessel's Equation of Order Zero.

   The differential equation

(6.101)
$$x^2\frac{d^2y}{dx^2} + x\frac{dy}{dx} + (x^2 - p^2)y = 0,$$

where p is a parameter, is called *Bessel's Equation of Order p.* Any solution of Bessel's Equation of Order p is called a *Bessel Function of Order p.* Bessel's Equation and Bessel Functions occur in connection with many problems of physics and engineering, and there is an extensive literature dealing with the theory and application of this equation and its solutions.

   If $p = 0$, Equation (6.101) is equivalent to the equation

(6.102)
$$x\frac{d^2y}{dx^2} + \frac{dy}{dx} + xy = 0,$$

which is called *Bessel's Equation of Order Zero.* We shall seek solutions of this equation which are valid in a deleted interval about $x = 0$. We observe at once that $x = 0$ is a regular singular point of (6.102), and hence we assume a solution

(6.103)
$$y = \sum_{n=0}^{\infty} c_n x^{n+r},$$

where $c_0 \neq 0$. Upon differentiating (6.103) twice and substituting into (6.102), we obtain

$$\sum_{n=0}^{\infty} (n + r)(n + r - 1)c_n x^{n+r-1} + \sum_{n=0}^{\infty} (n + r)c_n x^{n+r-1} + \sum_{n=0}^{\infty} c_n x^{n+r+1} = 0.$$

Simplifying, we write this in the form

$$\sum_{n=0}^{\infty} (n + r)^2 c_n x^{n+r-1} + \sum_{n=2}^{\infty} c_{n-2} x^{n+r-1} = 0$$

or

(6.104)
$$r^2 c_0 x^{r-1} + (1 + r)^2 c_1 x^r + \sum_{n=2}^{\infty} [(n + r)^2 c_n + c_{n-2}]x^{n+r-1} = 0.$$

Equating to zero the coefficient of the lowest power of x in (6.104), we obtain the indicial equation $r^2 = 0$, which has equal roots $r_1 = r_2 = 0$. Equating to zero the coefficients of the higher powers of x in (6.104) we obtain

(6.105)
$$(1 + r)^2 c_1 = 0$$

and the recurrence formula

(6.106)
$$(n + r)^2 c_n + c_{n-2} = 0, \quad n \geq 2.$$

Letting $r = 0$ in (6.105), we find at once that $c_1 = 0$. Letting $r = 0$ in (6.106) we obtain the recurrence formula in the form

$$n^2 c_n + c_{n-2} = 0, \quad n \geq 2,$$

or

$$c_n = -\frac{c_{n-2}}{n^2}, \quad n \geq 2.$$

From this we obtain successively

$$c_2 = -\frac{c_0}{2^2}, \quad c_3 = -\frac{c_1}{3^2} = 0 \text{ (since } c_1 = 0), \quad c_4 = -\frac{c_2}{4^2} = \frac{c_0}{2^2 \cdot 4^2}, \ \cdots$$

We note that all odd coefficients are zero and that the general even coefficient may be written

$$c_{2n} = \frac{(-1)^n c_0}{2^2 \cdot 4^2 \cdot 6^2 \cdots (2n)^2} = \frac{(-1)^n c_0}{(n!)^2 2^{2n}}, \quad n \geq 1.$$

Letting $r = 0$ in (6.103) and using these values of c_{2n}, we obtain the solution $y = y_1(x)$, where

$$y_1(x) = c_0 \sum_{n=0}^{\infty} \frac{(-1)^n}{(n!)^2} \left(\frac{x}{2}\right)^{2n}.$$

If we set the arbitrary constant $c_0 = 1$, we obtain an important particular solution of Equation (6.102). This particular solution defines a function denoted by J_0 and called the *Bessel Function of the First Kind of Order Zero*. That is, the function J_0 is the particular solution of Equation (6.102) defined by

(6.107)
$$J_0(x) = \sum_{n=0}^{\infty} \frac{(-1)^n}{(n!)^2} \left(\frac{x}{2}\right)^{2n}.$$

Writing out the first few terms of this series solution, we see that

(6.108)
$$J_0(x) = 1 - \frac{1}{(1!)^2}\left(\frac{x}{2}\right)^2 + \frac{1}{(2!)^2}\left(\frac{x}{2}\right)^4 - \frac{1}{(3!)^2}\left(\frac{x}{2}\right)^6 + \cdots$$
$$= 1 - \frac{x^2}{4} + \frac{x^4}{64} - \frac{x^6}{2304} + \cdots.$$

Since the roots of the indicial equation are equal, we know from Theorem 6.3 that a solution of Equation (6.102) which is linearly independent of J_0 must be of the form

$$y = \sum_{n=0}^{\infty} c_n^* x^n + CJ_0(x) \ln |x|,$$

where $C \neq 0$. Also, we know that such a linearly independent solution can be found by the method of Reduction of Order (Section 4.1). Indeed from Theorem 4.7 we know that this linearly independent solution y_2 is given by

$$y_2(x) = J_0(x) \int \frac{e^{-\int \frac{dx}{x}}}{[J_0(x)]^2} dx$$

and hence by

$$y_2(x) = J_0(x) \int \frac{dx}{x[J_0(x)]^2}.$$

From (6.108) we find that

$$[J_0(x)]^2 = 1 - \frac{x^2}{2} + \frac{3x^4}{32} - \frac{5x^6}{576} + \cdots$$

and hence

$$\frac{1}{[J_0(x)]^2} = 1 + \frac{x^2}{2} + \frac{5x^4}{32} + \frac{23x^6}{576} + \cdots.$$

Thus

$$\begin{aligned}
y_2(x) &= J_0(x) \int \left[\frac{1}{x} + \frac{x}{2} + \frac{5x^3}{32} + \frac{23x^5}{576} + \cdots \right] dx, \\
&= J_0(x) \left[\ln |x| + \frac{x^2}{4} + \frac{5x^4}{128} + \frac{23x^6}{3456} + \cdots \right], \\
&= J_0(x) \ln |x| + \left[1 - \frac{x^2}{4} + \frac{x^4}{64} - \frac{x^6}{2304} + \cdots \right] \left[\frac{x^2}{4} + \frac{5x^4}{128} + \frac{23x^6}{3456} + \cdots \right], \\
&= J_0(x) \ln |x| + \frac{x^2}{4} - \frac{3x^4}{128} + \frac{11x^6}{13824} + \cdots.
\end{aligned}$$

We thus obtain the first few terms of the "second" solution y_2 by the method of Reduction of Order. However, our computations give no information concerning the general coefficient c_{2n}^* in the above series. Indeed, it seems unlikely that an expression for the general coefficient can be found. However, let us observe that

$$(-1)^2 \frac{1}{2^2(1!)^2}(1) = \frac{1}{2^2} = \frac{1}{4},$$

$$(-1)^3 \frac{1}{2^4(2!)^2}\left(1 + \frac{1}{2}\right) = -\frac{3}{2^4 \cdot 2^2 \cdot 2} = -\frac{3}{128},$$

$$(-1)^4 \frac{1}{2^6(3!)^2}\left(1 + \frac{1}{2} + \frac{1}{3}\right) = \frac{11}{2^6 \cdot 6^2 \cdot 6} = \frac{11}{13824}.$$

Having observed these relations, we may express the solution y_2 in the following more systematic form

$$y_2(x) = J_0(x) \ln |x| + \frac{x^2}{2^2} - \frac{x^3}{2^4(2!)^2}\left(1 + \frac{1}{2}\right) + \frac{x^4}{2^6(3!)^2}\left(1 + \frac{1}{2} + \frac{1}{3}\right) + \cdots$$

Further, we would certainly suspect that the general coefficient c_{2n}^* is given by

$$c_{2n}^* = \frac{(-1)^{n+1}}{2^{2n}(n!)^2}\left(1 + \frac{1}{2} + \frac{1}{3} + \cdots + \frac{1}{n}\right), \quad n \geq 1.$$

It may be shown (though not without some difficulty) that this is indeed the case. This being true, we may express y_2 in the form

(6.109) $$y_2(x) = J_0(x) \ln |x| + \sum_{n=1}^{\infty} \frac{(-1)^{n+1}x^{2n}}{2^{2n}(n!)^2}\left(1 + \frac{1}{2} + \frac{1}{3} + \cdots + \frac{1}{n}\right).$$

Since the solution y_2 defined by (6.109) is linearly independent of J_0 we could write the general solution of the differential equation (6.102) as a general linear combination of J_0 and y_2. However, this is not usually done; instead, it has been customary to choose a certain special linear combination of J_0 and y_2 and take this special combination as the "second" solution of equation (6.102). This special combination is defined by

$$\frac{2}{\pi}[y_2(x) + (\gamma - \ln 2)J_0(x)],$$

where γ is a number called *Euler's Constant* and is defined by

$$\gamma = \lim_{n \to \infty} \left(1 + \frac{1}{2} + \frac{1}{3} + \cdots + \frac{1}{n} - \ln n\right) \approx 0.5772.$$

It is called the *Bessel Function of the second kind of order zero* (Weber's form) and is commonly denoted by Y_0. Thus the second solution of (6.102) is commonly taken as the function Y_0, where

$$Y_0(x) = \frac{2}{\pi}\left[J_0(x) \ln|x| + \sum_{n=1}^{\infty} \frac{(-1)^{n+1}x^{2n}}{2^{2n}(n!)^2}\left(1 + \frac{1}{2} + \frac{1}{3} + \cdots + \frac{1}{n}\right) + (\gamma - \ln 2)J_0(x)\right]$$

or

(6.110) $$Y_0(x) = \frac{2}{\pi}\left[\left(\ln\frac{|x|}{2} + \gamma\right)J_0(x) + \sum_{n=1}^{\infty} \frac{(-1)^{n+1}x^{2n}}{2^{2n}(n!)^2}\left(1 + \frac{1}{2} + \frac{1}{3} + \cdots + \frac{1}{n}\right)\right].$$

Therefore if we choose Y_0 as the second solution of the differential equation (6.102), the general solution of (6.102) is given by

(6.111) $$y = c_1 J_0(x) + c_2 Y_0(x),$$

where c_1 and c_2 are arbitrary constants, and J_0 and Y_0 are defined by (6.107) and (6.110), respectively.

The functions J_0 and Y_0 have been studied extensively and tabulated. Many of the interesting properties of these functions are indicated by their graphs, which are shown in Figure 6.1.

B. Bessel's Equation of Order p.

We now consider Bessel's Equation of order p, which we have already introduced at the beginning of Section 6.3A. This is the equation

$$(6.101) \qquad x^2\frac{d^2y}{dx^2} + x\frac{dy}{dx} + (x^2 - p^2)y = 0,$$

where we now assume that p is real and positive. We see at once that $x = 0$ is a regular singular point of equation (6.101), and hence we may assume a solution

$$(6.112) \qquad y = \sum_{n=0}^{\infty} c_n x^{n+r},$$

where $c_0 \neq 0$. Differentiating (6.112), substituting into (6.101), and simplifying as in our previous examples, we obtain

$$(6.113) \quad (r^2 - p^2)c_0 x^r + [(r + 1)^2 - p^2]c_1 x^{r+1} + \sum_{n=2}^{\infty} \{[(n + r)^2 - p^2]c_n + c_{n-2}\}x^{n+r} = 0.$$

Equating to zero the coefficient of each power of x in (6.113), we obtain

$$(6.114) \qquad r^2 - p^2 = 0,$$

$$(6.115) \qquad [(r + 1)^2 - p^2]c_1 = 0,$$

and

$$(6.116) \qquad [(n + r)^2 - p^2]c_n + c_{n-2} = 0, \quad n \geq 2.$$

Equation (6.114) is the indicial equation of the differential equation (6.101). Its roots are $r_1 = p > 0$ and $r_2 = -p$. If $r_1 - r_2 = 2p > 0$ is unequal to a positive integer, then from Theorem 6.3 we know that the differential equation (6.101) has *two* linearly independent solutions of the form (6.112). However, if $r_1 - r_2 = 2p$ is equal to a positive integer, we are only certain of a solution of this form corresponding to the *larger* root

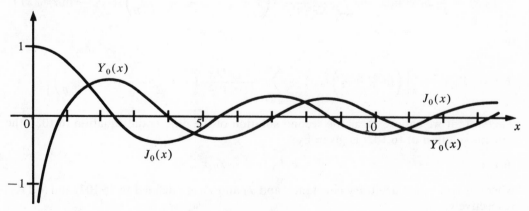

Figure 6.1

$r_1 = p$. We shall now proceed to obtain this one solution, the existence of which is always assured.

Letting $r = r_1 = p$ in (6.115), we obtain $(2p + 1) c_1 = 0$. Thus, since $p > 0$, we must have $c_1 = 0$. Letting $r = r_1 = p$ in (6.116), we obtain the recurrence formula

$$n(n + 2p)c_n + c_{n-2} = 0, \quad n \geq 2,$$

or

(6.117)
$$c_n = -\frac{c_{n-2}}{n(n + 2p)}, \quad n \geq 2,$$

corresponding to the larger root p. From this one finds that all odd coefficients are zero (since $c_1 = 0$) and that the general even coefficient is given by

$$c_{2n} = \frac{(-1)^n c_0}{[2 \cdot 4 \cdots (2n)][(2 + 2p)(4 + 2p) \cdots (2n + 2p)]}$$

$$= \frac{(-1)^n c_0}{2^{2n} n! [(1 + p)(2 + p) \cdots (n + p)]}, \quad n \geq 1.$$

Hence the solution of the differential equation (6.101) corresponding to the larger root p is given by $y = y_1(x)$, where

(6.118)
$$y_1(x) = c_0 \sum_{n=0}^{\infty} \frac{(-1)^n x^{2n+p}}{2^{2n} n! [(1 + p)(2 + p) \cdots (n + p)]}.$$

If p is a positive integer, we may write this in the form

(6.119)
$$y_1(x) = c_0 2^p p! \sum_{n=0}^{\infty} \frac{(-1)^n}{n!(n + p)!} \left(\frac{x}{2}\right)^{2n+p}.$$

If p is unequal to a positive integer, we need a generalization of the factorial function in order to express $y_1(x)$ in a form analogous to that given by (6.119). Such a generalization is provided by the so-called *Gamma Function*, which we now introduce.

For $N > 0$ the Gamma Function is defined by the convergent improper integral

(6.120)
$$\Gamma(N) = \int_0^{\infty} e^{-x} x^{N-1} dx.$$

If N is a positive integer, it can be shown that

(6.121)
$$N! = \Gamma(N + 1).$$

If N is positive but *not* an integer, we use (6.121) to *define* $N!$ The Gamma Function has been studied extensively. It can be shown that $\Gamma(N)$ satisfies the recurrence formula

(6.122)
$$\Gamma(N + 1) = N\Gamma(N), \quad (N > 0).$$

Values of $\Gamma(N)$ have been tabulated and are usually given for the range $1 \leq N \leq 2$. Using the tabulated values of $\Gamma(N)$ for $1 \leq N \leq 2$, one can evaluate $\Gamma(N)$ for all $N > 0$ by repeated application of formula (6.122). Suppose, for example, that we wish to evaluate $(3/2)!$. From the definition (6.121), we have $(3/2)! = \Gamma(5/2)$. Then from (6.122), we find that $\Gamma(5/2) = 3/2\ \Gamma(3/2)$. From tables one finds that $\Gamma(3/2) \approx 0.8862$, and thus $(3/2)! = \Gamma(5/2) \approx 1.3293$.

For $N < 0$ the integral (6.120) diverges, and thus $\Gamma(N)$ is not defined by (6.120) for negative values of N. We extend the definition of $\Gamma(N)$ to values of $N < 0$ by demanding that the recurrence formula (6.122) hold for *negative* (as well as positive) values of N. Repeated use of this formula thus defines $\Gamma(N)$ for every nonintegral negative value of N.

Thus $\Gamma(N)$ is defined for all $N \neq 0, -1, -2, -3, \ldots$. The graph of this function is shown in Figure 6.2. We now define $N!$ for all $N \neq -1, -2, -3, \ldots$ by the formula (6.121).

We now return to the solution y_1 defined by (6.118), for the case in which p is unequal to a positive integer. Applying the recurrence formula (6.122) successively with $N = n + p, n + p - 1, n + p - 2, \ldots, p + 1$, we obtain

$$\Gamma(n + p + 1) = (n + p)(n + p - 1)\cdots(p + 1)\Gamma(p + 1).$$

Thus for p unequal to a positive integer we may write the solution defined by (6.118) in the form

$$y_1(x) = c_0\Gamma(p + 1) \sum_{n=0}^{\infty} \frac{(-1)^n x^{2n+p}}{2^{2n}n!\Gamma(n + p + 1)}$$

(6.123)

$$= c_0 2^p \Gamma(p + 1) \sum_{n=0}^{\infty} \frac{(-1)^n}{n!\Gamma(n + p + 1)}\left(\frac{x}{2}\right)^{2n+p}.$$

Now using (6.121) with $N = p$ and $N = n + p$, we see that (6.123) takes the form (6.119). Thus the solution of the differential equation (6.101) corresponding to the larger root $p > 0$ is given by (6.119), where $p!$ and $(n + p)!$ are defined by $\Gamma(p + 1)$ and $\Gamma(n + p + 1)$, respectively, if p is not a positive integer.

If we set the arbitrary constant c_0 in (6.119) equal to the reciprocal of $2^p p!$, we obtain an important particular solution of (6.101). This particular solution defines a function denoted by J_p and called the *Bessel Function of the First Kind of Order p*. That is, the function J_p is the particular solution of equation (6.101) defined by

(6.124)
$$J_p(x) = \sum_{n=0}^{\infty} \frac{(-1)^n}{n!(n + p)!}\left(\frac{x}{2}\right)^{2n+p},$$

where $(n + p)!$ is defined by $\Gamma(n + p + 1)$ if p is not a positive integer.

Throughout this discussion we have assumed that $p > 0$ in (6.101) and hence that $p > 0$ in (6.124). If $p = 0$ in (6.101), then (6.101) reduces to the Bessel Equation of Order Zero given by (6.102) and the solution (6.124) reduces to the Bessel Function of the First Kind of Order Zero given by (6.107).

If $p = 1$ in (6.101), then equation (6.101) becomes

(6.125)
$$x^2\frac{d^2y}{dx^2} + x\frac{dy}{dx} + (x^2 - 1)y = 0,$$

which is Bessel's Equation of Order One. Letting $p = 1$ in (6.124) we obtain a solution of Equation (6.125) which is called the *Bessel Function of the First Kind of Order One* and

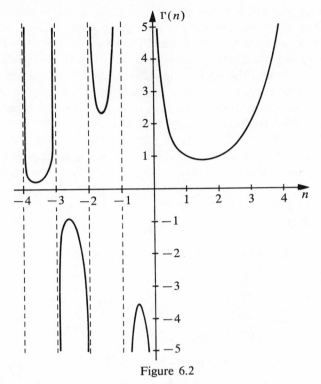

Figure 6.2

Graph of $\Gamma(N)$

is denoted by J_1. That is, the function J_1 is defined by

(6.126)
$$J_1(x) = \sum_{n=0}^{\infty} \frac{(-1)^n}{n!(n+1)!}\left(\frac{x}{2}\right)^{2n+1}$$

The graphs of the functions J_0, defined by (6.107), and J_1, defined by (6.126), are shown in Figure 6.3.

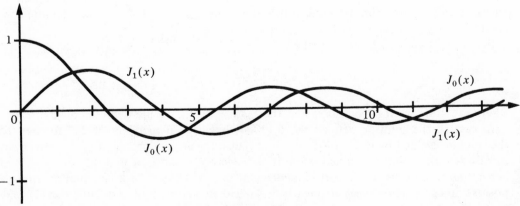

Figure 6.3

Several interesting properties of the Bessel Functions of the First Kind are suggested by these graphs. For one thing, they suggest that J_0 and J_1 each have a damped oscillatory behavior and that the positive zeros of J_0 and J_1 separate each other. This is indeed the case. In fact, it may be shown that for every $p \geq 0$ the function J_p has a damped oscillatory behavior as $x \to \infty$ and the positive zeros of J_p and J_{p+1} separate each other.

We now know that for every $p \geq 0$ one solution of Bessel's Equation of Order p (6.101) is given by (6.124). We now consider briefly the problem of finding a linearly independent solution of (6.101). We have already found such a solution for the case in which $p = 0$; it is given by (6.110). For $p > 0$, we have observed that if $2p$ is unequal to a positive integer, then the differential equation (6.101) has a linearly independent solution of the form (6.112) corresponding to the smaller root $r_2 = -p$. We now proceed to work with this smaller root.

Letting $r = r_2 = -p$ in (6.115), we obtain

$$(6.127) \qquad\qquad (-2p + 1)c_1 = 0.$$

Letting $r = r_2 = -p$ in (6.116) we obtain the recurrence formula

$$(6.128) \qquad\qquad n(n - 2p)c_n + c_{n-2} = 0, \quad n \geq 2,$$

or

$$(6.129) \qquad\qquad c_n = -\frac{c_{n-2}}{n(n - 2p)}, \quad n \geq 2, \quad n \neq 2p.$$

Using (6.127) and (6.128) or (6.129) one finds solutions $y = y_2(x)$, corresponding to the smaller root $-p$. Three distinct cases occur, leading to solutions of the following forms:

(i) If $2p \neq$ a positive integer,

$$(6.130) \qquad\qquad y_2(x) = c_0 x^{-p}\left[1 + \sum_{n=1}^{\infty} \alpha_{2n} x^{2n}\right],$$

where c_0 is an arbitrary constant and the α_{2n} $(n = 1, 2, \ldots)$ are definite constants.

(ii) If $2p =$ an *odd* positive integer,

$$(6.131) \qquad y_2(x) = c_0 x^{-p}\left[1 + \sum_{n=1}^{\infty} \beta_{2n} x^{2n}\right] + c_{2p} x^p\left[1 + \sum_{n=1}^{\infty} \gamma_{2n} x^{2n}\right],$$

where c_0 and c_{2p} are arbitrary constants and β_{2n} and γ_{2n} $(n = 1, 2, \ldots)$ are definite constants.

(iii) If $2p =$ an *even* positive integer,

$$(6.132) \qquad\qquad y_2(x) = c_{2p} x^p\left[1 + \sum_{n=1}^{\infty} \delta_{2n} x^{2n}\right],$$

where c_{2p} is an arbitrary constant and the $\delta_{2n}(n = 1, 2, \ldots)$ are definite constants.

In case (i) the solution defined by (6.130) is linearly independent of J_p. In case (ii) the solution defined by (6.131) with $c_{2p} = 0$ is also linearly independent of J_p. However, in case (iii) the solution defined by (6.132) is merely a constant multiple of $J_p(x)$, and hence this solution is *not* linearly independent of J_p. Thus if $2p$ is unequal to an *even* positive integer, there exists a linearly independent solution of the form (6.112) corresponding to the smaller root $-p$. In other words, if p is unequal to a positive integer, the differential equation (6.101) has a solution of the form $y = y_2(x)$, where

(6.133)
$$y_2(x) = \sum_{n=0}^{\infty} c_{2n}x^{2n-p},$$

and this solution y_2 is linearly independent of J_p.

It is easy to determine the coefficients c_{2n} in (6.133). We observe that the recurrence formula (6.129) corresponding to the smaller root $-p$ is obtained from the recurrence formula (6.117) corresponding to the larger root p simply by replacing p in (6.117) by $-p$. Hence a solution of the form (6.133) may be obtained from (6.124) simply by replacing p in (6.124) by $-p$. This leads at once to the solution denoted by J_{-p} and defined by

(6.134)
$$J_{-p}(x) = \sum_{n=0}^{\infty} \frac{(-1)^n}{n!(n-p)!}\left(\frac{x}{2}\right)^{2n-p},$$

where $(n - p)!$ is defined by $\Gamma(n - p + 1)$.

Thus if $p > 0$ is unequal to a positive integer, two linearly independent solutions of the differential equation (6.101) are J_p defined by (6.124), and J_{-p}, defined by (6.134). Hence, if $p > 0$ is unequal to a positive integer, the general solution of Bessel's Equation of order p is given by

$$y = C_1 J_p(x) + C_2 J_{-p}(x),$$

where J_p and J_{-p} are defined by (6.124) and (6.134), respectively, and C_1 and C_2 are arbitrary constants.

If p is a positive integer, the corresponding solution defined by (6.132) is *not* linearly independent of J_p, as we have already noted. Hence in this case a solution which is linearly independent of J_p must be given by $y = y_p(x)$, where

$$y_p(x) = x^{-p}\sum_{n=0}^{\infty} c_n^*x^n + CJ_p(x)\ln|x|,$$

where $C \neq 0$. Such a linearly independent solution y_p may be found by the method of Reduction of Order. Then the general solution of the differential equation (6.101) may be written as a general linear combination of J_p and y_p. However, as in the case of Bessel's Equation of Order Zero, it is customary to choose a certain special linear combination of J_p and y_p and take this special combination as the "second" solution of equation (6.101). This special combination is denoted by Y_p and defined by

(6.135)
$$Y_p(x) = \frac{2}{\pi}\left\{\left(\ln\frac{|x|}{2} + \gamma\right)J_p(x) - \frac{1}{2}\sum_{n=0}^{p-1} \frac{(p-n-1)!}{n!}\left(\frac{x}{2}\right)^{2n-p}\right.$$

$$\left. + \frac{1}{2}\sum_{n=0}^{\infty}(-1)^{n+1}\left[\sum_{k=1}^{n}\frac{1}{k} + \sum_{k=1}^{n+p}\frac{1}{k}\right]\left[\frac{1}{n!(n+p)!}\left(\frac{x}{2}\right)^{2n+p}\right]\right\},$$

where γ is Euler's constant. The solution Y_p is called the *Bessel Function of the second kind of order p* (Weber's form).

Thus if p is a positive integer, two linearly independent solutions of the differential equation (6.101) are J_p, defined by (6.124), and Y_p, defined by (6.135). Hence if p is a positive integer, the general solution of Bessel's Equation of Order p is given by

$$y = C_1 J_p(x) + C_2 Y_p(x),$$

where J_p and Y_p are defined by (6.124) and (6.135), respectively, and C_1 and C_2 are arbitrary constants.

Exercises

1. Show that $J_0(kx)$, where k is a constant, satisfies the differential equation

$$x\frac{d^2y}{dx^2} + \frac{dy}{dx} + k^2xy = 0.$$

2. Show that the transformation

$$y = \frac{u(x)}{\sqrt{x}}$$

reduces the Bessel Equation of order p, equation (6.101), to the form

$$\frac{d^2u}{dx^2} + \left[1 + \left(\frac{1}{4} - p^2\right)\frac{1}{x^2}\right]u = 0.$$

3. Use the result of Exercise 2 to obtain a solution of the Bessel Equation of order $\frac{1}{2}$.

4. Using the series definition (6.124) for J_p, show that

$$\frac{d}{dx}[x^p J_p(kx)] = kx^p J_{p-1}(kx)$$

and

$$\frac{d}{dx}[x^{-p} J_p(kx)] = -kx^{-p} J_{p+1}(kx),$$

where k is a constant.

5. Use the results of Exercise 4 to show that

$$\frac{d}{dx}[J_p(kx)] = kJ_{p-1}(kx) - \frac{p}{x}J_p(kx),$$

$$\frac{d}{dx}[J_p(kx)] = -kJ_{p+1}(kx) + \frac{p}{x}J_p(kx).$$

Hence show that

$$\frac{d}{dx}[J_p(kx)] = \frac{k}{2}[J_{p-1}(kx) - J_{p+1}(kx)],$$

$$J_p(kx) = \frac{kx}{2p}[J_{p-1}(kx) + J_{p+1}(kx)].$$

6. Using the results of Exercise 5,

    (a) express $J_1(x)$ and $\dfrac{d}{dx}[J_1(x)]$ in terms of $J_0(x)$ and $J_2(x)$;

    (b) express $J_{n+1/2}(x)$ in terms of $J_{n-1/2}(x)$ and $J_{n-3/2}(x)$.

SUGGESTED READING

I. Basic Theory and Methods:

    Agnew (1)   Hildebrand (22)
    Burkhill (8)   Kaplan (30)
    Coddington (12)   Martin and Reissner (38)
    Ford (17)   Rainville (45)

II. Further Material Concerning Bessel Functions:

    Churchill (10)   Wylie (57)
    Hochstadt (24)

III. Advanced Theory:

    Birkhoff and Rota (6)   Ince (26)
    Coddington and Levinson (13)

7

SYSTEMS OF
LINEAR DIFFERENTIAL EQUATIONS

In the previous chapters we have been concerned with one differential equation in one unknown function. Now we shall consider systems of two differential equations in two unknown functions. We shall restrict our attention to linear systems and begin by giving a brief survey of the basic theory of these systems. In this survey we shall introduce the relevant fundamental concepts and state without proof certain basic theorems. Then we shall consider various methods of solution. Finally, certain applications of linear systems will be considered.

7.1 Basic Theory of Linear Systems

A. Linear Systems and Their Solutions

We shall begin by considering a basic type of system of two linear differential equations in two unknown functions. This system is of the form

$$(7.1) \quad \begin{cases} \dfrac{dx}{dt} = a_{11}(t)x + a_{12}(t)y + b_1(t) \\ \dfrac{dy}{dt} = a_{21}(t)x + a_{22}(t)y + b_2(t). \end{cases}$$

We shall assume that the functions a_{11}, a_{12}, b_1, a_{21}, a_{22}, and b_2 are all continuous on a real interval $a \leq t \leq b$. If $b_1(t)$ and $b_2(t)$ are zero for all t, then the system (7.1) is called *homogeneous;* otherwise, the system is said to be *nonhomogeneous*.

Example 7.1.   The system

(7.2)
$$\begin{cases} \dfrac{dx}{dt} = 2x - y \\[2mm] \dfrac{dy}{dt} = 3x + 6y \end{cases}$$

is homogeneous; the system

(7.3)
$$\begin{cases} \dfrac{dx}{dt} = 2x - y - 5t \\[2mm] \dfrac{dy}{dt} = 3x + 6y - 4 \end{cases}$$

is nonhomogeneous.

DEFINITION.   By a *solution* of the system (7.1) we shall mean an ordered pair of real functions

(7.4) (f,g),

each having a continuous derivative on the real interval $a \leq t \leq b$, such that

$$\begin{cases} \dfrac{df(t)}{dt} = a_{11}(t)f(t) + a_{12}(t)g(t) + b_1(t) \\[2mm] \dfrac{dg(t)}{dt} = a_{21}(t)f(t) + a_{22}(t)g(t) + b_2(t) \end{cases}$$

for all t such that $a \leq t \leq b$.   In other words,

(7.5)
$$\begin{cases} x = f(t) \\ y = g(t) \end{cases}$$

simultaneously satisfy both equations of the system (7.1) identically for $a \leq t \leq b$.

Notation.   We shall use the notation

(7.5)
$$\begin{cases} x = f(t) \\ y = g(t) \end{cases}$$

to denote a solution of the system (7.1) and shall speak of "the solution

$$\begin{cases} x = f(t) \\ y = g(t). \end{cases}"$$

Whenever we do this, we must remember that the solution thus referred to is really the ordered pair of functions (f,g) such that (7.5) simultaneously satisfy both equations of the system (7.1) identically on $a \leq t \leq b$.

Example 7.2. The ordered pair of functions defined for all t by $(e^{5t}, -3e^{5t})$, which we denote by

(7.6)
$$\begin{cases} x = e^{5t} \\ y = -3e^{5t}, \end{cases}$$

is a solution of the system (7.2). That is,

(7.6)
$$\begin{cases} x = e^{5t} \\ y = -3e^{5t} \end{cases}$$

simultaneously satisfy both equations of the system (7.2). Let us verify this by directly substituting (7.6) into (7.2). We have

$$\begin{cases} \dfrac{d}{dt}(e^{5t}) = 2(e^{5t}) - (-3e^{5t}) \\ \dfrac{d}{dt}(-3e^{5t}) = 3(e^{5t}) + 6(-3e^{5t}) \end{cases}$$

or

$$\begin{cases} 5e^{5t} = 2e^{5t} + 3e^{5t} \\ -15e^{5t} = 3e^{5t} - 18e^{5t}. \end{cases}$$

Hence (7.6) is indeed a solution of the system (7.2). The reader should verify that the ordered pair of functions defined for all t by $(e^{3t}, -e^{3t})$, which we denote by

$$\begin{cases} x = e^{3t} \\ y = -e^{3t}, \end{cases}$$

is also a solution of the system (7.2).

We shall now proceed to survey the basic theory of linear systems. We shall observe a close analogy between this theory and that introduced in Section 4.1 for the single linear equation of higher order. Theorem 7.1 is the basic existence theorem dealing with the system (7.1).

THEOREM 7.1.

Hypothesis. Let the functions a_{11}, a_{12}, b_1, a_{21}, a_{22}, and b_2 in the system (7.1) all be continuous on the interval $a \le t \le b$. Let t_0 be any point of the interval $a \le t \le b$; and let c_1 and c_2 be two arbitrary constants.

Conclusion. There exists a unique solution

$$\begin{cases} x = f(t) \\ y = g(t) \end{cases}$$

of the system (7.1) such that

$$f(t_0) = c_1 \quad \text{and} \quad g(t_0) = c_2,$$

and this solution is defined on the entire interval $a \le t \le b$.

Example 7.3. Let us consider the system (7.3). The continuity requirements of the hypothesis of Theorem 7.1 are satisfied on every closed interval $a \leq t \leq b$. Hence, given any point t_0 and any two constants c_1 and c_2, there exists a unique solution $x = f(t)$, $y = g(t)$ of the system (7.3) which satisfies the conditions $f(t_0) = c_1$, $g(t_0) = c_2$. For example, there exists one and only one solution $x = f(t)$, $y = g(t)$ such that $f(2) = 5$, $g(2) = -7$.

B. Homogeneous Linear Systems

We shall now assume that $b_1(t)$ and $b_2(t)$ in the system (7.1) are both zero for all t and consider the basic theory of the resulting *homogeneous* linear system

(7.7)
$$\begin{cases} \dfrac{dx}{dt} = a_{11}(t)x + a_{12}(t)y \\ \dfrac{dy}{dt} = a_{21}(t)x + a_{22}(t)y. \end{cases}$$

Our first result concerning this system is the following.

THEOREM 7.2.

Hypothesis. Let

(7.8)
$$\begin{cases} x = f_1(t) \\ y = g_1(t) \end{cases} \quad \text{and} \quad \begin{cases} x = f_2(t) \\ y = g_2(t) \end{cases}$$

be two solutions of the homogeneous linear system (7.7). Let c_1 and c_2 be two arbitrary constants.

Conclusion. Then

(7.9)
$$\begin{cases} x = c_1 f_1(t) + c_2 f_2(t) \\ y = c_1 g_1(t) + c_2 g_2(t) \end{cases}$$

is also a solution of the system (7.7).

DEFINITION. The solution (7.9) is called a *linear combination* of the solutions (7.8). This definition enables us to express Theorem 7.2 in the following alternate form.

THEOREM 7.2 restated. Any linear combination of two solutions of the homogeneous linear system (7.7) is itself a solution of the system (7.7).

Example 7.4. We have already observed that

$$\begin{cases} x = e^{5t} \\ y = -3e^{5t} \end{cases} \quad \text{and} \quad \begin{cases} x = e^{3t} \\ y = -e^{3t} \end{cases}$$

are solutions of the homogeneous linear system (7.2). Theorem 7.2 tells us that

$$\begin{cases} x = c_1 e^{5t} + c_2 e^{3t} \\ y = -3c_1 e^{5t} - c_2 e^{3t}, \end{cases}$$

where c_1 and c_2 are arbitrary constants, is also a solution of the system (7.2). For example, if $c_1 = 4$ and $c_2 = -2$, we have the solution

$$\begin{cases} x = 4e^{5t} - 2e^{3t} \\ y = -12e^{5t} + 2e^{3t}. \end{cases}$$

DEFINITION.   Let

$$\begin{cases} x = f_1(t) \\ y = g_1(t) \end{cases} \quad \text{and} \quad \begin{cases} x = f_2(t) \\ y = g_2(t) \end{cases}$$

be two solutions of the homogeneous linear system (7.7). These two solutions are *linearly dependent* on the interval $a \le t \le b$ if there exist constants c_1 and c_2, *not both zero*, such that

(7.10) $$\begin{cases} c_1 f_1(t) + c_2 f_2(t) = 0 \\ c_1 g_1(t) + c_2 g_2(t) = 0 \end{cases}$$

for all t such that $a \le t \le b$.

DEFINITION.   Let

$$\begin{cases} x = f_1(t) \\ y = g_1(t) \end{cases} \quad \text{and} \quad \begin{cases} x = f_2(t) \\ y = g_2(t) \end{cases}$$

be two solutions of the homogeneous linear system (7.7). These two solutions are *linearly independent* on $a \le t \le b$ if they are not linearly dependent on $a \le t \le b$. That is, the solutions $x = f_1(t)$, $y = g_1(t)$ and $x = f_2(t)$, $y = g_2(t)$ are linearly independent on $a \le t \le b$ if

(7.11) $$\begin{cases} c_1 f_1(t) + c_2 f_2(t) = 0 \\ c_1 g_1(t) + c_2 g_2(t) = 0 \end{cases}$$

for all t such that $a \le t \le b$ implies that

$$c_1 = c_2 = 0.$$

Example 7.5.   The solutions

$$\begin{cases} x = e^{5t} \\ y = -3e^{5t} \end{cases} \quad \text{and} \quad \begin{cases} x = 2e^{5t} \\ y = -6e^{5t} \end{cases}$$

of the system (7.2) are linearly dependent on every interval $a \le t \le b$. For in this case the conditions (7.10) become

(7.12) $$\begin{cases} c_1 e^{5t} + 2c_2 e^{5t} = 0 \\ -3c_1 e^{5t} - 6c_2 e^{5t} = 0, \end{cases}$$

and clearly there exist constants c_1 and c_2, not both zero, such that the conditions (7.12) hold on $a \leq t \leq b$. For example, let $c_1 = 2$ and $c_2 = -1$.

On the other hand, the solutions

$$\begin{cases} x = e^{5t} \\ y = -3e^{5t} \end{cases} \quad \text{and} \quad \begin{cases} x = e^{3t} \\ y = -e^{3t} \end{cases}$$

of system (7.2) are linearly independent on $a \leq t \leq b$. For in this case the conditions (7.11) are

$$\begin{cases} c_1 e^{5t} + c_2 e^{3t} = 0 \\ -3c_1 e^{5t} - c_2 e^{3t} = 0. \end{cases}$$

If these conditions hold for all t such that $a \leq t \leq b$, then we must have $c_1 = c_2 = 0$.

We now state the following basic theorem concerning sets of linearly independent solutions of the homogeneous linear system (7.7).

THEOREM 7.3. There exist sets of two linearly independent solutions of the homogeneous linear system (7.7). Every solution of the system (7.7) can be written as a linear combination of a set of two linearly independent solutions of (7.7).

Example 7.6. We have seen that

$$\begin{cases} x = e^{5t} \\ y = -3e^{5t} \end{cases} \quad \text{and} \quad \begin{cases} x = e^{3t} \\ y = -e^{3t} \end{cases}$$

constitute a pair of linearly independent solutions of the system (7.2). This illustrates the first part of Theorem 7.3. The second part of the theorem tells us that every solution of the system (7.2) can be written in the form

$$\begin{cases} x = c_1 e^{5t} + c_2 e^{3t} \\ y = -3c_1 e^{5t} - c_2 e^{3t}, \end{cases}$$

where c_1 and c_2 are suitably chosen constants.

Recall that in Section 4.1 in connection with the single nth order homogeneous linear differential equation, we defined the general solution of such an equation to be a linear combination of n linearly independent solutions. As a result of Theorems 7.2 and 7.3 we now give an analogous definition of general solution for the homogeneous linear system (7.7).

DEFINITION. Let

$$\begin{cases} x = f_1(t) \\ y = g_1(t) \end{cases} \quad \text{and} \quad \begin{cases} x = f_2(t) \\ y = g_2(t) \end{cases}$$

be two linearly independent solutions of the homogeneous linear system (7.7). Let c_1

and c_2 be two arbitrary constants. Then the solution

$$\begin{cases} x = c_1 f_1(t) + c_2 f_2(t) \\ y = c_1 g_1(t) + c_2 g_2(t) \end{cases}$$

is called a *general solution* of the system (7.7).

Example 7.7.   Since

$$\begin{cases} x = e^{5t} \\ y = -3e^{5t} \end{cases} \quad \text{and} \quad \begin{cases} x = e^{3t} \\ y = -e^{3t} \end{cases}$$

are linearly independent solutions of the system (7.2), we may write the general solution of (7.2) in the form

$$\begin{cases} x = c_1 e^{5t} + c_2 e^{3t} \\ y = -3c_1 e^{5t} - c_2 e^{3t}, \end{cases}$$

where c_1 and c_2 are arbitrary constants.

As a criterion for the linear independence of two solutions of the system (7.7), we state the following theorem, which is analogous to the now familiar "Wronskian Theorem" of Section 4.1.

THEOREM 7.4.   Let

$$\begin{cases} x = f_1(t) \\ y = g_1(t) \end{cases} \quad \text{and} \quad \begin{cases} x = f_2(t) \\ y = g_2(t) \end{cases}$$

be two solutions of the homogeneous linear system (7.7). A necessary and sufficient condition that these two solutions be linearly independent on $a \leq t \leq b$ is that the determinant

(7.13)
$$\Delta(t) = \begin{vmatrix} f_1(t) & f_2(t) \\ g_1(t) & g_2(t) \end{vmatrix}$$

be different from zero for all t such that $a \leq t \leq b$.

Concerning this determinant, we also state the following result.

THEOREM 7.5.   The determinant $\Delta(t)$ of Theorem 7.4 either is identically zero or vanishes for no value of t on the interval $a \leq t \leq b$.

Example 7.8.   Let us employ Theorem 7.4 to verify the linear independence of the solutions

$$\begin{cases} x = e^{5t} \\ y = -3e^{5t} \end{cases} \quad \text{and} \quad \begin{cases} x = e^{3t} \\ y = -e^{3t} \end{cases}$$

of the system (7.2). We have

$$\Delta(t) = \begin{vmatrix} e^{5t} & e^{3t} \\ -3e^{5t} & -e^{3t} \end{vmatrix} = 2e^{8t} \neq 0$$

on every closed interval $a \leq t \leq b$. Thus by Theorem 7.4 the two solutions are indeed linearly independent on $a \leq t \leq b$.

C. Nonhomogeneous Linear Systems

Let us now return briefly to the nonhomogeneous system (7.1). A theorem and a definition, illustrated by a simple example, will suffice for our purposes here.

THEOREM 7.6.

Hypothesis. Let

$$\begin{cases} x = F(t) \\ y = G(t) \end{cases}$$

be any solution of the nonhomogeneous system (7.1), and let

$$\begin{cases} x = f(t) \\ y = g(t) \end{cases}$$

be any solution of the corresponding homogeneous system (7.7).

Conclusion. Then

$$\begin{cases} x = f(t) + F(t) \\ y = g(t) + G(t) \end{cases}$$

is also a solution of the nonhomogeneous system (7.1).

DEFINITION. Let

$$\begin{cases} x = F(t) \\ y = G(t) \end{cases}$$

be any solution of the nonhomogeneous system (7.1), and let

$$\begin{cases} x = f_1(t) \\ y = g_1(t) \end{cases} \quad \text{and} \quad \begin{cases} x = f_2(t) \\ y = g_2(t) \end{cases}$$

be two linearly independent solutions of the corresponding homogeneous system (7.7). Let c_1 and c_2 be two arbitrary constants. Then the solution

$$\begin{cases} x = c_1 f_1(t) + c_2 f_2(t) + F(t) \\ y = c_1 g_1(t) + c_2 g_2(t) + G(t) \end{cases}$$

will be called a *general solution* of the nonhomogeneous system (7.1).

Example 7.9. The student may verify that

$$\begin{cases} x = 2t + 1 \\ y = -t \end{cases}$$

is a solution of the nonhomogeneous system (7.3). The corresponding homogeneous system is the system (7.2), and we have already seen that

$$\begin{cases} x = e^{5t} \\ y = -3e^{5t} \end{cases} \quad \text{and} \quad \begin{cases} x = e^{3t} \\ y = -e^{3t} \end{cases}$$

are linearly independent solutions of this homogeneous system. Theorem 7.6 tells us, for example, that

$$\begin{cases} x = e^{5t} + 2t + 1 \\ y = -3e^{5t} - t \end{cases}$$

is a solution of the nonhomogeneous system (7.3). From the preceding definition we see that the general solution of (7.3) may be written in the form

$$\begin{cases} x = c_1 e^{5t} + c_2 e^{3t} + 2t + 1 \\ y = -3c_1 e^{5t} - c_2 e^{3t} - t, \end{cases}$$

where c_1 and c_2 are arbitrary constants.

Exercises

1. Consider the linear system

$$\begin{cases} \dfrac{dx}{dt} = 3x + 4y \\ \dfrac{dy}{dt} = 2x + y \end{cases}$$

(a) Show that

$$\begin{cases} x = 2e^{5t} \\ y = e^{5t} \end{cases} \quad \text{and} \quad \begin{cases} x = e^{-t} \\ y = -e^{-t} \end{cases}$$

are solutions of this system.

(b) Show that the two solutions of part (a) are linearly independent on every interval $a \le t \le b$, and write the general solution of the system.

(c) Find the solution

$$\begin{cases} x = f(t) \\ y = g(t) \end{cases}$$

of the system which is such that $f(0) = 1$ and $g(0) = 2$. Why is this solution unique? Over what interval is it defined?

2. Consider the linear system

$$\begin{cases} \dfrac{dx}{dt} = 5x + 3y \\[2mm] \dfrac{dy}{dt} = 4x + y. \end{cases}$$

(a) Show that

$$\begin{cases} x = 3e^{7t} \\ y = 2e^{7t} \end{cases} \quad \text{and} \quad \begin{cases} x = e^{-t} \\ y = -2e^{-t} \end{cases}$$

are solutions of this system.

   (b) Show that the two solutions of part (a) are linearly independent on every interval $a \le t \le b$, and write the general solution of the system.

   (c) Find the solution

$$\begin{cases} x = f(t) \\ y = g(t) \end{cases}$$

of the system which is such that $f(0) = 0$ and $g(0) = 8$.

3. (a) Show that

$$\begin{cases} x = 2e^{2t} \\ y = -3e^{2t} \end{cases} \quad \text{and} \quad \begin{cases} x = e^{7t} \\ y = e^{7t} \end{cases}$$

are solutions of the homogeneous linear system

$$\begin{cases} \dfrac{dx}{dt} = 5x + 2y \\[2mm] \dfrac{dy}{dt} = 3x + 4y. \end{cases}$$

   (b) Show that the two solutions defined in part (a) are linearly independent on every interval $a \le t \le b$, and write the general solution of the homogeneous system of part (a).

   (c) Show that

$$\begin{cases} x = t + 1 \\ y = -5t - 2 \end{cases}$$

is a particular solution of the nonhomogeneous linear system

$$\begin{cases} \dfrac{dx}{dt} = 5x + 2y + 5t \\[2mm] \dfrac{dy}{dt} = 3x + 4y + 17t, \end{cases}$$

and write the general solution of this system.

4. Let

$$\begin{cases} x = f_1(t) \\ y = g_1(t) \end{cases} \quad \text{and} \quad \begin{cases} x = f_2(t) \\ y = g_2(t) \end{cases}$$

be two linearly independent solutions of the homogeneous linear system (7.7), and let $\Delta(t)$ be the determinant defined by (7.13). Show that Δ satisfies the first-order differential equation

$$\frac{d\Delta}{dt} = [a_{11}(t) + a_{22}(t)]\Delta.$$

5. Prove Theorem 7.2.

6. Prove Theorem 7.6.

7. Consider the system

$$(A) \quad \begin{cases} \dfrac{dx}{dt} = a_{11}(t)x + a_{12}(t)y + a_{13}(t)z + b_1(t) \\[2mm] \dfrac{dy}{dt} = a_{21}(t)x + a_{22}(t)y + a_{23}(t)z + b_2(t) \\[2mm] \dfrac{dz}{dt} = a_{31}(t)x + a_{32}(t)y + a_{33}(t)z + b_3(t) \end{cases}$$

of three linear differential equations in three unknown functions, and extend the theory of this section to cover this type of system.

(a) In particular, guided by the definitions of solution, general solution, linear dependence, and linear independence in connection with systems (7.1) and (7.7) of the text, give appropriate analogous definitions in connection with the system (A) and the homogeneous system which corresponds to it.

(b) Further, state theorems dealing with the system (A) and the corresponding homogeneous system which are analogous to the various theorems of this section.

7.2 Homogeneous Linear Systems with Constant Coefficients

A. Introduction

In this section we shall be concerned with the homogeneous linear system

$$(7.14) \quad \begin{cases} \dfrac{dx}{dt} = a_1 x + b_1 y \\[2mm] \dfrac{dy}{dt} = a_2 x + b_2 y, \end{cases}$$

where the coefficients a_1, b_1, a_2, and b_2 are real constants. We seek solutions of this system; but how shall we proceed? Recall that in Section 4.2 we sought and found exponential solutions of the single nth order linear equation with constant coefficients. Remembering the analogy which exists between linear systems and single higher order linear equations, we might now attempt to find exponential solutions of the system (7.14). Let us therefore attempt to determine a solution of the form

$$(7.15) \quad \begin{cases} x = A e^{\lambda t} \\ y = B e^{\lambda t}, \end{cases}$$

where A, B, and λ are constants. If we substitute (7.15) into (7.14) we obtain

$$\begin{cases} A\lambda e^{\lambda t} = a_1 A e^{\lambda t} + b_1 B e^{\lambda t} \\ B\lambda e^{\lambda t} = a_2 A e^{\lambda t} + b_2 B e^{\lambda t}. \end{cases}$$

These equations lead at once to the system

(7.16)
$$\begin{cases} (a_1 - \lambda)A + b_1B = 0 \\ a_2A + (b_2 - \lambda)B = 0. \end{cases}$$

in the unknowns A and B. This system obviously has the trivial solution $A = B = 0$. But this would only lead to the trivial solution $x = 0$, $y = 0$ of the system (7.14). Thus we seek nontrivial solutions of the system (7.16). A necessary and sufficient condition (see Section 11.2, Theorem B) that this system have a nontrivial solution is that the determinant

(7.17)
$$\begin{vmatrix} a_1 - \lambda & b_1 \\ a_2 & b_2 - \lambda \end{vmatrix} = 0.$$

Expanding this determinant we are led at once to the quadratic equation

(7.18)
$$\lambda^2 - (a_1 + b_2)\lambda + (a_1b_2 - a_2b_1) = 0$$

in the unknown λ. This equation is called the *characteristic equation* associated with the system (7.14). Its roots λ_1 and λ_2 are called the *characteristic roots*. If the pair (7.15) is to be a solution of the system (7.14), then λ in (7.15) must be one of these roots. Suppose $\lambda = \lambda_1$. Then substituting $\lambda = \lambda_1$ into the algebraic system (7.16), we may obtain a nontrivial solution A_1, B_1, of this algebraic system. With these values A_1, B_1 we obtain the nontrivial solution

$$\begin{cases} x = A_1e^{\lambda_1 t} \\ y = B_1e^{\lambda_1 t} \end{cases}$$

of the given system (7.14).

Three cases must now be considered:
   (i) The roots λ_1 and λ_2 are real and distinct.
   (ii) The roots λ_1 and λ_2 are real and equal.
   (iii) The roots λ_1 and λ_2 are conjugate complex.

B. *Case (i). The Roots of the Characteristic Equation (7.18) are Real and Distinct*

If the roots λ_1 and λ_2 of the characteristic equation (7.18) are real and distinct, it appears that we should expect two distinct solutions of the form (7.15), one corresponding to each of the two distinct roots. This is indeed the case. Furthermore, these two distinct solutions are linearly independent. We summarize this case in the following theorem.

THEOREM 7.7.

Hypothesis. The roots λ_1 and λ_2, of the characteristic equation (7.18) associated with the system (7.14), are real and distinct.

Conclusion. The system (7.14) has two nontrivial linearly independent solutions of the form

$$\begin{cases} x = A_1e^{\lambda_1 t} \\ y = B_1e^{\lambda_1 t} \end{cases} \quad \text{and} \quad \begin{cases} x = A_2e^{\lambda_2 t} \\ y = B_2e^{\lambda_2 t}, \end{cases}$$

where A_1, B_1, A_2, and B_2 are definite constants. The general solution of the system (7.14) may thus be written

$$\begin{cases} x = c_1 A_1 e^{\lambda_1 t} + c_2 A_2 e^{\lambda_2 t} \\ y = c_1 B_1 e^{\lambda_1 t} + c_2 B_2 e^{\lambda_2 t}, \end{cases}$$

where c_1 and c_2 are arbitrary constants.

Example 7.10.

$$(7.19) \qquad \begin{cases} \dfrac{dx}{dt} = 6x - 3y \\[2mm] \dfrac{dy}{dt} = 2x + y \end{cases}$$

We assume a solution of the form (7.15):

$$(7.20) \qquad \begin{cases} x = A e^{\lambda t} \\ y = B e^{\lambda t}. \end{cases}$$

Substituting (7.20) into (7.19) we obtain

$$\begin{cases} A\lambda e^{\lambda t} = 6A e^{\lambda t} - 3B e^{\lambda t} \\ B\lambda e^{\lambda t} = 2A e^{\lambda t} + B e^{\lambda t}, \end{cases}$$

and this leads at once to the algebraic system

$$(7.21) \qquad \begin{cases} (6 - \lambda)A - 3B = 0 \\ 2A + (1 - \lambda)B = 0 \end{cases}$$

in the unknown λ. For nontrivial solutions of this system we must have

$$\begin{vmatrix} 6 - \lambda & -3 \\ 2 & 1 - \lambda \end{vmatrix} = 0.$$

Expanding this we obtain the characteristic equation

$$\lambda^2 - 7\lambda + 12 = 0.$$

Solving this, we find the roots $\lambda_1 = 3$, $\lambda_2 = 4$.
Setting $\lambda = \lambda_1 = 3$ in (7.21), we obtain

$$\begin{cases} 3A - 3B = 0 \\ 2A - 2B = 0. \end{cases}$$

A simple nontrivial solution of this system is obviously $A = B = 1$. With these values of A, B, and λ we find the nontrivial solution

$$(7.22) \qquad \begin{cases} x = e^{3t} \\ y = e^{3t} \end{cases}$$

Now setting $\lambda = \lambda_2 = 4$ in (7.21), we find

$$\begin{cases} 2A - 3B = 0 \\ 2A - 3B = 0. \end{cases}$$

A simple nontrivial solution of this system is $A = 3$, $B = 2$. Using these values of A, B, and λ we find the nontrivial solution

(7.23)
$$\begin{cases} x = 3e^{4t} \\ y = 2e^{4t}. \end{cases}$$

By Theorem 7.7 the solutions (7.22) and (7.23) are linearly independent (one may check this using Theorem 7.4) and the general solution of the system (7.19) may be written

$$\begin{cases} x = c_1e^{3t} + 3c_2e^{4t} \\ y = c_1e^{3t} + 2c_2e^{4t}, \end{cases}$$

where c_1 and c_2 are arbitrary constants.

C. Case (ii). *The Roots of the Characteristic Equation (7.18) are Real and Equal*

If the two roots of the characteristic equation (7.18) are real and equal, it would appear that we could find only one solution of the form (7.15). Except in trivial cases, this is indeed true. How shall we then proceed to find a second, linearly independent solution? Recall the analogous situation in which the auxiliary equation corresponding to a single nth-order linear equation has a double root. This would lead us to expect a second solution of the form

$$\begin{cases} x = Ate^{\lambda t} \\ y = Bte^{\lambda t}. \end{cases}$$

However, the situation here is not quite so simple. We must actually seek a second solution of the form

(7.24)
$$\begin{cases} x = (A_1t + A_2)e^{\lambda t} \\ y = (B_1t + B_2)e^{\lambda t}. \end{cases}$$

We shall illustrate this in Example 7.11. We first summarize case (ii) in the following theorem.

THEOREM 7.8.

Hypothesis. The roots λ_1 and λ_2 of the characteristic equation (7.18) associated with the system (7.14) are real and equal. Let λ denote their common value.

Conclusion. The system (7.14) has two linearly independent solutions of the form

$$\begin{cases} x = Ae^{\lambda t} \\ y = Be^{\lambda t} \end{cases} \quad \text{and} \quad \begin{cases} x = (A_1t + A_2)e^{\lambda t} \\ y = (B_1t + B_2)e^{\lambda t}, \end{cases}$$

where A, B, A_1, A_2, B_1, and B_2 are definite constants. The general solution of the system (7.14) may thus be written

$$x = c_1Ae^{\lambda t} + c_2(A_1t + A_2)e^{\lambda t}$$
$$y = c_1Be^{\lambda t} + c_2(B_1t + B_2)e^{\lambda t},$$

where c_1 and c_2 are arbitrary constants.

Example 7.11.

(7.25)
$$\begin{cases} \dfrac{dx}{dt} = 4x - y \\ \dfrac{dy}{dt} = x + 2y. \end{cases}$$

We assume a solution of the form (7.15):

(7.26)
$$\begin{cases} x = Ae^{\lambda t} \\ y = Be^{\lambda t}. \end{cases}$$

Substituting (7.26) into (7.25) we obtain

$$\begin{cases} A\lambda e^{\lambda t} = 4Ae^{\lambda t} - Be^{\lambda t} \\ B\lambda e^{\lambda t} = Ae^{\lambda t} + 2Be^{\lambda t}, \end{cases}$$

and this leads at once to the algebraic system

(7.27)
$$\begin{cases} (4 - \lambda)A - B = 0 \\ A + (2 - \lambda)B = 0 \end{cases}$$

in the unknown λ. For nontrivial solutions of this system we must have

$$\begin{vmatrix} 4 - \lambda & -1 \\ 1 & 2 - \lambda \end{vmatrix} = 0.$$

Expanding this we obtain the characteristic equation

(7.28)
$$\lambda^2 - 6\lambda + 9 = 0$$

or

$$(\lambda - 3)^2 = 0.$$

Thus the characteristic equation (7.28) has the real and equal roots 3, 3.

Setting $\lambda = 3$ in (7.27), we obtain

$$\begin{cases} A - B = 0 \\ A - B = 0. \end{cases}$$

A simple nontrivial solution of this system being $A = B = 1$, we obtain the nontrivial solution

(7.29)
$$\begin{cases} x = e^{3t} \\ y = e^{3t} \end{cases}$$

of the given system (7.25).

Since the roots of the characteristic equation are both equal to 3, we must seek a second solution of the form (7.24), with $\lambda = 3$. That is, we must determine $A_1, A_2, B_1,$ and B_2 (with A_1 and B_1 not both zero) such that

(7.30)
$$\begin{cases} x = (A_1 t + A_2)e^{3t} \\ y = (B_1 t + B_2)e^{3t} \end{cases}$$

is a solution of the system (7.25). Substituting (7.30) into (7.25), we obtain

$$\begin{cases} (3A_1t + 3A_2 + A_1)e^{3t} = 4(A_1t + A_2)e^{3t} - (B_1t + B_2)e^{3t} \\ (3B_1t + 3B_2 + B_1)e^{3t} = (A_1t + A_2)e^{3t} + 2(B_1t + B_2)e^{3t}. \end{cases}$$

These equations reduce at once to

$$\begin{cases} (A_1 - B_1)t + (A_2 - A_1 - B_2) = 0 \\ (A_1 - B_1)t + (A_2 - B_1 - B_2) = 0. \end{cases}$$

In order for these equations to be identities we must have

(7.31)
$$\begin{cases} A_1 - B_1 = 0, \quad A_2 - A_1 - B_2 = 0 \\ A_1 - B_1 = 0, \quad A_2 - B_1 - B_2 = 0. \end{cases}$$

Thus in order for (7.30) to be a solution of the system (7.25), the constants A_1, A_2, B_1, and B_2 must be chosen to satisfy the equations (7.31). From the equations $A_1 - B_1 = 0$, we see that $A_1 = B_1$. The other two equations of (7.31) show that A_2 and B_2 must satisfy

(7.32)
$$A_2 - B_2 = A_1 = B_1.$$

We may choose any convenient nonzero value for A_1 and B_1. We choose $A_1 = B_1 = 1$. Then (7.32) reduces to $A_2 - B_2 = 1$, and we can choose any convenient values for A_2 and B_2 which will satisfy this equation. We choose $A_2 = 1$, $B_2 = 0$. We are thus led to the solution

(7.33)
$$\begin{cases} x = (t + 1)e^{3t} \\ y = te^{3t}. \end{cases}$$

By Theorem 7.8 the solutions (7.29) and (7.33) are linearly independent. We may thus write the general solution of the system (7.25) in the form

$$\begin{cases} x = c_1e^{3t} + c_2(t + 1)e^{3t} \\ y = c_1e^{3t} + c_2te^{3t}, \end{cases}$$

where c_1 and c_2 are arbitrary constants.

D. Case (iii). *The Roots of the Characteristic Equation (7.18) are Conjugate Complex*
   If the roots λ_1 and λ_2 of the characteristic equation (7.18) are the conjugate complex numbers $a + bi$ and $a - bi$, then we obtain two distinct solutions

(7.34)
$$\begin{cases} x = A_1^*e^{(a+bi)t} \\ y = B_1^*e^{(a+bi)t} \end{cases} \quad \text{and} \quad \begin{cases} x = A_2^*e^{(a-bi)t} \\ y = B_2^*e^{(a-bi)t} \end{cases}$$

of the form (7.15), one corresponding to each of the complex roots. However, the solutions (7.34) are *complex* solutions. In order to obtain *real* solutions in this case we consider the first of the two solutions (7.34) and proceed as follows: We first express the complex constants A_1^* and B_1^* in this solution in the forms $A_1^* = A_1 + iA_2$ and $B_1^* = B_1 + iB_2$, where A_1, A_2, B_1, and B_2, are real. We then apply Euler's Formula $e^{i\theta} = \cos\theta + i\sin\theta$ and express the first solution (7.34) in the form

$$\begin{cases} x = (A_1 + iA_2)e^{at}(\cos bt + i\sin bt) \\ y = (B_1 + iB_2)e^{at}(\cos bt + i\sin bt). \end{cases}$$

Rewriting this, we have

$$(7.35) \qquad \begin{cases} x = e^{at}[(A_1\cos bt - A_2\sin bt) + i(A_2\cos bt + A_1\sin bt)] \\ y = e^{at}[(B_1\cos bt - B_2\sin bt) + i(B_2\cos bt + B_1\sin bt)]. \end{cases}$$

It can be shown that a pair $[f_1(t) + if_2(t), g_1(t) + ig_2(t)]$ of complex functions is a solution of the system (7.14) if and only if both the pair $[f_1(t), g_1(t)]$ consisting of their real parts and the pair $[f_2(t), g_2(t)]$ consisting of their imaginary parts are solutions of (7.14). Thus both the real part

$$(7.36) \qquad \begin{cases} x = e^{at}(A_1\cos bt - A_2\sin bt) \\ y = e^{at}(B_1\cos bt - B_2\sin bt) \end{cases}$$

and the imaginary part

$$(7.37) \qquad \begin{cases} x = e^{at}(A_2\cos bt + A_1\sin bt) \\ y = e^{at}(B_2\cos bt + B_1\sin bt) \end{cases}$$

of the solution (7.35) of the system (7.14) are also solutions of (7.14). Furthermore, the solutions (7.36) and (7.37) are linearly independent. We verify this by evaluating the determinant (7.13) for these solutions. We find

$$(7.38) \quad \Delta(t) = \begin{vmatrix} e^{at}(A_1\cos bt - A_2\sin bt) & e^{at}(A_2\cos bt + A_1\sin bt) \\ e^{at}(B_1\cos bt - B_2\sin bt) & e^{at}(B_2\cos bt + B_1\sin bt) \end{vmatrix} = e^{2at}(A_1B_2 - A_2B_1).$$

Now the constant B_1^* is a *nonreal* multiple of the constant A_1^*. If we assume that $A_1B_2 - A_2B_1 = 0$, then it follows that B_1^* is a *real* multiple of A_1^*, which contradicts the result stated in the previous sentence. Thus $A_1B_2 - A_2B_1 \neq 0$ and so the determinant $\Delta(t)$ in (7.38) is unequal to zero. Thus by Theorem 7.4 the solutions (7.36) and (7.37) are indeed linearly independent. Hence a linear combination of these two real solutions provides the general solution of the system (7.14) in this case. There is no need to consider the second of the two solutions (7.34). We summarize the above results in the following theorem:

THEOREM 7.9.

Hypothesis. The roots λ_1 and λ_2 of the characteristic equation (7.18) associated with the system (7.14) are the conjugate complex numbers $a \pm bi$.

Conclusion. The system (7.14) has two real linearly independent solutions of the form

$$\begin{cases} x = e^{at}(A_1\cos bt - A_2\sin bt) \\ y = e^{at}(B_1\cos bt - B_2\sin bt) \end{cases} \text{and} \begin{cases} x = e^{at}(A_2\cos bt + A_1\sin bt) \\ y = e^{at}(B_2\cos bt + B_1\sin bt), \end{cases}$$

where $A_1, A_2, B_1,$ and B_2 are definite real constants. The general solution of the system (7.14) may thus be written

$$\begin{cases} x = e^{at}[c_1(A_1\cos bt - A_2\sin bt) + c_2(A_2\cos bt + A_1\sin bt)] \\ y = e^{at}[c_1(B_1\cos bt - B_2\sin bt) + c_2(B_2\cos bt + B_1\sin bt)], \end{cases}$$

where c_1 and c_2 are arbitrary constants.

Example 7.12.

(7.39)
$$\begin{cases} \dfrac{dx}{dt} = 3x + 2y \\[2mm] \dfrac{dy}{dt} = -5x + y. \end{cases}$$

We assume a solution of the form (7.15):

(7.40)
$$\begin{cases} x = Ae^{\lambda t} \\ y = Be^{\lambda t}. \end{cases}$$

Substituting (7.40) into (7.39) we obtain

$$A\lambda e^{\lambda t} = 3Ae^{\lambda t} + 2Be^{\lambda t}$$
$$B\lambda e^{\lambda t} = -5Ae^{\lambda t} + Be^{\lambda t},$$

and this leads at once to the algebraic system

(7.41)
$$\begin{cases} (3 - \lambda)A + 2B = 0 \\ -5A + (1 - \lambda)B = 0 \end{cases}$$

in the unknown λ. For nontrivial solutions of this system we must have

$$\begin{vmatrix} 3 - \lambda & 2 \\ -5 & 1 - \lambda \end{vmatrix} = 0.$$

Expanding this, we obtain the characteristic equation

$$\lambda^2 - 4\lambda + 13 = 0.$$

The roots of this equation are the conjugate complex numbers $2 \pm 3i$.
   Setting $\lambda = 2 + 3i$ in (7.41), we obtain

$$\begin{cases} (1 - 3i)A + 2B = 0 \\ -5A + (-1 - 3i)B = 0. \end{cases}$$

A simple nontrivial solution of this system is $A = 2$, $B = -1 + 3i$. Using these values we obtain the complex solution

$$\begin{cases} x = 2e^{(2+3i)t} \\ y = (-1 + 3i)e^{(2+3i)t} \end{cases}$$

of the given system (7.39). Using Euler's formula this takes the form

$$\begin{cases} x = e^{2t}[(2\cos 3t) + i(2\sin 3t)] \\ y = e^{2t}[(-\cos 3t - 3\sin 3t) + i(3\cos 3t - \sin 3t)]. \end{cases}$$

Since both the real and imaginary parts of this solution of system (7.39) are themselves solutions of (7.39), we thus obtain the two real solutions

(7.42)
$$\begin{cases} x = 2e^{2t}\cos 3t \\ y = -e^{2t}(\cos 3t + 3\sin 3t) \end{cases}$$

and

(7.43)
$$\begin{cases} x = 2e^{2t}\sin3t \\ y = e^{2t}(3\cos3t - \sin3t). \end{cases}$$

Finally, since the two solutions (7.42) and (7.43) are linearly independent we may write the general solution of the system (7.39) in the form

$$\begin{cases} x = 2e^{2t}(c_1\cos3t + c_2\sin3t) \\ y = e^{2t}[c_1(-\cos3t - 3\sin3t) + c_2(3\cos3t - \sin3t)], \end{cases}$$

where c_1 and c_2 are arbitrary constants.

Exercises

Find the general solution of each of the linear systems in Exercises 1 through 22.

1. $\begin{cases} \dfrac{dx}{dt} = 5x - 2y \\ \dfrac{dy}{dt} = 4x - y \end{cases}$

2. $\begin{cases} \dfrac{dx}{dt} = 5x - y \\ \dfrac{dy}{dt} = 3x + y \end{cases}$

3. $\begin{cases} \dfrac{dx}{dt} = x + 2y \\ \dfrac{dy}{dt} = 3x + 2y \end{cases}$

4. $\begin{cases} \dfrac{dx}{dt} = 2x + 3y \\ \dfrac{dy}{dt} = -x - 2y \end{cases}$

5. $\begin{cases} \dfrac{dx}{dt} = 3x + y \\ \dfrac{dy}{dt} = 4x + 3y \end{cases}$

6. $\begin{cases} \dfrac{dx}{dt} = 6x - y \\ \dfrac{dy}{dt} = 3x + 2y \end{cases}$

7. $\begin{cases} \dfrac{dx}{dt} = 3x - 4y \\ \dfrac{dy}{dt} = 2x - 3y \end{cases}$

8. $\begin{cases} \dfrac{dx}{dt} = 2x - y \\ \dfrac{dy}{dt} = 9x + 2y \end{cases}$

9. $\begin{cases} \dfrac{dx}{dt} = x + 3y \\ \dfrac{dy}{dt} = 3x + y \end{cases}$

10. $\begin{cases} \dfrac{dx}{dt} = 3x + 2y \\ \dfrac{dy}{dt} = 6x - y \end{cases}$

11. $\begin{cases} \dfrac{dx}{dt} = 3x - y \\ \dfrac{dy}{dt} = 4x - y \end{cases}$

12. $\begin{cases} \dfrac{dx}{dt} = 4x - y \\ \dfrac{dy}{dt} = x + 2y \end{cases}$

13. $\begin{cases} \dfrac{dx}{dt} = 5x + 4y \\ \dfrac{dy}{dt} = -x + y \end{cases}$

14. $\begin{cases} \dfrac{dx}{dt} = x - 2y \\ \dfrac{dy}{dt} = 2x - 3y \end{cases}$

15. $\begin{cases} \dfrac{dx}{dt} = x - 4y \\[2mm] \dfrac{dy}{dt} = x + y \end{cases}$ 16. $\begin{cases} \dfrac{dx}{dt} = 2x - 3y \\[2mm] \dfrac{dy}{dt} = 3x + 2y \end{cases}$

17. $\begin{cases} \dfrac{dx}{dt} = x - 3y \\[2mm] \dfrac{dy}{dt} = 3x + y \end{cases}$ 18. $\begin{cases} \dfrac{dx}{dt} = 5x - 4y \\[2mm] \dfrac{dy}{dt} = 2x + y \end{cases}$

19. $\begin{cases} \dfrac{dx}{dt} = 4x - 2y \\[2mm] \dfrac{dy}{dt} = 5x + 2y \end{cases}$ 20. $\begin{cases} \dfrac{dx}{dt} = x - 5y \\[2mm] \dfrac{dy}{dt} = 2x - y \end{cases}$

21. $\begin{cases} \dfrac{dx}{dt} = 3x - 2y \\[2mm] \dfrac{dy}{dt} = 2x + 3y \end{cases}$ 22. $\begin{cases} \dfrac{dx}{dt} = 6x - 5y \\[2mm] \dfrac{dy}{dt} = x + 2y \end{cases}$

23. Consider the linear system

$$\begin{cases} t\dfrac{dx}{dt} = a_1 x + b_1 y \\[2mm] t\dfrac{dy}{dt} = a_2 x + b_2 y, \end{cases}$$

where a_1, b_1, a_2, and b_2 are real constants. Show that the transformation $t = e^w$ transforms this system into a linear system with constant coefficients.

24. Use the result of Exercise 23 to solve the system

$$\begin{cases} t\dfrac{dx}{dt} = x + y \\[2mm] t\dfrac{dy}{dt} = -3x + 5y. \end{cases}$$

25. Use the result of Exercise 23 to solve the system

$$\begin{cases} t\dfrac{dx}{dt} = 2x + 3y \\[2mm] t\dfrac{dy}{dt} = 2x + y. \end{cases}$$

26. Consider the linear system

$$\begin{cases} \dfrac{dx}{dt} = a_1 x + b_1 y \\[2mm] \dfrac{dy}{dt} = a_2 x + b_2 y \end{cases}$$

where a_1, b_1, a_2, and b_2 are real constants. Show that the condition $a_2 b_1 > 0$ is sufficient, but not necessary, for the system to have two real linearly independent solutions of the form

$$\begin{cases} x = Ae^{\lambda t} \\ y = Be^{\lambda t}. \end{cases}$$

Extend the methods of this section to solve the systems of three differential equations in Exercises 27 through 29.

27. $\begin{cases} \dfrac{dx}{dt} = x + y - z \\[2mm] \dfrac{dy}{dt} = 2x + 3y - 4z \\[2mm] \dfrac{dz}{dt} = 4x + y - 4z \end{cases}$
28. $\begin{cases} \dfrac{dx}{dt} = x - y - z \\[2mm] \dfrac{dy}{dt} = x + 3y + z \\[2mm] \dfrac{dz}{dt} = -3x - 6y + 6z \end{cases}$

29. $\begin{cases} \dfrac{dx}{dt} = x - y - z \\[2mm] \dfrac{dy}{dt} = x + 3y + z \\[2mm] \dfrac{dz}{dt} = -3x + y - z \end{cases}$

7.3 An Operator Method

A. Differential Operators

In this section we shall present a symbolic operator method for solving linear systems with constant coefficients. This method depends upon the use of so-called *differential operators*, which we now introduce.

Let x be an n-times differentiable function of the independent variable t. We denote the operation of differentiation with respect to t by the symbol D and call D a differential operator. In terms of this differential operator the derivative dx/dt is denoted by Dx. That is,

$$Dx \equiv dx/dt.$$

In like manner, we denote the second derivative of x with respect to t by D^2x. Extending this, we denote the nth derivative of x with respect to t by D^nx. That is,

$$D^nx = \frac{d^nx}{dt^n} \ (n = 1, 2, \cdots).$$

Further extending this operator notation, we write

$$(D + c)x \quad \text{to denote} \quad \frac{dx}{dt} + cx$$

and

$$(aD^n + bD^m)x \quad \text{to denote} \quad a\frac{d^nx}{dt^n} + b\frac{d^mx}{dt^m},$$

where a, b, and c are constants.

In this notation the general linear differential expression with constant coefficients $a_0, a_1, \ldots, a_{n-1}, a_n$,

$$a_0\frac{d^n x}{dt^n} + a_1\frac{d^{n-1}x}{dt^{n-1}} + \cdots + a_{n-1}\frac{dx}{dt} + a_n x,$$

is written

$$(a_0 D^n + a_1 D^{n-1} + \cdots + a_{n-1}D + a_n)x.$$

Observe carefully that the operators D^n, $D^{n-1}, \ldots, D$ in this expression do *not* represent quantities which are to be multiplied by the function x, but rather they indicate *operations* (differentiations) which are to be carried out upon this function. The expression

$$a_0 D^n + a_1 D^{n-1} + \cdots + a_{n-1}D + a_n$$

by itself, where $a_0, a_1, \ldots, a_{n-1}, a_n$ are constants, is called a linear differential operator with constant coefficients. Linear differential operators with variable coefficients are employed in Chapter 11, but we shall make no use of them in this chapter.

Example 7.13.   Consider the linear differential operator

$$3D^2 + 5D - 2.$$

If x is a differentiable function of t, then

$$(3D^2 + 5D - 2)x \quad \text{denotes} \quad 3\frac{d^2 x}{dt^2} + 5\frac{dx}{dt} - 2x.$$

For example, if $x = t^3$, we have

$$(3D^2 + 5D - 2)t^3 = 3\frac{d^2}{dt^2}(t^3) + 5\frac{d}{dt}(t^3) - 2(t^3) = 18t + 15t^2 - 2t^3.$$

We shall now discuss certain useful properties of the linear differential operator with constant coefficients. In order to facilitate our discussion, we shall let L denote this operator. That is,

$$L \equiv a_0 D^n + a_1 D^{n-1} + \cdots + a_{n-1}D + a_n,$$

where $a_0, a_1, \ldots, a_{n-1}, a_n$ are constants. Now suppose that f_1 and f_2 are both n-times differentiable functions of t and c_1 and c_2 are constants. Then it can be shown that

$$L[c_1 f_1 + c_2 f_2] = c_1 L[f_1] + c_2 L[f_2].$$

For example, if the operator $L \equiv 3D^2 + 5D - 2$ is applied to $3t^2 + 2\sin t$, then

$$L[3t^2 + 2\sin t] = 3L[t^2] + 2L[\sin t]$$

or

$$(3D^2 + 5D - 2)(3t^2 + 2\sin t) = 3(3D^2 + 5D - 2)t^2 + 2(3D^2 + 5D - 2)\sin t.$$

Now let $L_1 \equiv a_0 D^m + a_1 D^{m-1} + \cdots + a_{m-1}D + a_m$ and $L_2 \equiv b_0 D^n + b_1 D^{n-1} + \cdots + b_{n-1}D + b_n$ be two linear differential operators with constant coefficients $a_0, a_1, \ldots, a_{m-1}, a_m, b_0, b_1, \ldots, b_{n-1}, b_n$. Let

$$L_1(r) \equiv a_0 r^m + a_1 r^{m-1} + \cdots + a_{m-1}r + a_m$$

and

$$L_2(r) \equiv b_0 r^n + b_1 r^{n-1} + \cdots + b_{n-1} r + b_n$$

be the two polynomials in the quantity r obtained from the operators L_1 and L_2, respectively, by formally replacing D by r, D^2 by r^2, ..., D^k by r^k. Let us denote the product of the polynomials $L_1(r)$ and $L_2(r)$ by $L(r)$; that is,

$$L(r) = L_1(r)L_2(r).$$

Then, if f is a function possessing $n + m$ derivatives, it can be shown that

(7.44) $$L_1 L_2 f = L_2 L_1 f = Lf,$$

where L is the operator obtained from the "product polynomial" $L(r)$ by formally replacing r by D, r^2 by D^2, ..., r^{m+n} by D^{m+n}. The equation (7.44) indicates two important properties of linear differential operators with constant coefficients. First, it states the effect of first operating on f by L_2 and then operating on the resulting function by L_1 is the same as that which results from first operating on f by L_1 and then operating on this resulting function by L_2. Second, the equation (7.44) states that the effect of first operating on f by either L_1 or L_2 and then operating on the resulting function by the other is the same as that which results from operating on f by the "product operator" L. We illustrate these important properties in the following example.

Example 7.14. Let $L_1 \equiv D^2 + 1$, $L_2 \equiv 3D + 2$, $f(t) = t^3$. Then

$$L_1 L_2 f = (D^2 + 1)(3D + 2)t^3 = (D^2 + 1)(9t^2 + 2t^3) = 9(D^2 + 1)t^2 + 2(D^2 + 1)t^3$$
$$= 9(2 + t^2) + 2(6t + t^3) = 2t^3 + 9t^2 + 12t + 18$$

and

$$L_2 L_1 f = (3D + 2)(D^2 + 1)t^3 = (3D + 2)(6t + t^3) = 6(3D + 2)t + (3D + 2)t^3$$
$$= 6(3 + 2t) + (9t^2 + 2t^3) = 2t^3 + 9t^2 + 12t + 18.$$

Finally, $L \equiv 3D^3 + 2D^2 + 3D + 2$ and

$$Lf = (3D^3 + 2D^2 + 3D + 2)t^3 = 3(6) + 2(6t) + 3(3t^2) + 2t^3 = 2t^3 + 9t^2 + 12t + 18.$$

Now let $L \equiv a_0 D^n + a_1 D^{n-1} + \cdots + a_{n-1} D + a_n$, where $a_0, a_1, \ldots, a_{n-1}, a_n$ are constants; and let $L(r) \equiv a_0 r^n + a_1 r^{n-1} + \cdots + a_{n-1} r + a_n$ be the polynomial in r obtained from L by formally replacing D by r, D^2 by r^2, ..., D^n by r^n. Let $r_1, r_2, \ldots, r_n$ be the roots of the polynomial equation $L(r) = 0$. Then $L(r)$ may be written in the factored form

$$L(r) = a_0(r - r_1)(r - r_2)\cdots(r - r_n).$$

Now formally replacing r by D in the right member of this identity, we may express the operator $L \equiv a_0 D^n + a_1 D^{n-1} + \cdots + a_{n-1} D + a_n$ in the factored form

$$L = a_0(D - r_1)(D - r_2)\cdots(D - r_n).$$

We thus observe that linear differential operators with constant coefficients can be formally multiplied and factored exactly as if they were polynomials in the algebraic quantity D.

B. An Operator Method For Linear Systems with Constant Coefficients

We now proceed to explain a symbolic operator method for solving linear systems with constant coefficients. We shall outline the procedure of this method on a strictly formal basis and shall make no attempt to justify it.

We consider a linear system of the form

(7.45)
$$L_1 x + L_2 y = f_1(t)$$
$$L_3 x + L_4 y = f_2(t),$$

where L_1, L_2, L_3, and L_4 are linear differential operators with constant coefficients. That is, L_1, L_2, L_3, and L_4 are operators of the forms

$$L_1 \equiv a_0 D^m + a_1 D^{m-1} + \cdots + a_{m-1} D + a_m,$$
$$L_2 \equiv b_0 D^n + b_1 D^{n-1} + \cdots + b_{n-1} D + b_n,$$
$$L_3 \equiv \alpha_0 D^p + \alpha_1 D^{p-1} + \cdots + \alpha_{p-1} D + \alpha_p,$$
$$L_4 \equiv \beta_0 D^q + \beta_1 D^{q-1} + \cdots + \beta_{q-1} D + \beta_q,$$

where the a's, b's, α's, and β's are constants.

A simple example of a system which may be expressed in the form (7.45) is provided by

$$2\frac{dx}{dt} - 2\frac{dy}{dt} - 3x = t$$

$$2\frac{dx}{dt} + 2\frac{dy}{dt} + 3x + 8y = 2.$$

Introducing operator notation this system takes the form

$$(2D - 3)x - 2Dy = t$$
$$(2D + 3)x + (2D + 8)y = 2.$$

This is clearly of the form (7.45), where $L_1 \equiv 2D - 3$, $L_2 \equiv -2D$, $L_3 \equiv 2D + 3$, and $L_4 \equiv 2D + 8$.

Returning now to the general system (7.45), we apply the operator L_4 to the first equation of (7.45) and the operator L_2 to the second equation of (7.45), obtaining

$$L_4 L_1 x + L_4 L_2 y = L_4 f_1$$
$$L_2 L_3 x + L_2 L_4 y = L_2 f_2.$$

We now subtract the second of these equations from the first. Since $L_4 L_2 y = L_2 L_4 y$, we obtain

$$L_4 L_1 x - L_2 L_3 x = L_4 f_1 - L_2 f_2$$

or

(7.46)
$$(L_1 L_4 - L_2 L_3)x = L_4 f_1 - L_2 f_2.$$

The expression $L_1 L_4 - L_2 L_3$ in the left member of this equation is itself a linear differential operator with constant coefficients. We assume that it is neither zero nor a nonzero constant and denote it by L_5. If we further assume that the functions f_1 and f_2 are such that the right member $L_4f_1 - L_2f_2$ of (7.46) exists, then this member is some function, say g_1, of t. Then the equation (7.46) may be written

$$(7.47) \qquad\qquad\qquad L_5x = g_1.$$

Equation (7.47) is a linear differential equation with constant coefficients in the single dependent variable x. We thus observe that our procedure has eliminated the other dependent variable y. We now solve the differential equation (7.47) for x using the methods developed in Chapter 4. Suppose equation (7.47) is of order N. Then the general solution of (7.47) is of the form

$$(7.48) \qquad\qquad x = c_1u_1 + c_2u_2 + \cdots + c_Nu_N + U_1,$$

where $u_1, u_2, \ldots, u_N$ are N linearly independent solutions of the homogeneous linear equation $L_5x = 0$, $c_1, c_2, \ldots, c_N$ are arbitrary constants, and U_1 is a particular solution of $L_5x = g_1$.

We again return to the system (7.45) and this time apply the operators L_3 and L_1 to the first and second equations, respectively, of the system. We obtain

$$L_3L_1x + L_3L_2y = L_3f_1$$
$$L_1L_3x + L_1L_4y = L_1f_2.$$

Subtracting the first of these from the second, we obtain

$$(L_1L_4 - L_2L_3)y = L_1f_2 - L_3f_1.$$

Assuming that f_1 and f_2 are such that the right member $L_1f_2 - L_3f_1$ of this equation exists, we may express it as some function, say g_2, of t. Then this equation may be written

$$(7.49) \qquad\qquad\qquad L_5y = g_2,$$

where L_5 denotes the operator $L_1L_4 - L_2L_3$. Equation (7.49) is a linear differential equation with constant coefficients in the single dependent variable y. This time we have eliminated the dependent variable x. Solving the differential equation (7.49) for y, we obtain its general solution in the form

$$(7.50) \qquad\qquad y = k_1u_1 + k_2u_2 + \cdots + k_Nu_N + U_2,$$

where $u_1, u_2, \ldots, u_N$ are the N linearly independent solutions of $L_5y = 0$ (or $L_5x = 0$) which already appear in (7.48), $k_1, k_2, \ldots, k_N$ are arbitrary constants, and U_2 is a particular solution of $L_5y = g_2$.

We thus see that if x and y satisfy the linear system (7.45), then x satisfies the single linear differential equation (7.47) and y satisfies the single linear differential equation (7.49). Thus if x and y satisfy the system (7.45), then x is of the form (7.48) and y is of the form (7.50). However, the pairs of functions given by (7.48) and (7.50) do *not* satisfy the given system (7.45) for *all* choices of the constants $c_1, c_2, \ldots, c_N, k_1, k_2, \ldots, k_N$. In other words, in order for x given by (7.48) and y given by (7.50) to satisfy the given system (7.45), the $2N$ constants $c_1, c_2, \ldots, c_N, k_1, k_2, \ldots, k_N$ can not all be independent but rather certain of them must be functions of the others. It can be shown that the number of independent constants in the general solution of the linear system (7.45) is equal to the order of the operator $L_1L_4 - L_2L_3$ obtained from the determinant

$$\begin{vmatrix} L_1 & L_2 \\ L_3 & L_4 \end{vmatrix}$$

of the operator "coefficients" of x and y in (7.45), provided that this determinant is not zero. We have assumed that this operator is of order N. Thus in order for the pair (7.48) and (7.50) to satisfy the system (7.45) only N of the $2N$ constants in this pair can be independent. The remaining N constants must depend upon the N which are independent. In order to determine which of these $2N$ constants may be chosen as independent and how the remaining N then relate to the N so chosen, we must substitute x as given by (7.48) and y as given by (7.50) into the system (7.45). This determines the relations which must exist among the constants $c_1, c_2, \ldots, c_N, k_1, k_2, \ldots, k_N$ in order that the pair (7.48) and (7.50) constitute the general solution of (7.45).

We now illustrate the above procedure with an example.

Example 7.15.   Solve the system

(7.51)
$$2\frac{dx}{dt} - 2\frac{dy}{dt} - 3x = t$$
$$2\frac{dx}{dt} + 2\frac{dy}{dt} + 3x + 8y = 2.$$

We introduce operator notation and write this system in the form

(7.52)
$$(2D - 3)x - 2Dy = t$$
$$(2D + 3)x + (2D + 8)y = 2.$$

We apply the operator $(2D + 8)$ to the first equation of (7.52) and the operator $2D$ to the second equation of (7.52), obtaining

$$(2D + 8)(2D - 3)x - (2D + 8)2Dy = (2D + 8)t$$
$$2D(2D + 3)x + 2D(2D + 8)y = (2D)2.$$

Adding these two equations, we obtain

$$[(2D + 8)(2D - 3) + 2D(2D + 3)]x = (2D + 8)t + (2D)2$$

or

$$(8D^2 + 16D - 24)x = 2 + 8t + 0$$

or, finally,

(7.53)
$$(D^2 + 2D - 3)x = t + \frac{1}{4}.$$
$$(D+3)(D-1)$$

The general solution of the differential equation (7.53) is

(7.54)
$$x = c_1e^t + c_2e^{-3t} - \frac{1}{3}t - \frac{11}{36}.$$

We now return to the system (7.52) and apply the operator $(2D + 3)$ to the first equation of (7.52) and the operator $(2D - 3)$ to the second equation of (7.52). We obtain

$$(2D + 3)(2D - 3)x - (2D + 3)2Dy = (2D + 3)t$$
$$(2D - 3)(2D + 3)x + (2D - 3)(2D + 8)y = (2D - 3)2$$

Subtracting the first of these equations from the second, we have

$$[(2D - 3)(2D + 8) + (2D + 3)2D]y = (2D - 3)2 - (2D + 3)t$$

or

$$(8D^2 + 16D - 24)y = 0 - 6 - 2 - 3t$$

or, finally,

(7.55)
$$(D^2 + 2D - 3)y = -\frac{3}{8}t - 1.$$

The general solution of the differential equation (7.55) is

(7.56)
$$y = k_1 e^t + k_2 e^{-3t} + \frac{1}{8}t + \frac{5}{12}.$$

Thus if x and y satisfy the system (7.51), then x must be of the form (7.54) and y must be of the form (7.56) for some choice of the constants c_1, c_2, k_1, k_2. The determinant of the operator "coefficients" of x and y in (7.52) is

$$\begin{vmatrix} 2D - 3 & -2D \\ 2D + 3 & 2D + 8 \end{vmatrix} = 8D^2 + 16D - 24.$$

Since this is of order two, the number of independent constants in the general solution of the system (7.51) must also be two. Thus in order for the pair (7.54) and (7.56) to satisfy the system (7.51) only two of the four constants c_1, c_2, k_1, and k_2 can be independent. In order to determine the necessary relations which must exist among these constants, we substitute x as given by (7.54) and y as given by (7.56) into the system (7.51). Substituting into the first equation of (7.51), we have

$$\left[2c_1 e^t - 6c_2 e^{-3t} - \frac{2}{3} \right] - \left[2k_1 e^t - 6k_2 e^{-3t} + \frac{1}{4} \right] - \left[3c_1 e^t + 3c_2 e^{-3t} - t - \frac{11}{12} \right] = t$$

or

$$(-c_1 - 2k_1)e^t + (-9c_2 + 6k_2)e^{-3t} = 0.$$

Thus in order that the pair (7.54) and (7.56) satisfy the first equation of the system (7.51) we must have

(7.57)
$$-c_1 - 2k_1 = 0$$
$$-9c_2 + 6k_2 = 0.$$

Substitution of x and y into the second equation of the system (7.51) will lead to relations equivalent to (7.57). Hence in order for the pair (7.54) and (7.56) to satisfy the system (7.51), the relations (7.57) must be satisfied. Any two of the four constants in (7.57) may be chosen as independent. If we choose c_1 and c_2 as independent, then we have

$$k_1 = -\frac{1}{2}c_1 \quad \text{and} \quad k_2 = \frac{3}{2}c_2.$$

Using these values for k_1 and k_2 in (7.56), the resulting pair (7.54) and (7.56) constitute the general solution of the system (7.51). That is, the general solution of (7.51) is given by

$$x = c_1 e^t + c_2 e^{-3t} - \frac{1}{3}t - \frac{11}{36}$$

$$y = -\frac{1}{2}c_1 e^t + \frac{3}{2}c_2 e^{-3t} + \frac{1}{8}t + \frac{5}{12},$$

where c_1 and c_2 are arbitrary constants. If we had chosen k_1 and k_2 as the independent constants in (7.57), then the general solution of the system (7.51) would have been written

$$x = -2k_1 e^t + \frac{2}{3}k_2 e^{-3t} - \frac{1}{3}t - \frac{11}{36}$$

$$y = k_1 e^t + k_2 e^{-3t} + \frac{1}{8}t + \frac{5}{12}.$$

Exercises

Use the operator method described in this section to find the general solution of each of the following linear systems.

1. $\dfrac{dx}{dt} + \dfrac{dy}{dt} - 2x - 4y = e^t$

$\dfrac{dx}{dt} + \dfrac{dy}{dt} - y = e^{4t}$

2. $\dfrac{dx}{dt} + \dfrac{dy}{dt} - x = -2t$

$\dfrac{dx}{dt} + \dfrac{dy}{dt} - 3x - y = t^2$

3. $\dfrac{dx}{dt} + \dfrac{dy}{dt} - x - 3y = e^t$

$\dfrac{dx}{dt} + \dfrac{dy}{dt} + x = e^{3t}$

4. $\dfrac{dx}{dt} + \dfrac{dy}{dt} - x - 2y = 2e^t$

$\dfrac{dx}{dt} + \dfrac{dy}{dt} - 3x - 4y = e^{2t}$

5. $2\dfrac{dx}{dt} + \dfrac{dy}{dt} - x - y = e^{-t}$

$\dfrac{dx}{dt} + \dfrac{dy}{dt} + 2x + y = e^t$

6. $2\dfrac{dx}{dt} + \dfrac{dy}{dt} - 3x - y = t$

$\dfrac{dx}{dt} + \dfrac{dy}{dt} - 4x - y = e^t$

7. $\dfrac{dx}{dt} + \dfrac{dy}{dt} - x - 6y = e^{3t}$

$\dfrac{dx}{dt} + 2\dfrac{dy}{dt} - 2x - 6y = t$

8. $\dfrac{dx}{dt} + \dfrac{dy}{dt} - x - 3y = 3t$

$\dfrac{dx}{dt} + 2\dfrac{dy}{dt} - 2x - 3y = 1$

9. $\dfrac{dx}{dt} + \dfrac{dy}{dt} + 2y = \sin t$

$\dfrac{dx}{dt} + \dfrac{dy}{dt} - x - y = 0$

10. $\dfrac{dx}{dt} - \dfrac{dy}{dt} - 2x + 4y = t$

$\dfrac{dx}{dt} + \dfrac{dy}{dt} - x - y = 1$

11. $2\dfrac{dx}{dt} + \dfrac{dy}{dt} + x + 5y = 4t$

$\dfrac{dx}{dt} + \dfrac{dy}{dt} + 2x + 2y = 2$

12. $\dfrac{dx}{dt} + \dfrac{dy}{dt} - x + 5y = t^2$

$\dfrac{dx}{dt} + 2\dfrac{dy}{dt} - 2x + 4y = 2t + 1$

13. $2\dfrac{dx}{dt} + \dfrac{dy}{dt} + x + y = t^2 + 4t$

$\dfrac{dx}{dt} + \dfrac{dy}{dt} + 2x + 2y = 2t^2 - 2t$

14. $3\dfrac{dx}{dt} + 2\dfrac{dy}{dt} - x + y = t - 1$

$\dfrac{dx}{dt} + \dfrac{dy}{dt} - x = t + 2$

15. $2\dfrac{dx}{dt} + 4\dfrac{dy}{dt} + x - y = 3e^t$

$\dfrac{dx}{dt} + \dfrac{dy}{dt} + 2x + 2y = e^t$

16. $2\dfrac{dx}{dt} + \dfrac{dy}{dt} - x - y = -2t$

$\dfrac{dx}{dt} + \dfrac{dy}{dt} + x - y = t^2$

17. $2\dfrac{dx}{dt} + \dfrac{dy}{dt} - x - y = 1$

$\dfrac{dx}{dt} + \dfrac{dy}{dt} + 2x - y = t$

18. $\dfrac{d^2x}{dt^2} + \dfrac{dy}{dt} = e^{2t}$

$\dfrac{dx}{dt} + \dfrac{dy}{dt} - x - y = 0$

19. $\dfrac{d^2x}{dt^2} + \dfrac{dy}{dt} - x + y = 1$

$\dfrac{d^2y}{dt^2} + \dfrac{dx}{dt} - x + y = 0$

20. $\dfrac{d^2x}{dt^2} - \dfrac{dy}{dt} = e^t$

$\dfrac{dx}{dt} + \dfrac{dy}{dt} - 4x - y = 2e^t$

21. $\dfrac{d^2x}{dt^2} - \dfrac{dy}{dt} = t + 1$

$\dfrac{dx}{dt} + \dfrac{dy}{dt} - 3x + y = 2t - 1$

7.4 Applications

A. Applications to Mechanics

Systems of linear differential equations originate in the mathematical formulation of numerous problems in mechanics.   We consider one such problem in the following example. Another mechanics problem leading to a linear system is given in the exercises at the end of this section.

Example 7.16.   On a smooth horizontal plane BC (for example, a smooth table top) an object A_1 is connected to a fixed point P by a massless spring S_1 of natural length L_1. An object A_2 is then connected to A_1 by a massless spring S_2 of natural length L_2 in such a way that the fixed point P and the centers of gravity A_1 and A_2 all lie in a straight line (see Figure 7.1).

The object A_1 is then displaced a distance a_1 to the right or left of its equilibrium position O_1, the object A_2 is displaced a distance a_2 to the right or left of its equilibrium position O_2, and at time $t = 0$ the two objects are released (see Figure 7.2).   What are the positions of the two objects at any time $t > 0$?

Figure 7.1

Figure 7.2

Figure 7.3

Formulation. We assume first that the plane BC is so smooth that frictional forces may be neglected. We also assume that no external forces act upon the system. Suppose object A_1 has mass m_1 and object A_2 has mass m_2. Further suppose spring S_1 has spring constant k_1 and spring S_2 has spring constant k_2.

Let x_1 denote the displacement of A_1 from its equilibrium position O_1 at time $t > 0$ and assume that x_1 is positive when A_1 is to the right of O_1. In like manner, let x_2 denote the displacement of A_2 from its equilibrium position O_2 at time $t \geq 0$ and assume that x_2 is positive when A_2 is to the right of O_2 (see Figure 7.3).

Consider the forces acting on A_1 at time $t > 0$. There are two such forces, F_1 and F_2, where F_1 is exerted by spring S_1 and F_2 is exerted by spring S_2. By Hooke's Law (Section 5.1) the force F_1 is of magnitude $k_1 |x_1|$. Since this force is exerted toward the left when A_1 is to the right of O_1 and toward the right when A_1 is to the left of O_1, we have $F_1 = -k_1x_1$. Again using Hooke's Law, the force F_2 is of magnitude k_2s, where s is the elongation of S_2 at time t. Since $s = |x_2-x_1|$, we see that the magnitude of F_2 is $k_2 |x_2 - x_1|$. Further, since this force is exerted toward the left when $x_2 - x_1 < 0$ and toward the right when $x_2 - x_1 > 0$, we see that $F_2 = k_2(x_2 - x_1)$.

Now applying Newton's Second Law (Section 3.2) to the object A_1, we obtain the differential equation

(7.58)
$$m_1\frac{d^2x_1}{dt^2} = -k_1x_1 + k_2(x_2 - x_1).$$

We now turn to the object A_2 and consider the forces which act upon it at time $t > 0$. There is one such force, F_3, and this is exerted by spring S_2. Applying Hooke's Law once again, we observe that this force is also of magnitude $k_2 s = k_2 |x_2 - x_1|$. Since F_3 is exerted toward the left when $x_2 - x_1 > 0$ and toward the right when $x_2 - x_1 < 0$, we see that $F_3 = -k_2(x_2 - x_1)$. Applying Newton's Second Law to the object A_2, we obtain the differential equation

(7.59)
$$m_2 \frac{d^2 x_2}{dt^2} = -k_2(x_2 - x_1)$$

In addition to the differential equations (7.58) and (7.59), we see from the statement of the problem that the initial conditions are given by

(7.60)
$$x_1(0) = a_1, \ x_1'(0) = 0, \ x_2(0) = a_2, \ x_2'(0) = 0.$$

The mathematical formulation of the problem thus consists of the differential equations (7.58) and (7.59) and the initial conditions (7.60). Writing the differential equations in the form

(7.61)
$$\begin{cases} m_1 \dfrac{d^2 x_1}{dt^2} + (k_1 + k_2)x_1 - k_2 x_2 = 0 \\[2mm] m_2 \dfrac{d^2 x_2}{dt^2} - k_2 x_1 + k_2 x_2 = 0, \end{cases}$$

we see that they form a system of homogeneous linear differential equations with constant coefficients.

Solution of a Specific Case.   Rather than solve the general problem consisting of the system (7.61) and conditions (7.60), we shall carry through the solution in a particular case which was chosen to facilitate the work. Suppose the two objects A_1 and A_2 are each of unit mass, so that $m_1 = m_2 = 1$. Further, suppose that the springs S_1 and S_2 have spring constants $k_1 = 3$ and $k_2 = 2$, respectively. Also, we shall take $a_1 = -1$ and $a_2 = 2$. Then the system (7.61) reduces to

(7.62)
$$\begin{cases} \dfrac{d^2 x_1}{dt^2} + 5x_1 - 2x_2 = 0 \\[2mm] \dfrac{d^2 x_2}{dt^2} - 2x_1 + 2x_2 = 0, \end{cases}$$

and the initial conditions (7.60) become

(7.63)
$$x_1(0) = -1, \ x_1'(0) = 0, \ x_2(0) = 2, \ x_2'(0) = 0.$$

Writing the system (7.62) in operator notation, we have

(7.64)
$$\begin{cases} (D^2 + 5)x_1 - 2x_2 = 0 \\ -2x_1 + (D^2 + 2)x_2 = 0. \end{cases}$$

We apply the operator $(D^2 + 2)$ to the first equation of (7.64), multiply the second equation of (7.64) by 2, and add the two equations to obtain

$$[(D^2 + 2)(D^2 + 5) - 4]x_1 = 0$$

or

(7.65)
$$(D^4 + 7D^2 + 6)x_1 = 0.$$

The auxiliary equation corresponding to the fourth-order differential equation (7.65) is

$$m^4 + 7m^2 + 6 = 0 \quad \text{or} \quad (m^2 + 6)(m^2 + 1) = 0.$$

Thus the general solution of the differential equation (7.65) is

(7.66) $$x_1 = c_1\sin t + c_2\cos t + c_3\sin\sqrt{6}t + c_4\cos\sqrt{6}t.$$

We now multiply the first equation of (7.64) by 2, apply the operator $(D^2 + 5)$ to the second equation of (7.64), and add to obtain the differential equation

(7.67) $$(D^4 + 7D^2 + 6)x_2 = 0$$

for x_2. The general solution of (7.67) is clearly

(7.68) $$x_2 = k_1\sin t + k_2\cos t + k_3\sin\sqrt{6}t + k_4\cos\sqrt{6}t.$$

The determinant of the operator "coefficients" in the system (7.64) is

$$\begin{vmatrix} D^2 + 5 & -2 \\ -2 & D^2 + 2 \end{vmatrix} = D^4 + 7D^2 + 6.$$

Since this is a fourth-order operator, the general solution of (7.62) must contain four independent constants. We must substitute x_1 given by (7.66) and x_2 given by (7.68) into the equations of the system (7.62) to determine the relations which must exist among the constants $c_1, c_2, c_3, c_4, k_1, k_2, k_3,$ and k_4 in order that the pair (7.66) and (7.68) represent the general solution of (7.62). Substituting, we find that

$$k_1 = 2c_1, k_2 = 2c_2, k_3 = -\frac{1}{2}c_3, k_4 = -\frac{1}{2}c_4.$$

Thus the general solution of the system (7.62) is given by

$$x_1 = c_1\sin t + c_2\cos t + c_3\sin\sqrt{6}t + c_4\cos\sqrt{6}t$$

(7.69)

$$x_2 = 2c_1\sin t + 2c_2\cos t - \frac{1}{2}c_3\sin\sqrt{6}t - \frac{1}{2}c_4\cos\sqrt{6}t.$$

We now apply the initial conditions (7.63). Applying the conditions $x_1 = -1$, $dx_1/dt = 0$ at $t = 0$ to the first of the pair (7.69), we find

(7.70) $$\begin{cases} -1 = c_2 + c_4 \\ 0 = c_1 + \sqrt{6}c_3. \end{cases}$$

Applying the conditions $x_2 = 2$, $dx_2/dt = 0$ at $t = 0$ to the second of the pair (7.69), we obtain

(7.71) $$\begin{cases} 2 = 2c_2 - \dfrac{1}{2}c_4 \\ 0 = 2c_1 - \dfrac{\sqrt{6}}{2}c_3. \end{cases}$$

From the equations (7.70) and (7.71), we find that

$$c_1 = 0, c_2 = \frac{3}{5}, c_3 = 0, c_4 = -\frac{8}{5}.$$

Thus the particular solution of the specific problem consisting of the system (7.62) and the conditions (7.63) is

$$\begin{cases} x_1 = \dfrac{3}{5}\cos t - \dfrac{8}{5}\cos\sqrt{6}\,t \\[2mm] x_2 = \dfrac{6}{5}\cos t + \dfrac{4}{5}\cos\sqrt{6}\,t. \end{cases}$$

B. Applications to Electric Circuits

In Section 5.6 we considered the application of differential equations to electric circuits consisting of a single closed path. A closed path in an electrical network is called a *loop*. We shall now consider electrical networks which consist of several loops. For example, consider the network shown in Figure 7.4.

This network consists of the three loops *ABMNA*, *BJKMB*, and *ABJKMNA*. Points such as *B* and *M* at which two or more circuits join are called *junction points* or *branch points*. The direction of current flow has been arbitrarily assigned and indicated by arrows.

In order to solve problems involving multiple loop networks we shall need two fundamental laws of circuit theory. One of these is Kirchhoff's Voltage Law, which we have already stated and applied in Section 5.6. The other basic law which we shall employ is the following:

Kirchhoff's Current Law. In an electrical network the total current flowing into a junction point is equal to the total current flowing away from the junction point.

As an application of these laws we consider the following problem dealing with the circuit of Figure 7.4.

Example 7.17. Determine the currents in the electrical network of Figure 7.4, if *E* is an electromotive force of 30 V, R_1 is a resistor of 10 Ω, R_2 is a resistor of 20 Ω, L_1 is an inductor of 0.02 h, L_2 is an inductor of 0.04 h, and the currents are initially zero.

Formulation. The current flowing in the branch *MNAB* is denoted by i, that flowing on the branch *BM* by i_1, and that flowing on the branch *BJKM* by i_2.

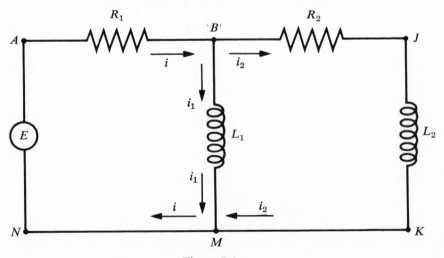

Figure 7.4

We now apply Kirchhoff's Voltage Law (Section 5.6) to each of the three loops *ABMNA*, *BJKMB*, and *ABJKMNA*.

For the loop *ABMNA* the voltage drops are as follows:

(1) Across the resistor R_1: $10i$.

(2) Across the inductor L_1: $0.02 \dfrac{di_1}{dt}$.

Thus applying the Voltage Law to the loop *ABMNA*, we have the equation

(7.72)
$$0.02\frac{di_1}{dt} + 10i = 30.$$

For the loop *BJKMB*, the voltage drops are as follows:

(1) Across the resistor R_2: $20i_2$.

(2) Across the inductor L_2: $0.04 \dfrac{di_2}{dt}$.

(3) Across the inductor L_1: $-0.02 \dfrac{di_1}{dt}$.

The minus sign enters into (3) since we traverse the branch *MB* in the direction opposite to that of the current i_1 as we complete the loop *BJKMB*. Since the loop *BJKMB* contains no electromotive force, upon applying the Voltage Law to this loop we obtain the equation

(7.73)
$$-0.02\frac{di_1}{dt} + 0.04\frac{di_2}{dt} + 20i_2 = 0.$$

For the loop *ABJKMNA*, the voltage drops are as follows:

(1) Across the resistor R_1: $10i$.

(2) Across the resistor R_2: $20i_2$.

(3) Across the inductor L_2: $0.04 \dfrac{di_2}{dt}$.

Applying the Voltage Law to this loop, we obtain the equation

(7.74)
$$10i + 0.04\frac{di_2}{dt} + 20i_2 = 30.$$

We observe that the three equations (7.72), (7.73), and (7.74) are not all independent. For example, we note that (7.73) may be obtained by subtracting (7.72) from (7.74). Thus we need to retain only the two equations (7.72) and (7.74).

We now apply Kirchhoff's Current Law to the junction point *B*. From this we see at once that

(7.75)
$$i = i_1 + i_2.$$

In accordance with this we replace i by $i_1 + i_2$ in (7.72) and (7.74) and thus obtain the linear system.

(7.76)
$$\begin{cases} 0.02\dfrac{di_1}{dt} + 10i_1 + 10i_2 = 30 \\[2mm] 10i_1 + 0.04\dfrac{di_2}{dt} + 30i_2 = 30. \end{cases}$$

Since the currents are initially zero, we have the initial conditions

(7.77)
$$i_1(0) = 0 \quad \text{and} \quad i_2(0) = 0.$$

Solution. We introduce operator notation and write the system (7.76) in the form

(7.78)
$$(0.02D + 10)i_1 + 10i_2 = 30$$
$$10i_1 + (0.04D + 30)i_2 = 30.$$

We apply the operator $(0.04D + 30)$ to the first equation of (7.78), multiply the second by 10, and subtract to obtain

$$[(0.04D + 30)(0.02D + 10) - 100]i_1 = (0.04D + 30)30 - 300$$

or

$$(0.0008D^2 + D + 200)i_1 = 600$$

or, finally,

(7.79) $$(D^2 + 1250D + 250{,}000)i_1 = 750{,}000.$$

We now solve the differential equation (7.79) for i_1. The auxiliary equation is

$$m^2 + 1250m + 250{,}000 = 0$$

or

$$(m + 250)(m + 1000) = 0.$$

Thus the complementary function of equation (7.79) is

$$i_{1,c} = c_1e^{-250t} + c_2e^{-1000t},$$

and a particular integral is obviously $i_{1,p} = 3$. Hence the general solution of the differential equation (7.79) is

(7.80) $$i_1 = c_1e^{-250t} + c_2e^{-1000t} + 3.$$

Now returning to the system (7.78), we multiply the first equation of the system by 10, apply the operator $(0.02D + 10)$ to the second equation, and subtract the first from the second. After simplifications we obtain the differential equation

$$(D^2 + 1250D + 250{,}000)i_2 = 0$$

for i_2. The general solution of this differential equation is clearly

(7.81) $$i_2 = k_1e^{-250t} + k_2e^{-1000t}.$$

Since the determinant of the operator "coefficients" in the system (7.78) is a second order operator, the general solution of the system (7.76) must contain two independent constants. We must substitute i_1 given by (7.80) and i_2 given by (7.81) into the equations of the system (7.76) to determine the relations which must exist among the constants c_1, c_2, k_1, k_2 in order that the pair (7.80) and (7.81) represent the general solution of (7.76). Substituting we find that

(7.82) $$k_1 = -\frac{1}{2}c_1, \; k_2 = c_2.$$

Thus the general solution of the system (7.76) is given by

(7.83)
$$i_1 = c_1e^{-250t} + c_2e^{-1000t} + 3$$
$$i_2 = -\frac{1}{2}c_1e^{-250t} + c_2e^{-1000t}.$$

Now applying the initial conditions (7.77), we find that $c_1 + c_2 + 3 = 0$ and $-\frac{1}{2}c_1 + c_2 = 0$ and hence $c_1 = -2$ and $c_2 = -1$. Thus the solution of the linear system (7.76) which satisfies the conditions (7.77) is

$$\begin{cases} i_1 = -2e^{-250t} - e^{-1000t} + 3 \\ i_2 = e^{-250t} - e^{-1000t}. \end{cases}$$

Finally, using (7.75) we find that

$$i = -e^{-250t} - 2e^{-1000t} + 3.$$

We observe that the current i_2 rapidly approaches zero. On the other hand, the currents, i_1 and $i = i_1 + i_2$ rapidly approach the value 3.

Exercises

1. Solve the problem of Example 7.16 for the case in which the object A_1 has mass $m_1 = 2$, the object A_2 has mass $m_2 = 1$, the spring S_1 has spring constant $k_1 = 4$, the spring S_2 has spring constant $k_2 = 2$, and the initial conditions are $x_1(0) = 1$, $x_1'(0) = 0$, $x_2(0) = 5$, and $x_2'(0) = 0$.

2. A projectile of mass m is fired into the air from a gun which is inclined at an angle θ with the horizontal, and suppose the initial velocity of the projectile is v_0 feet per second. Neglect all forces except that of gravity and the air resistance, and assume that this latter force (in pounds) is numerically equal to k times the velocity (in ft/sec).

(a) Taking the origin at the position of the gun, with the x axis horizontal and the y axis vertical, show that the differential equations of the resulting motion are

$$m\frac{d^2x}{dt^2} + k\frac{dx}{dt} = 0$$

$$m\frac{d^2y}{dt^2} + k\frac{dy}{dt} + mg = 0.$$

(b) Find the solution of the system of differential equations of part (a).

3. Determine the currents in the electrical network of Fig. 7.5 if E is an electromotive force of 100 V, R_1 is a resistor of 20 Ω, R_2 is a resistor of 40 Ω, L_1 is an inductor of 0.01 h, L_2 is an inductor of 0.02 h, and the currents are initially zero.

Figure 7.5

Figure 7.6

4. Set up differential equations for the currents in each of the electrical networks shown in Fig. 7.6. Do not solve the equations.

(a) For the network in Fig. 7.6(a) assume that E is an electromotive force of 15 V, R is a resistor of 20 Ω, L is an inductor of 0.02 h, and C is a capacitor of 10^{-4} farads.

(b) For the network in Fig. 7.6(b) assume that E is an electromotive force of $100\sin130t$ V, R_1 is a resistor of 20 Ω, R_2 is a resistor of 30 Ω, and L is an inductor of 0.05 h.

(c) For the network of Fig. 7.6(c), assume that E is an electromotive force of 100 V, R_1 is a resistor of 20 Ω, R_2 is a resistor of 10 Ω, C_1 is a capacitor of 10^{-4} farads, and C_2 is a capacitor of $2\cdot10^{-4}$ farads.

SELECTED READING

I. Basic Theory and Methods:
   Ford (17)   Martin and Reissner (38)
   Kaplan (30)

II. Advanced Theory:
   Bellman (4)   Hurewicz (25)
   Coddington and Levinson (13)   Ince (26)

PART II

Further Methods, Fundamental Theory, and Special Topics

8

APPROXIMATE METHODS OF SOLVING
FIRST-ORDER EQUATIONS

In Chapter 2 we considered certain special types of first-order differential equations having closed form solutions which can be obtained exactly. For a first-order differential equation which is not of one or another of these special types, it usually is not apparent how one should proceed in an attempt to obtain a solution exactly. Indeed, in most such cases the discovery of an exact closed form solution in terms of elementary functions would be an unexpected luxury! Therefore one considers the possibilities of obtaining approximate solutions of first-order differential equations. In this chapter we shall introduce several approximate methods. In the study of each method in this chapter our primary concern will be to obtain familiarity with the procedure itself and to develop skill in applying it. In general we shall not be concerned here with theoretical justifications and extended discussions of accuracy and error. We shall leave such matters, important as they are, to more specialized and advanced treatises and instead shall concentrate on the formal details of the various procedures.

8.1 Graphical Methods

A. Line Elements and Direction Fields

In Chapter 1 we considered briefly the geometric significance of the first-order differential equation

$$\frac{dy}{dx} = f(x,y), \tag{8.1}$$

where f is a real function of x and y. The explicit solutions of (8.1) are certain real functions, and the graphs of these solution functions are curves in the x,y-plane called the *integral curves* of (8.1). At each point (x,y) at which $f(x,y)$ is defined, the differential equation (8.1) defines the slope $f(x,y)$ at the point (x,y) of the integral curve of (8.1) which passes through this point. Thus we may construct the tangent to an integral curve of (8.1) at a given point (x,y) without actually knowing the solution function of which this integral curve is the graph.

We proceed to do this. Through the point (x,y) we draw a short segment of the tangent to the integral curve of (8.1) which passes through this point. That is, through (x,y) we construct a short segment the slope of which is $f(x,y)$, as given by the differential equation (8.1). Such a segment is called a *line element* of the differential equation (8.1).

For example, let us consider the differential equation

(8.2)
$$\frac{dy}{dx} = 2x + y.$$

Here $f(x,y) = 2x + y$, and the slope of the integral curve of (8.2) which passes through the point $(1,2)$ has at this point the value

$$f(1,2) = 4.$$

Thus through the point $(1,2)$ we construct a short segment of slope 4 or, in other words, of angle of inclination approximately $76°$ (see Figure 8.1). This short segment is the line element of the differential equation (8.2) at the point $(1,2)$. It is tangent to the integral curve of (8.2) which passes through this point.

Let us now return to the general equation (8.1). A line element of (8.1) can be constructed at every point (x,y) at which $f(x,y)$ in (8.1) is defined. Doing so for a selection of different points (x,y) leads to a configuration of selected line elements which indicates the directions of the integral curves at the various selected points. We shall refer to such a configuration as a *line element configuration*.

For each point (x,y) at which $f(x,y)$ is defined, the differential equation (8.1) thus defines a line segment with slope $f(x,y)$, or, in other words, a direction. Each such point, taken together with the corresponding direction so defined, constitutes the so-called

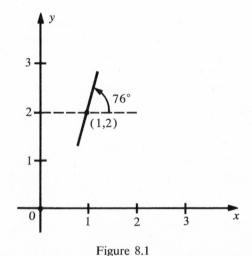

Figure 8.1

Line Element of Differential Equation (8.2) at Point (1,2).

direction field of the differential equation (8.1). We say that the differential equation (8.1) defines this direction field, and this direction field is represented graphically by a line element configuration. Clearly a more thorough and carefully constructed line element configuration gives a more accurate graphical representation of the direction field.

For a given differential equation of the form (8.1), let us assume that a "thorough and carefully constructed" line element configuration has been drawn. That is, we assume that line elements have been carefully constructed at a relatively large number of carefully chosen points. Then this resulting line element configuration will indicate the presence of a family of curves tangent to the various line elements constructed at the different points. This indicated family of curves is approximately the family of integral curves of the given differential equation. Actual smooth curves drawn tangent to the line elements as the configuration indicates will thus provide approximate graphs of the true integral curves.

Thus the construction of the line element configuration provides a procedure for approximately obtaining the solution of the differential equation in graphical form. We now summarize this basic graphical procedure and illustrate it with a simple example.

Summary of Basic Graphical Procedure.

(i) Carefully construct a line element configuration, proceeding until the family of "approximate integral curves" begins to appear.

(ii) Draw smooth curves as indicated by the configuration constructed in step (i).

Example 8.1.   Construct a line element configuration for the differential equation

$$(8.2) \qquad \frac{dy}{dx} = 2x + y,$$

and use this configuration to sketch the approximate integral curves.

Solution.   The slope of the exact integral curve of (8.2) at any point (x,y) is given by

$$f(x,y) = 2x + y.$$

We evaluate this slope at a number of selected points and so determine the approximate inclination of the corresponding line element at each point selected. We then construct the line elements so determined. From the resulting configuration we sketch several of the approximate integral curves. A few typical inclinations are listed in Table 8.1 and the completed configuration with the approximate integral curves appears in Figure 8.2.

Comments.   The basic graphical procedure outlined here is very general since it can be applied to any first order differential equation of the form (8.1). However, the method has several obvious disadvantages. For one thing, although it provides the approximate graphs of the integral curves, it does not furnish analytic expressions for the solutions, either exactly or approximately. Furthermore, it is extremely tedious and time-consuming. Finally, the graphs obtained are only approximations to the graphs of the exact integral curves, and the accuracy of these approximate graphs is uncertain. Of course, apparently better approximations can be obtained by constructing more complete and careful line element configurations, but this in turn increases the time and labor involved. We shall now consider a procedure by which the process may be speeded up considerably. This is the so-called *method of isoclines.*

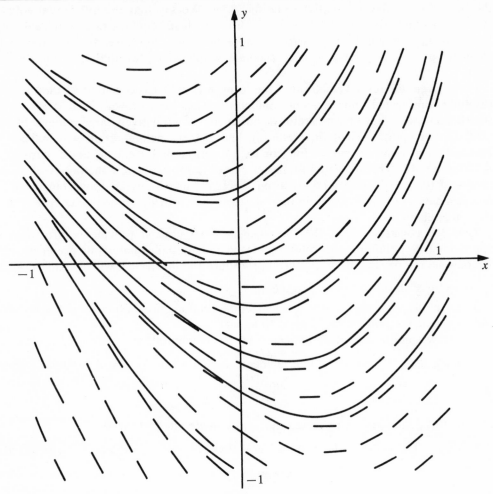

Figure 8.2

B. The Method of Isoclines

DEFINITION.   Consider the differential equation

(8.1)
$$\frac{dy}{dx} = f(x,y).$$

A curve along which the slope $f(x,y)$ has a constant value c is called an *isocline* of the differential equation (8.1). That is, the isoclines of (8.1) are the curves $f(x,y) = c$, for different values of the parameter c.

For example, the isoclines of the differential equation

(8.2)
$$\frac{dy}{dx} = 2x + y$$

Table 8.1

x	y	$\dfrac{dy}{dx}$ (slope)	approximate inclination of line element
$\dfrac{1}{2}$	$-\dfrac{1}{2}$	$\dfrac{1}{2}$	27°
$\dfrac{1}{2}$	0	1	45°
$\dfrac{1}{2}$	$\dfrac{1}{2}$	$\dfrac{3}{2}$	56°
$\dfrac{1}{2}$	1	2	63°
1	$-\dfrac{1}{2}$	$\dfrac{3}{2}$	56°
1	0	2	63°
1	$\dfrac{1}{2}$	$\dfrac{5}{2}$	68°
1	1	3	72°

are the straight lines $2x + y = c$. These are of course the straight lines $y = -2x + c$ of slope -2 and y-intercept c.

Caution. Note carefully that the isoclines of the differential equation (8.1) are *not* in general integral curves of (8.1). An isocline is merely a curve along which all of the line elements have a single, fixed inclination. This is precisely why isoclines are useful. Since the line elements along a given isocline all have the same inclination, a great number of line elements can be constructed with ease and speed, once the given isocline is drawn and *one* line element has been constructed upon it. This is exactly the procedure which we shall now outline.

Method of Isoclines Procedure.
(i) From the differential equation

(8.1)
$$\frac{dy}{dx} = f(x,y)$$

determine the family of isoclines

(8.3)
$$f(x,y) = c,$$

and carefully construct several members of this family.
(ii) Consider a particular isocline $f(x,y) = c_0$ of the family (8.3). At all points (x,y) on this isocline the line elements have the same slope c_0 and hence the same inclination

$\alpha_0 = \arctan c_0$, $0° \leq \alpha_0 < 180°$. At a series of points along this isocline construct line elements having this inclination α_0.

(iii) Repeat step (ii) for each of the isoclines of the family (8.3) constructed in step (i). In this way the line element configuration begins to take shape.

(iv) Finally, draw the smooth curves (the approximate integral curves) indicated by the line element configuration obtained in step (iii).

Example 8.2. Employ the method of isoclines to sketch the approximate integral curves of

(8.2) $$\frac{dy}{dx} = 2x + y$$

Solution. We have already noted that the isoclines of the differential equation (8.2) are the straight lines $2x + y = c$ or

(8.4) $$y = -2x + c.$$

Figure 8.3

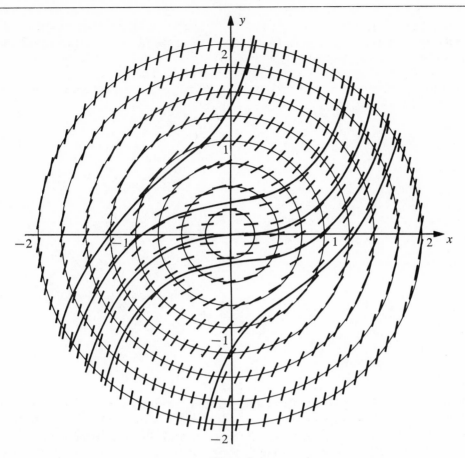

Figure 8.4

In Figure 8.3 we construct these lines for $c = -2, -3/2, -1, -1/2, 0, 1/2, 1, 3/2$, and
2. On each of these we then construct a number of line elements having the appropriate
inclination $\alpha = \text{arc tan } c$, $0° \leq \alpha < 180°$. For example for $c = 1$, the corresponding
isocline is $y = -2x + 1$, and on this line we construct line elements of inclination arc tan
$1 = 45°$. In the figure the isoclines are drawn with dashes and several of the approximate
integral curves are shown (drawn solidly).

Example 4.3.   Employ the method of isoclines to sketch the approximate integral
curves of

(8.5) $$\frac{dy}{dx} = x^2 + y^2.$$

Solution.   The isoclines of the differential equation (8.5) are the concentric circles
$x^2 + y^2 = c$, $c > 0$. In Figure 8.4 the circles for which $c = 1/16, 1/4, 9/16, 1, 25/16$,
$9/4, 49/16$, and 4 have been drawn with dashes, and several line elements having
the appropriate inclination have been drawn along each. For example, for $c = 4$, the
corresponding isocline is the circle $x^2 + y^2 = 4$ of radius 2, and along this circle the
line elements have inclination arctan $4 \approx 76°$. Several approximate integral curves are
shown (drawn solidly).

Exercises

Employ the method of isoclines to sketch the approximate integral curves of each of the differential equations in Exercises 1 through 12.

1. $\dfrac{dy}{dx} = 3x - y.$

2. $\dfrac{dy}{dx} = \dfrac{y}{x}.$

3. $\dfrac{dy}{dx} = \dfrac{y}{x^2}$

4. $\dfrac{dy}{dx} = x^2 + 2y^2$

5. $\dfrac{dy}{dx} = \dfrac{3x - y}{x + y}.$

6. $\dfrac{dy}{dx} = \sin x - y$

7. $\dfrac{dy}{dx} = y^3 - x^2$

8. $\dfrac{dy}{dx} = \dfrac{3x + 2y + x^2}{x + 2y}$

9. $\dfrac{dy}{dx} = \dfrac{3x + y + x^3}{5x - y}$

10. $\dfrac{dy}{dx} = \dfrac{\sin x + y}{x - y}$

11. $\dfrac{dy}{dx} = \dfrac{(1 - x^2)y - x}{y}$

12. $\dfrac{dy}{dx} = \dfrac{10(1 - x^2)y - x}{y}.$

8.2 Power Series Methods

A. Introduction

Although the graphical methods of the preceding section are very general, they suffer from several serious disadvantages. Not only are they tedious and subject to possible errors of construction, but they merely provide us with the approximate *graphs* of the solutions and do not furnish any analytic *expressions* for these solutions. Although we have now passed the naive state of searching for a closed form solution in terms of elementary functions, we might still hope for solutions which can be represented as some type of infinite series. In particular, we shall seek solutions which are representable as power series.

We point out that not all first order differential equations possess solutions which can be represented as power series, and it is beyond the scope of this book to consider conditions under which a first-order differential equation does possess such solutions. In order to explain the power series methods we shall *assume* that power series solutions actually do exist, realizing that this is an assumption which is not always justified.

Specifically, we consider the initial value problem consisting of the differential equation

(8.1) $$\frac{dy}{dx} = f(x,y)$$

and the initial condition

(8.6) $$y(x_0) = y_0$$

and *assume* that the differential equation (8.1) possesses a solution which is representable as a power series in powers of $(x - x_0)$. That is, we assume that the differential equation

(8.1) has a solution of the form

(8.7) $y = c_0 + c_1(x - x_0) + c_2(x - x_0)^2 + \cdots = \sum_{n=0}^{\infty} c_n(x - x_0)^n$

which is valid in some interval about the point x_0. We now consider methods of determining the coefficients $c_0, c_1, c_2, \ldots$ in (8.7) so that the series (8.7) actually does satisfy the differential equation (8.1).

B. The Taylor Series Method

We thus assume that the initial value problem consisting of the differential equation (8.1) and the initial condition (8.6) has a solution of the form (8.7) which is valid in some interval about x_0. Then by Taylor's Theorem, for each x in this interval the value $y(x)$ of this solution is given by

(8.8) $y(x) = y(x_0) + y'(x_0)(x - x_0) + \dfrac{y''(x_0)}{2!}(x - x_0)^2 + \cdots = \sum_{n=0}^{\infty} \dfrac{y^{(n)}(x_0)}{n!}(x - x_0)^n.$

From the initial condition (8.6), we have

$$y(x_0) = y_0,$$

and from the differential equation (8.1) itself,

$$y'(x_0) = f(x_0, y_0).$$

Substituting these values of $y(x_0)$ and $y'(x_0)$ into the series in (8.8), we obtain the first two coefficients of the desired series solution (8.7). Now differentiating the differential equation (8.1), we obtain

(8.9)
$$\frac{d^2y}{dx^2} = \frac{d}{dx}[f(x,y)] = f_x(x,y) + f_y(x,y)\frac{dy}{dx}$$
$$= f_x(x,y) + f_y(x,y)f(x,y),$$

where we use subscripts to denote partial differentiations. From this we obtain

$$y''(x_0) = f_x(x_0, y_0) + f_y(x_0, y_0)f(x_0, y_0).$$

Substituting this value of $y''(x_0)$ into (8.8), we obtain the third coefficient in the series solution (8.7). Proceeding in like manner, we differentiate (8.9) successively to obtain

$$\frac{d^3y}{dx^3}, \frac{d^4y}{dx^4}, \ldots, \frac{d^ny}{dx^n}, \ldots.$$

From these we obtain the values

$$y'''(x_0), y^{iv}(x_0), \cdots, y^{(n)}(x_0), \cdots.$$

Substituting these values into (8.8), we obtain the fourth and following coefficients in the series solution (8.7). Thus the coefficients in the series solution (8.7) are successively determined.

Example 8.4. Use the Taylor Series Method to obtain a power series solution of the initial value problem

(8.10)
$$\frac{dy}{dx} = x^2 + y^2$$

(8.11)
$$y(0) = 1,$$

in powers of x.

Solution. Since we seek a solution in powers of x, we set $x_0 = 0$ in (8.7) and thus assume a solution of the form

$$y = c_0 + c_1 x + c_2 x^2 + \cdots = \sum_{n=0}^{\infty} c_n x^n$$

By Taylor's Theorem, we know that for each x in the interval where this solution is valid

(8.12)
$$y(x) = y(0) + y'(0)x + \frac{y''(0)}{2!}x^2 + \cdots = \sum_{n=0}^{\infty} \frac{y^{(n)}(0)}{n!}x^n.$$

The initial condition (8.11) states that

(8.13)
$$y(0) = 1,$$

and from the differential equation (8.10) we see that

(8.14)
$$y'(0) = 0^2 + 1^2 = 1.$$

Differentiating (8.10) successively, we obtain

(8.15)
$$\frac{d^2y}{dx^2} = 2x + 2y\frac{dy}{dx},$$

(8.16)
$$\frac{d^3y}{dx^3} = 2 + 2y\frac{d^2y}{dx^2} + 2\left(\frac{dy}{dx}\right)^2,$$

(8.17)
$$\frac{d^4y}{dx^4} = 2y\frac{d^3y}{dx^3} + 6\frac{dy}{dx}\frac{d^2y}{dx^2}.$$

Substituting $x = 0$, $y = 1$, $\frac{dy}{dx} = 1$ into (8.15), we obtain

(8.18)
$$y''(0) = 2(0) + 2(1)(1) = 2.$$

Substituting $y = 1$, $\frac{dy}{dx} = 1$, $\frac{d^2y}{dx^2} = 2$ into (8.16), we obtain

(8.19)
$$y'''(0) = 2 + 2(1)(2) + 2(1)^2 = 8.$$

Finally, substituting $y = 1$, $\frac{dy}{dx} = 1$, $\frac{d^2y}{dx^2} = 2$, $\frac{d^3y}{dx^3} = 8$ into (8.17) , we find that

(8.20)
$$y^{iv}(0) = (2)(1)(8) + (6)(1)(2) = 28.$$

By successive differentiation of (8.17), we could proceed to determine

$$\frac{d^5y}{dx^5}, \frac{d^6y}{dx^6}, \cdots,$$

and hence obtain

$$y^{(v)}(0), y^{(vi)}(0), \cdots.$$

Now substituting the values given by (8.13), (8.14), (8.18), (8.19), and (8.20) into (8.12), we obtain the first five coefficients of the desired series solution. We thus find the solution

(8.21)
$$y = 1 + x + \frac{2}{2!}x^2 + \frac{8}{3!}x^3 + \frac{28}{4!}x^4 + \cdots$$

$$= 1 + x + x^2 + \frac{4}{3}x^3 + \frac{7}{6}x^4 + \cdots.$$

C. The Method of Undetermined Coefficients

We now consider an alternate method for obtaining the coefficients $c_0, c_1, c_2, \ldots$ in the assumed series solution

(8.7)
$$y = c_0 + c_1(x - x_0) + c_2(x - x_0)^2 + \cdots = \sum_{n=0}^{\infty} c_n(x - x_0)^n$$

of the problem consisting of the differential equation (8.1) with initial condition (8.6). We shall refer to this alternate method as the Method of Undetermined Coefficients. In order to apply it we assume that $f(x,y)$ in the differential equation (8.1) is representable in the form

(8.22)
$$f(x,y) = a_{00} + a_{10}(x - x_0) + a_{01}(y - y_0) + a_{20}(x - x_0)^2$$
$$+ a_{11}(x - x_0)(y - y_0) + a_{02}(y - y_0)^2 + \cdots.$$

The coefficients a_{ij} in (8.22) may be found by Taylor's Formula for functions of two variables, although in many simple cases the use of this formula is unnecessary. Using the representation (8.22) for $f(x,y)$, the differential equation (8.1) takes the form

(8.23)
$$\frac{dy}{dx} = a_{00} + a_{10}(x - x_0) + a_{01}(y - y_0) + a_{20}(x - x_0)^2$$
$$+ a_{11}(x - x_0)(y - y_0) + a_{02}(y - y_0)^2 + \cdots.$$

Now assuming that the series (8.7) converges in some interval $|x - x_0| < r$ $(r > 0)$ about x_0, we may differentiate (8.7) term-by-term and the resulting series will also converge on $|x - x_0| < r$ and represent $y'(x)$ there. Doing this we thus obtain

(8.24)
$$\frac{dy}{dx} = c_1 + 2c_2(x - x_0) + 3c_3(x - x_0)^2 + \cdots.$$

We note that in order for the series (8.7) to satisfy the initial condition (8.6) that $y = y_0$ at $x = x_0$, we must have $c_0 = y_0$ and hence

(8.25)
$$y - y_0 = c_1(x - x_0) + c_2(x - x_0)^2 + \cdots.$$

Now substituting (8.7) and (8.24) into the differential equation (8.23), and making use of (8.25), we find that

(8.26)
$$c_1 + 2c_2(x - x_0) + 3c_3(x - x_0)^2 + \cdots = a_{00} + a_{10}(x - x_0)$$
$$+ a_{01}[c_1(x - x_0) + c_2(x - x_0)^2 + \cdots] + a_{20}(x - x_0)^2$$
$$+ a_{11}(x - x_0)[c_1(x - x_0) + c_2(x - x_0)^2 + \cdots]$$
$$+ a_{02}[c_1(x - x_0) + c_2(x - x_0)^2 + \cdots]^2 + \cdots.$$

Performing the multiplications indicated in the right member of (8.26) and then combining like powers of $(x - x_0)$, we see that (8.26) takes the form

(8.27)
$$c_1 + 2c_2(x - x_0) + 3c_3(x - x_0)^2 + \cdots = a_{00} + (a_{10} + a_{01}c_1)(x - x_0)$$
$$+ (a_{01}c_2 + a_{20} + a_{11}c_1 + a_{02}c_1^2)(x - x_0)^2 + \cdots.$$

In order that (8.27) be satisfied for all values of x in the interval $|x - x_0| < r$, the coefficients of like powers of $(x - x_0)$ on both sides of (8.27) must be equal. Equating these coefficients, we obtain

(8.28)
$$c_1 = a_{00},$$
$$2c_2 = a_{10} + a_{01}c_1,$$
$$3c_3 = a_{01}c_2 + a_{20} + a_{11}c_1 + a_{02}c_1^2,$$
$$\cdot$$
$$\cdot$$
$$\cdot$$

From the conditions (8.28) we determine successively the coefficients $c_1, c_2, c_3, \ldots$ of the series solution (8.7). From the first of conditions (8.28) we first obtain c_1 as the known coefficient a_{00}. Then from the second of conditions (8.28) we obtain c_2 in terms of the known coefficients a_{10} and a_{01} and the coefficient c_1 just determined. Thus we obtain $c_2 = \frac{1}{2}(a_{10} + a_{01}a_{00})$. In like manner, we proceed to determine $c_3, c_4, \ldots$. We observe that in general each coefficient c_n is thus given in terms of the known coefficients a_{ij} in the expansion (8.22) and the previously determined coefficients $c_1, c_2, \ldots, c_{n-1}$.

Finally, we substitute the coefficients $c_0, c_1, c_2, \ldots$ so determined into the series (8.7) and thereby obtain the desired solution.

Example 8.5. Use the method of undetermined coefficients to obtain a power series solution of the initial-value problem

(8.10)
$$\frac{dy}{dx} = x^2 + y^2,$$

(8.11)
$$y(0) = 1,$$

in powers of x.

Solution. Since $x_0 = 0$, the assumed solution (8.7) is of the form

(8.29)
$$y = c_0 + c_1x + c_2x^2 + c_3x^3 + \cdots.$$

In order to satisfy the initial condition (8.11), we must have $c_0 = 1$ and hence the series (8.29) takes the form

(8.30)
$$y = 1 + c_1x + c_2x^2 + c_3x^3 + \cdots.$$

Differentiating (8.30), we obtain

$$(8.31) \qquad \frac{dy}{dx} = c_1 + 2c_2x + 3c_3x^2 + 4c_4x^3 + \cdots.$$

For the differential equation (8.10) we have $f(x,y) = x^2 + y^2$. Since $x_0 = 0$ and $y_0 = 1$, we must expand $x^2 + y^2$ in the form

$$\sum_{i,j=0}^{\infty} a_{ij}x^i(y-1)^j.$$

Since $y^2 = (y-1)^2 + 2(y-1) + 1$, the desired expansion is given by

$$x^2 + y^2 = 1 + 2(y-1) + x^2 + (y-1)^2.$$

Thus the differential equation (8.10) takes the form

$$(8.32) \qquad \frac{dy}{dx} = 1 + 2(y-1) + x^2 + (y-1)^2.$$

Now substituting (8.30) and (8.31) into the differential equation (8.32), we obtain

$$(8.33) \qquad c_1 + 2c_2x + 3c_3x^2 + 4c_4x^3 + \cdots = 1 + 2(c_1x + c_2x^2 + c_3x^3 + \cdots)$$
$$+ x^2 + (c_1x + c_2x^2 + \cdots)^2 + \cdots.$$

Performing the indicated multiplications and collecting like powers of x in the right member of (8.33), we see that it takes the form

$$(8.34) \qquad c_1 + 2c_2x + 3c_3x^2 + 4c_4x^3 + \cdots = 1 + 2c_1x + (2c_2 + 1 + c_1^2)x^2$$
$$+ (2c_3 + 2c_1c_2)x^3 + \cdots.$$

Equating the coefficients of the like powers of x in both members of (8.34), we obtain the conditions

$$(8.35) \qquad
\begin{aligned}
c_1 &= 1, \\
2c_2 &= 2c_1 \\
3c_3 &= 2c_2 + 1 + c_1^2 \\
4c_4 &= 2c_3 + 2c_1c_2
\end{aligned}$$

$$\vdots$$

From the conditions (8.35), we obtain successively

$$(8.36) \qquad
\begin{aligned}
c_1 &= 1, \\
c_2 &= c_1 = 1, \\
c_3 &= \frac{1}{3}(2c_2 + 1 + c_1^2) = \frac{4}{3}, \\
c_4 &= \frac{1}{4}(2c_3 + 2c_1c_2) = \frac{1}{4}\left(\frac{14}{3}\right) = \frac{7}{6}.
\end{aligned}$$

$$\vdots$$

Substituting the coefficients so determined in (8.36) into the series (8.30), we obtain the first five terms of the desired series solution. We thus find

$$y = 1 + x + x^2 + \frac{4}{3}x^3 + \frac{7}{6}x^4 + \cdots.$$

We note that this is of course the same series previously obtained by the Taylor Series Method and already given by (8.21).

Remark. We have made but little mention of the interval of convergence of the series involved in our discussion. We have merely assumed that a power series solution exists and converges on some interval $|x - x_0| < r$ $(r > 0)$ about the initial point x_0. In a practical problem the interval of convergence is of vital concern and should be determined, if possible. Another matter of great importance in a practical problem is the determination of the number of terms which have to be found in order to be certain of a sufficient degree of accuracy. We shall not consider these matters here. Our primary purpose has been merely to explain the details of the methods. We refer the reader to more advanced treatises for discussions of the important questions of convergence and accuracy.

Exercises

Obtain a power series solution in powers of x of each of the initial value problems in Exercises 1 through 7 by (a) the Taylor Series Method and (b) the method of undetermined coefficients.

1. $\dfrac{dy}{dx} = x + y,$

    $y(0) = 1.$

2. $\dfrac{dy}{dx} = x^2 + 2y^2,$

    $y(0) = 4.$

3. $\dfrac{dy}{dx} = 1 + xy^2,$

    $y(0) = 2.$

4. $\dfrac{dy}{dx} = x^3 + y^3,$

    $y(0) = 3.$

5. $\dfrac{dy}{dx} = x + \sin y,$

    $y(0) = 0.$

6. $\dfrac{dy}{dx} = 1 + x\sin y,$

    $y(0) = 0.$

7. $\dfrac{dy}{dx} = e^x + x\cos y,$

    $y(0) = 0.$

Obtain a power series solution in powers of $x - 1$ of each of the initial value problems in Exercises 8 through 12 by (a) the Taylor Series Method and (b) the method of undetermined coefficients.

8. $\dfrac{dy}{dx} = x^2 + y^2,$

    $y(1) = 4.$

9. $\dfrac{dy}{dx} = x^3 + y^2,$

    $y(1) = 1.$

10. $\dfrac{dy}{dx} = x + y + y^2,$ 11. $\dfrac{dy}{dx} = x + \cos y,$

   $y(1) = 1.$ $y(1) = \pi.$

12. $\dfrac{dy}{dx} = x^2 + x\sin y,$

   $y(1) = \dfrac{\pi}{2}.$

8.3   The Method of Successive Approximations

A. The Method

We again consider the initial value problem consisting of the differential equation

(8.1) $$\frac{dy}{dx} = f(x,y)$$

and the initial condition

(8.6) $$y(x_0) = y_0.$$

We now outline the Picard Method of Successive Approximations for finding a solution of this problem which is valid on some interval which includes the initial point x_0.

The first step of the Picard Method is quite unlike anything which we have done before and at first glance it appears to be rather fruitless. For the first step actually consists of making a guess at the solution! That is, we choose a function ϕ_0 and call it a "zeroth approximation" to the actual solution. How do we make this guess? In other words, what function do we choose? Actually, many different choices could be made. The only thing that we know about the actual solution is that in order to satisfy the initial condition (8.6) it must assume the value y_0 at $x = x_0$. Therefore it would seem reasonable to choose for ϕ_0 a function which assumes this value y_0 at $x = x_0$. Although this requirement is not essential, it certainly seems as sensible as anything else. In particular, it is often convenient to choose for ϕ_0 the constant function which has the value y_0 for all x. While this choice is certainly not essential, it is often the simplest, most reasonable choice which quickly comes to mind.

In summary, then, the first step of the Picard Method is to choose a function ϕ_0 which will serve as a "zeroth approximation."

Having thus chosen a "zeroth approximation" ϕ_0, we now determine a "first approximation" ϕ_1 in the following manner. We determine $\phi_1(x)$ so that (i) it satisfies the differential equation obtained from (8.1) by replacing y in $f(x,y)$ by $\phi_0(x)$, and (ii) it satisfies the initial condition (8.6). Thus ϕ_1 is determined such that

(8.37) $$\frac{d}{dx}[\phi_1(x)] = f[x, \phi_0(x)]$$

and

(8.38) $$\phi_1(x_0) = y_0.$$

We now assume that $f[x, \phi_0(x)]$ is continuous. Then ϕ_1 satisfies (8.37) and (8.38) if and only if

$$(8.39) \qquad \phi_1(x) = y_0 + \int_{x_0}^{x} f[t, \phi_0(t)]dt.$$

From this equation the "first approximation" ϕ_1 is determined.

We now determine the "second approximation" ϕ_2 in a similar manner. The function ϕ_2 is determined such that

$$(8.40) \qquad \frac{d}{dx}[\phi_2(x)] = f[x, \phi_1(x)]$$

and

$$(8.41) \qquad \phi_2(x_0) = y_0.$$

Assuming that $f[x, \phi_1(x)]$ is continuous, then ϕ_2 satisfies (8.40) and (8.41) if and only if

$$(8.42) \qquad \phi_2(x) = y_0 + \int_{x_0}^{x} f[t, \phi_1(t)]dt.$$

From this equation the "second approximation" ϕ_2 is determined.

We now proceed in like manner to determine a "third approximation" ϕ_3, a fourth approximation" ϕ_4, and so on. The "nth approximation" ϕ_n is determined from

$$(8.43) \qquad \phi_n(x) = y_0 + \int_{x_0}^{x} f[t, \phi_{n-1}(t)]dt,$$

where ϕ_{n-1} is the "$(n-1)$st approximation." We thus obtain a sequence of functions

$$\phi_0, \phi_1, \phi_2, \cdots, \phi_n, \cdots,$$

where ϕ_0 is chosen, ϕ_1 is determined from (8.39), ϕ_2 is determined from (8.42), . . . , and in general ϕ_n is determined from (8.43) for $n \geq 1$.

Now just how does this sequence of functions relate to the actual solution of the initial value problem under consideration? In Chapter 10 we shall prove under certain general conditions and for x restricted to a sufficiently small interval about the initial point x_0 that (i) as $n \to \infty$ the sequence of functions ϕ_n defined by (8.43) for $n \geq 1$ approaches a limit function ϕ, and (ii) this limit function ϕ satisfies both the differential equation (8.1) and the initial condition (8.6). That is, under suitable restrictions the function ϕ defined by

$$\phi = \lim_{n \to \infty} \phi_n$$

is the exact solution of the initial value problem under consideration. Furthermore, the error in approximating the exact solution ϕ by the nth approximation ϕ_n will be arbitrarily small provided that n is sufficiently large and that x is sufficiently close to the initial point x_0.

B. An Example; Remarks on The Method

We illustrate the Picard Method of Successive Approximations by applying it to the initial value problem of Examples 8.4 and 8.5.

Example 8.6.   Use the Method of Successive Approximations to find a sequence of functions which approaches the solution of the initial-value problem

(8.10)
$$\frac{dy}{dx} = x^2 + y^2,$$

(8.11)
$$y(0) = 1.$$

Solution.   Our first step is to choose a function for the "zeroth approximation" ϕ_0. Since the initial value of y is 1, it would seem reasonable to choose for ϕ_0 the constant function which has the value 1 for all x. Thus, we let ϕ_0 be such that

$$\phi_0(x) = 1$$

for all x. The "nth approximation" ϕ_n for $n \geq 1$ is given by formula (8.43). Since $f(x,y) = x^2 + y^2$ in the differential equation (8.10), the formula (8.43) becomes in this case

$$\phi_n(x) = 1 + \int_0^x \{t^2 + [\phi_{n-1}(t)]^2\}dt, \quad n \geq 1.$$

Using this formula for $n = 1, 2, 3, \ldots$, we obtain successively

$$\phi_1(x) = 1 + \int_0^x \{t^2 + [\phi_0(t)]^2\}dt = 1 + \int_0^x (t^2 + 1)dt = 1 + x + \frac{x^3}{3},$$

$$\phi_2(x) = 1 + \int_0^x \{t^2 + [\phi_1(t)]^2\}dt = 1 + \int_0^x \left[t^2 + \left(1 + t + \frac{t^3}{3}\right)^2\right]dt$$

$$= 1 + \int_0^x \left(1 + 2t + 2t^2 + \frac{2t^3}{3} + \frac{2t^4}{3} + \frac{t^6}{9}\right)dt$$

$$= 1 + x + x^2 + \frac{2x^3}{3} + \frac{x^4}{6} + \frac{2x^5}{15} + \frac{x^7}{63},$$

$$\phi_3(x) = 1 + \int_0^x \{t^2 + [\phi_2(t)]^2\}dt$$

$$= 1 + \int_0^x \left[t^2 + \left(1 + t + t^2 + \frac{2t^3}{3} + \frac{t^4}{6} + \frac{2t^5}{15} + \frac{t^7}{63}\right)^2\right]dt$$

$$= 1 + \int_0^x \left[1 + 2t + 4t^2 + \frac{10t^3}{3} + \frac{8t^4}{3} + \frac{29t^5}{15} + \frac{47t^6}{45} + \frac{164t^7}{315}\right.$$

$$\left. + \frac{299t^8}{1260} + \frac{8t^9}{105} + \frac{184t^{10}}{4725} + \frac{t^{11}}{189} + \frac{4t^{12}}{945} + \frac{t^{14}}{3969}\right]dt$$

$$= 1 + x + x^2 + \frac{4x^3}{3} + \frac{5x^4}{6} + \frac{8x^5}{15} + \frac{29x^6}{90} + \frac{47x^7}{315} + \frac{41x^8}{630} + \frac{299x^9}{11,340}$$

$$+ \frac{4x^{10}}{525} + \frac{184x^{11}}{51,975} + \frac{x^{12}}{2268} + \frac{4x^{13}}{12,285} + \frac{x^{15}}{59,535},$$

.
.
.

We have chosen the "zeroth approximation" ϕ_0 and then found the next three approximations ϕ_1, ϕ_2, and ϕ_3 explicitly. We could proceed in like manner to find ϕ_4, ϕ_5, ... explicitly and thus determine successively the members of the sequence $\{\phi_n\}$ which approaches the exact solution of the initial value problem under consideration. However, we believe that the procedure is now clear, and for rather obvious reasons we shall not proceed further with this problem.

Remarks. The greatest disadvantage of the Method of Successive Approximations is that it leads to tedious, involved, and sometimes impossible calculations. This is amply illustrated in Example 8.6. At best the calculations are usually very complicated, and in general it is impossible to carry through more than a few of the successive integrations exactly. Nevertheless, the method is of practical importance, for the first few approximations alone are sometimes quite accurate.

However, the principal use of the Method of Successive Approximations is in proving existence theorems. In Chapter 10 we shall employ the method to prove the basic existence theorem for first order initial value problems.

Exercises

For each of the initial-value problems in Exercises 1 through 8 use the Method of Successive Approximations to find the first three members ϕ_1, ϕ_2, ϕ_3 of a sequence of functions which approaches the exact solution of the problem.

1. $\dfrac{dy}{dx} = xy,$

   $y(0) = 1.$

2. $\dfrac{dy}{dx} = x + y,$

   $y(0) = 1.$

3. $\dfrac{dy}{dx} = x + y^2,$

   $y(0) = 0.$

4. $\dfrac{dy}{dx} = 1 + xy^2,$

   $y(0) = 0.$

5. $\dfrac{dy}{dx} = e^x + y^2,$

   $y(0) = 0.$

6. $\dfrac{dy}{dx} = \sin x + y^2,$

   $y(0) = 0.$

7. $\dfrac{dy}{dx} = 2x + y^3,$

   $y(0) = 0.$

8. $\dfrac{dy}{dx} = 1 + 6xy^4,$

   $y(0) = 0.$

8.4   Numerical Methods

A. Introduction; A Problem for Illustration

In this section we introduce certain basic numerical methods for approximating the solution of the initial value problem consisting of the differential equation

(8.1) $$\frac{dy}{dx} = f(x,y)$$

and the initial condition

(8.6)
$$y(x_0) = y_0.$$

Numerical methods employ the differential equation (8.1) and the condition (8.6) to obtain approximations to the values of the solution corresponding to various, selected values of x. To be more specific, let y denote the solution of the problem and let h denote a positive *increment* in x. The initial condition (8.6) tells us that $y = y_0$ at $x = x_0$. A numerical method will employ the differential equation (8.1) and the condition (8.6) to approximate successively the values of y at $x_1 = x_0 + h$, $x_2 = x_1 + h$, $x_3 = x_2 + h, \ldots$.

Let us denote these approximate values of y by $y_1, y_2, y_3, \ldots$, respectively. That is, we let y_n denote the approximate value of y at $x = x_n = x_0 + nh$, $n = 1, 2, 3, \ldots$. Now all that we know about y before starting is that $y = y_0$ at $x = x_0$. In order to get started we need a method which requires only the value y_n in order to obtain the next value y_{n+1}. For we can apply such a method with $n = 0$ and use the initial value y_0 to obtain the next value y_1. A method which uses only y_n to find y_{n+1}, and which therefore enables us to get started, is called a *starting method*. Once we have used a starting method to find y_1, we can repeat it with $n = 1$ to find y_2, with $n = 2$ to find y_3, and so forth. However, once we have several calculated values at our disposal, it is often convenient to change over to a method which uses both y_n and one or more *preceding* values y_{n-1}, $y_{n-2}, \ldots$ to find the next value y_{n+1}. Such a method, which enables us to continue once we have got sufficiently well started, is called a *continuing method*. Most of our attention in this text will be devoted to starting methods.

Our principal objective in this section is to present the actual details of certain basic numerical methods for solving first-order initial-value problems. In general, we shall not consider the theoretical justifications of these methods, nor shall we enter into detailed discussions of matters such as accuracy and error.

Before turning to the details of the numerical methods to be considered, we introduce a simple initial value problem which we shall use for purposes of illustration throughout this section. We consider the problem

(8.2)
$$\frac{dy}{dx} = 2x + y,$$

(8.44)
$$y(0) = 1.$$

We have already employed the differential equation (8.2) to illustrate the graphical methods of Section 8.1. We note at once that it is a linear differential equation and hence it can be solved exactly. Using the methods of Section 2.3, we find at once that its general solution is

(8.45)
$$y = -2(x + 1) + ce^x,$$

where c is an arbitrary constant. Applying the initial condition (8.44) to (8.45), we find that the exact solution of the initial-value problem consisting of (8.2) and (8.44) is

(8.46)
$$y = -2(x + 1) + 3e^x.$$

We have chosen the problem consisting of (8.2) and (8.44) for illustrative purposes for two reasons. First, the differential equation (8.2) is so simple, that numerical methods may be applied to it without introducing involved computations which might obscure the main steps of the method to a beginner. Second, since the exact solution (8.46) of the problem has been found, we can compare approximate solution values obtained numerically with this exact solution and thereby gain some insight into the accuracy of numerical methods.

Of course in practice we would not solve a simple linear differential equation such as (8.2) by a numerical method. The methods of this section are actually designed for equations which can *not* be solved exactly and for equations which, although solvable exactly, have exact solutions so unwieldy that they are practically useless.

B. The Euler Method

The Euler Method is very simple but not very practical. An understanding of it, however, paves the way for an understanding of the more practical (but also more complicated) methods which follow.

Let y denote the exact solution of the initial value problem which consists of the differential equation

$$(8.1) \qquad \frac{dy}{dx} = f(x,y)$$

and the initial condition

$$(8.6) \qquad y(x_0) = y_0.$$

Let h denote a positive increment in x and let $x_1 = x_0 + h$. Then

$$\int_{x_0}^{x_1} f(x,y)dx = \int_{x_0}^{x_1} \frac{dy}{dx}dx = y(x_1) - y(x_0).$$

Since y_0 denotes the value $y(x_0)$ of the exact solution y at x_0, we have

$$(8.47) \qquad y(x_1) = y_0 + \int_{x_0}^{x_1} f(x,y)dx.$$

If we assume that $f(x,y)$ varies slowly on the interval $x_0 \leq x \leq x_1$, then we can approximate $f(x,y)$ in (8.47) by its value $f(x_0,y_0)$ at the left end point x_0. Then

$$y(x_1) \approx y_0 + \int_{x_0}^{x_1} f(x_0,y_0)dx.$$

But

$$\int_{x_0}^{x_1} f(x_0,y_0)dx = f(x_0,y_0)(x_1 - x_0) = hf(x_0,y_0).$$

Thus

$$y(x_1) \approx y_0 + hf(x_0,y_0).$$

Thus we obtain the approximate value y_1 of y at $x_1 = x_0 + h$ by the formula

$$(8.48) \qquad y_1 = y_0 + hf(x_0,y_0).$$

Having obtained y_1 by formula (8.48), we proceed in like manner to obtain y_2 by the formula $y_2 = y_1 + hf(x_1,y_1)$, y_3 by the formula $y_3 = y_2 + hf(x_2,y_2)$, and so forth. In general we find y_{n+1} in terms of y_n by the formula

$$(8.49) \qquad y_{n+1} = y_n + hf(x_n,y_n).$$

Before illustrating the method, we give a useful geometric interpretation. The graph of the exact solution y is a curve C in the xy plane (see Figure 8.5). Let P denote the initial point (x_0, y_0) and let T be the tangent to C at P. Let Q be the point at which the line $x = x_1$ intersects C and let N be the point at which this line intersects T. Then the exact value of y at x_1 is represented by LQ. The approximate value y_1 is represented by LN, since $LN = LM + MN = y_0 + PM \tan \theta = y_0 + hf(x_0, y_0)$. The error in approximating the exact value of y at x_1 by y_1 is thus represented by NQ. The figure suggests that if h is sufficiently small, then this error NQ will also be small and hence that the approximation will be good.

It is clear that the Euler Method is indeed simple, but it should also be apparent from our discussion why it is not very practical. If the increment h is *not* very small, then the errors in the approximations generally will not be small and thus the method will lead to quite inaccurate results. If the increment h *is* very small, then the computations will be more lengthy and so the method will involve tedious and time-consuming labor.

Example 8.7.   Apply the Euler Method to the initial-value problem

(8.2) $$\frac{dy}{dx} = 2x + y,$$

(8.44) $$y(0) = 1.$$

Employ the method to approximate the value of the solution y at $x = 0.2, 0.4, 0.6, 0.8,$

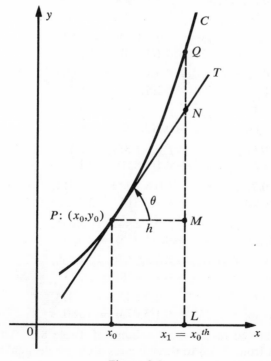

Figure 8.5

and 1 using (i) $h = 0.2$, and (ii) $h = 0.1$. Obtain results to three figures after the decimal point. Compare with the exact value determined from (8.46).

Solution. (i) We use formula (8.49) with $f(x,y) = 2x + y$ and $h = 0.2$. From the initial condition (8.44), we have $x_0 = 0$, $y_0 = 1$. We now proceed with the calculations.

(a) $x_1 = x_0 + h = 0.2$, $f(x_0,y_0) = f(0,1) = 1.000$,
$y_1 = y_0 + hf(x_0,y_0) = 1.000 + 0.2(1.000) = 1.200$.

(b) $x_2 = x_1 + h = 0.4$, $f(x_1,y_1) = f(0.2,1.200) = 1.600$,
$y_2 = y_1 + hf(x_1,y_1) = 1.200 + 0.2(1.600) = 1.520$.

(c) $x_3 = x_2 + h = 0.6$, $f(x_2,y_2) = f(0.4,1.520) = 2.320$,
$y_3 = y_2 + hf(x_2,y_2) = 1.520 + 0.2(2.320) = 1.984$.

(d) $x_4 = x_3 + h = 0.8$, $f(x_3,y_3) = f(0.6,1.984) = 3.184$,
$y_4 = y_3 + hf(x_3,y_3) = 1.984 + 0.2(3.184) = 2.621$,

(e) $x_5 = x_4 + h = 1.0$, $f(x_4,y_4) = f(0.8,2.621) = 4.221$,
$y_5 = y_4 + hf(x_4,y_4) = 2.621 + 0.2(4.221) = 3.465$.

These results, corresponding to the various values of x_n, are collected in the second column of Table 8.2.

(ii) We now use formula (8.49) with $f(x,y) = 2x + y$ and $h = 0.1$. Of course we again have $x_0 = 0$, $y_0 = 1$. The calculations follow.

(a) $x_1 = x_0 + h = 0.1$, $f(x_0,y_0) = f(0,1) = 1.000$,
$y_1 = y_0 + hf(x_0,y_0) = 1.000 + 0.1(1.000) = 1.100$.

(b) $x_2 = x_1 + h = 0.2$, $f(x_1,y_1) = f(0.1,1.100) = 1.300$,
$y_2 = y_1 + hf(x_1,y_1) = 1.100 + 0.1(1.300) = 1.230$.

(c) $x_3 = x_2 + h = 0.3$, $f(x_2,y_2) = f(0.2,1.230) = 1.630$,
$y_3 = y_2 + hf(x_2,y_2) = 1.230 + 0.1(1.630) = 1.393$.

(d) $x_4 = x_3 + h = 0.4$, $f(x_3,y_3) = f(0.3,1.393) = 1.993$,
$y_4 = y_3 + hf(x_3,y_3) = 1.393 + 0.1(1.993) = 1.592$.

(e) $x_5 = x_4 + h = 0.5$, $f(x_4,y_4) = f(0.4,1.592) = 2.392$,
$y_5 = y_4 + hf(x_4,y_4) = 1.592 + 0.1(2.392) = 1.831$.

(f) $x_6 = x_5 + h = 0.6$, $f(x_5,y_5) = f(0.5,1.831) = 2.831$,
$y_6 = y_5 + hf(x_5,y_5) = 1.831 + 0.1(2.831) = 2.114$.

(g) $x_7 = x_6 + h = 0.7$, $f(x_6,y_6) = f(0.6,2.114) = 3.314$,
$y_7 = y_6 + hf(x_6,y_6) = 2.114 + 0.1(3.314) = 2.445$.

(h) $x_8 = x_7 + h = 0.8$, $f(x_7,y_7) = f(0.7,2.445) = 3.845$,
$y_8 = y_7 + hf(x_7,y_7) = 2.445 + 0.1(3.845) = 2.830$.

(i) $x_9 = x_8 + h = 0.9$, $f(x_8,y_8) = f(0.8,2.830) = 4.430$,
$y_9 = y_8 + hf(x_8,y_8) = 2.830 + 0.1(4.430) = 3.273$.

(j) $x_{10} = x_9 + h = 1.0$, $f(x_9,y_9) = f(0.9,3.273) = 5.073$,
$y_{10} = y_9 + hf(x_9,y_9) = 3.273 + 0.1(5.073) = 3.780$.

These results are collected in the third column of Table 8.2. The values of the exact solution y, computed from (8.46) to three figures after the decimal point, are listed in the fourth column of Table 8.2.

Table 8.2

x_n	y_n using $h = 0.2$	y_n using $h = 0.1$	y
0.0	1.000	1.000	1.000
0.1	—	1.100	1.116
0.2	1.200	1.230	1.264
0.3	—	1.393	1.450
0.4	1.520	1.592	1.675
0.5	—	1.831	1.946
0.6	1.984	2.114	2.266
0.7	—	2.445	2.641
0.8	2.621	2.830	3.076
0.9	—	3.273	3.579
1.0	3.465	3.780	4.155

From this table we compute the errors involved in both approximations at $x = 0.2$, 0.4, 0.6, 0.8, and 1.0. These errors are tabulated in Table 8.3.

Table 8.3

x_n	Error using $h = 0.2$	Error using $h = 0.1$
0.2	0.064	0.034
0.4	0.155	0.083
0.6	0.282	0.152
0.8	0.455	0.246
1.0	0.690	0.375

A study of these tables illustrates two important facts concerning the Euler Method. First, for a fixed value of h, the error becomes greater and greater as we proceed over a larger and larger range away from the initial point. Second, for a fixed value of x_n, the error is smaller if the value of h is smaller.

Exercises

1. Consider the initial-value problem

$$\frac{dy}{dx} = x - 2y,$$

$$y(0) = 1.$$

   (a) Apply the Euler Method to approximate the values of the solution y at $x = 0.1, 0.2, 0.3$, and 0.4, using $h = 0.1$. Obtain results to three figures after the decimal point.
   (b) Proceed as in part (a) using $h = 0.05$.
   (c) Find the exact solution of the problem and determine its values at $x = 0.1, 0.2, 0.3$, and 0.4 (to three figures after the decimal point).
   (d) Compare the results obtained in parts (a), (b), and (c). Tabulate errors as in Table 4.3.

2. Proceed as in Exercise 1 for the initial-value problem

$$\frac{dy}{dx} = x + y,$$

$$y(0) = 2.$$

C. *The Modified Euler Method*

In Section B we observed that the value $y(x_1)$ of the exact solution y of the initial-value problem

(8.1) $$\frac{dy}{dx} = f(x,y),$$

(8.6) $$y(x_0) = y_0,$$

at $x_1 = x_0 + h$ is given by

(8.47) $$y(x_1) = y_0 + \int_{x_0}^{x_1} f(x,y)dx.$$

In the Euler Method we approximated $f(x,y)$ in (8.47) by its value $f(x_0,y_0)$ at the left end point of the interval $x_0 \le x \le x_1$ and thereby obtained the approximation

(8.48) $$y_1 = y_0 + hf(x_0,y_0)$$

for y at x_1. It seems reasonable that a more accurate value would be obtained if we were to approximate $f(x,y)$ by the *average* of its values at the left and right end points of $x_0 \le x \le x_1$, instead of simply by its value at the left end point x_0. This is essentially what is done in the modified Euler Method, which we shall now explain.

In order to approximate $f(x,y)$ by the average of its values at x_0 and x_1, we need to know its value $f[x_1, y(x_1)]$ at x_1. However, we do not know the value $y(x_1)$ of y at x_1. We must find a first approximation $y_1^{(1)}$ for $y(x_1)$, and to do this we proceed just as we did at the start of the Basic Euler Method. That is, we take

(8.50) $$y_1^{(1)} = y_0 + hf(x_0,y_0)$$

as the *first* approximation to the value of y at x_1. Then we approximate $f[x_1, y(x_1)]$ by $f(x_1,y_1^{(1)})$, using the value $y_1^{(1)}$ found by (8.50). From this we obtain

(8.51) $$\frac{f(x_0,y_0) + f(x_1,y_1^{(1)})}{2},$$

which is approximately the average of the values of $f(x,y)$ at the end points x_0, and x_1. We now replace $f(x,y)$ in (8.47) by (8.51) and thereby obtain

(8.52) $$y_1^{(2)} = y_0 + \frac{f(x_0,y_0) + f(x_1,y_1^{(1)})}{2}h$$

as the *second* approximation to the value of y at x_1.

We now use the second approximation $y_1^{(2)}$ to obtain a second approximation $f(x_1,y_1^{(2)})$ for the value of $f(x,y)$ at x_1. From this we proceed to obtain

$$(8.53) \qquad y_1^{(3)} = y_0 + \frac{f(x_0,y_0) + f(x_1,y_1^{(2)})}{2}h$$

as the *third* approximation to the value of y at x_1. Proceeding in this way we obtain a sequence of approximations

$$y_1^{(1)}, y_1^{(2)}, y_1^{(3)}, \cdots.$$

to the value of the exact solution y at x_1. We proceed to compute the successive members of the sequence until we encounter two consecutive members which have the same value to the number of decimal places required. We take the common value of these two consecutive members as our approximation to the value of the solution y at x_1 and denote it by y_1.

Having finally approximated y at x_1 by y_1, we now move on and proceed to approximate y at $x_2 = x_1 + h$. We proceed in exactly the same way as we did in finding y_1. We find successively

$$y_2^{(1)} = y_1 + hf(x_1,y_1),$$

$$y_2^{(2)} = y_1 + \frac{f(x_1,y_1) + f(x_2,y_2^{(1)})}{2}h,$$

$$(8.54) \qquad y_2^{(3)} = y_1 + \frac{f(x_1,y_1) + f(x_2,y_2^{(2)})}{2}h,$$

$$\vdots$$

until two consecutive members of this sequence agree, thereby obtaining an approximation y_2 to the value of y at x_2.

Proceeding further in like manner one obtains an approximation y_3 to the value of y at x_3, and so forth.

Example 8.8. Apply the Modified Euler Method to the initial-value problem

$$(8.2) \qquad \frac{dy}{dx} = 2x + y,$$

$$(8.44) \qquad y(0) = 1.$$

Employ the method to approximate the value of the solution y at $x = 0.2$ and $x = 0.4$ using $h = 0.2$. Obtain results to three figures after the decimal point. Compare with the results obtained using the basic Euler Method with $h = 0.1$ and with the exact values (Example 8.7, Table 8.2).

Solution. Here $f(x,y) = 2x + y$, $x_0 = 0$, and $y_0 = 1$, and we are to use $h = 0.2$. We begin by approximating the value of y at $x_1 = x_0 + h = 0.2$. A first approximation $y_1^{(1)}$ to this value is found using formula (8.50). Since $f(x_0,y_0) = f(0, 1) = 1.000$, we have

$$y_1^{(1)} = y_0 + hf(x_0,y_0) = 1.000 + 0.2(1.000) = 1.200.$$

We now use (8.52) to find a second approximation $y_1^{(2)}$ to the desired value. Since $f(x_1, y_1^{(1)}) = f(0.2, 1.200) = 1.600$, we have

$$y_1^{(2)} = y_0 + \frac{f(x_0, y_0) + f(x_1, y_1^{(1)})}{2} h = 1.000 + \frac{1.000 + 1.600}{2}(0.2) = 1.260.$$

We next employ (8.53) to find a third approximation $y_1^{(3)}$. Since $f(x_1, y_1^{(2)}) = f(0.2, 1.260) = 1.660$, we find

$$y_1^{(3)} = y_0 + \frac{f(x_0, y_0) + f(x_1, y_1^{(2)})}{2} h = 1.000 + \frac{1.000 + 1.660}{2}(0.2) = 1.266.$$

Proceeding in like manner, we obtain fourth and fifth approximations $y_1^{(4)}$ and $y_1^{(5)}$, respectively. We find

$$y_1^{(4)} = y_0 + \frac{f(x_0, y_0) + f(x_1, y_1^{(3)})}{2} h = 1.000 + \frac{1.000 + 1.666}{2}(0.2) = 1.267$$

and

$$y_1^{(5)} = y_0 + \frac{f(x_0, y_0) + f(x_1, y_1^{(4)})}{2} h = 1.000 + \frac{1.000 + 1.667}{2}(0.2) = 1.267.$$

Since the approximations $y_1^{(4)}$ and $y_1^{(5)}$ are the same to the number of decimal places required, we take their common value as the approximation y_1 to the value of the solution y at $x_1 = 0.2$. That is, we take

$$(8.55) \qquad\qquad y_1 = 1.267.$$

We now proceed to approximate the value of y at $x_2 = x_1 + h = 0.4$. For this purpose we employ the formulas (8.54), using $y_1 = 1.267$. We find successively

$$y_2^{(1)} = y_1 + hf(x_1, y_1) = 1.267 + 0.2(1.667) = 1.600,$$

$$y_2^{(2)} = y_1 + \frac{f(x_1, y_1) + f(x_2, y_2^{(1)})}{2} h = 1.267 + \frac{1.667 + 2.400}{2}(0.2) = 1.674,$$

$$y_2^{(3)} = y_1 + \frac{f(x_1, y_1) + f(x_2, y_2^{(2)})}{2} h = 1.267 + \frac{1.667 + 2.474}{2}(0.2) = 1.681,$$

$$y_2^{(4)} = y_1 + \frac{f(x_1, y_1) + f(x_2, y_2^{(3)})}{2} h = 1.267 + \frac{1.667 + 2.481}{2}(0.2) = 1.682,$$

$$y_2^{(5)} = y_1 + \frac{f(x_1, y_1) + f(x_2, y_2^{(4)})}{2} h = 1.267 + \frac{1.667 + 2.482}{2}(0.2) = 1.682.$$

Since the approximations $y_2^{(4)}$ and $y_2^{(5)}$ are both the same to the required number of decimal places, we take their common value as the approximation y_2 to the value of the solution y at $x_2 = 0.4$. That is, we take

$$(8.56) \qquad\qquad y_2 = 1.682.$$

We compare the results (8.55) and (8.56) with those obtained using the basic Euler method with $h = 0.1$ and with the exact values. For this purpose the various results and the corresponding errors are listed in Table 8.4.

Table 8.4

x_n	Exact value of y (to three decimal places)	Using basic Euler method with $h = 0.1$		Using modified Euler with $h = 0.2$	
		Approximation y_n	Error	Approximation y_n	Error
0.2	1.264	1.230	0.034	1.267	0.003
0.4	1.675	1.592	0.083	1.682	0.007

The principal advantage of the Modified Euler Method over the basic Euler Method is immediately apparent from a study of Table 8.4. The modified method is much more accurate. At $x = 0.4$ the error using the modified method with $h = 0.02$ is 0.007. The corresponding error 0.083 using the basic method with $h = 0.1$ is nearly twelve times as great, despite the fact that a smaller value of h was used in this case. Of course at each step the modified method involves more lengthy and complicated calculations than the basic method. We note, however, that the basic method would require many individual steps to give a result as accurate as that which the modified method can provide in a single step.

Exercises

1. Consider the initial-value problem

$$\frac{dy}{dx} = 3x + 2y,$$

$$y(0) = 1.$$

   (a) Apply the Modified Euler Method to approximate the values of the solution y at $x = 0.1$, 0.2, and 0.3 using $h = 0.1$. Obtain results to three figures after the decimal point.
   (b) Proceed as in part (a) using $h = 0.05$.
   (c) Find the exact solution of the problem and determine its values at $x = 0.1$, 0.2, and 0.3 (to three figures after the decimal point).
   (d) Compare the results obtained in parts (a), (b), and (c), and tabulate errors.

2. Proceed as in Exercise 1 for the initial-value problem

$$\frac{dy}{dx} = 2x - y,$$

$$y(0) = 3.$$

3. Consider the initial-value problem

$$\frac{dy}{dx} = x^2 + y^2,$$

$$y(0) = 1.$$

Apply the Modified Euler Method to approximate the values of the solution y at $x = 0.1, 0.2,$ and 0.3, using $h = 0.1$. Obtain results to three figures after the decimal point.

D. The Runge-Kutta Method

We now consider the so-called Runge-Kutta Method for approximating the values of the solution of the initial-value problem

(8.1)
$$\frac{dy}{dx} = f(x,y),$$

(8.6)
$$y(x_0) = y_0,$$

at $x_1 = x_0 + h$, $x_2 = x_1 + h$, and so forth. This method gives surprisingly accurate results without the need of using extremely small values of the interval h. We shall give no justification for the method but shall merely list the several formulas involved and explain how they are used.†

To approximate the value of the solution of the initial value problem under consideration at $x_1 = x_0 + h$ by the Runge-Kutta Method, we proceed in the following way. We calculate successively the numbers k_1, k_2, k_3, k_4, and K_0 defined by the formulas

(8.57)
$$k_1 = hf(x_0,y_0),$$
$$k_2 = hf\left(x_0 + \frac{h}{2}, y_0 + \frac{k_1}{2}\right),$$
$$k_3 = hf\left(x_0 + \frac{h}{2}, y_0 + \frac{k_2}{2}\right),$$
$$k_4 = hf(x_0 + h, y_0 + k_3),$$

and

$$K_0 = \frac{1}{6}(k_1 + 2k_2 + 2k_3 + k_4).$$

Then we set

(8.58)
$$y_1 = y_0 + K_0$$

and take this as the approximate value of the exact solution at $x_1 = x_0 + h$.

Having thus determined y_1, we proceed to approximate the value of the solution at $x_2 = x_1 + h$ in an exactly similar manner. Using $x_1 = x_0 + h$ and y_1 as determined by (8.58), we calculate successively the numbers k_1, k_2, k_3, k_4, and K_1 defined by

(8.59)
$$k_1 = hf(x_1,y_1),$$
$$k_2 = hf\left(x_1 + \frac{h}{2}, y_1 + \frac{k_1}{2}\right),$$
$$k_3 = hf\left(x_1 + \frac{h}{2}, y_1 + \frac{k_2}{2}\right),$$
$$k_4 = hf(x_1 + h, y_1 + k_3),$$

and

$$K_1 = \frac{1}{6}(k_1 + 2k_2 + 2k_3 + k_4).$$

†See Hildebrand (23), Chapter 6, and Levy and Baggott (37), Chapter 3.

Then we set

(8.60) $$y_2 = y_1 + K_1$$

and take this as the approximate value of the exact solution at $x_2 = x_1 + h$.

We proceed to approximate the value of the solution at $x_3 = x_2 + h$, $x_4 = x_3 + h$, and so forth, in an exactly similar manner. Letting y_n denote the approximate value obtained for the solution at $x_n = x_0 + nh$, we calculate successively k_1, k_2, k_3, k_4, and K_n defined by

$$k_1 = hf(x_n, y_n),$$

$$k_2 = hf\left(x_n + \frac{h}{2}, y_n + \frac{k_1}{2}\right),$$

$$k_3 = hf\left(x_n + \frac{h}{2}, y_n + \frac{k_2}{2}\right),$$

$$k_4 = hf(x_n + h, y_n + k_3),$$

and

$$K_n = \frac{1}{6}(k_1 + 2k_2 + 2k_3 + k_4).$$

Then we set

$$y_{n+1} = y_n + K_n$$

and take this as the approximate value of the exact solution at $x_{n+1} = x_n + h$.

Example 8.9.   Apply the Runge-Kutta Method to the initial value problem

(8.2) $$\frac{dy}{dx} = 2x + y,$$

(8.44) $$y(0) = 1.$$

Employ the method to approximate the value of the solution y at $x = 0.2$ and $x = 0.4$ using $h = 0.2$. Carry the intermediate calculations in each step to five figures after the decimal point, and round off the final results of each step to four such places. Compare with the exact value.

Solution.   Here $f(x,y) = 2x + y$, $x_0 = 0$, $y_0 = 1$, and we are to use $h = 0.2$. Using these quantities we calculate successively k_1, k_2, k_3, k_4, and K_0 defined by (8.57). We first find

$$k_1 = hf(x_0, y_0) = 0.2f(0,1) = 0.2(1) = 0.20000.$$

Then since

$$x_0 + \frac{h}{2} = 0 + \frac{1}{2}(0.2) = 0.1$$

and

$$y_0 + \frac{k_1}{2} = 1.00000 + \frac{1}{2}(0.20000) = 1.10000,$$

we find

$$k_2 = hf\left(x_0 + \frac{h}{2}, y_0 + \frac{k_1}{2}\right) = 0.2f(0.1,1.10000)$$
$$= 0.2(1.30000) = 0.26000.$$

Next, since $y_0 + \dfrac{k_2}{2} = 1.00000 + \dfrac{1}{2}(0.26000) = 1.13000$,

we find

$$k_3 = hf\left(x_0 + \frac{h}{2}, y_0 + \frac{k_2}{2}\right) = 0.2f(0.1,1.13000)$$
$$= 0.2(1.33000) = 0.26600.$$

Since $x_0 + h = 0.2$ and $y_0 + k_3 = 1.00000 + 0.26600 = 1.26600$, we obtain

$$k_4 = hf(x_0 + h, y_0 + k_3) = 0.2f(0.2,1.26600)$$
$$= 0.2(1.66600) = 0.33320.$$

Finally, we find

$$K_0 = \frac{1}{6}(k_1 + 2k_2 + 2k_3 + k_4) = \frac{1}{6}(0.20000 + 0.52000 + 0.53200 + 0.33320) = 0.26420.$$

Then by (8.58) the approximate value of the solution at $x_1 = 0.2$ is

$$(8.61) \qquad\qquad y_1 = 1 + 0.2642 = 1.2642.$$

Now using y_1 as given by (8.61), we calculate successively k_1, k_2, k_3, k_4, and K_1 defined by (8.59). We first find

$$k_1 = hf(x_1,y_1) = 0.2f(0.2,1.2642) = 0.2(1.6642) = 0.33284.$$

Then since

$$x_1 + \frac{h}{2} = 0.2 + \frac{1}{2}(0.2) = 0.3$$

and

$$y_1 + \frac{k_1}{2} = 1.26420 + \frac{1}{2}(0.33284) = 1.43062,$$

we find

$$k_2 = hf\left(x_1 + \frac{h}{2}, y_1 + \frac{k_1}{2}\right) = 0.2f(0.3,1.43062)$$
$$= 0.2(2.03062) = 0.40612.$$

Next, since $y_1 + \dfrac{k_2}{2} = 1.26420 + \dfrac{1}{2}(0.40612) = 1.46726$, we find

$$k_3 = hf\left(x_1 + \frac{h}{2}, y_1 + \frac{k_2}{2}\right) = 0.2f(0.3,1.46726)$$
$$= 0.2(2.06726) = 0.41345.$$

Since $x_1 + h = 0.4$ and $y_0 + k_3 = 1.26420 + 0.41345 = 1.67765$, we obtain

$$k_4 = hf(x_1 + h, y_1 + k_3) = 0.2f(0.4, 1.67765)$$

$$= 0.2(2.47765) = 0.49553.$$

Finally, we find

$$K_1 = \frac{1}{6}(k_1 + 2k_2 + 2k_3 + k_4)$$

$$= \frac{1}{6}(0.33284 + 0.81224 + 0.82690 + 0.49553) = 0.41125.$$

We round off K_1 according to the well-known rule of rounding off so as to leave the last digit retained an even one. Then by (8.60) we see that the approximate value of the solution at $x_2 = 0.4$ is

$$(8.62) \qquad\qquad y_2 = 1.2642 + 0.4112 = 1.6754.$$

As before, the exact values are determined using (8.46). Rounded off to four places after the decimal point, the exact values at $x = 0.2$ and $x = 0.4$ are 1.2642 and 1.6755, respectively. The approximate value at $x = 0.2$ as given by (8.61) is therefore correct to four places after the decimal point, and the approximate value at $x = 0.4$ as given by (8.62) differs from the exact value by only one unit in the fourth place after the point!

The remarkable accuracy of the Runge-Kutta Method in this problem is certainly apparent. In fact, if we employ the method to approximate the solution at $x = 0.4$ using $h = 0.4$ (that is, in only one step), we obtain the value 1.6752, which differs from the exact value 1.6755 by merely 0.0003.

Exercises

1. Consider the initial-value problem

$$\frac{dy}{dx} = 3x + 2y,$$

$$y(0) = 1.$$

(a) Apply the Runge-Kutta Method to approximate the values of the solution y at $x = 0.1, 0.2$, and 0.3, using $h = 0.1$. Carry the intermediate calculations in each step to five figures after the decimal point, and round off the final results of each step to four such places.

(b) Find the exact solution of the problem and compare the results obtained in part (a) with the exact values.

2. Proceed as in Exercise 1 for the initial-value problem

$$\frac{dy}{dx} = 2x - y,$$

$$y(0) = 3.$$

3. Proceed as in part (a) of Exercise 1 for initial-value problem

$$\frac{dy}{dx} = x^2 + y^2,$$

$$y(0) = 1.$$

E. The Milne Method

The Euler Method, the Modified Euler Method, and the Runge-Kutta Method are all *starting* methods for the numerical solution of an initial-value problem. As we have already pointed out, a starting method is a method which can be used to start the solution. In contrast, a *continuing* method is one which can not be used to start the solution but which can be used to continue it, once it is sufficiently well started. In this section we consider briefly a useful continuing method, the so-called Milne Method. We shall give no justification for this method but shall merely list the formulas involved and indicate how they are employed.†

The Milne Method can be used to approximate the value of the solution of the initial-value problem

(8.1) $$\frac{dy}{dx} = f(x,y),$$

(8.6) $$y(x_0) = y_0$$

at $x_{n+1} = x_0 + (n + 1)h$, provided the values at the four previous points x_{n-3}, x_{n-2}, x_{n-1}, and x_n have been determined. We assume that these four previous values have been found and denote them by y_{n-3}, y_{n-2}, y_{n-1}, and y_n, respectively. Then we can use (8.1) to determine dy/dx at x_{n-2}, x_{n-1}, and x_n. That is, we can determine $y'_{n-2} = f(x_{n-2}, y_{n-2})$, $y'_{n-1} = f(x_{n-1}, y_{n-1})$, and $y'_n = f(x_n, y_n)$. These various numbers being determined, the Milne Method proceeds as follows:

We first determine the number $y_{n+1}^{(1)}$ given by the formula

(8.63) $$y_{n+1}^{(1)} = y_{n-3} + \frac{4h}{3}(2y'_n - y'_{n-1} + 2y'_{n-2}).$$

Having thus determined $y_{n+1}^{(1)}$, we next determine the number $y'^{(1)}_{n+1}$ given by

(8.64) $$y'^{(1)}_{n+1} = f(x_{n+1}, y_{n+1}^{(1)}).$$

Finally, having determined $y'^{(1)}_{n+1}$, we proceed to determine the number $y_{n+1}^{(2)}$ given by

(8.65) $$y_{n+1}^{(2)} = y_{n-1} + \frac{h}{3}(y'^{(1)}_{n+1} + 4y'_n + y'_{n-1}).$$

If the numbers $y_{n+1}^{(1)}$ determined from (8.63) and $y_{n+1}^{(2)}$ determined from (8.65) are the same to the number of decimal places required, then we take this common value to be the approximate value of the solution at x_{n+1} and denote it by y_{n+1}.

If the numbers $y_{n+1}^{(1)}$ and $y_{n+1}^{(2)}$ so determined do not agree to the number of decimal places required and all of the calculations have been checked and appear to be correct,

†See Scarborough (47), Chapter 11.

then we proceed in the following way. We calculate the number

$$E = \frac{y_{n+1}^{(2)} - y_{n+1}^{(1)}}{29},$$

which is the principal part of the error in the formula (8.65). If E is negligible with respect to the number of decimal places required, then we take the number $y_{n+1}^{(2)}$ given by (8.65) as the approximate value of the solution at x_{n+1} and denote it by y_{n+1}. On the other hand, if E is so large that it is not negligible with respect to the number of decimal places required, then the value of h employed is too large and a smaller value must be used.

We observe that once the values y_0, y_1, y_2, and y_3 have been determined, we can use the Milne Formulas with $n = 3$ to determine y_4. Then when y_4 has been determined by the formulas, we can use them with $n = 4$ to determine y_5. Then proceeding in like manner, we can successively determine $y_6, y_7, \ldots$. But we must have y_0, y_1, y_2, and y_3 in order to start the Milne Method. Of course y_0 is given exactly by the initial condition (8.6), and we can find y_1, y_2, and y_3 by one of the previously explained starting methods (for example, by the Runge-Kutta Method).

Example 8.10. Apply the Milne Method to approximate the value at $x = 0.4$ of the solution y of the initial-value problem

(8.2) $$\frac{dy}{dx} = 2x + y,$$

(8.44) $$y(0) = 1,$$

assuming that the values at 0.1, 0.2, and 0.3 are 1.1155, 1.2642, and 1.4496, respectively.

Solution. We apply the formulas (8.63), (8.64), and (8.65) with $n = 3$. We set

$$x_0 = 0, \quad y_0 = 1.0000,$$
$$x_1 = 0.1, \ y_1 = 1.1155,$$
$$x_2 = 0.2, \ y_2 = 1.2642,$$
$$x_3 = 0.3, \ y_3 = 1.4496,$$

and $x_4 = 0.4$. Then using $f(x,y) = 2x + y$, we find

$$y_1' = f(x_1,y_1) = f(0.1,1.1155) = 1.3155,$$
$$y_2' = f(x_2,y_2) = f(0.2,1.2642) = 1.6642,$$
$$y_3' = f(x_3,y_3) = f(0.3,1.4496) = 2.0496.$$

We now use (8.63) with $n = 3$ and $h = 0.1$ to determine $y_4^{(1)}$. We have

$$y_4^{(1)} = y_0 + \frac{4(0.1)}{3}(2y_3' - y_2' + 2y_1')$$

$$= 1.000 + \frac{0.4}{3}(4.0992 - 1.6642 + 2.6310) = 1.6755.$$

Having thus determined $y_4^{(1)}$, we use (8.64) with $n = 3$ to determine $y_4'^{(1)}$. We find

$$y_4'^{(1)} = f(x_4,y_4^{(1)}) = f(0.4,1.6755) = 2.4755.$$

Finally, having determined $y_4'^{(1)}$, we use (8.65) with $n = 3$ and $h = 0.1$ to determine $y_4^{(2)}$.

We obtain

$$y_4^{(2)} = y_2 + \frac{0.1}{3}(y_4'^{(1)} + 4y_3' + y_2')$$

$$= 1.2642 + \frac{0.1}{3}(2.4755 + 8.1984 + 1.6642)$$

$$= 1.6755.$$

Since the numbers $y_4^{(1)}$ and $y_4^{(2)}$ agree to four decimal places, we take their common value as the approximate value of the solution at $x_4 = 0.4$ and denote it by y_4. That is, we set

$$y_4 = 1.6755.$$

Using (8.46), the exact value at $x = 0.4$, rounded off to four places after the decimal point, is also found to be 1.6755.

Exercises

1. Apply the Milne Method to approximate the value at $x = 0.4$ of the solution y of the initial-value problem

$$\frac{dy}{dx} = 3x + 2y,$$

$$y(0) = 1,$$

assuming that the values at 0.1, 0.2, and 0.3 are 1.2375, 1.5607, and 1.9887, respectively.

2. Apply the Milne Method to approximate the value at $x = 0.4$ of the solution y of the initial-value problem

$$\frac{dy}{dx} = 2x - y,$$

$$y(0) = 3,$$

assuming that the values at 0.1, 0.2, and 0.3 are 2.7242, 2.4937, and 2.3041, respectively.

SUGGESTED READING

I. Basic Methods:

Agnew (1)
Ford (17)
Hildebrand (22)
Kaplan (30)
Martin and Reissner (38)

II. Specialized and Advanced Topics:

Birkhoff and Rota (6)
Hildebrand (23)
Levy and Baggott (37)
Milne (41)
Scarborough (47)

9

THE LAPLACE TRANSFORM

In this chapter we shall introduce a concept which is especially useful in the solution of initial value problems. This concept is the so-called Laplace Transform, which transforms a suitable function F of a real variable t into a related function f of a real variable s. When this transform is applied in connection with an initial value problem involving a linear differential equation in an "unknown" function of t, it transforms the given initial value problem into an algebraic problem involving the variable s. In Section 9.2 we shall indicate just how this transformation is accomplished and how the resulting algebraic problem is then employed to find the solution of the given initial value problem. First, however, in Section 9.1 we shall introduce the Laplace Transform itself and develop certain of its most basic and useful properties.

9.1 Definition, Existence, and Basic Properties of the Laplace Transform

A. Definition and Existence

DEFINITION. Let F be a real-valued function of the real variable t, defined for $t > 0$. Let s be a variable which we shall assume to be real, and consider the function f defined by

$$(9.1) \qquad f(s) = \int_0^\infty e^{-st} F(t) dt,$$

for all values of s for which this integral exists. The function f defined by the integral (9.1) is called the *Laplace Transform* of the function F. We shall denote the Laplace Transform f of F by $\mathcal{L}\{F\}$ and shall denote $f(s)$ by $\mathcal{L}\{F(t)\}$.

In order to be certain that the integral (9.1) does exist for some range of values of s, we must impose suitable restrictions upon the function F under consideration. We shall do this shortly; however, first we shall directly determine the Laplace transforms of a few simple functions.

Example 9.1. Consider the function F defined by

$$F(t) = 1, \quad \text{for } t > 0.$$

Then

$$\mathcal{L}\{1\} = \int_0^\infty e^{-st} \cdot 1\,dt = \lim_{R \to \infty} \int_0^R e^{-st} \cdot 1\,dt = \lim_{R \to \infty} \left[\frac{-e^{-st}}{s}\right]_0^R = \lim_{R \to \infty} \left[\frac{1}{s} - \frac{e^{-sR}}{s}\right] = \frac{1}{s},$$

for all $s > 0$. Thus we have

(9.2)
$$\mathcal{L}\{1\} = \frac{1}{s}, \ (s > 0).$$

Example 9.2. Consider the function F defined by

$$F(t) = t, \quad \text{for } t > 0.$$

Then

$$\mathcal{L}\{t\} = \int_0^\infty e^{-st} \cdot t\,dt = \lim_{R \to \infty} \int_0^R e^{-st} \cdot t\,dt = \lim_{R \to \infty} \left[-\frac{e^{-st}}{s^2}(st + 1)\right]_0^R$$

$$= \lim_{R \to \infty} \left[\frac{1}{s^2} - \frac{e^{-sR}}{s^2}(sR + 1)\right] = \frac{1}{s^2}$$

for all $s > 0$. Thus

(9.3)
$$\mathcal{L}\{t\} = \frac{1}{s^2}, \ (s > 0).$$

Example 9.3. Consider the function f defined by

$$F(t) = e^{at}, \quad \text{for } t > 0.$$

$$\mathcal{L}\{e^{at}\} = \int_0^\infty e^{-st}e^{at}\,dt = \lim_{R \to \infty} \int_0^R e^{(a-s)t}\,dt = \lim_{R \to \infty} \left[\frac{e^{(a-s)t}}{a-s}\right]_0^R = \lim_{R \to \infty} \left[\frac{e^{(a-s)R}}{a-s} - \frac{1}{a-s}\right]$$

$$= -\frac{1}{a-s} = \frac{1}{s-a} \quad \text{for all } s > a.$$

Thus

(9.4)
$$\mathcal{L}\{e^{at}\} = \frac{1}{s-a}, \ (s > a).$$

Example 9.4. Consider the function F defined by

$$F(t) = \sin bt \quad \text{for } t > 0.$$

$$\mathcal{L}\{\sin bt\} = \int_0^\infty e^{-st} \cdot \sin bt\,dt = \lim_{R \to \infty} \int_0^R e^{-st} \cdot \sin bt\,dt = \lim_{R \to \infty} \left[-\frac{e^{-st}}{s^2 + b^2}(s\sin bt + b\cos bt)\right]_0^R$$

$$= \lim_{R \to \infty} \left[\frac{b}{s^2 + b^2} - \frac{e^{-sR}}{s^2 + b^2}(s\sin bR + b\cos bR)\right] = \frac{b}{s^2 + b^2} \quad \text{for all } s > 0.$$

Thus

(9.5) $$\mathcal{L}\{\sin bt\} = \frac{b}{s^2 + b^2}, \ (s > 0).$$

Example 9.5.   Consider the function F defined by

$$F(t) = \cos bt, \text{ for } t > 0.$$

$$\mathcal{L}\{\cos bt\} = \int_0^\infty e^{-st} \cdot \cos bt \, dt = \lim_{R \to \infty} \int_0^R e^{-st} \cos bt \, dt = \lim_{R \to \infty} \left[\frac{e^{-st}}{s^2 + b^2} (-s \cos bt + b \sin bt) \right]_0^R$$

$$= \lim_{R \to \infty} \left[\frac{e^{-sR}}{s^2 + b^2} (-s \cos bR + b \sin bR) + \frac{s}{s^2 + b^2} \right] = \frac{s}{s^2 + b^2} \text{ for all } s > 0.$$

Thus

(9.6) $$\mathcal{L}\{\cos bt\} = \frac{s}{s^2 + b^2}, \ (s > 0).$$

In each of the above examples we have seen directly that the integral (9.1) actually does exist for some range of values of s. We shall now determine a class of functions F for which this is always the case. To do so we first consider certain properties of functions.

DEFINITION. A function F is said to be *piecewise continuous* (or *sectionally continuous*) on a finite interval $a \le t \le b$ if this interval can be divided into a finite number of sub-intervals such that (i) F is continuous in the interior of each of these subintervals, and (ii) $F(t)$ approaches finite limits as t approaches either end point of each of the subintervals from its interior.

Suppose F is piecewise continuous on $a \le t \le b$, and t_0, $a < t_0 < b$, is an end point of one of the subintervals of the above definition. Then the finite limit approached by $F(t)$ as t approaches t_0 from the left (that is, through smaller values of t) is called the *left-hand limit* of $F(t)$ as t approaches t_0, denoted by $\lim_{t \to t_0^-} F(t)$ or by $F(t_0-)$. In like manner, the finite limit approached by $F(t)$ as t approaches t_0 from the right (through larger values) is called the *right-hand limit* of $F(t)$ as t approaches t_0, denoted by $\lim_{t \to t_0^+} F(t)$ or $F(t_0+)$. We emphasize that at such a point t_0, both $F(t_0-)$ and $F(t_0+)$ are finite but they are not in general equal.

We point out that if F is continuous on $a \le t \le b$ it is necessarily piecewise continuous on this interval. Also, we note that if F is piecewise continuous on $a \le t \le b$, then F is integrable on $a \le t \le b$.

Example 9.6.   Consider the function F defined by

$$F(t) = \begin{cases} -1, & 0 < t < 2, \\ 1, & t > 2. \end{cases}$$

F is piecewise continuous on every finite interval $0 \le t \le b$, for every positive number *b.* At $t = 2$, we have

$$F(2-) = \lim_{t \to 2-} F(t) = -1$$

$$F(2+) = \lim_{t \to 2+} F(t) = +1.$$

The graph of F is shown in Figure 9.1.

DEFINITION. A function F is said to be of *exponential order* if there exists a constant α and positive constants t_0 and M such that

(9.7) $$e^{-\alpha t}|F(t)| < M$$

for all $t > t_0$ at which $F(t)$ is defined. More explicitly, if F is of exponential order corresponding to some definite constant α in (9.7), then we say that F is of *exponential order* $e^{\alpha t}$.

In other words, we say that F is of exponential order if a constant α exists such that the product $e^{-\alpha t}|F(t)|$ is bounded for all sufficiently large values of t. From (9.7) we have

(9.8) $$|F(t)| < Me^{\alpha t}$$

for all $t > t_0$ at which $F(t)$ is defined. Thus if F is of exponential order and the values $F(t)$ of F become infinite as $t \to \infty$, these values can not become infinite more rapidly than a multiple M of the corresponding values $e^{\alpha t}$ of some exponential function. We note that if F is of exponential order $e^{\alpha t}$, then F is also of exponential order $e^{\beta t}$ for any $\beta > \alpha$.

Example 9.7. Every bounded function is of exponential order, with the constant $\alpha = 0$. Thus, for example, $\sin bt$ and $\cos bt$ are of exponential order.

Example 9.8. The function F such that $F(t) = e^{at} \sin bt$ is of exponential order, with the constant $\alpha = a$. For we then have

$$e^{-\alpha t}|F(t)| = e^{-at}e^{at}|\sin bt| = |\sin bt|,$$

which is bounded for all t.

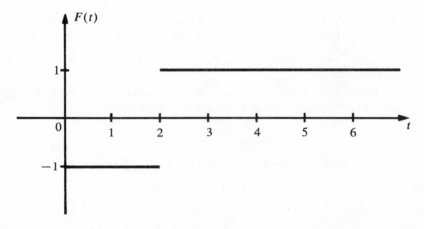

Figure 9.1

Example 9.9. Consider the function F such that $F(t) = t^n$, where $n > 0$. Then $e^{-\alpha t} |F(t)|$ is $e^{-\alpha t} t^n$. For any $\alpha > 0$, $\lim\limits_{t \to \infty} e^{-\alpha t} t^n = 0$. Thus there exists $M > 0$ and $t_0 > 0$ such that

$$e^{-\alpha t} |F(t)| = e^{-\alpha t} t^n < M$$

for $t > t_0$. Hence $F(t) = t^n$ is of exponential order, with the constant α equal to any positive number.

Example 9.10. The function F such that $F(t) = e^{t^2}$ is *not* of exponential order, for in this case $e^{-\alpha t} |F(t)|$ is $e^{t^2 - \alpha t}$ and this becomes unbounded as $t \to \infty$, no matter what is the value of α.

We shall now proceed to obtain a theorem giving conditions on F which are sufficient for the integral (9.1) to exist. To obtain the desired result we shall need the following two theorems from advanced calculus, which we state without proof.

THEOREM A.   Comparison Test for Improper Integrals.

Hypothesis.   (i) Let g and G be real functions such that

$$0 \le g(t) \le G(t) \text{ on } a \le t < \infty .$$

(ii) Suppose $\int_a^\infty G(t)\,dt$ exists.

(iii) Suppose g is integrable on every finite closed subinterval of $a \le t < \infty$.

Conclusion.   Then $\int_a^\infty g(t)\,dt$ exists.

THEOREM B.

Hypothesis.   (i) Suppose the real function g is integrable on every finite closed subinterval of $a \le t < \infty$.

(ii) Suppose $\int_a^\infty |g(t)|\,dt$ exists.

Conclusion.   Then $\int_a^\infty g(t)\,dt$ exists.

We now state and prove an existence theorem for Laplace Transforms.

THEOREM 9.1.

Hypothesis.   Let F be a real function which has the following properties:
(i) F is piecewise continuous in every finite closed interval $0 \le t \le b$ $(b > 0)$.

(ii) F is of exponential order; that is, there exists α, $M > 0$, and $t_0 > 0$ such that

$$e^{-\alpha t}|F(t)| < M \quad \text{for} \quad t > t_0.$$

Conclusion. The Laplace Transform

$$\int_0^\infty e^{-st}F(t)dt$$

of F exists for $s > \alpha$.

Proof. We have

$$\int_0^\infty e^{-st}F(t)dt = \int_0^{t_0} e^{-st}F(t)dt + \int_{t_0}^\infty e^{-st}F(t)dt.$$

By hypothesis (i), the first integral of the right member exists.
By hypothesis (ii),

$$e^{-st}|F(t)| < e^{-st}Me^{\alpha t} = Me^{-(s-\alpha)t}$$

for $t > t_0$. Also

$$\int_{t_0}^\infty Me^{-(s-\alpha)t}dt = \lim_{R \to \infty} \int_{t_0}^R Me^{-(s-\alpha)t}dt = \lim_{R \to \infty} \left[-\frac{Me^{-(s-\alpha)t}}{s-\alpha} \right]_{t_0}^R$$

$$= \lim_{R \to \infty} \left[\frac{M}{s-\alpha} \right][e^{-(s-\alpha)t_0} - e^{-(s-\alpha)R}] = \left[\frac{M}{s-\alpha} \right]e^{-(s-\alpha)t_0} \quad \text{if } s > \alpha.$$

Thus

$$\int_{t_0}^\infty Me^{-(s-\alpha)t}dt \text{ exists for } s > \alpha.$$

Finally, by hypothesis (i), $e^{-st}|F(t)|$ is integrable on every finite closed subinterval of $t_0 \le t < \infty$. Thus, applying Theorem A with $g(t) = e^{-st}|F(t)|$ and $G(t) = Me^{-(s-\alpha)t}$, we see that

$$\int_{t_0}^\infty e^{-st}|F(t)|dt \quad \text{exists if } s > \alpha.$$

In other words,

$$\int_{t_0}^\infty |e^{-st}F(t)|dt \quad \text{exists if } s > \alpha,$$

and so by Theorem B

$$\int_{t_0}^\infty e^{-st}F(t)dt$$

also exists if $s > \alpha$. Thus the Laplace Transform of F exists for $s > \alpha$. Q.E.D.

Let us look back at this proof for a moment. Actually we showed that if F satisfies the hypotheses stated, then

$$\int_{t_0}^{\infty} e^{-st}|F(t)|dt \quad \text{exists if } s > \alpha.$$

Further, hypothesis (i) shows that

$$\int_{0}^{t_0} e^{-st}|F(t)|dt \quad \text{exists.}$$

Thus

$$\int_{0}^{\infty} e^{-st}|F(t)|dt \quad \text{exists if } s > \alpha.$$

In other words, if F satisfies the hypotheses of Theorem 9.1, then not only does $\mathcal{L}\{F\}$ exist for $s > \alpha$, but also $\mathcal{L}\{|F|\}$ exists for $s > \alpha$. That is,

$$\int_{0}^{\infty} e^{-st}F(t)dt \quad \text{is absolutely convergent for } s > \alpha.$$

We point out that the conditions on F described in the hypothesis of Theorem 9.1 are not necessary for the existence of $\mathcal{L}\{F\}$. In other words, there exist functions F which do *not* satisfy the hypotheses of Theorem 9.1, but for which $\mathcal{L}\{F\}$ exists. For instance, suppose we replace hypothesis (i) by the following less restrictive condition. Let us suppose that F is piecewise continuous in every finite closed interval $a \leq t \leq b$, where $a > 0$, and is such that $|t^n F(t)|$ remains bounded as $t \to 0^+$ for some number n, where $0 < n < 1$. Then, provided hypothesis (ii) remains satisfied, it can be shown that $\mathcal{L}\{F\}$ still exists. Thus for example, if $F(t) = t^{-1/3}$, $t > 0$, $\mathcal{L}\{F\}$ exists. For although F does *not* satisfy hypothesis (i) of Theorem 9.1 ($F(t) \to \infty$ as $t \to 0^+$), it *does* satisfy the less restrictive requirement stated above (take $n = 2/3$), and F is of exponential order.

B. Basic Properties of the Laplace Transform

THEOREM 9.2. The Linear Property.

Let F_1 and F_2 be functions whose Laplace Transforms exist, and let c_1 and c_2 be constants. Then

(9.9) $$\mathcal{L}\{c_1 F_1(t) + c_2 F_2(t)\} = c_1 \mathcal{L}\{F_1(t)\} + c_2 \mathcal{L}\{F_2(t)\}.$$

Proof.   This follows directly from the definition (9.1).

Example 9.11.   Use Theorem 9.2 to find $\mathcal{L}\{\sin^2 at\}$.

Since $\sin^2 at = \dfrac{1 - \cos 2at}{2}$, we have

$$\mathcal{L}\{\sin^2 at\} = \mathcal{L}\left\{\frac{1}{2} - \frac{1}{2}\cos 2at\right\}.$$

By Theorem 9.2,

$$\mathcal{L}\left\{\frac{1}{2} - \frac{1}{2}\cos 2at\right\} = \frac{1}{2}\mathcal{L}\{1\} - \frac{1}{2}\mathcal{L}\{\cos 2at\}.$$

By (9.2), $\mathcal{L}\{1\} = \dfrac{1}{s}$, and by (9.6), $\mathcal{L}\{\cos 2at\} = \dfrac{s}{s^2 + 4a^2}$. Thus

$$(9.10) \qquad \mathcal{L}\{\sin^2 at\} = \frac{1}{2}\cdot\frac{1}{s} - \frac{1}{2}\cdot\frac{s}{s^2 + 4a^2} = \frac{2a^2}{s(s^2 + 4a^2)}.$$

THEOREM 9.3.

Hypothesis. (i) Let F be a real function which is continuous for $t \geq 0$ and of exponential order $e^{\alpha t}$.

(ii) Let F' (the derivative of F) be piecewise continuous in every finite closed interval $0 \leq t \leq b$.

Conclusion. Then $\mathcal{L}\{F'\}$ exists for $s > \alpha$; and

$$(9.11) \qquad \mathcal{L}\{F'(t)\} = s\mathcal{L}\{F(t)\} - F(0).$$

Proof. By definition of the Laplace Transform,

$$\mathcal{L}\{F'(t)\} = \lim_{R\to\infty}\int_0^R e^{-st}F'(t)\,dt,$$

provided this limit exists. In any closed interval $0 \leq t \leq R$, $F'(t)$ has at most a finite number of discontinuities; denote these by $t_1, t_2, \ldots, t_n$, where

$$0 < t_1 < t_2 < \cdots < t_n \leq R.$$

Then we may write

$$\int_0^R e^{-st}F'(t)\,dt = \int_0^{t_1} e^{-st}F'(t)\,dt + \int_{t_1}^{t_2} e^{-st}F'(t)\,dt + \cdots + \int_{t_n}^R e^{-st}F'(t)\,dt.$$

Now the integrand of each of the integrals on the right is continuous. We may therefore integrate each by parts. Doing so, we obtain

$$\int_0^R e^{-st}F'(t)\,dt = \left[e^{-st}F(t)\right]_0^{t_1-} + s\int_0^{t_1} e^{-st}F(t)\,dt + \left[e^{-st}F(t)\right]_{t_1+}^{t_2-}$$
$$+ s\int_{t_1}^{t_2} e^{-st}F(t)\,dt + \cdots + \left[e^{-st}F(t)\right]_{t_n+}^{R-} + s\int_{t_n}^R e^{-st}F(t)\,dt.$$

By hypothesis (i), F is continuous for $t \geq 0$. Thus $F(t_1-) = F(t_1+)$, $F(t_2-) = F(t_2+)$, $\ldots$, $F(t_n-) = F(t_n+)$. Thus all of the integrated "pieces" add out, except for $e^{-st}\,F(t)|_{t=0}$ and $e^{-st}F(t)|_{t=R-}$, and there remains only

$$\int_0^R e^{-st}F'(t)\,dt = -F(0) + e^{-sR}F(R) + s\int_0^R e^{-st}F(t)\,dt.$$

But by hypothesis (i) F is of exponential order $e^{\alpha t}$. Thus there exists $M > 0$ and $t_0 > 0$ such that $e^{-\alpha t}|F(t)| < M$ for $t > t_0$. Thus $|e^{-sR}F(R)| < Me^{-(s-\alpha)R}$ for $R > t_0$. Thus if $s > \alpha$,

$$\lim_{R \to \infty} e^{-sR}F(R) = 0.$$

Further,

$$\lim_{R \to \infty} s \int_0^R e^{-st}F(t)dt = s\mathcal{L}\{F(t)\}.$$

Thus, we have

$$\lim_{R \to \infty} \int_0^R e^{-st}F'(t)dt = -F(0) + s\mathcal{L}\{F(t)\},$$

and so $\mathcal{L}\{F'(t)\}$ exists for $s > \alpha$ and is given by (9.11).

Q.E.D.

Example 9.12.   Consider the function defined by $F(t) = \sin^2 at$. This function satisfies the hypotheses of Theorem 9.3. Since $F'(t) = 2a \sin at \cos at$ and $F(0) = 0$, equation (9.11) gives

$$\mathcal{L}\{2a \sin at \cos at\} = s\mathcal{L}\{\sin^2 at\}.$$

By (9.10),

$$\mathcal{L}\{\sin^2 at\} = \frac{2a^2}{s(s^2 + 4a^2)}.$$

Thus,

$$\mathcal{L}\{2a \sin at \cos at\} = \frac{2a^2}{s^2 + 4a^2}.$$

Since $2a \sin at \cos at = a \sin 2at$, we also have

$$\mathcal{L}\{\sin 2at\} = \frac{2a}{s^2 + 4a^2}.$$

Observe that this is the result (9.5), obtained in Example 9.4, with $b = 2a$.

We now generalize Theorem 9.3 and obtain the following result:

THEOREM 9.4.

Hypothesis.   (i) Let F be a real function having a continuous $(n-1)$st derivative $F^{(n-1)}$ (and hence $F, F', \ldots, F^{(n-2)}$ are also continuous) for $t \geq 0$; and assume that F, $F', \ldots, F^{(n-1)}$ are all of exponential order $e^{\alpha t}$.
  (ii) Suppose $F^{(n)}$ is piecewise continuous in every finite closed interval $0 \leq t \leq b$.

Conclusion. $\mathcal{L}\{F^{(n)}\}$ exists for $s > \alpha$ and

(9.12) $\mathcal{L}\{F^{(n)}(t)\} = s^n\mathcal{L}\{F(t)\} - s^{n-1}F(0) - s^{n-2}F'(0) - s^{n-3}F''(0) - \cdots - F^{(n-1)}(0).$

Outline of Proof. One first proceeds as in the proof of Theorem 9.3 to show that $\mathcal{L}\{F^{(n)}\}$ exists for $s > \alpha$ and is given by

$$\mathcal{L}\{F^{(n)}\} = s\mathcal{L}\{F^{(n-1)}\} - F^{(n-1)}(0).$$

One then completes the proof by mathematical induction.

Example 9.13. We apply Theorem 9.4, with $n = 2$, to find $\mathcal{L}\{\sin bt\}$, which we have already found directly and given by (9.5). Clearly the function F defined by $F(t) = \sin bt$ satisfies the hypotheses of the theorem with $\alpha = 0$. For $n = 2$, Equation (9.12) becomes

(9.13) $\mathcal{L}\{F''(t)\} = s^2\mathcal{L}\{F(t)\} - sF(0) - F'(0).$

We have $F'(t) = b\cos bt$, $F''(t) = -b^2\sin bt$, $F(0) = 0$, $F'(0) = b$. Substituting into Equation (9.13) we find

$$\mathcal{L}\{-b^2\sin bt\} = s^2\mathcal{L}\{\sin bt\} - b,$$

and so

$$(s^2 + b^2)\mathcal{L}\{\sin bt\} = b.$$

Thus,

$$\mathcal{L}\{\sin bt\} = \frac{b}{s^2 + b^2}, \; (s > 0),$$

which is the result (9.5), already found directly.

THEOREM 9.5.   Translation Property.

Hypothesis.   Suppose F is such that $\mathcal{L}\{F\}$ exists for $s > \alpha$.

Conclusion.   For any constant a,

(9.14) $\mathcal{L}\{e^{at}F(t)\} = f(s - a)$

for $s > \alpha + a$, where $f(s)$ denotes $\mathcal{L}\{F(t)\}$.

Proof. $f(s) = \mathcal{L}\{F(t)\} = \int_0^\infty e^{-st} F(t)dt.$
Replacing s by $s - a$, we have

$$f(s - a) = \int_0^\infty e^{-(s-a)t}F(t)dt = \int_0^\infty e^{-st}[e^{at}F(t)]dt = \mathcal{L}\{e^{at}F(t)\}. \qquad Q.E.D.$$

Example 9.14. Find $\mathcal{L}\{e^{at}t\}$.
We apply Theorem 9.5 with $F(t) = t$.

$$\mathcal{L}\{e^{at}t\} = f(s - a),$$

where $f(s) = \mathcal{L}\{F(t)\} = \mathcal{L}\{t\}$.

By (9.3), $\mathcal{L}\{t\} = \dfrac{1}{s^2}$, $(s > 0)$. That is, $f(s) = \dfrac{1}{s^2}$ and so $f(s - a) = \dfrac{1}{(s - a)^2}$. Thus

(9.15)
$$\mathcal{L}\{e^{at}t\} = \frac{1}{(s - a)^2}, \ (s > a).$$

Example 9.15. Find $\mathcal{L}\{e^{at}\mathrm{sin}bt\}$. We let $F(t) = \mathrm{sin}bt$. Then $\mathcal{L}\{e^{at}\mathrm{sin}bt\} = f(s - a)$, where $f(s) = \mathcal{L}\{\mathrm{sin}bt\} = \dfrac{b}{s^2 + b^2}$, $(s > 0)$. Thus

$$f(s - a) = \frac{b}{(s - a)^2 + b^2} \ \text{ and so}$$

(9.16)
$$\mathcal{L}\{e^{at}\mathrm{sin}bt\} = \frac{b}{(s - a)^2 + b^2}, \ (s > a).$$

THEOREM 9.6.

Hypothesis. Suppose F is a function satisfying the hypotheses of Theorem 9.1. with Laplace Transform f so that

$$f(s) = \int_0^\infty e^{-st}F(t)dt;$$

and G is the function defined as follows:

(9.17)
$$G(t) = \begin{cases} 0 & , 0 < t < a, \\ F(t - a), & t > a. \end{cases}$$

Conclusion.

(9.18)
$$\mathcal{L}\{G(t)\} = e^{-as}f(s)$$

Proof.

$$\mathcal{L}\{G(t)\} = \int_0^\infty e^{-st}G(t)dt = \int_0^a e^{-st} \cdot 0 dt + \int_a^\infty e^{-st}F(t - a)dt = \int_a^\infty e^{-st}F(t - a)dt.$$

Letting $t - a = \tau$, we obtain

$$\int_a^\infty e^{-st}F(t - a)dt = \int_0^\infty e^{-s(\tau + a)}F(\tau)d\tau = e^{-as}\int_0^\infty e^{-s\tau}F(\tau)d\tau = e^{-as}\mathcal{L}\{F(\tau)\}.$$

Thus

$$\mathcal{L}\{G(t)\} = e^{-as}f(s). \hspace{3cm} Q.E.D.$$

Example 9.16. Find $\mathcal{L}\{G(t)\}$ if

$$G(t) = \begin{cases} 0 & , 0 < t < \dfrac{\pi}{2}, \\ \mathrm{sin}t, & t > \dfrac{\pi}{2}. \end{cases}$$

Since $\sin t = \cos\left(t - \dfrac{\pi}{2}\right)$, we may write

$$G(t) = \begin{cases} 0 & , 0 < t < \dfrac{\pi}{2} \\ \cos\left(t - \dfrac{\pi}{2}\right), & t > \dfrac{\pi}{2}. \end{cases}$$

Thus Theorem 9.6 applies with $F(t) = \cos t$ and

$$\mathcal{L}\{G(t)\} = e^{-\frac{\pi}{2}s} f(s), \text{ where } f(s) = \mathcal{L}\{\cos t\} = \frac{s}{s^2 + 1}$$

(using (9.6) with $b = 1$).
Therefore, we have

$$\mathcal{L}\{G(t)\} = \frac{se^{-\frac{\pi}{2}s}}{s^2 + 1}.$$

THEOREM 9.7.

Hypothesis. Suppose F is a function satisfying the hypotheses of Theorem 9.1, with Laplace Transform f, where

(9.19)
$$f(s) = \int_0^\infty e^{-st} F(t)\,dt.$$

Conclusion.

(9.20)
$$\mathcal{L}\{t^n F(t)\} = (-1)^n \frac{d^n}{ds^n}[f(s)].$$

Proof. Differentiate both sides of Equation (9.19) n times with respect to s. This differentiation is justified in the present case and yields

$$f'(s) = (-1)^1 \int_0^\infty e^{-st} t F(t)\,dt,$$

$$f''(s) = (-1)^2 \int_0^\infty e^{-st} t^2 F(t)\,dt,$$

$$\vdots$$

$$f^{(n)}(s) = (-1)^n \int_0^\infty e^{-st} t^n F(t)\,dt,$$

from which the conclusion (9.20) is at once apparent.   *Q.E.D.*

Example 9.17. Find

$$\mathcal{L}\{t^2 \sin bt\}.$$

By Theorem 9.7,

$$\mathcal{L}\{t^2 \sin bt\} = (-1)^2 \frac{d^2}{ds^2}[f(s)],$$

where $f(s) = \mathcal{L}\{\sin bt\} = \dfrac{b}{s^2 + b^2}$ (using (9.5)).

From this,

$$\frac{d}{ds}[f(s)] = -\frac{2bs}{(s^2 + b^2)^2} \quad \text{and}$$

$$\frac{d^2}{ds^2}[f(s)] = \frac{6bs^2 - 2b^3}{(s^2 + b^2)^3}.$$

Thus,

$$\mathcal{L}\{t^2 \sin bt\} = \frac{6bs^2 - 2b^3}{(s^2 + b^2)^3}.$$

C. The Inverse Transform and the Convolution

Thus far in this chapter we have been concerned with the following problem: Given a function F, defined for $t > 0$, to find its Laplace Transform, which we denoted by $\mathcal{L}\{F\}$ or f. Now consider the inverse problem: Given a function f, to find a function F whose Laplace Transform is the given f. We introduce the notation $\mathcal{L}^{-1}\{f\}$ to denote such a function F, denote $\mathcal{L}^{-1}\{f(s)\}$ by $F(t)$, and call such a function an *inverse transform* of f. That is,

$$F(t) = \mathcal{L}^{-1}\{f(s)\}$$

means that $F(t)$ is such that

$$\mathcal{L}\{F(t)\} = f(s).$$

Three questions arise at once:
(a) Given a function f, does an inverse transform of f exist?
(b) Assuming f does have an inverse transform, is this inverse transform unique?
(c) How is an inverse transform found?

In answer to question (a) we shall say "not necessarily," for there exist functions f which are not Laplace Transforms of any function F. In order for f to be a transform it must possess certain continuity properties and also behave suitably as $s \to \infty$. To reassure the reader in a practical way we note that inverse transforms corresponding to numerous functions f have been determined and tabulated.

Now let us consider question (b). Assuming that f is a function which *does have* an inverse transform, in what sense, if any, is this inverse transform unique? We answer this question in a manner which us adequate for our purposes by stating without proof the following theorem.

THEOREM 9.8.

Hypothesis.   Let F and G be two functions which are continuous for $t \geq 0$ and which have the same Laplace Transform f.

Conclusion. $F(t) = G(t)$ for all $t \geq 0$.

Thus if it is known that a given function f has a *continuous* inverse transform F, then F is the *only* continuous inverse transform of f. Let us consider the following example.

Example 9.18.   By equation (9.2), $\mathcal{L}\{1\} = \dfrac{1}{s}$. Thus an inverse transform of the function f defined by $f(s) = \dfrac{1}{s}$ is the *continuous* function F defined for all t by $F(t) = 1$. Thus by Theorem 9.8 there is no other *continuous* inverse transform of the function f such that $f(s) = \dfrac{1}{s}$. However, discontinuous inverse transforms of this function f exist. For example, consider the function G defined as follows:

$$G(t) = \begin{cases} 1, 0 < t < 3, \\ 2, t = 3, \\ 1, t > 3. \end{cases}$$

Then

$$\mathcal{L}\{G(t)\} = \int_0^\infty e^{-st} G(t)\,dt = \int_0^3 e^{-st}\,dt + \int_3^\infty e^{-st}\,dt = \left[-\frac{e^{-st}}{s} \right]_0^3 + \lim_{R \to \infty} \left[-\frac{e^{-st}}{s} \right]_3^R$$

$$= \frac{1}{s} \quad \text{if } s > 0.$$

Thus this discontinuous function G is also an inverse transform of f defined by $f(s) = \dfrac{1}{s}$. However, we again emphasize that the only *continuous* inverse transform of f defined by $f(s) = \dfrac{1}{s}$ is F defined for all t by $F(t) = 1$. Indeed we write

$$\mathcal{L}^{-1}\left\{ \frac{1}{s} \right\} = 1,$$

with the understanding that F defined for all t by $F(t) = 1$ is the *unique continuous* inverse transform of f defined by $f(s) = \dfrac{1}{s}$.

Finally let us consider question (c). Assuming a unique continuous inverse transform of f exists, how is it actually found? The direct determination of inverse transforms will not be considered in this book. Our primary means of finding the inverse transform of a given f will be to make use of a table of transforms. As already indicated, extensive tables of transforms have been prepared. A short table of this kind appears on page 311.

In using a table of transforms to find the inverse transform of a given f, certain preliminary manipulations often have to be performed in order to put the given $f(s)$ in a form to which the various entries in the table apply. Among the various techniques available, the method of partial fractions is often very useful. We shall illustrate its use in Example 9.20.

Example 9.19. Using Table 9.1, find $\mathcal{L}^{-1}\left\{\dfrac{1}{s^2 + 6s + 13}\right\}$.

Solution. Looking in the $f(s)$ column of Table 9.1 we would first look for $(s)f = \dfrac{1}{as^2 + bs + c}$. However, we find no such $f(s)$; but we do find $f(s) = \dfrac{b}{(s + a)^2 + b^2}$ (number 11). We can put the given expression $\dfrac{1}{s^2 + 6s + 13}$ in this form as follows:

$$\frac{1}{s^2 + 6s + 13} = \frac{1}{(s + 3)^2 + 4} = \frac{1}{2}\cdot\frac{2}{(s + 3)^2 + 2^2}.$$

Thus, using number 11 of Table 9.1, we have

$$\mathcal{L}^{-1}\left\{\frac{1}{s^2 + 6s + 13}\right\} = \frac{1}{2}\mathcal{L}^{-1}\left\{\frac{2}{(s + 3)^2 + 2^2}\right\} = \frac{1}{2}e^{-3t}\sin 2t.$$

Example 9.20. Using Table 9.1, find $\mathcal{L}^{-1}\left\{\dfrac{1}{s(s^2 + 1)}\right\}$.

Solution. No entry of this form appears in the $f(s)$ column of Table 9.1. We employ the method of partial fractions. We have

$$\frac{1}{s(s^2 + 1)} = \frac{A}{s} + \frac{Bs + C}{s^2 + 1}$$

and hence

$$1 = (A + B)s^2 + Cs + A.$$

Thus

$$A + B = 0, C = 0, \text{ and } A = 1.$$

From these equations, we have the partial fractions decomposition

$$\frac{1}{s(s^2 + 1)} = \frac{1}{s} - \frac{s}{s^2 + 1}.$$

Thus

$$\mathcal{L}^{-1}\left\{\frac{1}{s(s^2 + 1)}\right\} = \mathcal{L}^{-1}\left\{\frac{1}{s}\right\} - \mathcal{L}^{-1}\left\{\frac{s}{s^2 + 1}\right\}.$$

By number 1 of Table 9.1, $\mathcal{L}^{-1}\left\{\dfrac{1}{s}\right\} = 1$ and by number 4, $\mathcal{L}^{-1}\left\{\dfrac{s}{s^2 + 1}\right\} = \cos t$. Thus

$$\mathcal{L}^{-1}\left\{\frac{1}{s(s^2 + 1)}\right\} = 1 - \cos t.$$

Another important procedure in connection with the use of tables of transforms is that furnished by the so-called Convolution Theorem which we shall state below. We first define the convolution of two functions F and G.

DEFINITION. Let F and G be two functions which are piecewise continuous on every finite closed interval $0 \leq t \leq b$ and of exponential order. The function denoted by $F * G$ and defined by

$$(9.21) \qquad F(t) * G(t) = \int_0^t F(\tau) G(t - \tau) d\tau$$

is called the *convolution* of the functions F and G.

Let us change the variable of integration in (9.21) by means of the substitution $u = t - \tau$. We have

$$F(t) * G(t) = \int_0^t F(\tau) G(t - \tau) d\tau = -\int_t^0 F(t - u) G(u) du$$

$$= \int_0^t G(u) F(t - u) du = G(t) * F(t).$$

Thus we have shown that

$$(9.22) \qquad F * G = G * F$$

Suppose that both F and G are piecewise continuous on every finite closed interval $0 \leq t \leq b$ and of exponential order e^{at}. Then it can be shown that $F * G$ is also piecewise continuous on every finite closed interval $0 \leq t \leq b$ and of exponential order $e^{(a+\epsilon)t}$, where ϵ is any positive number. Thus $\mathcal{L}\{F * G\}$ exists for s sufficiently large. More explicitly, it can be shown that $\mathcal{L}\{F * G\}$ exists for $s > a$.

We now prove the following important theorem concerning $\mathcal{L}\{F * G\}$.

THEOREM 9.9.

Hypothesis. Let the functions F and G be piecewise continuous on every finite closed interval $0 \leq t \leq b$ and of exponential order e^{at}.

Conclusion.

$$(9.23) \qquad \mathcal{L}\{F * G\} = \mathcal{L}\{F\}\mathcal{L}\{G\}$$

for $s > a$.

Proof. By definition of the Laplace Transform, $\mathcal{L}\{F * G\}$ is the function defined by

$$(9.24) \qquad \int_0^\infty e^{-st} \left[\int_0^t F(\tau) G(t - \tau) d\tau \right] dt.$$

The integral (9.24) may be expressed as the iterated integral

$$(9.25) \qquad \int_0^\infty \int_0^t e^{-st} F(\tau) G(t - \tau) d\tau dt.$$

Further, the iterated integral (9.25) is equal to the double integral

(9.26)
$$\iint_{R_1} e^{-st} F(\tau) G(t - \tau) d\tau dt,$$

where R_1 is the 45° wedge bounded by the lines $\tau = 0$ and $t = \tau$ (see Figure 9.2).

We now make the change of variable

(9.27)
$$\begin{cases} u = t - \tau \\ v = \tau \end{cases}$$

to transform the double integral (9.26). The change of variables (9.27) has Jacobian 1 and transforms the region R_1 in the τ, t plane into the first octant of the u,v plane. Thus the double integral (9.26) transforms into the double integral

(9.28)
$$\iint_{R_2} e^{-s(u+v)} F(v) G(u) du dv,$$

where R_2 is the quarter plane defined by $u > 0$, $v > 0$ (see Figure 9.3).

The double integral (9.28) is equal to the iterated integral

(9.29)
$$\int_0^\infty \int_0^\infty e^{-s(u+v)} F(v) G(u) du dv.$$

But the iterated integral (9.29) can be expressed in the form

(9.30)
$$\int_0^\infty e^{-sv} F(v) dv \int_0^\infty e^{-su} G(u) du.$$

But the left-hand integral in (9.30) defines $\mathcal{L}\{F\}$ and the right-hand integral defines $\mathcal{L}\{G\}$. Therefore the expression (9.30) is precisely $\mathcal{L}\{F\}\mathcal{L}\{G\}$.

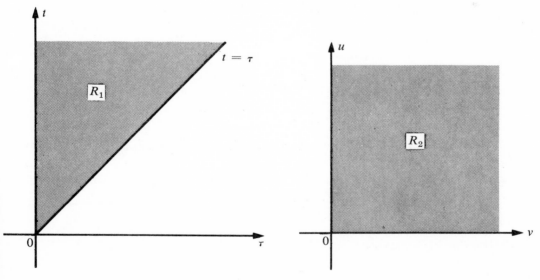

Figure 9.2   Figure 9.3

We note that since the integrals involved are absolutely convergent for $s > a$, the operations performed are indeed legitimate for $s > a$. Therefore we have shown that

$$\mathcal{L}\{F * G\} = \mathcal{L}\{F\}\mathcal{L}\{G\} \quad \text{for } s > a. \qquad\qquad Q.E.D.$$

Denoting $\mathcal{L}\{F\}$ by f and $\mathcal{L}\{G\}$ by g, we may write the conclusion (9.23) in the form

$$\mathcal{L}\{F(t) * G(t)\} = f(s)g(s).$$

Hence, we have

(9.31) $$\mathcal{L}^{-1}\{f(s)g(s)\} = F(t) * G(t) = \int_0^t F(\tau)G(t - \tau)d\tau,$$

and using (9.22), we also have

(9.32) $$\mathcal{L}^{-1}\{f(s)g(s)\} = G(t) * F(t) = \int_0^t G(\tau)F(t - \tau)d\tau.$$

Suppose we are given a function h and are required to determine $\mathcal{L}^{-1}\{h(s)\}$. If we can express $h(s)$ as a product $f(s)g(s)$, where $\mathcal{L}^{-1}\{f(s)\} = F(t)$ and $\mathcal{L}^{-1}\{g(s)\} = G(t)$ are known, then we can apply either (9.31) or (9.32) to determine $\mathcal{L}^{-1}\{h(s)\}$.

Example 9.21. Find $\mathcal{L}^{-1}\left\{\dfrac{1}{s(s^2 + 1)}\right\}$ using the convolution and Table 9.1.

Solution. We write $\dfrac{1}{s(s^2 + 1)}$ as the product $f(s)g(s)$, where $f(s) = \dfrac{1}{s}$ and $g(s) = \dfrac{1}{s^2 + 1}$. By Table 9.1, number 1, $F(t) = \mathcal{L}^{-1}\left\{\dfrac{1}{s}\right\} = 1$, and by number 3, $G(t) = \mathcal{L}^{-1}\left\{\dfrac{1}{s^2 + 1}\right\} = \sin t$. Thus by (9.31),

$$\mathcal{L}^{-1}\left\{\frac{1}{s(s^2 + 1)}\right\} = F(t) * G(t) = \int_0^t 1 \cdot \sin(t - \tau)d\tau,$$

and by (9.32),

$$\mathcal{L}^{-1}\left\{\frac{1}{s(s^2 + 1)}\right\} = G(t) * F(t) = \int_0^t \sin\tau \cdot 1 d\tau.$$

The second of these two integrals is slightly more simple. Evaluating it, we have

$$\mathcal{L}^{-1}\left\{\frac{1}{s(s^2 + 1)}\right\} = 1 - \cos t.$$

Observe that we obtained this result in Example 9.20 by means of partial fractions.

Exercises

1. Use the definition of the Laplace Transform to find:
   (a) $\mathcal{L}\{t^2\}$,
   (b) $\mathcal{L}\{\sinh bt\}$.
2. Use Theorem 9.2 to find:
   (a) $\mathcal{L}\{\cos^2 at\}$,
   (b) $\mathcal{L}\{\sin at \sin bt\}$.
3. Use Theorem 9.2 to find $\mathcal{L}\{\sin^3 at\}$ and then employ Theorem 9.3 to obtain $\mathcal{L}\{\sin^2 at \cos at\}$.
4. Use Theorem 9.2 to find $\mathcal{L}\{\cos^3 at\}$ and then employ Theorem 9.3 to obtain $\mathcal{L}\{\cos^2 at \sin at\}$.

Table 9.1 — Laplace Transforms

	$F(t)$	$f(s)$
1	1	$\dfrac{1}{s}$
2	e^{at}	$\dfrac{1}{s-a}$
3	$\sin bt$	$\dfrac{b}{s^2+b^2}$
4	$\cos bt$	$\dfrac{s}{s^2+b^2}$
5	$\sinh bt$	$\dfrac{b}{s^2-b^2}$
6	$\cosh bt$	$\dfrac{s}{s^2-b^2}$
7	$t^n\ (n=1,2,\ldots)$	$\dfrac{n!}{s^{n+1}}$
8	$t^n e^{at}\ (n=1,2,\ldots)$	$\dfrac{n!}{(s-a)^{n+1}}$
9	$t\sin bt$	$\dfrac{2bs}{(s^2+b^2)^2}$
10	$t\cos bt$	$\dfrac{s^2-b^2}{(s^2+b^2)^2}$
11	$e^{-at}\sin bt$	$\dfrac{b}{(s+a)^2+b^2}$
12	$e^{-at}\cos bt$	$\dfrac{s+a}{(s+a)^2+b^2}$
13	$\dfrac{\sin bt - bt\cos bt}{2b^3}$	$\dfrac{1}{(s^2+b^2)^2}$
14	$\dfrac{t\sin bt}{2b}$	$\dfrac{s}{(s^2+b^2)^2}$

5. Given that $\mathcal{L}\{t^2\} = \dfrac{2}{s^3}$, use Theorem 9.4 to find $\mathcal{L}\{t^4\}$.

6. Use Theorem 9.5 to find:
   (a) $\mathcal{L}\{e^{at}t^2\}$.
   (b) $\mathcal{L}\{e^{at}\sin^2 bt\}$.

7. Use Theorem 9.6 to find $\mathcal{L}\{G(t)\}$, where :

   (a) $G(t) = \begin{cases} 0, & 0 < t < \pi/2, \\ \cos t, & t > \pi/2. \end{cases}$

   (b) $G(t) = \begin{cases} 0, & 0 < t < 2, \\ t, & t > 2. \end{cases}$

8. Use Theorem 9.7 to find: (a) $\mathcal{L}\{t^2 \cos bt\}$.
   (b) $\mathcal{L}\{t^3 \sin bt\}$.
   (c) $\mathcal{L}\{t^4 e^{at}\}$.

Use Table 9.1 to find $\mathcal{L}^{-1}\{f(s)\}$ for each of the functions f defined in Exercises 9 through 18:

9. $f(s) = \dfrac{2}{s^2 + 9}$.

10. $f(s) = \dfrac{3s}{s^2 - 4}$.

11. $f(s) = \dfrac{5}{(s - 2)^4}$.

12. $f(s) = \dfrac{5s}{s^2 + 4s + 4}$.

13. $f(s) = \dfrac{s + 2}{s^2 + 4s + 7}$.

14. $f(s) = \dfrac{s + 10}{s^2 + 8s + 20}$.

15. $f(s) = \dfrac{1}{s^3 + 4s^2 + 3s}$.

16. $f(s) = \dfrac{s + 1}{s^3 + 2s}$.

17. $f(s) = \dfrac{s + 3}{(s^2 + 4)^2}$.

18. $f(s) = \dfrac{s + 5}{s^4 + 3s^3 + 2s^2}$.

9.2 Laplace Transform Solution of Linear Differential Equations with Constant Coefficients

A. The Method

We now consider how the Laplace Transform may be applied to solve the initial value problem consisting of the nth order linear differential equation with constant coefficients

$$(9.33) \qquad a_0 \frac{d^n Y}{dt^n} + a_1 \frac{d^{n-1} Y}{dt^{n-1}} + \cdots + a_{n-1} \frac{dY}{dt} + a_n Y = B(t),$$

plus the initial conditions

$$(9.34) \qquad Y(0) = c_0, \; Y'(0) = c_1, \ldots, Y^{(n-1)}(0) = c_{n-1}.$$

Theorem 4.1 (Chapter 4) assures us that this problem has a unique solution.

We now take the Laplace Transform of both members of Equation (9.33). By Theorem 9.2, we have

$$(9.35) \quad a_0 \mathcal{L}\left\{\frac{d^n Y}{dt^n}\right\} + a_1 \mathcal{L}\left\{\frac{d^{n-1} Y}{dt^{n-1}}\right\} + \cdots + a_{n-1} \mathcal{L}\left\{\frac{dY}{dt}\right\} + a_n \mathcal{L}\{Y(t)\} = \mathcal{L}\{B(t)\}.$$

We now apply Theorem 9.4 to $\mathcal{L}\left\{\dfrac{d^n Y}{dt^n}\right\}$, $\mathcal{L}\left\{\dfrac{d^{n-1} Y}{dt^{n-1}}\right\}$, $\ldots$, $\mathcal{L}\left\{\dfrac{dY}{dt}\right\}$ in the left member of equation (9.35). Using the initial conditions (9.34), we have

$$\mathcal{L}\left\{\frac{d^n Y}{dt^n}\right\} = s^n \mathcal{L}\{Y(t)\} - s^{n-1} Y(0) - s^{n-2} Y'(0) - \cdots - Y^{(n-1)}(0)$$

$$= s^n \mathcal{L}\{Y(t)\} - c_0 s^{n-1} - c_1 s^{n-2} - \cdots - c_{n-1},$$

$$\mathcal{L}\left\{\frac{d^{n-1} Y}{dt^{n-1}}\right\} = s^{n-1} \mathcal{L}\{Y(t)\} - s^{n-2} Y(0) - s^{n-3} Y'(0) - \cdots - Y^{(n-2)}(0)$$

$$= s^{n-1} \mathcal{L}\{Y(t)\} - c_0 s^{n-2} - c_1 s^{n-3} - \cdots - c_{n-2},$$

$$\cdots$$

$$\mathcal{L}\left\{\frac{dY}{dt}\right\} = s\mathcal{L}\{Y(t)\} - Y(0) = s\mathcal{L}\{Y(t)\} - c_0.$$

Thus, letting $y(s)$ denote $\mathcal{L}\{Y(t)\}$ and $b(s)$ denote $\mathcal{L}\{B(t)\}$, Equation (9.35) becomes

$$(9.36) \quad [a_0 s^n + a_1 s^{n-1} + \cdots + a_{n-1}s + a_n]y(s) - c_0[a_0 s^{n-1} + a_1 s^{n-2} + \cdots + a_{n-1}]$$
$$- c_1[a_0 s^{n-2} + a_1 s^{n-3} + \cdots + a_{n-2}] - \cdots - c_{n-2}[a_0 s + a_1] - c_{n-1}a_0 = b(s).$$

Since B is a known function of t, then b, assuming it exists and can be determined, is a known function of s. Thus Equation (9.36) is an algebraic equation in the "unknown" $y(s)$. We now solve the algebraic equation (9.36) to determine $y(s)$. Once $y(s)$ has been found, we then find the unique solution

$$Y(t) = \mathcal{L}^{-1}\{y(s)\}$$

of the given initial-value problem using the table of transforms.

We summarize this procedure as follows:
(a) Take the Laplace Transform of both sides of the differential equation (9.33), applying Theorem 9.4 and using the initial conditions (9.34) in the process, and equate the results to obtain the algebraic equation (9.36) in the "unknown" $y(s)$.
(b) Solve the algebraic equation (9.36) thus obtained to determine $y(s)$.
(c) Having found $y(s)$, employ the table of transforms to determine the solution $Y(t)$ $= \mathcal{L}^{-1}\{y(s)\}$ of the given initial-value problem.

B. Examples

We shall now consider several detailed examples which will illustrate the procedure outlined above.

Example 9.22. Solve the initial-value problem

$$(9.37) \qquad \qquad \frac{dY}{dt} - 2Y = e^{5t}$$

$$(9.38) \qquad \qquad Y(0) = 3$$

Step (a). Taking the Laplace Transform of both sides of the differential equation (9.37), we have

$$(9.39) \qquad \mathcal{L}\left\{\frac{dY}{dt}\right\} - 2\mathcal{L}\{Y(t)\} = \mathcal{L}\{e^{5t}\}.$$

Using Theorem 9.4 with $n = 1$ (or Theorem 9.3) and denoting $\mathcal{L}\{Y(t)\}$ by $y(s)$, we may express $\mathcal{L}\left\{\dfrac{dY}{dt}\right\}$ in terms of $y(s)$ and $Y(0)$ as follows:

$$\mathcal{L}\left\{\frac{dY}{dt}\right\} = sy(s) - Y(0).$$

Applying the initial condition (9.38), this becomes

$$\mathcal{L}\left\{\frac{dY}{dt}\right\} = sy(s) - 3.$$

Using this, the left member of Equation (9.39) becomes $sy(s) - 3 - 2y(s)$. From Table 9.1, number 2, $\mathcal{L}\{e^{5t}\} = \dfrac{1}{s-5}$. Thus Equation (9.39) reduces to the algebraic equation

$$(9.40) \qquad\qquad [s-2]y(s) - 3 = \frac{1}{s-5}$$

in the unknown $y(s)$.

Step (b). We now solve Equation (9.40) for $y(s)$. We have

$$[s-2]y(s) = \frac{3s-14}{s-5}$$

and so

$$y(s) = \frac{3s-14}{(s-2)(s-5)}.$$

Step (c). We must now determine

$$\mathcal{L}^{-1}\left\{\frac{3s-14}{(s-2)(s-5)}\right\}.$$

We employ partial fractions. We have

$$\frac{3s-14}{(s-2)(s-5)} = \frac{A}{s-2} + \frac{B}{s-5},$$

and so $3s - 14 = A(s-5) + B(s-2)$. From this we find that

$$A = \frac{8}{3} \quad \text{and} \quad B = \frac{1}{3},$$

and so

$$\mathcal{L}^{-1}\left\{\frac{3s-14}{(s-2)(s-5)}\right\} = \frac{8}{3}\mathcal{L}^{-1}\left\{\frac{1}{s-2}\right\} + \frac{1}{3}\mathcal{L}^{-1}\left\{\frac{1}{s-5}\right\}.$$

Using number 2 of Table 9.1,

$$\mathcal{L}^{-1}\left\{\frac{1}{s-2}\right\} = e^{2t} \quad \text{and} \quad \mathcal{L}^{-1}\left\{\frac{1}{s-5}\right\} = e^{5t}.$$

Thus the solution of the given initial-value problem is

$$Y = \frac{8}{3}e^{2t} + \frac{1}{3}e^{5t}.$$

Example 9.23. Solve the initial-value problem

$$(9.41)$$
$$(9.42)$$
$$(9.43)$$

$$\begin{cases} \dfrac{d^2Y}{dt^2} - 2\dfrac{dY}{dt} - 8Y = 0 \\[2mm] Y(0) = 3 \\[2mm] Y'(0) = 6 \end{cases}$$

Step (a). Taking the Laplace Transform of both sides of the differential equation (9.41), we have

(9.44) $$\mathcal{L}\left\{\frac{d^2Y}{dt^2}\right\} - 2\mathcal{L}\left\{\frac{dY}{dt}\right\} - 8\mathcal{L}\{Y(t)\} = \mathcal{L}\{0\}.$$

Since $\mathcal{L}\{0\} = 0$, the right member of equation (9.44) is simply 0. Denote $\mathcal{L}\{Y(t)\}$ by $y(s)$. Then, applying Theorem 9.4, we have the following expressions for $\mathcal{L}\left\{\frac{d^2Y}{dt^2}\right\}$ and $\mathcal{L}\left\{\frac{dY}{dt}\right\}$ in terms of $y(s)$, $Y(0)$, and $Y'(0)$:

$$\begin{cases} \mathcal{L}\left\{\dfrac{d^2Y}{dt^2}\right\} = s^2y(s) - sY(0) - Y'(0), \\[2mm] \mathcal{L}\left\{\dfrac{dY}{dt}\right\} = sy(s) - Y(0). \end{cases}$$

Applying the initial conditions (9.42) and (9.43) to these expressions, they become:

$$\begin{cases} \mathcal{L}\left\{\dfrac{d^2Y}{dt^2}\right\} = s^2y(s) - 3s - 6, \\[2mm] \mathcal{L}\left\{\dfrac{dY}{dt}\right\} = sy(s) - 3. \end{cases}$$

Now, using these expressions, Equation (9.44) becomes

$$s^2y(s) - 3s - 6 - 2sy(s) + 6 - 8y(s) = 0$$

or

(9.45) $$[s^2 - 2s - 8]y(s) - 3s = 0.$$

Step (b). We now solve Equation (9.45) for $y(s)$. We have at once

$$y(s) = \frac{3s}{(s-4)(s+2)}.$$

Step (c). We must now determine

$$\mathcal{L}^{-1}\left\{\frac{3s}{(s-4)(s+2)}\right\}.$$

We shall again employ partial fractions. From

$$\frac{3s}{(s-4)(s+2)} = \frac{A}{s-4} + \frac{B}{s+2}$$

we find that $A = 2$, $B = 1$. Thus

$$\mathcal{L}^{-1}\left\{\frac{3s}{(s-4)(s+2)}\right\} = 2\mathcal{L}^{-1}\left\{\frac{1}{s-4}\right\} + \mathcal{L}^{-1}\left\{\frac{1}{s+2}\right\}.$$

By Table 9.1, number 2, we find

$$\mathcal{L}^{-1}\left\{\frac{1}{s-4}\right\} = e^{4t} \quad \text{and} \quad \mathcal{L}^{-1}\left\{\frac{1}{s+2}\right\} = e^{-2t}.$$

Thus the solution of the given initial-value problem is

$$Y = 2e^{4t} + e^{-2t}.$$

Example 9.24.   Solve the initial-value problem

(9.46) $\dfrac{d^2Y}{dt^2} + Y = e^{-2t}\sin t,$

(9.47) $Y(0) = 0,$

(9.48) $Y'(0) = 0.$

Step (a).   Taking the Laplace Transform of both sides of the differential equation (9.46), we have

(9.49) $\mathcal{L}\left\{\dfrac{d^2Y}{dt^2}\right\} + \mathcal{L}\{Y(t)\} = \mathcal{L}\{e^{-2t}\sin t\}.$

Denoting $\mathcal{L}\{Y(t)\}$ by $y(s)$ and applying Theorem 9.4, we express $\mathcal{L}\left\{\dfrac{d^2Y}{dt^2}\right\}$ in terms of $y(s)$, $Y(0)$, and $Y'(0)$ as follows:

$$\mathcal{L}\left\{\dfrac{d^2Y}{dt^2}\right\} = s^2y(s) - sY(0) - Y'(0).$$

Applying the initial conditions (9.47) and (9.48) to this expression, it becomes simply

$$\mathcal{L}\left\{\dfrac{d^2Y}{dt^2}\right\} = s^2y(s);$$

and thus the left member of equation (9.49) becomes $s^2y(s) + y(s)$. By number 11, Table 9.1, the right member of equation (9.49) becomes

$$\frac{1}{(s+2)^2 + 1}.$$

Thus equation (9.49) reduces to the algebraic equation

(9.50) $(s^2 + 1)y(s) = \dfrac{1}{(s+2)^2 + 1}$

in the unknown $y(s)$.

Step (b).   Solving equation (9.50) for $y(s)$, we have

$$y(s) = \frac{1}{(s^2 + 1)[(s+2)^2 + 1]}.$$

Step (c).   We must now determine

$$\mathcal{L}^{-1}\left\{\frac{1}{(s^2 + 1)[(s+2)^2 + 1]}\right\}.$$

We may use either partial fractions or the convolution. We shall illustrate both methods.

(i)   *Use of Partial Fractions:*

We have

$$\frac{1}{(s^2 + 1)(s^2 + 4s + 5)} = \frac{As + B}{s^2 + 1} + \frac{Cs + D}{s^2 + 4s + 5}.$$

From this we find

$$1 = (As + B)(s^2 + 4s + 5) + (Cs + D)(s^2 + 1)$$
$$= (A + C)s^3 + (4A + B + D)s^2 + (5A + 4B + C)s + (5B + D).$$

Thus we obtain the equations

$$\begin{cases} A + C = 0, \\ 4A + B + D = 0, \\ 5A + 4B + C = 0, \\ 5B + D = 1. \end{cases}$$

From these equations we find that

$$A = -\frac{1}{8}, \quad B = \frac{1}{8}, \quad C = \frac{1}{8}, \quad D = \frac{3}{8}.$$

and so

(9.51) $$\mathcal{L}^{-1}\left\{\frac{1}{(s^2 + 1)(s^2 + 4s + 5)}\right\} = -\frac{1}{8}\mathcal{L}^{-1}\left\{\frac{s}{s^2 + 1}\right\} + \frac{1}{8}\mathcal{L}^{-1}\left\{\frac{1}{s^2 + 1}\right\}$$
$$+ \frac{1}{8}\mathcal{L}^{-1}\left\{\frac{s}{s^2 + 4s + 5}\right\} + \frac{3}{8}\mathcal{L}^{-1}\left\{\frac{1}{s^2 + 4s + 5}\right\}.$$

In order to determine

(9.52) $$\frac{1}{8}\mathcal{L}^{-1}\left\{\frac{s}{s^2 + 4s + 5}\right\} + \frac{3}{8}\mathcal{L}^{-1}\left\{\frac{1}{s^2 + 4s + 5}\right\},$$

we write

$$\frac{s}{s^2 + 4s + 5} = \frac{s + 2}{(s + 2)^2 + 1} - \frac{2}{(s + 2)^2 + 1}.$$

Thus the expression (9.52) becomes

$$\frac{1}{8}\mathcal{L}^{-1}\left\{\frac{s + 2}{(s + 2)^2 + 1}\right\} + \frac{1}{8}\mathcal{L}^{-1}\left\{\frac{1}{(s + 2)^2 + 1}\right\},$$

and so (9.51) may be written

$$\mathcal{L}^{-1}\left\{\frac{1}{(s^2 + 1)(s^2 + 4s + 5)}\right\} = -\frac{1}{8}\mathcal{L}^{-1}\left\{\frac{s}{s^2 + 1}\right\} + \frac{1}{8}\mathcal{L}^{-1}\left\{\frac{1}{s^2 + 1}\right\}$$
$$+ \frac{1}{8}\mathcal{L}^{-1}\left\{\frac{s + 2}{(s + 2)^2 + 1}\right\} + \frac{1}{8}\mathcal{L}^{-1}\left\{\frac{1}{(s + 2)^2 + 1}\right\}.$$

Now using Table 9.1, numbers 4, 3, 12, and 11, respectively, we obtain the solution

$$Y(t) = -\frac{1}{8}\cos t + \frac{1}{8}\sin t + \frac{1}{8}e^{-2t}\cos t + \frac{1}{8}e^{-2t}\sin t$$

or

(9.53) $$Y(t) = \frac{1}{8}(\sin t - \cos t) + \frac{e^{-2t}}{8}(\sin t + \cos t).$$

(ii) *Use of the Convolution:*

We write $\dfrac{1}{(s^2 + 1)[(s + 2)^2 + 1]}$ as the product $f(s)g(s)$, where $f(s) = \dfrac{1}{s^2 + 1}$ and $g(s)$

$= \dfrac{1}{(s + 2)^2 + 1}$. By Table 9.1, number 3, $F(t) = \mathcal{L}^{-1}\left\{\dfrac{1}{s^2 + 1}\right\} = \sin t$, and by number

11, $G(t) = \mathcal{L}^{-1}\left\{\dfrac{1}{(s + 2)^2 + 1}\right\} = e^{-2t}\sin t$. Thus by Theorem 9.9 using (9.31) or (9.32),

we have, respectively,

$$\mathcal{L}^{-1}\left\{\frac{1}{(s^2 + 1)[(s + 2)^2 + 1]}\right\} = F(t) * G(t) = \int_0^t \sin\tau \cdot e^{-2(t-\tau)}\sin(t - \tau)d\tau$$

or

$$\mathcal{L}^{-1}\left\{\frac{1}{(s^2 + 1)[(s + 2)^2 + 1]}\right\} = G(t) * F(t) = \int_0^t e^{-2\tau}\sin\tau \cdot \sin(t - \tau)d\tau.$$

The second of these integrals is slightly more simple; it reduces to

$$(\sin t)\int_0^t e^{-2\tau}\sin\tau\cos\tau d\tau - (\cos t)\int_0^t e^{-2\tau}\sin^2\tau d\tau.$$

Introducing double-angle formulas this becomes

$$\frac{\sin t}{2}\int_0^t e^{-2\tau}\sin 2\tau d\tau - \frac{\cos t}{2}\int_0^t e^{-2\tau}d\tau + \frac{\cos t}{2}\int_0^t e^{-2\tau}\cos 2\tau d\tau.$$

Carrying out the indicated integrations we find that this becomes

$$-\sin t\left[\frac{e^{-2\tau}}{8}(\sin 2\tau + \cos 2\tau)\right]_0^t + \frac{\cos t}{4}\left[e^{-2\tau}\right]_0^t + \cos t\left[\frac{e^{-2\tau}}{8}(\sin 2\tau - \cos 2\tau)\right]_0^t$$

$$= -\frac{e^{-2t}}{8}(\sin t \sin 2t + \sin t \cos 2t) + \frac{\sin t}{8} + \frac{e^{-2t}\cos t}{4} - \frac{\cos t}{4}$$

$$+ \frac{e^{-2t}}{8}(\cos t \sin 2t - \cos t \cos 2t) + \frac{\cos t}{8}.$$

Using double angle formulas and simplifying, this reduces to

$$\frac{1}{8}(\sin t - \cos t) + \frac{e^{-2t}}{8}(\sin t + \cos t),$$

which is the solution (9.53) obtained above using partial fractions.

Example 9.25. Solve the initial-value problem

(9.54)
$$\frac{d^3Y}{dt^3} + 4\frac{d^2Y}{dt^2} + 5\frac{dY}{dt} + 2Y = 10\cos t,$$

(9.55)
$$Y(0) = 0,$$

(9.56)
$$Y'(0) = 0,$$

(9.57)
$$Y''(0) = 3.$$

Step (a). Taking the Laplace Transform of both sides of the differential equation (9.54), we have

(9.58)
$$\mathscr{L}\left\{\frac{d^3Y}{dt^3}\right\} + 4\mathscr{L}\left\{\frac{d^2Y}{dt^2}\right\} + 5\mathscr{L}\left\{\frac{dY}{dt}\right\} + 2\mathscr{L}\{Y(t)\} = 10\mathscr{L}\{\cos t\}.$$

We denote $\mathscr{L}\{Y(t)\}$ by $y(s)$ and then apply Theorem 9.4 to express $\mathscr{L}\left\{\dfrac{d^3Y}{dt^3}\right\}$, $\mathscr{L}\left\{\dfrac{d^2Y}{dt^2}\right\}$,

and $\mathscr{L}\left\{\dfrac{dY}{dt}\right\}$ in terms of $y(s)$, $Y(0)$, $Y'(0)$, and $Y''(0)$. We thus obtain

$$\mathscr{L}\left\{\frac{d^3Y}{dt^3}\right\} = s^3y(s) - s^2Y(0) - sY'(0) - Y''(0),$$

$$\mathscr{L}\left\{\frac{d^2Y}{dt^2}\right\} = s^2y(s) - sY(0) - Y'(0), \text{ and}$$

$$\mathscr{L}\left\{\frac{dY}{dt}\right\} = sy(s) - Y(0).$$

Applying the initial conditions (9.55), (9.56), and (9.57), these expressions become

$$\mathscr{L}\left\{\frac{d^3Y}{dt^3}\right\} = s^3y(s) - 3$$

$$\mathscr{L}\left\{\frac{d^2Y}{dt^2}\right\} = s^2y(s), \text{ and}$$

$$\mathscr{L}\left\{\frac{dY}{dt}\right\} = sy(s).$$

Thus the left member of Equation (9.58) becomes

$$s^3y(s) - 3 + 4s^2y(s) + 5sy(s) + 2y(s)$$

or

$$[s^3 + 4s^2 + 5s + 2]y(s) - 3.$$

By number 4, Table 9.1,

$$10\mathscr{L}\{\cos t\} = \frac{10s}{s^2 + 1}.$$

Thus Equation (9.58) reduces to the algebraic equation

(9.59) $$(s^3 + 4s^2 + 5s + 2)y(s) - 3 = \frac{10s}{s^2 + 1}$$

in the unknown $y(s)$.

Step (b). We now solve Equation (9.59) for $y(s)$. We have

$$(s^3 + 4s^2 + 5s + 2)y(s) = \frac{3s^2 + 10s + 3}{s^2 + 1}$$

or

$$y(s) = \frac{3s^2 + 10s + 3}{(s^2 + 1)(s^3 + 4s^2 + 5s + 2)}.$$

Step (c). We must now determine

$$\mathcal{L}^{-1}\left\{\frac{3s^2 + 10s + 3}{(s^2 + 1)(s^3 + 4s^2 + 5s + 2)}\right\}.$$

Let us not despair! We can again employ partial fractions to put the expression for $y(s)$ into a form where Table 9.1 can be used, but the work will be rather involved. We proceed by writing

(9.60) $$\frac{3s^2 + 10s + 3}{(s^2 + 1)(s^3 + 4s^2 + 5s + 2)} = \frac{3s^2 + 10s + 3}{(s^2 + 1)(s + 1)^2(s + 2)}$$

$$= \frac{A}{s + 2} + \frac{B}{s + 1} + \frac{C}{(s + 1)^2} + \frac{Ds + E}{s^2 + 1}.$$

From this we find

(9.61) $$3s^2 + 10s + 3 = A(s + 1)^2(s^2 + 1) + B(s + 2)(s + 1)(s^2 + 1)$$
$$+ C(s + 2)(s^2 + 1) + (Ds + E)(s + 2)(s + 1)^2,$$

or

$$3s^2 + 10s + 3 = (A + B + D)s^4 + (2A + 3B + C + 4D + E)s^3$$
$$+ (2A + 3B + 2C + 5D + 4E)s^2$$
$$+ (2A + 3B + C + 2D + 5E)s + (A + 2B + 2C + 2E).$$

From this we obtain the system of equations

(9.62) $$\begin{cases} A + B + D = 0, \\ 2A + 3B + C + 4D + E = 0, \\ 2A + 3B + 2C + 5D + 4E = 3, \\ 2A + 3B + C + 2D + 5E = 10, \\ A + 2B + 2C + 2E = 3. \end{cases}$$

Letting $s = -1$ in equation (9.61), we find that $C = -2$; and letting $s = -2$ in this same equation results in $A = -1$. Using these values for A and C we find from the system (9.62) that

$$B = 2, D = -1, \text{ and } E = 2.$$

Substituting these values thus found for A, B, C, D, and E into Equation (9.60), we see that

$$\mathcal{L}^{-1}\left\{\frac{3s^2 + 10s + 3}{(s^2 + 1)(s^3 + 4s^2 + 5s + 2)}\right\} = -\mathcal{L}^{-1}\left\{\frac{1}{s+2}\right\} + 2\mathcal{L}^{-1}\left\{\frac{1}{s+1}\right\}$$
$$- 2\mathcal{L}^{-1}\left\{\frac{1}{(s+1)^2}\right\} - \mathcal{L}^{-1}\left\{\frac{s}{s^2+1}\right\} + 2\mathcal{L}^{-1}\left\{\frac{1}{s^2+1}\right\}.$$

Using Table 9.1, numbers 2, 2, 8, 4, and 3, respectively, we obtain the solution

$$Y(t) = -e^{-2t} + 2e^{-t} - 2te^{-t} - \cos t + 2\sin t.$$

Example 9.26.   Solve the initial-value problem

(9.63)
$$\frac{d^2Y}{dt^2} + 2\frac{dY}{dt} + 5Y = H(t),$$

(9.64)
$$\text{where } H(t) = \begin{cases} 1, & 0 < t < \pi, \\ 0, & t > \pi, \end{cases}$$

(9.65)
$$Y(0) = 0,$$

(9.66)
$$Y'(0) = 0.$$

Step (a).   We take the Laplace Transform of both sides of the differential equation (9.63) to obtain

(9.67)
$$\mathcal{L}\left\{\frac{d^2Y}{dt^2}\right\} + 2\mathcal{L}\left\{\frac{dY}{dt}\right\} + 5\mathcal{L}\{Y(t)\} = \mathcal{L}\{H(t)\}.$$

Denoting $\mathcal{L}\{Y(t)\}$ by $y(s)$, using Theorem 9.4 as in the previous examples, and then applying the initial conditions (9.65) and (9.66), we see that the left member of Equation (9.67) becomes $[s^2 + 2s + 5]y(s)$. By the definition of the Laplace Transform, from (9.64) we have

$$\mathcal{L}\{H(t)\} = \int_0^\infty e^{-st}H(t)dt = \int_0^\pi e^{-st}dt = \left[\frac{e^{-st}}{-s}\right]_0^\pi = \frac{1 - e^{-\pi s}}{s}.$$

Thus equation (9.67) becomes

(9.68)
$$[s^2 + 2s + 5]y(s) = \frac{1 - e^{-\pi s}}{s}.$$

Step (b).   We solve the algebraic equation (9.68) for $y(s)$ to obtain

$$y(s) = \frac{1 - e^{-\pi s}}{s(s^2 + 2s + 5)}.$$

Step (c).   We must now determine

$$\mathcal{L}^{-1}\left\{\frac{1 - e^{-\pi s}}{s(s^2 + 2s + 5)}\right\}.$$

Let us write this as

$$\mathcal{L}^{-1}\left\{\frac{1}{s(s^2 + 2s + 5)}\right\} - \mathcal{L}^{-1}\left\{\frac{e^{-\pi s}}{s(s^2 + 2s + 5)}\right\},$$

and apply partial fractions to determine the first of these two inverse transforms. Writing

$$\frac{1}{s(s^2 + 2s + 5)} = \frac{A}{s} + \frac{Bs + C}{s^2 + 2s + 5}, \text{ we find at once that } A = \frac{1}{5}, B = -\frac{1}{5}, C = -\frac{2}{5}.$$

Thus

$$\mathcal{L}^{-1}\left\{\frac{1}{s(s^2 + 2s + 5)}\right\} = \frac{1}{5}\mathcal{L}^{-1}\left\{\frac{1}{s}\right\} - \frac{1}{5}\mathcal{L}^{-1}\left\{\frac{s + 2}{(s + 1)^2 + 4}\right\} = \frac{1}{5}\mathcal{L}^{-1}\left\{\frac{1}{s}\right\}$$

$$- \frac{1}{5}\mathcal{L}^{-1}\left\{\frac{s + 1}{(s + 1)^2 + 4}\right\} - \frac{1}{10}\mathcal{L}^{-1}\left\{\frac{2}{(s + 1)^2 + 4}\right\} = \frac{1}{5} - \frac{1}{5}e^{-t}\cos 2t - \frac{1}{10}e^{-t}\sin 2t,$$

using Table 9.1, numbers 1, 12, and 11, respectively. Letting

$$f(s) = \frac{1}{s(s^2 + 2s + 5)}$$

and

$$F(t) = \frac{1}{5} - \frac{1}{5}e^{-t}\cos 2t - \frac{1}{10}e^{-t}\sin 2t,$$

we thus have

$$\mathcal{L}^{-1}\{f(s)\} = F(t).$$

We now consider

$$\mathcal{L}^{-1}\left\{\frac{e^{-\pi s}}{s(s^2 + 2s + 5)}\right\} = \mathcal{L}^{-1}\{e^{-\pi s}f(s)\}.$$

By Theorem 9.6,

$$\mathcal{L}^{-1}\{e^{-\pi s}f(s)\} = G(t),$$

where

$$G(t) = \begin{cases} 0 & , 0 < t < \pi, \\ F(t - \pi), & t > \pi. \end{cases}$$

Thus,

$$\mathcal{L}^{-1}\left\{\frac{e^{-\pi s}}{s(s^2 + 2s + 5)}\right\} = \begin{cases} 0, 0 < t < \pi, \\ \frac{1}{5} - \frac{1}{5}e^{-(t-\pi)}\cos 2(t - \pi) - \frac{1}{10}e^{-(t-\pi)}\sin 2(t - \pi), & t > \pi \end{cases}$$

$$= \begin{cases} 0, 0 < t < \pi, \\ \frac{1}{5} - \frac{1}{5}e^{-(t-\pi)}\cos 2t - \frac{1}{10}e^{-(t-\pi)}\sin 2t, & t > \pi. \end{cases}$$

Thus the solution is given by

$$Y(t) = \mathcal{L}^{-1}\left\{\frac{1 - e^{\pi s}}{s(s^2 + 2s + 5)}\right\} = F(t) - G(t)$$

$$= \begin{cases} \dfrac{1}{5} - \dfrac{1}{5}e^{-t}\cos2t - \dfrac{1}{10}e^{-t}\sin2t - 0, \quad 0 < t < \pi, \\ \dfrac{1}{5} - \dfrac{1}{5}e^{-t}\cos2t - \dfrac{1}{10}e^{-t}\sin2t - \dfrac{1}{5} + \dfrac{1}{5}e^{-(t-\pi)}\cos2t + \dfrac{1}{10}e^{-(t-\pi)}\sin2t, \quad t > \pi, \end{cases}$$

or

$$Y(t) = \begin{cases} \dfrac{1}{5}\left[1 - e^{-t}\left(\cos2t + \dfrac{1}{2}\sin2t\right)\right], \quad 0 < t < \pi, \\ \dfrac{e^{-t}}{5}\left[(e^\pi - 1)\cos2t + \left(\dfrac{e^\pi - 1}{2}\right)\sin2t\right], \quad t > \pi. \end{cases}$$

Exercises

Use Laplace Transforms to solve each of the initial-value problems in Exercises 1 through 10:

1. $\begin{cases} \dfrac{dY}{dt} - Y = e^{3t} \\ Y(0) = 2 \end{cases}$

2. $\begin{cases} \dfrac{dY}{dt} + Y = 2\sin t \\ Y(0) = -1 \end{cases}$

3. $\begin{cases} \dfrac{d^2Y}{dt^2} - 5\dfrac{dY}{dt} + 6Y = 0 \\ Y(0) = 1 \\ Y'(0) = 2 \end{cases}$

4. $\begin{cases} \dfrac{d^2Y}{dt^2} + \dfrac{dY}{dt} - 12Y = 0 \\ Y(0) = 4 \\ Y'(0) = -1 \end{cases}$

5. $\begin{cases} \dfrac{d^2Y}{dt^2} - \dfrac{dY}{dt} - 2Y = 18e^{-t}\sin3t \\ Y(0) = 0 \\ Y'(0) = 3 \end{cases}$

6. $\begin{cases} \dfrac{d^2Y}{dt^2} + 2\dfrac{dY}{dt} + Y = te^{-2t} \\ Y(0) = 1 \\ Y'(0) = 0 \end{cases}$

7. $\begin{cases} \dfrac{d^3Y}{dt^3} - 5\dfrac{d^2Y}{dt^2} + 7\dfrac{dY}{dt} - 3Y = \sin 20t \\[2mm] Y(0) = 0 \\[1mm] Y'(0) = 0 \\[1mm] Y''(0) = -2 \end{cases}$

8. $\begin{cases} \dfrac{d^3Y}{dt^3} - 6\dfrac{d^2Y}{dt^2} + 11\dfrac{dY}{dt} - 6Y = te^{-4t} \\[2mm] Y(0) = 1 \\[1mm] Y'(0) = 0 \\[1mm] Y''(0) = -1 \end{cases}$

9. $\begin{cases} \dfrac{d^2Y}{dt^2} - 3\dfrac{dY}{dt} + 2Y = H(t), \\[2mm] \text{where } H(t) = \begin{cases} 2, 0 < t < 4, \\ 0, t > 4, \end{cases} \\[2mm] Y(0) = 0, \\[1mm] Y'(0) = 0. \end{cases}$

10. $\begin{cases} \dfrac{d^2Y}{dt^2} + 4\dfrac{dY}{dt} + 5Y = H(t), \\[2mm] \text{where } H(t) = \begin{cases} 1, 0 < t < \dfrac{\pi}{2}, \\[2mm] 0, t > \dfrac{\pi}{2}, \end{cases} \\[2mm] Y(0) = 0, \\[1mm] Y'(0) = 1. \end{cases}$

11. Use Laplace Transforms to find the solution of the system

$$\begin{cases} \dfrac{dX}{dt} + Y = 3e^{2t} \\[2mm] \dfrac{dY}{dt} + X = 0 \end{cases}$$

which satisfies the initial conditions

$$X(0) = 2, \quad Y(0) = 0.$$

[*Outline of Procedure:* Let $x(s)$ denote $\mathcal{L}\{X(t)\}$ and let $y(s)$ denote $\mathcal{L}\{Y(t)\}$. Then for each equation of the system proceed as follows: Take the Laplace Transform of both sides, apply Theorem 9.3 and the initial conditions, and equate the results to obtain an algebraic equation in $x(s)$ and $y(s)$. Next solve the algebraic system in the two "unknowns" $x(s)$ and $y(s)$ to determine these two expressions. Finally, having found $x(s)$ and $y(s)$, use the table of transforms to find $X(t)$ and $Y(t)$.]

12. Use Laplace Transforms to find the solution of the system

$$\begin{cases} \dfrac{dX}{dt} - 2Y = 0 \\[2mm] \dfrac{dY}{dt} + X - 3Y = 2 \end{cases}$$

which satisfies the initial conditions

$$X(0) = 3, \quad Y(0) = 0.$$

[*Note:* Follow the outline of procedure described in Exercise 11.]

SUGGESTED READING

Agnew (1)
Churchill (11)
Holl, Maple, and Vinograde (21)

Hildebrand (22)
Widder (56)
Wylie (57)

10

THE THEORY OF FIRST-ORDER EQUATIONS

In certain of the preceding chapters we stated and illustrated several of the basic theorems of the theory of differential equations. However, in these earlier chapters our primary interest was in methods of solution, and our interest in theory was secondary. Now that we have become familiar with basic methods, we shall direct our attention to the more theoretical aspects of differential equations. In particular, in this chapter we shall state, prove, and illustrate an existence and uniqueness theorem for first order ordinary differential equations. In order to fully understand the proof of this theorem and those which follow, we shall need to be familiar with certain concepts of real function theory. Since the reader may not be familiar with all of these topics, our first section will be devoted to a brief survey of some of them.

10.1. Some Concepts From Real Function Theory

A. Uniform Convergence

We assume at once that the reader is familiar with the most basic concepts and results concerning functions of one real variable. To be specific, he should be familiar with continuous functions and their properties, and also with the basic theory of differentiation and integration.

This much assumed, let us recall the definition of convergence of a sequence $\{c_n\}$ of real numbers.

DEFINITION A. A sequence $\{c_n\}$ of real numbers is said to *converge* to the limit c if, given any $\epsilon > 0$, there exists a postive number N such that

$$|c_n - c| < \epsilon$$

for all $n > N$. We indicate this by writing $\lim_{n \to \infty} c_n = c$.

Example 10.1.   Let $c_n = \dfrac{n}{n+1}$, $n = 1, 2, 3, \ldots$.

Then $\lim\limits_{n\to\infty} \dfrac{n}{n+1} = 1$. For, given $\epsilon > 0$,

$$|c_n - c| = \left|\frac{n}{n+1} - 1\right| = \frac{1}{n+1} < \epsilon$$

provided $n > \dfrac{1}{\epsilon} - 1$. Thus, given $\epsilon > 0$, there exists $N = \dfrac{1}{\epsilon} - 1$ such that $\left|\dfrac{n}{n+1} - 1\right|$ $< \epsilon$ for all $n > N$. Hence we conclude that the given sequence converges to 1.

Let us now consider a sequence $\{f_n\}$ of real functions, each of which is defined on a real interval $a \le x \le b$. Now let x be a particular real number belonging to this interval. Then $\{f_n(x)\}$ is simply a sequence of real numbers. If this sequence $\{f_n(x)\}$ of real numbers converges to a limit $f(x)$, then we say that the sequence $\{f_n\}$ of functions converges at this particular x. If the sequence $\{f_n\}$ converges at *every* x such that $a \le x \le b$, then we say that the given sequence of functions *converges pointwise* on the interval $a \le x \le b$. More precisely, we have:

DEFINITION B.   Let $\{f_n\}$ be a sequence of real functions, each function of which is defined for all x on a real interval $a \le x \le b$. For each particular x such that $a \le x \le b$ consider the corresponding sequence of real numbers $\{f_n(x)\}$. Suppose that the sequence $\{f_n(x)\}$ converges for every x such that $a \le x \le b$, and let $f(x) = \lim\limits_{n\to\infty} f_n(x)$ for every $x \in [a,b]$. Then we say that the sequence of functions $\{f_n\}$ *converges pointwise* on the interval $a \le x \le b$, and the function f thus defined is called the *limit function* of the sequence $\{f_n\}$.

Example 10.2.   Consider the sequence of functions $\{f_n\}$ defined for all x on the real interval $0 \le x \le 1$ by

$$f_n(x) = \frac{nx}{nx+1}, \quad 0 \le x \le 1, \quad (n = 1, 2, 3, \ldots).$$

The first three terms of this sequence are the functions f_1, f_2, and f_3 defined, respectively, by

$$f_1(x) = \frac{x}{x+1}, \quad f_2(x) = \frac{2x}{2x+1}, \quad f_3(x) = \frac{3x}{3x+1}.$$

For $x = 0$, the corresponding sequence $\{f_n(0)\}$ of real numbers is simply $0, 0, 0, \ldots$, which obviously converges to the limit 0. For every x such that $0 < x \le 1$, the corresponding sequence of real numbers is $f_n(x) = \dfrac{nx}{nx+1}$. Since $\lim\limits_{n\to\infty} \dfrac{nx}{nx+1} = 1$ for every such x, we see that the sequence $\{f_n\}$ converges to f such that $f(x) = 1$ for $0 < x \le 1$. Thus the sequence $\{f_n\}$ converges pointwise on $0 \le x \le 1$, and the limit function is the function f defined by

$$\begin{cases} f(0) = 0, \\ f(x) = 1, \quad 0 < x \leq 1. \end{cases}$$

The graphs of the functions f_1, f_5, f_{10}, defined, respectively, by

$$f_1(x) = \frac{x}{x + 1}, \quad f_5(x) = \frac{5x}{5x + 1}, \quad \text{and} \quad f_{10}(x) = \frac{10x}{10x + 1},$$

as well as that of the limit function f, appear in Figure 10.1.

Now suppose that each term of a sequence $\{f_n\}$ of real functions which converges pointwise on $a \leq x \leq b$ is a *continuous* function on $a \leq x \leq b$. Can we conclude from this that the limit function f will also be continuous on $a \leq x \leq b$? The answer to this question is "no," for under such circumstances f might be continuous or it might not be. For instance, in Example 10.2 each f_n is continuous on $0 \leq x \leq 1$, and the sequence $\{f_n\}$ converges pointwise on $0 \leq x \leq 1$. However, the limit function f is such that $f(0) = 0$ but $f(x) = 1$ for $0 < x \leq 1$; thus this limit function is certainly *not* continuous on $0 \leq x \leq 1$. To be certain that the limit function of a sequence of continuous functions is itself continuous we shall need a "stronger" type of convergence than mere pointwise convergence. One such type of convergence is *uniform* convergence, which we shall now introduce.

In order to introduce the concept of uniform convergence, let us turn back to the definition of pointwise convergence and recast it in the more basic language of Definition A. We have:

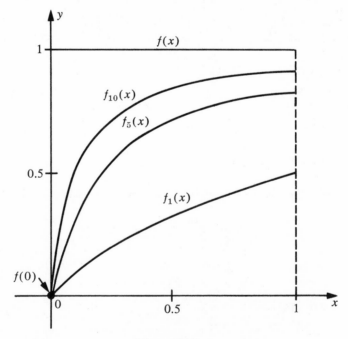

Figure 10.1

DEFINITION B'. Let $\{f_n\}$ be a sequence of real functions, each of which is defined on the real interval $a \leq x \leq b$. The sequence $\{f_n\}$ is said to *converge pointwise* to f on $a \leq x \leq b$, if, given any $\epsilon > 0$, for each x such that $a \leq x \leq b$ there exists a positive number N (in general depending both on ϵ and on x) such that

$$|f_n(x) - f(x)| < \epsilon$$

for every $n > N$.

Now observe carefully that in general the number N of this definition depends not only upon ϵ but also on x. For a given ϵ, different numbers $N(x)$ are in general required for different points x. However, if, given $\epsilon > 0$, there exists *one single* N such that

$$|f_n(x) - f(x)| < \epsilon$$

for *every* x such that $a \leq x \leq b$ for every $n > N$, then we say that the convergence is *uniform* on $a \leq x \leq b$. More precisely, we state:

DEFINITION C. Let $\{f_n\}$ be a sequence of real functions, each of which is defined on the real interval $a \leq x \leq b$. The sequence $\{f_n\}$ is said to *converge uniformly* to f on $a \leq x \leq b$ if, given any $\epsilon > 0$, there exists a positive number N (which depends *only upon* ϵ) such that

$$|f_n(x) - f(x)| < \epsilon$$

for all $n > N$ for every x such that $a \leq x \leq b$.

Geometrically, this means that given $\epsilon > 0$, the graphs of $y = f_n(x)$ for all $n > N$ all lie between the graphs of $y = f(x) + \epsilon$ and $y = f(x) - \epsilon$ for $a \leq x \leq b$ (See Figure 10.2).

Example 10.3. Consider the sequence of functions $\{f_n\}$ defined for all x on the real interval $0 \leq x \leq 1$ by

$$f_n(x) = \frac{nx^2}{nx + 1}, \quad 0 \leq x \leq 1, \quad (n = 1, 2, 3, \ldots).$$

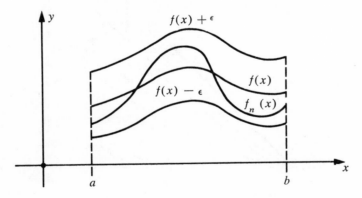

Figure 10.2

For $x = 0$, the corresponding sequence $\{f_n(0)\}$ of real numbers is $0,0,0, \ldots,$ and $\lim_{n \to \infty} f_n(0) = 0$. For every x such that $0 < x \leq 1$, we have

$$f_n(x) = \frac{nx^2}{nx + 1} \quad \text{and} \quad \lim_{n \to \infty} f_n(x) = x.$$

Thus the sequence $\{f_n\}$ converges pointwise on $0 \leq x \leq 1$ to the limit function f defined by $f(x) = x$, $0 \leq x \leq 1$. Further the convergence is uniform on $0 \leq x \leq 1$. To see this, consider

$$|f_n(x) - f(x)| = \left| \frac{nx^2}{nx + 1} - x \right| = \frac{x}{nx + 1}.$$

Given $\epsilon > 0$, we have $\dfrac{x}{nx + 1} < \epsilon$ provided $n > \dfrac{1}{\epsilon} - \dfrac{1}{x}$. But for x such that $0 \leq x \leq 1$, we have $\dfrac{1}{\epsilon} - \dfrac{1}{x} \leq \dfrac{1}{\epsilon} - 1$. Thus if we choose $N = \dfrac{1}{\epsilon} - 1$, we have $n > \dfrac{1}{\epsilon} - \dfrac{1}{x}$ for all $n > N$. Hence, given $\epsilon > 0$, there exists $N = \dfrac{1}{\epsilon} - 1$ (depending only upon ϵ and *not* on x) such that $|f_n(x) - f(x)| < \epsilon$ for all $n > N$ for *every* x such that $0 \leq x \leq 1$. In other words, the convergence is uniform on $0 \leq x \leq 1$. The graphs of the functions f_1, f_5, and f_{10} defined, respectively, by

$$f_1(x) = \frac{x^2}{x + 1}, \quad f_5(x) = \frac{5x^2}{5x + 1}, \quad \text{and} \quad f_{10}(x) = \frac{10x^2}{10x + 1},$$

as well as that of f, appear in Figure 10.3.

We now state and illustrate two important theorems on uniformly convergent sequences, which we shall use in the existence proof in Section 10.2. We shall not prove these

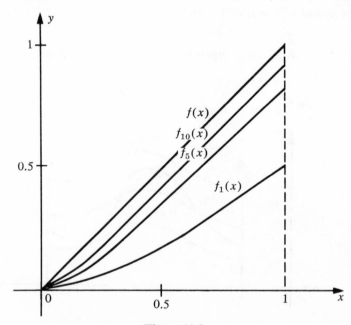

Figure 10.3

theorems here, since the proofs may be found in most texts on advanced calculus and real analysis.

THEOREM A.

Hypothesis. 1. Let $\{f_n\}$ be a sequence of real functions which converges uniformly to f on the interval $a \leq x \leq b$.

2. Suppose each function f_n $(n = 1, 2, 3, \ldots)$ is continuous on $a \leq x \leq b$.

Conclusion. The limit function f is continuous on $a \leq x \leq b$.

Example 10.4. In Example 10.3 we saw that the sequence of functions $\{f_n\}$ defined on the real interval $0 \leq x \leq 1$ by

$$f_n(x) = \frac{nx^2}{nx + 1}, \quad (n = 1, 2, 3, \ldots),$$

converges uniformly to a limit function f on $0 \leq x \leq 1$. Further, each function f_n $(n = 1, 2, 3, \ldots)$ is continuous on $0 \leq x \leq 1$. By Theorem A we conclude at once that the limit function f is also continuous on $0 \leq x \leq 1$. Indeed, in this example, the limit function f is that defined by $f(x) = x, 0 \leq x \leq 1$, and clearly this function f is continuous on $0 \leq x \leq 1$.

THEOREM B.

Hypothesis. 1. Let $\{f_n\}$ be a sequence of real functions which converges uniformly to f on the interval $a \leq x \leq b$.

2. Suppose each function f_n $(n = 1, 2, 3, \ldots)$ is continuous on $a \leq x \leq b$.

Conclusion. Then for every α and β such that $a \leq \alpha < \beta \leq b$,

$$\lim_{n \to \infty} \int_\alpha^\beta f_n(x)dx = \int_\alpha^\beta \lim_{n \to \infty} f_n(x)dx.$$

Example 10.5. We illustrate this theorem by again considering the sequence of functions $\{f_n\}$ discussed in Examples 10.3 and 10.4 and defined by

$$f_n(x) = \frac{nx^2}{nx + 1}, \quad 0 \leq x \leq 1, \quad (n = 1, 2, 3, \ldots).$$

The hypothesis of Theorem B is identical with that of Theorem A, and we have already noted in Example 10.4 that the sequence under consideration satisfies this hypothesis on $0 \leq x \leq 1$. Thus we can conclude that

$$\lim_{n \to \infty} \int_0^1 f_n(x)dx = \int_0^1 \lim_{n \to \infty} f_n(x)dx.$$

Since $\lim_{n \to \infty} f_n(x) = f(x) = x$ in this example, our conclusion here is that

$$\lim_{n \to \infty} \int_0^1 \frac{nx^2}{nx + 1}dx = \int_0^1 xdx.$$

We shall verify this directly.

$$\int_0^1 \frac{nx^2}{nx+1}dx = \int_0^1 \left[x - \frac{1}{n} + \frac{1}{n(nx+1)} \right]dx$$

$$= \frac{x^2}{2} - \frac{x}{n} + \frac{1}{n^2}\ln(nx+1)\Big|_0^1 = \frac{1}{2} - \frac{1}{n} + \frac{\ln(n+1)}{n^2}.$$

Thus

$$\lim_{n\to\infty} \int_0^1 \frac{nx^2}{nx+1}dx = \lim_{n\to\infty} \left[\frac{1}{2} - \frac{1}{n} + \frac{\ln(n+1)}{n^2} \right] = \frac{1}{2}.$$

Clearly $\int_0^1 xdx = \frac{1}{2}$ also, and our conclusion is thus verified.

Let us now consider briefly the uniform convergence of an infinite *series* of real functions, each of which is defined on a real interval $a \le x \le b$.

DEFINITION D. Consider the infinite series $\sum_{n=1}^{\infty} u_n$ of real functions u_n $(n = 1, 2, 3, \ldots)$, each of which is defined on a real interval $a \le x \le b$. Consider the sequence $\{f_n\}$ of so-called *partial sums* of this series, defined as follows:

$$\begin{cases} f_1 = u_1, \\ f_2 = u_1 + u_2, \\ f_3 = u_1 + u_2 + u_3, \\ \quad \cdot \quad \cdot \quad \cdot \quad \cdot \quad \cdot \\ f_n = u_1 + u_2 + u_3 + \cdots + u_n, \\ \quad \cdot \quad \cdot \quad \cdot \quad \cdot \quad \cdot \end{cases}$$

The infinite series $\sum_{n=1}^{\infty} u_n$ is said to *converge uniformly* to f on $a \le x \le b$ if its sequence of partial sums $\{f_n\}$ converges uniformly to f on $a \le x \le b$.

The following theorem gives a very useful test for uniform convergence of series.

THEOREM C. *Weierstrass M-Test.*

Hypothesis. 1. Let $\{M_n\}$ be a sequence of positive constants such that the series of constants $\sum_{n=1}^{\infty} M_n$ converges.

2. Let $\sum_{n=1}^{\infty} u_n$ be a series of real functions such that $|u_n(x)| \le M_n$ for all x such that $a \le x \le b$ and for each $n = 1, 2, 3, \ldots$.

Conclusion. The series $\sum_{n=1}^{\infty} u_n$ converges uniformly on $a \le x \le b$.

Example 10.6.   Consider the series $\sum\limits_{n=1}^{\infty} \dfrac{\sin nx}{n^2}$ on the interval $0 \leq x \leq 1$. The sequence $\left\{\dfrac{1}{n^2}\right\}$ is a sequence of positive constants which is such that the series $\sum\limits_{n=1}^{\infty} \dfrac{1}{n^2}$ is convergent. Let us take $M_n = \dfrac{1}{n^2}$ and observe that

$$|u_n(x)| = \left|\frac{\sin nx}{n^2}\right| \leq \frac{1}{n^2} = M_n$$

for all x such that $0 \leq x \leq 1$ and for each $n = 1, 2, 3, \ldots$. Thus by Theorem C the series $\sum\limits_{n=1}^{\infty} \dfrac{\sin nx}{n^2}$ converges uniformly on $0 \leq x \leq 1$.

B. Functions of Two Real Variables; the Lipschitz Condition.

DEFINITION E.   1. A set of points A of the xy plane will be called *connected* if any two points of A can be joined by a continuous curve which lies entirely in A.

2. A set of points A of the xy plane is called *open* if each point of A is the center of a circle whose interior lies entirely in A.

3. An open, connected set in the xy plane is called a *domain*.

4. A point P is called a *boundary point* of a domain D if every circle about P contains both points in D and points not in D.

5. A domain plus its boundary points will be called a *closed domain*.

Example 10.7.   The set of all points (x,y) lying *within* the ellipse $x^2 + 2y^2 = 1$ and characterized by $x^2 + 2y^2 < 1$ is a domain D. The boundary points of D are the points of the ellipse itself. The set of points (x,y) such that $x^2 + 2y^2 \leq 1$ *within and on* the ellipse is a closed domain.

We assume that the reader is at least somewhat familiar with functions f of two real variables x and y, defined on a domain of the xy plane or on such a domain plus its boundary. Let us recall a few useful concepts and results.

DEFINITION F.   Let f be a real function defined on a domain D of the xy plane, and let (x_0,y_0) be an (interior) point of D. The function f is said to be *continuous* at (x_0,y_0) if, given any $\epsilon > 0$ there exists a $\delta > 0$ such that

$$|f(x,y) - f(x_0,y_0)| < \epsilon$$

for all $(x,y) \in D$ such that

$$|x - x_0| < \delta \quad \text{and} \quad |y - y_0| < \delta.$$

DEFINITION G. Let f be a real function defined on D, where D is either a domain or a closed domain of the xy plane. The function f is said to be *bounded* on D if there exists a positive number M such that $|f(x,y)| \leq M$ for all (x,y) in D.

THEOREM D.

Hypothesis.   Let f be defined and continuous on a closed rectangle R: $a \leq x \leq b$, $c \leq y \leq d$.

Conclusion.   Then the function f is bounded on R.

Example 10.8.   The function f defined by $f(x,y) = x + y^2$ is continuous on the closed rectangle R: $0 \leq x \leq 1$, $0 \leq y \leq 2$. Thus by Theorem D, the function f is bounded on R. In fact, we have $|f(x,y)| = |x + y^2| \leq 5$ for all $(x,y) \in R$.

Having disposed of these preliminaries, we now introduce a concept which will be of paramount importance in the existence and uniqueness proof of Section 10.2.

DEFINITION H. Let f be defined on D, where D is either a domain or a closed domain of the xy plane. The function f is said to satisfy a *Lipschitz Condition* (with respect to y) in D if there exists a constant $k > 0$ such that

$$(10.1) \qquad\qquad |f(x,y_1) - f(x,y_2)| \leq k|y_1 - y_2|$$

for every (x,y_1) and (x,y_2) which belong to D. The constant k is called the *Lipschitz Constant.*

Let us investigate the geometric significance of the Lipschitz Condition. Let (x,y_1) and (x,y_2) be any two points in D having the same abscissa x. Consider the corresponding points

$$P_1 : [x,y_1,f(x,y_1)] \quad \text{and} \quad P_2 : [x,y_2,f(x,y_2)]$$

on the surface $z = f(x,y)$, and let α $(0 \leq \alpha \leq \frac{\pi}{2})$ denote the angle which the chord joining P_1 and P_2 makes with the xy plane. Then if condition (10.1) holds in D, $\tan \alpha$ is bounded in absolute value and so the chord joining P_1 and P_2 is bounded away from being perpendicular to the xy plane. Further, this bound is independent of x for points (x,y_1) and (x,y_2) belonging to D.

If f satisfies condition (10.1) in D, then for each fixed x the resulting function of y is a continuous function of y for (x,y) belonging to D. Note, however, that condition (10.1) implies nothing at all concerning the continuity of f with respect to x. For example, the function f defined by

$$f(x,y) = y + [x],$$

where $[x]$ denotes the greatest integer less than or equal to x, satisfies a Lipschitz Condition in any bounded domain D. For each fixed x, the resulting function of y is continuous. However, this function f is discontinuous with respect to x for every integral value of x.

Now suppose the function f is such that $\frac{\partial f}{\partial y}$ exists and is bounded for all $(x,y) \in D$. Then by the mean value theorem of differential calculus, for any (x,y_1) and $(x,y_2) \in D$ there exists ξ, where ξ is between y_1 and y_2, such that

$$f(x,y_1) - f(x,y_2) = (y_1 - y_2)\frac{\partial f(x,\xi)}{\partial y}.$$

Thus
$$|f(x,y_1) - f(x,y_2)| = |y_1 - y_2|\left|\frac{\partial f(x,\xi)}{\partial y}\right|$$

$$\leq \underset{(x,y) \in D}{\text{lub}} \left|\frac{\partial f(x,y)}{\partial y}\right| |y_1 - y_2|,$$

provided $(x,\xi) \in D$. Thus we have obtained the following very useful result.

THEOREM E.

Hypothesis. Let f be such that $\frac{\partial f}{\partial y}$ exists and is bounded for all $(x,y) \in D$, where D is a domain or closed domain such that the line segment joining any two points of D lies entirely within D.

Conclusion. Then f satisfies a Lipschitz Condition (with respect to y) in D, where the Lipschitz Constant is given by

$$k = \underset{(x,y) \in D}{\text{lub}} \left|\frac{\partial f(x,y)}{\partial y}\right|.$$

Example 10.9. Consider the function f defined by $f(x,y) = y^2$, where D is the rectangle defined by $|x| \leq a$, $|y| \leq b$. Then $\frac{\partial f(x,y)}{\partial y} = 2y$, and so $\frac{\partial f}{\partial y}$ exists and is bounded for all $(x,y) \in D$. Thus by Theorem E, the function f satisfies a Lipschitz Condition in D, where the Lipschitz Constant k is given by $2b$. If we directly apply the definition of Lipschitz Condition instead of Theorem E, we find that

$$|f(x,y_1) - f(x,y_2)| = |y_1^2 - y_2^2| = |y_1 + y_2||y_1 - y_2| \leq 2b|y_1 - y_2|$$

for all $(x,y_1), (x,y_2) \in D$.

Note that the sufficient condition of Theorem E is not necessary for f to satisfy a Lipschitz Condition in D. That is, there exist functions f such that f satisfies a Lipschitz Condition (with respect to y) in D but such that the hypothesis of Theorem E is not satisfied.

Example 10.10. Consider the function f defined by $f(x,y) = x|y|$, where D is the rectangle defined by $|x| \leq a$, $|y| \leq b$. We note that

$$|f(x,y_1) - f(x,y_2)| = \big|x|y_1| - x|y_2|\big| \leq |x||y_1 - y_2| \leq a|y_1 - y_2|$$

for all $(x,y_1), (x,y_2) \in D$. Thus f satisfies a Lipschitz Condition (with respect to y) in D.

However, the partial derivative $\dfrac{\partial f}{\partial y}$ does not exist at any point $(x,0) \in D$ for which $x \neq 0$.

Exercises

1. Consider the following sequences of functions $\{f_n\}$ which are defined for all x on the real interval $0 \leq x \leq 1$. Show that each of these sequences converges uniformly on $0 \leq x \leq 1$.

(a) $f_n(x) = \dfrac{1}{x+n},\ 0 \leq x \leq 1,\ (n = 1,2,3,\ldots)$.

(b) $f_n(x) = x - \dfrac{x^n}{n},\ 0 \leq x \leq 1,\ (n = 1,2,3,\ldots)$.

2. Consider the sequence of functions $\{f_n\}$ defined for all x on the real interval $0 \leq x \leq 1$ by

$$f_n(x) = \dfrac{1}{nx+1},\ 0 \leq x \leq 1,\ (n = 1,2,3,\ldots).$$

(a) Show that the sequence $\{f_n\}$ converges pointwise to a function f on $0 \leq x \leq 1$.
(b) Does f_n converge uniformly to f on $0 \leq x \leq 1$?
(c) Does f_n converge uniformly to f on $\frac{1}{2} \leq x \leq 1$?

3. (a) Prove the following theorem:

Hypothesis. Let $\{f_n\}$ be a sequence of real functions defined on $a \leq x \leq b$, and suppose f_n converges pointwise to a function f on $a \leq x \leq b$. Let $\{\phi_n\}$ be a sequence of positive real numbers such that $\lim\limits_{n \to \infty} \phi_n = 0$. Finally, suppose that for each $n = 1,2,3,\ldots$, $|f(x) - f_n(x)| \leq \phi_n$ for all $x \in [a,b]$.

Conclusion. Then $\{f_n\}$ converges uniformly to f on $a \leq x \leq b$.

(b) Use the theorem of part (a) to show that the sequence of functions $\{f_n\}$ defined by $f_n(x) = \dfrac{\sin nx}{n}$ converges uniformly on $0 \leq x \leq 1$.

4. Prove Theorem A.

5. Show that each of the following infinite series converges uniformly on every interval $-a \leq x \leq a$, where a is a positive number.

(a) $\displaystyle\sum_{n=1}^{\infty} \dfrac{x^n}{n!}$ (b) $\displaystyle\sum_{n=1}^{\infty} \dfrac{\cos nx}{n^2}$ (c) $\displaystyle\sum_{n=1}^{\infty} \dfrac{\sin 2nx}{(2n-1)(2n+1)}$

6. Show that each of the functions defined as follows satisfies a Lipschitz Condition in the rectangle D defined by $|x| \leq a$, $|y| \leq b$.

(a) $f(x,y) = x^2 + y^2$.
(b) $f(x,y) = x\sin y + y\cos x$.
(c) $f(x,y) = x^2 e^{x+y}$.
(d) $f(x,y) = A(x)y^2 + B(x)y + C(x)$, where A, B, and C are continuous on $|x| \leq a$.

7. Show that neither of the functions defined in (a) and (b) satisfies a Lipschitz Condition throughout any domain which includes the line $y = 0$.

(a) $f(x,y) = y^{2/3}$.

(b) $f(x,y) = \sqrt{|y|}$.

8. Consider the function f defined by $f(x,y) = x|y|$ for $(x,y) \in D$, where D is the rectangle defined by $|x| \leq a$, $|y| \leq b$. In Example 10.10 it is stated that $\dfrac{\partial f}{\partial y}$ does not exist for $(x,0) \in D$, where $x \neq 0$. Show that this statement is valid.

9. Consider the function f defined by

$$f(x,y) = \begin{cases} \dfrac{4x^3y}{x^4 + y^2}, & (x,y) \neq (0,0), \\ 0, & (x,y) = (0,0). \end{cases}$$

Show that f does not satisfy a Lipschitz Condition throughout any domain which includes $(0,0)$. [*Hint.* Let a and b be real constants and consider $|f(x,y_1) - f(x,y_2)|$ with $(x,y_1) = (x,ax^2)$ and $(x,y_2) = (x,bx^2)$.]

10.2 Existence and Uniqueness of Solutions

A. The Basic Problem and a Basic Lemma

We now formulate the basic problem with which this chapter is primarily concerned.

DEFINITION. Let D be a domain in the xy plane and let (x_0,y_0) be an (interior) point of D. Consider the differential equation

$$(10.2) \qquad \frac{dy}{dx} = f(x,y),$$

where f is a continuous real function defined on D. Consider the following problem. We wish to determine:

(1) an interval $\alpha \leq x \leq \beta$ of the real x axis such that $\alpha < x_0 < \beta$, and

(2) a differentiable real function ϕ defined on this interval $[\alpha,\beta]$ and satisfying the following three requirements:

(i) $[x, \phi(x)] \in D$, and thus $f[x,\phi(x)]$ is defined, for all $x \in [\alpha,\beta]$.

(ii) $\dfrac{d\phi(x)}{dx} = f[x,\phi(x)]$, and thus ϕ satisfies the differential equation (10.2), for all $x \in [\alpha,\beta]$.

(iii) $\phi(x_0) = y_0$.

We shall call this problem the *initial-value problem* associated with the differential equation (10.2) and the point (x_0,y_0). We shall denote it briefly by

$$(10.3) \qquad \begin{cases} \dfrac{dy}{dx} = f(x,y) \\ y(x_0) = y_0, \end{cases}$$

and call a function ϕ satisfying the above requirements on an interval $[\alpha,\beta]$ a *solution* of the problem on the interval $[\alpha,\beta]$.

If ϕ is a solution of the problem on $[\alpha,\beta]$, then requirement (ii) shows that ϕ has a continuous first derivative ϕ' on $[\alpha,\beta]$.

In order to investigate this problem we shall need the following basic lemma.

LEMMA.

Hypothesis.   1. Let f be a continuous function defined on a domain D of the xy plane.
2. Let ϕ be a continuous function defined on a real interval $\alpha \leq x \leq \beta$ and such that $[x,\phi(x)] \in D$ for all $x \in [\alpha,\beta]$.
3. Let x_0 be any real number such that $\alpha < x_0 < \beta$.

Conclusion.   Then ϕ is a solution of the differential equation $\dfrac{dy}{dx} = f(x,y)$ on $[\alpha,\beta]$ and is such that $\phi(x_0) = y_0$ if and and only if ϕ satisfies the *integral equation*

$$(10.4) \qquad\qquad \phi(x) = y_0 + \int_{x_0}^{x} f[t,\phi(t)]dt$$

for all $x \in [\alpha,\beta]$.

Proof.   If ϕ satisfies the differential equation $\dfrac{dy}{dx} = f(x,y)$ on $[\alpha,\beta]$, then $\dfrac{d\phi(x)}{dx} = f[x,\phi(x)]$ for all $x \in [\alpha,\beta]$ and integration yields at once

$$\phi(x) = \int_{x_0}^{x} f[t,\phi(t)]dt + c.$$

If also $\phi(x_0) = y_0$, then we have $c = y_0$ and so ϕ satisfies the integral equation (10.4) for all $x \in [\alpha,\beta]$.

Conversely, if ϕ satisfies the integral equation (10.4) for all $x \in [\alpha,\beta]$, then differentiation yields

$$\frac{d\phi(x)}{dx} = f[x,\phi(x)]$$

for all $x \in [\alpha,\beta]$ and so ϕ satisfies the differential equation $\dfrac{dy}{dx} = f(x,y)$ on $[\alpha,\beta]$; also equation (10.4) shows that $\phi(x_0) = y_0$.   *Q.E.D.*

B. The Existence and Uniqueness Theorem and Its Proof

We shall now state the main theorem of this chapter.

THEOREM 10.1.

Hypothesis.   1. Let D be a domain of the xy plane, and let f be a real function satisfying the following two requirements: (i) f is continuous in D; and (ii) f satisfies a Lipschitz

Condition (with respect to y) in D; that is, there exists a constant $k > 0$ such that

(10.1) $$|f(x,y_1) - f(x,y_2)| \leq k|y_1 - y_2|$$

for all (x,y_1), $(x,y_2) \in D$.

2. Let (x_0,y_0) be an (interior) point of D; let a and b be such that the rectangle R: $|x - x_0| \leq a$, $|y - y_0| \leq b$, lies in D; let $M = \max |f(x,y)|$ for $(x,y) \in R$; and let $h = \min\left(a,\dfrac{b}{M}\right)$.

Conclusion.   There exists a unique solution ϕ of the initial-value problem

(10.3) $$\begin{cases} \dfrac{dy}{dx} = f(x,y) \\[2mm] y(x_0) = y_0 \end{cases}$$

on the interval $|x - x_0| \leq h$. That is, there exists a unique differentiable real function ϕ defined on the interval $|x - x_0| \leq h$ which is such that

(i) $\dfrac{d\phi(x)}{dx} = f[x,\phi(x)]$ for all x on this interval,

and (ii) $\phi(x_0) = y_0$.

Remarks.   Since R lies in D, f satisfies the requirements (i) and (ii) of Hypothesis 1 in R. In particular, since f is thus continuous in the rectangular closed domain R, the constant M defined in Hypothesis 2 actually does exist. Let us examine more closely the number h defined in Hypothesis 2. If $a < \dfrac{b}{M}$, then $h = a$ and the solution ϕ is defined for all x in the interval $|x - x_0| \leq a$ used in defining the rectangle R. If, however, $\dfrac{b}{M} < a$, then $h = \dfrac{b}{M} < a$ and so the solution ϕ is assured only for all x in the *smaller* interval $|x - x_0| \leq h < a$ associated with the smaller rectangle R_1 defined by $|x - x_0| \leq h < a$, $|y - y_0| \leq b$.

Method of Proof.   We shall prove this theorem by the method of *successive approximations.* Let x be such that $|x - x_0| \leq h$. We define a sequence of functions

$$\phi_1, \phi_2, \phi_3, \ldots, \phi_n, \ldots$$

called the *successive approximations* (or *Picard Iterants*) as follows:

(10.5) $$\begin{cases} \phi_1(x) = y_0 + \displaystyle\int_{x_0}^{x} f[t,y_0]dt \\[4mm] \phi_2(x) = y_0 + \displaystyle\int_{x_0}^{x} f[t,\phi_1(t)]dt \\[4mm] \phi_3(x) = y_0 + \displaystyle\int_{x_0}^{x} f[t,\phi_2(t)]dt \\[2mm] \qquad \cdots\cdots\cdots \\[2mm] \phi_n(x) = y_0 + \displaystyle\int_{x_0}^{x} f[t,\phi_{n-1}(t)]dt. \end{cases}$$

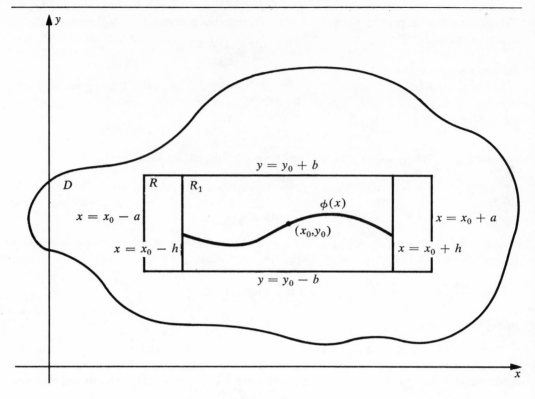

Figure 10.4

The case in which $\dfrac{b}{M} < a$ so that $h = \min\left(a, \dfrac{b}{M}\right) = \dfrac{b}{M}$.

We shall divide the proof into five main steps in which we shall show the following.

1. The functions $\{\phi_n\}$ defined by (10.5) actually exist, have continuous derivatives, and satisfy the inequality $|\phi_n(x) - y_0| \leq b$ on $|x - x_0| \leq h$; and thus $f[x, \phi_n(x)]$ is defined on this interval.

2. The functions $\{\phi_n\}$ satisfy the inequality

$$|\phi_n(x) - \phi_{n-1}(x)| \leq \frac{M}{k} \cdot \frac{(kh)^n}{n!} \quad \text{on} \quad |x - x_0| \leq h.$$

3. As $n \to \infty$, the sequence of functions $\{\phi_n\}$ converges uniformly to a continuous function ϕ on $|x - x_0| \leq h$.

4. The limit function ϕ satisfies the differential equation $\dfrac{dy}{dx} = f(x, y)$ on $|x - x_0| \leq h$ and is such that $\phi(x_0) = y_0$.

5. This function ϕ is the only differentiable function on $|x - x_0| \leq h$ which satisfies the differential equation $\dfrac{dy}{dx} = f(x, y)$ and is such that $\phi(x_0) = y_0$.

The Proof. Throughout the entire proof we shall consider the interval $[x_0, x_0 + h]$; similar arguments hold for the interval $[x_0 - h, x_0]$.

1. In this first step of the proof we use mathematical induction. Assume ϕ_{n-1} exists, has a continuous derivative, and is such that $|\phi_{n-1}(x) - y_0| \leq b$ for all x such that $x_0 \leq x \leq x_0 + h$. Thus $[x, \phi_{n-1}(x)]$ lies in the rectangle R and so $f[x, \phi_{n-1}(x)]$ is defined and continuous and satisfies

$$|f[x, \phi_{n-1}(x)]| \leq M \quad \text{on} \quad [x_0, x_0 + h].$$

Thus since

$$\phi_n(x) = y_0 + \int_{x_0}^{x} f[t, \phi_{n-1}(t)] dt,$$

we see that ϕ_n also exists and has a continuous derivative on $[x_0, x_0 + h]$. Also,

$$
\begin{aligned}
|\phi_n(x) - y_0| &= \left| \int_{x_0}^{x} f[t, \phi_{n-1}(t)] dt \right| \\
&\leq \int_{x_0}^{x} |f[t, \phi_{n-1}(t)]| dt \leq \int_{x_0}^{x} M dt \\
&= M(x - x_0) \leq Mh \leq b.
\end{aligned}
$$

Thus, also, $[x, \phi_n(x)]$ lies in R and hence $f[x, \phi_n(x)]$ is defined and continuous on $[x_0, x_0 + h]$. Clearly ϕ_1 defined by

$$\phi_1(x) = y_0 + \int_{x_0}^{x} f[t, y_0] dt$$

exists and has a continuous derivative on this interval. Also,

$$|\phi_1(x) - y_0| \leq \int_{x_0}^{x} |f[t, y_0]| dt \leq M(x - x_0) \leq b$$

and so $f[x, \phi_1(x)]$ is defined and continuous on the interval under consideration. Thus, by mathematical induction, each function ϕ_n of the sequence (10.5) possesses these desired properties on $[x_0, x_0 + h]$.

2. In this step we again employ mathematical induction. We assume that

(10.6) $$|\phi_{n-1}(x) - \phi_{n-2}(x)| \leq \frac{Mk^{n-2}}{(n-1)!}(x - x_0)^{n-1} \quad \text{on} \quad [x_0, x_0 + h].$$

Then

$$
\begin{aligned}
|\phi_n(x) - \phi_{n-1}(x)| &= \left| \int_{x_0}^{x} \{f[t, \phi_{n-1}(t)] - f[t, \phi_{n-2}(t)]\} dt \right| \\
&\leq \int_{x_0}^{x} |f[t, \phi_{n-1}(t)] - f[t, \phi_{n-2}(t)]| dt.
\end{aligned}
$$

Since by step (1), $|\phi_n(x) - y_0| \leq b$ for all n on $[x_0, x_0 + h]$, the Lipschitz Condition (10.1) applies with $y_1 = \phi_{n-1}(x)$ and $y_2 = \phi_{n-2}(x)$ and we have

$$|f[t, \phi_{n-1}(x)] - f[t, \phi_{n-2}(x)]| \leq k|\phi_{n-1}(x) - \phi_{n-2}(x)|.$$

Thus we have

$$|\phi_n(x) - \phi_{n-1}(x)| \leq \int_{x_0}^{x} k|\phi_{n-1}(t) - \phi_{n-2}(t)|dt.$$

Now using the assumption (10.6), we have

$$|\phi_n(x) - \phi_{n-1}(x)| \leq k \int_{x_0}^{x} \frac{Mk^{n-2}}{(n-1)!}(t - x_0)^{n-1}dt =$$

$$\frac{Mk^{n-1}}{(n-1)!} \int_{x_0}^{x} (t - x_0)^{n-1}dt = \frac{Mk^{n-1}}{(n-1)!} \left[\frac{(t - x_0)^n}{n} \right]\Big|_{x_0}^{x} = \frac{Mk^{n-1}}{n!}(x - x_0)^n.$$

That is, we now have

(10.7) $$|\phi_n(x) - \phi_{n-1}(x)| \leq \frac{Mk^{n-1}}{n!}(x - x_0)^n,$$

which is precisely inequality (10.6) with $(n-1)$ replaced by n. When $n = 1$, we have as in step (1):

$$|\phi_1(x) - y_0| \leq M(x - x_0).$$

This is inequality (10.7) when $n = 1$. Thus by induction the inequality (10.7) is satisfied on $[x_0, x_0 + h]$ for all n.

Since

$$\frac{Mk^{n-1}}{n!}(x - x_0)^n \leq \frac{Mk^{n-1}}{n!}h^n = \frac{M}{k} \frac{(kh)^n}{n!},$$

we have

(10.8) $$|\phi_n(x) - \phi_{n-1}(x)| \leq \frac{M}{k} \frac{(kh)^n}{n!}$$

for $n = 1, 2, 3, \ldots$ on $[x_0, x_0 + h]$.

3. Now the series of positive constants

$$\frac{M}{k} \sum_{n=1}^{\infty} \frac{(kh)^n}{n!} = \frac{M}{k} \frac{kh}{1!} + \frac{M}{k} \frac{(kh)^2}{2!} + \frac{M}{k} \frac{(kh)^3}{3!} + \cdots$$

converges to

$$\frac{M}{k}[e^{kh} - 1].$$

Also, the series

$$\sum_{i=1}^{\infty} [\phi_i(x) - \phi_{i-1}(x)]$$

is such that (10.8) is satisfied for all x on the interval $x_0 \leq x \leq x_0 + h$, for each n

$= 1, 2, 3, \ldots$. Thus by the Weierstrass M-Test (Theorem C), the series

$$y_0 + \sum_{i=1}^{\infty} [\phi_i(x) - \phi_{i-1}(x)]$$

converges uniformly on $[x_0, x_0 + h]$. Therefore its sequence of partial sums $\{S_n\}$ converges uniformly to a limit function ϕ on $[x_0, x_0 + h]$. But

$$S_n(x) = y_0 + \sum_{i=1}^{n} [\phi_i(x) - \phi_{i-1}(x)] = \phi_n(x).$$

In other words, the sequence ϕ_n converges uniformly to ϕ on $[x_0, x_0 + h]$. Thus, since each ϕ_n is continuous on $[x_0, x_0 + h]$, Theorem A shows that the limit function ϕ is also continuous on $[x_0, x_0 + h]$.

4. Since each ϕ_n satisfies $|\phi_n(x) - y_0| \leq b$ on $[x_0, x_0 + h]$, we also have $|\phi(x) - y_0| \leq b$ on $[x_0, x_0 + h]$. Thus $f[x, \phi(x)]$ is defined on this interval and we can further apply the Lipschitz condition (10.1) with $y_1 = \phi(x)$ and $y_2 = \phi_n(x)$. Doing so, we obtain

(10.9) $$|f[x, \phi(x)] - f[x, \phi_n(x)]| \leq k|\phi(x) - \phi_n(x)|$$

for $x \in [x_0, x_0 + h]$. By step 3, given $\epsilon > 0$, there exists $N > 0$ such that $|\phi(x) - \phi_n(x)| < \frac{\epsilon}{k}$ for all $n > N$ and all x on $[x_0, x_0 + h]$. Thus

(10.10) $$k|\phi(x) - \phi_n(x)| < k\left(\frac{\epsilon}{k}\right) = \epsilon$$

for all $n > N$ and all x on the interval under consideration. Thus from (10.9) and (10.10) we see that the sequence of functions defined for $n = 1, 2, 3, \ldots$ by $f[x, \phi_n(x)]$ converges uniformly to the function defined by $f[x, \phi(x)]$ on $[x_0, x_0 + h]$. Also, each function defined for $n = 1, 2, 3, \ldots$ by $f[x, \phi_n(x)]$ is continuous on this interval. Thus Theorem B applies and

$$\phi(x) = \lim_{n \to \infty} \phi_{n+1}(x) = y_0 + \lim_{n \to \infty} \int_{x_0}^{x} f[t, \phi_n(t)] dt$$

$$= y_0 + \int_{x_0}^{x} \lim_{n \to \infty} f[t, \phi_n(t)] dt = y_0 + \int_{x_0}^{x} f[t, \phi(t)] dt.$$

In short, the limit function ϕ satisfies the integral equation

$$\phi(x) = y_0 + \int_{x_0}^{x} f[t, \phi(t)] dt$$

on $[x_0, x_0 + h]$. Thus by the basic lemma, the limit function ϕ satisfies the differential equation $\frac{dy}{dx} = f(x, y)$ on $[x_0, x_0 + h]$ and is such that $\phi(x_0) = y_0$. We have thus proved the *existence* of a solution of the basic initial-value problem (10.3) on the interval $[x_0, x_0 + h]$.

5. We now prove that the solution ϕ is *unique*. Assume that ψ is *another* differentiable function defined on $[x_0, x_0 + h]$ such that

$$\frac{d\psi(x)}{dx} = f[x, \psi(x)]$$

and $\psi(x_0) = y_0$. Then certainly

(10.11) $$|\psi(x) - y_0| < b$$

on some interval $[x_0, x_0 + \delta]$. Let x_1 be such that $|\psi(x) - y_0| < b$ for $x_0 \leq x < x_1$ and $|\psi(x_1) - y_0| = b$. Suppose $x_1 < x_0 + h$. Then

$$M_1 = \left| \frac{\psi(x_1) - y_0}{x_1 - x_0} \right| = \frac{b}{x_1 - x_0} > \frac{b}{h} \geq M.$$

But by the mean-value theorem there exists ξ, where $x_0 < \xi < x_1$, such that

$$M_1 = |\psi'(\xi)| = |f[\xi, \psi(\xi)]| \leq M,$$

a contradiction. Thus $x_1 \geq x_0 + h$ and the inequality (10.11) holds for $x_0 \leq x < x_0 + h$, and so

(10.12) $$|\psi(x) - y_0| \leq b$$

on the interval $x_0 \leq x \leq x_0 + h$.

Since ψ is a solution of $\dfrac{dy}{dx} = f(x,y)$ on $[x_0, x_0 + h]$ such that $\psi(x_0) = y_0$, from the basic lemma we see that ψ satisfies the integral equation

(10.13) $$\psi(x) = y_0 + \int_{x_0}^{x} f[t, \psi(t)] dt$$

on $[x_0, x_0 + h]$. We shall now prove by mathematical induction that

(10.14) $$|\psi(x) - \phi_n(x)| \leq \frac{k^n b (x - x_0)^n}{n!}$$

on $[x_0, x_0 + h]$. We thus assume that

(10.15) $$|\psi(x) - \phi_{n-1}(x)| \leq \frac{k^{n-1} b (x - x_0)^{n-1}}{(n-1)!}$$

on $[x_0, x_0 + h]$. Then from (10.5) and (10.13) we have

$$|\psi(x) - \phi_n(x)| = \left| \int_{x_0}^{x} \{f[t, \psi(t)] dt - f[t, \phi_{n-1}(t)]\} dt \right|$$

$$\leq \int_{x_0}^{x} |f[t, \psi(t)] - f[t, \phi_{n-1}(t)]| dt.$$

By step 1 and Equation (10.12), respectively, the Lipschitz Condition (10.1) applies with $y_1 = \psi(x)$ and $y_2 = \phi_{n-1}(x)$. Thus we have

$$|\psi(x) - \phi_n(x)| \leq \int_{x_0}^{x} k |\psi(t) - \phi_{n-1}(t)| dt.$$

By the assumption (10.15) we then have

$$|\psi(x) - \phi_n(x)| \leq k \int_{x_0}^{x} \frac{k^{n-1} b (t - x_0)^{n-1}}{(n-1)!} dt$$

$$\leq \frac{k^n b}{(n-1)!} \left[\frac{(t - x_0)^n}{n} \right] \Big|_{x_0}^{x} = \frac{k^n b (x - x_0)^n}{n!},$$

which is (10.15) with $(n - 1)$ replaced by n. When $n = 1$, we have

$$|\psi(x) - \phi_1(x)| \leq \int_{x_0}^{x} |f[t,\psi(t)] - f[t,y_0]|dt$$

$$\leq k \int_{x_0}^{x} |\psi(t) - y_0|dt \leq kb(x - x_0),$$

which is (10.14) for $n = 1$. Thus by induction the inequality (10.14) holds for all n on $[x_0, x_0 + h]$. Hence, we have

(10.16) $$|\psi(x) - \phi_n(x)| \leq b\frac{(kh)^n}{n!}$$

for $n = 1, 2, 3, \ldots$, on $[x_0, x_0 + h]$.

Now the series $\sum_{n=0}^{\infty} b\frac{(kh)^n}{n!}$ converges, and so $\lim_{n \to \infty} b\frac{(kh)^n}{n!} = 0$. Thus from (10.16), $\psi(x) = \lim_{n \to \infty} \phi_n(x)$ on $[x_0, x_0 + h]$. But recall that $\phi(x) = \lim_{n \to \infty} \phi_n(x)$ on this interval. Thus,

$$\psi(x) = \phi(x)$$

on $[x_0, x_0 + h]$. Thus the solution ϕ of the basic initial value problem is unique on $[x_0, x_0 + h]$.

We have thus proved that the basic initial-value problem has a unique solution on $[x_0, x_0 + h]$. As we pointed out at the start of the proof, we can carry through similar arguments on the interval $[x_0 - h, x_0]$. We thus conclude that the differential equation $\frac{dy}{dx} = f(x,y)$ has a unique solution ϕ such that $\phi(x_0) = y_0$ on $|x - x_0| \leq h$.

Q.E.D.

C. Remarks and Examples

Notice carefully that Theorem 10.1 is both an existence theorem and a uniqueness theorem. It tells us that

if (i) f is continuous, and

(ii) f satisfies a Lipschitz Condition (with respect to y) in the rectangle R,

then (a) there *exists* a solution ϕ of $\frac{dy}{dx} = f(x,y)$, defined on $|x - x_0| \leq h$, which is such that $\phi(x_0) = y_0$; and

(b) this solution ϕ is the *unique* solution satisfying these conditions.

Let us first concern ourselves with the *existence* aspect, conclusion (a). Although the above proof made use of both hypotheses (i) and (ii) in obtaining this first conclusion, other methods of proof can be employed to obtain conclusion (a) under hypothesis (i) alone. In other words, the continuity of f in R is a sufficient condition for the *existence* of solutions as described in conclusion (a).

We now turn to the *uniqueness* aspect, conclusion (b). The continuity of f alone is *not* sufficient to assure us of a unique solution of the problem. That is, the function f must satisfy some additional condition besides the continuity requirement in order to obtain the uniqueness conclusion (b). One such additional condition which is sufficient for the uniqueness is of course the Lipschitz Condition. Other less restrictive conditions are also known, however. For example, the Lipschitz Condition (ii) could be replaced by the condition

$$|f(x,y_1) - f(x,y_2)| < k|y_1 - y_2| \ln \frac{1}{|y_1 - y_2|}$$

for all (x,y_1) and (x,y_2) in a sufficiently small rectangle about (x_0,y_0), and uniqueness would still be assured.

Example 10.11. Consider the initial-value problem

$$(10.17) \qquad \begin{cases} \dfrac{dy}{dx} = y^{1/3} \\ y(0) = 0. \end{cases}$$

Here $f(x,y) = y^{1/3}$ is continuous in the rectangle R: $|x| \le a$, $|y| \le b$ about the origin. Thus there *exists* at least one solution of $\dfrac{dy}{dx} = y^{1/3}$ on $|x| \le h$ such that $y(0) = 0$.

Existence of a solution of problem (10.17) being thus assured, let us examine the uniqueness aspect. If f satisfies a Lipschitz Condition in R, then Theorem 10.1 will apply and uniqueness will also be assured. We have

$$\left| \frac{f(x,y_1) - f(x,y_2)}{y_1 - y_2} \right| = \left| \frac{y_1^{1/3} - y_2^{1/3}}{y_1 - y_2} \right|.$$

If we choose $y_1 = \delta > 0$ and $y_2 = -\delta$, this becomes

$$\left| \frac{\delta^{1/3} - (-\delta)^{1/3}}{\delta - (-\delta)} \right| = \frac{1}{\delta^{2/3}}.$$

Since this becomes unbounded as δ approaches zero, we see that f does *not* satisfy a Lipschitz Condition throughout any domain containing the line $y = 0$, and hence not in R. Thus we can *not* apply Theorem 10.1 to obtain a uniqueness conclusion here. On the other hand we must not conclude that uniqueness is impossible simply because a Lipschitz Condition is not satisfied. The simple truth is that at this point we can draw no conclusion one way or the other about uniqueness in this problem.

In fact, the problem does *not* have a *unique* solution; for we can actually exhibit *two* solutions. Indeed, the functions ϕ_1 and ϕ_2 defined, respectively, by $\phi_1(x) = 0$ for all x, and

$$\phi_2(x) = \begin{cases} \left(\dfrac{2}{3}x\right)^{3/2}, & x \ge 0, \\ 0, & x \le 0, \end{cases}$$

are both solutions of problem (10.17) on the interval $-\infty < x < \infty$.

We further observe that Theorem 10.1 is a "local" existence theorem or an existence theorem "in the small." For it states that if f satisfies the given hypothesis in a domain D

and if (x_0,y_0) is a point of D, then there exists a solution ϕ of

$$\begin{cases} \dfrac{dy}{dx} = f(x,y) \\ y(x_0) = y_0, \end{cases}$$

defined on an interval $|x - x_0| \leq h$, where h is *sufficiently small*. It does *not* assert that ϕ is defined for *all* x, even if f satisfies the given hypotheses for all (x,y). Existence "in the large" can not be asserted unless additional, very specialized restrictions are placed upon f. If f is linear in y, then an existence theorem in the large may be proved.

   Example 10.12.   Consider the initial-value problem

(10.18)
$$\begin{cases} \dfrac{dy}{dx} = y^2 \\ y(1) = -1. \end{cases}$$

Here $f(x,y) = y^2$ and $\dfrac{\partial f(x,y)}{\partial y} = 2y$ are both continuous for all (x,y). Thus using Theorem E we observe that f satisfies the hypothesis of Theorem 10.1 in every rectangle R,

$$|x - 1| \leq a, \quad |y + 1| \leq b,$$

about the point $(1, -1)$.

As in Theorem 10.1, let $M = \max|f(x,y)|$ for $(x,y) \in R$, and $h = \min\left(a, \dfrac{b}{M}\right)$. Then Theorem 10.1 asserts that the initial-value problem (10.18) possesses a unique solution defined on $|x - 1| \leq h$.
   Now in this case $M = (-1 - b)^2 = (b + 1)^2$ and so

$$h = \min\left[a, \frac{b}{(b + 1)^2}\right].$$

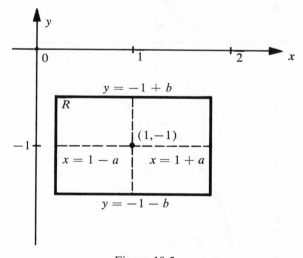

Figure 10.5

Now consider $F(b) = \dfrac{b}{(b+1)^2}$. From $F'(b) = \dfrac{1-b}{(b+1)^3}$, we see that the maximum value

of $F(b)$ for $b > 0$ occurs at $b = 1$; and we find $F(1) = \frac{1}{4}$. Thus if $a \ge \frac{1}{4}$, $\dfrac{b}{(b+1)^2} \le a$ for

all $b > 0$ and so $h = \dfrac{b}{(b+1)^2} \le \frac{1}{4}$, regardless of the value of a. If, however, $a < \frac{1}{4}$, then

certainly $h < \frac{1}{4}$. Thus in any case $h \le \frac{1}{4}$. For $b = 1$, $a \ge \frac{1}{4}$, $h = \min \left[a, \dfrac{b}{(b+1)^2} \right] =$

$\min (a,\frac{1}{4}) = \frac{1}{4}$.

This is the "best possible" h, according to the theorem. That is, at best Theorem 10.1 assures us that the initial-value problem (10.18) possesses a unique solution on the interval $\frac{3}{4} \le x \le \frac{5}{4}$. Thus, although the hypotheses of Theorem 10.1 are satisfied for *all* (x,y), the theorem only assures us of a solution to our problem on the "small" interval $|x - 1| \le \frac{1}{4}$.

On the other hand, this does *not* necessarily mean that the actual solution of problem (10.18) is defined only on this small interval and nowhere outside of it. It may actually be defined on a much larger interval which includes the "small" interval $|x - 1| \le \frac{1}{4}$ on which it is guaranteed by the theorem. Indeed, the solution of problem (10.18) is readily

found to be $y = -\dfrac{1}{x}$, and this is actually defined and possesses a continuous derivative

on the interval $0 < x < \infty$ (see Figure 10.6).

D. *Continuation of Solutions*

Example 10.12 brings up another point worthy of consideration. In this problem, the

solution $y = -\dfrac{1}{x}$ was actually defined on the interval $0 < x < \infty$, while Theorem 10.1

guaranteed its existence only for $\frac{3}{4} \le x \le \frac{5}{4}$. We might thus inquire whether there is

Figure 10.6

any way in which our theory could be applied to assure us that a solution is actually defined over a larger interval than that guaranteed by the basic application of Theorem 10.1.

Suppose then that f satisfies the hypotheses of Theorem 10.1 in D and that $(x_0,y_0) \in D$. Let $R: |x - x_0| \leq a, |y - y_0| \leq b$ be a rectangle lying in D which gives rise to the "best possible" h of the conclusion of Theorem 10.1. Then a single application of the Theorem 10.1 asserts that the initial value problem

(10.19)
$$\begin{cases} \dfrac{dy}{dx} = f(x,y) \\ y(x_0) = y_0 \end{cases}$$

possesses a unique solution ϕ_0 on $|x - x_0| \leq h$, but nothing is implied about ϕ_0 *outside* this interval. Now let us consider the extreme right-hand point for which we are thus assured that ϕ_0 is defined. This is the point (x_1,y_1), where $x_1 = x_0 + h$, $y_1 = \phi_0(x_1)$. Since this point is a point of R, it is certainly a point of the domain D in which the hypotheses of Theorem 10.1 are satisfied. Thus we can re-apply Theorem 10.1 at the point (x_1,y_1) to conclude that the differential equation $\dfrac{dy}{dx} = f(x,y)$ possesses a unique solution ϕ_1 such that $\phi_1(x_1) = y_1$, which is defined on some interval $x_1 \leq x \leq x_1 + h_1$, where $h_1 > 0$.

Now let us define ϕ as follows:

$$\phi(x) = \begin{cases} \phi_0(x), & x_0 - h \leq x \leq x_0 + h = x_1, \\ \phi_1(x), & x_1 \leq x \leq x_1 + h_1. \end{cases}$$

We now assert that ϕ is a solution of problem (10.19) on the extended interval $x_0 - h \leq x \leq x_1 + h_1$ (see Figure 10.7).

The function ϕ is continuous on this interval and is such that $\phi(x_0) = y_0$. For $x_0 - h \leq x \leq x_0 + h$ we have

$$\phi_0(x) = y_0 + \int_{x_0}^{x} f[t,\phi_0(t)]dt$$

and hence

(10.20)
$$\phi(x) = y_0 + \int_{x_0}^{x} f[t,\phi(t)]dt$$

on this interval. On the interval $x_0 + h < x \leq x_1 + h_1$, we have

$$\phi_1(x) = y_1 + \int_{x_1}^{x} f[t,\phi_1(t)]dt,$$

or

$$\phi(x) = y_1 + \int_{x_1}^{x} f[t,\phi(t)]dt.$$

Since $y_1 = \phi_0(x_1) = y_0 + \int_{x_0}^{x_1} f[t,\phi(t)]dt,$

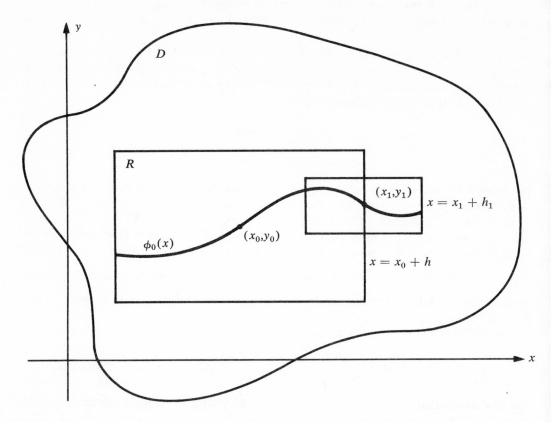

Figure 10.7

we thus have

(10.21)
$$\phi(x) = y_0 + \int_{x_0}^{x} f[t,\phi(t)]dt$$

on the interval $x_0 + h < x \leq x_1 + h_1$. Thus, combining the results of (10.20) and (10.21) we see that ϕ satisfies the integral equation (10.21) on the extended interval $x_0 - h \leq x \leq x_1 + h_1$. Since ϕ is continuous on this interval, so is $f[x,\phi(x)]$. Thus,

$$\frac{d\phi(x)}{dx} = f[x,\phi(x)]$$

on $[x_0 - h, x_1 + h_1]$. Therefore ϕ is a solution of problem (10.19) on this larger interval.

The function ϕ so defined is called a *continuation* of the solution ϕ_0 to the interval $[x_0 - h, x_1 + h_1]$. If we now apply Theorem 10.1 again at the point $[x_1 + h_1, \phi(x_1 + h_1)]$, we may thus obtain the continuation over the still longer interval $x_0 - h \leq x \leq x_2 + h_2$ where $x_2 = x_1 + h_1$ and h_2 is positive. Repeating this process further, we may continue the solution over successively longer intervals $x_0 - h \leq x \leq x_n + h_n$ extending farther and farther to the right of $x_0 + h$. Also, in like manner, it may be continued over successively longer intervals extending farther and farther to the left of $x_0 - h$.

Thus repeating the process indefinitely on both the left and the right, we continue the solution to successively longer intervals $[a_n, b_n]$, where

$$[x_0 - h, x_0 + h] = [a_0, b_0] \subset [a_1, b_1] \subset [a_2, b_2] \subset \cdots \subset [a_n, b_n] \subset \cdots.$$

Let $a = \lim_{n \to \infty} a_n$ and $b = \lim_{n \to \infty} b_n$.

We thus obtain a largest open interval $a < x < b$ over which the solution ϕ such that $\phi(x_0) = y_0$ may be defined. It is clear that two cases are possible:

(i) $a = -\infty$ and $b = +\infty$, in which case ϕ is defined for all x, $-\infty < x < +\infty$.

(ii) Either a is finite or b is finite or both.

Note carefully that even if f is continuous and satisfies a Lipschitz Condition in every *bounded* domain D, we still can not conclude that (i) will necessarily be the case. The initial-value problem $\dfrac{dy}{dx} = y^2$, $y(1) = -1$ of Example 10.12 illustrates this. The solution of this problem (given by $y = -\dfrac{1}{x}$) is defined for $0 < x < \infty$ and so $a = 0$, despite the fact that f such that $f(x,y) = y^2$ is continuous and satisfies a Lipschitz Condition in every *bounded* domain. Note, however, that this f does *not* satisfy a Lipschitz Condition in any *unbounded* domain defined by $a < x < b$, $-\infty < y < +\infty$.

On the other hand, suppose that for the initial value problem $\dfrac{dy}{dx} = f(x,y)$, $y(x_0) = y_0$, the function f is continuous and *does* satisfy a Lipschitz Condition in an *unbounded* domain $a < x < b$, $-\infty < y < +\infty$ which includes (x_0, y_0). Then we can be more definite concerning the largest open interval over which the solution of this initial-value problem is defined. In this connection we state without proof the following theorem.

THEOREM 10.2.

Hypothesis. 1. Let f be continuous in the *unbounded* domain D: $a < x < b$, $-\infty < y < +\infty$.

2. Let f satisfy a Lipschitz Condition (with respect to y) in this unbounded domain. That is, assume there exists $k > 0$ such that

$$|f(x,y_1) - f(x,y_2)| \leq k|y_1 - y_2|$$

for *all* (x,y_1), $(x,y_2) \in D$.

Conclusion. A solution ϕ of $\dfrac{dy}{dx} = f(x,y)$ such that $\phi(x_0) = y_0$, where (x_0, y_0) is any point of D, is defined on the entire open interval $a < x < b$. In particular, if $a = -\infty$ and $b = +\infty$, then ϕ is defined for all x, $-\infty < x < +\infty$.

For example, a solution of the initial-value problem

$$\frac{dy}{dx} = F(x)y, \quad y(x_0) = y_0,$$

where F is continuous for $-\infty < x < +\infty$, is defined for all x, $-\infty < x < +\infty$.

Exercises

1. Consider the initial-value problem

$$\frac{dy}{dx} = y^{4/3}, \quad y(x_0) = y_0.$$

(a) Discuss the existence of a solution of this problem.

(b) Discuss the uniqueness of a solution of this problem.

2. For each of the following initial-value problems show that there exists a unique solution of the problem if $y_0 \neq 0$. In each case discuss the existence and uniqueness of a solution if $y_0 = 0$.

(a) $\dfrac{dy}{dx} = y^{2/3}, \quad y(x_0) = y_0.$

(b) $\dfrac{dy}{dx} = \sqrt{|y|}, \quad y(x_0) = y_0.$

3. For each of the following initial-value problems find the largest interval $|x| \leq h$ on which Theorem 10.1 guarantees the existence of a unique solution. In each case find the unique solution and show that it actually exists over a larger interval than that guaranteed by the theorem.

(a) $\dfrac{dy}{dx} = 1 + y^2, \quad y(0) = 0.$

(b) $\dfrac{dy}{dx} = e^{2y}, \quad y(0) = 0.$

4. Show that Theorem 10.1 guarantees the existence of a unique solution of the initial-value problem

$$\frac{dy}{dx} = x^2 + y^2, \quad y(0) = 0$$

on the interval $|x| \leq \dfrac{\sqrt{2}}{2}$.

10.3   Dependence of Solutions on Initial Conditions and on the Function f

We now consider how the solution of the differential equation $\dfrac{dy}{dx} = f(x,y)$ depends upon a slight change in the initial conditions or upon a slight change in the function f. It would seem that such slight changes would cause only slight changes in the solution. We shall show that under suitable restrictions this is indeed the case.

We first consider the result of a slight change in the initial condition $y(x_0) = y_0$. Let f be continuous and satisfy a Lipschitz Condition with respect to y in a domain D, and let (x_0,y_0) be a fixed point of D. Then by Theorem 10.1 the initial-value problem

$$\begin{cases} \dfrac{dy}{dx} = f(x,y) \\ y(x_0) = y_0 \end{cases}$$

has a unique solution ϕ defined on some sufficiently small interval $|x - x_0| \leq h_0$. Now suppose the initial y value is changed from y_0 to Y_0. Our first concern is whether or not the new initial-value problem

(10.22)
$$\begin{cases} \dfrac{dy}{dx} = f(x,y) \\ y(x_0) = Y_0 \end{cases}$$

also has a unique solution on some sufficiently small interval $|x - x_0| \leq h_1$. If Y_0 is such that $|Y_0 - y_0|$ is sufficiently small then we can be certain that the problem (10.22) does possess a unique solution on some such interval $|x - x_0| \leq h_1$. In fact, let the rectangle $R: |x - x_0| \leq a, |y - y_0| \leq b$, lie in D and let Y_0 be such that $|Y_0 - y_0| \leq \dfrac{b}{2}$. Then an application of Theorem 10.1 to problem (10.22) shows that this problem has a unique solution ψ which is defined and contained in R for $|x - x_0| \leq h_1$, where $h_1 = \min$ $(a, \dfrac{b}{2M})$ and $M = \max|f(x,y)|$ for $(x,y) \in R$. Thus we may assume that there exists $\delta > 0$ and $h > 0$ such that for each Y_0 satisfying $|Y_0 - y_0| \leq \delta$ problem (10.22) possesses a unique solution $\phi(x,Y_0)$ on $|x - x_0| \leq h$ (see Figure 10.8).

We are now in a position to state the basic theorem concerning the dependence of solutions on initial conditions.

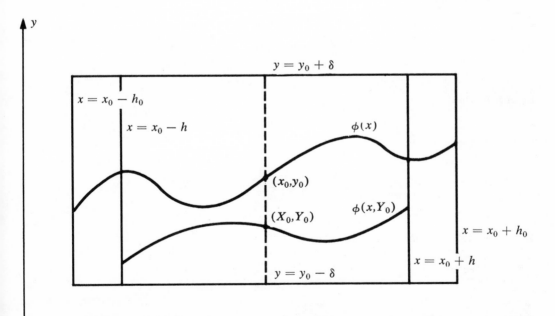

Figure 10.8

THEOREM 10.3.

Hypothesis. 1. Let f be continuous and satisfy a Lipschitz Condition with respect to y, with Lipschitz Constant k, in a domain D of the xy plane; and let (x_0,y_0) be a fixed point of D.

        2. Assume there exists $\delta > 0$ and $h > 0$ such that for each Y_0 satisfying $|Y_0 - y_0| \leq \delta$ the initial-value problem

(10.22)
$$\begin{cases} \dfrac{dy}{dx} = f(x,y) \\ y(x_0) = Y_0 \end{cases}$$

possesses a unique solution $\phi(x,Y_0)$ defined and contained in D on $|x - x_0| \leq h$.

Conclusion.   If ϕ denotes the unique solution of (10.22) when $Y_0 = y_0$, and $\bar{\phi}$ denotes the unique solution of (10.22) when $Y_0 = \bar{y}_0$, where $|\bar{y}_0 - y_0| = \delta_1 \leq \delta$, then

$$|\bar{\phi}(x) - \phi(x)| \leq \delta_1 e^{kh} \quad \text{on} \quad |x - x_0| \leq h.$$

Thus the solution $\phi(x,Y_0)$ of problem (10.22) is a continuous function of the initial value Y_0 at $Y_0 = y_0$.

Proof.   From Theorem 10.1 we know that

$$\phi = \lim_{n \to \infty} \phi_n,$$

where

$$\phi_n(x) = y_0 + \int_{x_0}^x f[t,\phi_{n-1}(t)]dt, \quad (n = 1,2,3,\ldots),$$

and $\phi_0(x) = y_0$; $|x - x_0| \leq h$.

In like manner,

$$\bar{\phi} = \lim_{n \to \infty} \bar{\phi}_n,$$

where

$$\bar{\phi}_n(x) = \bar{y}_0 + \int_{x_0}^x f[t,\bar{\phi}_{n-1}(t)]dt, \quad (n = 1,2,3,\ldots),$$

and $\bar{\phi}_0(x) = \bar{y}_0$; $|x - x_0| \leq h$.

We shall show by induction that

(10.23)
$$|\bar{\phi}_n(x) - \phi_n(x)| \leq \delta_1 \sum_{j=0}^{n} \frac{k^j(x - x_0)^j}{j!}$$

on $[x_0,x_0 + h]$, where k is the Lipschitz Constant. We thus assume that on $[x_0,x_0 + h]$,

(10.24)
$$|\bar{\phi}_{n-1}(x) - \phi_{n-1}(x)| \leq \delta_1 \sum_{j=0}^{n-1} \frac{k^j(x - x_0)^j}{j!}.$$

Then

$$\left| \tilde{\phi}_n(x) - \phi_n(x) \right| = \left| \tilde{y}_0 + \int_{x_0}^{x} f[t, \tilde{\phi}_{n-1}(t)] dt - y_0 - \int_{x_0}^{x} f[t, \phi_{n-1}(t)] dt \right|$$

$$\leq |\tilde{y}_0 - y_0| + \int_{x_0}^{x} |f[t, \tilde{\phi}_{n-1}(t)] - f[t, \phi_{n-1}(t)]| dt.$$

Applying the Lipschitz Condition, we have

$$|f[x, \tilde{\phi}_{n-1}(x)] - f[x, \phi_{n-1}(x)]| \leq k|\tilde{\phi}_{n-1}(x) - \phi_{n-1}(x)|;$$

and so, since $|\tilde{y}_0 - y_0| = \delta_1$,

$$\left| \tilde{\phi}_n(x) - \phi_n(x) \right| \leq \delta_1 + k \int_{x_0}^{x} |\tilde{\phi}_{n-1}(t) - \phi_{n-1}(t)| dt.$$

Using the assumption (10.24), we have

$$\left| \tilde{\phi}_n(x) - \phi_n(x) \right| \leq \delta_1 + k \int_{x_0}^{x} \delta_1 \sum_{j=0}^{n-1} \frac{k^j (t - x_0)^j}{j!} dt =$$

$$\delta_1 + k\delta_1 \sum_{j=0}^{n-1} \frac{k^j}{j!} \int_{x_0}^{x} (t - x_0)^j dt = \delta_1 \left[1 + \sum_{j=0}^{n-1} \frac{k^{j+1}(x - x_0)^{j+1}}{(j+1)!} \right].$$

Since

$$\delta_1 \left[1 + \sum_{j=0}^{n-1} \frac{k^{j+1}(x - x_0)^{j+1}}{(j+1)!} \right] = \delta_1 \sum_{j=0}^{n} \frac{k^j (x - x_0)^j}{j!},$$

we have

$$\left| \tilde{\phi}_n(x) - \phi_n(x) \right| \leq \delta_1 \sum_{j=0}^{n} \frac{k^j (x - x_0)^j}{j!},$$

which is (10.24) with $(n - 1)$ replaced by n.
Also, on $[x_0, x_0 + h]$, we have

$$\left| \tilde{\phi}_1(x) - \phi_1(x) \right| = \left| \tilde{y}_0 + \int_{x_0}^{x} f[t, \tilde{y}_0] dt - y_0 - \int_{x_0}^{x} f[t, y_0] dt \right|$$

$$\leq |\tilde{y}_0 - y_0| + \int_{x_0}^{x} |f[t, \tilde{y}_0] - f[t, y_0]| dt$$

$$\leq \delta_1 + \int_{x_0}^{x} k|\tilde{y}_0 - y_0| dt = \delta_1 + k\delta_1 (x - x_0).$$

Thus (10.23) holds for $n = 1$. Hence the induction is complete and (10.23) holds on $[x_0, x_0 + h]$. Using similar arguments on $[x_0 - h, x_0]$, we have

$$\left| \tilde{\phi}_n(x) - \phi_n(x) \right| \leq \delta_1 \sum_{j=0}^{n} \frac{k^j |x - x_0|^j}{j!} \leq \delta_1 \sum_{j=0}^{n} \frac{(kh)^j}{j!}$$

for all x on $|x - x_0| \leq h$, $n = 1, 2, 3, \ldots$. Letting $n \to \infty$, we have

$$|\bar{\phi}(x) - \phi(x)| \leq \delta_1 \sum_{j=0}^{\infty} \frac{(kh)^j}{j!}.$$

But $\sum_{j=0}^{\infty} \frac{(kh)^j}{j!} = e^{kh}$; and so we have the desired inequality

$$|\bar{\phi}(x) - \phi(x)| \leq \delta_1 e^{kh} \quad \text{on} \quad |x - x_0| \leq h.$$

The remaining statement of the conclusion is now obvious.

Q.E.D.

Thus under the conditions stated, if the initial values of the two solutions ϕ and $\bar{\phi}$ differ by a sufficiently small amount, then their values will differ by an arbitrarily small amount at every point of $|x - x_0| \leq h$. Geometrically, this means that if the corresponding integral curves are sufficiently close to each other initially, then they will be arbitrarily close to each other for all x such that $|x - x_0| \leq h$.

We now consider how the solution of $\frac{dy}{dx} = f(x,y)$ will change if the function f is slightly changed. In this connection we have the following theorem.

THEOREM 10.4.

Hypothesis. 1. In a domain D of the xy plane, assume that
      (i) f is continuous and satisfies a Lipschitz Condition with respect to y, with Lipschitz constant k.
      (ii) F is continuous.
      (iii) $|F(x,y) - f(x,y)| \leq \epsilon$ for $(x,y) \in D$.
   2. Let (x_0, y_0) be a point of D; and let
      (i) ϕ be the solution of the initial-value problem

$$\begin{cases} \dfrac{dy}{dx} = f(x,y), \\ y(x_0) = y_0, \end{cases}$$

      (ii) ψ be a solution of the initial-value problem

$$\begin{cases} \dfrac{dy}{dx} = F(x,y), \\ y(x_0) = y_0, \end{cases}$$

      (iii) $[x,\phi(x)]$ and $[x,\psi(x)] \in D$ for $|x - x_0| \leq h$.

Conclusion. Then

$$|\phi(x) - \psi(x)| \leq \frac{\epsilon}{k}(e^{kh} - 1) \quad \text{on} \quad |x - x_0| \leq h.$$

Proof. Let $\bar{\phi}_0(x) = \psi(x)$ and define a sequence of functions $\{\bar{\phi}_n\}$ by

$$\bar{\phi}_n(x) = y_0 + \int_{x_0}^{x} f[t, \bar{\phi}_{n-1}(t)]dt, \quad n = 1, 2, 3, \ldots; \quad |x - x_0| \leq h.$$

Then $\bar{\phi} = \lim_{n \to \infty} \bar{\phi}_n$ is a solution of $\dfrac{dy}{dx} = f(x,y)$ such that $\bar{\phi}(x_0) = y_0$ on $|x - x_0| \leq h$. By hypothesis 1(i) the initial-value problem $\dfrac{dy}{dx} = f(x,y)$, $y(x_0) = y_0$, has a *unique* solution on $|x - x_0| \leq h$. Thus from hypothesis 2(i) $\bar{\phi}(x) = \phi(x)$ on $|x - x_0| \leq h$, and so $\lim_{n \to \infty} \bar{\phi}_n = \phi$.

From hypothesis 2(ii) we have

$$\psi(x) = y_0 + \int_{x_0}^{x} F[t, \psi(t)]dt, \quad |x - x_0| \leq h.$$

We shall show by induction that

(10.25)
$$|\bar{\phi}_n(x) - \psi(x)| \leq \epsilon \sum_{j=1}^{n} \frac{k^{j-1}(x - x_0)^j}{j!}$$

on $[x_0, x_0 + h]$. We thus assume that on this interval

(10.26)
$$|\bar{\phi}_{n-1}(x) - \psi(x)| \leq \epsilon \sum_{j=1}^{n-1} \frac{k^{j-1}(x - x_0)^j}{j!}.$$

Then

$$|\bar{\phi}_n(x) - \psi(x)| = \left| y_0 + \int_{x_0}^{x} f[t, \bar{\phi}_{n-1}(t)]dt - y_0 - \int_{x_0}^{x} F[t, \psi(t)]dt \right|$$

$$\leq \int_{x_0}^{x} |f[t, \bar{\phi}_{n-1}(t)] - F[t, \psi(t)]|dt.$$

We now write $F(x,y) = f(x,y) + \delta(x,y)$. Then

$$|\bar{\phi}_n(x) - \psi(x)| \leq \int_{x_0}^{x} |f[t, \bar{\phi}_{n-1}(t)] - f[t, \psi(t)] - \delta[t, \psi(t)]|dt.$$

Applying the inequality $|A - B| \leq |A| + |B|$ and then the Lipschitz Condition satisfied by f, we have

$$|\bar{\phi}_n(x) - \psi(x)| \leq \int_{x_0}^{x} |f[t, \bar{\phi}_{n-1}(t)] - f[t, \psi(t)]|dt + \int_{x_0}^{x} |\delta[t, \psi(t)]|dt$$

$$\leq k \int_{x_0}^{x} |\bar{\phi}_{n-1}(t) - \psi(t)|dt + \int_{x_0}^{x} |\delta[t, \psi(t)]|dt.$$

Now using the assumption (10.26) and the fact that

$$|\delta(x,y)| = |F(x,y) - f(x,y)| \leq \epsilon,$$

we obtain

$$|\bar{\phi}_n(x) - \psi(x)| \leq k\,\epsilon \sum_{j=1}^{n-1} \frac{k^{j-1}}{j!} \int_{x_0}^x (t - x_0)^j dt + \int_{x_0}^x \epsilon\, dt$$

$$= \epsilon \sum_{j=1}^{n-1} \frac{k^j (x - x_0)^{j+1}}{(j+1)!} + \epsilon\,(x - x_0) = \epsilon \sum_{j=1}^{n} \frac{k^{j-1}(x - x_0)^j}{j!}.$$

Thus (10.26) holds with $(n - 1)$ replaced by n. Also hypothesis 1(iii) shows that

$$|\bar{\phi}_1(x) - \psi(x)| \leq \int_{x_0}^x |f[t,\psi(t)] - F[t,\psi(t)]|dt \leq \int_{x_0}^x \epsilon\, dt = \epsilon(x - x_0)$$

on $[x_0, x_0 + h]$. Thus (10.25) holds for $n = 1$. Thus the induction is complete and so (10.25) holds on $[x_0, x_0 + h]$ for $n = 1, 2, 3, \ldots$.
Using similar arguments on $[x_0 - h, x_0]$, we thus have

$$|\bar{\phi}_n(x) - \psi(x)| \leq \epsilon \sum_{j=1}^{n} \frac{k^{j-1}|x - x_0|^j}{j!} \leq \frac{\epsilon}{k} \sum_{j=1}^{n} \frac{(kh)^j}{j!}$$

for all x on $|x - x_0| \leq h$, $n = 1, 2, 3, \ldots$.
Letting $n \to \infty$, we obtain

$$|\phi(x) - \psi(x)| \leq \frac{\epsilon}{k} \sum_{j=1}^{\infty} \frac{(kh)^j}{j!}.$$

But $\displaystyle\sum_{j=1}^{\infty} \frac{(kh)^j}{j!} = e^{kh} - 1$. Thus we obtain the desired inequality

$$|\phi(x) - \psi(x)| \leq \frac{\epsilon}{k}(e^{kh} - 1) \quad \text{on} \quad |x - x_0| \leq h.$$

$$Q.E.D.$$

Thus, under the hypotheses stated, if ϵ is sufficiently small, the difference between the solutions ϕ and ψ will be arbitrarily small on $|x - x_0| \leq h$. The following example illustrates how this result can be used to advantage.

Example 10.13.   Consider the initial-value problem

(10.27)
$$\begin{cases} \dfrac{dy}{dx} = x^2 + y^2 + y + 1, \\ y(0) = 0. \end{cases}$$

The differential equation of this problem can not be solved explicitly by any of the methods which we have studied, but the differential equation $\dfrac{dy}{dx} = y + 1$ can be. If x and y are sufficiently small, the difference $|(x^2 + y^2 + y + 1) - (y + 1)| = |x^2 + y^2|$ will be less than or equal to any given $\epsilon > 0$. Thus the solution of problem (10.27) will differ from that of the problem

(10.28)
$$\begin{cases} \dfrac{dy}{dx} = y + 1, \\ y(0) = 0 \end{cases}$$

by an arbitrarily small amount if x and y are sufficiently small. We can thus use the explicit solution of problem (10.28) to obtain information about the solution of problem (10.27) in a sufficiently small neighborhood of $(0,0)$.

Exercise

1. The differential equation $\dfrac{dy}{dx} = \sin(xy)$ can not be solved explicitly by any of our methods, but the differential equation $\dfrac{dy}{dx} = xy$ can be. Explain why and how we can use the explicit solution of the initial value problem

$$\begin{cases} \dfrac{dy}{dx} = xy \\ y(0) = 0 \end{cases}$$

to obtain information about the solution of the initial-value problem

$$\begin{cases} \dfrac{dy}{dx} = \sin(xy) \\ y(0) = 0, \end{cases}$$

if x and y are sufficiently small.

SUGGESTED READING

I. Concerning Uniform Convergence:

    Apostol (3)   Rudin (46)
    Brand (7)   Widder (56)

II. Basic Theory:

    Agnew (1)   Ford (17)
    Burkhill (8)   Greenspan (20)
    Coddington (12)   Kaplan (30)

III. Advanced Theory:

    Birkhoff and Rota (6)   Ince (26)
    Coddington and Levinson (13)   Kamke (29)
    Hurewicz (25)   Lefschetz (35)

11

THE THEORY OF
LINEAR DIFFERENTIAL EQUATIONS

At the beginning of Chapter 4 we stated and illustrated certain basic theorems on linear differential equations. Our main purpose in introducing them there was to have them available as background material for the methods which followed. In this chapter the theory itself is of primary concern. We shall restate and also prove the various theorems already introduced and shall then proceed to obtain further theorems on linear differential equations.

11.1. The Basic Existence Theorem

Our first concern is the basic existence theorem for an initial value problem involving the nth order linear differential equation

$$(11.1) \qquad a_0(x)\frac{d^n y}{dx^n} + a_1(x)\frac{d^{n-1} y}{dx^{n-1}} + \cdots + a_{n-1}(x)\frac{dy}{dx} + a_n(x)y = b(x),$$

where $a_0, a_1, \ldots, a_{n-1}, a_n$, and b are continuous on a real interval $a \leq x \leq b$, and $a_0(x) \neq 0$ on $a \leq x \leq b$. Recall that in Chapter 10 we obtained an existence theorem for the general first-order initial value problem $\frac{dy}{dx} = f(x,y)$, $y(x_0) = y_0$, by means of the method of successive approximations. As a first step toward obtaining an existence theorem for the initial-value problem associated with the linear equation (11.1) we shall extend the above-mentioned existence theorem of Chapter 10 to obtain a similar theorem concerning a system of n first-order differential equations in n unknowns.

Specifically, we consider a system of n first-order differential equations of the form

$$(11.2) \quad \begin{cases} \dfrac{dy_1}{dx} = f_1(x, y_1, y_2, \ldots, y_n) \\[2mm] \dfrac{dy_2}{dx} = f_2(x, y_1, y_2, \ldots, y_n) \\[2mm] \qquad \vdots \\[2mm] \dfrac{dy_n}{dx} = f_n(x, y_1, y_2, \ldots, y_n) \end{cases}$$

in the n unknowns $y_1, y_2, \ldots, y_n$, where $f_1, f_2, \ldots, f_n$ are n continuous real functions defined in some domain D of real $(n + 1)$-dimensional $x, y_1, y_2, \ldots, y_n$ space.

DEFINITION.   By a *solution* of the system (11.2) we shall mean an ordered set of n differentiable real functions

$$(\phi_1, \phi_2, \ldots, \phi_n)$$

defined on some real x interval $a \le x \le b$ such that

$$[x, \phi_1(x), \phi_2(x), \ldots, \phi_n(x)] \in D$$

and

$$\begin{cases} \dfrac{d\phi_1(x)}{dx} = f_1[x, \phi_1(x), \phi_2(x), \ldots, \phi_n(x)] \\[2mm] \dfrac{d\phi_2(x)}{dx} = f_2[x, \phi_1(x), \phi_2(x), \ldots, \phi_n(x)] \\[2mm] \qquad \vdots \\[2mm] \dfrac{d\phi_n(x)}{dx} = f_n[x, \phi_1(x), \phi_2(x), \ldots, \phi_n(x)] \end{cases}$$

for all x such that $a \le x \le b$.

Corresponding to Theorem 10.1 we have the following theorem dealing with the system (11.2). Since its proof parallels that of Theorem 10.1 we shall merely outline the major steps of the proof and omit the details.

THEOREM 11.1.

Hypothesis.   1. Let the functions $f_1, f_2, \ldots, f_n$ be continuous in the $(n + 1)$-dimensional rectangle R defined by

$$|x - x_0| \leq a, |y_1 - c_1| \leq b_1, \ldots, |y_n - c_n| \leq b_n,$$

where $(x_0, c_1, \ldots, c_n)$ is a point of real $(n + 1)$-dimensional $(x, y_1, \ldots, y_n)$ space and $a, b_1, \ldots, b_n$ are positive constants.

Let M be such that

$|f_i(x, y_1, y_2, \ldots, y_n)| \leq M$ for $i = 1, 2, \ldots, n$ for all $(x, y_1, y_2, \ldots, y_n) \in R$. Let $h = \min\left(a, \dfrac{b_1}{M}, \dfrac{b_2}{M}, \ldots, \dfrac{b_n}{M}\right).$

2. Let the functions f_i $(i = 1, 2, \ldots, n)$ satisfy a Lipschitz condition with Lipschitz constant k in R. That is, assume there exists a constant $k > 0$ such that

$$(11.3) \qquad \begin{aligned} |f_i(x, \bar{y}_1, \bar{y}_2, \ldots, \bar{y}_n) - f_i(x, \tilde{y}_1, \tilde{y}_2, \ldots, \tilde{y}_n)| \\ \leq k(|\bar{y}_1 - \tilde{y}_1| + |\bar{y}_2 - \tilde{y}_2| + \cdots + |\bar{y}_n - \tilde{y}_n|) \end{aligned}$$

for any two points $(x, \bar{y}_1, \bar{y}_2, \ldots, \bar{y}_n)$, $(x, \tilde{y}_1, \tilde{y}_2, \ldots, \tilde{y}_n) \in R$, and for $i = 1, 2, \ldots, n$.

Conclusion.   There exists a unique solution

$$\phi_1, \phi_2, \ldots, \phi_n$$

of the system

$$(11.2) \qquad \begin{cases} \dfrac{dy_1}{dx} = f_1(x, y_1, y_2, \ldots, y_n) \\[2mm] \dfrac{dy_2}{dx} = f_2(x, y_1, y_2, \ldots, y_n) \\[2mm] \qquad \vdots \\[2mm] \dfrac{dy_n}{dx} = f_n(x, y_1, y_2, \ldots, y_n), \end{cases}$$

such that

$$\phi_1(x_0) = c_1, \quad \phi_2(x_0) = c_2, \quad \ldots, \quad \phi_n(x_0) = c_n,$$

defined for $|x - x_0| \leq h$.

Outline of Proof.   We first define functions $\phi_{i,j}$ by

$$\phi_{i,0}(x) = c_i \quad (i = 1, 2, \ldots, n)$$

and

$$(11.4) \qquad \phi_{i,j}(x) = c_i + \int_{x_0}^{x} f_i[t, \phi_{1,j-1}(t), \ldots, \phi_{n,j-1}(t)]dt$$

$(i = 1, 2, \ldots, n; j = 1, 2, 3, \ldots)$.

We then prove by mathematical induction that all of the functions $\phi_{i,j}$ so defined are continuous and satisfy the relations

$$|\phi_{i,j}(x) - c_i| \leq b_i \quad (i = 1, 2, \ldots, n; \quad j = 1, 2, 3, \ldots)$$

on $|x - x_0| \leq h$. This much assured, the formulas (11.4) and the Lipschitz condition (11.3) can be used to obtain the following inequality by another induction:

$$|\phi_{i,j}(x) - \phi_{i,j-1}(x)| \leq \frac{M(kn)^{j-1}|x - x_0|^j}{j!},$$

$(i = 1, 2, \ldots, n; j = 1, 2, 3, \ldots; |x - x_0| \leq h)$. Thus also

(11.5)
$$|\phi_{i,j}(x) - \phi_{i,j-1}(x)| \leq \frac{M}{kn} \frac{(knh)^j}{j!}$$

$(i = 1, 2, \ldots, n; j = 1, 2, 3, \ldots)$. This enables us to conclude that for each $i = 1, 2, \ldots, n$, the sequence $\{\phi_{i,j}\}$ defined by

$$\phi_{i,j}(x) = \phi_{i,0}(x) + \sum_{p=1}^{j} [\phi_{i,p}(x) - \phi_{i,p-1}(x)], \, (j = 1, 2, 3, \ldots)$$

converges uniformly to a continuous function ϕ_i. We may then show that each ϕ_i $(i = 1, 2, \ldots, n)$ satisfies the integral equation

$$\phi_i(x) = c_i + \int_{x_0}^{x} f_i[t, \phi_1(t), \ldots, \phi_n(t)]dt,$$

on $|x - x_0| \leq h$. From this we have at once that

$$\frac{d\phi_i(x)}{dx} = f_i[t, \phi_1(t), \ldots, \phi_n(t)]$$

on $|x - x_0| \leq h$ and $\phi_i(x_0) = c_1$ $(i = 1, 2, \ldots, n)$.

Our outline of the existence proof is thus completed. It is clear that it parallels that for the case $n = 1$ given for Theorem 10.1. The proof of the uniqueness in the present case also parallels that of Theorem 10.1, and we shall leave it to the reader to make the necessary changes and complete the present outline.

Theorem 11.1 can be used to obtain an existence and uniqueness theorem for the basic initial-value problem associated with an nth order differential equation of the form

(11.6)
$$\frac{d^n y}{dx^n} = f\left[x, y, \frac{dy}{dx}, \ldots, \frac{d^{n-1}y}{dx^{n-1}}\right].$$

DEFINITION. Consider the differential equation

(11.6)
$$\frac{d^n y}{dx^n} = f\left[x, y, \frac{dy}{dx}, \ldots, \frac{d^{n-1}y}{dx^{n-1}}\right],$$

where f is a continuous real function defined in a domain D of real $(n+1)$-dimensional $(x, y, y', \ldots, y^{(n-1)})$-space. By a *solution* of the equation (11.6) we mean a real function ϕ having an nth derivative (and hence all lower ordered derivatives) on a real interval

$a \leq x \leq b$ such that

$$f[x, \phi(x), \phi'(x), \ldots, \phi^{(n-1)}(x)] \in D$$

and $\phi^{(n)}(x) = f[x, \phi(x), \phi'(x), \ldots, \phi^{(n-1)}(x)]$ for all x such that $a \leq x \leq b$.

THEOREM 11.2.

Hypothesis. Consider the differential equation

(11.6) $$\frac{d^n y}{dx^n} = f\left[x, y, \frac{dy}{dx}, \ldots, \frac{d^{n-1}y}{dx^{n-1}}\right],$$

where the function f is continuous and satisfies a Lipschitz Condition of the form (11.3) in a domain D of real $(n + 1)$-dimensional $(x, y, y', \ldots, y^{(n-1)})$-space. Let $(x_0, c_0, c_1, \ldots, c_{n-1})$ be a point of D.

Conclusion. There exists a unique solution ϕ of the nth-order differential equation (11.6) such that

(11.7) $$\phi(x_0) = c_0, \quad \phi'(x_0) = c_1, \quad \ldots, \quad \phi^{(n-1)}(x_0) = c_{n-1},$$

defined on some interval $|x - x_0| \leq h$ about $x = x_0$.

Proof.

$$\text{Let } y_1 = y, \quad y_2 = \frac{dy}{dx}, \quad \cdots, \quad y_n = \frac{d^{n-1}y}{dx^{n-1}}.$$

Then the nth-order differential equation (11.6) is equivalent to the system of n first-order equations

(11.8)
$$\begin{cases}
\dfrac{dy_1}{dx} = y_2 \\[2mm]
\dfrac{dy_2}{dx} = y_3 \\[1mm]
\quad \vdots \\[1mm]
\dfrac{dy_{n-1}}{dx} = y_n \\[2mm]
\dfrac{dy_n}{dx} = f[x, y_1, y_2, \ldots, y_n].
\end{cases}$$

If ϕ is a solution of (11.6) which satisfies the conditions (11.7), then the ordered set of functions $\phi_1, \phi_2, \ldots, \phi_n$, where $\phi_1 = \phi, \phi_2 = \phi', \ldots, \phi_n = \phi^{(n-1)}$, is a solution of the system (11.8) which satisfies the conditions

(11.9) $$\phi_1(x_0) = c_0, \quad \phi_2(x_0) = c_1, \quad \ldots, \quad \phi_n(x_0) = c_{n-1}.$$

Conversely, if $\phi_1, \phi_2, \ldots, \phi_n$ is a solution of (11.8) which satisfies conditions (11.9), then the function ϕ, where $\phi = \phi_1$, is a solution of the differential equation (11.6) which satisfies condition (11.7).

Since $(x_0, c_0, c_1, \ldots, c_{n-1})$ is a point of D, there exists an $(n + 1)$-dimensional rectangle R about this point such that the function f satisfies the stated hypotheses in R. Thus the system (11.8) satisfies all the hypotheses of Theorem 11.1 in R. Hence there exists a unique solution $\phi_1, \phi_2, \ldots, \phi_n$ of system (11.8) which satisfies the conditions (11.9) and is defined on some sufficiently small interval $|x - x_0| \leq h$ about $x = x_0$. Thus if we set $\phi = \phi_1$, the above-noted equivalence of (11.6) and (11.7) with (11.8) and (11.9) gives the desired conclusion.   *Q.E.D.*

We now consider the linear system

(11.10)
$$\begin{cases} \dfrac{dy_1}{dx} = a_{11}(x)y_1 + a_{12}(x)y_2 + \cdots + a_{1n}(x)y_n + b_1(x) \\[2mm] \dfrac{dy_2}{dx} = a_{21}(x)y_1 + a_{22}(x)y_2 + \cdots + a_{2n}(x)y_n + b_2(x) \\[2mm] \qquad \cdots\cdots\cdots\cdots \\[2mm] \dfrac{dy_n}{dx} = a_{n1}(x)y_1 + a_{n2}(x)y_2 + \cdots + a_{nn}(x)y_n + b_n(x), \end{cases}$$

where the coefficients a_{ij} and the functions b_i are continuous on the interval $a \leq x \leq b$. We first prove a lemma.

LEMMA.

Hypothesis.   Let the functions a_{ij} and b_i $(i = 1, 2, \ldots, n; j = 1, 2, \ldots, n)$ be continuous on the interval $a \leq x \leq b$.

Conclusion.   Then the functions f_i defined by

$$f_i(x, y_1, y_2, \ldots, y_n) = a_{i1}(x)y_1 + a_{i2}(x)y_2 + \cdots + a_{in}(x)y_n + b_i(x),$$

$(i = 1, 2, \ldots, n)$, satisfy a Lipschitz Condition on

$$a \leq x \leq b, \ -\infty < y_i < +\infty \ (i = 1, 2, \ldots, n).$$

That is, there exists a constant $k > 0$ such that

$$|f_i(x, \bar{y}_1, \bar{y}_2, \ldots, \bar{y}_n) - f_i(x, \tilde{y}_1, \tilde{y}_2, \ldots, \tilde{y}_n)| \leq k(|\bar{y}_1 - \tilde{y}_1| + |\bar{y}_2 - \tilde{y}_2| + \cdots + |\bar{y}_n - \tilde{y}_n|)$$

for all x such that $a \leq x \leq b$ and any two sets of real numbers $\bar{y}_1, \bar{y}_2, \ldots, \bar{y}_n$ and $\tilde{y}_1, \tilde{y}_2, \ldots, \tilde{y}_n$ $(i = 1, 2, 3, \ldots, n)$.

Proof.   Since each of the functions a_{ij} is continuous on $a \leq x \leq b$, corresponding to each of these functions there exists a constant k_{ij} such that $|a_{ij}(x)| \leq k_{ij}$ for $x \in [a,b]$, $(i = 1, 2, \ldots, n; j = 1, 2, \ldots, n)$. Let $k = \max \{k_{ij}\}$ for $i = 1, 2, \ldots, n; j = 1, 2, \ldots, n$. Then $|a_{ij}(x)| \leq k$ for $x \in [a,b]$. Then for every $x \in [a,b]$ and any two sets of real numbers $\bar{y}_1, \bar{y}_2, \ldots, \bar{y}_n$ and $\tilde{y}_1, \tilde{y}_2, \ldots, \tilde{y}_n$, we have

$$|f_i(x, \bar{y}_1, \bar{y}_2, \ldots, \bar{y}_n) - f(x, \tilde{y}_1, \tilde{y}_2, \ldots, \tilde{y}_n)|$$
$$= |a_{i1}(x)\bar{y}_1 + a_{i2}(x)\bar{y}_2 + \cdots + a_{in}(x)\bar{y}_n + b_i(x)$$
$$\quad - a_{i1}(x)\tilde{y}_1 - a_{i2}(x)\tilde{y}_2 - \cdots - a_{in}(x)\tilde{y}_n - b_i(x)|$$
$$= |a_{i1}(x)[\bar{y}_1 - \tilde{y}_1] + a_{i2}(x)[\bar{y}_2 - \tilde{y}_2] + \cdots + a_{in}(x)[\bar{y}_n - \tilde{y}_n]|$$
$$\leq |a_{i1}(x)| \, |\bar{y}_1 - \tilde{y}_1| + |a_{i2}(x)| \, |\bar{y}_2 - \tilde{y}_2| + \cdots + |a_{in}(x)| \, |\bar{y}_n - \tilde{y}_n|$$
$$\leq k(|\bar{y}_1 - \tilde{y}_1| + |\bar{y}_2 - \tilde{y}_2| + \cdots + |\bar{y}_n - \tilde{y}_n|). \qquad\qquad Q.E.D.$$

We now obtain the basic existence theorem concerning the linear system (11.10).

THEOREM 11.3.

Hypothesis.   1. Let the coefficients a_{ij} and the functions b_i, $(i, j = 1, 2, \ldots, n)$ in the linear system

(11.10)
$$\begin{cases} \dfrac{dy_1}{dx} = a_{11}(x)y_1 + a_{12}(x)y_2 + \cdots + a_{1n}(x)y_n + b_1(x) \\[2mm] \dfrac{dy_2}{dx} = a_{21}(x)y_1 + a_{22}(x)y_2 + \cdots + a_{2n}(x)y_n + b_2(x) \\[2mm] \qquad\qquad \cdots\cdots \\[2mm] \dfrac{dy_n}{dx} = a_{n1}(x)y_1 + a_{n2}(x)y_2 + \cdots + a_{nn}(x)y_n + b_n(x) \end{cases}$$

be continuous on the real interval $a \leq x \leq b$.

2. Let x_0 be a point of the interval $a \leq x \leq b$, and let $c_1, c_2, \ldots, c_n$ be a set of n real constants.

Conclusion.   There exists a unique solution

$$\phi_1, \phi_2, \ldots, \phi_n$$

of the system (11.10) such that

$$\phi_1(x_0) = c_1, \quad \phi_2(x_0) = c_2, \quad \ldots, \phi_n(x_0) = c_n,$$

and this solution is defined on the entire interval $a \leq x \leq b$.

Outline of Proof.   The system (11.10) is a special case of the system (11.2) with which Theorem 11.1 is concerned, and the present outline of proof parallels that given for Theorem 11.1. We first define functions $\phi_{i,j}$ by

$$\phi_{i,0}(x) = c_i \quad (i = 1, 2, \ldots, n)$$

and

(11.11) $$\phi_{i,j}(x) = c_i + \int_{x_0}^{x} [a_{i1}(t)\phi_{1,j-1}(t) + \cdots + a_{in}(t)\phi_{n,j-1}(t) + b_i(t)]dt$$

$(i = 1, 2, \ldots, n; j = 1, 2, 3, \ldots)$ on $a \leq x \leq b$.

The functions $\phi_{i,j}$ so defined are continuous on the entire interval $a \leq x \leq b$. Also, by hypothesis there exists $M > 0$ such that $|a_{i1}(x)c_1 + \cdots + a_{in}(x)c_n + b_i(x)| \leq M$, $(i = 1, 2, \ldots, n)$, $a \leq x \leq b$.

By the lemma the functions defined by

$$a_{i1}(x)y_1 + a_{i2}(x)y_2 + \cdots + a_{in}(x)y_n + b_i(x)$$

satisfy a Lipschitz condition on $a \leq x \leq b$. We can thus use the formulas (11.11) and this Lipschitz condition to obtain by induction the inequality

$$|\phi_{i,j}(x) - \phi_{i,j-1}(x)| \leq \frac{M(kn)^{j-1}|x - x_0|^j}{j!},$$

$(i = 1, 2, \ldots, n; j = 1, 2, 3, \ldots)$ on the entire interval $a \leq x \leq b$. Thus also

(11.12) $$|\phi_{i,j}(x) - \phi_{i,j-1}(x)| \leq \frac{M}{kn}\frac{(knH)^j}{j!},$$

$(i = 1, 2, \ldots, n; j = 1, 2, 3, \ldots)$, $a \le x \le b$, where $H = \max(|a - x_0|, |b - x_0|)$. The inequality (11.12) here corresponds to the inequality (11.5) in the proof of Theorem 11.1. The remainder of the proof outlined for Theorem 11.1 now carries over to the present case for $a \le x \le b$ and we obtain the desired conclusion.

Now we are in a position to obtain the basic existence theorem for the initial value problem associated with the nth-order linear differential equation (11.1).

THEOREM 11.4.

Hypothesis. Consider the differential equation

$$(11.1) \qquad a_0(x)\frac{d^n y}{dx^n} + a_1(x)\frac{d^{n-1} y}{dx^{n-1}} + \cdots + a_{n-1}(x)\frac{dy}{dx} + a_n(x)y = b(x),$$

where $a_0, a_1, \ldots, a_{n-1}, a_n$, and b are continuous on the interval $a \le x \le b$ and $a_0(x) \ne 0$ on $a \le x \le b$.
2. Let x_0 be a point of the interval $a \le x \le b$, and let $c_0, c_1, \ldots, c_{n-1}$ be a set of n real constants.

Conclusion. There exists a unique solution ϕ of (11.1) such that

$$(11.13) \qquad \phi(x_0) = c_0, \quad \phi'(x_0) = c_1, \quad \ldots, \phi^{(n-1)}(x_0) = c_{n-1},$$

and this solution is defined over the entire interval $a \le x \le b$.

Proof. As in the proof of Theorem 11.2, we let

$$y_1 = y, \quad y_2 = \frac{dy}{dx}, \quad \cdots, y_n = \frac{d^{n-1} y}{dx^{n-1}}.$$

Then the nth order linear differential equation (11.1) is equivalent to the linear system

$$(11.14) \qquad \begin{cases} \dfrac{dy_1}{dx} = y_2 \\[2mm] \dfrac{dy_2}{dx} = y_3 \\[2mm] \qquad \vdots \\[2mm] \dfrac{dy_{n-1}}{dx} = y_n \\[2mm] \dfrac{dy_n}{dx} = -\dfrac{a_n(x)}{a_0(x)}y_1 - \dfrac{a_{n-1}(x)}{a_0(x)}y_2 - \cdots - \dfrac{a_1(x)}{a_0(x)}y_n + \dfrac{b(x)}{a_0(x)}. \end{cases}$$

If ϕ is a solution of (11.1) which satisfies the conditions (11.13), then the ordered set of functions $\phi_1, \phi_2, \ldots, \phi_n$, where $\phi_1 = \phi$, $\phi_2 = \phi'$, $\ldots, \phi_n = \phi^{(n-1)}$, is a solution of the linear system (11.14) which satisfies the conditions

$$(11.15) \qquad \phi_1(x_0) = c_0, \quad \phi_2(x_0) = c_1, \quad \ldots, \phi_n(x_0) = c_{n-1}.$$

Conversely, if $\phi_1 \ldots, \phi_n$ is a solution of (11.14) which satisfies (11.15), then the function $\phi = \phi_1$ is a solution of the differential equation (11.1) which satisfies conditions (11.13).

The system (11.14) is simply a special case of the linear system (11.10) to which Theorem 11.3 applies. Thus the system (11.14) possesses a unique solution $\phi_1, \ldots, \phi_n$ defined on the entire interval $a \leq x \leq b$ which satisfies the conditions (11.15). Thus if we set $\phi = \phi_1$, the above-noted equivalence of (11.1) and (11.13) with (11.14) and (11.15) gives the desired conclusion. *Q.E.D.*

Observe that this is the basic existence theorem which was first stated without proof at the beginning of Chapter 4 (Theorem 4.1). Two examples illustrating it were given in that chapter (page 83) and it has been tacitly employed in the intervening pages whenever initial value problems were solved. We give one further example.

Example 11.1. Consider the initial-value problem:

$$\begin{cases} (x^2 - x - 6)\dfrac{d^2y}{dx^2} + (x^2 + 4)\dfrac{dy}{dx} + \dfrac{1}{2x + 3}y = e^{-x} \\ y(2) = 0 \\ y'(2) = 4. \end{cases}$$

The coefficient of y is continuous except at $x = -3/2$. The remaining coefficients and the non-homogeneous term are continuous for all values of x, $-\infty < x < \infty$. The leading coefficient $(x^2 - x - 6)$ equals zero at $x = -2$ and $x = 3$. Thus the hypothesis of Theorem 11.4 is satisfied in every closed interval $a \leq x \leq b$ such that $-3/2 < a < x_0 = 2 < b < 3$. Therefore the given initial-value problem has a unique solution, and we are assured that this solution is defined over every such closed interval $a \leq x \leq b$.

In Chapter 4 we stated an important corollary to this theorem concerning the homogeneous equation

$$(11.16) \qquad a_0(x)\frac{d^ny}{dx^n} + a_1(x)\frac{d^{n-1}y}{dx^{n-1}} + \cdots + a_{n-1}(x)\frac{dy}{dx} + a_n(x)y = 0.$$

We now restate this corollary, which will soon be very useful to us, and give its proof.

COROLLARY.

Hypothesis. The function ϕ is a solution of the homogeneous equation (11.16) such that

$$(11.17) \qquad \phi(x_0) = 0, \quad \phi'(x_0) = 0, \quad \ldots, \phi^{(n-1)}(x_0) = 0,$$

where x_0 is a point of an interval $a \leq x \leq b$ on which the coefficients $a_0, a_1, \ldots, a_n$ are all continuous and $a_0(x) \neq 0$.

Conclusion. $\phi(x) = 0$ for all x such that $a \leq x \leq b$.

Proof. First note that ϕ such that $\phi(x) = 0$ for all $x \in [a,b]$ is indeed *a* solution of the differential equation (11.16) which satisfies the initial conditions (11.17). But by Theorem 11.4 the initial-value problem composed of Equation (11.16) and conditions (11.17) has a *unique* solution on $a \leq x \leq b$. Hence the stated conclusion follows.

Exercises

1. Consider the third-order differential equation

$$\frac{d^3y}{dx^3} = x^2 + y\frac{dy}{dx} + \left(\frac{d^2y}{dx^2}\right)^2$$

of the form (11.6) of the text.
   (a) Does there exist a unique solution ϕ of the given equation such that

$$\phi(0) = 1, \phi'(0) = -3, \phi''(0) = 0?$$

Explain precisely why or why not.
   (b) Find the system of three first-order equations of the form (11.8) to which the given third-order equation is equivalent.

2. Does there exist a solution of the initial-value problem

$$\begin{cases} (x^2 - 4)\dfrac{d^4y}{dx^4} + 2x\dfrac{d^2y}{dx^2} + (\sin x)y = 0, \\ y(0) = 0, \, y'(0) = 1, \, y''(0) = 1, \, y'''(0) = -1? \end{cases}$$

If so, is the solution unique and over what interval are we assured that it is defined? Explain precisely.

3. Given that each of the functions f_1 and f_2 defined for all x by

$$f_1(x) = \sin x \quad \text{and} \quad f_2(x) = \sum_{n=1}^{\infty} \frac{(-1)^{n+1}x^{2n-1}}{(2n-1)!}$$

are solutions of the initial-value problem

$$\begin{cases} \dfrac{d^2y}{dx^2} + y = 0 \\ y(0) = 0, \, y'(0) = 1 \end{cases}$$

for all x, $-\infty < x < \infty$, what theorem enables us to conclude that $f_1(x) = f_2(x)$ for all x, $-\infty < x < \infty$? Explain.

4. Consider the differential equation

(A) $$a_0(x)\frac{d^2y}{dx^2} + a_1(x)\frac{dy}{dx} + a_2(x)y = 0,$$

where a_0, a_1, and a_2 are continuous for all x, $-\infty < x < \infty$, and $a_0(x) \neq 0$ for all values of x.
   (a) Let f be a nontrivial solution of differential equation (A), let f' denote the derivative of f, and let $x_0 \in [a,b]$. Prove that if $f(x_0) = 0$, then $f'(x_0) \neq 0$.
   (b) Let f and g be two distinct solutions of differential equation (A), and suppose there exists $x_0 \in [a,b]$ such that $f(x_0) = g(x_0) = 0$. Prove that there exists a constant c such that $f = cg$.

[*Hint.* Observe that the function h defined by $h(x) = Af(x) - Bg(x)$, where $A = g'(x_0)$ and $B = f'(x_0)$, is also a solution of differential equation (A).]

5. Complete the details of the proof of Theorem 11.1.

6. Complete the details of the proof of Theorem 11.3.

11.2 Basic Theory of the Homogeneous Linear Equation; Linear Independence and Fundamental Systems

Throughout this and the following section we shall be concerned with the nth order homogeneous linear differential equation

$$(11.18) \qquad a_0(x)\frac{d^n y}{dx^n} + a_1(x)\frac{d^{n-1}y}{dx^{n-1}} + \cdots + a_{n-1}(x)\frac{dy}{dx} + a_n(x)y = 0,$$

where $a_0, a_1, \ldots, a_{n-1}, a_n$ are continuous on an interval $a \leq x \leq b$ and $a_0(x) \neq 0$ on $a \leq x \leq b$. Let L_n denote the formal nth-order linear differential operator defined by

$$(11.19) \qquad L_n = a_0(x)\frac{d^n}{dx^n} + a_1(x)\frac{d^{n-1}}{dx^{n-1}} + \cdots + a_{n-1}(x)\frac{d}{dx} + a_n(x).$$

Then the equation (11.18) may be written

$$(11.20) \qquad\qquad\qquad\qquad L_n y = 0.$$

If we divide through by $a_0(x)$ on $a \leq x \leq b$, we obtain the equation

$$\frac{d^n y}{dx^n} + \frac{a_1(x)}{a_0(x)}\frac{d^{n-1}y}{dx^{n-1}} + \cdots + \frac{a_{n-1}(x)}{a_0(x)}\frac{dy}{dx} + \frac{a_n(x)}{a_0(x)}y = 0.$$

This equation, in which the coefficient of $\dfrac{d^n y}{dx^n}$ is 1, is said to be *normalized*.

The basic theorem concerning equation (11.18), already stated and frequently used in Chapter 4, is the following:

THEOREM 11.5.

Hypothesis. Let the functions $f_1, f_2, \ldots, f_m$ be any m solutions of the homogeneous linear differential equation (11.18) on $a \leq x \leq b$.

Conclusion. Then the function $c_1 f_1 + c_2 f_2 + \cdots + c_m f_m$, where $c_1, c_2, \ldots, c_m$ are m arbitrary constants, is also a solution of (11.18) on $a \leq x \leq b$.

Proof. Using the notation (11.19) the equation (11.18) may be written in the form (11.20),

$$L_n y = 0.$$

Then for all $x \in [a,b]$, we have:

$$L_n[c_1 f_1(x) + c_2 f_2(x) + \cdots + c_m f_m(x)] = \sum_{i=0}^{n} a_i(x)\frac{d^{n-i}}{dx^{n-i}}[c_1 f_1(x) + c_2 f_2(x) + \cdots + c_m f_m(x)]$$

$$= c_1 \sum_{i=0}^{n} a_i(x)\frac{d^{n-i}}{dx^{n-i}}f_1(x) + c_2 \sum_{i=0}^{n} a_i(x)\frac{d^{n-i}}{dx^{n-i}}f_2(x) + \cdots + c_m \sum_{i=0}^{n} a_i(x)\frac{d^{n-i}}{dx^{n-i}}f_m(x)$$

$$= c_1 L_n[f_1(x)] + c_2 L_n[f_2(x)] + \cdots + c_m L_n[f_m(x)].$$

By hypothesis $f_1, f_2, \ldots, f_m$ are solutions of $L_n y = 0$ on $a \leq x \leq b$; that is,

$$L_n[f_1(x)] = L_n[f_2(x)] = \cdots = L_n[f_m(x)] = 0 \text{ for all } x \in [a,b].$$

Thus

$$L_n[c_1 f_1(x) + c_2 f_2(x) + \cdots + c_m f_m(x)] = 0 \text{ for all } x \in [a,b];$$

that is, the function

$$c_1 f_1 + c_2 f_2 + \cdots + c_m f_m$$

is a solution of (11.18) on $a \leq x \leq b$.

Q.E.D.

Before proceeding, we state without proof three theorems from algebra which we shall employ in the following pages.

THEOREM A. If $n < m$, a system of n homogeneous linear algebraic equations in m unknowns always has non-trivial solutions.

THEOREM B. A necessary and sufficient condition that n homogeneous linear algebraic equations in n unknowns have a non-trivial solution is that the determinant of coefficients of the system be equal to zero.

THEOREM C. A necessary and sufficient condition that n linear algebraic equations in n unknowns have a unique solution is that the determinant of coefficients of the system be unequal to zero.

We shall now proceed to obtain further basic results concerning the homogeneous linear differential equation (11.18). Many of these have already been stated without proof, illustrated, and used in Chapter 4. Recall first the following definitions which were first introduced in that chapter.

DEFINITION. If $f_1, f_2, \ldots, f_n$ are n functions, and $c_1, \ldots, c_n$ are n constants, the expression

$$c_1 f_1 + c_2 f_2 + \cdots + c_n f_n$$

is called a *linear combination* of $f_1, f_2, \ldots, f_n$.

DEFINITION. The n functions $f_1, f_2, \ldots, f_n$ are called *linearly dependent* on $a \leq x \leq b$ if and only if there exist constants $c_1, c_2, \ldots, c_n$ *not all zero*, such that

$$c_1 f_1(x) + c_2 f_2(x) + \cdots + c_n f_n(x) = 0$$

for all x such that $a \leq x \leq b$.

DEFINITION. The n functions $f_1, f_2, \ldots, f_n$ are called *linearly independent* on $a \leq x \leq b$ if and only if they are *not* linearly dependent there. That is, the functions

$$f_1, f_2, \ldots, f_n$$

are linearly independent on $a \leq x \leq b$ if and only if

$$c_1 f_1(x) + c_2 f_2(x) + \cdots + c_n f_n(x) = 0$$

for all x such that $a \leq x \leq b$ implies that

$$c_1 = c_2 = \cdots = c_n = 0.$$

Examples illustrating these concepts have already appeared in Chapter 4 and we shall not give additional illustrations here. We now have the following theorem.

THEOREM 11.6.

Hypothesis. Consider the nth order homogeneous linear differential equation

$$(11.18) \qquad a_0(x)\frac{d^n y}{dx^n} + a_1(x)\frac{d^{n-1}y}{dx^{n-1}} + \cdots + a_{n-1}(x)\frac{dy}{dx} + a_n(x)y = 0,$$

where $a_0, a_1, \ldots a_{n-1}, a_n$ are continuous on $a \leq x \leq b$, and $a_0(x) \neq 0$ on $a \leq x \leq b$.

Conclusions. (i). There exists a set of n solutions of Equation (11.18) such that the n solutions of this set are linearly independent on $a \leq x \leq b$.

(ii). If a set of solutions of Equation (11.18) has m members, where $m > n$, then the m solutions of this set are linearly dependent on $a \leq x \leq b$.

Proof. (i). We shall obtain conclusion (i) by actually exhibiting a set of n solutions of (11.18) which are linearly independent on $a \leq x \leq b$. Let x_0 be a point of the interval $a \leq x \leq b$ and define the n solutions $f_1, f_2, \ldots, f_n$ such that

$$(11.21) \qquad
\begin{cases}
f_1(x_0) = 1 \\
f_1'(x_0) = 0 \\
f_1''(x_0) = 0 \\
\cdots \\
f_1^{(n-2)}(x_0) = 0 \\
f_1^{(n-1)}(x_0) = 0
\end{cases}
\begin{cases}
f_2(x_0) = 0 \\
f_2'(x_0) = 1 \\
f_2''(x_0) = 0 \\
\cdots \\
f_2^{(n-2)}(x_0) = 0 \\
f_2^{(n-1)}(x_0) = 0
\end{cases}
\cdots
\begin{cases}
f_n(x_0) = 0 \\
f_n'(x_0) = 0 \\
f_n''(x_0) = 0 \\
\cdots \\
f_n^{(n-2)}(x_0) = 0 \\
f_n^{(n-1)}(x_0) = 1,
\end{cases}
$$

that is, in general, such that $f_i^{(j)}(x_0) = \begin{cases} 0, j \neq i - 1 \\ 1, j = i - 1 \end{cases} (i = 1, 2, \ldots, n; j = 0, 1, \ldots, n-1)$.
Observe that the existence and uniqueness of these solutions on $a \leq x \leq b$ is guaranteed by Theorem 11.4.

We now show that $f_1, f_2, \ldots, f_n$ defined by (11.21) are indeed linearly independent on $a \leq x \leq b$. Suppose they were not. Then from the definition of linear dependence, there would exist constants $c_1, c_2, \ldots, c_n$, *not all zero*, such that

$$(11.22) \qquad c_1 f_1(x) + c_2 f_2(x) + \cdots + c_n f_n(x) = 0$$

for all x such that $a \leq x \leq b$. Then also

(11.23)
$$\begin{cases} c_1 f_1'(x) + c_2 f_2'(x) + \cdots + c_n f_n'(x) = 0 \\ \qquad \cdots \cdots \\ c_1 f_1^{(n-1)}(x) + c_2 f_2^{(n-1)}(x) + \cdots + c_n f_n^{(n-1)}(x) = 0 \end{cases}$$

on $a \leq x \leq b$. The identities (11.22) and (11.23) hold at $x = x_0$, giving

$$\begin{cases} c_1 f_1(x_0) + c_2 f_2(x_0) + \cdots + c_n f_n(x_0) = 0 \\ c_1 f_1'(x_0) + c_2 f_2'(x_0) + \cdots + c_n f_n'(x_0) = 0 \\ \qquad \cdots \cdots \\ c_1 f_1^{(n-1)}(x_0) + c_2 f_2^{(n-1)}(x_0) + \cdots + c_n f_n^{(n-1)}(x_0) = 0. \end{cases}$$

Apply conditions (11.21) to this set of equations; we see that $c_1 = c_2 = \cdots = c_n = 0$, which is a contradiction. Thus the solutions $f_1, f_2, \ldots, f_n$ defined by (11.21) are linearly independent on $a \leq x \leq b$.

(ii) To obtain the second conclusion, let $f_1, f_2, \ldots, f_m$ be a set of m solutions of Equation (11.18) on $a \leq x \leq b$, where $m > n$. Let x_0 be a point of the interval $a \leq x \leq b$ and consider the following system of n homogeneous linear algebraic equations in the m unknowns $k_1, k_2, \ldots, k_m$.

(11.24)
$$\begin{cases} k_1 f_1(x_0) + k_2 f_2(x_0) + \cdots + k_m f_m(x_0) = 0 \\ k_1 f_1'(x_0) + k_2 f_2'(x_0) + \cdots + k_m f_m'(x_0) = 0 \\ \qquad \cdots \cdots \\ k_1 f_1^{(n-1)}(x_0) + k_2 f_2^{(n-1)}(x_0) + \cdots + k_m f_m^{(n-1)}(x_0) = 0. \end{cases}$$

By Theorem A this system has a solution

$$k_1 = c_1, \, k_2 = c_2, \ldots, k_m = c_m,$$

where $c_1, c_2, \ldots, c_m$ are *not all zero*. Now consider the function f defined by

(11.25)
$$f(x) = c_1 f_1(x) + c_2 f_2(x) + \cdots + c_m f_m(x)$$

for all x on $a \leq x \leq b$. The function f is a linear combination of the solutions $f_1, f_2,$ $\ldots, f_m$. Hence by Theorem 11.5 the function f is also a solution of Equation (11.18) on $a \leq x \leq b$.

Now differentiate (11.25) $(n - 1)$ times and let $x = x_0$ in (11.25) and the $(n - 1)$ derivatives so obtained. We have

$$\begin{cases} f(x_0) = c_1 f_1(x_0) + c_2 f_2(x_0) + \cdots + c_m f_m(x_0) \\ f'(x_0) = c_1 f_1'(x_0) + c_2 f_2'(x_0) + \cdots + c_m f_m'(x_0) \\ \qquad \cdots \cdots \\ f^{(n-1)}(x_0) = c_1 f_1^{(n-1)}(x_0) + c_2 f_2^{(n-1)}(x_0) + \cdots + c_m f_m^{(n-1)}(x_0). \end{cases}$$

The right members of these expressions are precisely the left members of equations (11.24) with the unknowns k_i replaced by c_i, $i = 1, 2, \ldots, m$. Since $c_1, c_2, \ldots, c_m$ is a solution of the system (11.24), we see at once that the solution f of equation (11.18) is such that

$$f(x_0) = f'(x_0) = \cdots = f^{(n-1)}(x_0) = 0.$$

Thus by the Corollary to Theorem 11.4 we conclude that $f(x) = 0$ for all x such that

$a \leq x \leq b$. Thus from (11.25) we have

$$c_1 f_1(x) + c_2 f_2(x) + \cdots + c_m f_m(x) = 0,$$

$a \leq x \leq b$, where $c_1, c_2, \ldots, c_m$ are *not all zero*. Thus the solutions $f_1, f_2, \ldots, f_m$ are linearly dependent on $a \leq x \leq b$.

Q.E.D.

The proof of Theorem 11.6 shows that any n solutions $f_1, f_2, \ldots, f_n$ of equation (11.18) which satisfy conditions of the form (11.21) at some point x_0 of $a \leq x \leq b$ are linearly independent on $a \leq x \leq b$. However, there are also sets of n linearly independent solutions of Equation (11.18) which do *not* satisfy conditions of the form (11.21) at any one point x_0 of $a \leq x \leq b$. For example, the functions f_1 and f_2 defined respectively by $f_1(x) = \sin x$, $f_2(x) = \sin x + \cos x$ are a set of linearly independent solutions of $\frac{d^2y}{dx^2} + y = 0$ on every closed interval $a \leq x \leq b$, but there is no point x_0 such that $f_1(x_0) = 1, f_1'(x_0) = 0, f_2(x_0) = 0, f_2'(x_0) = 1$.

DEFINITION. Let $f_1, f_2, \ldots, f_n$ be n real functions, each of which has an $(n-1)$st derivative on $a \leq x \leq b$. The determinant

$$\begin{vmatrix} f_1 & f_2 & \cdots & f_n \\ f_1' & f_2' & \cdots & f_n' \\ \cdots\cdots\cdots\cdots\cdots \\ f_1^{(n-1)} & f_2^{(n-1)} & \cdots & f_n^{(n-1)} \end{vmatrix}$$

where the primes denote derivatives, is called the *Wronskian* of the n functions $f_1, f_2, \ldots, f_n$. We denote it by $W(f_1, f_2, \ldots, f_n)$ and denote its value at x by $W(f_1, f_2, \ldots, f_n)(x)$.

THEOREM 11.7. A necessary and sufficient condition that n solutions $f_1, f_2, \ldots, f_n$ of equation (11.18) be linearly dependent on $a \leq x \leq b$ is that the value of the Wronskian of $f_1, f_2, \ldots, f_n$ be zero for all x on $a \leq x \leq b$:

$$W(f_1, f_2, \ldots, f_n)(x) = 0 \text{ for all } x \in [a,b].$$

Proof. (*i*) *Sufficiency proof.* We must show that if

$$W(f_1, f_2, \ldots, f_n)(x) = 0$$

for all x on $a \leq x \leq b$, then $f_1, f_2, \ldots, f_n$ are linearly dependent on $a \leq x \leq b$. We thus assume that

$$W(f_1, f_2, \ldots, f_n)(x) = \begin{vmatrix} f_1(x) & f_2(x) & \cdots & f_n(x) \\ f_1'(x) & f_2'(x) & \cdots & f_n'(x) \\ \cdots\cdots\cdots \\ f_1^{(n-1)}(x) & f_2^{(n-1)}(x) & \cdots & f_n^{(n-1)}(x) \end{vmatrix} = 0$$

for all $x \in [a,b]$.

Then at any particular $x_0 \in [a,b]$, we have

$$\begin{vmatrix} f_1(x_0) & f_2(x_0) & \cdots & f_n(x_0) \\ f_1'(x_0) & f_2'(x_0) & \cdots & f_n'(x_0) \\ & & \cdots \cdots & \\ f_1^{(n-1)}(x_0) & f_2^{(n-1)}(x_0) & \cdots & f_n^{(n-1)}(x_0) \end{vmatrix} = 0.$$

Now, appealing to Theorem B, there exist constants $c_1, c_2, \ldots, c_n$, *not all zero*, such that

(11.26)
$$\begin{cases} c_1 f_1(x_0) + c_2 f_2(x_0) + \cdots + c_n f_n(x_0) = 0 \\ c_1 f_1'(x_0) + c_2 f_2'(x_0) + \cdots + c_n f_n'(x_0) = 0 \\ \qquad\qquad \cdots\cdots \\ c_1 f_1^{(n-1)}(x_0) + c_2 f_2^{(n-1)}(x_0) + \cdots + c_n f_n^{(n-1)}(x_0) = 0. \end{cases}$$

Now consider the solution f of Equation (11.18) defined by

$$f(x) = c_1 f_1(x) + c_2 f_2(x) + \cdots + c_n f_n(x), \quad a \le x \le b$$

From (11.26) we have

$$f(x_0) = f'(x_0) = \cdots = f^{(n-1)}(x_0) = 0.$$

Thus by the corollary to Theorem 11.4,

$$f(x) = 0 \quad \text{for all } x \text{ on} \quad a \le x \le b.$$

That is,

$$c_1 f_1(x) + c_2 f_2(x) + \cdots + c_n f_n(x) = 0$$

for all x on $a \le x \le b$, where $c_1, c_2, \ldots, c_n$ are *not all zero*. Thus the solutions $f_1, f_2, \ldots, f_n$ are linearly dependent on $a \le x \le b$.

(*ii*)   *Necessity Proof.*   We must now show that if $f_1, f_2, \ldots, f_n$ are linearly dependent on $a \le x \le b$, then their Wronskian has the value zero for all x on this interval.

We thus assume that $f_1, f_2, \ldots, f_n$ are linearly dependent on $a \le x \le b$. Then there exist constants $c_1, c_2, \ldots, c_n$, *not all zero*, such that

(11.27)
$$c_1 f_1(x) + c_2 f_2(x) + \cdots + c_n f_n(x) = 0$$

for all x on $a \le x \le b$. From (11.27) we obtain

(11.28)
$$\begin{cases} c_1 f_1'(x) + c_2 f_2'(x) + \cdots + c_n f_n'(x) = 0 \\ \qquad\qquad \cdots\cdots \\ c_1 f_1^{(n-1)}(x) + c_2 f_2^{(n-1)}(x) + \cdots + c_n f_n^{(n-1)}(x) = 0 \end{cases}$$

for all $x \in [a,b]$. Now let $x = x_0$ be an arbitrary point of $a \le x \le b$. Then (11.27) and (11.28) hold at $x = x_0$. In other words, the relations (11.26) hold, where $c_1, c_2, \ldots, c_n$ are not all zero. Thus, applying Theorem B, we have

$$\begin{vmatrix} f_1(x_0) & f_2(x_0) & \cdots & f_n(x_0) \\ f_1'(x_0) & f_2'(x_0) & \cdots & f_n'(x_0) \\ & & \cdots\cdots & \\ f_1^{(n-1)}(x_0) & f_2^{(n-1)}(x_0) & \cdots & f_n^{(n-1)}(x_0) \end{vmatrix} = 0.$$

But this determinant is the value of the Wronskian of $f_1, f_2, \ldots, f_n$ at $x = x_0$, and x_0 is an *arbitrary* point of $[a,b]$. Hence

$$W(f_1, f_2, \ldots, f_n)(x) = 0$$

for all $x \in [a,b]$.

$$Q.E.D$$

THEOREM 11.8. *Abel's Identity or Liouville's Formula.*

Hypothesis. Let $f_1, f_2, \ldots, f_n$ be a set of n linearly independent solutions of equation. (11.18) on $a \leq x \leq b$; let W denote the Wronskian of $f_1, f_2, \ldots, f_n$; and let $x_0 \in [a,b]$.

Conclusion. Then

$$W(x) = W(x_0)e^{-\int_{x_0}^{x} \frac{a_1(t)}{a_0(t)}\, dt}$$

for all x on $a \leq x \leq b$.

Proof. We differentiate

$$W(x) = \begin{vmatrix} f_1(x) & f_2(x) & \cdots & f_n(x) \\ f_1'(x) & f_2'(x) & \cdots & f_n'(x) \\ f_1''(x) & f_2''(x) & \cdots & f_n''(x) \\ & & \cdots\cdots \\ f_1^{(n-1)}(x) & f_2^{(n-1)}(x) & \cdots & f_n^{(n-1)}(x) \end{vmatrix}$$

to obtain

$$W'(x) = \begin{vmatrix} f_1'(x) & f_2'(x) & \cdots & f_n'(x) \\ f_1'(x) & f_2'(x) & \cdots & f_n'(x) \\ f_1''(x) & f_2''(x) & \cdots & f_n''(x) \\ & & \cdots\cdots \\ f_1^{(n-1)}(x) & f_2^{(n-1)}(x) & \cdots & f_n^{(n-1)}(x) \end{vmatrix} + \begin{vmatrix} f_1(x) & f_2(x) & \cdots & f_n(x) \\ f_1''(x) & f_2''(x) & \cdots & f_n''(x) \\ f_1''(x) & f_2''(x) & \cdots & f_n''(x) \\ & & \cdots\cdots \\ f_1^{(n-1)}(x) & f_2^{(n-1)}(x) & \cdots & f_n^{(n-1)}(x) \end{vmatrix}$$

$$+ \cdots + \begin{vmatrix} f_1(x) & f_2(x) & \cdots & f_n(x) \\ f_1'(x) & f_2'(x) & \cdots & f_n'(x) \\ & & \cdots\cdots \\ f_1^{(n-1)}(x) & f_2^{(n-1)}(x) & \cdots & f_n^{(n-1)}(x) \\ f_1^{(n-1)}(x) & f_2^{(n-1)}(x) & \cdots & f_n^{(n-1)}(x) \end{vmatrix} + \begin{vmatrix} f_1(x) & f_2(x) & \cdots & f_n(x) \\ f_1'(x) & f_2'(x) & \cdots & f_n'(x) \\ & & \cdots\cdots \\ f_1^{(n-2)}(x) & f_2^{(n-2)}(x) & \cdots & f_n^{(n-2)}(x) \\ f_1^{(n)}(x) & f_2^{(n)}(x) & \cdots & f_n^{(n)}(x) \end{vmatrix}$$

(11.29)

$$= \begin{vmatrix} f_1(x) & f_2(x) & \cdots & f_n(x) \\ f_1'(x) & f_2'(x) & \cdots & f_n'(x) \\ & & \cdots\cdots \\ f_1^{(n-2)}(x) & f_2^{(n-2)}(x) & \cdots & f_n^{(n-2)}(x) \\ f_1^{(n)}(x) & f_2^{(n)}(x) & \cdots & f_n^{(n)}(x) \end{vmatrix}.$$

Now since $f_1, f_2, \ldots, f_n$ are all solutions of the differential equation (11.18), we have:

$$
\begin{cases}
f_1^{(n)}(x) = -\dfrac{a_1(x)}{a_0(x)}f_1^{(n-1)}(x) - \cdots - \dfrac{a_n(x)}{a_0(x)}f_1(x) \\[2ex]
f_2^{(n)}(x) = -\dfrac{a_1(x)}{a_0(x)}f_2^{(n-1)}(x) - \cdots - \dfrac{a_n(x)}{a_0(x)}f_2(x) \\[2ex]
f_n^{(n)}(x) = -\dfrac{a_1(x)}{a_0(x)}f_n^{(n-1)}(x) - \cdots - \dfrac{a_n(x)}{a_0(x)}f_n(x).
\end{cases}
$$

Substitute these expressions for $f_1^{(n)}(x), f_2^{(n)}(x), \ldots, f_n^{(n)}(x)$ into the last row of the sole determinant which remains in the right member of (11.29). One obtains

$$
\begin{vmatrix}
f_1(x) & f_2(x) & \cdots & f_n(x) \\
f_1'(x) & f_2'(x) & \cdots & f_n'(x) \\
\vdots & \vdots & \vdots & \vdots \\
f_1^{(n-2)}(x) & f_2^{(n-2)}(x) & \cdots & f_n^{(n-2)}(x) \\
-\sum\limits_{i=1}^{n}\dfrac{a_i(x)}{a_0(x)}f_1^{(n-i)}(x) & -\sum\limits_{i=1}^{n}\dfrac{a_i(x)}{a_0(x)}f_2^{(n-i)}(x) & \cdots & -\sum\limits_{i=1}^{n}\dfrac{a_i(x)}{a_0(x)}f_n^{(n-i)}(x)
\end{vmatrix}
$$

$$
=
\begin{vmatrix}
f_1(x) & f_2(x) & \cdots & f_n(x) \\
f_1'(x) & f_2'(x) & \cdots & f_n'(x) \\
\vdots & \vdots & \vdots & \vdots \\
f_1^{(n-2)}(x) & f_2^{(n-2)}(x) & \cdots & f_n^{(n-2)}(x) \\
-\dfrac{a_1(x)}{a_0(x)}f_1^{(n-1)}(x) & -\dfrac{a_1(x)}{a_0(x)}f_2^{(n-1)}(x) & \cdots & -\dfrac{a_1(x)}{a_0(x)}f_n^{(n-1)}(x)
\end{vmatrix}
$$

$$
+ D_1 + D_2 + \cdots + D_{n-1},
$$

where each D_i $(i = 1, 2, \ldots, n-1)$ denotes a determinant having two proportional rows. Thus we have

$$
W'(x) = -\frac{a_1(x)}{a_0(x)}
\begin{vmatrix}
f_1(x) & f_2(x) & \cdots & f_n(x) \\
f_1'(x) & f_2'(x) & \cdots & f_n'(x) \\
\cdots & \cdots & \cdots & \cdots \\
f_1^{(n-1)}(x) & f_2^{(n-1)}(x) & \cdots & f_n^{(n-1)}(x)
\end{vmatrix}
= -\frac{a_1(x)}{a_0(x)}W(x).
$$

Thus W satisfies the first-order homogeneous linear differential equation

$$
\frac{dW}{dx} + \frac{a_1(x)}{a_0(x)}W = 0.
$$

Integrating this, we obtain

$$
W(x) = ce^{-\int_{x_0}^{x}\frac{a_1(t)}{a_0(t)}dt}.
$$

Letting $x = x_0$, we find that $c = W(x_0)$ and hence obtain the desired formula of the conclusion,

$$W(x) = W(x_0)e^{-\int_{x_0}^{x} \frac{a_1(t)}{a_0(t)}dt}.$$

$Q.E.D.$

THEOREM 11.9.

Hypothesis. Let $f_1, f_2, \ldots, f_n$ be a set of n solutions of equation (11.18) on $a \leq x \leq b$; and let W denote the Wronskian of $f_1, f_2, \ldots, f_n$.

Conclusion. Either $W(x)$ is zero for all x on $a \leq x \leq b$ or $W(x)$ is zero for no x on $a \leq x \leq b$.

Proof. If $f_1, f_2, \ldots, f_n$ are linearly dependent on $a \leq x \leq b$, then by Theorem 11.7, $W(x)$ is zero for all x on $a \leq x \leq b$.

If $f_1, f_2, \ldots, f_n$ are linearly independent on $a \leq x \leq b$, then by Theorem 11.8,

$$W(x) = W(x_0)e^{-\int_{x_0}^{x} \frac{a_1(t)}{a_0(t)}dt}, a \leq x \leq b,$$

where x_0 is an arbitrary point of the interval $a \leq x \leq b$. Now suppose $W(x_0) = 0$. Then by the above formula, $W(x) = 0$ for all x such that $a \leq x \leq b$. Hence by Theorem 11.7, $f_1, f_2, \ldots, f_n$ must be linearly dependent on $a \leq x \leq b$. But this is a contradiction. Therefore the assumption that $W(x_0) = 0$ is false, and so $W(x_0) \neq 0$. But x_0 is an *arbitrary* point of $a \leq x \leq b$. Hence $W(x)$ is zero for no x on this interval.

$Q.E.D.$

THEOREM 11.10. A necessary and sufficient condition that n solutions $f_1, f_2, \ldots, f_n$ of the nth order homogeneous linear differential equation (11.18) be linearly independent on $a \leq x \leq b$ is that the value of the Wronskian of $f_1, f_2, \ldots, f_n$ be unequal to zero for all x on $a \leq x \leq b$:

$$W(f_1, f_2, \ldots, f_n)(x) \neq 0 \text{ for all } x \in [a,b].$$

Proof. By Theorem 11.7, the solutions $f_1, f_2, \ldots, f_n$ are linearly independent on $a \leq x \leq b$ if and only if $W(f_1, f_2, \ldots, f_n)(x_0) \neq 0$ for *some* $x_0 \in [a,b]$. By Theorem 11.9, either $W(f_1, f_2, \ldots, f_n)(x) = 0$ for *all* $x \in [a,b]$ or $W(f_1, f_2, \ldots, f_n)(x) \neq 0$ for *all* $x \in [a,b]$. Thus $W(f_1, f_2, \ldots, f_n)(x_0) \neq 0$ for *some* $x_0 \in [a,b]$ if and only if $W(f_1, f_2, \ldots, f_n)(x) \neq 0$ for *all* $x \in [a,b]$. Thus $f_1, f_2, \ldots, f_n$ are linearly independent on $a \leq x \leq b$ if and only if $W(f_1, f_2, \ldots, f_n)(x) \neq 0$ for all $x \in [a,b]$.

$Q.E.D.$

Example 11.2. The coefficients $x^2 + 1$ and $2x$ in the differential equation

$$(x^2 + 1)\frac{d^2y}{dx^2} + 2x\frac{dy}{dx} = 0$$

are continuous for all x, $-\infty < x < \infty$, and $x^2 + 1 \neq 0$ for all real x. The reader can verify that f_1 and f_2 defined, respectively, by

$$f_1(x) = 1 \quad \text{and} \quad f_2(x) = \arctan x$$

are solutions of equation (11.30) on $-\infty < x < \infty$. Since

$$W(f_1, f_2)(x) = \begin{vmatrix} 1 & \arctan x \\ 0 & \dfrac{1}{1+x^2} \end{vmatrix} = \frac{1}{1+x^2} \neq 0$$

on every finite closed interval $a \leq x \leq b$, we conclude that f_1 and f_2 are a set of linearly independent solutions of Equation (11.30) on every such interval. In this case Abel's Identity

$$W(x) = W(x_0) e^{-\int_{x_0}^{x} \frac{a_1(t)}{a_0(t)} dt}$$

becomes

$$\frac{1}{1+x^2} = \frac{1}{1+x_0^2} e^{-\int_{x_0}^{x} \frac{2t}{t^2+1} dt}$$

for all $x \in [a,b]$.

Example 11.3.   The coefficients in the differential equation

$$(11.31) \qquad\qquad x\frac{d^2y}{dx^2} - 2\frac{dy}{dx} + 9x^5 y = 0$$

are continuous for all values of x, $-\infty < x < \infty$; but the leading coefficient x is zero for $x = 0$. Thus the closed interval $a \leq x \leq b$ of Theorems 11.8, 11.9, and 11.10 is any finite closed interval which does *not* include zero. The reader can verify that f_1 and f_2 defined, respectively, by

$$f_1(x) = \sin(x^3) \quad \text{and} \quad f_2(x) = \cos(x^3)$$

are solutions of the differential equation on $-\infty < x < \infty$. Since

$$W(f_1, f_2)(x) = \begin{vmatrix} \sin(x^3) & \cos(x^3) \\ 3x^2\cos(x^3) & -3x^2\sin(x^3) \end{vmatrix} = -3x^2 \neq 0$$

for $x \neq 0$, we conclude that f_1 and f_2 are linearly independent solutions on every finite closed interval $a \leq x \leq b$ which does not contain the origin. For example, we may say that they constitute a set of linearly independent solutions on every interval $[a,b]$, where $0 < a \leq x \leq b < \infty$. Observe carefully that the conclusion of Theorem 11.9 does indeed hold on such an interval.

THEOREM 11.11.

Hypothesis.   Let

$$(11.32) \qquad\qquad f_1, f_2, \ldots, f_n$$

be *any* set of n linearly independent solutions of (11.18) on $a \leq x \leq b$.

Conclusion. Every solution f of (11.18) can be expressed as a suitable linear combination

$$c_1 f_1 + c_2 f_2 + \cdots + c_n f_n$$

of the n linearly independent solutions (11.32).

Proof. Let $x_0 \in [a,b]$ and consider the following system of n equations in the n unknowns $k_1, k_2, \ldots, k_n$:

$$(11.33) \quad \begin{cases} k_1 f_1(x_0) + k_2 f_2(x_0) + \cdots + k_n f_n(x_0) = f(x_0) \\ k_1 f_1'(x_0) + k_2 f_2'(x_0) + \cdots + k_n f_n'(x_0) = f'(x_0) \\ \qquad \vdots \\ k_1 f_1^{(n-1)}(x_0) + k_2 f_2^{(n-1)}(x_0) + \cdots + k_n f_n^{(n-1)}(x_0) = f^{(n-1)}(x_0). \end{cases}$$

Since the solutions (11.32) are linearly independent on $a \le x \le b$, we know by Theorem 11.10 that $W(f_1, f_2, \ldots, f_n)(x) \ne 0$ for all x on this interval. Hence $W(f_1, f_2, \ldots, f_n)(x_0) \ne 0$; that is,

$$\begin{vmatrix} f_1(x_0) & f_2(x_0) & \cdots & f_n(x_0) \\ f_1'(x_0) & f_2'(x_0) & \cdots & f_n'(x_0) \\ & \cdots\cdots \\ f_1^{(n-1)}(x_0) & f_2^{(n-1)}(x_0) & \cdots & f_n^{(n-1)}(x_0) \end{vmatrix} \ne 0.$$

Thus by Theorem C the system (11.33) has a unique solution $c_1, c_2, \ldots, c_n$. Thus for $k_1 = c_1, k_2 = c_2, \ldots, k_n = c_n$ each left member

$$(11.34) \quad c_1 f_1^{(i)}(x_0) + c_2 f_2^{(i)}(x_0) + \cdots + c_n f_n^{(i)}(x_0),$$

$i = 0, 1, 2, \ldots, n - 1$, of the system (11.33) has the same value as the corresponding right member $f^{(i)}(x_0)$, $i = 0, 1, 2, \ldots, n - 1$. But these left members (11.34) are the values of the solution

$$c_1 f_1 + c_2 f_2 + \cdots + c_n f_n$$

of equation (11.18) and its first $(n - 1)$ derivatives at x_0; while the corresponding right members are the values of the solution f and its first $(n - 1)$ derivatives at x_0. Thus the two solutions

$$c_1 f_1 + c_2 f_2 + \cdots + c_n f_n \quad \text{and} \quad f$$

have equal values and their ith derivatives $(i = 1, 2, \ldots, n - 1)$ have equal values at x_0. Hence by Theorem 11.4, they are identical throughout $[a,b]$; that is,

$$f(x) = c_1 f_1(x) + c_2 f_2(x) + \cdots + c_n f_n(x)$$

for all x on $a \le x \le b$.

$$Q.E.D.$$

Example 11.4.   Every solution f of

$$\frac{d^2y}{dx^2} + y = 0$$

can be expressed as a linear combination of *any* two linearly independent solutions f_1 and f_2. For example, if $f(x) = 2\sin x + 4\cos x$, $f_1(x) = \sin x$, and $f_2(x) = \cos x$, we have $f(x) = 2f_1(x) + 4f_2(x)$; while if $f_1(x) = \sin x$ and $f_2(x) = \sin x + \cos x$, we have $f(x) = -2f_1(x) + 4f_2(x)$.

The property of a set of n linearly independent solutions proved in Theorem 11.11 has led to the terminology introduced in the following definition:

DEFINITION.   A set of n linearly independent solutions of Equation (11.18) is called a *fundamental system* (or *fundamental set*) of Equation (11.18).

Exercises

1. Consider the third-order homogeneous linear differential equation

$$\frac{d^3y}{dx^3} - \frac{d^2y}{dx^2} + \frac{dy}{dx} - y = 0.$$

   (a) Find the three linearly independent solutions f_1, f_2, f_3 of this equation which are such that

$$\begin{cases} f_1(0) = 1 \\ f_1'(0) = 0 \\ f_1''(0) = 0, \end{cases} \quad \begin{cases} f_2(0) = 0 \\ f_2'(0) = 1 \\ f_2''(0) = 0, \end{cases} \quad \begin{cases} f_3(0) = 0 \\ f_3'(0) = 0 \\ f_3''(0) = 1, \end{cases}$$

respectively.

   (b) Express the solution

$$2\sin x + 3\cos x + 5e^x$$

as a linear combination of the three linearly independent solutions f_1, f_2, and f_3 defined in part (a).

2. (a) Show that e^x, $e^x(x - 1)$, and $2e^x - e^{2x}$ are linearly independent solutions of

$$\frac{d^3y}{dx^3} - 4\frac{d^2y}{dx^2} + 5\frac{dy}{dx} - 2y = 0.$$

   (b) Express the solution $2e^x + 3xe^x + 4e^{2x}$ as a linear combination of the three linearly independent solutions of part (a).

   (c) Find another set of three linearly independent solutions of the given equation.

3. (a) Show that x, x^2, and x^3 is a fundamental system of the differential equation

$$x^3\frac{d^3y}{dx^3} - 3x^2\frac{d^2y}{dx^2} + 6x\frac{dy}{dx} - 6y = 0$$

on every closed interval $[a,b]$, where $0 < a < b < \infty$.

   (b) Verify the truth of Abel's Identity (Theorem 11.8) for this fundamental system.

4. Consider the second order homogeneous linear differential equation

(A) $$a_0(x)\frac{d^2y}{dx^2} + a_1(x)\frac{dy}{dx} + a_2(x)y = 0,$$

where a_0, a_1, and a_2 are continuous on an interval $a \leq x \leq b$, and $a_0(x) \neq 0$ on this interval. Let f and g be distinct solutions of differential equation (A) on $a \leq x \leq b$, and suppose $g(x) \neq 0$ for all $x \in [a,b]$.

(a) Show that

$$\frac{d}{dx}\left[\frac{f(x)}{g(x)}\right] = -\frac{W[f(x),g(x)]}{[g(x)]^2} \quad \text{for all } x \in [a,b].$$

(b) Use the result of part (a) to show that if $W[f(x),g(x)] = 0$ for all $x \in [a,b]$, then the solutions f and g are linearly dependent on this interval.

(c) Suppose the solutions f and g are linearly independent on $a \leq x \leq b$, and let h be the function defined by $h(x) = f(x)/g(x)$, $a \leq x \leq b$. Show that h is a monotonic function on $a \leq x \leq b$.

5. Let f and g be two solutions of the second-order homogeneous linear differential equation (A) of Exercise 4.

(a) Show that if f and g have a common zero at $x_0 \in [a,b]$, then f and g are linearly dependent on $a \leq x \leq b$.

(b) Show that if f and g have relative maxima at a common point $x_0 \in [a,b]$, then f and g are linearly dependent on $a \leq x \leq b$.

6. Consider the second-order homogeneous linear differential equation (A) of Exercise 4.

(a) Let f and g be two solutions of this equation. Show that if f and g are linearly independent on $a \leq x \leq b$ and A_1, A_2, B_1, and B_2 are constants such that $A_1B_2 - A_2B_1 \neq 0$, then the solutions $A_1f + A_2g$ and $B_1f + B_2g$ of (A) are also linearly independent on $a \leq x \leq b$.

(b) Let $\{f,g\}$ and $\{\phi,\psi\}$ be two fundamental systems of differential equation (A) on $a \leq x \leq b$. Show that there exists a constant $c \neq 0$ such that $W(f,g)(x) = cW(\phi,\psi)(x)$ for all $x \in [a,b]$.

7. Let f and g be two solutions of the second-order homogeneous linear differential equation (A) of Exercise 4. Show that if f and g are linearly independent on $a \leq x \leq b$ and are such that $f''(x_0) = g''(x_0) = 0$ at some point $x_0 \in [a,b]$, then $a_1(x_0) = a_2(x_0) = 0$.

8. (a) Show that the substitution

$$y = ue^{-\frac{1}{2}\int P_1(x)dx}$$

transforms the second-order homogeneous linear differential equation

(A) $$\frac{d^2y}{dx^2} + P_1(x)\frac{dy}{dx} + P_2(x)y = 0$$

into the second-order homogeneous linear differential equation

(B) $$\frac{d^2u}{dx^2} + \{P_2(x) - \tfrac{1}{2}P_1'(x) - \tfrac{1}{4}[P_1(x)]^2\}u = 0$$

in which the first derivative term is missing.

(b) If $g_1(x)$ and $g_2(x)$ is a fundamental system of Equation (B) on an interval $a \leq x \leq b$, show that

$$f_1(x) = g_1(x)e^{-\frac{1}{2}\int P_1(x)dx} \quad \text{and} \quad f_2(x) = g_2(x)e^{-\frac{1}{2}\int P_1(x)dx}$$

is a fundamental system of Equation (A) on this interval.

9. Use the substitution given in problem 8(a) to transform the differential equation

(C) $$\frac{d^2y}{dx^2} + (2x + 1)\frac{dy}{dx} + (x^2 + x + \tfrac{1}{4})y = 0$$

into an equation (D) of the form (B) (of problem 8) in which the first derivative term is missing. Obtain a fundamental system of the equation (D) which thus results, and use this fundamental system to obtain a fundamental system of the given equation (C).

11.3. Further Properties of the Homogeneous Linear Equation; Reduction of Order

In Theorem 11.7 we obtained a necessary and sufficient condition that n solutions of the nth order homogeneous linear differential equation

(11.18) $$a_0(x)\frac{d^ny}{dx^n} + a_1(x)\frac{d^{n-1}y}{dx^{n-1}} + \cdots + a_{n-1}(x)\frac{dy}{dx} + a_n(x)y = 0$$

be linearly dependent on $a \leq x \leq b$. This condition is that the value of the Wronskian of the n solutions be zero for all x on $a \leq x \leq b$. We now inquire whether or not this condition remains both necessary and sufficient if the n functions involved are not necessarily solutions of an nth order homogeneous linear differential equation but are merely functions having a continuous $(n-1)$st derivative on $a \leq x \leq b$. The following theorem tells us that the condition is still necessary.

THEOREM 11.12.

Hypothesis. 1. Let each of the functions $f_1, f_2, \ldots, f_n$ have a continuous $(n-1)$st derivative on $a \leq x \leq b$.
2. Let the functions $f_1, f_2, \ldots, f_n$ be linearly dependent on $a \leq x \leq b$.

Conclusion. $W(f_1, f_2, \ldots, f_n)(x) = 0$ for all x on $a \leq x \leq b$.

Proof. In the necessity proof of Theorem 11.7 no use was made of the fact that the functions $f_1, f_2, \ldots, f_n$ were solutions of a homogeneous linear differential equation. Hence the entire necessity proof of that theorem applies to the present case and the stated conclusion is established.

$Q.E.D.$

We now consider whether or not the condition $W(f_1, f_2, \ldots, f_n)(x) = 0$ for all x on $a \leq x \leq b$ is still sufficient for linear dependence in the present case. The following example shows that it is *not*.

Example 11.5. Consider the functions f_1, f_2, and f_3 defined, respectively, by

$$f_1(x) = x^3, \qquad f_2(x) = 1, \qquad f_3(x) = |x|^3.$$

Each of these functions has a continuous second derivative on every interval $a \leq x \leq b$. Further,

$$W(f_1, f_2, f_3)(x) = \begin{vmatrix} x^3 & 1 & |x|^3 \\ 3x^2 & 0 & 3x|x| \\ 6x & 0 & 6|x| \end{vmatrix} = 0, \quad a \leq x \leq b.$$

But the functions f_1, f_2, and f_3 are *not* linearly dependent on any interval $a \leq x \leq b$ which includes $x = 0$.

Thus we see that the condition $W(f_1, f_2, \ldots, f_n)(x) = 0$ for all x on $a \leq x \leq b$ is not sufficient for linear dependence in general. However, we shall obtain the following result.

THEOREM 11.13.

Hypothesis. 1. Let each of the functions $f_1, f_2, \ldots, f_n$ have a continuous $(n - 1)$st derivative on $a \leq x \leq b$.

2. Suppose $W(f_1, f_2, \ldots, f_n)(x) = 0$ for all x on a $\leq x \leq b$.

3. Suppose the Wronskian of some $(n - 1)$ of the functions $f_1, f_2, \ldots, f_n$ is unequal to zero for all x on $a \leq x \leq b$. That is, without loss in generality, suppose that $W(f_1, f_2, \ldots, f_{n-1})(x) \neq 0$ for all x on $a \leq x \leq b$.

Conclusion. Then the functions $f_1, f_2, \ldots, f_n$ are linearly dependent on $a \leq x \leq b$.

Proof. The equation

$$W[f_1(x), f_2(x), \ldots, f_{n-1}(x), y] = 0,$$

that is,

(11.35)
$$\begin{vmatrix} f_1(x) & f_2(x) & \cdots & f_{n-1}(x) & y \\ f_1'(x) & f_2'(x) & \cdots & f_{n-1}'(x) & y' \\ & & \cdots\cdots\cdots & & \\ f_1^{(n-1)}(x) & f_2^{(n-1)}(x) & \cdots & f_{n-1}^{(n-1)}(x) & y^{(n-1)} \end{vmatrix} = 0$$

is a homogeneous linear differential equation of order $(n - 1)$. By Hypothesis 1 the coefficients are continuous on $a \leq x \leq b$. The coefficient of $\dfrac{d^{n-1}y}{dx^{n-1}}$ is $W(f_1, f_2, \ldots, f_{n-1})(x)$, and by Hypothesis 3 this is never zero on $a \leq x \leq b$. If any one of $f_1(x), f_2(x), \ldots, f_{n-1}(x)$ is substituted for y in equation (11.35), the resulting determinant will have two identical columns. Thus each of the functions $f_1, f_2, \ldots, f_{n-1}$ is a solution of the differential equation (11.35) on $a \leq x \leq b$. By Hypothesis 2 the function f_n is also a solution of Equation (11.35) on $a \leq x \leq b$. Thus on $a \leq x \leq b$ the n functions $f_1, f_2, \ldots, f_{n-1}, f_n$ are all solutions of the differential equation (11.35). Since this differential equation is of order $(n - 1)$, we know from Conclusion (ii) of Theorem 11.6 that no set of n solutions of it can be linearly independent. Thus the functions $f_1, f_2, \ldots, f_n$ are linearly dependent on $a \leq x \leq b$.

Q.E.D.

Example 11.6. Although the functions f_1, f_2, f_3 of Example 11.5 are *not* linearly dependent on any interval $a \leq x \leq b$ *including* $x = 0$, it is clear that they *are* linearly dependent on every interval $a \leq x \leq b$ which does *not* include $x = 0$. Observe that on any such interval not including $x = 0$ the hypothesis of Theorem 11.13 are indeed satisfied. In particular, note that Hypothesis 3 holds, since

$$W(f_1, f_2,)(x) = \begin{vmatrix} x^3 & 1 \\ 3x^2 & 0 \end{vmatrix} = -3x^2 \neq 0 \text{ for } x \neq 0.$$

Theorem 11.6 showed that every nth-order homogeneous linear differential equation (11.18) possesses sets of n linearly independent solutions on $a \leq x \leq b$, and Theorem 11.10 showed that the value of the Wronskian of such a set is unequal to zero on $a \leq x \leq b$. Now, given a set of n functions having continuous nth derivatives and a nonzero Wronskian on $a \leq x \leq b$, does there exist an nth order homogeneous linear differential equation for which this set of n functions constitutes a fundamental system (set of n linearly independent solutions) on $a \leq x \leq b$? In answer to this we shall obtain the following theorem.

THEOREM 11.14.

Hypothesis.   1. Let $f_1, f_2, \ldots, f_n$ be a set of n functions each of which has a continuous nth derivative on $a \leq x \leq b$.

2. Suppose $W(f_1, f_2, \ldots, f_n)(x) \neq 0$ for all x on $a \leq x \leq b$.

Conclusion.   There exists a unique normalized (coefficient of $\dfrac{d^n y}{dx^n}$ is unity) homogeneous linear differential equation of order n (with continuous coefficients) which has $f_1, f_2, \ldots, f_n$ as a fundamental system on $a \leq x \leq b$. This equation is

$$(11.36) \qquad \frac{W[f_1(x), f_2(x), \ldots, f_n(x), y]}{W[f_1(x), f_2(x), \ldots, f_n(x)]} = 0.$$

Proof.   The differential equation (11.36) is actually

$$(11.37) \qquad \frac{\begin{vmatrix} f_1(x) & f_2(x) & \cdots & f_n(x) & y \\ f_1'(x) & f_2'(x) & \cdots & f_n'(x) & y' \\ \cdots\cdots\cdots \\ f_1^{(n)}(x) & f_2^{(n)}(x) & \cdots & f_n^{(n)}(x) & y^{(n)} \end{vmatrix}}{\begin{vmatrix} f_1(x) & f_2(x) & \cdots & f_n(x) \\ f_1'(x) & f_2'(x) & \cdots & f_n'(x) \\ \cdots\cdots\cdots \\ f_1^{(n-1)}(x) & f_2^{(n-1)}(x) & \cdots & f_n^{(n-1)}(x) \end{vmatrix}} = 0.$$

This is of the form

$$\frac{d^n y}{dx^n} + p_1(x)\frac{d^{n-1} y}{dx^{n-1}} + \cdots + p_{n-1}(x)\frac{dy}{dx} + p_n(x)y = 0,$$

and so is a normalized homogeneous linear differential equation of order n. Also, by Hypotheses 1 and 2 the coefficients p_i ($i = 1, 2, \ldots, n$) are continuous on $a \leq x \leq b$. If any one of $f_1(x), f_2(x), \ldots, f_n(x)$ is substituted for y in Equation (11.37), the resulting determinant in the numerator will have two identical columns. Thus each of the functions $f_1, f_2, \ldots, f_n$ is a solution of Equation (11.36) on $a \leq x \leq b$; and by Theorem 11.10, we see from Hypothesis 2 that these solutions are linearly independent on $a \leq x \leq b$. Thus Equation (11.36) is indeed an equation of the required type having $f_1, f_2, \ldots, f_n$ as a fundamental system.

We must now show that Equation (11.36) is the *only* normalized nth order homogeneous linear differential equation with continuous coefficients which has this property. Suppose there are two such equations

(11.38)
$$\frac{d^n y}{dx^n} + q_1(x)\frac{d^{n-1}y}{dx^{n-1}} + \cdots + q_{n-1}(x)\frac{dy}{dx} + q_n(x)y = 0$$

$$\frac{d^n y}{dx^n} + r_1(x)\frac{d^{n-1}y}{dx^{n-1}} + \cdots + r_{n-1}(x)\frac{dy}{dx} + r_n(x)y = 0.$$

Then the equation

(11.39)
$$[q_1(x) - r_1(x)]\frac{d^{n-1}y}{dx^{n-1}} + \cdots + [q_n(x) - r_n(x)]y = 0$$

is a homogeneous linear differential equation of order at most $(n - 1)$, and the coefficients in Equation (11.39) are continuous on $a \leq x \leq b$. Further, since $f_1, f_2, \ldots, f_n$ satisfy both of Equations (11.38), these n functions are all solutions of Equation (11.39) on $a \leq x \leq b$.

We shall show that $q_1(x) - r_1(x) = 0$ for all x on $a \leq x \leq b$. To do so, let x_0 be a point of the interval $a \leq x \leq b$ and suppose that $q_1(x_0) - r_1(x_0) \neq 0$. Then there exists a subinterval I, $\alpha \leq x \leq \beta$, of $a \leq x \leq b$ containing x_0 such that $q_1(x) - r_1(x) \neq 0$ on I. Since the n solutions $f_1, f_2, \ldots, f_n$ of Equation (11.39) are linearly independent on $a \leq x \leq b$, they are also linearly independent on I. Thus on I the equation (11.39), of order at most $(n - 1)$, has a set of n linearly independent solutions. But this contradicts Conclusion (ii) of Theorem 11.6. Thus there exists no $x_0 \in [a,b]$ such that $q_1(x_0) - r_1(x_0) \neq 0$. In other words, $q_1(x) - r_1(x) = 0$ for all x on $a \leq x \leq b$.

In like manner, one shows that $q_k(x) - r_k(x) = 0$, $k = 2, 3, \ldots, n$, for all x on $a \leq x \leq b$. Thus the equations (11.38) are identical on $a \leq x \leq b$ and the uniqueness is proved.
                                                                              Q.E.D.

Example 11.7. Consider the functions f_1 and f_2 defined, respectively, by $f_1(x) = x$ and $f_2(x) = xe^x$. We note that

$$W(f_1, f_2)(x) = \begin{vmatrix} x & xe^x \\ 1 & xe^x + e^x \end{vmatrix} = x^2 e^x \neq 0 \text{ for } x \neq 0.$$

Thus by Theorem 11.14 on every closed interval $a \leq x \leq b$ not including $x = 0$ there exists a unique normalized second order homogeneous linear differential equation with continuous coefficients which has f_1 and f_2 as a fundamental system. Indeed, Theorem 11.14 states that this equation is

$$\frac{W[x, xe^x, y]}{W[x, xe^x]} = 0.$$

Writing out the two Wronskians involved, this becomes

$$\frac{\begin{vmatrix} x & xe^x & y \\ 1 & xe^x + e^x & y' \\ 0 & xe^x + 2e^x & y'' \end{vmatrix}}{\begin{vmatrix} x & xe^x \\ 1 & xe^x + e^x \end{vmatrix}} = 0.$$

Since

$$\begin{vmatrix} x & x & y \\ 1 & x+1 & y' \\ 0 & x+2 & y'' \end{vmatrix} = x^2\frac{d^2y}{dx^2} - x(x+2)\frac{dy}{dx} + (x+2)y \quad \text{and} \quad \begin{vmatrix} x & x \\ 1 & x+1 \end{vmatrix} = x^2,$$

we see that this differential equation is

$$\frac{d^2y}{dx^2} - \left(\frac{x+2}{x}\right)\frac{dy}{dx} + \left(\frac{x+2}{x^2}\right)y = 0.$$

Reduction of Order. In Chapter 4 we introduced the process of reduction of order of an nth order homogeneous linear differential equation. There we stated the basic theorem without proof and went on to consider the second order case in greater detail. We employed the process in Chapter 4 and later in Chapter 6. We shall now restate the basic theorem, give its proof, and indicate further how it may be employed.

THEOREM 11.15.

Hypothesis. Let f be a nontrivial solution of the nth order homogeneous linear differential equation

(11.18) $$a_0(x)\frac{d^ny}{dx^n} + a_1(x)\frac{d^{n-1}y}{dx^{n-1}} + \cdots + a_{n-1}(x)\frac{dy}{dx} + a_n(x)y = 0.$$

Conclusion. The transformation

(11.40) $$y = f(x)u$$

reduces the equation (11.18) to an $(n-1)$st-order homogeneous linear differential equation in the dependent variable w, where $w = \dfrac{du}{dx}.$

Proof. Let $y = f(x)u$.
Then

$$\frac{dy}{dx} = f(x)\frac{du}{dx} + f'(x)u,$$

$$\frac{d^2y}{dx^2} = f(x)\frac{d^2u}{dx^2} + 2f'(x)\frac{du}{dx} + f''(x)u,$$

$$\begin{array}{c} \cdot \\ \cdot \\ \cdot \end{array}$$

$$\frac{d^ny}{dx^n} = f(x)\frac{d^nu}{dx^n} + nf'(x)\frac{d^{n-1}u}{dx^{n-1}} + \frac{n(n-1)}{2!}f''(x)\frac{d^{n-2}u}{dx^{n-2}} + \cdots + f^{(n)}(x)u.$$

Substituting these expressions into the differential equation (11.18), we have

$$a_0(x)\left[f(x)\frac{d^nu}{dx^n} + nf'(x)\frac{d^{n-1}u}{dx^{n-1}} + \cdots + f^{(n)}(x)u \right] +$$

$$a_1(x)\left[f(x)\frac{d^{n-1}u}{dx^{n-1}} + (n-1)f'(x)\frac{d^{n-2}u}{dx^{n-2}} + \cdots + f^{(n-1)}(x)u \right]$$

$$+ \cdots + a_{n-1}(x)\left[f(x)\frac{du}{dx} + f'(x)u \right] + a_n(x)f(x)u = 0$$

or

(11.41) $$a_0(x)f(x)\frac{d^n u}{dx^n} + [na_0(x)f'(x) + a_1(x)f(x)]\frac{d^{n-1}u}{dx^{n-1}} + \cdots$$

$$+ [na_0(x)f^{(n-1)}(x) + \cdots + a_{n-1}(x)f(x)]\frac{du}{dx}$$

$$+ [a_0(x)f^{(n)}(x) + a_1(x)f^{(n-1)}(x) + \cdots + a_{n-1}(x)f'(x) + a_n(x)f(x)]u = 0.$$

Now since f is a solution of Equation (11.18), the coefficient of u is zero. Then, letting $w = \frac{du}{dx}$, Equation (11.41) reduces to the $(n-1)$st-order equation in w,

(11.42) $$A_0(x)\frac{d^{n-1}w}{dx^{n-1}} + A_1(x)\frac{d^{n-2}w}{dx^{n-2}} + \cdots + A_{n-1}(x)w = 0,$$

where $$A_0(x) = a_0(x)\,f(x), \quad A_1(x) = na_0(x)\,f'(x) + a_1(x)\,f(x), \ldots ,$$
$$A_{n-1}(x) = na_0(x)\,f^{(n-1)}(x) + \cdots + a_{n-1}(x)\,f(x).$$

Q.E.D.

Now suppose that $w_1, w_2, \ldots , w_{n-1}$ is a known fundamental system of equation (11.42). Then $u_1, u_2, \ldots , u_{n-1}$ defined by

$$u_1(x) = \int w_1(x)dx, \quad u_2(x) = \int w_2(x)dx, \quad \ldots \quad , u_{n-1}(x) = \int w_{n-1}(x)dx$$

is a set of $(n-1)$ solutions of Equation (11.41). Also, the function u_n such that $u_n(x) = 1$ for all x is a solution of Equation (11.41). These n solutions $u_1, u_2, \ldots , u_n$ of Equation (11.41) are linearly independent. Then, using (11.40), we obtain n solutions f_i, where $f_i(x) = f(x)u_i(x)$ $(i = 1, 2, \ldots , n)$ of the original nth-order Equation (11.18). The n solutions f_i so defined are also linearly independent and thus constitute a fundamental system of Equation (11.18).

One may extend Theorem 11.15 to show that if m (where $m < n$) linearly independent solutions of Equation (11.18) are known, then Equation (11.18) may be reduced to a homogeneous linear equation of order $(n - m)$.

Exercises

1. Let f and g be defined, respectively, by $f(x) = \begin{cases} x^2, x \geq 0 \\ 0, x < 0, \end{cases}$ and $g(x) = \begin{cases} 0, x \geq 0 \\ x^2, x < 0. \end{cases}$

Show that $W(f,g)(x) = 0$ for all x but that f and g are not linearly dependent on any interval $a \leq x \leq b$ which includes $x = 0$.

2. In each case find the unique normalized homogeneous linear differential equation of order 3 (with continuous coefficients) which has the given set as a fundamental system.

(a) x, x^2, e^x.

(b) $x, \sin x, \cos x$.

3. The differential equation

$$(x^3 - 2x^2)\frac{d^2y}{dx^2} - (x^3 + 2x^2 - 6x)\frac{dy}{dx} + (3x^2 - 6)y = 0$$

has a solution of the form x^n, where n is an integer.

(a) Find this solution of the form x^n.

(b) Using the solution found in part (a) reduce the order and find the general solution of the given differential equation.

4. Given that the differential equation

$$x^3\frac{d^3y}{dx^3} - (x + 3)x^2\frac{d^2y}{dx^2} + 2x(x + 3)\frac{dy}{dx} - 2(x + 3)y = 0$$

has two linearly independent solutions of the form x^n, where n is an integer, find the general solution.

5. Consider the normalized nth-order homogeneous linear differential equation

(A)
$$\frac{d^ny}{dx^n} + P_1(x)\frac{d^{n-1}y}{dx^{n-1}} + \cdots + P_{n-1}(x)\frac{dy}{dx} + P_n(x)y = 0,$$

where P_i, $i = 1, 2, \ldots, n$, are continuous on $a \le x \le b$. Let $f_1, f_2, \ldots, f_n$ be a fundamental system of this equation on $a \le x \le b$. By the uniqueness result of Theorem 11.14 the differential equation (A) may be written

(B)
$$\frac{W[f_1(x), f_2(x), \ldots, f_n(x), y]}{W[f_1(x), f_2(x), \ldots, f_n(x)]} = 0,$$

and the coefficients of $\dfrac{d^{n-1}y}{dx^{n-1}}$ in the two expressions (A) and (B) for the differential equation must be identical. Equate these coefficients to show that $W(f_1, f_2, \ldots f_n)$ satisfies the first-order differential equation

$$\frac{dW}{dx} + P_1(x)W = 0.$$

Note that this paves the way for the proof of the Abel Identity (Theorem 11.8) in the case of the normalized nth-order equation.

11.4   The Nonhomogeneous Equation

In this section we consider briefly the nonhomogeneous equation

(11.1)
$$a_0(x)\frac{d^ny}{dx^n} + a_1(x)\frac{d^{n-1}y}{dx^{n-1}} + \cdots + a_{n-1}(x)\frac{dy}{dx} + a_n(x)y = b(x).$$

Using the operator notation already introduced in Section 11.2 of this chapter, we may write this as

(11.43)
$$L_ny = b(x),$$

where, as before,

$$L_n = a_0(x)\frac{d^n}{dx^n} + a_1(x)\frac{d^{n-1}}{dx^{n-1}} + \cdots + a_{n-1}(x)\frac{d}{dx} + a_n(x).$$

We now prove the basic theorem dealing with Equation (11.43).

THEOREM 11.16.

Hypothesis.   1. Let v be any solution of the nonhomogeneous equation (11.43).
2. Let u be any solution of the corresponding homogeneous equation

(11.44) $L_n y = 0.$

Conclusion.   Then $u + v$ is also a solution of the nonhomogeneous equation (11.43).

Proof.   We have

$$L_n[u(x) + v(x)] = a_0(x)\frac{d^n}{dx^n}[u(x) + v(x)] + a_1(x)\frac{d^{n-1}}{dx^{n-1}}[u(x) + v(x)]$$

$$+ \cdots + a_{n-1}(x)\frac{d}{dx}[u(x) + v(x)] + a_n(x)[u(x) + v(x)]$$

$$= a_0(x)\frac{d^n}{dx^n}u(x) + a_1(x)\frac{d^{n-1}}{dx^{n-1}}u(x) + \cdots + a_{n-1}(x)\frac{d}{dx}u(x) + a_n(x)u(x)$$

$$+ a_0(x)\frac{d^n}{dx^n}v(x) + a_1(x)\frac{d^{n-1}}{dx^{n-1}}v(x) + \cdots + a_{n-1}(x)\frac{d}{dx}v(x) + a_n(x)v(x)$$

$$= L_n[u(x)] + L_n[v(x)].$$

Now by Hypothesis 1, $L_n[v(x)] = b(x)$; and by Hypothesis 2, $L_n[u(x)] = 0$. Thus $L_n[u(x) + v(x)] = b(x)$; that is, $u + v$ is a solution of Equation (11.43)

                                                                      Q.E.D.

In particular, if $f_1, f_2, \ldots, f_n$ is a fundamental system of the homogeneous equation (11.44) and v is any particular solution of the nonhomogeneous equation (11.43), then

$$c_1 f_1 + c_2 f_2 + \cdots + c_n f_n + v$$

is also a solution of the nonhomogeneous equation (11.43). If a fundamental system $f_1, f_2, \ldots, f_n$ of the corresponding homogeneous equation (11.44) is known, then a particular solution of the nonhomogeneous equation (11.43) can always be found by the method of *variation of parameters*. This method was introduced in Chapter 4, Section 4.4. In that section we gave a detailed development of the method for the case of the second order equation and considered several illustrative examples. We now state and prove the relevant theorem for the general nth order equation.

THEOREM 11.17.

Hypothesis.   1. Let $f_1, f_2, \ldots, f_n$ be a fundamental system of the homogeneous equation

(11.44) $L_n y = 0$

on the interval $a \leq x \leq b.$

2. Let v be a function defined by

(11.45) $$v(x) = v_1(x)f_1(x) + v_2(x)f_2(x) + \cdots + v_n(x)f_n(x),$$

$a \leq x \leq b$, where $v_1, v_2, \ldots, v_n$ are functions such that

$$v_1'(x)f_1(x) + v_2'(x)f_2(x) + \cdots + v_n'(x)f_n(x) = 0,$$
$$v_1'(x)f_1'(x) + v_2'(x)f_2'(x) + \cdots + v_n'(x)f_n'(x) = 0,$$

(11.46)

$$v_1'(x)f_1^{(n-2)}(x) + v_2'(x)f_2^{(n-2)}(x) + \cdots + v_n'(x)f_n^{(n-2)}(x) = 0,$$
$$v_1'(x)f_1^{(n-1)}(x) + v_2'(x)f_2^{(n-1)}(x) + \cdots + v_n'(x)f_n^{(n-1)}(x) = \frac{b(x)}{a_0(x)},$$

for $a \leq x \leq b$.

Conclusion.   Each such function v is a particular solution of the nonhomogeneous equation

(11.43) $$L_n y = b(x)$$

on $a \leq x \leq b$.

Proof.   We first consider the linear algebraic system (11.46) in the n unknowns $v_1'(x)$, $v_2'(x), \ldots, v_n'(x)$. The determinant of coefficients of this system is $W(f_1, f_2, \ldots f_n)(x)$. Since $f_1, f_2, \ldots, f_n$ is a fundamental system of the homogeneous equation (11.44), on $a \leq x \leq b$ this determinant is different from zero for all $x \in [a,b]$. Therefore the system (11.46) uniquely determines $v_1'(x), v_2'(x), \ldots, v_n'(x)$, $a \leq x \leq b$, and hence $v_1(x), v_2(x)$, $\ldots, v_n(x)$ may be determined by antidifferentiation.

In this manner functions v are indeed defined by (11.45). We must now show that any such function v satisfies the nonhomogeneous equation (11.43).

Differentiating (11.45), we obtain

$$v'(x) = v_1(x)f_1'(x) + v_2(x)f_2'(x) + \cdots + v_n(x)f_n'(x)$$
$$+ v_1'(x)f_1(x) + v_2'(x)f_2(x) + \cdots + v_n'(x)f_n(x);$$

and using the first equation of (11.46), this reduces to

(11.47) $$v'(x) = v_1(x)f_1'(x) + v_2(x)f_2'(x) + \cdots + v_n(x)f_n'(x).$$

Differentiating (11.47), we obtain

$$v''(x) = v_1(x)f_1''(x) + v_2(x)f_2''(x) + \cdots + v_n(x)f_n''(x)$$
$$+ v_1'(x)f_1'(x) + v_2'(x)f_2'(x) + \cdots + v_n'(x)f_n'(x);$$

and using the second equation of (11.46), this reduces to

(11.48) $$v''(x) = v_1(x)f_1''(x) + v_2(x)f_2''(x) + \cdots + v_n(x)f_n''(x).$$

Proceeding in like manner, we also obtain

$$(11.49) \quad \begin{cases} v'''(x) = v_1(x)f_1'''(x) + v_2(x)f_2'''(x) + \cdots + v_n(x)f_n'''(x), \\ \qquad\qquad\qquad \vdots \\ v^{(n-1)}(x) = v_1(x)f_1^{(n-1)}(x) + v_2(x)f_2^{(n-1)}(x) + \cdots + v_n(x)f_n^{(n-1)}(x), \\ v^{(n)}(x) = v_1(x)f_1^{(n)}(x) + v_2(x)f_2^{(n)}(x) + \cdots + v_n(x)f_n^{(n)}(x) + \dfrac{b(x)}{a_0(x)}. \end{cases}$$

We now substitute (11.45), (11.47), (11.48), and (11.49) into the nonhomogeneous differential equation (11.43). We obtain

$$a_0(x)\left[v_1(x)f_1^{(n)}(x) + v_2(x)f_2^{(n)}(x) + \cdots + v_n(x)f_n^{(n)}(x) + \frac{b(x)}{a_0(x)} \right]$$

$$+ a_1(x)[v_1(x)f_1^{(n-1)}(x) + v_2(x)f_2^{(n-1)}(x) + \cdots + v_n(x)f_n^{(n-1)}(x)]$$

$$+ \cdots + a_n(x)[v_1(x)f_1(x) + v_2(x)f_2(x) + \cdots + v_n(x)f_n(x)] = b(x).$$

or

$$(11.50) \quad v_1(x)[a_0(x)f_1^{(n)}(x) + a_1(x)f_1^{(n-1)}(x) + \cdots + a_n(x)f_1(x)]$$

$$+ v_2(x)[a_0(x)f_2^{(n)}(x) + a_1(x)f_2^{(n-1)}(x) + \cdots + a_n(x)f_2(x)]$$

$$+ \cdots + v_n(x)[a_0(x)f_n^{(n)}(x) + a_1(x)f_n^{(n-1)}(x) + \cdots + a_n(x)f_n(x)] + b(x) = b(x).$$

Since $f_1, f_2, \ldots, f_n$ are solutions of the homogeneous equation (11.44) on $a \le x \le b$, each of the expressions in brackets in (11.50) is equal to zero for all $x \in [a,b]$. Therefore (11.50) reduces to $b(x) = b(x)$ and thus the function v satisfies the nonhomogeneous differential equation (11.43) on $a \le x \le b$.

Q.E.D.

We now prove the so-called superposition principle for particular solutions of equation (11.43).

THEOREM 11.18.

Hypothesis. 1. Let $L_n y = F_i(x)$, $i = 1, 2, \ldots, m$, be m different nonhomogeneous linear equations, each of which has the same left member

$$L_n y = a_0(x)\frac{d^n y}{dx^n} + a_1(x)\frac{d^{n-1}y}{dx^{n-1}} + \cdots + a_n(x)y.$$

2. Let f_i be a particular solution of $L_n y = F_i(x)$, $i = 1, 2, \ldots, m$.

Conclusion. Then

$$\sum_{i=1}^{m} k_i f_i \text{ is a particular solution of the equation}$$

$$L_n y = \sum_{i=1}^{m} k_i F_i(x),$$

where $k_1, k_2, \ldots, k_m$ are constants.

Proof.   We have

$$L_n\left[\sum_{i=1}^{m} k_i f_i(x)\right] = a_0(x)\frac{d^n}{dx^n}\left[\sum_{i=1}^{m} k_i f_i(x)\right] + \cdots + a_n(x)\left[\sum_{i=1}^{m} k_i f_i(x)\right]$$

$$= k_1\left[a_0(x)\frac{d^n}{dx^n}f_1(x) + \cdots + a_n(x)f_1(x)\right] + \cdots + k_m\left[a_0(x)\frac{d^n}{dx^n}f_m(x) + \cdots + a_n(x)f_m(x)\right]$$

$$= k_1 L_n[f_1(x)] + \cdots + k_m L_n[f_m(x)].$$

By hypothesis 2, f_i satisfies $L_n y = F_i(x)$, $i = 1, 2, \cdots, m$. Thus $L_n[f_1(x)] = F_1(x)$, $\ldots$, $L_n[f_m(x)] = F_m(x)$, and so $L_n\left[\sum_{i=1}^{m} k_i f_i(x)\right] = k_1 F_1(x) + \cdots + k_m F_m(x)$. That is, $\sum_{i=1}^{m} k_i f_i$ is a solution of $L_n y = \sum_{i=1}^{m} k_i F_i(x)$.   *Q.E.D.*

Exercises

1. Show that Theorem 11.16 does not in general apply to nonlinear equations by showing that although f such that $f(x) = x$ is solution of

$$\frac{d^2y}{dx^2} - x^2\frac{dy}{dx} + y^2 = 0$$

and g such that $g(x) = 1$ is a solution of

$$\frac{d^2y}{dx^2} - x^2\frac{dy}{dx} + y^2 = 1,$$

the sum $f + g$ is *not* a solution of

$$\frac{d^2y}{dx^2} - x^2\frac{dy}{dx} + y^2 = 1.$$

2. Apply the superposition principle for particular solutions (Theorem 11.18) to find a particular solution of

$$\frac{d^2y}{dx^2} - y = \sum_{k=1}^{m} \frac{\sin kx}{k^2}.$$

11.5   The Adjoint Equation

DEFINITION.   Consider the nth-order linear differential operator

$$L_n = a_0(x)\frac{d^n}{dx^n} + a_1(x)\frac{d^{n-1}}{dx^{n-1}} + \cdots + a_{n-1}(x)\frac{d}{dx} + a_n(x)$$

and the corresponding nth-order linear differential equation

$$L_n y = 0.$$

The nth order linear operator

$$\bar{L}_n = (-1)^n\frac{d^n}{dx^n}[a_0(x)\cdot] + (-1)^{n-1}\frac{d^{n-1}}{dx^{n-1}}[a_1(x)\cdot] + \cdots - \frac{d}{dx}[a_{n-1}(x)\cdot] + a_n(x)$$

is called the *adjoint operator* of the operator L_n, and the differential equation

$$\bar{L}_n y = 0$$

is called the *adjoint equation* to the equation $L_n y = 0$. That is, the adjoint equation to

$$(11.18) \qquad a_0(x)\frac{d^n y}{dx^n} + a_1(x)\frac{d^{n-1} y}{dx^{n-1}} + \cdots + a_{n-1}(x)\frac{dy}{dx} + a_n(x)y = 0$$

is the equation

$$(11.51) \quad (-1)^n\frac{d^n}{dx^n}[a_0(x)y] + (-1)^{n-1}\frac{d^{n-1}}{dx^{n-1}}[a_1(x)y] + \cdots - \frac{d}{dx}[a_{n-1}(x)y] + a_n(x)y = 0.$$

Note. In our previous study of Equation (11.18) we have assumed that $a_0, a_1, \ldots,$ a_{n-1}, a_n are all continuous on an interval $a \leq x \leq b$ and that $a_0(x) \neq 0$ on $a \leq x \leq b$. In order that the adjoint Equation (11.51) shall also possess such continuity properties on $a \leq x \leq b$ we must now further assume that the coefficients a_k in Equation (11.18) have continuous $(n - k)$th derivatives $(k = 0, 1, \ldots, n - 1)$ on $a \leq x \leq b$.

The Second-Order Case. We consider in particular the second-order linear differential operator

$$L_2 = a_0(x)\frac{d^2}{dx^2} + a_1(x)\frac{d}{dx} + a_2(x)$$

and the corresponding second-order linear differential equation

$$(11.52) \qquad a_0(x)\frac{d^2 y}{dx^2} + a_1(x)\frac{dy}{dx} + a_2(x)y = 0.$$

From Equation (11.51) the adjoint equation to Equation (11.52) is

$$(-1)^2\frac{d^2}{dx^2}[a_0(x)y] + (-1)^1\frac{d}{dx}[a_1(x)y] + a_2(x)y = 0.$$

This reduces to

$$(11.53) \qquad a_0(x)\frac{d^2 y}{dx^2} + [2a_0'(x) - a_1(x)]\frac{dy}{dx} + [a_0''(x) - a_1'(x) + a_2(x)]y = 0,$$

where the primes denote differentiations with respect to x. Thus the adjoint equation to the second-order Equation (11.52) is the equation (11.53).

Example 11.8. Consider

$$(11.54) \qquad x^2\frac{d^2 y}{dx^2} + 7x\frac{dy}{dx} + 8y = 0.$$

Here $a_0(x) = x^2$, $a_1(x) = 7x$, $a_2(x) = 8$. By (11.53) the adjoint equation to equation (11.54) is

$$x^2\frac{d^2 y}{dx^2} + [4x - 7x]\frac{dy}{dx} + [2 - 7 + 8]y = 0$$

or simply

$$(11.55) \qquad x^2\frac{d^2y}{dx^2} - 3x\frac{dy}{dx} + 3y = 0.$$

Of course we could have obtained equation (11.55) directly from (11.51) without using the special result given in (11.53).

THEOREM 11.19. *Lagrange Identity.*

Hypothesis.   1. Let the coefficients a_k in

$$L_n = a_0(x)\frac{d^n}{dx^n} + a_1(x)\frac{d^{n-1}}{dx^{n-1}} + \cdots + a_{n-1}(x)\frac{d}{dx} + a_n(x)$$

have continuous $(n - k)$th derivatives, $(k = 0, 1, 2, \ldots, n)$ on the interval $a \leq x \leq b$.
2. Let u and v be any two functions having nth derivatives on $a \leq x \leq b$.

Conclusion.

$$(11.56) \qquad vL_n[u] - u\bar{L}_n[v] = \frac{d}{dx}[P(u,v)],$$

where

$$(11.57) \qquad P(u,v) = \sum_{k=1}^{n}\left[\sum_{j=1}^{k}(-1)^{j-1}u^{(k-j)}(va_{n-k})^{(j-1)}\right].$$

Note.   We shall refer to the form $P(u,v)$ as the *bilinear concomitant* associated with L_n. The notation $u^{(k-j)}$ denotes the $(k - j)$th derivative of u with respect to x, and in like manner $(va_{n-k})^{(j-1)}$ denotes the $(j - 1)$st x derivative of va_{n-k}.

Proof.   By differentiating the expression

$$U^{(k-1)}V - U^{(k-2)}V' + \cdots + (-1)^{k-2}U'V^{(k-2)} + (-1)^{k-1}UV^{(k-1)}$$

one obtains the formula

$$(11.58) \qquad VU^{(k)} = (-1)^kV^{(k)}U$$
$$+ \frac{d}{dx}[U^{(k-1)}V - U^{(k-2)}V' + \cdots + (-1)^{k-2}U'V^{(k-2)} + (-1)^{k-1}UV^{(k-1)}]$$

$(k = 0, 1, 2, \ldots, n)$. Apply the formula (11.58) with $U = u$ and $V = va_0, va_1, \ldots, va_{n-1}$, successively, in

$$vL_n[u] = va_0\frac{d^nu}{dx^n} + va_1\frac{d^{n-1}u}{dx^{n-1}} + \cdots + va_{n-1}\frac{du}{dx} + va_nu.$$

We obtain

$$vL_n[u] = (-1)^n(va_0)^{(n)}u + \frac{d}{dx}[u^{(n-1)}(va_0) - u^{(n-2)}(va_0)' + \cdots + (-1)^{n-1}u(va_0)^{(n-1)}]$$

$$+ (-1)^{n-1}(va_1)^{(n-1)}u + \frac{d}{dx}[u^{(n-2)}(va_1) - u^{(n-3)}(va_1)' + \cdots + (-1)^{n-2}u(va_1)^{(n-2)}]$$

$$+ \cdots + (-1)^1(va_{n-1})'u + \frac{d}{dx}[uva_{n-1}] + va_n u$$

$$= u \sum_{k=0}^{n}(-1)^{n-k}(va_k)^{(n-k)} + \frac{d}{dx}\left[\sum_{j=1}^{n}(-1)^{j-1}u^{(n-j)}(va_0)^{(j-1)}\right]$$

$$+ \frac{d}{dx}\left[\sum_{j=1}^{n-1}(-1)^{j-1}u^{(n-1-j)}(va_1)^{(j-1)}\right] + \cdots + \frac{d}{dx}\left[\sum_{j=1}^{1}(-1)^{j-1}u^{(1-j)}(va_{n-1})^{(j-1)}\right].$$

But

$$\sum_{k=0}^{n}(-1)^{n-k}(va_k)^{(n-k)} = \bar{L}_n[v].$$

Thus

$$vL_n[u] - u\bar{L}_n[v] = \sum_{k=1}^{n}\frac{d}{dx}\left[\sum_{j=1}^{k}(-1)^{j-1}u^{(k-j)}(va_{n-k})^{(j-1)}\right]$$

and hence

$$vL_n[u] - u\bar{L}_n[v] = \frac{d}{dx}\sum_{k=1}^{n}\left[\sum_{j=1}^{k}(-1)^{j-1}u^{(k-j)}(va_{n-k})^{(j-1)}\right].$$

Q.E.D.

COROLLARY. *Green's Formula.*

Hypothesis. Exactly as in Theorem 11.19.

Conclusion. For any two points x_1 and x_2 of $a \leq x \leq b$,

$$\int_{x_1}^{x_2}\{vL_n[u] - u\bar{L}_n[v]\}dx = P(u,v)|_{x=x_2} - P(u,v)|_{x=x_1}.$$

Proof. Merely integrate the Lagrange Identity (11.56) from x_1 to x_2.

The Second-Order Case. Let us consider the Lagrange Identity (11.56) in the second-order case. In this case

$$L_2 = a_0(x)\frac{d^2}{dx^2} + a_1(x)\frac{d}{dx} + a_2(x)$$

and from (11.53) we see that the adjoint operator L_2 may be written

$$L_2 = a_0(x)\frac{d^2}{dx^2} + [2a_0'(x) - a_1(x)]\frac{d}{dx} + [a_0''(x) - a_1'(x) + a_2(x)].$$

Thus the left member $vL_2[u] - uL_2[v]$ of the Lagrange Identity reduces to

(11.59) $a_0vu'' + a_1vu' - a_0uv'' - 2a_0'uv' + a_1uv' - a_0''uv + a_1'uv,$

where the primes denote differentiations with respect to x. Now the right member of the identity is $\frac{d}{dx}[P(u,v)]$, where in this case

$$P(u,v) = \sum_{k=1}^{2}\left[\sum_{j=1}^{k} (-1)^{j-1}u^{(k-j)}(va_{2-k})^{(j-1)} \right]$$

$$= \sum_{j=1}^{1}(-1)^{j-1}u^{(1-j)}(va_1)^{(j-1)} + \sum_{j=1}^{2}(-1)^{j-1}u^{(2-j)}(va_0)^{(j-1)}.$$

This reduces to

$$P(u,v) = uva_1 + u'(va_0) - u(va_0)'$$

or

(11.60) $P(u,v) = a_0vu' + (a_1 - a_0')vu - a_0v'u.$

Thus the right member of (11.56) in the second-order case is

(11.61) $\frac{d}{dx}[a_0vu' + (a_1 - a_0')vu - a_0v'u].$

The student should perform the indicated differentiation in (11.61) and observe that the result is indeed the expression given by (11.59).

THEOREM 11.20.   **A necessary and sufficient condition that f be a solution of the nth-order linear differential equation $L_ny = 0$ is that f be a solution of the $(n - 1)$st-order linear differential equation**

(11.62) $P[y,g(x)] = c,$

where $P(u,v)$ is the bilinear concomitant associated with L_n, the function g is a non-trivial solution of the adjoint equation $\bar{L}_ny = 0$, and c is an arbitrary constant.

Proof.   Since g is a solution of $\bar{L}_ny = 0$, $\bar{L}_n[g(x)] = 0$ and the Lagrange Identity (11.56) with $u = y$, $v = g(x)$ becomes

(11.63) $g(x)L_n[y] = \frac{d}{dx}\{P[y,g(x)]\}.$

If f is a solution of $L_ny = 0$, then $L_n[f(x)] = 0$. Thus letting $y = f(x)$ in (11.63), we see that (11.63) reduces to

$$\frac{d}{dx}\{P[f(x),g(x)]\} = 0.$$

Thus

$$P[f(x),g(x)] = c,$$

where c is an arbitrary constant. Thus if f is a solution of $L_n y = 0$, then it also satisfies the equation $P[y,g(x)] = c$, which is actually an $(n - 1)$st-order linear differential equation in the dependent variable y.

Conversely, suppose f satisfies $P[y,g(x)] = c$, where c is an arbitrary constant. Then $P[f(x), g(x)] = c$ and $\frac{d}{dx}\{P[f(x), g(x)]\} = 0$. Then (11.63) gives $g(x)L_n[f(x)] = 0$. Since g is a *nontrivial* solution of $\bar{L}_n y = 0$, we see that f is a solution of $L_n y = 0$. Thus if f satisfies $P[y, g(x)] = c$, it also satisfies $L_n y = 0$.   Q.E.D.

The Second-Order Case. The bilinear concomitant $P(u,v)$ associated with the second-order linear operator L_2 has been given explicitly in (11.60). Using this, we find that in the second-order case

$$P[y,g(x)] = a_0(x)g(x)\frac{dy}{dx} + \{[a_1(x) - a_0'(x)]g(x) - a_0(x)g'(x)\}y.$$

Hence f is a solution of the second-order linear equation

(11.64) $$a_0(x)\frac{d^2y}{dx^2} + a_1(x)\frac{dy}{dx} + a_2(x)y = 0$$

if and only if it is a solution of the first-order linear equation

(11.65) $$a_0(x)g(x)\frac{dy}{dx} + \{[a_1(x) - a_0'(x)]g(x) - a_0(x)g'(x)\}y = c,$$

where g is a solution of the adjoint equation to (11.64) and c is an arbitrary constant.

Example 11.9. Solve

(11.66) $$x^2\frac{d^2y}{dx^2} + 7x\frac{dy}{dx} + 8y = 0$$

by finding a solution of its adjoint equation by inspection.

Solution. The adjoint equation to the given equation is given by (11.55). It is

$$x^2\frac{d^2y}{dx^2} - 3x\frac{dy}{dx} + 3y = 0.$$

Clearly g such that $g(x) = x$ is a solution of this equation. In Equation (11.66) $a_0(x) = x^2$, $a_1(x) = 7x$, and $a_2(x) = 8$. Thus in this case Equation (11.65) becomes

$$x^2 \cdot x\frac{dy}{dx} + \{[7x - 2x] \cdot x - x^2 \cdot 1\}y = c$$

or simply

(11.67)
$$x^3\frac{dy}{dx} + 4x^2y = c.$$

Writing this first-order linear equation in the standard form introduced in Chapter 2, we see that x^4 is an integrating factor. Thus the equation (11.67) reduces to

$$\frac{d}{dx}[x^4y] = cx.$$

Integrating, we find

$$x^4y = \frac{cx^2}{2} + c_2$$

or

$$y = c_1x^{-2} + c_2x^{-4},$$

where c_1 and c_2 are arbitrary constants.

Thus f defined by $f(x) = c_1x^{-2} + c_2x^{-4}$ is a solution of (11.66), where c_1 and c_2 are arbitrary constants. In other words, we have obtained the general solution of equation (11.66) by finding a solution of its adjoint and then solving the related first order equation (11.67).

Remarks. The solution of Equation (11.66) by this procedure was merely for illustrative purposes. We hope that no one who has studied sec. 4.5 of Chapter 4 would solve Equation (11.66) by the present method under any other circumstances. Also, the success of the present method in any case depends upon obtaining a solution of the adjoint equation to the given equation. Obtaining such a solution may be impossible; the adjoint equation may be much more formidable than the given equation.

THEOREM 11.21.

Hypothesis.   Let $\bar{L}_n$ be the adjoint operator of L_n.

Conclusion.   Then L_n is the adjoint operator of $\bar{L}_n$.

Proof.   Let $\bar{\bar{L}}_n$ denote the adjoint operator of $\bar{L}_n$. Then

$$u\bar{L}_n[v] - v\bar{\bar{L}}_n[u] = \frac{d}{dx}\{\bar{P}(v,u)\},$$

where $\bar{P}(v,u)$ is the bilinear concomitant associated with the operator $\bar{L}_n$. By hypothesis,

$$vL_n[u] - u\bar{L}_n[v] = \frac{d}{dx}\{P(u,v)\},$$

where $P(u,v)$ is the bilinear concomitant associated with L_n. Thus

(11.68)
$$v\{L_n[u] - \bar{\bar{L}}_n[u]\} = \frac{d}{dx}\{P(u,v) + \bar{P}(v,u)\}.$$

Now (11.57) shows that the bilinear concomitant associated with an nth order linear differential operator is a homogeneous linear form in $v, v', \ldots, v^{(n-1)}$. Thus

(11.69) $$P(u,v) + \bar{P}(v,u) = c_1 v^{(n-1)} + c_2 v^{(n-2)} + \cdots + c_n v,$$

where the coefficients $c_i(i = 1, \ldots, n)$ are functions of $u, u', \ldots, u^{(n-1)}$, the various coefficients in the operators under consideration, and certain derivatives of these various coefficients. Thus $\frac{d}{dx}\{P(u,v) + \bar{P}(v,u)\}$ is the homogeneous linear form

(11.70) $$c_1 v^{(n)} + [c_1' + c_2]v^{(n-1)} + \cdots + [c_{n-1}' + c_n]v' + c_n'v,$$

in $v, v', \ldots, v^{(n)}$. Thus by (11.68) we see that

$$v\{L_n[u] - \bar{L}_n[u]\} \text{ is equal to the form (11.70).}$$

Thus the coefficients of $v^{(n)}, v^{(n-1)}, \ldots, v'$ in (11.70) must be zero. From this it follows at once that $c_1 = c_2 = \cdots = c_n = 0$, and hence (11.69) shows that $P(u,v) + \bar{P}(v,u) = 0$. Thus from (11.68) we see that $\bar{\bar{L}}_n[u] = L_n[u]$. Thus the adjoint operator of the adjoint operator $\bar{L}_n$ is the original operator L_n.

Q.E.D.

Thus if $L_n y = 0$ is a given nth order homogeneous linear equation and $\bar{L}_n y = 0$ is the adjoint equation to $L_n y = 0$, then the adjoint equation to $\bar{L}_n y = 0$ is the original equation $L_n y = 0$.

Example 11.10. We have already seen in Example 11.8 that the adjoint equation to

(11.71) $$x^2\frac{d^2y}{dx^2} + 7x\frac{dy}{dx} + 8y = 0$$

is

(11.72) $$x^2\frac{d^2y}{dx^2} - 3x\frac{dy}{dx} + 3y = 0.$$

In Equation (11.72), $a_0(x) = x^2$, $a_1(x) = -3x$, and $a_2(x) = 3$. Using (11.53) we find that the adjoint equation to (11.72) is

$$x^2\frac{d^2y}{dx^2} + [4x + 3x]\frac{dy}{dx} + [2 + 3 + 3]y = 0,$$

which is the original equation (11.71).

DEFINITION. An nth order homogeneous linear differential equation $L_n y = 0$ is called *self-adjoint* if it is identical with its adjoint equation $\bar{L}_n y = 0$.

In what follows we shall be concerned with self-adjoint equations of the second order. In this connection we have the following theorem.

THEOREM 11.22. Consider the second-order linear differential equation

(11.73) $$a_0(x)\frac{d^2y}{dx^2} + a_1(x)\frac{dy}{dx} + a_2(x)y = 0,$$

where a_0 has a continuous second derivative, a_1 has a continuous first derivative, a_2 is continuous, and $a_0(x) \neq 0$ on $a \leq x \leq b$. A necessary and sufficient condition that equation (11.73) be self-adjoint is that

(11.74) $$\frac{d}{dx}[a_0(x)] = a_1(x)$$

on $a \leq x \leq b$.

Proof.   From Equation (11.53) the adjoint equation to Equation (11.73) is

(11.75) $$a_0(x)\frac{d^2y}{dx^2} + [2a_0'(x) - a_1(x)]\frac{dy}{dx} + [a_0''(x) - a_1'(x) + a_2(x)]y = 0.$$

If condition (11.74) is satisfied, then

$$2a_0'(x) - a_1(x) = a_1(x)$$

and

$$a_0''(x) - a_1'(x) + a_2(x) = a_2(x).$$

These relations show that Equations (11.73) and (11.75) are identical; that is, equation (11.73) is self-adjoint.

Conversely, if Equations (11.73) and (11.75) are identical then

$$2a_0'(x) - a_1(x) = a_1(x)$$

and

$$a_0''(x) - a_1'(x) + a_2(x) = a_2(x).$$

The second of these conditions shows that $a_0'(x) = a_1(x) + c$, where c is an arbitrary constant. From the first condition we see that $a_0'(x) = a_1(x)$. Thus $c = 0$ and we have the condition (11.74).   *Q.E.D.*

COROLLARY.

Hypothesis.   Suppose the second-order equation

(11.73) $$a_0(x)\frac{d^2y}{dx^2} + a_1(x)\frac{dy}{dx} + a_2(x)y = 0$$

is self-adjoint.

Conclusion.   Then Equation (11.73) can be written in the form

(11.76) $$\frac{d}{dx}\left[a_0(x)\frac{dy}{dx}\right] + a_2(x)y = 0.$$

Proof.   Since Equation (11.73) is self-adjoint, condition (11.74) is satisfied. Thus Equation (11.73) may be written

$$a_0(x)\frac{d^2y}{dx^2} + a_0'(x)\frac{dy}{dx} + a_2(x)y = 0$$

or

$$\frac{d}{dx}\left[a_0(x)\frac{dy}{dx}\right] + a_2(x)y = 0.$$

Q.E.D.

Example 11.11. Legendre's Equation

$$(1 - x^2)\frac{d^2y}{dx^2} - 2x\frac{dy}{dx} + n(n + 1)y = 0$$

is self-adjoint, for $a_0(x) = 1 - x^2$, $a_1(x) = -2x$ and $\frac{d}{dx}(1 - x^2) = -2x$. Written in the form (11.76), it is

$$\frac{d}{dx}\left[(1 - x^2)\frac{dy}{dx}\right] + n(n + 1)y = 0.$$

THEOREM 11.23.

Hypothesis. The coefficients a_0, a_1, and a_2 in the differential equation

$$(11.73) \qquad a_0(x)\frac{d^2y}{dx^2} + a_1(x)\frac{dy}{dx} + a_2(x)y = 0$$

are continuous on $a \leq x \leq b$, and $a_0(x) \neq 0$ on $a \leq x \leq b$.

Conclusion. Equation (11.73) can be transformed into the equivalent self-adjoint equation

$$(11.77) \qquad \frac{d}{dx}\left[P(x)\frac{dy}{dx}\right] + Q(x)y = 0$$

on $a \leq x \leq b$, where

$$(11.78) \qquad P(x) = e^{\int \frac{a_1(x)}{a_0(x)}dx}, \; Q(x) = \frac{a_2(x)}{a_0(x)}e^{\int \frac{a_1(x)}{a_0(x)}dx},$$

by multiplication throughout by the factor

$$(11.79) \qquad \frac{1}{a_0(x)}e^{\int \frac{a_1(x)}{a_0(x)}dx}.$$

Proof. Multiplying Equation (11.73) through by the factor (11.79) we obtain

$$e^{\int \frac{a_1(x)}{a_0(x)}dx}\frac{d^2y}{dx^2} + \frac{a_1(x)}{a_0(x)}e^{\int \frac{a_1(x)}{a_0(x)}dx}\frac{dy}{dx} + \frac{a_2(x)}{a_0(x)}e^{\int \frac{a_1(x)}{a_0(x)}dx}y = 0.$$

This equation is clearly self-adjoint and may be written as

$$\frac{d}{dx}\left[e^{\int \frac{a_1(x)}{a_0(x)}dx}\frac{dy}{dx}\right] + \frac{a_2(x)}{a_0(x)}e^{\int \frac{a_1(x)}{a_0(x)}dx}y = 0$$

or

$$\frac{d}{dx}\left[P(x)\frac{dy}{dx}\right] + Q(x)y = 0,$$

where P and Q are given by (11.78).   *Q.E.D.*

Example 11.12.   Consider the equation

(11.80)
$$x^2\frac{d^2y}{dx^2} - 2x\frac{dy}{dx} + 2y = 0.$$

Here $a_0(x) = x^2$, $a_1(x) = -2x$, $a_2(x) = 2$. Since $a_0'(x) = 2x \neq -2x = a_1(x)$, Equation (11.80) is *not* self-adjoint. Let us form the factor (11.79) for this equation. We have

$$\frac{1}{a_0(x)}e^{\int\frac{a_1(x)}{a_0(x)}dx} = \frac{1}{x^2}e^{\int\frac{-2x}{x^2}dx} = \frac{1}{x^4}.$$

Multiplying Equation (11.80) by $\frac{1}{x^4}$ on any interval $a \le x \le b$ which does not include $x = 0$, we obtain

$$\frac{1}{x^2}\frac{d^2y}{dx^2} - \frac{2}{x^3}\frac{dy}{dx} + \frac{2}{x^4}y = 0.$$

Since $\frac{d}{dx}\left(\frac{1}{x^2}\right) = -\frac{2}{x^3}$, this equation is self-adjoint and may be written in the form

$$\frac{d}{dx}\left[\frac{1}{x^2}\frac{dy}{dx}\right] + \frac{2}{x^4}y = 0.$$

Exercises

1. Find the adjoint equation to each of the following equations:

(a) $x^2\frac{d^2y}{dx^2} + 3x\frac{dy}{dx} + 3y = 0.$

(b) $(2x + 1)\frac{d^2y}{dx^2} + x^3\frac{dy}{dx} + y = 0.$

(c) $x^3\frac{d^3y}{dx^3} + x^2\frac{d^2y}{dx^2} + x\frac{dy}{dx} + y = 0.$

(d) $\frac{d^4y}{dx^4} + x\frac{d^3y}{dx^3} + x^2\frac{d^2y}{dx^2} + x^3\frac{dy}{dx} + x^3y = 0.$

2. Consider the differential equation $L_n[y] = 0$, where

$$L_n[y] = x^2\frac{d^2y}{dx^2} + 9x\frac{dy}{dx} + 12y.$$

(a) Find the adjoint equation $\bar{L}_n[y] = 0$ and the bilinear concomitant $P(u,v)$ associated with L_n, and verify the truth of the Lagrange Identity [Equation (11.56)] in this case.

(b) Solve the equation $L_n[y] = 0$ by finding by inspection a solution of the adjoint equation $\bar{L}_n[y] = 0$.

3. Solve

$$x^2\frac{d^2y}{dx^2} + (2x^3 + 7x)\frac{dy}{dx} + (8x^2 + 8)y = 0$$

by finding a simple solution of its adjoint equation by inspection.

4. Show that each of the following equations is self-adjoint and write each in the form (11.76).

(a) $x^3\frac{d^2y}{dx^2} + 3x^2\frac{dy}{dx} + y = 0$.

(b) $\sin x\frac{d^2y}{dx^2} + \cos x\frac{dy}{dx} + 2y = 0$.

(c) $\left(\frac{x+1}{x}\right)\frac{d^2y}{dx^2} - \frac{1}{x^2}\frac{dy}{dx} + \frac{1}{x^3}y = 0$.

5. Transform each of the following equations into an equivalent self-adjoint equation:

(a) $x^2\frac{d^2y}{dx^2} + x\frac{dy}{dx} + y = 0$

(b) $(x^4 + x^2)\frac{d^2y}{dx^2} + 2x^3\frac{dy}{dx} + 3y = 0$

(c) $\frac{d^2y}{dx^2} - \tan x\frac{dy}{dx} + y = 0$

(d) $f(x)\frac{d^2y}{dx^2} + g(x)y = 0$.

6. (a) A first-order differential equation of the form

$$\frac{dy}{dx} + a(x)y + b(x)y^2 + c(x) = 0$$

is called a Riccati Equation. Show that the transformation

$$u = \frac{P(x)\frac{dy}{dx}}{y}$$

transforms the self-adjoint second-order equation

$$\frac{d}{dx}\left[P(x)\frac{dy}{dx}\right] + Q(x)y = 0$$

into the special Riccati equation

$$\frac{du}{dx} + \frac{1}{P(x)}u^2 + Q(x) = 0.$$

(b) Use the result of part (a) to transform the self-adjoint equation

(A)
$$\frac{d}{dx}\left[x\frac{dy}{dx}\right] + (1 - x)y = 0$$

into a Riccati equation. For this Riccati equation find a solution of the form cx^n. Then employ the transformation of part (a) to find a solution of Equation (A). Finally, use the method of reduction of order to obtain the general solution of Equation (A).

11.6 The Sturm Theory

In this section we consider the equation

(11.81)
$$\frac{d}{dx}\left[P(x)\frac{dy}{dx}\right] + Q(x)y = 0,$$

where P has a continuous derivative, Q is continuous, and $P(x)$ is > 0 on $a \leq x \leq b$.

In order to obtain our first result we shall need a well-known theorem on point sets which is known as the Bolzano-Weierstrass Theorem. Suppose E is a set of points on the x axis. A point x_0 is called a *limit point* of E if there exists a sequence of distinct points $x_1, x_2, x_3, \ldots$ of E such that $\lim_{n \to \infty} x_n = x_0$. The Bolzano-Weierstrass Theorem states that every bounded infinite set E has at least one limit point.

We now proceed to study Equation (11.81).

THEOREM 11.24.

Hypothesis.   1. Let f be a solution of

(11.81)
$$\frac{d}{dx}\left[P(x)\frac{dy}{dx}\right] + Q(x)y = 0,$$

having first derivative f' on $a \leq x \leq b$.
2. Suppose f has an infinite number of zeros on $a \leq x \leq b$.

Conclusion.   Then $f(x) = 0$ for all x on $a \leq x \leq b$.

Proof.   Since f has an infinite number of zeros on $[a,b]$, by the Bolzano-Weierstrass Theorem the set of zeros has a limit point x_0, where $x_0 \in [a,b]$. Thus there exists a sequence $\{x_n\}$ of zeros which converges to x_0 (where $x_n \neq x_0$). Since f is continuous, $\lim_{x \to x_0} f(x) = f(x_0)$, where $x \to x_0$ through any sequence of points on $[a,b]$. Let $x \to x_0$ through the sequence of zeros $\{x_n\}$. Then

$$\lim_{x \to x_0} f(x) = 0 = f(x_0).$$

Now since $f'(x_0)$ exists,

$$f'(x_0) = \lim_{x \to x_0} \frac{f(x) - f(x_0)}{x - x_0},$$

where $x \to x_0$ through the sequence $\{x_n\}$. For such points

$$\frac{f(x) - f(x_0)}{x - x_0} = 0 \quad \text{and thus } f'(x_0) = 0.$$

Thus f is a solution of Equation (11.81) such that $f(x_0) = f'(x_0) = 0$. Hence by the Corollary to Theorem 11.4 we conclude that

$$f(x) = 0 \text{ for all } x \text{ on } a \leq x \leq b.$$

Q.E.D.

THEOREM 11.25. *Abel's Formula.*

Hypothesis. Let f and g be any two solutions of

$$\frac{d}{dx}\left[P(x)\frac{dy}{dx} \right] + Q(x)y = 0 \tag{11.81}$$

on the interval $a \leq x \leq b$.

Conclusion. Then for all x on $a \leq x \leq b$,

$$P(x)[f(x)g'(x) - f'(x)g(x)] = k, \tag{11.82}$$

where k is a constant.

Proof. Since f and g are solutions of (11.81) on $a \leq x \leq b$, we have

$$\frac{d}{dx}[P(x)f'(x)] + Q(x)f(x) = 0 \tag{11.83}$$

and

$$\frac{d}{dx}[P(x)g'(x)] + Q(x)g(x) = 0 \tag{11.84}$$

for all $x \in [a,b]$.
Multiply (11.83) by $-g(x)$ and (11.84) by $f(x)$ and add to obtain

$$f(x)\frac{d}{dx}[P(x)g'(x)] - g(x)\frac{d}{dx}[P(x)f'(x)] = 0. \tag{11.85}$$

Now integrate both sides of (11.85) from a to x. Using integration by parts, we obtain

$$f(t)P(t)g'(t)\Big|_a^x - \int_a^x P(t)g'(t)f'(t)dt$$

$$-g(t)P(t)f'(t)\Big|_a^x + \int_a^x P(t)f'(t)g'(t)dt = 0,$$

which reduces to

$$P(x)[f(x)g'(x) - f'(x)g(x)] = P(a)[f(a)g'(a) - f'(a)g(a)]\cdot$$

The right member is a constant k, and thus we have Abel's Formula (11.82).

Q.E.D.

THEOREM 11.26.

A. Hypothesis.   Let f and g be two solutions of

(11.81)
$$\frac{d}{dx}\left[P(x)\frac{dy}{dx}\right] + Q(x)y = 0$$

such that f and g have a common zero on $a \leq x \leq b$.

Conclusion.   Then f and g are linearly dependent on $a \leq x \leq b$.

B. Hypothesis.   Let f and g be nontrivial linearly dependent solutions of equation (11.81) on $a \leq x \leq b$, and suppose $f(x_0) = 0$, where x_0 is such that $a \leq x_0 \leq b$.

Conclusion.   Then $g(x_0) = 0$.

Proof. A.   We apply Abel's Formula

(11.82)
$$P(x)[f(x)g'(x) - f'(x)g(x)] = k.$$

Let $x_0 \in [a,b]$ be the common zero of f and g. Letting $x = x_0$ in the formula (11.82) we obtain $k = 0$. Thus

$$P(x)[f(x)g'(x) - f'(x)g(x)] = 0 \quad \text{for all } x \in [a,b].$$

Since we have assumed throughout that $P(x) > 0$ on $a \leq x \leq b$, the quantity in brackets above must be zero for all x on $a \leq x \leq b$. But this quantity is $W(f,g)(x)$. Thus by Theorem 11.7, the solutions f and g are linearly dependent on $a \leq x \leq b$.

B. Since f and g are linearly dependent on $a \leq x \leq b$, there exist constants c_1 and c_2, not both zero, such that

(11.86)
$$c_1 f(x) + c_2 g(x) = 0,$$

for all x on $a \leq x \leq b$. Now by hypothesis neither f nor g is zero for *all* x on $a \leq x \leq b$. If $c_1 = 0$, then $c_2 g(x) = 0$ for *all* x on $a \leq x \leq b$. Since g is not zero for *all* x on $[a,b]$, we must have $c_2 = 0$, which is a contradiction. Thus $c_1 \neq 0$, and likewise $c_2 \neq 0$. Thus neither c_1 nor c_2 in (11.86) is zero. Since $f(x_0) = 0$, letting $x = x_0$ in (11.86), we have $c_2 g(x_0) = 0$. Thus $g(x_0) = 0$.   *Q.E.D.*

Example 11.13.   The equation

$$\frac{d^2y}{dx^2} + y = 0$$

is of the type (11.81) where $P(x) = Q(x) = 1$ on every interval $a \leq x \leq b$. The linearly dependent solutions $A \sin x$ and $B \sin x$ have the common zeros $x = \pm n\pi$ $(n = 0, 1, 2, \ldots)$ and no other zeros.

THEOREM 11.27.   *Sturm Separation Theorem.*

Hypothesis.   Let f and g be real linearly independent solutions of

(11.81)
$$\frac{d}{dx}\left[P(x)\frac{dy}{dx}\right] + Q(x)y = 0$$

on the interval $a \leq x \leq b$.

Conclusion.   Between any two consecutive zeros of f there is precisely one zero of g.

Proof.   Let x_1 and x_2 be two consecutive zeros of f on $[a,b]$. Then by Theorem 11.26, Part A, we know that $g(x_1) \neq 0$ and $g(x_2) \neq 0$. Now assume that g has *no* zero in the open interval $x_1 < x < x_2$. Then since the solutions f and g have continuous derivatives on $[a,b]$, the quotient $\dfrac{f}{g}$ has a continuous derivative on the interval $x_1 \leq x \leq x_2$. Further $\dfrac{f(x)}{g(x)}$ is zero at the end points of this interval. Thus by Rolle's Theorem there exists ξ, where $x_1 < \xi < x_2$, such that $\dfrac{d}{dx}\left[\dfrac{f(x)}{g(x)}\right]\Big|_{x=\xi} = 0$. But

$$\frac{d}{dx}\left[\frac{f(x)}{g(x)}\right] = \frac{W(g,f)(x)}{[g(x)]^2};$$

and thus since f and g are linearly independent on $a \leq x \leq b$,

$$\frac{d}{dx}\left[\frac{f(x)}{g(x)}\right] \neq 0 \quad \text{on } x_1 < x < x_2.$$

This contradiction shows that g has *at least one* zero in $x_1 < x < x_2$.

Now suppose g has *more than one* zero in $x_1 < x < x_2$, and let x_3 and x_4 be two such consecutive zeros of g. Then interchanging f and g, the preceding paragraph shows that f must have at least one zero x_5 in the open interval $x_3 < x < x_4$. Then $x_1 < x_5 < x_2$, and so x_1 and x_2 would not be *consecutive* zeros of f, contrary to our assumption concerning x_1 and x_2. Thus g has *precisely one* zero in the open interval $x_1 < x < x_2$.

$$\text{Q.E.D.}$$

We may restate Theorem 11.27 in the following form: The zeros of one of two real linearly independent solutions of Equation (11.81) separate the zeros of the other solution (See Figure 11.1).

Example 11.14.   We have already observed that the equation $\dfrac{d^2y}{dx^2} + y = 0$ is of the type (11.81). The functions f and g defined, respectively, by $f(x) = \sin x$ and $g(x) = \cos x$ are linearly independent solutions of this equation. Between any two consecutive zeros of one of these two linearly independent solutions there is indeed precisely one zero of the other solution.

THEOREM 11.28.   *Sturm's Fundamental Comparison Theorem.*

Hypothesis.   On the interval $a \leq x \leq b$,
(1) Let f be a real solution of

$$(11.87) \qquad\qquad \frac{d}{dx}\left[P(x)\frac{dy}{dx}\right] + Q_1(x)y = 0,$$

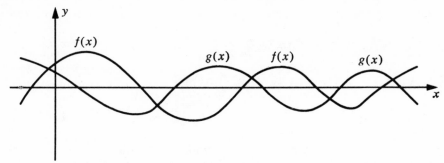

Figure 11.1

(2) Let g be a real solution of

(11.88)
$$\frac{d}{dx}\left[P(x)\frac{dy}{dx}\right] + Q_2(x)y = 0,$$

(3) Let P have a continuous derivative and be such that $P(x) > 0$, and let Q_1 and Q_2 be continuous and such that $Q_2(x) > Q_1(x)$.

Conclusion.   If x_1 and x_2 are successive zeros of f on $[a,b]$, then g has a zero at some point of the open interval $x_1 < x < x_2$.

Proof.   Assume that g does *not* have a zero on the open interval $x_1 < x < x_2$. Then without loss in generality we can assume that $f(x) > 0$ and $g(x) > 0$ on $x_1 < x < x_2$. By hypothesis, we have

(11.89)
$$\frac{d}{dx}[P(x)f'(x)] + Q_1(x)f(x) = 0$$

(11.90)
$$\frac{d}{dx}[P(x)g'(x)] + Q_2(x)g(x) = 0$$

for all $x \in [a,b]$. Multiply (11.89) by $g(x)$ and (11.90) by $f(x)$, and subtract, to obtain

(11.91) $$g(x)\frac{d}{dx}[P(x)f'(x)] - f(x)\frac{d}{dx}[P(x)g'(x)] = [Q_2(x) - Q_1(x)]f(x)g(x).$$

Since

$$g(x)\frac{d}{dx}[P(x)f'(x)] - f(x)\frac{d}{dx}[P(x)g'(x)] = \frac{d}{dx}\{P(x)[f'(x)g(x) - f(x)g'(x)]\},$$

the identity (11.91) reduces to

$$\frac{d}{dx}\{P(x)[f'(x)g(x) - f(x)g'(x)]\} = [Q_2(x) - Q_1(x)]f(x)g(x).$$

We now integrate this from x_1 to x_2 to obtain

$$\int_{x_1}^{x_2} \frac{d}{dx}\{P(x)[f'(x)g(x) - f(x)g'(x)]\}dx$$

$$= \int_{x_1}^{x_2} [Q_2(x) - Q_1(x)]f(x)g(x)dx$$

or

$$(11.92) \qquad P(x)[f'(x)g(x) - f(x)g'(x)]\Big|_{x_1}^{x_2} = \int_{x_1}^{x_2} [Q_2(x) - Q_1(x)]f(x)g(x)dx.$$

Since $f(x_1) = f(x_2) = 0$, the equality (11.92) becomes

$$(11.93) \quad P(x_2)f'(x_2)g(x_2) - P(x_1)f'(x_1)g(x_1) = \int_{x_1}^{x_2} [Q_2(x) - Q_1(x)]f(x)g(x)dx.$$

By hypothesis $P(x_2) > 0$. Since $f(x_2) = 0$ and $f(x) > 0$ on $x_1 < x < x_2$, we have $f'(x_2) < 0$. Since $g(x) > 0$ on $x_1 < x < x_2$, we have $g(x_2) \geq 0$. Thus $P(x_2)f'(x_2)g(x_2) \leq 0$. In like manner, we have $P(x_1)f'(x_1)g(x_1) \geq 0$. Thus, the left member of (11.93) is *not* positive.

But by hypothesis $Q_2(x) - Q_1(x) > 0$ on $x_1 \leq x \leq x_2$, and so the right member of (11.93) *is* positive. Thus the assumption that g does *not* have a zero on the open interval $x_1 < x < x_2$ leads to a contradiction, and so g has a zero at some point of this open interval. $\qquad$ *Q.E.D.*

As a particular case of importance, suppose that the hypotheses of Theorem 11.28 are satisfied and that x_1 is a zero of *both* f and g. Then if x_2 and ξ are the "next" zeros of f and g, respectively, we must have $\xi < x_2$ (See Figure 11.2).

Example 11.15. Consider the equations

$$(11.94) \qquad\qquad \frac{d^2y}{dx^2} + A^2y = 0$$

and

$$(11.95) \qquad\qquad \frac{d^2y}{dx^2} + B^2y = 0,$$

where A and B are constants such that $B > A > 0$. The functions f and g defined respectively by $f(x) = \sin Ax$ and $g(x) = \sin Bx$ are real solutions of these respective equations. Consecutive zeros of $\sin Ax$ are $\frac{n\pi}{A}$ and $\frac{(n+1)\pi}{A}$ ($n = 0, \pm 1, \pm 2, \ldots$). Theorem 11.28 applies, and so we are assured that $\sin Bx$ has at least one zero ξ_n such that

$$\frac{n\pi}{A} < \xi_n < \frac{(n+1)\pi}{A} \quad (n = 0, \pm 1, \pm 2, \ldots).$$

In particular, $x = 0$ is a zero of both $\sin Ax$ and $\sin Bx$. The "next" zero of $\sin Ax$ is $\frac{\pi}{A}$, while the "next" zero of $\sin Bx$ is $\frac{\pi}{B}$; and clearly $\frac{\pi}{B} < \frac{\pi}{A}$.

Exercises

1. Use the Sturm Separation Theorem to show that between any two consecutive zeros of $\sin 2x + \cos 2x$ there is precisely one zero of $\sin 2x - \cos 2x$.

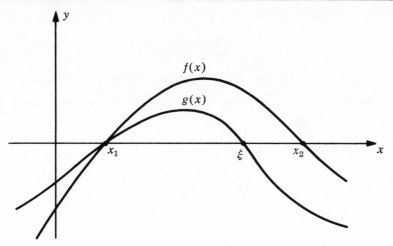

Figure 11.2

2. (a) Show that every real solution of

$$\frac{d^2y}{dx^2} + (x + 1)y = 0$$

has an infinite number of positive zeros.

(b) More generally, show that if q is continuous and such that $q(x) > 0$ for $x > 0$ and k is a positive constant, then every real solution of

$$\frac{d^2y}{dx^2} + [q(x) + k^2]y = 0$$

has an infinite number of positive zeros.

3. Show that if q is continuous and $q(x) < 0$ throughout $a \leq x \leq b$, then no nontrivial solutions of

$$\frac{d^2y}{dx^2} + q(x)y = 0$$

can have more than one zero on $a \leq x \leq b$.

4. Consider the equation

(A) $$\frac{d^2y}{dx^2} + q(x)y = 0,$$

where q is continuous on $a \leq x \leq b$ and such that $0 < m < q(x) < M$. Let f be a solution of equation (A) having consecutive zeros at x_1 and x_2 (where $a \leq x_1 < x_2 \leq b$). Show that

$$\frac{\pi}{\sqrt{M}} < x_2 - x_1 < \frac{\pi}{\sqrt{m}}.$$

[*Hint.* Consider a solution g of $\dfrac{d^2y}{dx^2} + My = 0$ which is such that $g(x_1) = 0$, and apply Theorem 11.28.]

5. Consider the differential equation

(A)
$$\frac{d^2y}{dx^2} + q(x)y = 0,$$

where q is continuous and $q(x) > 0$ on $a \leq x \leq b$. Let q_m denote the minimum value of $q(x)$ on $a \leq x \leq b$. Show that if $q_m > \dfrac{k^2\pi^2}{(b-a)^2}$, then every real solution of Equation (A) has at least k zeros on $a \leq x \leq b$.

[*Hint.* Consider the zeros of the real solutions of

$$\frac{d^2y}{dx^2} + \frac{k^2\pi^2}{(b-a)^2}y = 0$$

and apply Theorem 11.28.]

6. Consider the Bessel Differential Equation

(A)
$$x^2\frac{d^2y}{dx^2} + x\frac{dy}{dx} + (x^2 - p^2)y = 0,$$

where p is a parameter. Suppose $x > 0$; and let $[a, a + \pi]$, where $a > 0$, be an arbitrary interval of length π on the positive x axis. Prove the following result:

If $p = 0$, every such interval $[a, a + \pi]$ contains at least one zero of any solution of the Bessel Differential Equation (A) of order zero; and if $p > \frac{1}{2}$, every such interval $[a, a + \pi]$ contains at most one zero of any nontrivial solution of the Bessel Differential Equation of order p.

[*Hint.* According to the result stated in Exercise 2 of Section 6.3 the transformation

$$y = \frac{u(x)}{\sqrt{x}}$$

reduces the equation (A) to the form

$$\frac{d^2u}{dx^2} + \left[1 + \left(\frac{1}{4} - p^2\right)\frac{1}{x^2}\right]u = 0$$

or, equivalently,

(B)
$$\frac{d^2u}{dx^2} + \left[1 - \frac{4p^2 - 1}{4x^2}\right]u = 0.$$

Note that if a solution of an equation of the form (B) has a zero at $x_0 > 0$, then the solution g such that $g(x) = f(x)/\sqrt{x}$ of the corresponding Bessel Equation (A) also has a zero at x_0. Then apply Theorem 11.28 to compare the number of zeros of solutions of Equation (B) to the number of zeros of solutions of

$$\frac{d^2u}{dx^2} + u = 0.]$$

7. Consider the differential equations

(A)
$$\frac{d}{dx}\left[P(x)\frac{dy}{dx}\right] + Q_1(x)y = 0$$

and

(B)
$$\frac{d}{dx}\left[P(x)\frac{dy}{dx}\right] + Q_2(x)y = 0,$$

where P has a continuous derivative and is such that $P(x) > 0$, and Q_1 and Q_2 are continuous and such that $Q_2(x) > Q_1(x)$ on $a \le x \le b$. Let x_0 and x_1 be such that $a \le x_0 < x_1 \le b$. Let f be the solution of equation (A) such that $f(x_0) = c_0$, $f'(x_0) = c_1$, and let g be the solution of Equation (B) such that $g(x_0) = c_0$ and $g'(x_0) = c_1$, where $c_0 \ge 0$ and $c_1 > 0$ if $c_0 = 0$. Suppose that $g(x) > 0$ for $x_0 < x < x_1$.

Show that $f(x) > g(x)$ for $x_0 < x < x_1$.

[*Hint.* Proceed as in the proof of Theorem 11.28 to show that $P(x)[f'(x)g(x) - f(x)g'(x)] = \int_{x_0}^{x} [Q_2(x) - Q_1(x)]f(x)g(x)dx$ for all $x \in [a,b]$. Thus show that the function h such that $h(x) = \dfrac{f(x)}{g(x)}$ is increasing for $x_0 < x < x_1$, and observe the value $h(x_0)$.]

SUGGESTED READING

I. Basic Theory:
    Burkhill (8)   Greenspan (20)
    Coddington (12)

II. Advanced Theory:
    Bellman (4)   Coddington and Levinson (13)
    Bieberbach (5)   Hurewicz (25)
    Birkhoff and Rota (6)   Ince (26)
    Cesari (9)   Kamke (29)

12

STURM-LIOUVILLE PROBLEMS
AND FOURIER SERIES

In Chapter 1 we encountered boundary value problems consisting of a second order linear differential equation and two supplementary conditions which the solution of the equation must satisfy. In this chapter we shall consider a special kind of boundary value problem known as a *Sturm-Liouville Problem*. Our study of this type of problem will introduce us to several important concepts including *characteristic function, orthogonality*, and *Fourier Series*. These concepts are frequently employed in the applications of differential equations to physics and engineering. In Chapter 14 we shall use them to obtain solutions of boundary value problems which involve partial differential equations.

12.1 Sturm-Liouville Problems

A. Definition and Examples

Our first concern in this chapter is a study of the special type of two-point boundary-value problem given in the following definition:

DEFINITION. We consider a boundary value problem which consists of
(i) a second-order homogeneous linear differential equation of the form

$$(12.1) \qquad \frac{d}{dx}\left[p(x)\frac{dy}{dx}\right] + [q(x) + \lambda r(x)]y = 0,$$

where p, q, and r are real functions such that p has a continuous derivative, q and r are continuous, and $p(x) > 0$ and $r(x) > 0$ for all x on a real interval $a \leq x \leq b$; and λ is a parameter independent of x; and

(ii) two supplementary conditions

(12.2)
$$A_1 y(a) + A_2 y'(a) = 0,$$
$$B_1 y(b) + B_2 y'(b) = 0,$$

where A_1, A_2, B_1 and B_2 are real constants such that A_1 and A_2 are not both zero and B_1 and B_2 are not both zero.

This type of boundary-value problem is called a *Sturm-Liouville Problem* (or *Sturm-Liouville System*).

Two important special cases are those in which the supplementary conditions (12.2) are either of the form

(12.3) $$y(a) = 0, \quad y(b) = 0$$

or of the form

(12.4) $$y'(a) = 0, \quad y'(b) = 0.$$

Example 12.1.   The boundary-value problem

(12.5) $$\frac{d^2 y}{dx^2} + \lambda y = 0,$$

(12.6) $$y(0) = 0, \quad y(\pi) = 0$$

is a Sturm-Liouville problem. The differential equation (12.5) may be written

$$\frac{d}{dx}\left[1 \cdot \frac{dy}{dx}\right] + [0 + \lambda \cdot 1]y = 0$$

and hence is of the form (12.1), where $p(x) = 1$, $q(x) = 0$, and $r(x) = 1$. The supplementary conditions (12.6) are of the special form (12.3) of (12.2).

Example 12.2.   The boundary-value problem

(12.7) $$\frac{d}{dx}\left[x \frac{dy}{dx}\right] + [2x^2 + \lambda x^3]y = 0,$$

(12.8)
$$3y(1) + 4y'(1) = 0,$$
$$5y(2) - 3y'(2) = 0,$$

is a Sturm-Liouville Problem. The differential equation (12.7) is of the form (12.1), where $p(x) = x$, $q(x) = 2x^2$, and $r(x) = x^3$. The conditions (12.8) are of the form (12.2), where $a = 1$, $b = 2$, $A_1 = 3$, $A_2 = 4$, $B_1 = 5$, and $B_2 = -3$.

Let us now see what is involved in solving a Sturm-Liouville Problem. We must find a function f which satisfies both the differential equation (12.1) and the two supplementary conditions (12.2). Clearly one solution of *any* problem of this type is the *trivial* solution ϕ such that $\phi(x) = 0$ for all values of x. Equally clear is the fact that this trivial solution is not very useful. We shall therefore focus our attention on the search for *nontrivial* solutions of the problem. That is, we shall attempt to find functions, *not identically zero*, which satisfy both the differential equation (12.1) and the two conditions (12.2). We shall see that the existence of such nontrivial solutions depends upon the value of the parameter λ in the differential equation (12.1). To illustrate this, let us return to the Sturm-Liouville Problem of Example 12.1 and attempt to find nontrivial solutions.

Example 12.3. Find nontrivial solutions of the Sturm-Liouville Problem

$$\frac{d^2y}{dx^2} + \lambda y = 0,$$
(12.5)

$$y(0) = 0, \quad y(\pi) = 0.$$
(12.6)

Solution. We shall consider separately the three cases $\lambda = 0$, $\lambda < 0$, and $\lambda > 0$. In each case we shall first find the general solution of the differential equation (12.5). We shall then attempt to determine the two arbitrary constants in this solution so that the supplementary conditions (12.6) will also be satisfied.

Case (i): $\lambda = 0$. In this case the differential equation (12.5) reduces at once to

$$\frac{d^2y}{dx^2} = 0$$

and so the general solution is

$$y = c_1 + c_2 x.$$
(12.9)

We now apply the conditions (12.6) to the solution (12.9). Applying the first condition $y(0) = 0$, we obtain $c_1 = 0$. Applying the second condition $y(\pi) = 0$, we find that $c_1 + c_2\pi = 0$. Hence, since $c_1 = 0$, we must also have $c_2 = 0$. Thus in order for the solution (12.9) to satisfy the conditions (12.6), we must have $c_1 = c_2 = 0$. But then the solution (12.9) becomes the solution y such that $y(x) = 0$ for all values of x. Thus if the parameter $\lambda = 0$, the only solution of the given problem is the trivial solution.

Case (ii): $\lambda < 0$. The auxiliary equation of the differential equation (12.5) is $m^2 + \lambda = 0$ and has the roots $\pm \sqrt{-\lambda}$. Since in this case $\lambda < 0$, these roots are real and unequal. Denoting $\sqrt{-\lambda}$ by α, we see that for $\lambda < 0$ the general solution of (12.5) is of the form

$$y = c_1 e^{\alpha x} + c_2 e^{-\alpha x}.$$
(12.10)

We now apply the conditions (12.6) to the solution (12.10). Applying the first condition $y(0) = 0$, we obtain

$$c_1 + c_2 = 0.$$
(12.11)

Applying the second condition $y(\pi) = 0$, we find that

$$c_1 e^{\alpha\pi} + c_2 e^{-\alpha\pi} = 0.$$
(12.12)

We must thus determine c_1 and c_2 such that the system consisting of (12.11) and (12.12) is satisfied. Thus in order for the solution (12.10) to satisfy the conditions (12.6), the constants c_1 and c_2 must satisfy the system of Equations (12.11) and (12.12). Obviously $c_1 = c_2 = 0$ is a solution of this system; but these values of c_1 and c_2 would only give the trivial solution of the given problem. We must therefore seek nonzero values of c_1 and c_2 which satisfy (12.11) and (12.12). By Theorem B of Chapter 11 this system has nonzero solutions only if the determinant of coefficients is zero. Therefore we must have

$$\begin{vmatrix} 1 & 1 \\ e^{\alpha\pi} & e^{-\alpha\pi} \end{vmatrix} = 0.$$

But this implies that $e^{\alpha\pi} = e^{-\alpha\pi}$ and hence that $\alpha = 0$. Thus in order for a nontrivial function of the form (12.10) to satisfy the conditions (12.6) we must have $\alpha = 0$. Since $\alpha = \sqrt{-\lambda}$, we must then have $\lambda = 0$. But $\lambda < 0$ in this case. Thus there are no nontrivial solutions of the given problem in the case $\lambda < 0$.

Case (iii): $\lambda > 0$. Since $\lambda > 0$ here, the roots $\pm\sqrt{-\lambda}$ of the auxiliary equation of (12.5) are the conjugate complex numbers $\pm\sqrt{\lambda}i$. Thus in this case the general solution of (12.5) is of the form

(12.13) $$y = c_1\sin\sqrt{\lambda}x + c_2\cos\sqrt{\lambda}x.$$

We now apply the conditions (12.6) to this general solution. Applying the first condition $y(0) = 0$, we obtain

$$c_1\sin 0 + c_2\cos 0 = 0$$

and hence $c_2 = 0$. Applying the second condition $y(\pi) = 0$, we find that

$$c_1\sin\sqrt{\lambda}\pi + c_2\cos\sqrt{\lambda}\pi = 0.$$

Since $c_2 = 0$, this reduces at once to

(12.14) $$c_1\sin\sqrt{\lambda}\pi = 0$$

We must therefore satisfy (12.14). At first glance it appears that we can do this in either of two ways: we can set $c_1 = 0$ or we can set $\sin\sqrt{\lambda}\pi = 0$. However, if we set $c_1 = 0$, then (since $c_2 = 0$ also) the solution (12.13) reduces immediately to the unwanted trivial solution. Thus to obtain a *nontrivial* solution we can *not* set $c_1 = 0$ but rather we *must* set

(12.15) $$\sin\sqrt{\lambda}\pi = 0.$$

If $k > 0$, then $\sin k\pi = 0$ only if k is a positive integer $n = 1, 2, 3, \ldots$. Thus in order to satisfy (12.15), we must have $\sqrt{\lambda} = n$, where $n = 1, 2, 3, \ldots$. Therefore, in order that the differential equation (12.5) have a nontrivial solution of the form (12.13) satisfying the conditions (12.6), we must have

(12.16) $$\lambda = n^2, \quad \text{where } n = 1, 2, 3, \ldots.$$

In other words, the parameter λ in (12.5) must be a member of the infinite sequence

$$1, 4, 9, 16, \ldots, n^2, \ldots.$$

Let us summarize our results. If $\lambda \leq 0$, the Sturm-Liouville Problem consisting of (12.5) and (12.6) does *not* have a nontrivial solution; if $\lambda > 0$, a nontrivial solution can exist only if λ is one of the values given by (12.16). We now note that if λ *is* one of the values (12.16), then the problem *does have* nontrivial solutions. Indeed, from (12.13) we see that nontrivial solutions corresponding to $\lambda = n^2$ ($n = 1, 2, 3, \ldots$) are given by

(12.17) $$y = c_n\sin nx \ (n = 1, 2, 3, \ldots),$$

where c_n ($n = 1, 2, 3, \ldots$) is an arbitrary nonzero constant. That is, the functions defined by $c_1 \sin x$, $c_2 \sin 2x$, $c_3 \sin 3x$, ..., where $c_1, c_2, c_3, \ldots$ are arbitrary nonzero constants, are nontrivial solutions of the given problem.

B. Characteristic Values and Characteristic Functions

Example 12.3 shows that the existence of nontrivial solutions of a Sturm-Liouville Problem does indeed depend upon the value of the parameter λ in the differential equation of the problem. Those values of the parameter for which nontrivial solutions do exist, as well as the corresponding nontrivial solutions themselves, are singled out by the following definition:

DEFINITION.   Consider the Sturm-Liouville Problem consisting of the differential equation (12.1) and the supplementary conditions (12.2). *The values of the parameter λ in (12.1) for which there exist nontrivial solutions of the problem are called the character-istic values of the problem. The corresponding nontrivial solutions themselves are called the characteristic functions of the problem.†*

Example 12.4.   Consider again the Sturm-Liouville Problem

(12.5)
$$\frac{d^2y}{dx^2} + \lambda y = 0,$$

(12.6)
$$y(0) = 0, \quad y(\pi) = 0.$$

In Example 12.3 we found that the values of λ in (12.5) for which there exist nontrivial solutions of this problem are the values

(12.16) $\lambda = n^2$,   where $n = 1, 2, 3, \ldots$.

These then are the characteristic values of the problem under consideration. The character-istic functions of the problem are the corresponding nontrivial solutions

(12.17) $y = c_n \sin nx$ $(n = 1, 2, 3, \ldots)$,

where c_n $(n = 1, 2, 3, \ldots)$ is an arbitrary nonzero constant.

Example 12.5.   Find the characteristic values and characteristic functions of the Sturm-Liouville Problem

(12.18)
$$\frac{d}{dx}\left[x\frac{dy}{dx} \right] + \frac{\lambda}{x}y = 0,$$

(12.19) $y'(1) = 0, \quad y'(e^{2\pi}) = 0,$

where we assume that the parameter λ in (12.18) is nonnegative.

Solution.   We consider separately the cases $\lambda = 0$ and $\lambda > 0$. If $\lambda = 0$, the differential equation (12.18) reduces to

$$\frac{d}{dx}\left[x\frac{dy}{dx} \right] = 0.$$

The general solution of this differential equation is

$$y = C \ln |x| + C_0,$$

---

†The characteristic values are also called *characteristic numbers* or *eigenvalues;* and the characteristic functions are also called *eigenfunctions.*

where C and C_0 are arbitrary constants. If we apply the conditions (12.19) to this general solution, we find that both of them require that $C = 0$ but neither of them imposes any restriction upon C_0. Thus for $\lambda = 0$ we obtain the solutions $y = C_0$, where C_0 is an arbitrary constant. These are nontrivial solutions for all choices of $C_0 \neq 0$. Thus $\lambda = 0$ is a characteristic value and the corresponding characteristic functions are given by $y = C_0$, where C_0 is an arbitrary nonzero constant.

If $\lambda > 0$, we see that for $x \neq 0$ this equation is equivalent to the Cauchy-Euler Equation

(12.20) $$x^2\frac{d^2y}{dx^2} + x\frac{dy}{dx} + \lambda y = 0.$$

Letting $x = e^t$, the equation (12.20) transforms into

(12.21) $$\frac{d^2y}{dt^2} + \lambda y = 0.$$

Since $\lambda > 0$, the general solution of (12.21) is of the form

$$y = c_1\sin\sqrt{\lambda}t + c_2\cos\sqrt{\lambda}t.$$

Thus for $\lambda > 0$ and $x > 0$ the general solution of (12.18) may be written

(12.22) $$y = c_1\sin(\sqrt{\lambda}\ln x) + c_2\cos(\sqrt{\lambda}\ln x).$$

We now apply the supplementary conditions (12.19). From (12.22) we find that

(12.23) $$\frac{dy}{dx} = \frac{c_1\sqrt{\lambda}}{x}\cos(\sqrt{\lambda}\ln x) - \frac{c_2\sqrt{\lambda}}{x}\sin(\sqrt{\lambda}\ln x)$$

for $x > 0$. Applying the first condition $y'(1) = 0$ of (12.19) to (12.23), we have

$$c_1\sqrt{\lambda}\cos(\sqrt{\lambda}\ln 1) - c_2\sqrt{\lambda}\sin(\sqrt{\lambda}\ln 1) = 0$$

or simply $c_1\sqrt{\lambda} = 0$. Thus we must have

(12.24) $$c_1 = 0.$$

Applying the second condition $y'(e^{2\pi}) = 0$ of (12.19) to (12.23), we obtain

$$c_1\sqrt{\lambda}e^{-2\pi}\cos(\sqrt{\lambda}\ln e^{2\pi}) - c_2\sqrt{\lambda}e^{-2\pi}\sin(\sqrt{\lambda}\ln e^{2\pi}) = 0.$$

Since $c_1 = 0$ by (12.24) and $\ln e^{2\pi} = 2\pi$, this reduces at once to

$$c_2\sqrt{\lambda}e^{-2\pi}\sin(2\pi\sqrt{\lambda}) = 0.$$

Since $c_1 = 0$, the choice $c_2 = 0$ would lead to the trivial solution. Thus we must have $\sin(2\pi\sqrt{\lambda}) = 0$ and hence $2\pi\sqrt{\lambda} = n\pi$, where $n = 1, 2, 3, \ldots$. Thus in order to satisfy the second condition (12.19) nontrivially we must have

(12.25) $$\lambda = \frac{n^2}{4}, \quad (n = 1, 2, 3, \ldots).$$

Corresponding to these values of λ we obtain for $x > 0$ the nontrivial solutions

(12.26) $$y = C_n\cos\left(\frac{n\ln x}{2}\right), \quad (n = 1, 2, 3, \ldots),$$

where the C_n $(n = 1, 2, 3, \ldots)$ are arbitrary nonzero constants.

Thus the values

$$\lambda = 0, \frac{1}{4}, 1, \frac{9}{4}, 4, \frac{25}{4}, \cdots, \frac{n^2}{4}, \cdots,$$

given by (12.25) for $n \geq 0$, are the characteristic values of the given problem. The functions

$$C_0, \ C_1\cos\left(\frac{\ln x}{2}\right), \ C_2\cos(\ln x), \ C_3\cos\left(\frac{3\ln x}{2}\right), \cdots,$$

given by (12.26) for $n \geq 0$, where $C_0, C_1, C_2, C_3, \ldots$ are arbitrary nonzero constants, are the corresponding characteristic functions.

For each of the Sturm-Liouville Problems of Examples 12.3 and 12.5 we found an infinite number of characteristic values. We observe that in each of these problems the infinite set of characteristic values thus found can be arranged in a monotonic increasing sequence†

$$\lambda_1 < \lambda_2 < \lambda_3 < \cdots$$

such that $\lambda_n \to +\infty$ as $n \to +\infty$. For example, the characteristic values of the problem of Example 12.3 can be arranged in the monotonic increasing sequence

(12.27) $$1 < 4 < 9 < 16 < \cdots$$

such that $\lambda_n = n^2 \to +\infty$ as $n \to +\infty$. We also note that in each problem there is a one-parameter family of characteristic functions corresponding to each characteristic value, and any two characteristic functions corresponding to the same characteristic value are merely nonzero constant multiples of each other. For example, in the problem of Example 12.3 the one-parameter family of characteristic functions corresponding to the characteristic value n^2 is $c_n\sin nx$, where $c_n \neq 0$ is the parameter.

We might now inquire whether or not all Sturm-Liouville Problems of the type under consideration possess characteristic values and characteristic functions having the properties noted in the preceding paragraph. We can answer in the affirmative by stating the following important theorem.

THEOREM 12.1.

Hypothesis. Consider the Sturm-Liouville Problem consisting of
(i) the differential equation

(12.1) $$\frac{d}{dx}\left[p(x)\frac{dy}{dx}\right] + [q(x) + \lambda r(x)]y = 0,$$

where p, q, and r are real functions such that p has a continuous derivative, q and r are continuous, and $p(x) > 0$ and $r(x) > 0$ for all x on a real interval $a \leq x \leq b$; and λ is a parameter independent of x; and

---

†An infinite sequence $\{x_n\}$ is said to be monotonic increasing if $x_{n+1} \geq x_n$ for every n.

(ii) the conditions

(12.2)
$$A_1 y(a) + A_2 y'(a) = 0$$
$$B_1 y(b) + B_2 y'(b) = 0,$$

where A_1, A_2, B_1, and B_2 are real constants such that A_1 and A_2 are not both zero and B_1 and B_2 are not both zero.

Conclusions. (i)   There exists an infinite number of characteristic values λ_n of the given problem. These characteristic values λ_n can be arranged in a monotonic increasing sequence

$$\lambda_1 < \lambda_2 < \lambda_3 < \cdots$$

such that $\lambda_n \to + \infty$ as $n \to + \infty$.

(ii)   Corresponding to each characteristic value λ_n there exists a one-parameter family of characteristic functions ϕ_n. Each of these characteristic functions is defined on $a \leq x \leq b$, and any two characteristic functions corresponding to the same characteristic value are nonzero constant multiples of each other.

(iii)   Each characteristic function ϕ_n corresponding to the characteristic value λ_n ($n = 1, 2, 3, \ldots$) has exactly $(n - 1)$ zeros in the *open* interval $a < x < b$.

We regard the proof of this theorem as beyond the scope of this book and refer the reader to *Kamke*, Reference (29), where a proof is given for a stronger theorem which includes Theorem 12.1 as a special case.

Example 12.6.   Consider again the Sturm-Liouville Problem of Examples 12.3 and 12.4,

(12.5)
$$\frac{d^2 y}{dx^2} + \lambda y = 0,$$

(12.6)
$$y(0) = 0, \quad y(\pi) = 0.$$

We have already noted the validity of conclusions (i) and (ii) of Theorem 12.1 for this problem. The infinite number of characteristic values $\lambda_n = n^2$ ($n = 1, 2, 3, \ldots$) can be arranged in the unbounded monotonic increasing sequence indicated by (12.27); and the characteristic functions $c_n \sin nx$ ($c_n \neq 0$), corresponding to $\lambda_n = n^2$ possess the properties stated.

We now illustrate conclusion (iii) by showing that each characteristic function $c_n \sin nx$ corresponding to $\lambda_n = n^2$ has exactly $(n - 1)$ zeros in the open interval $0 < x < \pi$. We know that $\sin nx = 0$ if and only if $nx = k\pi$, where k is an integer. Thus the zeros of $c_n \sin nx$ are given by

(12.28)
$$x = \frac{k\pi}{n}, \ (n = 0, \pm 1, \pm 2, \ldots)$$

The zeros (12.28) which lie in the open interval $0 < x < \pi$ are precisely those for which $k = 1, 2, 3, \ldots, n - 1$. Thus, just as conclusion (iii) asserts, each characteristic function $c_n \sin nx$ has precisely $(n - 1)$ zeros in the open interval $0 < x < \pi$.

Exercises

Find the characteristic values and characteristic functions of each of the following Sturm-Liouville Problems.

1. $\dfrac{d^2y}{dx^2} + \lambda y = 0$,

     $y(0) = 0$,

     $y\left(\dfrac{\pi}{2}\right) = 0$.

2. $\dfrac{d^2y}{dx^2} + \lambda y = 0$,

     $y(0) = 0$,

     $y'(\pi) = 0$.

3. $\dfrac{d^2y}{dx^2} + \lambda y = 0$,

     $y(0) = 0$,

     $y(L) = 0$, where $L > 0$.

4. $\dfrac{d^2y}{dx^2} + \lambda y = 0$,

     $y'(0) = 0$,

     $y'(L) = 0$, where $L > 0$.

5. $\dfrac{d^2y}{dx^2} + \lambda y = 0$,

     $y(0) = 0$,

     $y(\pi) - y'(\pi) = 0$.

6. $\dfrac{d^2y}{dx^2} + \lambda y = 0$,

     $y(0) - y'(0) = 0$,

     $y(\pi) - y'(\pi) = 0$.

7. $\dfrac{d}{dx}\left[x\dfrac{dy}{dx}\right] + \dfrac{\lambda}{x}y = 0$,

     $y(1) = 0$,

     $y(e^{\pi}) = 0$.

8. $\dfrac{d}{dx}\left[x\dfrac{dy}{dx}\right] + \dfrac{\lambda}{x}y = 0$,

     $y(1) = 0$,

     $y'(e^{\pi}) = 0$.

9. $\dfrac{d}{dx}\left[(x^2 + 1)\dfrac{dy}{dx}\right] + \dfrac{\lambda}{x^2 + 1}y = 0$,

     $y(0) = 0$,

     $y(1) = 0$.

[*Hint.* Let $x = \tan t$.]

10. $\dfrac{d}{dx}\left[\dfrac{1}{3x^2 + 1}\dfrac{dy}{dx}\right] + \lambda(3x^2 + 1)y = 0$,

     $y(0) = 0$,

     $y(\pi) = 0$.

[*Hint.* Let $t = x^3 + x$.]

12.2   Orthogonality of Characteristic Functions

A. Orthogonality.

     We now introduce the concept of orthogonality of functions in the following definition.

DEFINITION. Two functions f and g are called *orthogonal* with respect to the *weight* function r on the interval $a \leq x \leq b$ if and only if

$$\int_a^b f(x)g(x)r(x)dx = 0.$$

Example 12.7. The functions $\sin x$ and $\sin 2x$ are orthogonal with respect to the weight function having the constant value 1 on the interval $0 \leq x \leq \pi$, for

$$\int_0^\pi (\sin x)(\sin 2x)(1)dx = \frac{2\sin^3 x}{3}\Big|_0^\pi = 0.$$

DEFINITION. Let $\{\phi_n\}$, $n = 1, 2, 3, \ldots$, be an infinite set of functions defined on the interval $a \leq x \leq b$. The set $\{\phi_n\}$ is called an *orthogonal system* with respect to the weight function r on $a \leq x \leq b$ if every two distinct functions of the set are orthogonal with respect to r on $a \leq x \leq b$. That is, the set $\{\phi_n\}$ is orthogonal with respect to r on $a \leq x \leq b$ if

$$\int_a^b \phi_m(x)\phi_n(x)r(x)dx = 0 \quad \text{for } m \neq n.$$

Example 12.8. Consider the infinite set of functions $\{\phi_n\}$, where $\phi_n(x) = \sin nx$, $n = 1, 2, 3, \ldots$, on the interval $0 \leq x \leq \pi$. The set $\{\phi_n\}$ is an orthogonal system with respect to the weight function having the constant value 1 on the interval $0 \leq x \leq \pi$, for

$$\int_0^\pi (\sin mx)(\sin nx)(1)dx = \frac{\sin(m-n)x}{2(m-n)} - \frac{\sin(m+n)x}{2(m+n)}\Big|_0^\pi = 0 \quad \text{for } m \neq n.$$

B. Orthogonality of Characteristic Functions

We now state and prove a basic theorem concerning the orthogonality of characteristic functions of a Sturm-Liouville Problem.

THEOREM 12.2.

Hypothesis. Consider the Sturm-Liouville Problem consisting of

(i) the differential equation

(12.1)
$$\frac{d}{dx}\left[p(x)\frac{dy}{dx}\right] + [q(x) + \lambda r(x)]y = 0,$$

where p, q, and r are real functions such that p has a continuous derivative, q and r are continuous, and $p(x) > 0$ and $r(x) > 0$ for all x on a real interval $a \leq x \leq b$; and λ is a parameter independent of x; and
   (ii) the conditions

(12.2)
$$A_1 y(a) + A_2 y'(a) = 0$$
$$B_1 y(b) + B_2 y'(b) = 0,$$

where A_1, A_2, B_1, and B_2 are real constants such that A_1 and A_2 are not both zero and B_1 and B_2 are not both zero.

Let λ_m and λ_n be any two distinct characteristic values of this problem. Let ϕ_m be a characteristic function corresponding to λ_m and let ϕ_n be a characteristic function corresponding to λ_n.

Conclusion. The characteristic functions ϕ_m and ϕ_n are orthogonal with respect to the weight function r on the interval $a \leq x \leq b$.

Proof. Since ϕ_m is a characteristic function corresponding to λ_m, the function ϕ_m satisfies the differential equation (12.1) with $\lambda = \lambda_m$; and since ϕ_n is a characteristic function corresponding to λ_n, the function ϕ_n satisfies the differential equation (12.1) with $\lambda = \lambda_n$. Thus, denoting the derivatives of ϕ_m and ϕ_n by ϕ'_m and ϕ'_n, respectively, we have

$$(12.29) \qquad \frac{d}{dx}[p(x)\phi'_m(x)] + [q(x) + \lambda_m r(x)]\phi_m(x) = 0,$$

$$(12.30) \qquad \frac{d}{dx}[p(x)\phi'_n(x)] + [q(x) + \lambda_n r(x)]\phi_n(x) = 0,$$

for all x such that $a \leq x \leq b$. Multiplying both sides of (12.29) by $\phi_n(x)$ and both sides of (12.30) by $\phi_m(x)$ and then subtracting the results we obtain

$$\phi_n(x)\frac{d}{dx}[p(x)\phi'_m(x)] + \lambda_m \phi_m(x)\phi_n(x)r(x) - \phi_m(x)\frac{d}{dx}[p(x)\phi'_n(x)] - \lambda_n \phi_m(x)\phi_n(x)r(x) = 0,$$

and hence

$$(\lambda_m - \lambda_n)\phi_m(x)\phi_n(x)r(x) = \phi_m(x)\frac{d}{dx}[p(x)\phi'_n(x)] - \phi_n(x)\frac{d}{dx}[p(x)\phi'_m(x)].$$

We now integrate both members of this identity from a to b to obtain

$$(12.31) \qquad (\lambda_m - \lambda_n)\int_a^b \phi_m(x)\phi_n(x)r(x)dx$$
$$= \int_a^b \phi_m(x)\frac{d}{dx}[p(x)\phi'_n(x)]dx - \int_a^b \phi_n(x)\frac{d}{dx}[p(x)\phi'_m(x)]dx.$$

Applying integration by parts to each integral in the right member of (12.31), this right member becomes

$$\phi_m(x)p(x)\phi'_n(x)\Big|_a^b - \int_a^b p(x)\phi'_n(x)\phi'_m(x)dx - \phi_n(x)p(x)\phi'_m(x)\Big|_a^b + \int_a^b p(x)\phi'_m(x)\phi'_n(x)dx$$

or simply

$$\left\{p(x)\Big[\phi_m(x)\phi'_n(x) - \phi_n(x)\phi'_m(x)\Big]\right\}\Big|_a^b$$

Therefore the identity (12.31) becomes

$$(12.32) \quad (\lambda_m - \lambda_n) \int_a^b \phi_m(x)\phi_n(x)r(x)dx$$
$$= p(b)[\phi_m(b)\phi_n'(b) - \phi_n(b)\phi_m'(b)] - p(a)[\phi_m(a)\phi_n'(a) - \phi_n(a)\phi_m'(a)].$$

Since ϕ_m and ϕ_n are characteristic functions of the problem under consideration, they satisfy the supplementary conditions (12.2) of the problem. If $A_2 = B_2 = 0$ in (12.2), these conditions reduce to $y(a) = 0$, $y(b) = 0$. Then in this case $\phi_m(a) = 0$, $\phi_m(b) = 0$, $\phi_n(a) = 0$, and $\phi_n(b) = 0$, and so the right member of (12.32) is equal to zero.

If $A_2 = 0$ but $B_2 \neq 0$ in (12.2), these conditions reduce to $y(a) = 0$, $\beta y(b) + y'(b) = 0$, where $\beta = B_1/B_2$. Then the second bracket in the right member of (12.32) is again equal to zero. Also, the first bracket in this member may then be written

$$[\beta\phi_n(b) + \phi_n'(b)]\phi_m(b) - [\beta\phi_m(b) + \phi_m'(b)]\phi_n(b),$$

and so it is also equal to zero. Thus in this case the right member of (12.32) is equal to zero.

In like manner, if either $A_2 \neq 0$, $B_2 = 0$ or $A_2 \neq 0$, $B_2 \neq 0$ in (12.2), then the right member of (12.32) is equal to zero. Thus in all cases the right member of (12.32) is equal to zero and so

$$(\lambda_m - \lambda_n) \int_a^b \phi_m(x)\phi_n(x)r(x)dx = 0.$$

Since λ_m and λ_n are *distinct* characteristic values, their difference $\lambda_m - \lambda_n \neq 0$. Therefore we must have

$$\int_a^b \phi_m(x)\phi_n(x)r(x)dx = 0,$$

and so ϕ_m and ϕ_n are orthogonal with respect to r on $a \leq x \leq b$.   **Q.E.D.**

Let $\{\lambda_n\}$ be the infinite set of characteristic values of a Sturm-Liouville Problem, arranged in a monotonic increasing sequence $\lambda_1 < \lambda_2 < \lambda_3 < \cdots$. For each $n = 1, 2, 3, \ldots$, let ϕ_n be one of the characteristic functions corresponding to the characteristic value λ_n. Then Theorem 12.2 implies at once that the infinite set of characteristic functions $\phi_1, \phi_2, \phi_3, \ldots$ is an orthogonal system with respect to the weight function r on $a \leq x \leq b$.

Example 12.9. Consider once more the Sturm-Liouville Problem

$$(12.5) \qquad \frac{d^2y}{dx^2} + \lambda y = 0,$$

$$(12.6) \qquad y(0) = 0, \quad y(\pi) = 0,$$

which we have already investigated in Examples 12.3, 12.4, and 12.6. Corresponding to each characteristic value $\lambda_n = n^2$, $n = 1, 2, 3, \ldots$, we found the characteristic functions $c_n\sin nx$, $n = 1, 2, 3, \ldots$, where c_n $(n = 1, 2, 3, \ldots)$ is an arbitrary nonzero constant. Let $\{\phi_n\}$ denote the infinite set of characteristic functions for which $c_n = 1, n = 1, 2, 3, \ldots$.

That is,

$$\phi_n(x) = \sin nx, \ 0 \leq x \leq \pi, (n = 1, 2, 3, \ldots).$$

Then by Theorem 12.2, the infinite set $\{\phi_n\}$ is an orthogonal system with respect to the weight function r, where $r(x) = 1$ for all x, on the interval $0 \leq x \leq \pi$. That is, Theorem 12.2 shows that

$$(12.33) \qquad\qquad \int_0^\pi (\sin mx)(\sin nx)(1)dx = 0$$

for $m = 1, 2, 3, \ldots ; n = 1, 2, 3, \ldots ; m \neq n$. We have already noted the validity of (12.33) in Example 12.8.

Exercises

Directly verify the validity of the conclusion of Theorem 12.2 for the characteristic functions of each of the Sturm-Liouville Problems in Exercises 1, 2, and 3.

1. $\dfrac{d^2y}{dx^2} + \lambda y = 0,$

   $y(0) = 0,$
   $y(\pi/2) = 0.$ (See Exercise 1 at the end of Section 12.1.)

2. $\dfrac{d^2y}{dx^2} + \lambda y = 0,$

   $y'(0) = 0,$

   $y'(L) = 0,$ where $L > 0.$ (See Exercise 4 at the end of Section 12.1.)

3. $\dfrac{d}{dx}\left[x\dfrac{dy}{dx}\right] + \dfrac{\lambda}{x}y = 0,$

   $y'(1) = 0,$

   $y'(e^{2\pi}) = 0.$ (See Example 12.5 of the text).

4. Let $\{P_n\}$, $n = 0, 1, 2, \ldots$, be an infinite set of polynomial functions such that
   (i) P_n is of degree n, $n = 0, 1, 2, \ldots$,
   (ii) $P_n(1) = 1$, $n = 0, 1, 2, \ldots$, and
   (iii) the set $\{P_n\}$ is an orthogonal system with respect to the weight function r such that $r(x) = 1$ on the interval $-1 \leq x \leq 1$.

Construct consecutively the members P_0, P_1, P_2, and P_3 of this set by writing

$$P_0(x) = a_0,$$
$$P_1(x) = b_0x + b_1,$$
$$P_2(x) = c_0x^2 + c_1x + c_2,$$
$$P_3(x) = d_0x^3 + d_1x^2 + d_2x + d_3,$$

and determining the constants in each expression so that it has the value 1 at $x = 1$ and is orthogonal to each of the preceding expressions with respect to r on $-1 \leq x \leq 1$.

12.3   The Expansion of a Function in a Series of Orthonormal Functions

A. Orthonormal Systems

We proceed to introduce the concept of an orthonormal system.

DEFINITION.   A function f is called *normalized* with respect to the weight function r on the interval $a \leq x \leq b$ if and only if

$$\int_a^b [f(x)]^2 r(x)dx = 1.$$

Example 12.10.   The function f such that $f(x) = \sqrt{2/\pi} \sin x$ is normalized with respect to the weight function having the constant value 1 on the interval $0 \leq x \leq \pi$, for

$$\int_0^\pi \left(\sqrt{\frac{2}{\pi}}\sin x\right)^2 (1)dx = \frac{2}{\pi}\int_0^\pi \sin^2 x dx = \frac{2}{\pi}\cdot\frac{\pi}{2} = 1.$$

DEFINITION.   Let $\{\phi_n\}$, $n = 1, 2, 3, \ldots$, be an infinite set of functions defined on the interval $a \leq x \leq b$. The set $\{\phi_n\}$ is called an *orthonormal system* with respect to the weight function r on $a \leq x \leq b$ if (i) it is an orthogonal system with respect to r on $a \leq x \leq b$ and (ii) every function of the system is normalized with respect to r on $a \leq x \leq b$. That is, the set $\{\phi_n\}$ is orthonormal with respect to r on $a \leq x \leq b$ if

$$\int_a^b \phi_m(x)\phi_n(x)r(x)dx = \begin{cases} 0 \text{ for } m \neq n \\ 1 \text{ for } m = n. \end{cases}$$

Example 12.11.   Consider the infinite set of functions $\{\phi_n\}$, where $\phi_n(x) = \sqrt{\frac{2}{\pi}} \sin nx$, $n = 1, 2, 3, \ldots$, on the interval $0 \leq x \leq \pi$. The set $\{\phi_n\}$ is an orthogonal system with respect to the weight function having the constant value 1 on the interval $0 \leq x \leq \pi$, for

$$\int_0^\pi \left(\sqrt{\frac{2}{\pi}}\sin mx\right)\left(\sqrt{\frac{2}{\pi}}\sin nx\right)(1)dx = 0 \text{ for } m \neq n.$$

Further, every function of the system is normalized with respect to this weight function on $0 \leq x \leq \pi$, for

$$\int_0^\pi \left(\sqrt{\frac{2}{\pi}}\sin nx\right)^2 (1)dx = 1.$$

Thus the set $\{\phi_n\}$ is an orthonormal system with respect to the weight function having the constant value 1 on $0 \leq x \leq \pi$.

Now consider the Sturm-Liouville Problem consisting of the differential equation (12.1) and the supplementary conditions (12.2). Let $\{\lambda_n\}$ be the infinite set of characteristic values of this problem, arranged in a monotonic increasing sequence $\lambda_1 < \lambda_2 < \lambda_3 < \cdots$. If ϕ_n $(n = 1, 2, 3, \ldots)$ is one of the characteristic functions corresponding to the characteristic value λ_n, then we know from Theorem 12.2 that the infinite set of characteristic functions ϕ_1, ϕ_2, ϕ_3, ... is an orthogonal system with respect to the weight function r on $a \leq x \leq b$. But this set of characteristic functions is not necessarily orthonormal with respect to r on $a \leq x \leq b$.

Now recall that if ϕ_n is one of the characteristic functions corresponding to λ_n, then $k_n\phi_n$, where k_n is an arbitrary nonzero constant, is also a characteristic function corresponding to λ_n. Thus from the given set of characteristic functions ϕ_1, ϕ_2, ϕ_3, ... , we can form a set of "new" characteristic functions $k_1\phi_1$, $k_2\phi_2$, $k_3\phi_3$, ... ; and this "new" set is also orthogonal with respect to r on $a \leq x \leq b$. Now if we can choose the constants k_1, k_2, k_3, ... in such a way that every characteristic function of the "new" set is also *normalized* with respect to r on $a \leq x \leq b$, then the "new" set of characteristic functions $k_1\phi_1$, $k_2\phi_2$, $k_3\phi_3$, ... , will be an *orthonormal* system with respect to r on $a \leq x \leq b$.

We now show that the constants k_1, k_2, k_3, ... can indeed be chosen so that the set $k_1\phi_1$, $k_2\phi_2$, $k_3\phi_3$, ... *is* orthonormal. Recall that the function r in the differential equation (12.1) is such that $r(x) > 0$ for all x on the interval $a \leq x \leq b$. Also recall that by definition no characteristic function ϕ_n $(n = 1, 2, 3, \ldots)$ is identically zero on $a \leq x \leq b$. Therefore

$$\int_a^b [\phi_n(x)]^2 r(x)dx = K_n > 0, (n = 1, 2, 3, \ldots),$$

and so

$$\int_a^b \left[\frac{1}{\sqrt{K_n}}\phi_n(x) \right]^2 r(x)dx = 1, (n = 1, 2, 3, \ldots).$$

Thus the set $\dfrac{1}{\sqrt{K_1}} \phi_1$, $\dfrac{1}{\sqrt{K_2}} \phi_2$, $\dfrac{1}{\sqrt{K_3}} \phi_3$, ... is an orthonormal set with respect to r on $a \leq x \leq b$. We have thus shown that from a given set of orthogonal characteristic functions ϕ_1, ϕ_2, ϕ_3, ... , we can always form the set of *orthonormal* characteristic functions $k_1\phi_1$, $k_2\phi_2$, $k_3\phi_3$, ... , where

$$(12.34) \qquad k_n = \frac{1}{\sqrt{K_n}} = \frac{1}{\sqrt{\int_a^b [\phi_n(x)]^2 r(x)dx}}, (n = 1, 2, 3, \ldots).$$

Example 12.12. The Sturm-Liouville Problem consisting of the differential equation (12.5) and the conditions (12.6) has the set of orthogonal characteristic functions $\{\phi_n\}$, where $\phi_n(x) = c_n \sin nx$, $n = 1, 2, 3, \ldots, 0 \leq x \leq \pi$, and c_n $(n = 1, 2, 3, \ldots)$ is a nonzero constant. We now form the sequence of *orthonormal* characteristic functions $\{k_n\phi_n\}$, where k_n is given by (12.34). We have

$$K_n = \int_0^\pi (c_n \sin nx)^2 (1)dx = \frac{c_n^2 \pi}{2},$$

$$k_n = \frac{1}{\sqrt{K_n}} = \frac{1}{c_n} \sqrt{\frac{2}{\pi}},$$

$$k_n\phi_n(x) = \left(\frac{1}{c_n} \sqrt{\frac{2}{\pi}} \right)(c_n \sin nx) = \sqrt{\frac{2}{\pi}}\sin nx, (n = 1, 2, 3, \ldots).$$

Thus the Sturm-Liouville Problem under consideration has the set of orthonormal characteristic functions $\{\psi_n\}$, where $\psi_n(x) = \sqrt{\dfrac{2}{\pi}} \sin nx$, $n = 1, 2, 3, \ldots$, $0 \leq x \leq \pi$. We observe that this is the set of orthonormal functions considered in Example 12.11.

B. The Expansion Problem

We now consider a problem which has many applications and has led to the development of a vast amount of advanced mathematical analysis. Let $\{\phi_n\}$ be an orthonormal system with respect to a weight function r on an interval $a \leq x \leq b$, and let f be an "arbitrary" function. The basic problem under consideration is to expand the function f in an infinite series of the orthonormal functions $\phi_1, \phi_2, \phi_3, \ldots$.

Let us first assume that such an expansion exists. That is, we assume that

$$(12.35) \qquad\qquad f(x) = \sum_{n=1}^{\infty} c_n \phi_n(x)$$

for each x in the interval $a \leq x \leq b$. Now assuming that this expansion does exist, how do we determine the coefficients c_n ($n = 1, 2, 3, \ldots$)? Let us proceed formally for the moment, without considering questions of convergence. We multiply both sides of (12.35) by $\phi_k(x)r(x)$, where r is the weight function and ϕ_k is the kth function of the system $\{\phi_n\}$, thereby obtaining

$$f(x)\phi_k(x)r(x) = \sum_{n=1}^{\infty} c_n \phi_n(x)\phi_k(x)r(x).$$

We now integrate both sides of this equation from a to b and obtain

$$\int_a^b f(x)\phi_k(x)r(x)\,dx = \int_a^b \left[\sum_{n=1}^{\infty} c_n \phi_n(x)\phi_k(x)r(x)\right]dx = \sum_{n=1}^{\infty} \int_a^b c_n \phi_n(x)\phi_k(x)r(x)\,dx,$$

assuming that the integral of the sum in the middle member is the sum of the integrals in the right member. Under this assumption we thus have

$$(12.36) \qquad\qquad \int_a^b f(x)\phi_k(x)r(x)\,dx = \sum_{n=1}^{\infty} c_n \int_a^b \phi_n(x)\phi_k(x)r(x)\,dx.$$

But $\{\phi_n\}$ is an orthonormal set with respect to r on $a \leq x \leq b$, and so

$$\int_a^b \phi_n(x)\phi_k(x)r(x)\,dx = \begin{cases} 0 & \text{for } n \neq k, \\ 1 & \text{for } n = k. \end{cases}$$

Therefore every term except the kth term in the series in the right member of (12.36) is zero, and the kth term is simply $c_k \cdot 1 = c_k$. Thus (12.36) reduces to

$$\int_a^b f(x)\phi_k(x)r(x)\,dx = c_k.$$

This is a formula for the kth coefficient ($k = 1, 2, 3, \ldots$) in the assumed series expansion (12.35). Thus under suitable convergence conditions the coefficients c_n in the expansion

(12.35) are given by the formula

$$(12.37) \qquad c_n = \int_a^b f(x)\phi_n(x)r(x)dx, \ (n = 1, 2, 3, \ldots).$$

In particular, we note that *if* the series $\sum_{n=1}^{\infty} c_n\phi_n(x)$ converges *uniformly* to $f(x)$ on $a \leq x \leq b$, then the above formal procedure is justified and we are assured that the coefficients c_n are given by the formula (12.37).

Now, given an orthonormal system $\{\phi_n\}$ and a function f, we can form the series

$$(12.38) \qquad \sum_{n=1}^{\infty} c_n\phi_n,$$

where $c_n, (n = 1, 2, 3, \ldots)$ is given by formula (12.37). But note carefully that this formula was obtained under the *assumption* that f *is* representable by an expansion of the form (12.38). Therefore in general the expansion (12.38) obtained using formula (12.37) is indeed a strictly *formal* expansion. That is, in general we have no assurance that the series (12.38) determined by (12.37) converges *pointwise* on $[a,b]$. Further, if this series *does* converge at a point x on $[a,b]$, we have no assurance that it converges to $f(x)$ at this point. To be assured that the formal expansion (12.38) *does* converge to $f(x)$ at every point x of $[a,b]$, the functions f and $\{\phi_n\}$ must satisfy certain restrictive conditions. It is beyond the scope of this book to attempt to give a detailed discussion of the various conditions on f and $\{\phi_n\}$ which are sufficient for the convergence of this expansion. However, we shall state without proof one basic convergence theorem concerned with the case in which the system $\{\phi_n\}$ is the system of orthonormal characteristic functions of a Sturm-Liouville Problem.

THEOREM 12.3.

Hypothesis. (*i*).　Consider the Sturm-Liouville Problem

$$\frac{d}{dx}\left[p(x)\frac{dy}{dx}\right] + [q(x) + \lambda r(x)]y = 0,$$

$$A_1 y(a) + A_2 y'(a) = 0,$$

$$B_1 y(b) + B_2 y'(b) = 0,$$

where p, q, and r are real functions such that p has a continuous derivative, q and r are continuous, and $p(x) > 0$ and $r(x) > 0$ for all x on the real interval $a \leq x \leq b$. Let $\{\lambda_n\}$ $(n = 1, 2, 3, \ldots)$ be the infinite set of characteristic values of this problem, arranged in a monotonic increasing sequence $\lambda_1 < \lambda_2 < \lambda_3 < \cdots$. Let $\{\phi_n\}$, $(n = 1, 2, 3, \ldots)$, be the corresponding set of orthonormal characteristic functions of the given problem.

(ii) Let f be a function which is continuous on the interval $a \leq x \leq b$, has a piecewise continuous derivative f' on $a \leq x \leq b$, and is such that $f(a) = 0$ if $\phi_1(a) = 0$ and $f(b) = 0$ if $\phi_1(b) = 0$.

Conclusion.   The series

$$\sum_{n=1}^{\infty} c_n \phi_n,$$

where

$$c_n = \int_a^b f(x)\phi_n(x)r(x)dx, \quad (n = 1, 2, 3, \ldots),$$

converges uniformly and absolutely to f on the interval $a \le x \le b$.

Example 12.13.   Obtain the formal expansion of the function f, where $f(x) = \pi x - x^2$, $0 \le x \le \pi$, in the series of orthonormal characteristic functions $\{\phi_n\}$ of the Sturm-Liouville problem

(12.5)
$$\frac{d^2y}{dx^2} + \lambda y = 0,$$

(12.6)
$$y(0) = 0, \, y(\pi) = 0.$$

Discuss the convergence of this formal expansion.

Solution.   In Example 12.12 we found that the orthonormal characteristic functions $\{\phi_n\}$ of the problem under consideration are given by

$$\phi_n(x) = \sqrt{\frac{2}{\pi}}\sin nx, \quad n = 1, 2, 3, \ldots, \quad 0 \le x \le \pi.$$

We now form the series

(12.39)
$$\sum_{n=1}^{\infty} c_n \phi_n(x),$$

where for each $n = 1, 2, 3, \ldots$,

$$
\begin{aligned}
c_n &= \int_a^b f(x)\phi_n(x)r(x)dx \\
&= \int_0^\pi (\pi x - x^2)\left(\sqrt{\frac{2}{\pi}}\sin nx\right)(1)dx \\
&= \sqrt{\frac{2}{\pi}}\left[\pi\int_0^\pi x\sin nx\,dx - \int_0^\pi x^2\sin nx\,dx\right] \\
&= \sqrt{\frac{2}{\pi}}\left[\left(\frac{\pi}{n^2}\sin nx - \frac{\pi x}{n}\cos nx\right)\Big|_0^\pi - \left(\frac{2x}{n^2}\sin nx + \frac{2}{n^3}\cos nx - \frac{x^2}{n}\cos nx\right)\Big|_0^\pi\right] \\
&= \sqrt{\frac{2}{\pi}}\left[\left(-\frac{\pi^2}{n}\cos n\pi\right) - \left(\frac{2}{n^3}\cos n\pi - \frac{\pi^2}{n}\cos n\pi - \frac{2}{n^3}\right)\right] \\
&= \sqrt{\frac{2}{\pi}}\frac{2}{n^3}(1 - \cos n\pi) \\
&= \begin{cases} \sqrt{\dfrac{2}{\pi}}\cdot\dfrac{4}{n^3} & \text{if } n \text{ is odd,} \\ 0 & \text{if } n \text{ is even.} \end{cases}
\end{aligned}
$$

Thus the series (12.39) becomes

(12.40)
$$\sum_{\substack{n=1 \\ (n \text{ odd})}}^{\infty} \frac{8}{\pi n^3} \sin nx \quad \text{or} \quad \frac{8}{\pi} \sum_{n=1}^{\infty} \frac{\sin(2n-1)x}{(2n-1)^3}.$$

We write

$$\pi x - x^2 \sim \frac{8}{\pi} \sum_{n=1}^{\infty} \frac{\sin(2n-1)x}{(2n-1)^3}, \quad 0 \leq x \leq \pi,$$

to denote that the series (12.40) is the *formal* expansion of f in terms of the orthonormal characteristic functions $\{\phi_n\}$. We note that the first few terms of this expansion are

$$\frac{8}{\pi}\left[\frac{\sin x}{1^3} + \frac{\sin 3x}{3^3} + \frac{\sin 5x}{5^3} + \cdots \right].$$

Let us now discuss the convergence of this formal expansion. We note first that the coefficients p, q, and r in the differential equation (12.5) satisfy hypothesis (i) of Theorem 12.3. Let us now see if the function f satisfies hypothesis (ii). Since f is a polynomial function, it certainly satisfies the requirements of continuity and a piecewise continuous derivative on $0 \leq x \leq \pi$. Hypothesis (ii) also requires that $f(0) = 0$ if $\phi_1(0) = 0$ and $f(\pi) = 0$ if $\phi_1(\pi) = 0$. These requirements are also fulfilled, for

$$\phi_1(0) = \sqrt{\frac{2}{\pi}} \sin 0 = 0, \quad f(0) = 0,$$

$$\phi_1(\pi) = \sqrt{\frac{2}{\pi}} \sin \pi = 0, \quad \text{and} \quad f(\pi) = \pi^2 - \pi^2 = 0.$$

Thus all the hypotheses of Theorem 12.3 are satisfied and we conclude that the series (12.40) converges uniformly and absolutely to $\pi x - x^2$ on the interval $0 \leq x \leq \pi$. Thus we may write

$$\pi x - x^2 = \frac{8}{\pi} \sum_{n=1}^{\infty} \frac{\sin(2n-1)x}{(2n-1)^3}, \quad 0 \leq x \leq \pi.$$

Exercises

1. Consider the set of functions $\{\phi_n\}$, where

$$\phi_1(x) = \frac{1}{\sqrt{\pi}}$$

$$\phi_{n+1}(x) = \sqrt{\frac{2}{\pi}} \cos nx, \ (n = 1, 2, 3, \ldots),$$

on the interval $0 \leq x \leq \pi$. Show that this set $\{\phi_n\}$ is an orthonormal system with respect to the weight function having the constant value 1 on $0 \leq x \leq \pi$.

2. Obtain the formal expansion of the function f defined by $f(x) = x$, $0 \le x \le \pi$, in a series of orthonormal characteristic functions $\{\phi_n\}$ of the Sturm-Liouville Problem

$$\frac{d^2y}{dx^2} + \lambda y = 0,$$

$$y(0) = 0,$$

$$y(\pi) = 0.$$

3. Obtain the formal expansion of the function f defined by $f(x) = 1$, $1 \le x \le e^\pi$, in a series of orthonormal characteristic functions $\{\phi_n\}$ of the Sturm-Liouville Problem

$$\frac{d}{dx}\left[x\frac{dy}{dx}\right] + \frac{\lambda}{x}y = 0,$$

$$y(1) = 0,$$

$$y(e^\pi) = 0.$$

(See Exercise 7 at the end of Section 12.1.)

4. Obtain the formal expansion of the function f defined by $f(x) = \ln x$, $1 \le x \le e^{2\pi}$, in a series of orthonormal characteristic functions $\{\phi_n\}$ of the Sturm-Liouville Problem

$$\frac{d}{dx}\left[x\frac{dy}{dx}\right] + \frac{\lambda}{x}y = 0,$$

$$y'(1) = 0,$$

$$y'(e^{2\pi}) = 0,$$

where $\lambda \ge 0$ (See Example 12.5 of the text).

12.4   Trigonometric Fourier Series

A. Definition of Trigonometric Fourier Series

In Section 12.3 we introduced the problem of expanding a function f in a series of the form

$$(12.38) \qquad\qquad \sum_{n=1}^{\infty} c_n\phi_n,$$

where $\{\phi_n\}$, $(n = 1, 2, 3, \ldots)$, is an orthonormal system with respect to a weight function r on $a \le x \le b$. We first assumed that an expansion for f of the form (12.38) does indeed exist. Then, assuming suitable convergence, we found that the coefficients c_n in (12.38) are given by

$$(12.37) \qquad\qquad c_n = \int_a^b f(x)\phi_n(x)r(x)dx, \quad (n = 1, 2, 3, \ldots).$$

We noted that in general this is a strictly formal expansion and that certain restrictions must be imposed upon f and $\{\phi_n\}$ in order to be assured that the series (12.38) thus formed does indeed converge to f on $a \leq x \leq b$. Nevertheless, assuming that the functions involved in (12.37) are integrable, we can determine the formal expansion (12.38) and give it a name, even though we have no assurance in advance that it actually represents the given function f in any sense. This is essentially what we do in the following definition.

DEFINITION. Let $\{\phi_n\}$, $(n = 1, 2, 3, \ldots)$, be an orthonormal system with respect to a weight function r on $a \leq x \leq b$. Let f be a function such that for each $n = 1, 2, 3, \ldots$, the product $f\phi_n r$ is integrable on $a \leq x \leq b$. Then the series

$$(12.38) \qquad \sum_{n=1}^{\infty} c_n \phi_n,$$

where

$$(12.37) \qquad c_n = \int_a^b f(x)\phi_n(x)r(x)dx, \quad (n = 1, 2, 3, \ldots),$$

is called the *Fourier Series* of f relative to the system $\{\phi_n\}$; the coefficients c_n are called the *Fourier Coefficients* of f relative to $\{\phi_n\}$; and we write

$$f(x) \sim \sum_{n=1}^{\infty} c_n \phi_n(x), \qquad a \leq x \leq b.$$

We now proceed to introduce an important special class of Fourier Series. For this purpose, consider the system of functions $\{\psi_n\}$ defined by

$$\psi_1(x) = 1,$$

$$\psi_{2n}(x) = \cos\frac{n\pi x}{L}, \quad (n = 1, 2, 3, \ldots)$$

$$\psi_{2n+1}(x) = \sin\frac{n\pi x}{L}, \quad (n = 1, 2, 3, \ldots)$$

for all x on the interval $-L \leq x \leq L$, where L is a positive constant. Since

$$\int_{-L}^{L} \cos\frac{m\pi x}{L}\cos\frac{n\pi x}{L}dx = 0, \quad (m, n = 0, 1, 2, \ldots; \ m \neq n),$$

$$\int_{-L}^{L} \sin\frac{m\pi x}{L}\sin\frac{n\pi x}{L}dx = 0, \quad (m, n = 1, 2, 3, \ldots; \ m \neq n),$$

$$\int_{-L}^{L} \cos\frac{m\pi x}{L}\sin\frac{n\pi x}{L}dx = 0, \quad (m = 0, 1, 2, \ldots; \ n = 1, 2, 3, \ldots),$$

we see that the system (12.41) is orthogonal with respect to the weight function r defined by $r(x) = 1$ on $-L \leq x \leq L$. Now note that

$$\int_{-L}^{L} (1)^2 dx = 2L,$$

$$\int_{-L}^{L} \cos^2\left(\frac{n\pi x}{L}\right)dx = L, \quad (n = 1, 2, 3, \ldots),$$

and

$$\int_{-L}^{L} \sin^2\left(\frac{n\pi x}{L}\right)dx = L, \quad (n = 1, 2, 3, \ldots).$$

Thus the corresponding *orthonormal* system is the system of functions $\{\phi_n\}$ defined by

$$\phi_1(x) = \frac{1}{\sqrt{2L}}$$

$$\phi_{2n}(x) = \frac{1}{\sqrt{L}}\cos\frac{n\pi x}{L}, \quad (n = 1, 2, 3, \ldots),$$

$$\phi_{2n+1}(x) = \frac{1}{\sqrt{L}}\sin\frac{n\pi x}{L}, \quad (n = 1, 2, 3, \ldots),$$

on the interval $-L \leq x \leq L$.

Now suppose f is a function such that the product $f\phi_n$ is integrable for each function ϕ_n of the system (12.42) on the interval $-L \leq x \leq L$. Then we can form the Fourier Series of f relative to the orthonormal system $\{\phi_n\}$ defined by (12.42). This is of the form (12.38), where the coefficients c_n are given by (12.37). Thus using (12.37), with $r(x) = 1$, we find the Fourier coefficients

$$(12.43) \quad \begin{aligned} c_1 &= \int_a^b f(x)\phi_1(x)dx = \frac{1}{\sqrt{2L}}\int_{-L}^{L} f(x)dx, \\ c_{2n} &= \int_a^b f(x)\phi_{2n}(x)dx = \frac{1}{\sqrt{L}}\int_{-L}^{L} f(x)\cos\frac{n\pi x}{L}dx, \\ c_{2n+1} &= \int_a^b f(x)\phi_{2n+1}(x)dx = \frac{1}{\sqrt{L}}\int_{-L}^{L} f(x)\sin\frac{n\pi x}{L}dx, \end{aligned}$$

$(n = 1, 2, 3, \ldots)$. Thus the Fourier Series of f relative to the orthonormal system $\{\phi_n\}$ defined by (12.42) is

$$\sum_{n=1}^{\infty} c_n\phi_n,$$

where c_n $(n = 1, 2, 3, \ldots)$ is given by (12.43) and ϕ_n $(n = 1, 2, 3, \ldots)$ is of course given by (12.42). We now write this series in the form

$$c_1\phi_1 + \sum_{n=1}^{\infty} (c_{2n}\phi_{2n} + c_{2n+1}\phi_{2n+1}).$$

Substituting c_n $(n = 1, 2, 3, \ldots)$ given by (12.43) and ϕ_n $(n = 1, 2, 3, \ldots)$ given by (12.42) into this series, it takes the form

$$\left[\frac{1}{\sqrt{2L}}\int_{-L}^{L} f(x)dx\right]\left[\frac{1}{\sqrt{2L}}\right] + \sum_{n=1}^{\infty}\left\{\left[\frac{1}{\sqrt{L}}\int_{-L}^{L} f(x)\cos\frac{n\pi x}{L}dx\right]\left[\frac{1}{\sqrt{L}}\cos\frac{n\pi x}{L}\right]\right.$$
$$\left. + \left[\frac{1}{\sqrt{L}}\int_{-L}^{L} f(x)\sin\frac{n\pi x}{L}dx\right]\left[\frac{1}{\sqrt{L}}\sin\frac{n\pi x}{L}\right]\right\}.$$

Rewriting this slightly, it assumes the form

$$\frac{1}{2}\left[\frac{1}{L}\int_{-L}^{L}f(x)dx\right] + \sum_{n=1}^{\infty}\left\{\left[\frac{1}{L}\int_{-L}^{L}f(x)\cos\frac{n\pi x}{L}dx\right]\cos\frac{n\pi x}{L}\right.$$

$$\left. + \left[\frac{1}{L}\int_{-L}^{L}f(x)\sin\frac{n\pi x}{L}dx\right]\sin\frac{n\pi x}{L}\right\}.$$

Thus the Fourier Series of f relative to system (12.42) may be written as

$$\frac{1}{2}a_0 + \sum_{n=1}^{\infty}\left(a_n\cos\frac{n\pi x}{L} + b_n\sin\frac{n\pi x}{L}\right),$$

where

$$a_n = \frac{1}{L}\int_{-L}^{L}f(x)\cos\frac{n\pi x}{L}dx, \quad (n = 0, 1, 2, 3, \ldots),$$

$$b_n = \frac{1}{L}\int_{-L}^{L}f(x)\sin\frac{n\pi x}{L}dx, \quad (n = 1, 2, 3, \ldots).$$

This special type of Fourier Series is singled out in the following definition.

DEFINITION. Let f be a function which is defined on the interval $-L < x < L$ and is such that the integrals

$$\int_{-L}^{L}f(x)\cos\frac{n\pi x}{L}dx \quad \text{and} \quad \int_{-L}^{L}f(x)\sin\frac{n\pi x}{L}dx,$$

$(n = 0, 1, 2, \ldots)$, exist. Then the series

(12.44)
$$\frac{1}{2}a_0 + \sum_{n=1}^{\infty}\left(a_n\cos\frac{n\pi x}{L} + b_n\sin\frac{n\pi x}{L}\right),$$

where

(12.45)
$$a_n = \frac{1}{L}\int_{-L}^{L}f(x)\cos\frac{n\pi x}{L}dx, \quad (n = 0, 1, 2, \ldots),$$

$$b_n = \frac{1}{L}\int_{-L}^{L}f(x)\sin\frac{n\pi x}{L}dx, \quad (n = 1, 2, 3, \ldots),$$

is called the *trigonometric Fourier Series* of f on the interval $-L \leq x \leq L$. We denote this by writing

$$f(x) \sim \frac{1}{2}a_0 + \sum_{n=1}^{\infty}\left(a_n\cos\frac{n\pi x}{L} + b_n\sin\frac{n\pi x}{L}\right), \quad -L \leq x \leq L.$$

The numbers a_n, $(n = 0, 1, 2, \ldots)$, and b_n, $(n = 1, 2, 3, \ldots)$, defined by (12.45) will be called simply the *Fourier Coefficients* of f.

Thus to find the trigonometric Fourier Series of a function f having the required integrability properties on $-L \le x \le L$, we determine the Fourier Coefficients from (12.45) and substitute these coefficients into the series (12.44). There are two important special cases in which the determination of the Fourier Coefficients is considerably simplified. These are the cases in which f is either a so-called *even* function or a so-called *odd* function.

A function F is said to be an *even* function if $F(-x) = F(x)$ for every x. If F is an even function, the graph of $y = F(x)$ is symmetric with respect to the y axis and

$$\int_{-c}^{c} F(x)dx = 2\int_{0}^{c} F(x)dx$$

for every $c > 0$. A function F is said to be an *odd* function if $F(-x) = -F(x)$ for every x. If F is an odd function, the graph of $y = F(x)$ is symmetric with respect to the origin and

$$\int_{-c}^{c} F(x)dx = 0$$

for every $c > 0$.

Now suppose we wish to find the trigonometric Fourier Series of an *even* function f. Then each function F_n defined by $F_n(x) = f(x)\cos\dfrac{n\pi x}{L}$, $(n = 0, 1, 2, \ldots)$, is also even, since $F_n(-x) = f(-x) \cos\left(-\dfrac{n\pi x}{L}\right) = f(x)\cos\dfrac{n\pi x}{L} = F_n(x)$.

Therefore

$$\int_{-L}^{L} F_n(x)dx = 2\int_{0}^{L} F_n(x)dx, \quad (n = 0, 1, 2, \ldots),$$

and so

$$a_n = \frac{1}{L}\int_{-L}^{L} f(x)\cos\frac{n\pi x}{L}dx = \frac{2}{L}\int_{0}^{L} f(x)\cos\frac{n\pi x}{L}dx, \quad (n = 0, 1, 2, \ldots).$$

Further, each function G_n defined by $G_n(x) = f(x)\sin\dfrac{n\pi x}{L}$, $(n = 1, 2, 3, \ldots)$, is odd, since

$$G_n(-x) = f(-x)\sin\left(-\frac{n\pi x}{L}\right) = -f(x)\sin\frac{n\pi x}{L} = -G_n(x).$$

Therefore

$$\int_{-L}^{L} G_n(x)dx = 0, \quad (n = 1, 2, 3, \ldots),$$

and so

$$b_n = \frac{1}{L}\int_{-L}^{L} f(x)\sin\frac{n\pi x}{L}dx = 0, \quad (n = 1, 2, 3, \ldots).$$

Thus the trigonometric Fourier Series of an *even* function f on the interval $-L \leq x \leq L$ is given by

(12.46)
$$\frac{1}{2}a_0 + \sum_{n=1}^{\infty} a_n \cos\frac{n\pi x}{L},$$

where

(12.47)
$$a_n = \frac{2}{L}\int_0^L f(x)\cos\frac{n\pi x}{L}dx, \quad (n = 0, 1, 2, \ldots).$$

In like manner, one finds that the trigonometric Fourier Series of an *odd* function f on the interval $-L \leq x \leq L$ is given by

(12.48)
$$\sum_{n=1}^{\infty} b_n \sin\frac{n\pi x}{L},$$

where

(12.49)
$$b_n = \frac{2}{L}\int_0^L f(x)\sin\frac{n\pi x}{L}dx, \quad (n = 1, 2, 3, \ldots).$$

We note that in general the trigonometric Fourier Series of a function f is a strictly formal expansion, for we have said nothing concerning its convergence. We shall discuss this important matter briefly in part D of this Section. In the meantime, let us gain some facility in finding trigonometric Fourier Series by considering the following examples.

B. Examples of Trigonometric Fourier Series

Example 12.14. Find the trigonometric Fourier Series of the function f defined by
$$f(x) = |x|, \quad -\pi \leq x \leq \pi,$$
on the interval $-\pi \leq x \leq \pi$ (See Figure 12.1).

Solution. In this problem $L = \pi$. Since $f(-x) = |-x| = |x| = f(x)$ for all x, the function f is an *even* function. Therefore the trigonometric Fourier Series of f on $-\pi \leq x \leq \pi$ is given by (12.46) with $L = \pi$, where the coefficients a_n are given by (12.47)

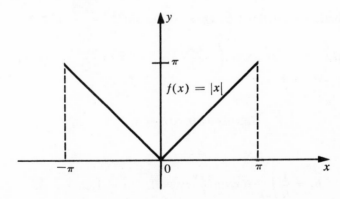

Figure 12.1

with $L = \pi$. Thus, since $|x| = x$ for $0 \le x \le \pi$, we have

$$a_0 = \frac{2}{\pi} \int_0^\pi f(x)dx = \frac{2}{\pi} \int_0^\pi xdx = \pi,$$

and

$$a_n = \frac{2}{\pi} \int_0^\pi f(x) \cos nx \, dx = \frac{2}{\pi} \int_0^\pi x \cos nx \, dx = \frac{2}{\pi}\left[\frac{\cos nx}{n^2} + \frac{x \sin nx}{n} \right]_0^\pi$$

$$= \frac{2}{\pi}\left[\frac{\cos n\pi - 1}{n^2} \right] = \frac{2}{\pi}\left[\frac{(-1)^n - 1}{n^2} \right] = \begin{cases} -\dfrac{4}{\pi n^2}, & n \text{ odd}, \\ 0, & n \text{ even}, \end{cases}$$

$$(n = 1, 2, 3, \ldots).$$

Thus the required series is

$$\frac{\pi}{2} - \frac{4}{\pi} \sum_{\substack{n=1 \\ (n \text{ odd})}}^{\infty} \frac{\cos nx}{n^2} = \frac{\pi}{2} - \frac{4}{\pi} \sum_{n=1}^{\infty} \frac{\cos(2n-1)x}{(2n-1)^2} = \frac{\pi}{2} - \frac{4}{\pi}\left[\frac{\cos x}{1^2} + \frac{\cos 3x}{3^2} + \frac{\cos 5x}{5^2} + \cdots \right]$$

and we write

$$|x| \sim \frac{\pi}{2} - \frac{4}{\pi} \sum_{n=1}^{\infty} \frac{\cos(2n-1)x}{(2n-1)^2}, \quad -\pi \le x \le \pi.$$

Example 12.15.   Find the trigonometric Fourier Series of the function f defined by

$$f(x) = x, \quad -4 \le x \le 4,$$

on the interval $-4 \le x \le 4$ (see Figure 12.2).

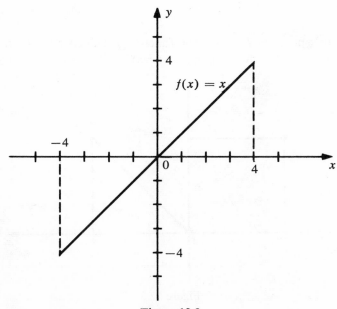

Figure 12.2

Solution. In this problem $L = 4$. Since $f(-x) = -x = -f(x)$ for all x, the function is an *odd* function. Therefore the trigonometric Fourier Series of f on $-4 \leq x \leq 4$ is given by (12.48) with $L = 4$, where the coefficients b_n are given by (12.49) with $L = 4$. Thus we have

$$b_n = \frac{2}{4}\int_0^4 f(x)\sin\frac{n\pi x}{4}dx = \frac{1}{2}\int_0^4 x\sin\frac{n\pi x}{4}dx = \frac{1}{2}\left[\frac{16}{n^2\pi^2}\sin\frac{n\pi x}{4} - \frac{4x}{n\pi}\cos\frac{n\pi x}{4}\right]_0^4$$

$$= -\frac{8}{n\pi}\cos n\pi = -\frac{8(-1)^n}{n\pi} = \frac{8(-1)^{n+1}}{n\pi}, \quad (n = 1, 2, 3, \ldots).$$

Thus the required series is

$$\frac{8}{\pi}\sum_{n=1}^\infty \frac{(-1)^{n+1}}{n}\sin\frac{n\pi x}{4} = \frac{8}{\pi}\left[\sin\frac{\pi x}{4} - \frac{1}{2}\sin\frac{\pi x}{2} + \frac{1}{3}\sin\frac{3\pi x}{4} - \cdots\right]$$

and we write

$$x \sim \frac{8}{\pi}\sum_{n=1}^\infty \frac{(-1)^{n+1}}{n}\sin\frac{n\pi x}{4}, \quad -4 \leq x \leq 4.$$

Example 12.16. Find the trigonometric Fourier Series of the function f defined by

(12.50)
$$f(x) = \begin{cases} \pi, & -\pi \leq x < 0, \\ x, & 0 \leq x \leq \pi, \end{cases}$$

on the interval $-\pi \leq x \leq \pi$ (see Figure 12.3).

Solution. In this problem $L = \pi$. The function f defined by (12.50) is neither even nor odd. Therefore the trigonometric Fourier Series of this function on $-\pi \leq x \leq \pi$ is

Figure 12.3

given by (12.44) with $L = \pi$, where the coefficients a_n and b_n are given by (12.45) with $L = \pi$. We find

$$a_0 = \frac{1}{\pi} \int_{-\pi}^{\pi} f(x)dx = \frac{1}{\pi} \left[\int_{-\pi}^{0} \pi dx + \int_{0}^{\pi} xdx \right] = \frac{3\pi}{2};$$

$$a_n = \frac{1}{\pi} \int_{-\pi}^{\pi} f(x) \cos nx\, dx = \frac{1}{\pi} \left[\int_{-\pi}^{0} \pi \cos nx\, dx + \int_{0}^{\pi} x \cos nx\, dx \right]$$

$$= \frac{1}{\pi} \left\{ \left[\frac{\pi \sin nx}{n} \right]_{-\pi}^{0} + \left[\frac{\cos nx}{n^2} + \frac{x \sin nx}{n} \right]_{0}^{\pi} \right\}$$

$$= \frac{1}{\pi} \left[\frac{\cos n\pi - 1}{n^2} \right] = \frac{(-1)^n - 1}{\pi n^2} = \begin{cases} -\dfrac{2}{\pi n^2}, & n \text{ odd,} \\ 0, & n \text{ even,} \end{cases}$$

$$(n = 1, 2, 3, \ldots);$$

$$b_n = \frac{1}{\pi} \int_{-\pi}^{\pi} f(x) \sin nx\, dx = \frac{1}{\pi} \left[\int_{-\pi}^{0} \pi \sin nx\, dx + \int_{0}^{\pi} x \sin nx\, dx \right]$$

$$= \frac{1}{\pi} \left\{ \left[-\frac{\pi \cos nx}{n} \right]_{-\pi}^{0} + \left[\frac{\sin nx}{n^2} - \frac{x \cos nx}{n} \right]_{0}^{\pi} \right\}$$

$$= \frac{1}{\pi} \left(-\frac{\pi}{n} \right) = -\frac{1}{n}, \quad (n = 1, 2, 3, \ldots).$$

Thus the required series is

$$\frac{3\pi}{4} + \sum_{n=1}^{\infty} \left[\frac{(-1)^n - 1}{\pi n^2} \cos nx - \frac{1}{n} \sin nx \right]$$

$$= \frac{3\pi}{4} - \left(\frac{2}{\pi} \cos x + \sin x \right) - \frac{1}{2} \sin 2x$$

$$- \left(\frac{2}{9\pi} \cos 3x + \frac{1}{3} \sin 3x \right) - \frac{1}{4} \sin 4x - \cdots.$$

Now that we have gained some familiarity with the actual details of finding trigonometric Fourier Series, we call attention to a matter which is of considerable importance in this connection. Suppose f is a function defined and integrable on an interval $a \le x \le b$, and suppose g is a function such that $g(x) = f(x)$ for all except a finite number of points of the interval $a \le x \le b$. Then it is shown in advanced calculus that

$$\int_{a}^{b} g(x)dx = \int_{a}^{b} f(x)dx.$$

Now suppose f is a function which is defined on the interval $-L \le x \le L$ and is such that the integrals

$$\int_{-L}^{L} f(x) \cos \frac{n\pi x}{L} dx \quad \text{and} \quad \int_{-L}^{L} f(x) \sin \frac{n\pi x}{L} dx,$$

($n = 0, 1, 2, \ldots$), exist, and suppose g is a function such that $g(x) = f(x)$ for all except a finite number of points of $-L \leq x \leq L$.
Then

$$\frac{1}{L}\int_{-L}^{L} g(x)\cos\frac{n\pi x}{L}dx = \frac{1}{L}\int_{-L}^{L} f(x)\cos\frac{n\pi x}{L}dx, \quad (n = 0, 1, 2, \ldots),$$

$$\frac{1}{L}\int_{-L}^{L} g(x)\sin\frac{n\pi x}{L}dx = \frac{1}{L}\int_{-L}^{L} f(x)\sin\frac{n\pi x}{L}dx, \quad (n = 1, 2, 3, \ldots).$$

The left members of these two identities are the Fourier Coefficients of g, and the right members are the Fourier Coefficients of f. Thus f and g have the same Fourier Coefficients (12.45) and hence the same trigonometric Fourier Series (12.44). We thus see that if f and g are two functions which have the same values at all except a finite number of points of the interval $-L \leq x \leq L$, then f and g have the same trigonometric Fourier Series on $-L \leq x \leq L$, assuming that the Fourier Coefficients of either of these functions exist.

Example 12.17. In Example 12.16 we found the trigonometric Fourier Series of the function f defined by

(12.50)
$$f(x) = \begin{cases} \pi, & -\pi \leq x < 0, \\ x, & 0 \leq x \leq \pi, \end{cases}$$

on the interval $-\pi \leq x \leq \pi$ (see Figure 12.3 again). The series is

(12.51)
$$\frac{3\pi}{4} + \sum_{n=1}^{\infty}\left[\frac{(-1)^n - 1}{\pi n^2}\cos nx - \frac{1}{n}\sin nx\right].$$

Now consider the function g defined by

$$g(x) = \begin{cases} \pi, & -\pi \leq x < 0, \\ \dfrac{\pi}{2}, & x = 0, \\ x, & 0 < x \leq \pi. \end{cases}$$

(See Figure 12.4 and compare with Figure 12.3.)

The functions f and g have the same values *except* at $x = 0$; for $f(x) = g(x) = \pi$, $-\pi \leq x < 0$, and $f(x) = g(x) = x$, $0 < x \leq \pi$, but $f(0) = 0$ and $g(0) = \pi/2$. Thus, since f and g have the same values at all except a finite number (in this case, one) of points of $-\pi \leq x \leq \pi$, they have the same trigonometric Fourier Series on this interval. Thus the trigonometric Fourier Series of the function g on $-\pi \leq x \leq \pi$ is also the series (12.51).

Exercises

For each of the functions f defined in Exercises 1 through 8 find the trigonometric Fourier Series of f on $-\pi \leq x \leq \pi$.

1. $f(x) = x$, $-\pi \leq x \leq \pi$.

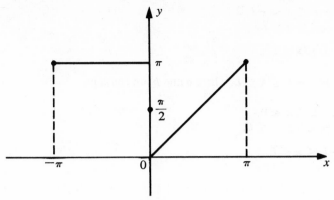

Figure 12.4

2. $f(x) = x^2, -\pi \leq x \leq \pi$.

3. $f(x) = \begin{cases} -2, -\pi \leq x < 0, \\ 2, 0 \leq x \leq \pi. \end{cases}$

4. $f(x) = \begin{cases} 0, -\pi \leq x < 0, \\ 2, 0 < x \leq \pi. \end{cases}$

5. $f(x) = \begin{cases} 0, -\pi \leq x < 0, \\ x^2, 0 \leq x \leq \pi. \end{cases}$

6. $f(x) = \begin{cases} 0, -\pi \leq x < -\pi/2, \\ 1, -\pi/2 \leq x < 0, \\ 2, 0 \leq x < \pi/2, \\ 3, \pi/2 \leq x \leq \pi. \end{cases}$

7. $f(x) = x|x|, -\pi \leq x \leq \pi$.

8. $f(x) = e^x, -\pi \leq x \leq \pi$.

For each of the functions f defined in Exercises 9 through 16 find the trigonometric Fourier Series of f on the interval stated.

9. $f(x) = |x|, -6 \leq x \leq 6$.

10. $f(x) = 2x + 1, -1 \leq x \leq 1$.

11. $f(x) = \begin{cases} 0, -3 \leq x < 0, \\ 1, \quad 0 \leq x \leq 3, \end{cases}$

on the interval $-3 \leq x \leq 3$.

12. $f(x) = \begin{cases} -2, -4 \leq x < 0, \\ \quad 0, x = 0, \\ \quad 2, 0 < x \leq 4, \end{cases}$

on the interval $-4 \leq x \leq 4$.

13. $f(x) = \begin{cases} 0, -L \leq x < 0, \\ L, \quad 0 \leq x \leq L, \end{cases}$

on the interval $-L \leq x \leq L$.

14. $f(x) = \begin{cases} 0, & -L \leq x < -L/2, \\ 1, & L/2 \leq x \leq L, \end{cases}$

on the interval $-L \leq x \leq L$.

15. $f(x) = ax + b$, $-L \leq x \leq L$, where a and b are constants.

16. $f(x) = \begin{cases} 1, & -L \leq x < 0, \\ L - x, & 0 \leq x \leq L, \end{cases}$

on the interval $-L \leq x \leq L$.

C. Fourier Sine Series and Fourier Cosine Series

In Example 12.12 we noted that the Sturm-Liouville Problem

$$(12.5) \qquad \qquad \frac{d^2y}{dx^2} + \lambda y = 0,$$

$$(12.6) \qquad \qquad y(0) = 0, \quad y(\pi) = 0$$

has the set of orthonormal characteristic functions $\{\psi_n\}$ defined by

$$\psi_n(x) = \sqrt{\frac{2}{\pi}} \sin nx, \quad (n = 1, 2, 3, \ldots), \quad 0 \leq x \leq \pi.$$

If we replace the second condition (12.6) by the more general condition $y(L) = 0$, where $L > 0$, we obtain the problem

$$\frac{d^2y}{dx^2} + \lambda y = 0,$$

$$y(0) = 0, \quad y(L) = 0.$$

This problem has the set of orthonormal characteristic functions $\{\phi_n\}$ defined by

$$(12.52) \qquad \phi_n(x) = \sqrt{\frac{2}{L}} \sin\frac{n\pi x}{L}, \quad (n = 1, 2, 3, \ldots), \quad 0 \leq x \leq L.$$

Let us now consider the problem of expanding an "arbitrary" function f which is defined on $0 \leq x \leq L$ in a series of these orthonormal functions $\{\phi_n\}$. In other words, given a function f defined on $0 \leq x \leq L$, let us find the Fourier Series of f relative to the orthonormal system $\{\phi_n\}$ defined by (12.52). From the definition of Fourier Series we see that the desired series is of the form

$$\sum_{n=1}^{\infty} c_n\phi_n,$$

where ϕ_n, $(n = 1, 2, 3, \ldots)$, is given by (12.52) and

$$c_n = \int_a^b f(x)\phi_n(x)r(x)dx = \int_0^L f(x)\sqrt{\frac{2}{L}}\sin\frac{n\pi x}{L}dx, \quad (n = 1, 2, 3, \ldots).$$

Thus the series takes the form

$$\sum_{n=1}^{\infty}\left[\sqrt{\frac{2}{L}}\int_0^L f(x)\sin\frac{n\pi x}{L}dx\right]\left[\sqrt{\frac{2}{L}}\sin\frac{n\pi x}{L}\right]$$

or

$$\sum_{n=1}^{\infty} b_n\sin\frac{n\pi x}{L},$$

where

$$b_n = \frac{2}{L}\int_0^L f(x)\sin\frac{n\pi x}{L}dx, \quad (n = 1, 2, 3, \ldots).$$

This special type of Fourier Series is identified in the following definition.

DEFINITION.   Let f be a function which is defined on the interval $0 \leq x \leq L$ and is such that the integrals

$$\int_0^L f(x)\sin\frac{n\pi x}{L}dx, \quad (n = 1, 2, 3, \ldots), \quad \text{exist.}$$

Then the series

(12.53) $$\sum_{n=1}^{\infty} b_n\sin\frac{n\pi x}{L},$$

where

(12.54) $$b_n = \frac{2}{L}\int_0^L f(x)\sin\frac{n\pi x}{L}dx, \quad (n = 1, 2, 3, \ldots),$$

is called the *Fourier Sine Series* of f on the interval $0 \leq x \leq L$. We indicate this by writing

$$f(x) \sim \sum_{n=1}^{\infty} b_n\sin\frac{n\pi x}{L}, \quad 0 \leq x \leq L.$$

We thus see that a function f having the required integrability properties on $0 \leq x \leq L$ can be formally expanded into a sine series of the form (12.53) with coefficients given by (12.54). We observe that this expansion is identical with the trigonometric Fourier Series (12.48) of the *odd* function which is defined on $-L \leq x \leq L$ and which coincides with f on $0 \leq x \leq L$.

Now suppose that we wish to expand a function f defined on $0 \leq x \leq L$ into a series of cosines instead of a series of sines. If we consider the Sturm-Liouville Problem

$$\frac{d^2y}{dx^2} + \lambda y = 0,$$

$$y'(0) = 0, \quad y'(L) = 0, \quad \text{(where } L > 0\text{)},$$

we find that the set of orthonormal characteristic functions of this problem is the set $\{\phi_n\}$ defined by

$$\phi_1(x) = \frac{1}{\sqrt{L}},$$

$$\phi_{n+1}(x) = \sqrt{\frac{2}{L}}\cos\frac{n\pi x}{L}, \quad (n = 1, 2, 3, \ldots), \quad 0 \leq x \leq L.$$

Using the definition of Fourier Series one finds that the Fourier Series of a function f relative to this orthonormal system is the series identified in the following definition.

DEFINITION. Let f be a function which is defined on the interval $0 \leq x \leq L$ and is such that the integrals

$$\int_0^L f(x)\cos\frac{n\pi x}{L}dx, \quad (n = 0, 1, 2, \ldots), \quad \text{exist}.$$

Then the series

(12.55) $$\frac{1}{2}a_0 + \sum_{n=1}^{\infty} a_n\cos\frac{n\pi x}{L},$$

where

(12.56) $$a_n = \frac{2}{L}\int_0^L f(x)\cos\frac{n\pi x}{L}dx, \quad (n = 0, 1, 2, \ldots),$$

is called the *Fourier Cosine Series* of f on the interval $0 \leq x \leq L$. We indicate this by writing

$$f(x) \sim \frac{1}{2}a_0 + \sum_{n=1}^{\infty} a_n\cos\frac{n\pi x}{L}, \quad 0 \leq x \leq L.$$

Note that this expansion is identical with the trigonometric Fourier Series (12.46) of the *even* function which is defined on $-L \leq x \leq L$ and which coincides with f on $0 \leq x \leq L$.

Example 12.18. Consider the function f defined by

$$f(x) = 2x, \quad 0 \leq x \leq \pi \quad \text{(See Figure 12.5.)}$$

Figure 12.5

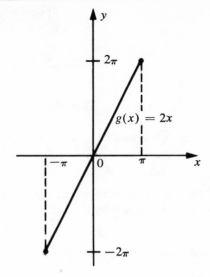

Figure 12.6

Find (a) the Fourier sine series of f on $0 \leq x \leq \pi$, and (b) the Fourier cosine series of f on $0 \leq x \leq \pi$.

Solution (a).   In this problem $L = \pi$. The Fourier sine series of f on $0 \leq x \leq \pi$ is given by (12.53) with $L = \pi$, where the coefficients b_n are given by (12.54) with $L = \pi$. We find

$$
\begin{aligned}
b_n &= \frac{2}{\pi} \int_0^\pi f(x) \sin nx \, dx = \frac{2}{\pi} \int_0^\pi 2x \sin nx \, dx \\
&= \frac{4}{\pi} \left[\frac{\sin nx}{n^2} - \frac{x \cos nx}{n} \right]_0^\pi \\
&= -\frac{4 \cos n\pi}{n} = \frac{(-1)^{n+1} 4}{n}, \quad (n = 1, 2, 3, \ldots).
\end{aligned}
$$

Thus the Fourier sine series of f on $0 \leq x \leq \pi$ is

$$
4 \sum_{n=1}^{\infty} \frac{(-1)^{n+1}}{n} \sin nx = 4 \left[\sin x - \frac{1}{2} \sin 2x + \frac{1}{3} \sin 3x - \cdots \right].
$$

This expansion is identical with the trigonometric Fourier series (12.48) of the odd function g defined by

$$
g(x) = 2x, \qquad -\pi \leq x \leq \pi,
$$

on the interval $-\pi \leq x \leq \pi$ (see Figure 12.6).

(b).   The Fourier cosine series of f on $0 \leq x \leq \pi$ is given by (12.55) with $L = \pi$, where the coefficients a_n are given by (12.56) with $L = \pi$. We find

$$
a_0 = \frac{2}{\pi} \int_0^\pi f(x) \, dx = \frac{2}{\pi} \int_0^\pi 2x \, dx = 2\pi;
$$

$$
a_n = \frac{2}{\pi} \int_0^\pi f(x) \cos nx \, dx = \frac{2}{\pi} \int_0^\pi 2x \cos nx \, dx
$$

$$= \frac{4}{\pi} \left[\frac{\cos nx}{n^2} + \frac{x \sin nx}{n} \right]_0^\pi = \frac{4}{\pi n^2}(\cos n\pi - 1)$$

$$= \frac{4}{\pi n^2}[(-1)^n - 1] = \begin{cases} -\dfrac{8}{\pi n^2}, & n \text{ odd}, \\ 0, & n \text{ even}, \end{cases}$$

$(n = 1, 2, 3, \ldots)$. Thus the Fourier cosine series of f on $0 \le x \le \pi$ is

$$\pi - \frac{8}{\pi} \sum_{\substack{n=1 \\ (n \text{ odd})}}^\infty \frac{\cos nx}{n^2} = \pi - \frac{8}{\pi} \sum_{n=1}^\infty \frac{\cos(2n-1)x}{(2n-1)^2} = \pi - \frac{8}{\pi} \left[\frac{\cos x}{1^2} + \frac{\cos 3x}{3^2} + \frac{\cos 5x}{5^2} + \cdots \right].$$

This expansion is identical with the trigonometric Fourier Series (12.46) of the even function h defined by

$$h(x) = |2x|, \quad -\pi \le x \le \pi,$$

on the interval $-\pi \le x \le \pi$ (see Figure 12.7).

Exercises

For each of the functions f defined in Exercises 1 through 6 find (a) the Fourier sine series of f on $0 \le x \le \pi$, and (b) the Fourier cosine series of f on $0 \le x \le \pi$.

1. $f(x) = 1, 0 \le x \le \pi$.

2. $f(x) = x, 0 \le x \le \pi$.

3. $f(x) = \begin{cases} 0, 0 \le x < \pi/2, \\ 2, \pi/2 \le x \le \pi. \end{cases}$

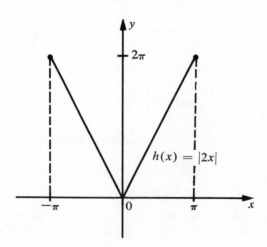

Figure 12.7

4. $f(x) = \begin{cases} x, 0 \le x < \pi/2, \\ \pi - x, \pi/2 \le x \le \pi. \end{cases}$

5. $f(x) = \sin x, 0 \le x \le \pi.$

6. $f(x) = e^x, 0 \le x \le \pi.$

For each of the functions f defined in Exercises 7 through 12 find (a) the Fourier sine series of f on $0 \le x \le L$, and (b) the Fourier cosine series of f on $0 \le x \le L$.

7. $f(x) = 2L, 0 \le x \le L.$

8. $f(x) = 4x, 0 \le x \le L.$

9. $f(x) = \begin{cases} 0, 0 \le x < L/2, \\ L^2, L/2 \le x \le L. \end{cases}$

10. $f(x) = \begin{cases} \dfrac{x}{10}, 0 \le x < L/2, \\[2mm] \dfrac{L-x}{10}, L/2 \le x \le L. \end{cases}$

11. $f(x) = Lx - x^2, 0 \le x \le L.$

12. $f(x) = \begin{cases} x^2, 0 \le x < \dfrac{3L}{4}, \\[2mm] \dfrac{9L^2}{4} - \dfrac{9Lx}{4}, \dfrac{3L}{4} \le x \le L. \end{cases}$

D. *Convergence of Trigonometric Fourier Series*

In part A of this section we defined the trigonometric Fourier series of a function f on the interval $-L \le x \le L$. According to our definition one finds the trigonometric Fourier series of f by first determining certain constants (the Fourier coefficients of f) from the formulas

(12.45)

$$a_n = \frac{1}{L} \int_{-L}^{L} f(x) \cos\frac{n\pi x}{L} dx, \quad (n = 0, 1, 2, \ldots),$$

$$b_n = \frac{1}{L} \int_{-L}^{L} f(x) \sin\frac{n\pi x}{L} dx, \quad (n = 1, 2, 3, \ldots),$$

and then substituting these constants into the series

(12.44)

$$\frac{1}{2}a_0 + \sum_{n=1}^{\infty} \left(a_n \cos\frac{n\pi x}{L} + b_n \sin\frac{n\pi x}{L} \right).$$

We have already pointed out that this development is a formal expansion since no mention of convergence is made. Thus the following questions arise concerning the trigonometric Fourier Series (12.44) of the function f.

(a) Is the trigonometric Fourier series of f convergent for some or all values of x in the interval $-L \leq x \leq L$?

(b) If the trigonometric Fourier Series of f converges at a certain point x of this interval, does it converge to $f(x)$?

In this section we shall state a theorem which will enable us to answer these questions in a manner which is satisfactory for our purposes.

As a first step toward stating this theorem, let us consider a general trigonometric series of the form (12.44). We shall say that a function F is *periodic of period P* if there exists a constant $P > 0$ such that $F(x + P) = F(x)$ for every x for which F is defined. In particular, the functions defined by $\sin \frac{n\pi x}{L}$ and $\cos \frac{n\pi x}{L}$ are periodic of period $2L/n$. Now observe that if F is periodic of period P, then F is also periodic of period nP, where n is a positive integer. Hence for every positive integer n, the functions defined by $\sin \frac{n\pi x}{L}$ and $\cos \frac{n\pi x}{L}$ are also periodic of period $2L$. We thus see that every term in the series (12.44) is periodic of period $2L$. Therefore if the series converges for all x, then the function defined by the series must be periodic of period $2L$.

In particular, suppose that the series (12.44) is the triogonometric Fourier Series of a function f defined on $-L \leq x \leq L$ and *assume* that this series converges for every x in this interval. Then this series will also converge for every value of x $(-\infty < x < \infty)$ and the function so defined will be periodic of period $2L$. This suggests that a trigonometric Fourier Series of the form (12.44) might possibly be employed to represent a periodic function of period $2L$ for *all* values of x. Such a representation is indeed possible for a periodic function which satisfies suitable additional conditions. The convergence theorem which we shall state gives one set of such conditions. In order to state this theorem as simply as possible, we introduce the following definition.

DEFINITION. A function f is said to be *piecewise smooth* (or *sectionally smooth*) on a finite interval $a \leq x \leq b$ if this interval can be divided into a finite number of subintervals such that (i) f has a continuous derivative f' in the interior of each of these subintervals, and (ii) both $f(x)$ and $f'(x)$ approach finite limits as x approaches either end point of each of these subintervals from its interior. In other words, we may say that f is piecewise smooth on $a \leq x \leq b$ if both f and f' are piecewise continuous on $a \leq x \leq b$.

Example 12.19. The function f defined on the interval $0 \leq x \leq 5$ by

$$f(x) = \begin{cases} x^2 & ,0 \leq x < 1, \\ 2 - x, & 1 \leq x < 3, \\ 1 & ,3 \leq x < 4, \\ x - 4, & 4 \leq x \leq 5, \end{cases}$$

is piecewise smooth on this interval (see Figure 12.8).

We now state the convergence theorem for trigonometric Fourier Series on the interval $-L \leq x \leq L$.

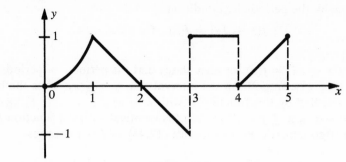

Figure 12.8

THEOREM 12.4.

Hypothesis.   Let f be a function such that
(i) f is periodic of period $2L$, and
(ii) f is piecewise smooth on the interval $-L \leq x \leq L$.

Conclusion.   The trigonometric Fourier Series of f,

(12.44)
$$\frac{1}{2}a_0 + \sum_{n=1}^{\infty}\left(a_n\cos\frac{n\pi x}{L} + b_n\sin\frac{n\pi x}{L}\right),$$

where

(12.45)
$$a_n = \frac{1}{L}\int_{-L}^{L} f(x)\cos\frac{n\pi x}{L}dx, \quad (n = 0, 1, 2, \ldots),$$

$$b_n = \frac{1}{L}\int_{-L}^{L} f(x)\sin\frac{n\pi x}{L}dx, \quad (n = 1, 2, 3, \ldots),$$

converges at every point x to the value

(12.57)
$$\frac{f(x+) + f(x-)}{2},$$

where $f(x+)$ is the right-hand limit of f at x and $f(x-)$ is the left-hand limit of f at x.
    In particular, if f is also continuous at x, the value (12.57) reduces to $f(x)$ and the trigonometric Fourier Series of f at x converges to $f(x)$.

    We observe that the value (12.57) is the arithmetic mean ("average") of the right-hand and left-hand limits of f at x.

Example 12.20.   Consider the function f defined for x in the interval $-\pi \leq x \leq \pi$ by

(12.58)
$$f(x) = \begin{cases} \pi, & -\pi \leq x < 0, \\ x, & 0 \leq x \leq \pi, \end{cases}$$

and for all other x by the periodicity condition

(12.59) $f(x + 2\pi) = f(x)$ for all x.

(See Figure 12.9)

The condition $f(x + 2\pi) = f(x)$ for all x states that f is periodic of period 2π. Further, the function f is piecewise smooth on the interval $-\pi \leq x \leq \pi$. Thus the hypothesis of Theorem 12.4 is satisfied by this function f (with $L = \pi$).

On the interval $-\pi \leq x \leq \pi$ the function f is identical with the function f of Example 12.16. Thus the trigonometric Fourier Series (12.44) of f is the series

(12.51) $$\frac{3\pi}{4} + \sum_{n=1}^{\infty}\left[\frac{(-1)^n - 1}{\pi n^2}\cos nx - \frac{1}{n}\sin nx\right]$$

which was determined in Example 12.16.

The conclusion of Theorem 12.4 assures us that the series (12.51) converges to

(12.57) $$\frac{f(x +) + f(x -)}{2}$$

at every point x, $-\infty < x < \infty$. Further, since f is continuous at every x except $x = \pm 2n\pi$, $(n = 0, 1, 2, \dots)$, the series (12.51) converges to $f(x)$ at every x except $x = \pm 2n\pi, (n = 0, 1, 2, \dots)$. For example, at $x = \pi$, the series (12.51) is

$$\frac{3\pi}{4} + \sum_{n=1}^{\infty}\frac{1 - (-1)^n}{\pi n^2} = \frac{3\pi}{4} + \frac{2}{\pi}\sum_{n=1}^{\infty}\frac{1}{(2n-1)^2} = \frac{3\pi}{4} + \frac{2}{\pi}\left[\frac{1}{1^2} + \frac{1}{3^2} + \frac{1}{5^2} + \cdots\right]$$

and this converges to $f(\pi) = \pi$. Thus we may write

$$\pi = \frac{3\pi}{4} + \frac{2}{\pi}\left[\frac{1}{1^2} + \frac{1}{3^2} + \frac{1}{5^2} + \cdots\right],$$

from which we obtain the interesting result

(12.60) $$\frac{\pi^2}{8} = \frac{1}{1^2} + \frac{1}{3^2} + \frac{1}{5^2} + \cdots + \frac{1}{(2n-1)^2} + \cdots.$$

At each point $x = \pm 2n\pi$, $(n = 0, 1, 2, \dots)$, at which f is discontinuous, we find that $f(x +) = f(0 +) = 0, f(x -) = f(0 -) = \pi$, and hence

$$\frac{f(x +) + f(x -)}{2} = \frac{\pi}{2}.$$

Figure 12.9

Figure 12.10

Thus at $x = \pm 2n\pi$, $(n = 0, 1, 2, \ldots)$, the series (12.51) converges to the value $\pi/2$. For example, at $x = 0$, the series is

$$\frac{3\pi}{4} + \sum_{n=1}^{\infty} \frac{(-1)^n - 1}{\pi n^2} = \frac{3\pi}{4} - \frac{2}{\pi} \sum_{n=1}^{\infty} \frac{1}{(2n - 1)^2}$$

and this converges to $\pi/2$. Thus we may write

$$\frac{\pi}{2} = \frac{3\pi}{4} - \frac{2}{\pi} \sum_{n=1}^{\infty} \frac{1}{(2n - 1)^2},$$

and this again leads to the result (12.60).

In summary, we see that the trigonometric Fourier Series (12.51) of the function f defined by (12.58) and (12.59) converges for all x to the function g defined by

(12.61)
$$g(x) = \begin{cases} \pi, & -\pi \leq x < 0, \\ \dfrac{\pi}{2}, & x = 0, \\ x, & 0 < x \leq \pi, \end{cases}$$

$$g(x + 2\pi) = g(x) \quad \text{for all } x.$$

(See Figure 12.10) and compare with Figure 12.9.)

Concerning the convergence of Fourier sine and Fourier cosine series on the interval $0 \leq x \leq L$, we state the following theorem.

THEOREM 12.5.

Hypothesis.   Let f be a function which is piecewise smooth on the interval $0 \leq x \leq L$.

Conclusions. (i).   The Fourier sine series of f,

(12.53)
$$\sum_{n=1}^{\infty} b_n \sin\frac{n\pi x}{L},$$

where

(12.54) $$b_n = \frac{2}{L} \int_0^L f(x) \sin\frac{n\pi x}{L} dx, \quad (n = 1, 2, 3, \ldots),$$

converges to the value

$$\frac{f(x+) + f(x-)}{2}$$

for every x such that $0 < x < \pi$.

In particular, if f is also continuous at x, $0 < x < L$, the Fourier sine series of f at x converges to $f(x)$.

The Fourier sine series of f converges to zero at $x = 0$ and $x = L$.

The Fourier sine series of f converges at every point x to the value

$$\frac{g(x+) + g(x-)}{2},$$

where g is the odd, periodic function of period $2L$ which coincides with f in the interval $0 < x < L$ and is such that $g(0) = g(L) = 0$.

(ii) The Fourier cosine series of f,

(12.55) $$\frac{1}{2}a_0 + \sum_{n=1}^{\infty} a_n \cos\frac{n\pi x}{L},$$

where

(12.56) $$a_n = \frac{2}{L} \int_0^L f(x) \cos\frac{n\pi x}{L} dx, \quad (n = 0, 1, 2, \ldots),$$

converges to the value

$$\frac{f(x+) + f(x-)}{2}$$

for every x such that $0 < x < \pi$.

In particular, if f is also continuous at x, $0 < x < L$, the Fourier cosine series of f at x converges to $f(x)$.

The Fourier cosine series of f converges to $f(0+)$ at $x = 0$ and to $f(L-)$ at $x = L$.

The Fourier cosine series of f converges at every point x to the value

$$\frac{h(x+) + h(x-)}{2},$$

where h is the even, periodic function of period $2L$ which coincides with f in the interval $0 \le x \le L$.

Example 12.21. Consider the function f defined by

$$f(x) = x, \quad 0 \le x \le \pi.$$

The Fourier sine and cosine series of f on $0 \leq x \leq \pi$ are readily found to be

(12.62)
$$2 \sum_{n=1}^{\infty} \frac{(-1)^{n+1} \sin nx}{n}$$

and

(12.63)
$$\frac{\pi}{2} - \frac{4}{\pi} \sum_{n=1}^{\infty} \frac{\cos(2n-1)x}{(2n-1)^2},$$

respectively.

The function f is piecewise smooth on $0 \leq x \leq \pi$; in fact, it is continuous on this interval. Therefore, applying Theorem 12.5, we see that the Fourier sine series (12.62) and the Fourier cosine series (12.63) of f both converge to $f(x)$ at every x such that $0 < x < \pi$. Further, the sine series (12.62) converges to zero at $x = 0$ and $x = \pi$; and the cosine series (12.63) converges to $f(0+) = 0$ at $x = 0$ and to $f(\pi -) = \pi$ at $x = \pi$.

The sine series (12.62) converges at every point x to the value

$$\frac{g(x+) + g(x-)}{2},$$

where g is the odd, periodic function of period 2π which coincides with f in the interval $0 < x < \pi$ and is such that $g(0) = g(\pi) = 0$. This function g is defined by

(12.64)
$$\begin{cases} g(x) = x, 0 \leq x < \pi, \\ g(x) = 0, x = \pi, \\ g(-x) = -g(x) \text{ for all } x, \\ g(x + 2\pi) = g(x) \text{ for all } x. \end{cases}$$

Its graph is shown in Figure 12.11. For this function g we see that

$$\frac{g(x+) + g(x-)}{2} = g(x)$$

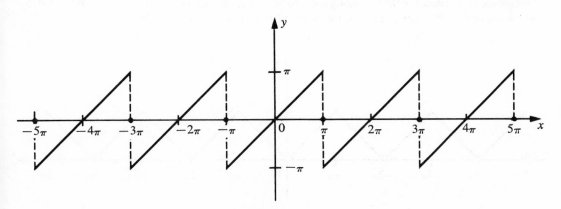

Figure 12.11

for every x. Thus the sine series (12.62) converges at every point x to the value $g(x)$ given by (12.64).

The cosine series (12.63) converges at every point x to the value

$$\frac{h(x+) + h(x-)}{2},$$

where h is the even, periodic function of period 2π which coincides with f in the interval $0 \leq x \leq \pi$. This function h is defined by

(12.65)
$$\begin{cases} h(x) = x, 0 \leq x \leq \pi, \\ h(-x) = h(x) \text{ for all } x, \\ h(x + 2\pi) = h(x) \text{ for all } x. \end{cases}$$

Its graph is shown in Figure 12.12. For this function h we see that

$$\frac{h(x+) + h(x-)}{2} = h(x)$$

for every x. Thus the cosine series (12.63) converges at every point x to the value $h(x)$ given by (12.65).

Exercises

1. Consider the function f defined for x on the interval $-\pi \leq x < \pi$ by

$$f(x) = \begin{cases} 0, -\pi \leq x < 0, \\ x + 1, 0 \leq x < \pi/2, \\ 2x, \pi/2 \leq x < \pi, \end{cases}$$

and for all other x by the periodicity condition

$$f(x + 2\pi) = f(x) \quad \text{for all } x.$$

Discuss the convergence of the trigonometric Fourier Series of f. In particular, determine the value to which the series converges at each of the points $x = 0$, $x = \pi/2$, and $x = \pi$.

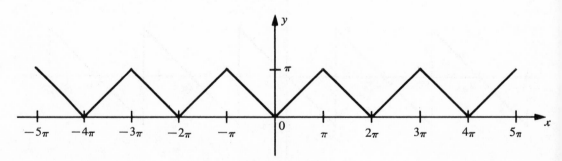

Figure 12.12

2. Consider the function f defined on the interval $-\pi \leq x < \pi$ by

$$f(x) = \begin{cases} (x + \pi)^2, & -\pi \leq x < 0, \\ \pi^2, & 0 \leq x < \pi/3, \\ 8, & \pi/3 \leq x < 2\pi/3, \\ 5, & 2\pi/3 \leq x < \pi, \end{cases}$$

and for all other x by the periodicity condition

$$f(x + 2\pi) = f(x) \quad \text{for all } x.$$

Discuss the convergence of the trigonometric Fourier Series of f. Determine those values of x in $-\pi \leq x \leq \pi$ at which this series does *not* converge to $f(x)$ and determine the value to which the series *does* converge at each of these points.

SUGGESTED READING

I. Basic Theory, Methods, and Applications:

Agnew (1)   Rainville (45)
Churchill (10)   Wylie (57)
Hildebrand (22)

II. Advanced Theory:

Bieberbach (5)   Kamke (29)
Birkhoff and Rota (6)   Tricomi (54)
Coddington and Levinson (13)   Yosida (58)
Ince (26)

13

NONLINEAR DIFFERENTIAL EQUATIONS

The mathematical formulation of numerous physical problems results in differential equations which are actually nonlinear. In many cases it is possible to replace such a non-linear equation by a related linear equation which approximates the actual nonlinear equation closely enough to give useful results. However, such a "linearization" is not always feasible; and when it is not, the original nonlinear equation itself must be considered. While the general theory and methods of linear equations are highly developed, very little of a general character is known about nonlinear equations. The study of nonlinear equations is generally confined to a variety of rather special cases, and one must resort to various methods of approximation. In this chapter we shall give a brief introduction to certain of these methods.

13.1 Phase Plane, Paths, and Critical Points

A. Basic Concepts and Definitions

In this chapter we shall be concerned with second-order nonlinear differential equations of the form

(13.1)
$$\frac{d^2x}{dt^2} = F\left(x, \frac{dx}{dt}\right).$$

As a specific example of such an equation we list the important van der Pol equation

(13.2)
$$\frac{d^2x}{dt^2} + \mu(x^2 - 1)\frac{dx}{dt} + x = 0,$$

where μ is a positive constant. We shall consider this equation at a later stage of our study. For the time being, we merely note that (13.2) may be put in the form (13.1), where

$$F\left(x, \frac{dx}{dt}\right) = -\mu(x^2 - 1)\frac{dx}{dt} - x.$$

Let us suppose that the differential equation (13.1) describes a certain dynamical system having one degree of freedom. The state of this system at time t is determined by the values of x (position) and dx/dt (velocity). The plane of the variables x and dx/dt is called a *phase plane*.

If we let $y = dx/dt$, we can replace the second-order equation (13.1) by the equivalent system

(13.3)
$$\begin{cases} \dfrac{dx}{dt} = y \\[2mm] \dfrac{dy}{dt} = F(x,y). \end{cases}$$

We can determine information about the equation (13.1) from a study of the system (13.3). In particular we shall be interested in the configurations formed by the curves which the solutions of (13.3) define. We shall regard t as a parameter so that these curves will appear in the xy plane. Since $y = dx/dt$, this xy plane is simply the $x, dx/dt$-phase plane mentioned in the preceding paragraph.

More generally, we shall consider systems of the form

(13.4)
$$\begin{cases} \dfrac{dx}{dt} = P(x,y) \\[2mm] \dfrac{dy}{dt} = Q(x,y) \end{cases}$$

where P and Q have continuous first partial derivatives for all (x,y). Such a system, in which the independent variable t appears only in the differentials dt of the left members and not explicitly in the functions P and Q on the right, is called an *autonomous system*. We shall now proceed to study the configurations formed in the xy-phase plane by the curves which are defined by the solutions of (13.4).

From the existence theory of Chapter 11, Section 11.1, it follows that given any number t_0 and any pair (x_0, y_0) of real numbers, there exists a unique solution

(13.5)
$$\begin{cases} x = f(t) \\ y = g(t) \end{cases}$$

of the system (13.4) such that

$$\begin{cases} f(t_0) = x_0 \\ g(t_0) = y_0. \end{cases}$$

If f and g are not both constant functions, then (13.5) defines a curve in the xy plane which we shall call a *path*† of the system (13.4).

If the ordered pair of functions defined by (13.5) is a solution of (13.4) and t_1 is any real number, then it is easy to see that the ordered pair of functions defined by

(13.6)
$$\begin{cases} x = f(t - t_1) \\ y = g(t - t_1) \end{cases}$$

is also a solution of (13.4). Assuming that f and g in (13.5) are not both constant functions and that $t_1 \neq 0$, the solutions defined by (13.5) and (13.6) are two *different solutions*

†The terms *trajectory* and *characteristic* are also used.

of (13.4). However, these two *different solutions* are simply different parameterizations of the *same path*. We thus observe that the terms *solution* and *path* are not synonymous. On the one hand, a *solution* of (13.4) is an ordered *pair of functions* (f,g) such that $x = f(t), y = g(t)$ simultaneously satisfy the two equations of the system (13.4) identically; on the other hand, a *path* of (13.4) is a *curve* in the xy-phase plane, which may be defined parametrically by more than one solution of (13.4).

Through any point of the xy-phase plane there passes at most one path of (13.4). Let C be a path of (13.4) and consider the totality of different solutions of (13.4) which define this path C parametrically. For each of these defining solutions, C is traced out in the *same direction* as the parameter t increases. Thus with each path C there is associated a definite direction, the direction of increase of the parameter t in the various possible parametric representations of C by the corresponding solutions of the system. In our figures we shall use arrows to indicate this direction associated with a path.

Eliminating t between the two equations of the system (13.4), we obtain the equation

$$(13.7) \qquad \frac{dy}{dx} = \frac{Q(x,y)}{P(x,y)}.$$

This equation gives the slope of the tangent to the path of (13.4) passing through the point (x,y), provided the functions P and Q are not both zero at this point. The general solution of (13.7) thus provides the one-parameter family of paths of (13.4). However, the description (13.7) does not indicate the directions associated with these paths.

At a point (x_0,y_0) at which both P and Q are zero, the slope of the tangent to the path, as defined by (13.7), is indeterminate. Such points are singled out in the following definition.

DEFINITION. Given the autonomous system

$$(13.4) \qquad \begin{cases} \dfrac{dx}{dt} = P(x,y) \\[2mm] \dfrac{dy}{dt} = Q(x,y), \end{cases}$$

a point (x_0,y_0) at which both

$$P(x_0,y_0) = 0 \qquad \text{and} \qquad Q(x_0,y_0) = 0$$

is called a *critical point*† of (13.4).

Example 13.1.   Consider the linear autonomous system

$$(13.8) \qquad \begin{cases} \dfrac{dx}{dt} = y \\[2mm] \dfrac{dy}{dt} = -x. \end{cases}$$

Using the methods developed in Chapter 7, we find that the general solution of this system may be written

$$\begin{cases} x = c_1 \sin t - c_2 \cos t \\ y = c_1 \cos t + c_2 \sin t, \end{cases}$$

where c_1 and c_2 are arbitrary constants. The solution satisfying the conditions $x(0) = 0$,

†The terms *equilibrium point* and *singular point* are also used.

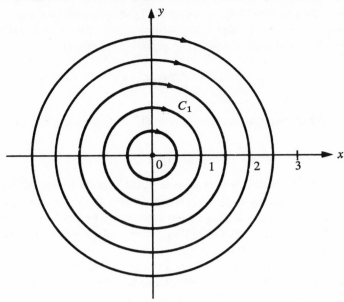

Figure 13.1

$y(0) = 1$ is readily found to be

(13.9)
$$\begin{cases} x = \sin t \\ y = \cos t. \end{cases}$$

This solution defines a path C_1 in the xy plane. The solution satisfying the conditions $x(0) = -1$, $y(0) = 0$ is

(13.10)
$$\begin{cases} x = \sin(t - \pi/2) \\ y = \cos(t - \pi/2). \end{cases}$$

The solution (13.10) is different from the solution (13.9), but (13.10) also defines the same path C_1. That is, the ordered pairs of functions defined by (13.9) and (13.10) are two *different solutions* of (13.8) which are different parametrizations of the *same path* C_1. Eliminating t from either (13.9) or (13.10) we obtain the equation $x^2 + y^2 = 1$ of the path C_1 in the xy phase plane. Thus the path C_1 is the circle with center at $(0,0)$ and radius 1. From either (13.9) or (13.10) we see that the direction associated with C_1 is the *clockwise* direction.

Eliminating t between the equations of the system (13.8) we obtain the differential equation

(13.11)
$$\frac{dy}{dx} = -\frac{x}{y},$$

which gives the slope of the tangent to the path of (13.8) passing through the point (x,y), provided $(x,y) \neq (0,0)$.

The general solution

$$x^2 + y^2 = c^2$$

of equation (13.11) gives the one-parameter family of paths in the xy-phase plane. Several of these are shown in Figure 13.1. The path C_1 referred to above is of course that for which $c = 1$.

Looking back at the system (13.8), we see that $P(x,y) = y$ and $Q(x,y) = -x$. Therefore the only critical point of the system is the origin $(0,0)$. Given any real number t_0, the solution $x = f(t)$, $y = g(t)$ such that $f(t_0) = g(t_0) = 0$ is simply

$$\begin{cases} x = 0 \\ y = 0 \end{cases} \text{ for all } t.$$

We can also interpret the autonomous system (13.4) as defining a *velocity vector field V*, where

$$V(x,y) = [P(x,y), Q(x,y)].$$

The x component of this velocity vector at a point (x,y) is given by $P(x,y)$, and the y component there is given by $Q(x,y)$. This vector is the velocity vector of a representative point R describing a path of (13.4) defined parametrically by a solution $x = f(t)$, $y = g(t)$. At a critical point both components of this vector velocity are zero, and hence at a critical point the point R is at rest.

In particular, let us consider the special case (13.3) which arises from a dynamical system described by the differential equation (13.1). At a critical point of (13.3) both $\dfrac{dx}{dt}$ and $\dfrac{dy}{dt}$ are zero. Since $\dfrac{dy}{dt} = \dfrac{d^2x}{dt^2}$, we thus see that at such a point the velocity and acceleration of the dynamical system described by (13.1) are both zero. Thus the critical points of (13.3) are equilibrium points of the dynamical system described by (13.1).

We now introduce certain basic concepts dealing with critical points and paths.

DEFINITION. *A critical point* (x_0,y_0) *of the system* (13.4) *is called* isolated *if there exists a circle*

$$(x - x_0)^2 + (y - y_0)^2 = r^2$$

about the point (x_0,y_0) *such that* (x_0,y_0) *is the only critical point of* (13.4) *within this circle.*

In what follows we shall assume that every critical point is isolated.

DEFINITION. *Let C be a path of the system* (13.4), *and let* $x = f(t)$, $y = g(t)$ *be a solution of* (13.4) *which represents C parametrically. Let* (x_0,y_0) *be a critical point of* (13.4). *We shall say that the path C* approaches the critical point (x_0,y_0) as $t \to +\infty$ *if*

(13.12)
$$\lim_{t \to +\infty} f(t) = x_0, \quad \lim_{t \to +\infty} g(t) = y_0.$$

Thus when we say that a path C defined parametrically by $x = f(t)$, $y = g(t)$ approaches a critical point (x_0,y_0) as $t \to +\infty$, we understand the following: a point R tracing out C according to the equations $x = f(t)$, $y = g(t)$ will approach the point (x_0,y_0) as $t \to +\infty$. This approach of a path C to a critical point (x_0,y_0) is independent of the solution actually used to represent C. That is, if C approaches (x_0,y_0) as $t \to +\infty$, then (13.12) is true for all solutions $x = f(t)$, $y = g(t)$ representing C.

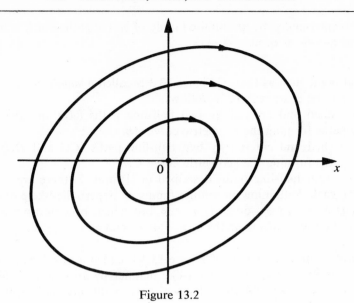

Figure 13.2

In like manner, a path C_1 approaches a critical point (x_0, y_0) as $t \to - \infty$ if

$$\lim_{t \to - \infty} f_1(t) = x_0, \quad \lim_{t \to - \infty} g_1(t) = y_0,$$

where $x = f_1(t)$, $y = g_1(t)$ is a solution defining the path C_1.

DEFINITION.   Let C be a path of the system (13.4) which approaches the critical point (x_0, y_0) as $t \to + \infty$, and let $x = f(t)$, $y = g(t)$ be a solution of (13.4) which represents C parametrically.   We say that *C enters the critical point (x_0, y_0) as $t \to + \infty$* if

(13.13) $$\lim_{t \to + \infty} \frac{g(t) - y_0}{f(t) - x_0}$$

exists or if the quotient in (13.13) becomes either positively or negatively infinite as $t \to + \infty$.

We observe that the quotient in (13.13) represents the slope of the line joining (x_0, y_0) and a point R with coordinates $[f(t), g(t)]$ on C.   Thus when we say that a path C enters a critical point (x_0, y_0) as $t \to + \infty$ we mean that the line joining (x_0, y_0) and a point R tracing out C tends to a definite direction as $t \to + \infty$.

B. Types of Critical Points; Stability

We shall now give geometric descriptions of certain types of critical points which we shall encounter, making use of appropriate figures in our discussions.   In each figure we shall take the critical point to be the origin $(0,0)$.

1. A critical point such as that of Figure 13.2 is called a *center*.

Such a point is surrounded by an infinite family of *closed* paths but it is not approached by any path as $t \to +\infty$ or as $t \to -\infty$.

2. A critical point such as that of Figure 13.3 is called a *saddle point*.
Such a point may be characterized as follows:

(1) It is approached and entered by two half-line paths (*AO* and *BO*) as $t \to +\infty$, these two paths forming the geometric curve *AB*.

(2) It is approached and entered by two half-line paths (*CO* and *DO*) as $t \to -\infty$, these two paths forming the geometric curve *CD*.

(3) Between the four half-line paths described in (1) and (2) there are four regions R_1, R_2, R_3, R_4, each containing an infinite family of hyperbolic-like paths which do not approach *O* as $t \to +\infty$ or as $t \to -\infty$ but which become asymptotic to one or another of the four half-line paths as $t \to +\infty$ and as $t \to -\infty$.

3. A critical point such as that of Figure 13.4 is called a *spiral point* (or *focal point*).
Such a point is approached in a spiral-like manner by an infinite family of paths as $t \to +\infty$ (or as $t \to -\infty$). Observe that while the paths *approach O*, they do not *enter* it. That is, a point *R* tracing such a path *C* approaches *O* as $t \to +\infty$ (or as $t \to -\infty$) but the line *OR* does not tend to a definite direction, since the path constantly winds about *O*.

4. A critical point such as that of Figure 13.5 is called a *node* (or *nodal point*).
Such a point is not only approached but also *entered* by an infinite family of paths as $t \to +\infty$ (or as $t \to -\infty$). That is, a point *R* tracing such a path not only approaches

Figure 13.3

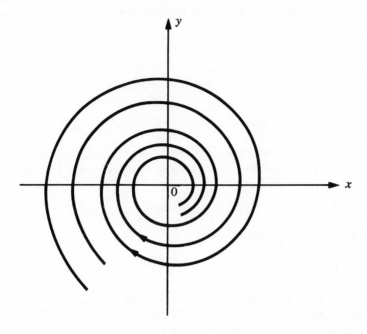

Figure 13.4

O but does so in such a way that the line OR tends to a definite direction as $t \to + \infty$ (or as $t \to - \infty$). For the node shown in Figure 13.5 there are four rectilinear paths AO, BO, CO, and DO. All other paths are like "semi-parabolas." As each of these semi-parabolic-like paths approaches O its slope approaches that of the line AB.

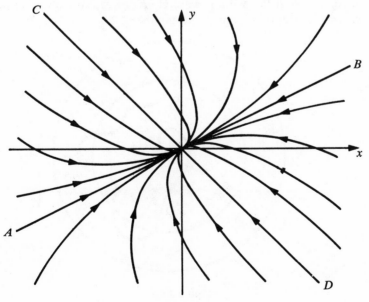

Figure 13.5

We close this introductory section by introducing the concept of *stability* as applied to a critical point.

DEFINITION. Let (x_0, y_0) be a critical point of the system (13.4); let C be a path of (13.4); and let $x = f(t)$, $y = g(t)$ be a solution of (13.4) representing C parametrically. Let

$$(13.14) \qquad D(t) = \sqrt{[f(t) - x_0]^2 + [g(t) - y_0]^2}$$

denote the distance between (x_0, y_0) and the point R: $[f(t), g(t)]$ on C. The critical point (x_0, y_0) is called *stable* if for every number $\epsilon > 0$, there exists a number $\delta > 0$ such that the following is true: Every path C for which

$$(13.15) \qquad D(t_0) < \delta \text{ for some value } t_0$$

is defined for all $t \geq t_0$ and is such that

$$(13.16) \qquad D(t) < \epsilon \text{ for } t_0 \leq t < \infty.$$

Let us try to analyze this definition, making use of Figure 13.6 as we do so. The critical point (x_0, y_0) is said to be stable if corresponding to every positive number ϵ, we can find another positive number δ which does "something" for us. Now what is this "something?" To answer this we must understand what the inequalities in (13.15) and (13.16) mean. According to (13.14), the inequality $D(t_0) < \delta$ for some value t_0 in (13.15) means that the distance between the critical point (x_0, y_0) and the point R on the path C must be less than δ at $t = t_0$. This means that at $t = t_0$, R lies within the circle K_1 of radius δ about (x_0, y_0) (see Figure 13.6). Likewise the inequality $D(t) < \epsilon$ for $t_0 \leq t < \infty$ in (13.16) means that the distance between (x_0, y_0) and R is less than ϵ for all $t \geq t_0$, and hence that for $t \geq t_0$ R lies within the circle K_2 of radius ϵ about (x_0, y_0). Now we can understand the "something" which the number δ does for us. If (x_0, y_0) is stable,

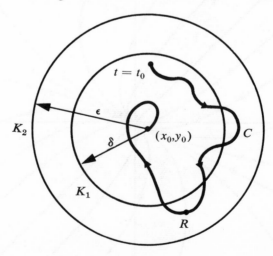

Figure 13.6

then *every* path C which is inside the circle K_1 of radius δ at $t = t_0$ will remain inside the circle K_2 of radius ϵ for all $t \geq t_0$. Roughly speaking, if every path C stays as close to (x_0, y_0) as we want it to (that is, within distance ϵ) after it once gets close enough (that is, within distance δ), then (x_0, y_0) is stable.

As examples of stable critical points, we point out that the center in Figure 13.2, the spiral point in Figure 13.4, and the node in Figure 13.5 are all stable. If the directions of the paths in Figures 13.4 and 13.5 had been reversed, then the spiral point and the node of these respective figures would have both been unstable. The saddle point of Figure 13.3 is unstable.

Exercises

For each of the autonomous systems in Exercises 1 and 2, (i) find the real critical points of the system, (ii) obtain the differential equation which gives the slope of the tangent to the paths of the system, and (iii) solve this differential equation to obtain the one-parameter family of paths.

1. $\begin{cases} \dfrac{dx}{dt} = x - y^2 \\[2mm] \dfrac{dy}{dt} = x^2 - y \end{cases}$

   2. $\begin{cases} \dfrac{dx}{dt} = y \\[2mm] \dfrac{dy}{dt} = \sin x \end{cases}$

3. Consider the linear autonomous system

$$\begin{cases} \dfrac{dx}{dt} = x \\[2mm] \dfrac{dy}{dt} = x + y. \end{cases}$$

(a) Find the solution of this system which satisfies the conditions $x(0) = 1$, $y(0) = 3$.

(b) Find the solution of this system which satisfies the conditions $x(4) = e$, $y(4) = 4e$.

(c) Show that the two *different* solutions found in (a) and (b) both represent the *same* path.

(d) Find the differential equation which gives the slope of the tangent to the paths, and solve it to obtain the one-parameter family of paths.

13.2   Critical Points and Paths of Linear Systems

A. Basic Theorems

Our main purpose in this chapter is the study of nonlinear differential equations and the corresponding nonlinear autonomous systems of the form (13.4). We shall be interested in classifying the critical points of such nonlinear systems. In Section 13.3 we shall see that under appropriate circumstances we may replace a given nonlinear system by a related linear system and then employ this linear system to determine the nature of the critical point of the given system. Thus in this section we shall first investigate the critical points of a linear autonomous system.

We consider the linear system

(13.17)
$$
\begin{cases}
\dfrac{dx}{dt} = ax + by \\[2mm]
\dfrac{dy}{dt} = cx + dy,
\end{cases}
$$

where a, b, c, and d (in the right member of the second equation) are real constants. The origin $(0,0)$ is clearly a critical point of (13.17). We assume that

(13.18)
$$
\begin{vmatrix} a & b \\ c & d \end{vmatrix} \neq 0,
$$

and hence $(0,0)$ is the *only* critical point of (13.17).

Recall that in Chapter 7 we sought and found solutions of (13.17) of the form

(13.19)
$$
\begin{cases}
x = Ae^{\lambda t} \\
y = Be^{\lambda t}.
\end{cases}
$$

We saw there that if (13.19) is to be a solution of (13.17), then λ must satisfy the quadratic equation

(13.20)
$$
\lambda^2 - (a + d)\lambda + (ad - bc) = 0,
$$

called the *characteristic equation* of (13.17). Note that by condition (13.18) zero can not be a root of the equation (13.20) in the problem under discussion.

Let λ_1 and λ_2 be the roots of the characteristic equation (13.20). We shall prove that the nature of the critical point $(0,0)$ of the system (13.17) depends upon the nature of the roots λ_1 and λ_2. We would expect three possibilities, according as λ_1 and λ_2 are real and distinct, real and equal, or conjugate complex. But actually the situation here is not quite so simple and we must consider the following five cases:

(1) λ_1 and λ_2 are real, unequal, and of the same sign.
(2) λ_1 and λ_2 are real, unequal, and of opposite sign.
(3) λ_1 and λ_2 are real and equal.
(4) λ_1 and λ_2 are conjugate complex but not pure imaginary.
(5) λ_1 and λ_2 are pure imaginary.

Case (1).

THEOREM 13.1.

Hypothesis. The roots λ_1 and λ_2 of the characteristic equation (13.20) are real, unequal, and of the same sign.

Conclusion.   The critical point (0,0) of the linear system (13.17) is a *node*.

Proof.   We first assume that λ_1 and λ_2 are both negative and take $\lambda_1 < \lambda_2 < 0$. By Theorem 7.7 of Chapter 7 the general solution of the system (13.17) may then be written

$$(13.21) \qquad \begin{cases} x = c_1 A_1 e^{\lambda_1 t} + c_2 A_2 e^{\lambda_2 t} \\ y = c_1 B_1 e^{\lambda_1 t} + c_2 B_2 e^{\lambda_2 t}, \end{cases}$$

where A_1, B_1, A_2, and B_2 are definite constants and $A_1 B_2 \neq A_2 B_1$, and where c_1 and c_2 are arbitrary constants. Choosing $c_2 = 0$ we obtain the solutions

$$(13.22) \qquad \begin{cases} x = c_1 A_1 e^{\lambda_1 t} \\ y = c_1 B_1 e^{\lambda_1 t}; \end{cases}$$

and choosing $c_1 = 0$ we obtain the solutions

$$(13.23) \qquad \begin{cases} x = c_2 A_2 e^{\lambda_2 t} \\ y = c_2 B_2 e^{\lambda_2 t}. \end{cases}$$

For any $c_1 > 0$, the solutions (13.22) represent a path consisting of "half" of the line $B_1 x = A_1 y$ of slope $\dfrac{B_1}{A_1}$. For any $c_1 < 0$, they represent a path consisting of the "other half" of this line. Since $\lambda_1 < 0$, both of these half-line paths approach (0,0) as $t \to +\infty$. Also, since $\dfrac{y}{x} = \dfrac{B_1}{A_1}$, these two paths *enter* (0,0) with slope $\dfrac{B_1}{A_1}$.

In like manner, for any $c_2 > 0$ the solutions (13.23) represent a path consisting of "half" of the line $B_2 x = A_2 y$; while for any $c_2 < 0$, the path so represented consists of the "other half" of this line. These two half-line paths also approach (0,0) as $t \to +\infty$ and enter it with slope $\dfrac{B_2}{A_2}$.

Thus the solutions (13.22) and (13.23) provide us with four half-line paths which all approach and enter (0,0) as $t \to +\infty$.

If $c_1 \neq 0$ and $c_2 \neq 0$, the general solution (13.21) represents nonrectilinear paths. Again, since $\lambda_1 < \lambda_2 < 0$, all of these paths approach (0,0) as $t \to +\infty$. Further since

$$\frac{y}{x} = \frac{c_1 B_1 e^{\lambda_1 t} + c_2 B_2 e^{\lambda_2 t}}{c_1 A_1 e^{\lambda_1 t} + c_2 A_2 e^{\lambda_2 t}} = \frac{\dfrac{c_1 B_1}{c_2} e^{(\lambda_1 - \lambda_2) t} + B_2}{\dfrac{c_1 A_1}{c_2} e^{(\lambda_1 - \lambda_2) t} + A_2},$$

we have $\displaystyle \lim_{t \to \infty} \frac{y}{x} = \frac{B_2}{A_2}$ and so all of these paths *enter* (0,0) with limiting slope $\dfrac{B_2}{A_2}$.

Thus all the paths (both rectilinear and nonrectilinear) *enter* (0,0) as $t \to +\infty$, and all except the two rectilinear ones defined by (13.22) enter with slope $\dfrac{B_2}{A_2}$. A qualitative

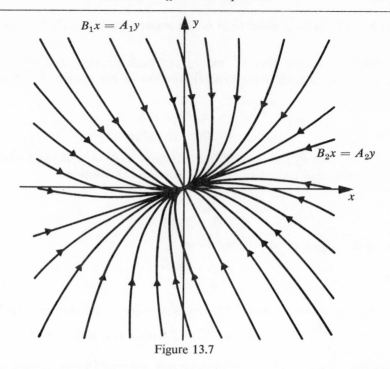

Figure 13.7

picture of the paths appears in Figure 13.7. According to our discussion of section 13.1, the situation is that which characterizes a node. Without further apologies, then, we say that the critical point (0,0) is a *node*. It is clearly *stable*.

If now λ_1 and λ_2 are both positive and we take $\lambda_1 > \lambda_2 > 0$, we see that the general solution of (13.17) is still of the form (13.21) and particular solutions of the forms (13.22) and (13.23) still exist. The situation is the same as before, except all the paths approach and enter (0,0) as $t \rightarrow -\infty$. The qualitative picture of Figure 13.7 is unchanged, except that all the arrows now point in the opposite directions. The critical point (0,0) is again a *node*, but in this case it is clearly *unstable*.

Case (2)

THEOREM 13.2.

Hypothesis.   The roots λ_1 and λ_2 of the characteristic equation (13.20) are real, unequal, and of opposite sign.

Conclusion.   The critical point (0,0) of the linear system (13.17) is a *saddle point*.

Proof.   We assume that $\lambda_1 < 0 < \lambda_2$. The general solution of the system (13.17) may again be written in the form (13.21) and particular solutions of the forms (13.22) and (13.23) are again present.

For any $c_1 > 0$, the solutions (13.22) again represent a path consisting of "half" the line $B_1 x = A_1 y$; while for any $c_1 < 0$, they again represent a path consisting of the "other half" of this line. Also, since $\lambda_1 < 0$, both of these half-line paths still approach and enter (0,0) as $t \rightarrow +\infty$.

Also, for any $c_2 > 0$, the solutions (13.23) represent a path consisting of half the line $B_2x = A_2y$; and for any $c_2 < 0$, the path which they represent consists of the "other half" of this line. But in this case, since $\lambda_2 > 0$, both of these half-line paths now approach and enter $(0,0)$ as $t \to -\infty$.

Once again, if $c_1 \neq 0$ and $c_2 \neq 0$, the general solution (13.21) represents nonrectilinear paths. But here since $\lambda_1 < 0 < \lambda_2$, none of these paths can approach $(0,0)$ as $t \to +\infty$ or as $t \to -\infty$. Further, none of them pass through $(0,0)$ for any t_0 such that $-\infty < t_0 < +\infty$. As $t \to +\infty$, we see from (13.21) that each of these nonrectilinear paths becomes asymptotic to one of the half-line paths defined by (13.23). As $t \to -\infty$, each of them becomes asymptotic to one of the paths defined by (13.22).

Thus there are two half-line paths which approach and enter $(0,0)$ as $t \to +\infty$ and two other half-line paths which approach and enter $(0,0)$ as $t \to -\infty$. All other paths are nonrectilinear paths which do not approach $(0,0)$ as $t \to +\infty$ or as $t \to -\infty$ but which become asymptotic to one or another of the four half-line paths as $t \to +\infty$ and as $t \to -\infty$. A qualitative picture of the paths appears in Figure 13.8. The situation is that of a saddle point. We thus say that in this case the critical point $(0,0)$ is a *saddle point*. It is clearly *unstable*.

Case (3).

THEOREM 13.3.

Hypothesis.   The roots λ_1 and λ_2 of the characteristic equation (13.20) are real and equal.

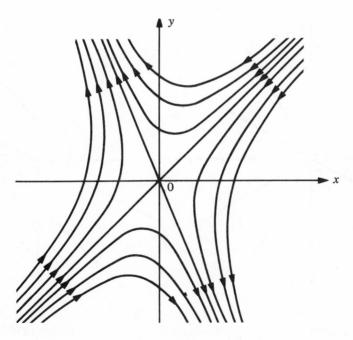

Figure 13.8

Conclusion.   The critical point (0,0) of the linear system (13.17) is a *node*.

Proof.   Let us first assume that $\lambda_1 = \lambda_2 = \lambda < 0$. We consider two subcases:
(3a) $a = d \neq 0, b = c = 0$.
(3b) All other possibilities leading to a double root.
We consider first the special case (3a). The characteristic equation (13.20) becomes

$$\lambda^2 - 2a\lambda + a^2 = 0$$

and hence $\lambda = a = d$. The system (13.17) itself is thus simply

$$\begin{cases} \dfrac{dx}{dt} = \lambda x \\[2mm] \dfrac{dy}{dt} = \lambda y. \end{cases}$$

The general solution of this system is clearly

(13.24) $$\begin{cases} x = c_1 e^{\lambda t} \\ y = c_2 e^{\lambda t}, \end{cases}$$

where c_1 and c_2 are arbitrary constants. The paths defined by (13.24) for the various values of c_1 and c_2 are half-lines of all possible slopes. Since $\lambda < 0$, we see that each of these half-lines approaches and enters (0,0) as $t \to +\infty$. The situation is that pictured in Figure 13.9. Since all paths actually enter (0,0) as $t \to +\infty$ we are justified in classifying (0,0) as a *node*. It is clearly *stable*.

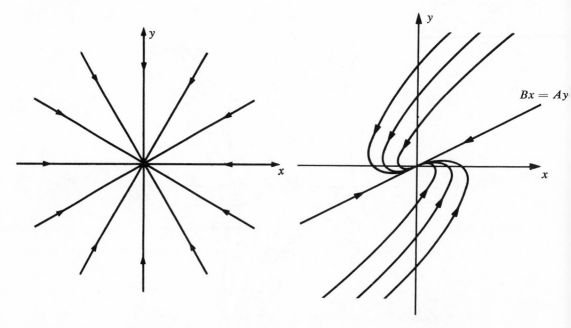

Figure 13.9   Figure 13.10

If $\lambda > 0$, the situation is the same except that the paths enter (0,0) as $t \to -\infty$, the arrows in Figure 13.9 are all reversed, and (0,0) is unstable.

Let us now consider case (3b). Here the characteristic equation has the double root $\lambda < 0$, but we exclude the special circumstances of case (3a). By Theorem 7.8 of Chapter 7 the general solution of the system (13.17) may in this case be written

$$(13.25) \qquad \begin{cases} x = c_1 A e^{\lambda t} + c_2(A_1 t + A_2)e^{\lambda t} \\ y = c_1 B e^{\lambda t} + c_2(B_1 t + B_2)e^{\lambda t}, \end{cases}$$

where the A's and B's are definite constants and c_1 and c_2 are arbitrary constants. Further it may be shown that in this subcase $\dfrac{B_1}{A_1} = \dfrac{B}{A}$. Choosing $c_2 = 0$ in (13.25) we obtain solutions

$$(13.26) \qquad \begin{cases} x = c_1 A e^{\lambda t} \\ y = c_1 B e^{\lambda t}. \end{cases}$$

For any $c_1 > 0$, the solutions (13.26) represent a path consisting of "half" of the line $Bx = Ay$ of slope $\dfrac{B}{A}$; and for any $c_1 < 0$, they represent a path which consists of the "other half" of this line. Since $\lambda < 0$, both of these half-line paths approach (0,0) as $t \to +\infty$. Further, since $\dfrac{y}{x} = \dfrac{B}{A}$ both paths *enter* (0,0) with slope $\dfrac{B}{A}$.

If $c_2 \neq 0$, the general solution (13.25) represents nonrectilinear paths. Since $\lambda < 0$ we see from (13.25) that

$$\lim_{t \to +\infty} x = 0, \qquad \lim_{t \to +\infty} y = 0.$$

Thus the nonrectilinear paths defined by (13.25) all approach (0,0) as $t \to +\infty$. Also, since

$$\frac{y}{x} = \frac{c_1 B e^{\lambda t} + c_2(B_1 t + B_2)e^{\lambda t}}{c_1 A e^{\lambda t} + c_2(A_1 t + A_2)e^{\lambda t}} = \frac{\dfrac{c_1 B}{c_2} + B_2 + B_1 t}{\dfrac{c_1 A}{c_2} + A_2 + A_1 t},$$

we see that

$$\lim_{t \to +\infty} \frac{y}{x} = \frac{B_1}{A_1} = \frac{B}{A}.$$

Thus all the nonrectilinear paths *enter* (0,0) with limiting slope $\dfrac{B}{A}$.

Thus all the paths (both rectilinear and nonrectilinear) *enter* (0,0) as $t \to +\infty$ with slope $\dfrac{B}{A}$. A qualitative picture of the paths appears in Figure 13.10. Since all the paths enter (0,0) we say that (0,0) is a *node*. It is *stable*.

If $\lambda > 0$, the situation is again the same except that the paths enter (0,0) as $t \to -\infty$, the arrows in Figure 13.10 are reversed, and (0,0) is unstable.

Case (4).

THEOREM 13.4.

Hypothesis. The roots λ_1 and λ_2 of the characteristic equation (13.20) are conjugate complex with real part not zero (that is, not pure imaginary).

Conclusion. The critical point (0,0) of the linear system (13.17) is a *spiral point*.

Proof. Since λ_1 and λ_2 are conjugate complex with real part not zero, we may write these roots as $\alpha \pm i\beta$, where α and β are both real and unequal to zero. Then by Theorem 7.9 of Chapter 7, the general solution of the system (13.17) may be written

$$(13.27) \quad \begin{cases} x = e^{\alpha t}[c_1(A_1\cos\beta t - A_2\sin\beta t) + c_2(A_2\cos\beta t + A_1\sin\beta t)] \\ y = e^{\alpha t}[c_1(B_1\cos\beta t - B_2\sin\beta t) + c_2(B_2\cos\beta t + B_1\sin\beta t)], \end{cases}$$

where A_1, A_2, B_1, and B_2 are definite real constants and c_1 and c_2 are arbitrary constants.

Let us first assume that $\alpha < 0$. Then from (13.27) we see that

$$\lim_{t \to +\infty} x = 0 \qquad \text{and} \qquad \lim_{t \to +\infty} y = 0$$

and hence all paths defined by (13.27) approach (0,0) as $t \to +\infty$. We may rewrite (13.27) in the form

$$(13.28) \quad \begin{cases} x = e^{\alpha t}(c_3\cos\beta t + c_4\sin\beta t) \\ y = e^{\alpha t}(c_5\cos\beta t + c_6\sin\beta t), \end{cases}$$

where $c_3 = c_1A_1 + c_2A_2$, $c_4 = c_2A_1 - c_1A_2$, $c_5 = c_1B_1 + c_2B_2$, and $c_6 = c_2B_1 - c_1B_2$. Assuming c_1 and c_2 are real, the solutions (13.28) represent all paths in the real xy-phase plane. We may now put these solutions in the form

$$(13.29) \quad \begin{cases} x = K_1e^{\alpha t}\cos(\beta t + \phi_1) \\ y = K_2e^{\alpha t}\cos(\beta t + \phi_2), \end{cases}$$

where $K_1 = \sqrt{c_3^2 + c_4^2}$, $K_2 = \sqrt{c_5^2 + c_6^2}$ and ϕ_1 and ϕ_2 are defined by the equations

$$\begin{cases} \cos\phi_1 = \dfrac{c_3}{K_1} \\[2mm] \sin\phi_1 = -\dfrac{c_4}{K_1} \end{cases} \qquad \begin{cases} \cos\phi_2 = \dfrac{c_5}{K_2} \\[2mm] \sin\phi_2 = -\dfrac{c_6}{K_2}. \end{cases}$$

Let us now consider

$$(13.30) \quad \frac{y}{x} = \frac{K_2e^{\alpha t}\cos(\beta t + \phi_2)}{K_1e^{\alpha t}\cos(\beta t + \phi_1)}.$$

Letting $K = \dfrac{K_2}{K_1}$ and $\phi_3 = \phi_1 - \phi_2$, this becomes

$$(13.31) \quad \frac{y}{x} = \frac{K\cos(\beta t + \phi_1 - \phi_3)}{\cos(\beta t + \phi_1)} = K\left[\frac{\cos(\beta t + \phi_1)\cos\phi_3 + \sin(\beta t + \phi_1)\sin\phi_3}{\cos(\beta t + \phi_1)}\right]$$

$$= K[\cos\phi_3 + \sin\phi_3\tan(\beta t + \phi_1)],$$

provided $\cos(\beta t + \phi_1) \neq 0$. As a result of the periodicity of the trigonometric functions involved in (13.30) and (13.31) we conclude from these expressions that $\lim\limits_{t \to +\infty} \dfrac{y}{x}$ does not exist and so the paths *do not enter* (0,0). Instead, it follows from (13.30) and (13.31) that the paths approach (0,0) in a spiral-like manner. A qualitative picture of the paths appears in Figure 13.11. The situation is that of a spiral point. Thus we say that the critical point (0,0) is a *spiral point*. It is *stable*.

If $\alpha > 0$, the situation is the same except that the paths approach (0,0) as $t \to -\infty$. The arrows in Figure 13.11 are reversed, and the critical point (0,0) is unstable.

Case (5).

THEOREM 13.5.

Hypothesis. The roots λ_1 and λ_2 of the characteristic equation (13.20) are pure imaginary.

Conclusion. The critical point (0,0) of the linear system (13.17) is a *center*.

Proof. Since λ_1 and λ_2 are pure imaginary we may write them as $\alpha \pm \beta i$, where $\alpha = 0$ but β is real and unequal to zero. Then the general solution of the system (13.17) is of the form (13.27), where $\alpha = 0$. In the notation of (13.29) all real solutions may be written in the form

(13.32)
$$\begin{cases} x = K_1\cos(\beta t + \phi_1) \\ y = K_2\cos(\beta t + \phi_2), \end{cases}$$

Figure 13.11

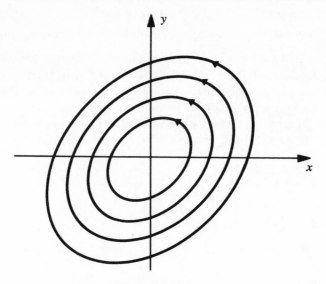

Figure 13.12

where K_1, K_2, ϕ_1, and ϕ_2 are defined as before. The solutions (13.32) define the paths in the real xy-phase plane. Since the trigonometric functions in (13.32) oscillate indefinitely between ± 1 as $t \to + \infty$ or as $t \to - \infty$, the paths do not approach (0,0) as $t \to + \infty$ or as $t \to - \infty$. Rather it is clear from (13.32) that x and y are periodic functions of t and hence the paths are closed curves surrounding (0,0). Indeed they are ellipses with center at (0,0). Figure 13.12 gives a qualitative picture of the paths. The situation is that of a center. Thus we say that the critical point (0,0) is a *center*. Even though the paths do not approach (0,0), nevertheless the critical point is *stable*.

We summarize our results in Table 13.1.

The stability results of column 3 of this table lead at once to the following result:

THEOREM 13.6. The critical point (0,0) of the linear system

$$\begin{cases} \dfrac{dx}{dt} = ax + by \\[2mm] \dfrac{dy}{dt} = cx + dy \end{cases} \quad \text{, where} \quad \begin{vmatrix} a & b \\ c & d \end{vmatrix} \neq 0,$$

is stable if and only if both roots of the characteristic equation (13.20) have negative or zero real parts.

B. Examples and Applications

Example 13.2. Determine the nature of the critical point (0,0) of the system

(13.33)
$$\begin{cases} \dfrac{dx}{dt} = 2x - 7y \\[2mm] \dfrac{dy}{dt} = 3x - 8y \end{cases}$$

and determine whether or not the point is stable.

Table 13.1

Nature of roots λ_1 and λ_2 of characteristic equation $\lambda^2 - (a + d)\lambda + (ad - bc) = 0$	Nature of critical point (0,0) of linear system $\begin{cases} \dfrac{dx}{dt} = ax + by \\[2mm] \dfrac{dy}{dt} = cx + dy \end{cases}$	Stability of critical point (0,0)
real, unequal, and of same sign	node	stable if roots are negative; unstable if roots are positive.
real, unequal, and of opposite sign	saddle point	unstable
real and equal	node	stable if roots are negative; unstable if roots are positive.
conjugate complex but not pure imaginary	spiral point	stable if real part of roots is negative; unstable if real part of roots is positive.
pure imaginary	center	stable

Solution.   The system (13.33) is of the form (13.17) where $a = 2$, $b = -7$, $c = 3$, and $d = -8$. The characteristic equation (13.20) is

$$\lambda^2 + 6\lambda + 5 = 0.$$

Hence the roots of the characteristic equation are $\lambda_1 = -5$, $\lambda_2 = -1$. Since the roots are real, unequal, and of the same sign (both negative), we conclude that the critical point (0,0) of (13.33) is a *node*. Since the roots are negative, the point is *stable*.

Example 13.3.   Determine the nature of the critical point (0,0) of the system

(13.34)
$$\begin{cases} \dfrac{dx}{dt} = 2x + 4y \\[2mm] \dfrac{dy}{dt} = -2x + 6y \end{cases}$$

and determine whether or not the point is stable.

Solution.   Here $a = 2$, $b = 4$, $c = -2$, and $d = 6$. The characteristic equation is

$$\lambda^2 - 8\lambda + 20 = 0$$

and its roots are $4 \pm 2i$. Since these roots are conjugate complex but not pure imaginary, we conclude that the critical point (0,0) of (13.34) is a *spiral point*. Since the real part of the roots is positive, the point is *unstable*.

Application to Dynamics. Recall that in Chapter 5 we studied the free vibrations of a mass on a coil spring. The differential equation for the motion was

(13.35) $$m\frac{d^2x}{dt^2} + \alpha\frac{dx}{dt} + kx = 0,$$

where $m > 0$, $\alpha \geq 0$, and $k > 0$ are constants denoting the mass, damping coefficient, and spring constant, respectively. We use α instead of a for the damping coefficient here to avoid confusion with the coefficient a of the system (13.17).

The dynamical equation (13.35) is equivalent to the system

(13.36) $$\begin{cases} \dfrac{dx}{dt} = y \\ \dfrac{dy}{dt} = -\dfrac{k}{m}x - \dfrac{\alpha}{m}y. \end{cases}$$

The solutions of the system (13.36) define the paths (phase trajectories) associated with the dynamical equation (13.35) in the $x,y = \dfrac{dx}{dt}$ phase plane. From (13.36) the differential equation of these paths is

$$\frac{dy}{dx} = -\frac{kx + \alpha y}{my}.$$

We observe that $(0,0)$ is the only critical point of the system (13.36).

The auxiliary equation of the differential equation (13.35) is

(13.37) $$mr^2 + \alpha r + k = 0,$$

while the characteristic equation of the system (13.36) is

(13.38) $$\lambda^2 + \frac{\alpha}{m}\lambda + \frac{k}{m} = 0.$$

The two equations (13.37) and (13.38) clearly have the same roots λ_1 and λ_2. We summarize the possible situations in Table 13.2, which gives the form of the solution of the dynamical equation, the phase plane analysis of the critical point, and a brief interpretation.

Exercises

Determine the nature of the critical point $(0,0)$ of each of the linear autonomous systems in Exercises 1 through 8. Also, determine whether or not the critical point is stable.

1. $\dfrac{dx}{dt} = x + 3y$

   $\dfrac{dy}{dt} = 3x + y$

2. $\dfrac{dx}{dt} = 3x + 2y$

   $\dfrac{dy}{dt} = x + 2y$

3. $\dfrac{dx}{dt} = 3x + 4y$

   $\dfrac{dy}{dt} = 3x + 2y$

4. $\dfrac{dx}{dt} = 2x + 5y$

   $\dfrac{dy}{dt} = x - 2y$

Table 13.2

Damping factor α	Nature of roots of auxiliary and characteristic equations	Form of solution of dynamical equation. $\omega = \sqrt{\dfrac{k}{m}}, \beta = \dfrac{\alpha}{2m}.$	Nature of critical point $(0,0)$ in x,y-phase plane.	Interpretation.
$\alpha = 0$ (no damping)	pure imaginary	$x = c\cos(\omega t + \phi)$	(stable) center	oscillatory motion. displacement and velocity are periodic functions of time.
$\alpha < 2\sqrt{km}$ (under-damped)	conjugate complex with negative real parts	$x = ce^{-\beta t}\cos(\omega_1 t + \phi)$, where $\omega_1 = \sqrt{\omega^2 - \beta^2}$.	stable spiral point	damped oscillatory motion. displacement and velocity $\to 0$ through smaller and smaller oscillations.
$\alpha = 2\sqrt{km}$ (critically damped)	real, equal and negative	$x = (c_1 + c_2 t)e^{-\beta t}$	stable node	displacement and velocity $\to 0$ without oscillating.
$\alpha > 2\sqrt{km}$ (over-damped)	real, unequal, and negative	$x = c_1 e^{r_1 t} + c_2 e^{r_2 t}$, where $r_1 = -\beta + \sqrt{\beta^2 - \omega^2}$ $r_2 = -\beta - \sqrt{\beta^2 - \omega^2}$	stable node	displacement and velocity $\to 0$ without oscillating.

5. $\dfrac{dx}{dt} = 2x - 4y$

   $\dfrac{dy}{dt} = 2x - 2y$

6. $\dfrac{dx}{dt} = x - 2y$

   $\dfrac{dy}{dt} = 4x + 5y$

7. $\dfrac{dx}{dt} = x - y$

   $\dfrac{dy}{dt} = x + 5y$

8. $\dfrac{dx}{dt} = x + 7y$

   $\dfrac{dy}{dt} = 3x + 5y$

9. Consider the linear autonomous system

$$\frac{dx}{dt} = x + y$$

$$\frac{dy}{dt} = 3x - y.$$

(a) Determine the nature of the critical point (0,0) of this system.

(b) Find the general solution of this system.

(c) Find the differential equation of the paths in the xy plane and obtain the general solution of this differential equation.

(d) Using the equation of the family of paths [the general solution obtained in part (c)], carefully plot the paths which pass through each of the following points: (1,1), (−1,−1), (1,−3), (−1,3), (0,2), (0,−2), (0,4), (0,−4), (1,−1), (−1,1), (2,−2), (−2,2). Does the configuration thus obtained agree with your answer to part (a)? Comment.

10. Consider the linear autonomous system

(A)
$$\begin{cases} \dfrac{dx}{dt} = ax + by, \\[2mm] \dfrac{dy}{dt} = cx + dy, \end{cases}$$

where $a,b,c,$ and d are real constants.

(a) Show that if $a = d$, and b and c are of opposite sign, then the critical point (0,0) of system (A) is a spiral point.

(b) Show that if $a = d$, and either b or $c = 0$, then the critical point (0,0) of (A) is a node.

(c) Show that if $a = d$, and b and c are of the same sign and such that $\sqrt{bc} < |a|$, then the critical point (0,0) of (A) is a node.

(d) Show that if $a = d$, and b and c are of the same sign and such that $\sqrt{bc} > |a|$, then the critical point (0,0) of (A) is a saddle point.

(e) Show that if $a = -d$ and $ad > bc$, then the critical point (0,0) of (A) is a center.

(f) Show that if $a = -d$, and b and c are of the same sign, then the critical point (0,0) of (A) is a saddle point.

13.3 Critical Points and Paths of Nonlinear Systems

A. Basic Theorems on Nonlinear Systems

We now consider the nonlinear real autonomous system

(13.4)
$$\begin{cases} \dfrac{dx}{dt} = P(x,y) \\[2mm] \dfrac{dy}{dt} = Q(x,y). \end{cases}$$

We assume that the system (13.4) has an isolated critical point which we shall choose to be the origin (0,0). We now assume further that the functions P and Q in the right members of (13.4) are such that $P(x,y)$ and $Q(x,y)$ can be written in the form

(13.39)
$$\begin{cases} P(x,y) = ax + by + P_1(x,y) \\ Q(x,y) = cx + dy + Q_1(x,y), \end{cases}$$

where (i) a, b, c, and d, are real constants,

$$\text{and } \begin{vmatrix} a & b \\ c & d \end{vmatrix} \neq 0,$$

and (ii) P_1 and Q_1 have continuous first partial derivatives for all (x,y), and are such that

(13.40)
$$\lim_{(x,y)\to(0,0)} \frac{P_1(x,y)}{\sqrt{x^2 + y^2}} = \lim_{(x,y)\to(0,0)} \frac{Q_1(x,y)}{\sqrt{x^2 + y^2}} = 0.$$

Thus the system under consideration may be written in the form

(13.41)
$$\begin{cases} \dfrac{dx}{dt} = ax + by + P_1(x,y) \\ \dfrac{dy}{dt} = cx + dy + Q_1(x,y), \end{cases}$$

where a, b, c, d, P_1 and Q_1 satisfy the requirements (i) and (ii) above.

If $P(x,y)$ and $Q(x,y)$ in (13.4) can be expanded in power series about $(0,0)$, the system (13.4) takes the form

(13.42)
$$\begin{cases} \dfrac{dx}{dt} = \left[\dfrac{\partial P}{\partial x}\right]_{(0,0)} x + \left[\dfrac{\partial P}{\partial y}\right]_{(0,0)} y + a_{12}x^2 + a_{22}xy + a_{21}y^2 + \cdots \\ \dfrac{dy}{dt} = \left[\dfrac{\partial Q}{\partial x}\right]_{(0,0)} x + \left[\dfrac{\partial Q}{\partial y}\right]_{(0,0)} y + b_{12}x^2 + b_{22}xy + b_{21}y^2 + \cdots \end{cases}$$

This system is of the form (13.41), where $P_1(x,y)$ and $Q_1(x,y)$ are the terms of higher degree in the right members of the equations. The requirements (i) and (ii) will be met, provided the Jacobian $\left.\dfrac{\partial(P,Q)}{\partial(x,y)}\right|_{(0,0)} \neq 0$. Observe that the constant terms are missing in the expansions in the right members of (13.42), since $P(0,0) = Q(0,0) = 0$.

Example 13.4.   The system

$$\begin{cases} \dfrac{dx}{dt} = x + 2y + x^2 \\ \dfrac{dy}{dt} = -3x - 4y + 2y^2 \end{cases}$$

is of the form (13.41) and satisfies the requirements (i) and (ii). Here $a = 1$, $b = 2$, $c = -3$, $d = -4$, and

$$\begin{vmatrix} a & b \\ c & d \end{vmatrix} = 2 \neq 0.$$

Further $P_1(x,y) = x^2$, $Q_1(x,y) = 2y^2$, and hence

$$\lim_{(x,y)\to(0,0)} \frac{P_1(x,y)}{\sqrt{x^2 + y^2}} = \lim_{(x,y)\to(0,0)} \frac{x^2}{\sqrt{x^2 + y^2}} = 0$$

and

$$\lim_{(x,y)\to(0,0)} \frac{Q_1(x,y)}{\sqrt{x^2 + y^2}} = \lim_{(x,y)\to(0,0)} \frac{2y^2}{\sqrt{x^2 + y^2}} = 0.$$

By the requirement (ii) the nonlinear terms $P_1(x,y)$ and $Q_1(x,y)$ in (13.41) tend to zero more rapidly than the linear terms $ax + by$ and $cx + dy$. Hence one would suspect that the behavior of the paths of the system (13.41) near (0,0) would be similar to that of the paths of the related linear system

(13.17)
$$\begin{cases} \dfrac{dx}{dt} = ax + by \\ \dfrac{dy}{dt} = cx + dy, \end{cases}$$

obtained from (13.41) by neglecting the nonlinear terms. In other words, it would seem that the nature of the critical point (0,0) of the nonlinear system (13.41) should be similar to that of the linear system (13.17). In general this is actually the case. We now state without proof the main theorem regarding this relation.

THEOREM 13.7.

Hypothesis. Consider the nonlinear system

(13.41)
$$\begin{cases} \dfrac{dx}{dt} = ax + by + P_1(x,y) \\ \dfrac{dy}{dt} = cx + dy + Q_1(x,y), \end{cases}$$

where a, b, c, d, P_1 and Q_1 satisfy the requirements (i) and (ii) above. Consider also the corresponding linear system

(13.17)
$$\begin{cases} \dfrac{dx}{dt} = ax + by \\ \dfrac{dy}{dt} = cx + dy, \end{cases}$$

obtained from (13.41) by neglecting the nonlinear terms $P_1(x,y)$ and $Q_1(x,y)$. Both systems have an isolated critical point at (0,0). Let λ_1 and λ_2 be the roots of the characteristic equation

(13.20) $\lambda^2 - (a + d)\lambda + (ad - bc) = 0$

of the linear system (13.17).

Conclusions. (a) The critical point (0,0) of the nonlinear system (13.41) is of the same type as that of the linear system (13.17) in the following cases:

(i) If λ_1 and λ_2 are real, unequal, and of the same sign, then not only is (0,0) a node of (13.17), but also (0,0) is a node of (13.41).

(ii) If λ_1 and λ_2 are real, unequal, and of opposite sign, then not only is (0,0) a saddle point of (13.17), but also (0,0) is a saddle point of (13.41).

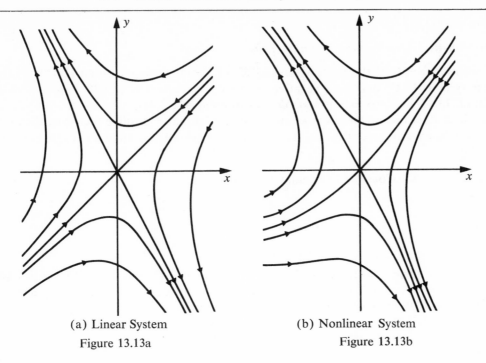

(a) Linear System

Figure 13.13a

(b) Nonlinear System

Figure 13.13b

(iii)   If λ_1 and λ_2 are real and equal and the system (13.17) is *not* such that $a = d \neq 0$, $b = c = 0$, then not only is (0,0) a node of (13.17), but also (0,0) is a node of (13.41).

(iv)   If λ_1 and λ_2 are conjugate complex with real part not zero, then not only is (0,0) a spiral point of (13.17), but also (0,0) is a spiral point of (13.41).

(b)   The critical point (0,0) of the nonlinear system (13.41) is not necessarily of the same type as that of the linear system (13.17) in the following cases:

(v)   If λ_1 and λ_2 are real and equal and the system (13.17) is such that $a = d \neq 0$, $b = c = 0$, then although (0,0) is a node of (13.17), the point (0,0) may be either a node or a spiral point of (13.41).

(vi)   If λ_1 and λ_2 are pure imaginary, then although (0,0) is a center of (13.17), the point (0,0) may be either a center or a spiral point of (13.41).

Although the critical point (0,0) of the nonlinear system (13.41) is of the same type as that of the linear system (13.17) in cases (i), (ii), (iii), and (iv) of the conclusion, the actual appearance of the paths is somewhat different. For example, if (0,0) is a saddle point of the linear system (13.17), then we know that there are four half-line paths entering (0,0), two for $t \rightarrow + \infty$ and two for $t \rightarrow - \infty$. However, at the saddle point of the nonlinear system (13.41), we have four nonrectilinear curves entering (0,0), two for $t \rightarrow + \infty$ and two for $t \rightarrow - \infty$, in place of the half-line paths of the linear case (see Figure 13.13).

Theorem 13.7 deals with the *type* of the critical point (0,0) of the nonlinear system (13.41). Concerning the *stability* of this point, we state without proof the following theorem of Liapounoff.

THEOREM 13.8.

Hypothesis.   Exactly as in Theorem 13.7.

Conclusions.   (a) If the roots λ_1 and λ_2 of the characteristic equation (13.20) of the linear system (13.17) both have negative real parts, then not only is (0,0) a *stable* critical point of (13.17) but also (0,0) is a *stable* critical point of (13.41).

(b) If at least one of the roots λ_1 and λ_2 of (13.20) has a positive real part, then not only is (0,0) an *unstable* critical point of (13.17), but also (0,0) is an *unstable* critical point of (13.41).

Example 13.5.   Consider the nonlinear system

(13.43)
$$\begin{cases} \dfrac{dx}{dt} = x + 4y - x^2 \\[2mm] \dfrac{dy}{dt} = 6x - y + 2xy. \end{cases}$$

This is of the form (13.41), where $P_1(x,y) = -x^2$ and $Q_1(x,y) = 2xy$. We see at once that the hypotheses of Theorems 13.7 and 13.8 are satisfied. Hence to investigate the critical point (0,0) of (13.43), we consider the linear system

(13.44)
$$\begin{cases} \dfrac{dx}{dt} = x + 4y \\[2mm] \dfrac{dy}{dt} = 6x - y \end{cases}$$

of the form (13.17). The characteristic equation (13.20) of this system is

$$\lambda^2 - 25 = 0.$$

Hence the roots are $\lambda_1 = 5$, $\lambda_2 = -5$. Since the roots are real, unequal, and of opposite sign, we see from conclusion (ii) of Theorem 13.7 that the critical point (0,0) of the nonlinear system (13.43) is a *saddle point*. From conclusion (b) of Theorem 13.8 we further conclude that this point is *unstable*.

Eliminating dt from equations (13.43), we obtain the differential equation

(13.45)
$$\frac{dy}{dx} = \frac{6x - y + 2xy}{x + 4y - x^2},$$

which gives the slope of the paths in the xy-phase plane defined by the solutions of (13.43). The first order equation (13.45) is exact. Its general solution is readily found to be

(13.46)
$$x^2y + 3x^2 - xy - 2y^2 + c = 0,$$

where c is an arbitrary constant. Equation (13.46) is the equation of the family of paths in the xy-phase plane. Several of these are shown in Figure 13.14.

Example 13.6.   Consider the nonlinear system

(13.47)
$$\begin{cases} \dfrac{dx}{dt} = \sin x - 4y \\[2mm] \dfrac{dy}{dt} = \sin 2x - 5y. \end{cases}$$

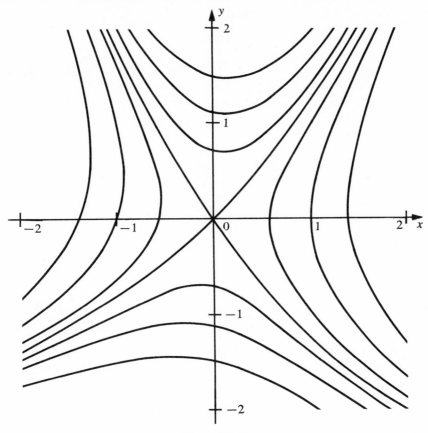

Figure 13.14

Using the expansion

$$\sin x = x - \frac{x^3}{3!} + \frac{x^5}{5!} - \cdots,$$

we write this system in the form

(13.48)
$$\begin{cases} \dfrac{dx}{dt} = x - 4y - \dfrac{x^3}{6} + \dfrac{x^5}{120} + \cdots \\ \dfrac{dy}{dt} = 2x - 5y - \dfrac{4x^3}{3} + \dfrac{4x^5}{15} - \cdots \end{cases}$$

The hypotheses of Theorems 13.7 and 13.8 are satisfied. Thus to investigate the critical point (0,0) of (13.47) (or (13.48)), we consider the linear system

(13.49)
$$\begin{cases} \dfrac{dx}{dt} = x - 4y \\ \dfrac{dy}{dt} = 2x - 5y. \end{cases}$$

The characteristic equation of this system is

$$\lambda^2 + 4\lambda + 3 = 0.$$

Thus the roots are $\lambda_1 = -3$, $\lambda_2 = -1$. Since the roots are real, unequal, and of the same sign, we see from conclusion (i) of Theorem 13.7 that the critical point $(0,0)$ of the nonlinear system (13.47) is a *node*. From conclusion (a) of Theorem 13.8 we conclude that this node is *stable*.

Example 13.7. Consider the two nonlinear systems

(13.50)
$$\begin{cases} \dfrac{dx}{dt} = -y - x^2 \\ \dfrac{dy}{dt} = x \end{cases}$$

and

(13.51)
$$\begin{cases} \dfrac{dx}{dt} = -y - x^3 \\ \dfrac{dy}{dt} = x. \end{cases}$$

The point $(0,0)$ is a critical point for each of these systems. The hypotheses of Theorem 13.7 are satisfied in each case, and in each case the corresponding linear system to be investigated is

(13.52)
$$\begin{cases} \dfrac{dx}{dt} = -y \\ \dfrac{dy}{dt} = x. \end{cases}$$

The characteristic equation of the system (13.52) is

$$\lambda^2 + 1 = 0$$

with the pure imaginary roots $\pm i$. Thus the critical point $(0,0)$ of the linear system (13.52) is a center. However, Theorem 13.7 does not give us definite information concerning the nature of this point for either of the nonlinear systems (13.50) or (13.51). Conclusion (vi) of Theorem 13.7 tells us that in each case $(0,0)$ is *either* a center *or* a spiral point; but this is all that this theorem tells us concerning the two systems under consideration.

Hurewicz, Reference (25), p. 99, shows that the critical point $(0,0)$ of the system (13.50) is a *center*, while the same point for the system (13.51) is a *spiral point*.

B. Nonlinear Conservative Systems

Let us consider a dynamical system in which the dissipation of energy is so slow that it may be neglected. Thus neglecting this slow dissipation, we assume the law of conservation of energy, namely, that the sum of the kinetic energy and the potential energy is a constant. In other words, the system is regarded as *conservative*.

Specifically, we consider a particle of mass m in rectilinear motion under the action of restoring force F which is a function of the displacement x only. The differential equation of motion is thus

(13.53)
$$m\frac{d^2x}{dt^2} = F(x).$$

The differential equation (13.53) is equivalent to the nonlinear autonomous system

(13.54)
$$\begin{cases} \dfrac{dx}{dt} = y \\[2mm] \dfrac{dy}{dt} = \dfrac{F(x)}{m}. \end{cases}$$

Eliminating dt we obtain the differential equation of the paths defined by the solutions of (13.54) in the $x,y = \dfrac{dx}{dt}$ phase plane:

(13.55)
$$\frac{dy}{dx} = \frac{F(x)}{my}.$$

Separating variables in this equation, we obtain

$$my\,dy = F(x)dx.$$

Suppose $x = x_0$ and $y\,(= dx/dt) = y_0$ at $t = t_0$.
Then, integrating we find

$$\frac{1}{2}my^2 - \frac{1}{2}my_0^2 = \int_{x_0}^{x} F(x)dx$$

or

(13.56)
$$\frac{1}{2}my^2 - \int_0^x F(x)dx = \frac{1}{2}my_0^2 - \int_0^{x_0} F(x)dx.$$

But $\dfrac{1}{2}m\left(\dfrac{dx}{dt}\right)^2 = \dfrac{1}{2}\,my^2$ is the kinetic energy of the system and $V(x) = -\displaystyle\int_0^x F(x)dx$ is the potential energy. Thus the equation (13.56) expresses the law of conservation of energy,

(13.57)
$$\frac{1}{2}my^2 + V(x) = h,$$

where $h = \frac{1}{2}\,my_0^2 + V(x_0)$ is the total energy of the system.

Since equation (13.57) was obtained by integrating (13.55), we see that (13.57) gives the family of paths in the xy-phase plane. For a given value of h the path given by (13.57) is a curve of constant energy in this plane.

The critical points of the system (13.54) are the points with coordinates $(x_c,0)$, where x_c are the roots of the equation $F(x) = 0$. These are equilibrium points of the given dynamical system. From the differential equation (13.55) we see that the paths cross the x axis at right angles and have horizontal tangents along the lines $x = x_c$. From equation (13.57) we observe that the paths are symmetrical with respect to the x axis.

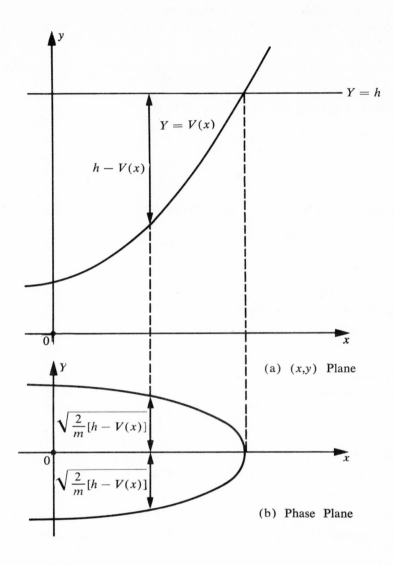

Figure 13.15a   Figure 13.15b

From the equation (13.57) of the paths we find at once

(13.58)
$$y = \pm\sqrt{\frac{2}{m}[h - V(x)]}.$$

This may be used to construct the paths in the following convenient way.

(i) On a rectangular (x,Y) plane construct the graph of $Y = V(x)$ and the lines $Y = h$, for various values of h [(see Figure 13.15(a)] where one such line is shown). For each fixed value h this shows the difference $h - V(x)$ for each x.

(ii) Directly below the (x,Y) plane draw the xy-phase plane, with the y axis on the same vertical line as the Y axis [see Figure 13.15(b)]. For each x multiply the difference $h - V(x)$ obtained from the graph in step (i) by the constant factor $\dfrac{2}{m}$ and use (13.58) to plot the corresponding y value on the phase plane.

Example 13.8.   Suppose $F(x) = 4x^3 - 4x$ and $m = 1$. Then the differential equation (13.53) of motion is

$$\frac{d^2x}{dt^2} = 4x^3 - 4x.$$

The equivalent nonlinear system (13.54) is

(13.59)
$$\begin{cases} \dfrac{dx}{dt} = y \\[2mm] \dfrac{dy}{dt} = 4x^3 - 4x. \end{cases}$$

The critical points of this system are $(0,0)$, $(1,0)$, and $(-1,0)$. The differential equation (13.55) of the paths in the xy-phase plane is

$$\frac{dy}{dx} = \frac{4x^3 - 4x}{y}.$$

Integrating this we obtain the family of paths

$$\frac{1}{2}y^2 - x^4 + 2x^2 = h.$$

This is of the form (13.57), where

$$V(x) = -\int_0^x F(x)\,dx = -x^4 + 2x^2$$

is the potential energy.

We now construct the xy-phase plane diagram by first constructing the curve $Y = V(x)$ and the lines $Y = h$ for various values of h in the (x,Y) plane [see Figure 13.16(a)]. From this (x,Y) plane we read off the values $h - V(x) = h + x^4 - 2x^2$ and plot the paths in the xy-phase plane directly below [see Figure 13.16(b)] using

$$y = \pm\sqrt{2(h + x^4 - 2x^2)}.$$

From the diagram we see that if the total energy h is less than 1 and x is initially between -1 and $+1$, then the corresponding paths are closed and hence the motion is periodic. If, however, $h > 1$, the paths are not closed and the motion is not periodic. The value $h = 1$ clearly separates the motions of one type (periodic) from those of another (non-periodic). For this reason the corresponding path is called a *separatrix*. We observe the nature of the critical points from the phase plane diagram. The point $(0,0)$ is clearly a *center*, while the points $(1,0)$ and $(-1,0)$ are *saddle points*.

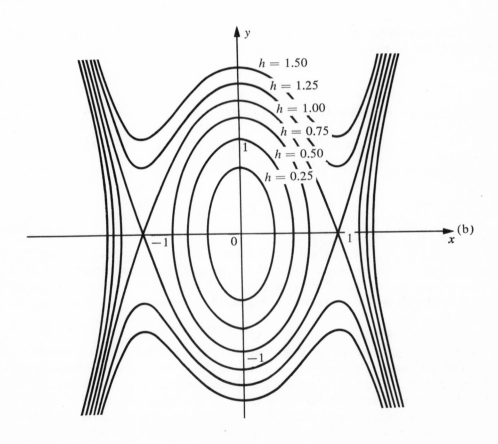

Figure 13.16

Exercises

Determine the type and stability of the critical point $(0,0)$ of each of the nonlinear autonomous systems in Exercises 1 through 6.

1. $\dfrac{dx}{dt} = x + x^2 - 3xy$

    $\dfrac{dy}{dt} = -2x + y + 3y^2$

2. $\dfrac{dx}{dt} = x + 4y + 3x^4$

    $\dfrac{dy}{dt} = 2x - 3y - y^2 + 2x^3$

3. $\dfrac{dx}{dt} = x + y + x^2y$

    $\dfrac{dy}{dt} = 3x - y + 2xy^3$

4. $\dfrac{dx}{dt} = y + \tan x$

    $\dfrac{dy}{dt} = y\cos x$

5. $\dfrac{dx}{dt} = (y + 1)^2 - \cos x$

    $\dfrac{dy}{dt} = \sin(x + y)$

6. $\dfrac{dx}{dt} = x - 2y + e^{xy} - \cos^2 x$

    $\dfrac{dy}{dt} = \sin(x + y)$

7. Consider the autonomous system

$$\frac{dx}{dt} = ye^x$$

$$\frac{dy}{dt} = e^x - 1.$$

(a) Determine the type of the critical point $(0,0)$.

(b) Obtain the differential equation of the paths and find its general solution.

(c) Carefully plot several of the paths found in step (b) to obtain a phase plane diagram which clearly exhibits the nature of the critical point $(0,0)$.

(d) Obtain the differential equation of the paths of the corresponding reduced linear system and find its general solution.

(e) Proceed as in step (c) for the paths found in step (d).

(f) Compare the results of the two phase plane diagrams constructed in steps (c) and (e). Comment.

8. Consider the autonomous system

$$\frac{dx}{dt} = 10x + x^2$$

$$\frac{dy}{dt} = 20y + x^3,$$

and proceed as in Exercise 7.

9. The differential equation

$$\frac{d^2x}{dt^2} = x^5 - 5x^4 + 5x^3 + 5x^2 - 6x$$

is of the form $\frac{d^2x}{dt^2} = F(x)$ and may be considered as the differential equation of a nonlinear conservative dynamical system.

(a) Obtain the equivalent nonlinear autonomous system and find its critical points.

(b) Obtain the differential equation of the paths in the $x,y = \frac{dx}{dt}$ phase plane and show that its general solution is $\frac{1}{2}y^2 + V(x) = h$, where $V(x) = -\int_0^x F(x)dx$.

(c) Carefully construct the graph of $Y = V(x)$ along with the lines $Y = h$ for several well-chosen values of h in an auxiliary (x,Y) plane. Then use this auxiliary diagram to sketch the paths $\frac{1}{2}y^2 + V(x) = h$ in the xy phase plane.

(d) Use the phase plane diagram constructed in part (c) to determine the type of each of the critical points found in step (a). Also use the diagram to draw conclusions concerning the motion described by the second-order nonlinear equation of the problem.

10. Proceed as in Exercise 9 for the differential equation

$$\frac{d^2x}{dt^2} = -\sin x.$$

11. Proceed as in Exercise 9 for the differential equation

$$\frac{d^2x}{dt^2} = x^5 - 3x^4 + x^3 + 3x^2 - 2x.$$

12. Find the real critical points of each of the following systems, and determine the type and stability of each critical point found.

(a) $\begin{cases} \dfrac{dx}{dt} = y - x^2 \\[2mm] \dfrac{dy}{dt} = 8x - y^2 \end{cases}$
  (b) $\begin{cases} \dfrac{dx}{dt} = 2x - y + x^2 \\[2mm] \dfrac{dy}{dt} = -12x + y + y^2 \end{cases}$

13. Consider the differential equation

$$\frac{d^2x}{dt^2} = x^2 - 6x + \lambda,$$

where λ is a real parameter independent of x and t.

(a) Obtain the equivalent nonlinear autonomous system. Show that for $\lambda < 9$ this system has two real critical points, that for $\lambda = 9$ it has only one real critical point, and that for $\lambda > 9$ it has no real critical points.

(b) Let $\lambda = 0$. Find the critical points in this case, sketch the paths in the xy phase plane, and determine the type of each of the critical points.

(c) Let $\lambda = 5$, and proceed as in step (b).

(d) Let $\lambda = 8$, and proceed as in step (b).

(e) Let $\lambda = 9$. Find the one real critical point in this case, and sketch the paths in the xy phase plane. What is the nature of the critical point?

(f) Compare the diagrams obtained in steps (b), (c), (d), and (e), and comment on the dependence of the critical points and paths on the parameter λ. The value 9 is called the *critical value* of the parameter λ. Can you give any good reasons why such a designation is appropriate?

13.4   Limit Cycles and Periodic Solutions

A. *Limit Cycles*

We have already encountered autonomous systems having closed paths. For example, the system (13.59) of Section 13.3B has a center at (0,0) and in the neighborhood of this center there is an infinite family of closed paths resembling ellipses (see Figure 13.16). In this example the closed paths about (0,0) form a continuous family in the sense that arbitrarily near to any one of the closed paths of this family there is always another closed path of the family. Now we shall consider systems having closed paths which are isolated in the sense that there are no other closed paths of the system arbitrarily near to a given closed path of the system.

What is the significance of a closed path? Given an autonomous system

(13.4)
$$\begin{cases} \dfrac{dx}{dt} = P(x,y) \\[2mm] \dfrac{dy}{dt} = Q(x,y), \end{cases}$$

one is often most interested in determining the existence of *periodic* solutions of this system. It is easy to see that periodic solutions and closed paths of (13.4) are very closely related. For, in the first place, if $x = f_1(t)$, $y = g_1(t)$, where f_1 and g_1 are not both constant functions, is a periodic solution of (13.4), then the path which this solution defines is a *closed* path. On the other hand, let C be a closed path of (13.4) defined by a solution $x = f(t)$, $y = g(t)$ of (13.4), and suppose $f(t_0) = x_0$, $g(t_0) = y_0$. Since C is closed, there exists a value $t_1 = t_0 + T$, where $T > 0$, such that $f(t_1) = x_0$, $g(t_1) = y_0$. Now the pair $x = f(t + T)$, $y = g(t + T)$ is also a solution of (13.4). At $t = t_0$, this latter solution also assumes the values $x = x_0$, $y = y_0$. Thus by the uniqueness theorem of Chapter 11, the two solutions $x = f(t)$, $y = g(t)$ and $x = f(t + T)$, $y = g(t + T)$ are identical for all t. In other words, $f(t + T) = f(t)$, $g(t + T) = g(t)$ for all t, and so the solution $x = f(t)$, $y = g(t)$ defining the closed path C is a *periodic* solution. Thus, the search for periodic solutions of (13.4) falls back on the search for closed paths.

Now suppose the system (13.4) has a closed path C. Further, suppose (13.4) possesses a non-closed path C_1 defined by a solution $x = f(t)$, $y = g(t)$ of (13.4) and having the following property: As a point R traces out C_1 according to the equations $x = f(t)$, $y = g(t)$, the path C_1 spirals and the distance between R and the nearest point on the closed path C approaches zero either as $t \to +\infty$ or as $t \to -\infty$. In other words, the nonclosed path C_1 spirals closer and closer around the closed path C either from the inside of C or from the outside either as $t \to + \infty$ or as $t \to - \infty$ (see Figure 13.17 where C_1 approaches C from the outside).

In such a case we call the closed path C a *limit cycle*, according to the following definition:

DEFINITION. A closed path C of the system (13.4) which is approached spirally from either the inside or the outside by a nonclosed path C_1 of (13.4) either as $t \to + \infty$ or as $t \to - \infty$ is called a *limit cycle* of (13.4).

Example 13.9. The following well-known example of a system having a limit cycle will illustrate the above discussion and definition.

$$(13.60) \qquad \begin{cases} \dfrac{dx}{dt} = y + x(1 - x^2 - y^2) \\ \dfrac{dy}{dt} = -x + y(1 - x^2 - y^2). \end{cases}$$

To study this system we shall introduce polar coordinates (r,θ), where

$$(13.61) \qquad \begin{cases} x = r\cos\theta \\ y = r\sin\theta. \end{cases}$$

From these relations we find that

$$(13.62) \qquad \begin{cases} x\dfrac{dx}{dt} + y\dfrac{dy}{dt} = r\dfrac{dr}{dt} \\ x\dfrac{dy}{dt} - y\dfrac{dx}{dt} = r^2\dfrac{d\theta}{dt}. \end{cases}$$

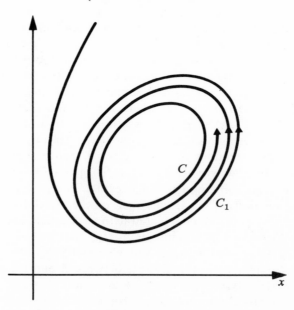

Figure 13.17

Now, multiplying the first equation of (13.60) by x and the second by y and adding, we obtain

$$x\frac{dx}{dt} + y\frac{dy}{dt} = (x^2 + y^2)(1 - x^2 - y^2).$$

Introducing the polar coordinates defined by (13.61), and making use of (13.62), this becomes

$$r\frac{dr}{dt} = r^2(1 - r^2).$$

For $r \neq 0$, we may thus write

$$\frac{dr}{dt} = r(1 - r^2).$$

Now multiplying the first equation of (13.60) by y and the second by x and subtracting, we obtain

$$y\frac{dx}{dt} - x\frac{dy}{dt} = y^2 + x^2.$$

Again using (13.62), this becomes

$$-r^2\frac{d\theta}{dt} = r^2,$$

and so for $r \neq 0$ we may write

$$\frac{d\theta}{dt} = -1.$$

Thus in polar coordinates the system (13.60) becomes

(13.63)
$$\begin{cases} \dfrac{dr}{dt} = r(1 - r^2) \\ \dfrac{d\theta}{dt} = -1. \end{cases}$$

From the second of these equations we find at once that

$$\theta = -t + t_0,$$

where t_0 is an arbitrary constant. The first of the equations (13.63) is separable. Separating variables, we have

$$\frac{dr}{r(1 - r^2)} = dt,$$

and an integration using partial fractions yields

$$\ln r^2 - \ln |1 - r^2| = 2t + \ln |c_0|.$$

After some manipulations we obtain

$$r^2 = \frac{c_0 e^{2t}}{1 + c_0 e^{2t}}.$$

Thus we may write

$$r = \frac{1}{\sqrt{1 + ce^{-2t}}}, \quad \text{where } c = \frac{1}{c_0}.$$

Thus, the solution of the system (13.63) may be written

$$\begin{cases} r = \dfrac{1}{\sqrt{1 + ce^{-2t}}} \\ \theta = -t + t_0, \end{cases}$$

where c and t_0 are arbitrary constants. We may choose $t_0 = 0$. Then $\theta = -t$; and using (13.61), the solution of the system (13.60) becomes

(13.64)
$$\begin{cases} x = \dfrac{\cos t}{\sqrt{1 + ce^{-2t}}} \\ y = -\dfrac{\sin t}{\sqrt{1 + ce^{-2t}}}. \end{cases}$$

The solutions (13.64) of (13.60) define the paths of (13.60) in the xy plane. Examining these paths for various values of c, we note the following conclusions:

(i) If $c = 0$, the path defined by (13.64) is the circle $x^2 + y^2 = 1$, described in the clockwise direction.

(ii) If $c \neq 0$, the paths defined by (13.64) are *not* closed paths but rather paths having a spiral behavior. If $c > 0$, the paths are spirals lying inside the circle $x^2 + y^2 = 1$. As $t \to +\infty$, they approach this circle; while as $t \to -\infty$, they approach the critical point $(0,0)$ of (13.60). If $c < 0$, the paths lie outside the circle $x^2 + y^2 = 1$. These "outer" paths also approach this circle as $t \to +\infty$; while as $t \to \ln \sqrt{|c|}$, both $|x|$ and $|y|$ become infinite.

Since the closed path $x^2 + y^2 = 1$ is approached spirally from both the inside and the outside by nonclosed paths as $t \to +\infty$, we conclude that this circle is a limit cycle of the system (13.60). (See Figure 13.18).

B. Existence and Nonexistence of Limit Cycles

In Example 13.9 the existence of a limit cycle was ascertained by actually finding this limit cycle. In general such a procedure is of course impossible. Given the autonomous system (13.4) we need a theorem giving sufficient conditions for the existence of a limit cycle of (13.4). One of the few general theorems of this nature is the Poincaré-Bendixson Theorem, which we shall state below (Theorem 13.10). First, however, we shall state and prove a theorem on the *nonexistence* of closed paths of the system (13.4).

THEOREM 13.9. *Bendixson's Nonexistence Criterion.*

Hypothesis. Let D be a domain in the xy plane. Consider the autonomous system

(13.4)
$$\begin{cases} \dfrac{dx}{dt} = P(x,y) \\ \dfrac{dy}{dt} = Q(x,y), \end{cases}$$

where P and Q have continuous first partial derivatives in D. Suppose that $\dfrac{\partial P}{\partial x} + \dfrac{\partial Q}{\partial y}$ has the same sign throughout D.

Conclusion. The system (13.4) has no closed path in the domain D.

Proof. We shall use Green's Theorem in the plane.† Let C be a closed curve in D, let R be the region bounded by C, and apply Green's Theorem. We have

$$\int_C (Pdy - Qdx) = \iint_R \left(\frac{\partial P}{\partial x} + \frac{\partial Q}{\partial y}\right)ds,$$

where the line integral is taken in the positive sense. Assume C is a closed path of (13.4). Then we can write

$$\int_C (Pdy - Qdx) = \int_0^T \left(P\frac{dy}{dt} - Q\frac{dx}{dt}\right)dt = \int_0^T (PQ - QP)dt = 0,$$

where T denotes the period of the solution defining C. Thus

$$\iint_R \left(\frac{\partial P}{\partial x} + \frac{\partial Q}{\partial y}\right)ds = 0.$$

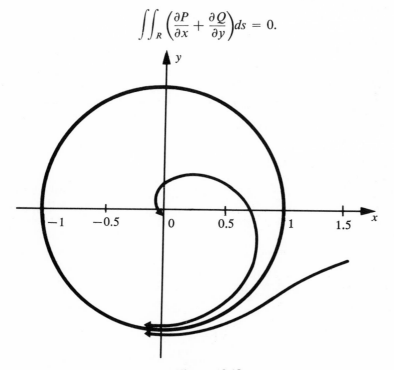

Figure 13.18

†See, for example, Widder, Reference (56), p. 223.

But this double integral can be zero only if $\dfrac{\partial P}{\partial x} + \dfrac{\partial Q}{\partial y}$ changes sign. This is a contradiction. Thus C is not a path of (13.4) and hence (13.4) possesses no closed path in D.   *Q.E.D.*

Example 13.10.

$$(13.65) \qquad \begin{cases} \dfrac{dx}{dt} = 2x + y + x^3, \\[2mm] \dfrac{dy}{dt} = 3x - y + y^3. \end{cases}$$

Here $P(x,y) = 2x + y + x^3$, $Q(x,y) = 3x - y + y^3$, and $\dfrac{\partial P(x,y)}{\partial x} + \dfrac{\partial Q(x,y)}{\partial y} = 3(x^2 + y^2) + 1$. Since this expression is positive throughout every domain D in the xy plane, the system (13.65) has no closed path in any such domain. In particular, then, the system (13.65) has no limit cycles and hence no periodic solutions.

Having considered this nonexistence result, we now turn to the Poincaré-Bendixson Existence Theorem. The proof of this theorem is outside the scope of this book, and we refer the reader to References (13) and (25). We shall merely state the theorem and indicate its significance. In order to make the statement of the theorem less involved, we introduce two further concepts.

DEFINITION. Let C be a path of the system (13.4) and let $x = f(t)$, $y = g(t)$ be a solution of (13.4) defining C. Then we shall call the set of all points of C for $t \geq t_0$, where t_0 is some value of t, a *half-path* of (13.4). In other words, by a half-path of (13.4) we mean the set of all points with coordinates $[f(t), g(t)]$ for $t_0 \leq t < +\infty$. We denote a half-path of (13.4) by C^+.

DEFINITION. Let C^+ be a half-path of (13.4) defined by $x = f(t)$, $y = g(t)$ for $t \geq t_0$. Let (x_1, y_1) be a point in the xy plane. If there exists a sequence of real numbers $\{t_n\}$, $n = 1, 2, \ldots$, such that $t_n \to +\infty$ and $[f(t_n), g(t_n)] \to (x_1, y_1)$ as $n \to +\infty$, then we call (x_1, y_1) a *limit point* of C^+. The set of all limit points of a half-path C^+ will be called the *limit set* of C^+ and will be denoted by $L(C^+)$.

Example 13.11. The paths of the system (13.60) are given by Equations (13.64). Letting $c = 1$ we obtain the path C defined by

$$(13.66) \qquad \begin{cases} x = \dfrac{\cos t}{\sqrt{1 + e^{-2t}}} \\[4mm] y = -\dfrac{\sin t}{\sqrt{1 + e^{-2t}}}. \end{cases}$$

The set of all points of C for $t \geq 0$ is a half-path C^+. That is, C^+ is the set of all points with coordinates

$$\left[\frac{\cos t}{\sqrt{1 + e^{-2t}}}, \quad -\frac{\sin t}{\sqrt{1 + e^{-2t}}}\right], \quad 0 \leq t < +\infty.$$

Consider the sequence $0, 2\pi, 4\pi, \ldots, 2n\pi, \ldots$, tending to $+\infty$ as $n \to +\infty$. The corresponding sequence of points on C^+ is

$$\left[\frac{\cos 2n\pi}{\sqrt{1 + e^{-4n\pi}}}, \quad -\frac{\sin 2n\pi}{\sqrt{1 + e^{-4n\pi}}}\right], \quad (n = 0, 1, 2, \ldots),$$

and this sequence approaches the point $(1,0)$ as $n \to +\infty$.

Thus $(1,0)$ is a *limit point* of the half-path C^+.

The set of *all* limit points of C^+ is the set of points such that $x^2 + y^2 = 1$. In other words, the circle $x^2 + y^2 = 1$ is the *limit set of* C^+.

We are now in a position to state the Poincaré-Bendixson Theorem.

THEOREM 13.10. *Poincaré-Bendixson Theorem; "strong" form.*

Hypothesis. (i).   Consider the autonomous system

(13.4)
$$\begin{cases} \dfrac{dx}{dt} = P(x,y) \\ \dfrac{dy}{dt} = Q(x,y), \end{cases}$$

where P and Q have continuous first partial derivatives in a domain D of the xy plane. Let D_1 be a bounded subdomain of D, and let R denote D_1 plus its boundary.

(ii) Let C^+ defined by $x = f(t)$, $y = g(t)$, $t \geq t_0$, be a half-path of (13.4) contained entirely in R. Suppose the limit set $L(C^+)$ of C^+ contains no critical points of (13.4).

Conclusion. Either (i) The half-path C^+ is itself a closed path (in this case C^+ and and $L(C^+)$ are identical), or (ii) $L(C^+)$ is a closed path which C^+ approaches spirally from either the inside or the outside (in this case $L(C^+)$ is a limit cycle). Thus in either case, there exists a closed path of (13.4) in R.

A slightly weaker but somewhat more practical form of this theorem may be seen at once. If the region R of hypothesis (i) contains no critical points of (13.4), then the limit set $L(C^+)$ will contain no critical points of (13.4) and so the second statement of hypothesis (ii) will automatically be satisfied. Thus we may state:

THEOREM 13.10A. *Poincaré-Bendixson Theorem; "weak" form.*

Hypothesis. (i)   Exactly as in Theorem 13.10.   (ii)   Suppose R contains no critical points of (13.4).

Conclusion.   If R contains a half-path of (13.4), then R also contains a closed path of (13.4).

Let us indicate how this theorem may be applied to determine the existence of a closed path of (13.4). Suppose the continuity requirements concerning the derivatives of $P(x,y)$ and $Q(x,y)$ are satisfied for all (x,y). Further suppose that (13.4) has a critical point at (x_0,y_0) but no other critical points within some circle K: $(x - x_0)^2 + (y - y_0)^2 = r^2$ about (x_0,y_0) (see Figure 13.19). Then an annular region whose boundary consists of two smaller circles K_1: $(x - x_0)^2 + (y - y_0)^2 = r_1^2$ and K_2: $(x - x_0)^2 + (y - y_0)^2 = r_2^2$, where $0 < r_1 < r_2 < r$, about (x_0,y_0) may be taken as a region R containing no critical points of (13.4). If we can then show that a half-path C^+ of (13.4) (for $t \geq$ some t_0) is entirely contained in this annular region R, then we can conclude at once that a closed path C_0 of (13.4) is also contained in R.

The difficulty in applying Theorem 13.10A usually comes in being able to show that a half-path C^+ is entirely contained in R. If one can show that the vector $[P(x,y), Q(x,y)]$ determined by (13.4) points *into* R at *every* point of the boundary of R, then a path C entering R at $t = t_0$ will remain in R for $t \geq t_0$ and hence provide the needed half-path C^+.

Example 13.12. Consider again the system (13.60) with critical point $(0,0)$. The annular region R bounded by $x^2 + y^2 = \frac{1}{4}$ and $x^2 + y^2 = 4$ contains no critical points of (13.60). If we can show that R contains a half-path of (13.60), the Poincaré-Bendixson Theorem ("weak" form) will apply.

In our previous study of this system we found that

$$\frac{dr}{dt} = r(1 - r^2)$$

for $r > 0$, where $r = \sqrt{x^2 + y^2}$. On the circle $x^2 + y^2 = \frac{1}{4}$, $\frac{dr}{dt} > 0$ and hence $r = \sqrt{x^2 + y^2}$ is increasing. Thus the vector $[P(x,y), Q(x,y)]$ points *into* R at *every* point of this inner circle. On the circle $x^2 + y^2 = 4$, $\frac{dr}{dt} < 0$ and hence $r = \sqrt{x^2 + y^2}$ is decreasing. Thus the vector $[P(x,y), Q(x,y)]$ also points *into* R at *every* point of this outer circle (See Figure 13.20, in which this situation is illustrated qualitatively). Hence a path C entering R at $t = t_0$ will remain in R for $t \geq t_0$, and this provides us with the needed half-path contained in R.

Thus by the Poincaré-Bendixson Theorem ("weak" form), we know that R contains a closed path C_0. We have already seen that the circle $x^2 + y^2 = 1$ is indeed such a closed path of (13.60).

C. The Index of a Critical Point

We again consider the system (13.4), where P and Q have continuous first partial derivatives for all (x,y), and assume that all of the critical points of (13.4) are isolated. Now consider a simple closed curve† C [not necessarily a path of (13.4)] which passes

---

†By a simple closed curve we mean a closed curve having no double points; for example, a circle is a simple closed curve, but a "figure eight" is not.

Figure 13.19

Figure 13.20

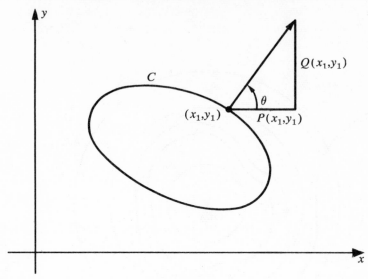

Figure 13.21

through no critical points of (13.4). Consider a point (x_1, y_1) on C and the vector $[P(x_1, y_1), Q(x_1, y_1)]$ defined by (13.4) at the point (x_1, y_1). Let θ denote the angle from the positive x direction to this vector (see Figure 13.21).

Now let (x_1, y_1) describe the curve C once in the counterclockwise direction and return to its original position. As (x_1, y_1) describes C, the vector $[P(x_1, y_1), Q(x_1, y_1)]$ changes continuously and consequently the angle θ also varies continuously. When (x_1, y_1) reaches its original position, the angle θ will have changed by an amount $\Delta\theta$. We are now prepared to define the index of the curve C.

DEFINITION. Let θ denote the angle from the positive x direction to the vector $[P(x_1, y_1), Q(x_1, y_1)]$ defined by (13.4) at (x_1, y_1). Let $\Delta\theta$ denote the total change in θ as (x_1, y_1) describes the simple closed curve C once in the counterclockwise direction. We call the number

$$I = \frac{\Delta\theta}{2\pi}$$

the *index* of the curve C with respect to the system (13.4).

Clearly $\Delta\theta$ is either equal to zero or a positive or negative integral multiple of 2π and hence I is either zero or a positive or negative integer. If $[P(x_1, y_1), Q(x_1, y_1)]$ merely oscillates but does not make a complete rotation as (x_1, y_1) describes C, then I is zero. If the net change $\Delta\theta$ in θ is a decrease, then I is negative.

Now let (x_0, y_0) be an isolated critical point of (13.4). It can be shown that all simple closed curves enclosing (x_0, y_0) but containing no other critical point of (13.4) have the same index. This leads us to make the following definition.

DEFINITION. By the *index* of an isolated critical point (x_0, y_0) of (13.4) we mean the index of a simple closed curve C which encloses (x_0, y_0) but no other critical points of (13.4).

From an examination of Figure 13.22 we may reach the following conclusion intuitively: The index of a node, a center, or a spiral point is $+1$, while the index of a saddle point is -1.

We now list several interesting results concerning the index of a simple closed curve C and then point out several important consequences of these results. Most of these results are intuitively obvious, but few are easy to prove rigorously. In each case when we say index we shall mean the index with respect to the system (13.4) where $P(x, y)$ and $Q(x, y)$ have continuous first partial derivatives for all (x, y) and (13.4) has only isolated critical points.

(i) The index of a simple closed curve which neither passes through a critical point of (13.4) nor has a critical point of (13.4) in its interior is zero.

(ii) The index of a simple closed curve which surrounds a finite number of critical points of (13.4) is equal to the sum of the indices of these critical points.

(iii) The index of a closed path of (13.4) is $+1$.

From these results the following conclusions follow at once.

(a) A closed path of (13.4) contains at least one critical point of (13.4) in its interior (for otherwise, by (i), the index of such a closed path would be zero; and this would contradict (iii)).

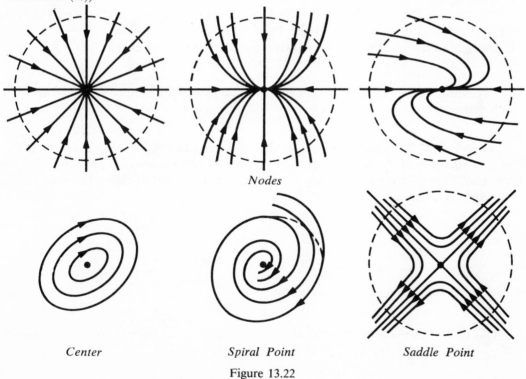

Nodes

Center   Spiral Point   Saddle Point

Figure 13.22

(b) A closed path of (13.4) may contain in its interior a finite number of critical points of (13.4), the sum of the indices of which is $+1$ (this follows at once from (ii) and (iii)).

D. The Lienard-Levinson-Smith Theorem and the van der Pol Equation

Throughout this chapter we have stated a number of important results without proof. We have done this because we feel that every serious student of differential equations should become aware of these results as soon as possible, even though their proofs are definitely beyond our scope and properly belong to a more advanced study of our subject. In keeping with this philosophy, we close this section by stating without proof an important theorem dealing with the existence of periodic solutions for a class of second order nonlinear equations. We shall then apply this theorem to the famous van der Pol Equation already introduced at the beginning of the chapter.

THEOREM 13.11. *Lienard-Levinson-Smith.*

Hypothesis. Consider the differential equation

(13.67) $$\frac{d^2x}{dt^2} + f(x)\frac{dx}{dt} + g(x) = 0,$$

where f, g, F defined by $F(x) = \int_0^x f(u)du$, and G defined by $G(x) = \int_0^x g(u)du$ are real functions having the following properties:
   (i) f is even and is continuous for all x.
   (ii) There exists a number $x_0 > 0$ such that $F(x) < 0$ for $0 < x < x_0$ and $F(x) > 0$ and monotonic increasing for $x > x_0$. Further, $F(x) \to \infty$ as $x \to \infty$.
   (iii) g is odd, has a continuous derivative for all x, and is such that $g(x) > 0$ for $x > 0$.
   (iv) $G(x) \to \infty$ as $x \to \infty$.

Conclusion. The equation (13.67) possesses an essentially unique nontrivial periodic solution.

Remark. By "essentially unique" in the above conclusion we mean that if $x = \phi(t)$ is a nontrivial periodic solution of (13.67), then all other nontrivial periodic solutions of (13.67) are of the form $x = \phi(t - t_1)$, where t_1 is a real number. In other words, the equivalent autonomous system

$$\begin{cases} \dfrac{dx}{dt} = y \\[2mm] \dfrac{dy}{dt} = -f(x)y - g(x) \end{cases}$$

has a unique closed path in the xy plane.

One of the most important examples of an equation of the form (13.67) which satisfies the hypotheses of Theorem 13.11 is the van der Pol Equation

(13.2) $$\frac{d^2x}{dt^2} + \mu(x^2 - 1)\frac{dx}{dt} + x = 0,$$

where μ is a positive constant. Here $f(x) = \mu(x^2 - 1)$, $g(x) = x$,

$$F(x) = \int_0^x \mu(u^2 - 1)du = \mu\left(\frac{x^3}{3} - x\right), \quad \text{and}$$

$$G(x) = \int_0^x udu = \frac{x^2}{2}.$$

We check that the hypotheses of Theorem 13.11 are indeed satisfied:

(i) Since $f(-x) = \mu(x^2 - 1) = f(x)$, the function f is even. Clearly it is continuous for all x.

(ii) $F(x) = \mu\left(\dfrac{x^3}{3} - x\right)$ is negative for $0 < x < \sqrt{3}$. For $x > \sqrt{3}$, $F(x)$ is positive and monotonic increasing (it is in fact monotonic increasing for $x > 1$). Clearly $F(x) \to \infty$ as $x \to \infty$.

(iii) Since $g(-x) = -x = -g(x)$, the function g is odd. Since $g'(x) = 1$, the derivative of g is continuous for all x. Obviously $g(x) > 0$ for $x > 0$.

(iv) Obviously $G(x) \to \infty$ as $x \to \infty$.

Thus the conclusion of Theorem 13.11 is valid, and we conclude that the van der Pol Equation (13.2) has an essentially unique nontrivial periodic solution. In other words, the equivalent autonomous system

(13.68)
$$\begin{cases} \dfrac{dx}{dt} = y \\ \dfrac{dy}{dt} = \mu(1 - x^2)y - x \end{cases}$$

has a unique closed path in the xy plane.

The differential equation of the paths of the system (13.68) is

(13.69)
$$\frac{dy}{dx} = \frac{\mu(1 - x^2)y - x}{y}.$$

Using the method of isoclines (Section 8.1B) one can obtain the paths defined by (13.69) in the xy plane. The results for $\mu = 0.1$, $\mu = 1$, and $\mu = 10$ are shown in Figure 13.23, (a), (b), and (c), respectively. The limit cycle C in each of these figures is the unique closed path whose existence we have already ascertained on the basis of Theorem 13.11. For $\mu = 0.1$ we note that this limit cycle is very nearly a circle of radius 2. For $\mu = 1$, it has lost its circle-like form and appears rather "baggy"; while for $\mu = 10$, it is very long and narrow.

Exercises

1. Consider the nonlinear autonomous system

$$\frac{dx}{dt} = 4x - 4y - x(x^2 + y^2)$$

$$\frac{dy}{dt} = 4x + 4y - y(x^2 + y^2).$$

(a) Introduce polar coordinates (r,θ) and transform the system to polar coordinate form.

(a) $\mu = 0.1$

(c) $\mu = 10$

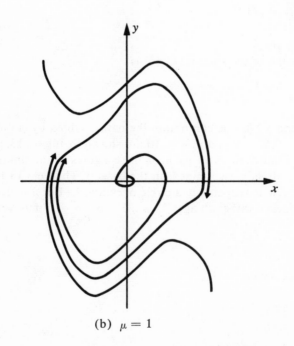

(b) $\mu = 1$

Figure 13.23

(b) Apply the Poincaré-Bendixson Theorem to show that there exists a limit cycle between the circles

$$x^2 + y^2 = 1/4 \quad \text{and} \quad x^2 + y^2 = 16.$$

(c) Find the explicit solutions $x = f(t)$, $y = g(t)$ of the original system. In particular, find "the" periodic solution corresponding to the limit cycle whose existence was ascertained in step (b).

(d) Sketch the limit cycle and at least one of the nonclosed paths.

2. Proceed as in Exercise 1 for the system

$$\frac{dx}{dt} = y + \frac{x}{\sqrt{x^2 + y^2}}[1 - (x^2 + y^2)]$$

$$\frac{dy}{dt} = -x + \frac{y}{\sqrt{x^2 + y^2}}[1 - (x^2 + y^2)].$$

Consider the nonlinear differential equations in Exercises 3 through 7. In each case apply one of the theorems of this section to determine whether or not the differential equation has periodic solutions.

3. $\dfrac{d^2x}{dt^2} + x^4\dfrac{dx}{dt} - \dfrac{dx}{dt} + x = 0.$

4. $\dfrac{d^2x}{dt^2} + \dfrac{dx}{dt} + \left(\dfrac{dx}{dt}\right)^3 + x = 0.$

5. $\dfrac{d^2x}{dt^2} + (x^4 + x^2)\dfrac{dx}{dt} + (x^3 + x) = 0.$

6. $\dfrac{d^2x}{dt^2} + (5x^4 - 6x^2)\dfrac{dx}{dt} + x^3 = 0.$

7. $\dfrac{d^2x}{dt^2} + (x^2 + 1)\dfrac{dx}{dt} + x^3 = 0.$

8. Consider the nonlinear autonomous system

$$\frac{dx}{dt} = x - x^2$$

$$\frac{dy}{dt} = 2y - y^2.$$

(a) Locate, classify (as to type), and list the index of each of the critical points.

(b) Find the equation of the paths of the system in the xy phase plane and sketch several of these paths.

(c) Determine the index of each of the following simple closed curves with respect to the given system. In each case explain how the index was determined.

   (i) $4(x^2 + y^2) = 1$.
   (ii) $100(x^2 + y^2) = 441$.
   (iii) $x^2 + y^2 = 9$.
   (iv) $4(x^2 + y^2) - 8(x + 2y) + 11 = 0$.

13.5   The Method of Kryloff and Bogoliuboff

A. *The First Approximation of Kryloff and Bogoliuboff*

In this section we consider a method of finding an approximate solution of an equation of the form

$$(13.70) \qquad \frac{d^2x}{dt^2} + \omega^2 x + \mu f\left(x, \frac{dx}{dt}\right) = 0,$$

where μ is a sufficiently small parameter so that the nonlinear term $\mu f\left(x, \dfrac{dx}{dt}\right)$ is relatively small. The method which we shall discuss is due to the Russian scientists Kryloff and Bogoliuboff, and it is basically a method of variation of parameters.

If $\mu = 0$ in Equation (13.70), then Equation (13.70) reduces to the linear equation

$$(13.71) \qquad \frac{d^2x}{dt^2} + \omega^2 x = 0.$$

The solution of equation (13.71) may be written

$$(13.72) \qquad x = a\sin(\omega t + \phi),$$

where a and ϕ are constants. The derivative of the solution (13.72) of (13.71) is

$$(13.73) \qquad \frac{dx}{dt} = a\omega\cos(\omega t + \phi).$$

If $\mu \neq 0$ but sufficiently small (that is, $|\mu| << 1$), one might reasonably assume that the nonlinear equation (13.70) also has a solution of the *form* (13.72) with derivative of the *form* (13.73), provided that a and ϕ now be regarded as functions of t rather than constants. This is precisely what we shall do in applying the Kryloff-Bogoliuboff method. That is, we assume a solution of (13.70) of the form

$$(13.74) \qquad x = a(t)\sin[\omega t + \phi(t)],$$

where a and ϕ are functions of t to be determined, such that the derivative of the solution (13.74) is of the form

$$(13.75) \qquad \frac{dx}{dt} = \omega a(t)\cos[\omega t + \phi(t)].$$

Differentiating the assumed solution (13.74), we obtain

$$(13.76) \quad \frac{dx}{dt} = \omega a(t)\cos[\omega t + \phi(t)] + a(t)\frac{d\phi}{dt}\cos[\omega t + \phi(t)] + \frac{da}{dt}\sin[\omega t + \phi(t)].$$

In order for $\dfrac{dx}{dt}$ to be of the desired form (13.75), we see from (13.76) that we must have

$$(13.77) \qquad a(t)\frac{d\phi}{dt}\cos[\omega t + \phi(t)] + \frac{da}{dt}\sin[\omega t + \phi(t)] = 0.$$

Now differentiating the assumed derivative (13.75), we obtain

$$(13.78) \quad \frac{d^2x}{dt^2} = -\omega^2 a(t)\sin[\omega t + \phi(t)] - \omega a(t)\frac{d\phi}{dt}\sin[\omega t + \phi(t)] + \omega\frac{da}{dt}\cos[\omega t + \phi(t)].$$

Substituting the assumed solution (13.74), its assumed derivative (13.75), and the second derivative given by (13.78) into the differential equation (13.70), we obtain

$$-\omega^2 a(t)\sin[\omega t + \phi(t)] - \omega a(t)\frac{d\phi}{dt}\sin[\omega t + \phi(t)] + \omega\frac{da}{dt}\cos[\omega t + \phi(t)]$$

$$+w^2 a(t)\sin[\omega t + \phi(t)] + \mu f\{a(t)\sin[\omega t + \phi(t)], \omega a(t)\cos[\omega t + \phi(t)]\} = 0$$

or

(13.79)
$$\omega\frac{da}{dt}\cos[\omega t + \phi(t)] - \omega a(t)\frac{d\phi}{dt}\sin[\omega t + \phi(t)]$$

$$= -\mu f\{a(t)\sin[\omega t + \phi(t)], \omega a(t)\cos[\omega t + \phi(t)]\}.$$

Let $\theta(t)$ denote $\omega t + \phi(t)$. Then the equations (13.77) and (13.79) may be written

(13.80)
$$\begin{cases} \sin\theta(t)\dfrac{da}{dt} + a(t)\cos\theta(t)\dfrac{d\phi}{dt} = 0 \\[2mm] \omega\cos\theta(t)\dfrac{da}{dt} - \omega a(t)\sin\theta(t)\dfrac{d\phi}{dt} = -\mu f[a(t)\sin\theta(t), \omega a(t)\cos\theta(t)]. \end{cases}$$

Solving the system (13.80) for $\dfrac{da}{dt}$ and $\dfrac{d\phi}{dt}$, we obtain the following equations:

(13.81)
$$\begin{cases} \dfrac{da}{dt} = -\dfrac{\mu}{\omega}f[a(t)\sin\theta(t), \omega a(t)\cos\theta(t)]\cos\theta(t) \\[3mm] \dfrac{d\phi}{dt} = \dfrac{\mu}{\omega a(t)}f[a(t)\sin\theta(t), \omega a(t)\cos\theta(t)]\sin\theta(t). \end{cases}$$

These are the *exact* equations for the functions a and ϕ in the solution of the form (13.74) with derivative of the form (13.75). Note that they are nonlinear and nonautonomous and hence are quite complicated, to say the least. In order to make these equations tractable, we now apply the first approximation of Kryloff and Bogoliuboff.

From Equations (13.81) we see that $\dfrac{da}{dt}$ and $\dfrac{d\phi}{dt}$ are both proportional to the *small* parameter μ. Hence although a and ϕ *are* functions of t, they are *slowly varying functions* of t during a period $T = \dfrac{2\pi}{\omega}$ of t. That is, in a time interval of length $\dfrac{2\pi}{\omega}$, $a(t)$ and $\phi(t)$ are almost constant, while $\theta(t) = \omega t + \phi(t)$ increases by approximately 2π. Thus in the right members of (13.81) we regard $a(t)$ and $\phi(t)$ as constant during an interval of 2π in θ and then replace the functions of the right members of (13.81) by their mean-values over such an interval in θ. This leads to the equations

(13.82)
$$\begin{cases} \dfrac{da}{dt} = -\dfrac{\mu}{2\pi\omega}\int_0^{2\pi} f(a\sin\theta, \omega a\cos\theta)\cos\theta\, d\theta \\[3mm] \dfrac{d\phi}{dt} = \dfrac{\mu}{2\pi\omega a}\int_0^{2\pi} f(a\sin\theta, \omega a\cos\theta)\sin\theta\, d\theta. \end{cases}$$

These are the equations of the *first approximation* of Kryloff and Bogoliuboff for the functions a and ϕ of the solution (13.74). We hasten to point out that we have not rigorously justified this procedure. For a more complete account the reader may consult

Reference (31) or (42). Assuming that the procedure is justifiable for the problem under consideration, a first approximation to the solution of Equation (13.70) is thus given by

(13.74) $$x = a(t)\sin[\omega t + \phi(t)],$$

where $a(t)$ and $\phi(t)$ are determined by equations (13.82).

B. Two Special Cases

Case (i). The term $f\left(x, \dfrac{dx}{dt}\right)$ *depends upon x only.* If $f\left(x, \dfrac{dx}{dt}\right)$ in Equation (13.70) depends upon x only, then the equation reduces to

(13.83) $$\frac{d^2x}{dt^2} + \omega^2 x + \mu f(x) = 0.$$

Then $f(a\sin\theta, \omega a\cos\theta)$ becomes simply $f(a\sin\theta)$, and the Equations (13.82) reduce at once to

(13.84) $$\begin{cases} \dfrac{da}{dt} = -\dfrac{\mu}{2\pi\omega} \displaystyle\int_0^{2\pi} f(a\sin\theta)\cos\theta d\theta \\[3mm] \dfrac{d\phi}{dt} = \dfrac{\mu}{2\pi\omega a} \displaystyle\int_0^{2\pi} f(a\sin\theta)\sin\theta d\theta. \end{cases}$$

Consider the integral in the right member of the first equation of (13.84). Letting $u = a\sin\theta$, we have

$$\int_0^{2\pi} f(a\sin\theta)\cos\theta d\theta = \frac{1}{a}\int_0^0 f(u)du = 0.$$

Thus from the first equation of (13.84) we see that $\dfrac{da}{dt} = 0$, and so the amplitude $a(t)$ is a constant a_0. The second equation of (13.84) now reduces to

(13.85) $$\frac{d\phi}{dt} = F(a_0),$$

where

(13.86) $$F(a_0) = \frac{\mu}{2\pi\omega a_0}\int_0^{2\pi} f(a_0\sin\theta)\sin\theta d\theta.$$

Thus from (13.85), $\phi(t) = F(a_0)t + \phi_0$, where ϕ_0 is a constant of integration.

Hence the first approximation to the solution of (13.83) is given by

(13.87) $$x = a_0\sin\{[F(a_0) + \omega]t + \phi_0\},$$

where the constant $F(a_0)$ is given by (13.86).

Therefore in the special case (13.83) in which the nonlinear term $f(x)$ depends upon x only $\left(\text{and not on } \dfrac{dx}{dt}\right)$, the first approximation to a solution is a periodic oscillation the period of which depends upon the amplitude.

Case (ii). The term $f\left(x, \dfrac{dx}{dt}\right)$ *depends upon* $\dfrac{dx}{dt}$ *only.* In this case Equation (13.70) reduces to

(13.88)
$$\frac{d^2x}{dt^2} + \omega^2x + \mu f\left(\frac{dx}{dt}\right) = 0.$$

Thus $f(a\sin\theta, \omega a\cos\theta)$ becomes simply $f(\omega a\cos\theta)$, and the Equations (13.82) now reduce to

(13.89)
$$\begin{cases} \dfrac{da}{dt} = -\dfrac{\mu}{2\pi\omega}\displaystyle\int_0^{2\pi} f(\omega a\cos\theta)\cos\theta\, d\theta \\[3mm] \dfrac{d\phi}{dt} = \dfrac{\mu}{2\pi\omega a}\displaystyle\int_0^{2\pi} f(\omega a\cos\theta)\sin\theta\, d\theta. \end{cases}$$

Letting $u = \omega a\cos\theta$ in the integral in the right member of the second equation of (13.89), we have

$$\int_0^{2\pi} f(\omega a\cos\theta)\sin\theta\, d\theta = -\frac{1}{\omega a}\int_{\omega a}^{\omega a} f(u)\, du = 0.$$

Thus from the second equation of (13.89) we see that $\dfrac{d\phi}{dt} = 0$, and so $\phi(t)$ is a constant ϕ_0.

Hence the first approximation to the solution of (13.88) is given by

(13.90)
$$x = a(t)\sin[\omega t + \phi_0],$$

where $a(t)$ is given by the first equation of (13.89).

Therefore in the special case (13.88) in which the nonlinear term $f(dx/dt)$ depends upon dx/dt only (and not on x), the first approximation to a **solution** is a nonperiodic oscillation of variable "amplitude" having the same frequency $\left(\dfrac{\omega}{2\pi}\right)$ as that of solution (13.72) of the related linear equation (13.71).

C. Examples

We now apply the equations of the first approximation of Kryloff and Bogoliuboff to several differential equations of the form (13.70).

Example 13.13.   Consider the differential equation

(13.91)
$$\frac{d^2x}{dt^2} + \omega^2x + \mu x^3 = 0,$$

where μ is a small parameter. Here $f(x, dx/dt) = f(x) = x^3$, and hence Equation (13.91) is of the special form (13.83) in which the nonlinear term depends upon x only. Thus the first approximation to the solution of (13.91) is given by (13.87), where $F(a_0)$ is determined by (13.86). Since $f(a_0\sin\theta) = a_0^3 \sin^3\theta$, we see from (13.86) that

$$F(a_0) = \frac{\mu}{2\pi\omega a_0}\int_0^{2\pi} a_0^3 \sin^3\theta \sin\theta\, d\theta$$

$$= \frac{\mu a_0^2}{2\pi\omega}\int_0^{2\pi} \sin^4\theta\, d\theta = \frac{\mu a_0^2}{2\pi\omega}\left(\frac{3\pi}{4}\right) = \frac{3\mu a_0^2}{8\omega}.$$

Thus the first approximation to the solution of Equation (13.91) is given by

(13.92)
$$x = a_0\sin\left[\left(\frac{3\mu a_0^2}{8\omega} + \omega\right)t + \phi_0\right],$$

where a_0 (the amplitude) and ϕ_0 are arbitrary constants. Observe that the period

$$\frac{2\pi}{\dfrac{3\mu a_0^2}{8\omega} + \omega}$$

of the oscillation (13.92) is a function of the amplitude.

Example 13.14. Consider the differential equation

(13.93) $$\frac{d^2x}{dt^2} + \omega^2 x + \mu\left[\left(\frac{dx}{dt}\right)^2 + \left(\frac{dx}{dt}\right)^3\right] = 0,$$

where μ is a small parameter. Here

$$\left(x, \frac{dx}{dt}\right) = f\left(\frac{dx}{dt}\right) = \left(\frac{dx}{dt}\right)^2 + \left(\frac{dx}{dt}\right)^3,$$

and hence equation (13.93) is of the special form (13.88) in which the nonlinear term depends upon $\dfrac{dx}{dt}$ only. Thus the first approximation to the solution of (13.93) is given by (13.90) where the amplitude $a(t)$ is determined from the first equation of (13.89). Since $f(\omega a \cos\theta) = \omega^2 a^2 \cos^2\theta + \omega^3 a^3 \cos^3\theta$, this equation is

$$\frac{da}{dt} = -\frac{\mu}{2\pi\omega}\int_0^{2\pi} (\omega^2 a^2 \cos^2\theta + \omega^3 a^3 \cos^3\theta)\cos\theta\, d\theta$$

or

$$\frac{da}{dt} = -\frac{\mu\omega a^2}{2\pi}\left[\int_0^{2\pi}\cos^3\theta\, d\theta + \omega a\int_0^{2\pi}\cos^4\theta\, d\theta\right].$$

Since

$$\int_0^{2\pi}\cos^3\theta\, d\theta = 0 \quad\text{and}\quad \int_0^{2\pi}\cos^4\theta\, d\theta = \frac{3\pi}{4},$$

this reduces at once to

(13.94) $$\frac{da}{dt} = -\frac{3\mu\omega^2 a^3}{8}.$$

Separating variables in (13.94) and integrating, we obtain

$$\frac{1}{2a^2} = \frac{3\mu\omega^2}{8}t + c,$$

where c is an arbitrary constant. If $a(0) = a_0$, then $c = \dfrac{1}{2a_0^2}$.

We thus have

$$\frac{1}{2a^2} = \frac{3\mu\omega^2}{8}t + \frac{1}{2a_0^2},$$

and so

$$a = 2\sqrt{\frac{a_0^2}{4 + 3\mu\omega^2 a_0^2 t}}.$$

Thus the first approximation to the solution of Equation (13.93) is given by

$$x = 2\sqrt{\frac{a_0^2}{4 + 3\mu\omega^2 a_0^2 t}}\sin[\omega t + \phi_0].$$

Assuming $\mu > 0$, the amplitude of this oscillation tends to zero as $t \to \infty$

Example 13.15. Consider the van der Pol Equation

(13.2)
$$\frac{d^2x}{dt^2} + \mu(x^2 - 1)\frac{dx}{dt} + x = 0,$$

where $0 < \mu << 1$.
This equation is of neither of the special forms (13.83) or (13.88) considered above but rather of the more general form (13.70) where $\omega^2 = 1$ and

$$f\left(x, \frac{dx}{dt}\right) = (x^2 - 1)\frac{dx}{dt}.$$

Therefore the first approximation to the solution of (13.2) is given by (13.74), where $a(t)$ and $\phi(t)$ are determined by Equations (13.82) and where $\omega = 1$.
Since $f(a\sin\theta, a\cos\theta) = (a^2\sin^2\theta - 1) a\cos\theta$, the Equations (13.82) become

$$\begin{cases} \dfrac{da}{dt} = -\dfrac{\mu}{2\pi}\displaystyle\int_0^{2\pi} (a^2\sin^2\theta - 1)a\cos^2\theta d\theta \\[2mm] \dfrac{d\phi}{dt} = \dfrac{\mu}{2\pi a}\displaystyle\int_0^{2\pi} (a^2\sin^2\theta - 1)\, a\cos\theta \sin\theta\, d\theta. \end{cases}$$

Since

$$\int_0^{2\pi} \sin^2\theta \cos^2\theta\, d\theta = \frac{\pi}{4}, \quad \int_0^{2\pi} \cos^2\theta d\theta = \pi,$$

$$\int_0^{2\pi} \sin^3\theta \cos\theta\, d\theta = 0, \quad \text{and} \quad \int_0^{2\pi} \cos\theta \sin\theta\, d\theta = 0,$$

these equations reduce at once to

(13.95)
$$\begin{cases} \dfrac{da}{dt} = \dfrac{\mu a}{2}\left(1 - \dfrac{a^2}{4}\right) \\[2mm] \dfrac{d\phi}{dt} = 0. \end{cases}$$

From the second of Equations (13.95) we see at once that $\phi(t) = \phi_0$, a constant. Thus by (13.74) the first approximation to the solution is given by

$$x = a(t)\sin(t + \phi_0),$$

where $a(t)$ is to be found from the first of Equations (13.95). Separating variables in this equation we obtain

$$\text{(13.96)} \qquad\qquad \frac{da}{a(a^2 - 4)} = -\frac{\mu}{8}dt.$$

Integrating and simplifying we find that

$$\frac{a^2 - 4}{a^2} = ce^{-\mu t}$$

and hence

$$a^2 = \frac{4}{1 - ce^{-\mu t}}.$$

If $a(0) = a_0 > 0$, then $c = \dfrac{a_0^2 - 4}{a_0^2}$

and hence

$$a^2 = \frac{4}{1 - \left(\dfrac{a_0^2 - 4}{a_0^2}\right)e^{-\mu t}} = \frac{a_0^2 e^{\mu t}}{1 + \dfrac{a_0^2}{4}(e^{\mu t} - 1)}.$$

Thus the first approximation to the solution of the van der Pol Equation (13.2) for $0 < \mu << 1$ is given by

$$\text{(13.97)} \qquad\qquad x = \frac{a_0 e^{\frac{\mu}{2}t}}{\sqrt{1 + \dfrac{a_0^2}{4}(e^{\mu t} - 1)}} \sin(t + \phi_0),$$

where a_0 is the initial value of the amplitude.

If $a_0 = 2$, the first approximation (13.97) reduces to the *periodic* function defined by

$$\text{(13.98)} \qquad\qquad x = 2\sin(t + \phi_0)$$

with constant amplitude 2.

If $0 < a_0 < 2$ or if $a_0 > 2$, we see that

$$\lim_{t \to \infty} a(t) = \lim_{t \to \infty} \frac{a_0 e^{\frac{\mu}{2}t}}{\sqrt{1 + \dfrac{a_0^2}{4}(e^{\mu t} - 1)}} = 2.$$

Thus for any finite $a_0 > 0$ except $a_0 = 2$ the nonperiodic oscillation given by (13.97) tends to the periodic oscillation given by (13.98) as $t \to \infty$.

Now we must remember that the formula (13.97) is only a first *approximation* to the exact solution of equation (13.2). Hence our above observations give only an approximate appraisal of the actual situation. Nevertheless, if $0 < \mu << 1$, they indicate the actual situation quite well. The equation (13.2) has only *one* type of nontrivial periodic solutions, and these periodic solutions are given approximately by (13.98). All other nontrivial solutions of equation (13.2) are nonperiodic oscillations which tend to one of the aforementioned periodic solutions as $t \to \infty$. These nonperiodic solutions are of course given approximately by (13.97).

In the previous section of this chapter we studied the phase plane paths associated with the van der Pol equation (13.2). We recall that there is a unique closed path, a limit cycle which all nonclosed paths approach as $t \to \infty$. For $0 < \mu << 1$, this limit cycle is approximately a circle of radius 2, and the nonclosed paths approach this nearly circular path spirally as $t \to \infty$. The limit cycle is represented approximately by the periodic oscillations (13.98) above, while the spiral paths are represented approximately by the nonperiodic oscillations (13.97).

Exercises

Use the method of Kryloff and Bogoliuboff to find a first approximation to the solution of each of the differential equations in Exercises 1 through 6. In each case assume that $0 < \mu << 1$ and that the initial value of the "amplitude" $a(t)$ of the "solution" is given by $a_0 > 0$.

1. $\dfrac{d^2x}{dt^2} + \omega^2 x + \mu x^5 = 0.$

2. $\dfrac{d^2x}{dt^2} + x + \mu \dfrac{dx}{dt} \left| \dfrac{dx}{dt} \right| = 0.$

3. $\dfrac{d^2x}{dt^2} + \mu \left[\left(\dfrac{dx}{dt} \right)^3 + x^3 \right] + \omega^2 x = 0.$

4. $\dfrac{d^2x}{dt^2} + \omega^2 x + \mu(x^2 + 1)\dfrac{dx}{dt} = 0.$

5. $\dfrac{d^2x}{dt^2} + \omega^2 x + \mu \left(x^3 + \dfrac{dx}{dt} \right) = 0.$

6. $\dfrac{d^2x}{dt^2} + x + \mu \left(\dfrac{8}{9}x^4 - 1 \right)\dfrac{dx}{dt} = 0.$

SUGGESTED READING

I. Basic Theory:
   Kaplan (30)

II. Theory, Methods, and Applications:
   Andronow and Chaikin (2)   McLachlan (39)
   Cunningham (15)   Minorsky (42)
   Kryloff and Bogoliuboff (31)   Stoker (51)
   Ku (32)   Struble (52)
   Lawden (33)

III. Advanced Theory:
   Birkhoff and Rota (6)   Hurewicz (25)
   Cesari (9)   Lefschetz (35)
   Coddington and Levinson (13)   Nemytskii and Stepanov (43)
   Friedrichs (18)   Tricomi (54)

14

PARTIAL DIFFERENTIAL EQUATIONS

In the previous chapters of this text we have concentrated upon ordinary differential equations. In this final chapter we shall give a brief introduction to partial differential equations. The subject of partial differential equations is a vast one, and an entire book of this size could be devoted to an introduction to it. In this short chapter we shall merely introduce certain basic concepts of partial differential equations and present a basic method of solution which is very useful in many applied problems.

14.1 Some Basic Concepts and Examples

A. Partial Differential Equations and Their Solutions

Let us first recall that a partial differential equation is a differential equation which involves partial derivatives of one or more dependent variables with respect to one or more independent variables. We shall say that a *solution* of a partial differential equation is an explicit or implicit relation between the variables which does not contain derivatives and which identically satisfies the equation. In certain very simple cases a solution can be obtained immediately.

For example, consider the first-order partial differential equation

$$(14.1) \qquad \frac{\partial u}{\partial x} = x^2 + y^2,$$

in which u is the dependent variable and x and y are independent variables. We have already solved equations of this type in Chapter 2. The solution is

$$u = \int (x^2 + y^2)\partial x + \phi(y),$$

where $\int (x^2 + y^2)\partial x$ indicates a "partial integration" with respect to x, holding y constant, and ϕ is an arbitrary function of y only. Thus the solution of Equation (14.1) is

(14.2) $$u = \frac{x^3}{3} + xy^2 + \phi(y),$$

where ϕ is an arbitrary function of y.

As a second example, consider the second-order partial differential equation

(14.3) $$\frac{\partial^2 u}{\partial y \partial x} = x^3 - y.$$

We first write this in the form

$$\frac{\partial}{\partial y}\left(\frac{\partial u}{\partial x}\right) = x^3 - y$$

and integrate partially with respect to y, holding x constant, to obtain

$$\frac{\partial u}{\partial x} = x^3 y - \frac{y^2}{2} + \phi(x),$$

where ϕ is an arbitrary function of x. We now integrate this result partially with respect to x, holding y constant, and so obtain the solution of Equation (14.3) in the form

(14.4) $$u = \frac{x^4 y}{4} - \frac{xy^2}{2} + f(x) + g(y),$$

where f defined by $f(x) = \int \phi(x)dx$ is an arbitrary function of x and g is an arbitrary function of y.

As a result of these two simple examples, we note that whereas ordinary differential equations have solutions which involve arbitrary *constants*, partial differential equations have solutions which involve arbitrary *functions*. In particular, we note that the solution (14.2) of the *first-order* partial differential equation (14.1) contains *one* arbitrary function, and the solution (14.4) of the *second-order* partial differential equation (14.3) contains *two* arbitrary functions.

Let us now consider the nature of a typical mathematical problem which involves a partial differential equation and which originated in the mathematical formulation of some physical problem. Such a problem involves not only the partial differential equation itself, but also certain supplementary conditions (so-called *boundary conditions* or *initial conditions* or both). The number and nature of these conditions depend upon the nature of the physical problem from which the mathematical problem originated. The solution of the problem must satisfy both the partial differential equation and these supplementary conditions. In other words, the solution of the whole problem (differential equation plus conditions) is a *particular* solution of the differential equation of the problem. In Section 2 of this chapter we shall consider a basic method which may be employed to obtain this partcular solution in certain cases. First, however, we consider briefly the class of partial differential equations which most frequently occurs in such problems. This is the class of so-called linear partial differential equations of the second order.

B. *Linear Partial Differential Equations of the Second-Order*

The general linear partial differential equation of the second order in two independent variables x and y is an equation of the form

$$(14.5) \qquad A\frac{\partial^2 u}{\partial x^2} + B\frac{\partial^2 u}{\partial x \partial y} + C\frac{\partial^2 u}{\partial y^2} + D\frac{\partial u}{\partial x} + E\frac{\partial u}{\partial y} + Fu = G,$$

where A, B, C, D, E, F, and G are functions of x and y. If $G(x,y) = 0$ for all (x,y), the equation (14.5) reduces to

$$(14.6) \qquad A\frac{\partial^2 u}{\partial x^2} + B\frac{\partial^2 u}{\partial x \partial y} + C\frac{\partial^2 u}{\partial y^2} + D\frac{\partial u}{\partial x} + E\frac{\partial u}{\partial y} + Fu = 0.$$

Concerning solutions of the equation (14.6), we state the following basic theorem, which is analogous to Theorem 11.5 for linear ordinary differential equations.

THEOREM 14.1.

Hypothesis. Let $f_1, f_2, \ldots, f_n$ be n solutions of Equation (14.6) in a region R of the xy plane.

Conclusion. The linear combination $c_1 f_1 + c_2 f_2 + \cdots + c_n f_n$, where $c_1, c_2, \ldots, c_n$ are arbitrary constants, is also a solution of Equation (14.6) in the region R.

Extending this, it may be shown that the following theorem is also valid.

THEOREM 14.2.

Hypothesis. (*i*). Let $f_1, f_2, \ldots, f_n, \ldots$ be an infinite set of solutions of Equation (14.6) in a region R of the xy plane.
(ii) Suppose the infinite series

$$\sum_{n=1}^{\infty} f_n = f_1 + f_2 + \cdots + f_n + \cdots.$$

converges to f in R, and suppose this series may be differentiated term by term in R to obtain the various derivatives (of f) which appear in the equation (14.6).

Conclusion. The function f (defined by $f = \sum_{n=1}^{\infty} f_n$) is also a solution of equation (14.6) in R.

We now consider an important special class of second-order linear partial differential equations, the so-called *homogeneous* linear equations of the second order *with constant coefficients.* An equation of this class is of the form

$$(14.7) \qquad a\frac{\partial^2 u}{\partial x^2} + b\frac{\partial^2 u}{\partial x \partial y} + c\frac{\partial^2 u}{\partial y^2} = 0,$$

where a, b, and c are constants. The word *homogeneous* here refers to the fact that all terms in (14.7) contain derivatives of the *same* order (the second).

We shall seek solutions of (14.7) of the form

(14.8) $$u = f(y + mx),$$

where f is an arbitrary function of its argument and m is a constant. Differentiating (14.8), we obtain

(14.9)
$$\frac{\partial^2 u}{\partial x^2} = m^2 f''(y + mx),$$

$$\frac{\partial^2 u}{\partial x \partial y} = m f''(y + mx),$$

$$\frac{\partial^2 u}{\partial y^2} = f''(y + mx).$$

Substituting (14.9) into the equation (14.7), we obtain

$$am^2 f''(y + mx) + bm f''(y + mx) + c f''(y + mx) = 0$$

or

$$f''(y + mx)[am^2 + bm + c] = 0.$$

Thus $f(y + mx)$ will be a solution of (14.7) if m satisfies the quadratic equation

(14.10) $$am^2 + bm + c = 0.$$

We now consider the following four cases of Equation (14.7).
(i) $a \neq 0$, and the roots of the quadratic equation (14.10) are distinct.
(ii) $a \neq 0$, and the roots of (14.10) are equal.
(iii) $a = 0$, $b \neq 0$.
(iv) $a = 0$, $b = 0$, $c \neq 0$.

In case (i) let the distinct roots of (14.10) be m_1 and m_2. Then the equation (14.7) has the solutions

$$f(y + m_1 x) \quad \text{and} \quad g(y + m_2 x),$$

where f and g are arbitrary functions of their respective arguments. Applying Theorem 14.1, we see that

(14.11) $$f(y + m_1 x) + g(y + m_2 x)$$

is a solution of equation (14.7).

In case (ii), let the double root of (14.10) be m_1. Then the equation (14.7) has the solution $f(y + m_1 x)$, where f is an arbitrary function of its argument. Further, it can be shown that in this case Equation (14.7) also has the solution $xg(y + m_1 x)$, where g is an arbitrary function of its argument. Hence by Theorem 14.1 we see that

(14.12) $$f(y + m_1 x) + xg(y + m_1 x)$$

is a solution of (14.7).

In case (iii), the quadratic equation (14.10) reduces to $bm + c = 0$ and hence has only one root. Denoting this root by m_1, Equation (14.7) has the solution $f(y + m_1 x)$, where *f* is an arbitrary function of its argument. Further, it can be verified at once that in this case *g*(*x*), where *g* is an arbitrary function of *x* only, is also a solution of Equation (14.7). Thus by Theorem 14.1, we see that

(14.13) $$f(y + m_1 x) + g(x)$$

is a solution of (14.7).

Finally, in case (iv), the equation (14.10) reduces to *c* = 0, which is impossible. Thus in this case there exist no solutions of the form (14.8). However, in this case the differential equation (14.7) is simply

$$c\frac{\partial^2 u}{\partial y^2} = 0 \quad \text{or} \quad \frac{\partial}{\partial y}\left(\frac{\partial u}{\partial y}\right) = 0.$$

Integrating partially with respect to *y* twice in succession, we obtain $u = f(x) + yg(x)$, where *f* and *g* are arbitrary functions of *x* only. Thus in this case

(14.14) $$f(x) + yg(x)$$

is a solution of (14.7).

In each of the four cases under consideration we have obtained a solution of (14.7) which involves two arbitrary functions. Every equation of the form (14.7) with constant coefficients is in one and only one of the four categories covered by cases (i) through (iv). Thus the equation (14.7) always has a solution which involves two arbitrary functions. This solution is given by (14.11) in case (i), by (14.12) in case (ii), by (14.13) in case (iii), and by (14.14) in case (iv).

We now consider two simple examples.

Example 14.1. Find a solution of

(14.15) $$\frac{\partial^2 u}{\partial x^2} - 5\frac{\partial^2 u}{\partial x \partial y} + 6\frac{\partial^2 u}{\partial y^2} = 0$$

which contains two arbitrary functions.

Solution. The quadratic equation (14.10) corresponding to the differential equation (14.15) is

$$m^2 - 5m + 6 = 0,$$

and this equation has the distinct roots $m_1 = 2$ and $m_2 = 3$. Therefore this is an example of case (i). Hence using (14.11) we see that

$$u = f(y + 2x) + g(y + 3x)$$

is a solution of (14.15) which contains two arbitrary functions.

Example 14.2. Find a solution of

(14.16) $$\frac{\partial^2 u}{\partial x^2} - 4\frac{\partial^2 u}{\partial x \partial y} + 4\frac{\partial^2 u}{\partial y^2} = 0$$

which contains two arbitrary functions.

Solution.   The quadratic equation (14.10) corresponding to the differential equation (14.16) is

$$m^2 - 4m + 4 = 0,$$

and this equation has the double root $m_1 = 2$. Therefore this is an example of case (ii). Hence using (14.12) we see that

$$u = f(y + 2x) + xg(y + 2x)$$

is a solution of (14.16) which contains two arbitrary functions.

We close this section by classifying equations of the form (14.6) in the special case in which the coefficients A, B, C, D, E, and F are real constants. We shall illustrate this classification with certain of the famous equations of mathematical physics.

DEFINITION.   The second-order linear partial differential equation

(14.6) $$A\frac{\partial^2 u}{\partial x^2} + B\frac{\partial^2 u}{\partial x \partial y} + C\frac{\partial^2 u}{\partial y^2} + D\frac{\partial u}{\partial x} + E\frac{\partial u}{\partial y} + Fu = 0,$$

where A, B, C, D, E, and F are real constants is said to be
   (i)   *hyperbolic* if $B^2 - 4AC > 0$,
   (ii)   *parabolic* if $B^2 - 4AC = 0$,
and
   (iii)   *elliptic* if $B^2 - 4AC < 0$.

Example 14.3.   The equation

(14.17) $$\frac{\partial^2 u}{\partial x^2} - \frac{\partial^2 u}{\partial y^2} = 0$$

is hyperbolic, since $A = 1$, $B = 0$, $C = -1$, and $B^2 - 4AC = 4 > 0$. Equation (14.17) is a special case of the so-called one-dimensional *wave equation*, which is satisfied by the small transverse displacements of the points of a vibrating string. Observing that Equation (14.17) is a homogeneous linear equation with constant coefficients, we find at once that it has the solution

$$u = f(y + x) + g(y - x),$$

where f and g are arbitrary functions of their respective arguments.

Example 14.4.   The equation

(14.18) $$\frac{\partial^2 u}{\partial x^2} - \frac{\partial u}{\partial y} = 0$$

is parabolic, since $A = 1$, $B = C = 0$, and $B^2 - 4AC = 0$. Equation (14.18) is a special case of the one-dimensional *heat equation* (or *diffusion equation*), which is satisfied by the temperature at a point of a homogeneous rod. We observe that Equation (14.18) is not homogeneous.

Example 14.5. The equation

(14.19) $$\frac{\partial^2 u}{\partial x^2} + \frac{\partial^2 u}{\partial y^2} = 0$$

is elliptic, since $A = 1$, $B = 0$, $C = 1$, and $B^2 - 4AC = -4 < 0$. Equation (14.19) is the so-called two-dimensional *Laplace Equation*, which is satisfied by the steady-state temperature at points of a thin rectangular plate. Observing that Equation (14.19) is a homogeneous linear equation with constant coefficients, we find at once that it has the solution

$$u = f(y + ix) + g(y - ix),$$

where f and g are arbitrary functions of their respective arguments.

Exercises

For each of the differential equations in Exercises 1 through 10 find a solution which contains two arbitrary functions. In each case determine whether the equation is hyperbolic, parabolic, or elliptic.

1. $\dfrac{\partial^2 u}{\partial x^2} - 7\dfrac{\partial^2 u}{\partial x \partial y} + \dfrac{\partial^2 u}{\partial y^2} = 0.$

2. $\dfrac{\partial^2 u}{\partial x^2} + \dfrac{\partial^2 u}{\partial x \partial y} - 6\dfrac{\partial^2 u}{\partial y^2} = 0.$

3. $\dfrac{\partial^2 u}{\partial x^2} + 6\dfrac{\partial^2 u}{\partial x \partial y} + 9\dfrac{\partial^2 u}{\partial y^2} = 0.$

4. $4\dfrac{\partial^2 u}{\partial x^2} - 4\dfrac{\partial^2 u}{\partial x \partial y} + \dfrac{\partial^2 u}{\partial y^2} = 0.$

5. $\dfrac{\partial^2 u}{\partial x^2} + \dfrac{\partial^2 u}{\partial y^2} = 0.$

6. $2\dfrac{\partial^2 u}{\partial x \partial y} + 3\dfrac{\partial^2 u}{\partial y^2} = 0.$

7. $\dfrac{\partial^2 u}{\partial x^2} - 2\dfrac{\partial^2 u}{\partial x \partial y} = 0.$

8. $\dfrac{\partial^2 u}{\partial x^2} + 2\dfrac{\partial^2 u}{\partial x \partial y} + 5\dfrac{\partial^2 u}{\partial y^2} = 0.$

9. $8\dfrac{\partial^2 u}{\partial x^2} - 2\dfrac{\partial^2 u}{\partial x \partial y} - 3\dfrac{\partial^2 u}{\partial y^2} = 0.$

10. $2\dfrac{\partial^2 u}{\partial x^2} - 2\dfrac{\partial^2 u}{\partial x \partial y} + 5\dfrac{\partial^2 u}{\partial y^2} = 0.$

11. Consider the equation

$$A\frac{\partial^2 u}{\partial x^2} + B\frac{\partial^2 u}{\partial x \partial y} + C\frac{\partial^2 u}{\partial y^2} + D\frac{\partial u}{\partial x} + E\frac{\partial u}{\partial y} + Fu = 0,$$

where A, B, C, D, E, and F are functions of x and y. Extending the definition of the text, we say that this equation is

(i) hyperbolic at all points at which $B^2 - 4AC > 0$,
(ii) parabolic at all points at which $B^2 - 4AC = 0$, and
(iii) elliptic at all points at which $B^2 - 4AC < 0$.

(a) Show that the equation

$$(x^2 - 1)\frac{\partial^2 u}{\partial x^2} + 2y\frac{\partial^2 u}{\partial x \partial y} - \frac{\partial^2 u}{\partial y^2} = 0$$

is hyperbolic for all (x,y) outside the region bounded by the circle $x^2 + y^2 = 1$, parabolic on the boundary of this region, and elliptic for all (x,y) inside this region.

(b) Determine all points (x,y) at which the equation

$$\frac{\partial^2 u}{\partial x^2} + x\frac{\partial^2 u}{\partial x \partial y} + y\frac{\partial^2 u}{\partial y^2} - xy\frac{\partial u}{\partial x} = 0$$

(i) is hyperbolic,
(ii) is parabolic,
(iii) is elliptic.

14.2   The Method of Separation of Variables

A. Introduction

In this section we introduce the so-called *method of separation of variables*. This is a basic method which is very powerful for obtaining solutions of certain problems involving partial differential equations. Although the class of problems to which the method applies is relatively small, it nevertheless includes many problems of great physical interest.

We have already pointed out that the mathematical statement of such a problem involves (i) a partial differential equation and (ii) certain supplementary conditions. The solution of the problem is a function which satisfies both the equation and the various conditions, and the task before us is to find such a function. Let us recall a common procedure in solving analogous problems involving *ordinary* differential equations and supplementary conditions. In such a problem we first find the general solution of the ordinary differential equation and then apply the supplementary conditions, one at a time, to obtain the particular solution which satisfies them. Should we attempt to follow a similar procedure in problems in which the differential equation is *partial* instead of ordinary? Generally speaking, the answer is "no." In the first place, it is often impossible to obtain a "general" solution of the partial differential equation; and in the second place, even if such a solution can be found, it is usually impossible to apply the supplementary conditions to it. How then should we proceed? Instead of first finding the most general solution and then specializing it to obtain the particular solution desired, we shall first find particular solutions which satisfy *some* of the supplementary conditions and then combine these particular solutions in some manner to obtain a solution which satisfies *all* of the supplementary conditions. That is, instead of "breaking down" to the desired particular solution, the method of separation of variables in partial differential equations is one of "building up" to it.

In attempting to apply the method of separation of variables, to a partial differential equations problem, one makes a certain basic assumption at the outset. If the partial differential equation involves n independent variables $x_1, x_2, \ldots, x_n$, one first *assumes* that the equation possesses product solutions of the form $X_1 X_2 \ldots X_n$, where X_i is a function of x_i only, $(i = 1, 2, \ldots, n)$. If the method actually does apply to the problem, then this basic assumption will produce n ordinary differential equations, one in each of the unknown functions X_i, $(i = 1, 2, \ldots, n)$. Certain of the supplementary conditions of the problem lead to supplementary conditions which must be satisfied by certain of the functions X_i. Thus at this stage of the method, one must solve n problems in ordinary differential equations, some of which involve initial or boundary conditions. The solutions of these n problems produce *particular* solutions of the form $X_1 X_2 \ldots X_n$ which satisfy *some* of the supplementary conditions of the original problem. One must now attempt to combine these particular solutions in some manner to produce a solution which satisfies *all* of the original supplementary conditions. One does this by first applying Theorem 14.2 to obtain a series solution and then applying the remaining supplementary conditions to this series solution.

We point out that the procedure outlined in the preceding paragraph is a strictly formal one. We shall illustrate it in considerable detail in parts B, C, and D of this section, and our treatment there will again be of a strictly formal nature. We have not made, and shall not make, any attempt to justify the procedure; but at least we should be aware of some of the questions with which a rigorous treatment would be concerned. In the first place, there is the question of *existence*. Does a solution of the given partial differential equations problem actually exist? In analogous problems involving ordinary differential equations we have seen that existence theorems are available which often enable us to answer questions of this type. Existence theorems for problems in partial differential equations are also known (See Greenspan, Reference (19), for example), and these theorems can often be applied to answer the existence question. But even if such a theorem answers this question in the affirmative, how do we know that a solution can be "built up" by the method which we have outlined? Even if the method seems "to work" formally, the various steps require justification. In particular, questions of convergence enter the problem, and a rigorous justification of the method involves a careful study of these convergence questions. Finally, assuming that each step can be justified and that the final result is indeed a solution, the question of *uniqueness* enters the picture. Is the solution obtained the *only* solution of the problem? Uniqueness theorems are known which can often be applied to answer this question.

In summary, our treatment of the method of separation of variables is a *formal* one. In a rigorous treatment one must show (i) that the formal "solution" obtained actually does satisfy both the partial differential equation and all of the supplementary conditions, and (ii) that the solution thus justified is the only solution of the problem.

B. Example: The Vibrating String Problem

We now illustrate the method of separation of variables by applying it to obtain a formal solution of the so-called *vibrating string problem*.

The Physical Problem.   Consider a tightly stretched elastic string the ends of which are fixed on the x axis at $x = 0$ and $x = L$. Suppose that for each x in the interval $0 < x < L$

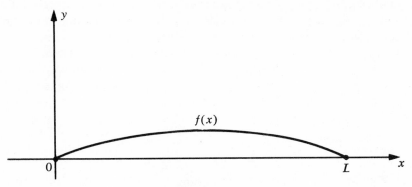

Figure 14.1

the string is displaced into the xy plane and that for each such x the displacement from the x axis is given by $f(x)$, where f is a known function of x (see Figure 14.1).

Suppose that at $t = 0$ the string is released from the initial position defined by $f(x)$ with an initial velocity given at each point of the interval $0 \leq x \leq L$ by $g(x)$, where g is a known function of x. Obviously the string will vibrate, and its displacement in the y direction at any point x at any time t will be a function of both x and t. We seek to find this displacement as a function of x and t; we denote it by y or $y(x,t)$.

We now make certain assumptions concerning the string, its vibrations, and its surroundings. To begin with, we assume that the string is perfectly flexible, is of constant linear density ρ, and is of•constant tension T at all times. Concerning the vibrations, we assume that the motion is confined to the xy plane and that each point on the string moves on a straight line perpendicular to the x axis as the string vibrates. Further, we assume that the displacement y at each point of the string is small compared to the length L and that the angle between the string and the x axis at each point is also sufficiently small. Finally, we assume that no external forces (such as damping forces, for example) act upon the string.

Although these assumptions are not actually valid in any physical problem, nevertheless they are approximately satisfied in many cases. They are made in order to make the resulting mathematical problem more tractable. With these assumptions, then, the problem is to find the displacement y as a function of x and t.

The Mathematical Problem.   Under the assumptions stated it can be shown that the displacement y satisfies the *partial differential equation,*

(14.20)
$$\alpha^2 \frac{\partial^2 y}{\partial x^2} = \frac{\partial^2 y}{\partial t^2},$$

where $\alpha^2 = T/\rho$. This is the one-dimensional wave equation, a special case of which we have already studied in Example 14.3. Since our primary concern here is to illustrate the method of separation of variables, we omit the derivation of the equation.†

Since the ends of the string are fixed at $x = 0$ and $x = L$ for all time t, the displacement y must satisfy the *boundary conditions*

(14.21)
$$y(0,t) = 0, \quad 0 \leq t < \infty;$$
$$y(L,t) = 0, \quad 0 \leq t < \infty.$$

†See, for example, Miller, Reference (40).

At $t = 0$ the string is released from the initial position defined by $f(x)$, $0 \leq x \leq L$, with initial velocity given by $g(x)$, $0 \leq x \leq L$. Thus the displacement y must also satisfy the *initial conditions*

(14.22)
$$y(x,0) = f(x), \qquad 0 \leq x \leq L;$$
$$\frac{\partial y(x,0)}{\partial t} = g(x), \qquad 0 \leq x \leq L.$$

This, then, is our problem. We must find a function y of x and t which satisfies the partial differential equation (14.20), the boundary conditions (14.21), and the initial conditions (14.22).

Solution. We apply the method of separation of variables. We first make the basic assumption that the differential equation (14.20) has product solutions of the form XT, where X is a function of x only and T is a function of t only. To emphasize this, we write

(14.23)
$$y(x,t) = X(x)T(t).$$

We now differentiate (14.23) and substitute into the differential equation (14.20). Differentiating, we find

$$\frac{\partial^2 y}{\partial x^2} = T\frac{d^2X}{dx^2} \quad \text{and} \quad \frac{\partial^2 y}{\partial t^2} = X\frac{d^2T}{dt^2};$$

and substituting, we obtain

$$\alpha^2 T\frac{d^2X}{dx^2} = X\frac{d^2T}{dt^2}.$$

From this we obtain at once

(14.24)
$$\alpha^2 \frac{\dfrac{d^2X}{dx^2}}{X} = \frac{\dfrac{d^2T}{dt^2}}{T}.$$

Since X is a function of x only, the left member of (14.24) is also a function of x only and hence is independent of t. Further, since T is a function of t only, the right member of (14.24) is also a function of t only and hence is independent of x. Since one of the two equal expressions in (14.24) is independent of t and the other one is independent of x, both of them must be equal to a constant k. That is, we have

$$\alpha^2 \frac{\dfrac{d^2X}{dx^2}}{X} = k \quad \text{and} \quad \frac{\dfrac{d^2T}{dt^2}}{T} = k.$$

From this we obtain the two ordinary differential equations

(14.25)
$$\frac{d^2X}{dx^2} - \frac{k}{\alpha^2}X = 0$$

and

(14.26)
$$\frac{d^2T}{dt^2} - kT = 0.$$

Let us now consider the boundary conditions (14.21). Since $y(x,t) = X(x)T(t)$, we see that $y(0,t) = X(0)T(t)$ and $y(L,t) = X(L)T(t)$. Thus the boundary conditions (14.21) take the forms

$$X(0)T(t) = 0, \qquad 0 \leq t < \infty ;$$
$$X(L)T(t) = 0, \qquad 0 \leq t < \infty .$$

Since $T(t) = 0$, $0 \leq t < \infty$, would reduce the assumed solution (14.23) to the trivial solution of (14.20), we must have

(14.27) $X(0) = 0$ and $X(L) = 0.$

Thus the function X in the assumed solution (14.23) must satisfy both the ordinary differential equation (14.25) and the boundary conditions (14.27). That is, the function X must be a nontrivial solution of the Sturm-Liouville Problem

(14.25) $$\frac{d^2X}{dx^2} - \frac{k}{\alpha^2}X = 0,$$

(14.27) $$X(0) = 0, \quad X(L) = 0.$$

We have already solved a special case of this problem in Example 12.3 of Chapter 12. Our procedure here will parallel the treatment in that example. We must first find the general solution of the differential equation (14.25). The form of this general solution depends upon whether $k = 0$, $k > 0$, or $k < 0$.

If $k = 0$, the general solution of (14.25) is of the form

(14.28) $$X = c_1 + c_2 x.$$

We apply the boundary conditions (14.27) to the solution (14.28). The condition $X(0) = 0$ requires that $c_1 = 0$. The condition $X(L) = 0$ becomes $c_1 + c_2 L = 0$. Since $c_1 = 0$, this requires that $c_2 = 0$ also. Thus the solution (14.28) reduces to the trivial solution.

If $k > 0$, the general solution of (14.25) is of the form

(14.29) $$X = c_1 e^{\frac{\sqrt{k}x}{\alpha}} + c_2 e^{-\frac{\sqrt{k}x}{\alpha}}.$$

Applying the boundary conditions (14.27) to the solution (14.29), we obtain the system of equations

(14.30) $$c_1 + c_2 = 0,$$
$$c_1 e^{\frac{\sqrt{k}L}{\alpha}} + c_2 e^{-\frac{\sqrt{k}L}{\alpha}} = 0.$$

To obtain nontrivial solutions of this system, we must have

$$\begin{vmatrix} 1 & 1 \\ e^{\frac{\sqrt{k}L}{\alpha}} & e^{-\frac{\sqrt{k}L}{\alpha}} \end{vmatrix} = 0.$$

But this implies that $e^{\frac{\sqrt{k}L}{\alpha}} = e^{-\frac{\sqrt{k}L}{\alpha}}$ and hence that $k = 0$, contrary to our assumption in this case. Thus the system (14.30) has no nontrivial solutions, and so the solution (14.29) also reduces to the trivial solution.

Finally, if $k < 0$, the general solution of (14.25) is of the form

$$(14.31) \qquad X = c_1\sin\frac{\sqrt{-k}x}{\alpha} + c_2\cos\frac{\sqrt{-k}x}{\alpha}.$$

Applying the boundary conditions (14.27) to the solution (14.31), we obtain

$$c_2 = 0$$

and

$$c_1\sin\frac{\sqrt{-k}L}{\alpha} + c_2\cos\frac{\sqrt{-k}L}{\alpha} = 0.$$

Since $c_2 = 0$, the latter condition reduces to

$$c_1\sin\frac{\sqrt{-k}L}{\alpha} = 0.$$

Thus to obtain nontrivial solutions of the form (14.31), we must have

$$\frac{\sqrt{-k}L}{\alpha} = n\pi, \qquad (n = 1, 2, 3, \ldots),$$

and so

$$(14.32) \qquad k = -\frac{n^2\pi^2\alpha^2}{L^2}, \qquad (n = 1, 2, 3, \ldots).$$

We thus find that the constant k must be a negative number of the form (14.32). We recognize these values of k as the characteristic values of the Sturm-Liouville Problem under consideration. The corresponding nontrivial solutions (the characteristic functions) of the problem are then

$$(14.33) \qquad X_n = c_n\sin\frac{n\pi x}{L}, \qquad (n = 1, 2, 3, \ldots),$$

where the c_n, $(n = 1, 2, 3, \ldots)$, are arbitrary constants. We thus find that the function X in the assumed solution (14.23) must be of the form (14.33). That is, corresponding to each positive integral value of n, we obtain functions X_n of the form (14.33) which will serve as the function X in the product solution (14.23).

Let us now return to the differential equation (14.26) which the function T in (14.23) must satisfy. Since k must be of the form (14.32), the differential equation (14.26) becomes

$$\frac{d^2T}{dt^2} + \frac{n^2\pi^2\alpha^2}{L^2}T = 0,$$

where $n = 1, 2, 3, \ldots$. For each such value of n, this differential equation has solutions of the form

$$(14.34) \qquad T_n = c_{n,1}\sin\frac{n\pi\alpha t}{L} + c_{n,2}\cos\frac{n\pi\alpha t}{L}, \qquad (n = 1, 2, 3, \ldots),$$

where the $c_{n,1}$ and $c_{n,2}$, $(n = 1, 2, 3, \ldots)$, are arbitrary constants. Thus the function T in the assumed solution (14.23) must be of the form (14.34). That is, corresponding to each positive integral value of n, we obtain functions T_n of the form (14.34) which will serve as the function T in the product solution (14.23).

Therefore, corresponding to each positive integral value of n, $(n = 1, 2, 3, \ldots)$, we obtain solutions

$$X_n T_n = \left[c_n \sin\frac{n\pi x}{L} \right]\left[c_{n,1}\sin\frac{n\pi\alpha t}{L} + c_{n,2}\cos\frac{n\pi\alpha t}{L} \right]$$

which have the product form (14.23).

We set $a_n = c_n c_{n,1}$ and $b_n = c_n c_{n,2}$, $(n = 1, 2, 3, \ldots)$, and write these solutions as

$$(14.35) \qquad y_n(x,t) = \left[\sin\frac{n\pi x}{L} \right]\left[a_n\sin\frac{n\pi\alpha t}{L} + b_n\cos\frac{n\pi\alpha t}{L} \right], \qquad (n = 1, 2, 3, \ldots).$$

We point out that each one of these solutions (14.35) satisfies both the partial differential equation (14.20) and the two boundary conditions (14.21) for all values of the constants a_n and b_n.

We must now try to satisfy the two initial conditions (14.22). In general no single one of the solutions (14.35) will satisfy these conditions. For example, if we apply the first initial condition (14.22) to a solution of the form (14.35) we must have

$$b_n\sin\frac{n\pi x}{L} = f(x), \qquad 0 \le x \le L,$$

where n is some positive integer; and this is clearly impossible unless f happens to be a sine function of the form $A\sin\frac{n\pi x}{L}$ for some positive integer n.

What can we do now? By Theorem 14.1 every finite linear combination of solutions of (14.20) is also a solution of (14.20); and by Theorem 14.2, assuming appropriate convergence, an infinite series of solutions of (14.20) is also a solution of (14.20). This suggests that we should form either a finite linear combination or an infinite series of the solutions (14.35) and attempt to apply the initial conditions (14.22) to the "more general" solution thus obtained. In general no finite linear combination will satisfy these conditions, and we must resort to an infinite series.

We therefore form an infinite series

$$\sum_{n=1}^{\infty} y_n(x,t) = \sum_{n=1}^{\infty} \left[\sin\frac{n\pi x}{L} \right]\left[a_n\sin\frac{n\pi\alpha t}{L} + b_n\cos\frac{n\pi\alpha t}{L} \right]$$

of the solutions (14.35). Assuming appropriate convergence, Theorem 14.2 applies and assures us that the sum of this series is also a solution of the differential equation (14.20). Denoting this sum by $y(x,t)$, we write

$$(14.36) \qquad y(x,t) = \sum_{n=1}^{\infty} \left[\sin\frac{n\pi x}{L} \right]\left[a_n\sin\frac{n\pi\alpha t}{L} + b_n\cos\frac{n\pi\alpha t}{L} \right].$$

We note that $y(0,t) = 0$ and $y(L,t) = 0$. Thus, assuming appropriate convergence, the function y given by (14.36) satisfies both the differential equation (14.20) and the two boundary conditions (14.21).

Let us now apply the initial conditions (14.22) to the series solution (14.36). The first condition $y(x,0) = f(x)$, $0 \leq x \leq L$, reduces (14.36) to

$$(14.37) \qquad \sum_{n=1}^{\infty} b_n \sin\frac{n\pi x}{L} = f(x), \quad 0 \leq x \leq L.$$

Thus to satisfy the first initial condition (14.22), we must determine the coefficients b_n so that (14.37) is satisfied. We recognize this as a problem in Fourier Sine Series (See Section 12.4, C). Using (12.54) we find that the coefficients b_n are given by

$$(14.38) \qquad b_n = \frac{2}{L} \int_0^L f(x)\sin\frac{n\pi x}{L}dx, \quad (n = 1, 2, 3, \ldots).$$

Thus in order for the series solution (14.36) to satisfy the initial condition $y(x,0) = f(x)$, $0 \leq x \leq L$, the coefficients b_n in the series must be given by (14.38).

The only condition which remains to be satisfied is the second initial condition (14.22), which is

$$\frac{\partial y(x,0)}{\partial t} = g(x), \quad 0 \leq x \leq L.$$

From (14.36), we find that

$$\frac{\partial y(x,t)}{\partial t} = \sum_{n=1}^{\infty} \left[\frac{n\pi\alpha}{L}\right]\left[\sin\frac{n\pi x}{L}\right]\left[a_n\cos\frac{n\pi\alpha t}{L} - b_n\sin\frac{n\pi\alpha t}{L}\right].$$

The second initial condition reduces this to

$$\sum_{n=1}^{\infty} \frac{a_n n\pi\alpha}{L}\sin\frac{n\pi x}{L} = g(x), \quad 0 \leq x \leq L.$$

Letting $A_n = \frac{a_n n\pi\alpha}{L}$, $(n = 1, 2, 3, \ldots)$, this takes the form

$$(14.39) \qquad \sum_{n=1}^{\infty} A_n \sin\frac{n\pi x}{L} = g(x), \quad 0 \leq x \leq L.$$

Thus to satisfy the second initial condition (14.22), we must determine the coefficients A_n so that (14.39) is satisfied. This is another problem in Fourier Sine Series. Using (12.54) again, we find that the coefficients A_n are given by

$$A_n = \frac{2}{L} \int_0^L g(x)\sin\frac{n\pi x}{L}dx, \quad (n = 1, 2, 3, \ldots).$$

Since $A_n = \frac{a_n n\pi\alpha}{L}$, $(n = 1, 2, 3, \ldots)$, we find that

$$(14.40) \qquad a_n = \frac{L}{n\pi\alpha}A_n = \frac{2}{n\pi\alpha} \int_0^L g(x)\sin\frac{n\pi x}{L}dx, \quad (n = 1, 2, 3, \ldots).$$

Thus in order for the series solution (14.36) to satisfy the second initial condition (14.22), the coefficients a_n in the series must be given by (14.40).

Therefore, the formal solution of the problem consisting of the partial differential equation (14.20), the two boundary conditions (14.21), and the two initial conditions (14.22) is

(14.36)
$$y(x,t) = \sum_{n=1}^{\infty} \left[\sin\frac{n\pi x}{L} \right] \left[a_n\sin\frac{n\pi\alpha t}{L} + b_n\cos\frac{n\pi\alpha t}{L} \right],$$

where

(14.40)
$$a_n = \frac{2}{n\pi\alpha} \int_0^L g(x)\sin\frac{n\pi x}{L}dx, \quad (n = 1, 2, 3, \ldots)$$

and

(14.38)
$$b_n = \frac{2}{L} \int_0^L f(x)\sin\frac{n\pi x}{L}dx, \quad (n = 1, 2, 3, \ldots).$$

Summary.   We briefly summarize the principal steps in the solution of this problem. The initial step was to assume the product solution XT given by (14.23). This led to the ordinary differential equation (14.25) for the function X and the ordinary differential equation (14.26) for the function T. We then considered the boundary conditions (14.21) and found that they reduced to the boundary conditions (14.27) on the function X. Thus the function X had to be a nontrivial solution of the Sturm-Liouville Problem consisting of (14.25) and (14.27). The next step was to solve this Sturm-Liouville problem. We did this and obtained for solutions the functions X_n given by (14.33). We then returned to the differential equation (14.26) for the function T and obtained the solutions T_n given by (14.34). Thus, for each positive integral value of n, we found the product solutions X_nT_n denoted by y_n and given by (14.35). Each of these solutions y_n satisfied both the partial differential equation (14.20) and the boundary conditions (14.21), but no one of them satisfied the initial conditions (14.22). In order to satisfy these initial conditions, we formed an infinite series of the solutions y_n. We thus obtained the formal solution y given by (14.36), in which the coefficients a_n and b_n were arbitrary. We applied the initial conditions to this series solution and thereby determined the coefficients a_n and b_n. We thus obtained the formal solution y given by (14.36), in which the coefficients a_n and b_n are given by (14.40) and (14.38), respectively. We emphasize that this solution is a formal one, for in the process of obtaining it we made assumptions of convergence which we did not justify.

A Special Case.   As a particular case of the vibrating string problem, we consider the problem of the so-called *plucked string*. Let us suppose that the string is such that the constant $\alpha^2 = 2500$ and that the ends of the string are fixed on the x axis at $x = 0$ and $x = 1$. Suppose the midpoint of the string is displaced into the xy plane a distance 0.01 in the direction of the positive y axis (see Figure 14.2).

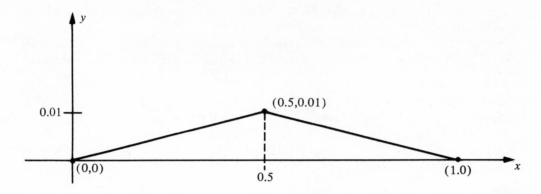

Figure 14.2

Then the displacement from the x axis on the interval $0 \leq x \leq 1$ is given by $f(x)$ where

(14.41)
$$f(x) = \begin{cases} \dfrac{x}{50}, & 0 \leq x \leq \dfrac{1}{2}; \\[2mm] -\dfrac{x}{50} + \dfrac{1}{50}, & \dfrac{1}{2} \leq x \leq 1. \end{cases}$$

Suppose that at $t = 0$ the string is released from rest from the initial position defined by $f(x)$, $0 \leq x \leq 1$. Let us find the formal expression (14.36) for the displacement $y(x,t)$ in the y direction, in this special case.

The coefficients a_n and b_n in the expression (14.36) are given by (14.40) and (14.38), respectively. In the special case under consideration we have $\alpha = 50$, $L = 1$, and $f(x)$ given by (14.41). Further, since the string is released from rest, the initial velocity is given by $g(x) = 0$, $0 \leq x \leq 1$. Therefore from (14.40) we find that

$$a_n = 0, \quad (n = 1, 2, 3, \ldots).$$

Using (14.38), we find that

$$\begin{aligned} b_n &= 2 \int_0^1 f(x) \sin n\pi x \, dx \\ &= 2 \int_0^{1/2} \frac{x}{50} \sin n\pi x \, dx + 2 \int_{1/2}^1 \left(-\frac{x}{50} + \frac{1}{50} \right) \sin n\pi x \, dx \\ &= \frac{2}{25 n^2 \pi^2} \sin \frac{n\pi}{2}, \quad (n = 1, 2, 3, \ldots). \end{aligned}$$

Hence the even coefficients $b_{2n} = 0$, $(n = 1, 2, 3, \ldots)$, and the odd coefficients are given by

$$b_{2n-1} = \frac{(-1)^{n-1} 2}{25 \pi^2 (2n - 1)^2}, \quad (n = 1, 2, 3, \ldots).$$

Therefore in the special case under consideration the expression (14.36) for the displacement is

$$y(x,t) = \frac{2}{25 \pi^2} \sum_{n=1}^{\infty} \frac{(-1)^{n-1}}{(2n - 1)^2} \sin n\pi x \cos 50 n\pi t.$$

C. An Example Involving the Laplace Equation

We now consider a second example of the application of the method of separation of variables to a partial differential equations problem. The problem which we shall consider originated from a problem of physics, but we shall not enter into a discussion of this related physical problem. Our sole purpose in presenting this second example is to help the reader to gain greater familiarity with the various details of the method under consideration.

Problem.   Apply the method of separation of variables to obtain a formal solution $u(x,y)$ of the problem which consists of the two-dimensional Laplace Equation

$$\text{(14.42)} \qquad\qquad \frac{\partial^2 u}{\partial x^2} + \frac{\partial^2 u}{\partial y^2} = 0$$

and the four boundary conditions

$$\text{(14.43)} \qquad\qquad u(0,y) = 0, \qquad 0 \le y \le b;$$

$$\text{(14.44)} \qquad\qquad u(a,y) = 0, \qquad 0 \le y \le b;$$

$$\text{(14.45)} \qquad\qquad u(x,0) = 0, \qquad 0 \le x \le a;$$

$$\text{(14.46)} \qquad\qquad u(x,b) = f(x), \quad 0 \le x \le a.$$

We point out that the numbers a and b are definite positive constants and the function f is a specified function of x, $0 \le x \le a$.

Formal Solution.   We first make the basic assumption that the differential equation (14.42) has product solutions of the form XY, where X is a function of x only and Y is a function of y only. That is, we assume solutions

$$\text{(14.47)} \qquad\qquad u(x,y) = X(x)Y(y).$$

We now differentiate (14.47) and substitute into the differential equation (14.42). Differentiating, we find

$$\frac{\partial^2 u}{\partial x^2} = Y\frac{d^2 X}{dx^2} \quad \text{and} \quad \frac{\partial^2 u}{\partial y^2} = X\frac{d^2 Y}{dy^2};$$

and substituting, we obtain

$$Y\frac{d^2 X}{dx^2} + X\frac{d^2 Y}{dy^2} = 0.$$

From this we obtain at once

$$\text{(14.48)} \qquad\qquad \frac{\dfrac{d^2 X}{dx^2}}{X} = -\frac{\dfrac{d^2 Y}{dy^2}}{Y}.$$

The left member of (14.48) is a function of x only and so is independent of y. The right member of (14.48) is a function of y only and so is independent of x. Therefore the two equal expressions in (14.48) must both be equal to a constant k. Setting each member of (14.48) equal to this constant k, we obtain the two ordinary differential equations

$$\frac{d^2X}{dx^2} - kX = 0$$

and

$$\frac{d^2Y}{dy^2} + kY = 0.$$

Let us now consider the four boundary conditions (14.43) through (14.46). The first three of these are homogeneous, but the fourth one is not. Let us attempt to satisfy the three homogeneous conditions first. Since $u(x,y) = X(x)Y(y)$, we see that the three homogeneous conditions (14.43), (14.44) and (14.45) reduce to

$$X(0)Y(y) = 0, \quad 0 \leq y \leq b;$$
$$X(a)Y(y) = 0, \quad 0 \leq y \leq b;$$

and

$$X(x)Y(0) = 0, \quad 0 \leq x \leq a; \quad \text{respectively.}$$

Since either $X(x) = 0$, $0 \leq x \leq a$, or $Y(y) = 0$, $0 \leq y \leq b$, would reduce the assumed solution (14.47) to the trivial solution of (14.42), we must have

$$X(0) = 0, \quad X(a) = 0, \quad \text{and} \quad Y(0) = 0.$$

Thus the function X in the assumed solution (14.47) must be a nontrivial solution of the Sturm-Liouville Problem

$$(14.49) \qquad\qquad \frac{d^2X}{dx^2} - kX = 0,$$

$$(14.50) \qquad\qquad X(0) = 0, \quad X(a) = 0.$$

Further, the function Y in (14.47) must be a nontrivial solution of the problem

$$(14.51) \qquad\qquad \frac{d^2Y}{dy^2} + kY = 0,$$

$$(14.52) \qquad\qquad Y(0) = 0.$$

The Sturm-Liouville problem (14.49) and (14.50) is essentially the same as the problem (14.25) and (14.27) which we encountered and solved in connection with the Vibrating String Problem in part B of this section. Indeed, the present problem (14.49) and (14.50) is merely the special case of the problem (14.25) and (14.27) in which $\alpha^2 = 1$ and $L = a$. Thus if we set $\alpha^2 = 1$ and $L = a$ in the results (14.32) and (14.33) of the problem (14.25) and (14.27), we shall obtain the desired results for the present problem (14.49) and (14.50). Doing this, we first find from (14.32) that the constant k in (14.49) must be given by

$$(14.53) \qquad\qquad k = -\frac{n^2\pi^2}{a^2}, \quad (n = 1, 2, 3, \ldots).$$

Then from (14.33) we find that the corresponding nontrivial solutions of the problem (14.49) and (14.50) are

(14.54)
$$X_n = c_n \sin\frac{n\pi x}{a}, \quad (n = 1, 2, 3, \ldots),$$

where the c_n, $(n = 1, 2, 3, \ldots)$, are arbitrary constants. That is, corresponding to each positive integral value of n, we obtain functions X_n of the form (14.54) which will serve as the function X in the product solution (14.47).

We now return to the problem (14.51) and (14.52) involving the function Y. Since k must be of the form (14.53), the differential equation (14.51) becomes

$$\frac{d^2Y}{dy^2} - \frac{n^2\pi^2}{a^2}Y = 0,$$

where $n = 1, 2, 3, \ldots$. For each such value of n, this differential equation has the general solution

$$Y_n = c_{n,1}e^{\frac{n\pi y}{a}} + c_{n,2}e^{-\frac{n\pi y}{a}}, \quad (n = 1, 2, 3, \ldots),$$

where $c_{n,1}$ and $c_{n,2}$, $(n = 1, 2, 3, \ldots)$, are arbitrary constants. In order to satisfy the condition (14.52), we must have

$$c_{n,1} + c_{n,2} = 0, \quad (n = 1, 2, 3, \ldots).$$

Thus nontrivial solutions of the problem (14.51) and (14.52) are

$$Y_n = c_{n,1}(e^{\frac{n\pi y}{a}} - e^{-\frac{n\pi y}{a}}), \quad (n = 1, 2, 3, \ldots),$$

where the $c_{n,1}$, $(n = 1, 2, 3, \ldots)$, are arbitrary constants. Using the identity $e^\theta - e^{-\theta} = 2\sinh\theta$, we may put these solutions in the form

(14.55)
$$Y_n = c'_{n,1}\sinh\frac{n\pi y}{a}, \quad (n = 1, 2, 3, \ldots),$$

where the $c'_{n,1}$, $(n = 1, 2, 3, \ldots)$, are arbitrary constants. Thus, corresponding to each positive integral value of n, we obtain functions Y_n of the form (14.55) which will serve as the function Y in the product solution (14.47).

Hence, corresponding to each positive integral value of n, $(n = 1, 2, 3, \ldots)$, we obtain solutions

$$X_nY_n = \left[c_n\sin\frac{n\pi x}{a}\right]\left[c'_{n,1}\sinh\frac{n\pi y}{a}\right]$$

which have the product form (14.47). We set $C_n = c_n c'_{n,1}$, $(n = 1, 2, 3, \ldots)$, and write these solutions as

(14.56)
$$u_n(x,y) = C_n\sin\frac{n\pi x}{a}\sinh\frac{n\pi y}{a}, \quad (n = 1, 2, 3, \ldots).$$

Each one of these solutions (14.56) satisfies both the partial differential equation (14.42) and the three homogeneous boundary conditions (14.43), (14.44), and (14.45) for all values of the constant C_n.

We must now apply the nonhomogeneous boundary condition (14.46). In order to do this, we form an infinite series

$$\sum_{n=1}^{\infty} u_n(x,y) = \sum_{n=1}^{\infty} C_n \sin\frac{n\pi x}{a} \sinh\frac{n\pi y}{a}$$

of the solutions (14.56). Assuming appropriate convergence, Theorem 14.2 applies and assures us that the sum of this series is also a solution of the differential equation (14.42). Denoting this sum by $u(x,y)$, we write

(14.57) $$u(x,y) = \sum_{n=1}^{\infty} C_n \sin\frac{n\pi x}{a} \sinh\frac{n\pi y}{a}.$$

We observe that $u(0,y) = 0$, $u(a,y) = 0$, and $u(x,0) = 0$. Thus, assuming appropriate convergence, the function u given by (14.57) satisfies both the differential equation (14.42) and the three homogeneous boundary conditions (14.43), (14.44), and (14.45).

We now apply the nonhomogeneous boundary condition (14.46) to the series solution (14.57). Doing so, we obtain at once

$$\sum_{n=1}^{\infty} c_n \sin\frac{n\pi x}{a} \sinh\frac{n\pi b}{a} = f(x), \quad 0 \le x \le a.$$

Letting $A_n = C_n \sinh\dfrac{n\pi b}{a}$, $(n = 1, 2, 3, \ldots)$, this takes the form

(14.58) $$\sum_{n=1}^{\infty} A_n \sin\frac{n\pi x}{a} = f(x), \quad 0 \le x \le a.$$

Thus in order to satisfy the condition (14.46), we must determine the coefficients A_n so that (14.58) is satisfied. This is a problem in Fourier Sine Series. Using (12.56), we find that the coefficients A_n are given by

$$A_n = \frac{2}{a} \int_0^a f(x) \sin\frac{n\pi x}{a} dx, \quad (n = 1, 2, 3, \ldots).$$

Since $A_n = C_n \sinh\dfrac{n\pi b}{a}$, $(n = 1, 2, 3, \ldots)$, we find that

(14.59) $$C_n = \frac{A_n}{\sinh\dfrac{n\pi b}{a}} = \frac{2}{a \sinh\dfrac{n\pi b}{a}} \int_0^a f(x) \sin\frac{n\pi x}{a} dx, \quad (n = 1, 2, 3, \ldots).$$

Thus in order for the series solution (14.57) to satisfy the nonhomogeneous boundary condition (14.46), the coefficients C_n in the series must be given by (14.59).

Therefore the formal solution of the problem consisting of the partial differential equation (14.42) and the four boundary conditions (14.43) through (14.46) is

(14.57) $$u(x,y) = \sum_{n=1}^{\infty} c_n \sin\frac{n\pi x}{a} \sinh\frac{n\pi y}{a},$$

where

(14.59)
$$C_n = \frac{2}{a \sinh\dfrac{n\pi b}{a}} \int_0^a f(x)\sin\frac{n\pi x}{a}dx, \quad (n = 1, 2, 3, \ldots).$$

D. An Example Involving Bessel Functions

In this example we shall apply the method of separation of variables to a problem in which the partial differential equation has a variable coefficient. As a result of this variable coefficient we shall encounter certain difficulties which were not present in the two previous examples. Further, we shall need to know a few results which we have not yet proved. Whenever such a result is needed, we shall state it without proof.

Problem. Apply the method of separation of variables to obtain a formal solution $u(x,t)$ of the problem which consists of the partial differential equation

(14.60)
$$\frac{\partial^2 u}{\partial x^2} + \frac{1}{x}\frac{\partial u}{\partial x} = \frac{\partial u}{\partial t}$$

and the three conditions

(14.61)   (i) $u(L,t) = 0, \quad t > 0;$

(14.62)   (ii) $u(x,0) = f(x), \quad 0 < x < L,$

where f is a prescribed function of x, $0 < x < L$;

and

(14.63)   (iii) $\lim_{t \to \infty} u(x,t) = 0$

for each x, $0 \le x \le L$.

Formal Solution. We begin by making the basic assumption that the differential equation (14.60) has product solutions of the form

(14.64)
$$u(x,t) = X(x)T(t),$$

where X is a function of x only and T is a function of t only. Upon differentiating (14.64) and substituting into the differential equation (14.60), we obtain

$$T\frac{d^2X}{dx^2} + \frac{1}{x}T\frac{dX}{dx} = X\frac{dT}{dt}.$$

From this we obtain at once

(14.65)
$$\frac{1}{X}\left(\frac{d^2X}{dx^2} + \frac{1}{x}\frac{dX}{dx}\right) = \frac{1}{T}\frac{dT}{dt}.$$

The left member of (14.65) is a function of x only and so is independent of t. The right member of (14.65) is a function of t only and so is independent of x. Therefore the two equal expressions in (14.65) must both be equal to a constant k. Setting each member of (14.65) equal to this constant k, we obtain the two ordinary differential equations

(14.66)
$$\frac{d^2X}{dx^2} + \frac{1}{x}\frac{dX}{dx} - kX = 0$$

and

(14.67)
$$\frac{dT}{dt} - kT = 0.$$

The effect of the variable coefficient $(1/x)$ in the partial differential equation (14.60) appears here, for the ordinary differential equation (14.66) also has this same variable coefficient.

We shall need the general solutions of both of the ordinary differential equations (14.66) and (14.67). The equation (14.67) is the more promising of the two; let us work with it first. We find at once that the general solution of (14.67) is of the form

(14.68)
$$T = Ce^{kt},$$

where C is an arbitrary constant.

Let us now examine the three conditions (14.61), (14.62), and (14.63) to see if any of them will lead to further information about the solution (14.68). The first two of these conditions lead to conditions on the function X. Let us therefore examine the third condition (14.63). Since $u(x,t) = X(x)T(t)$, this condition reduces to

$$X(x)[\lim_{t\to\infty} T(t)] = 0$$

for each x, $0 \le x \le L$. Hence we require that

$$\lim_{t\to\infty} T(t) = 0.$$

From this we see that the constant k in (14.68) must be a negative number. Therefore we set $k = -\lambda^2$, where λ is real and positive. The general solution (14.68) of the differential equation (14.67) now takes the form

(14.69)
$$T = Ce^{-\lambda^2 t},$$

where C is an arbitrary constant.

Let us now return to the differential equation (14.66) for X. Since $k = -\lambda^2$ it now takes the form

$$\frac{d^2X}{dx^2} + \frac{1}{x}\frac{dX}{dx} + \lambda^2 X = 0$$

or equivalently,

(14.70)
$$x^2\frac{d^2X}{dx^2} + x\frac{dX}{dx} + \lambda^2 x^2 X = 0.$$

The transformation $\theta = \lambda x$ reduces (14.70) to the equation

$$\theta^2\frac{d^2X}{d\theta^2} + \theta\frac{dX}{d\theta} + \theta^2 X = 0.$$

We readily recognize this equation as the Bessel Equation of Order Zero. Its general solution may be written

$$X = c_1 J_0(\theta) + c_2 Y_0(\theta),$$

where J_0 and Y_0 are the Bessel Functions of Order Zero of the first and second kind, respectively, and c_1 and c_2 are arbitrary constants (see Section 6.3). Thus the general solution of (14.70) may be written

(14.71) $$X = c_1 J_0(\lambda x) + c_2 Y_0(\lambda x),$$

where c_1 and c_2 are arbitrary constants.

   Let us now return to the condition (14.63). This condition requires that

$$\lim_{t \to \infty} u(x,t) = 0$$

for *each* x, $0 \le x \le L$. For $x = 0$ this becomes

$$\lim_{t \to \infty} u(0,t) = 0$$

or

$$X(0)[\lim_{t \to \infty} T(t)] = 0.$$

In order to satisfy this condition we must require that $X(0)$ be finite. We recall that $J_0(0) = 1$. However, it can be shown that

$$\lim_{x \to 0} Y_0(\lambda x) = - \infty.$$

Thus in order for $X(0)$ to be finite we must set $c_2 = 0$. Thus the solution (14.71) reduces to

(14.72) $$X = c_1 J_0(\lambda x).$$

   Let us now consider the condition (14.61). We have already noticed that this condition leads to a condition on X. Indeed, it reduces to

$$X(L)T(t) = 0, \quad t > 0; \quad \text{and}$$

thus we must have $X(L) = 0$. Applying this to the solution (14.72), we see that λ must satisfy the equation

(14.73) $$J_0(\lambda L) = 0.$$

In Section 6.3B we pointed out that the function J_0 has a damped oscillatory behavior as $x \to + \infty$. Thus the equation $J_0(x) = 0$ has an infinite sequence of positive roots x_n, ($n = 1, 2, 3, \ldots$). Let us arrange these positive roots such that $x_n < x_{n+1}$, ($n = 1, 2, 3, \ldots$). Then there exists a monotonic increasing sequence of positive numbers

$$\lambda_n = \frac{x_n}{L}, \quad (n = 1, 2, 3, \ldots),$$

each of which satisfies equation (14.73). Thus corresponding to each positive integer n, the differential equation (14.70) has solutions which satisfy the condition (14.61). These solutions are of the form

(14.74) $$X_n = c_{1,n} J_0(\lambda_n x), \quad (n = 1, 2, 3, \ldots),$$

where the $c_{1,n}$, $(n = 1, 2, 3, \ldots)$, are arbitrary constants and the λ_n, $(n = 1, 2, 3, \ldots)$, are the positive roots of equation (14.73). That is, corresponding to each positive integer n, we obtain functions X_n of the form (14.74) which will serve as the function X in the product solution (14.64).

Let us now return to the solution (14.69) of the differential equation (14.67). We see that, corresponding to each positive integer n, the differential equation (14.67) has solutions of the form

$$(14.75) \qquad T_n = c_{2,n} e^{-\lambda_n^2 t}, \quad (n = 1, 2, 3, \ldots),$$

where the $c_{2,n}$, $(n = 1, 2, 3, \ldots)$, are arbitrary constants and the λ_n, $(n = 1, 2, 3, \ldots)$, are the positive roots of Equation (14.73). That is, corresponding to each positive integer n, we obtain functions T_n of the form (14.75) which will serve as the function T in the product solution (14.64).

Hence, corresponding to each positive integral value of n, $(n = 1, 2, 3, \ldots)$, we obtain product solutions of the form

$$(14.76) \qquad u_n(x,t) = A_n J_0(\lambda_n x) e^{-\lambda_n^2 t}, \quad (n = 1, 2, 3, \ldots),$$

where the $A_n = c_{1,n} c_{2,n}$, $(n = 1, 2, 3, \ldots)$, are arbitrary constants. Each one of these solutions (14.76) satisfies the partial differential equation (14.60) and the conditions (14.61) and (14.63) for all values of the constant A_n.

We must now apply the initial condition (14.62). In order to do this, we form an infinite series of the solutions (14.76). Assuming appropriate convergence, the sum of this series is also a solution of the partial differential equation (14.60). We denote this sum by $u(x,t)$ and thus write

$$(14.77) \qquad u(x,t) = \sum_{n=1}^{\infty} A_n J_0(\lambda_n x) e^{-\lambda_n^2 t}.$$

Applying the initial condition (14.62) to the series solution (14.77), we obtain

$$(14.78) \qquad \sum_{n=1}^{\infty} A_n J_0(\lambda_n x) = f(x), \quad 0 < x < L.$$

Thus in order to satisfy the initial condition (14.62), the coefficients A_n must be determined so that (14.78) is satisfied. In other words, we must expand the function f in a series of Bessel Functions of the first kind of order zero, valid on the interval $0 < x < L$.

Here we have encountered a new difficulty, and this difficulty leads to matters which are outside the scope of this book. Nevertheless, we shall indicate briefly what can be done. This is one place where we need to know certain of the results which we referred to at the beginning of this section. Let us state them and get on with the problem! In the first place, it can be shown that if the numbers λ_n, $(n = 1, 2, 3, \ldots)$, are the positive roots of the equation $J_0(\lambda L) = 0$, then the set of functions defined by $\{J_0(\lambda_n x)\}$, $(n = 1, 2, 3, \ldots)$, is an orthogonal system with respect to the weight function r such that $r(x) = x$ on the interval $0 \leq x \leq L$. Therefore,

$$\int_0^L x J_0(\lambda_m x) J_0(\lambda_n x) dx = 0, \quad (m = 1, 2, 3, \ldots; n = 1, 2, 3, \ldots; m \neq n).$$

Further, if $m = n$, we have

(14.79)
$$\int_0^L x[J_0(\lambda_n x)]^2 dx = \Gamma_n > 0, \quad (n = 1, 2, 3, \ldots).$$

In Section 12.3A we learned how to form a set of *orthonormal* functions from a set of orthogonal characteristic functions of a Sturm-Liouville Problem. Applying this procedure to the orthogonal set defined by $\{J_0(\lambda_n x)\}$, we obtain the corresponding orthonormal system $\{\phi_n\}$, where

(14.80)
$$\phi_n(x) = \frac{J_0(\lambda_n x)}{\sqrt{\Gamma_n}}, \quad (n = 1, 2, 3, \ldots),$$

and $\Gamma_n, (n = 1, 2, 3, \ldots)$, is given by (14.79). Let us now recall the results of Section 12.3B concerning the formal expansion of a function f in a series

$$\sum_{n=1}^{\infty} c_n \phi_n$$

of orthonormal functions $\{\phi_n\}$. According to (12.37) the coefficients c_n in the expansion of f in the series of orthonormal function ϕ_n defined by (14.80) are given by

$$c_n = \frac{1}{\sqrt{\Gamma_n}} \int_0^L x f(x) J_0(\lambda_n x) dx, \quad (n = 1, 2, 3, \ldots).$$

Thus this expansion takes the form

$$\sum_{n=1}^{\infty} \left[\frac{1}{\sqrt{\Gamma_n}} \int_0^L x f(x) J_0(\lambda_n x) dx \right] \frac{J_0(\lambda_n x)}{\sqrt{\Gamma_n}},$$

and we write formally

(14.81)
$$f(x) = \sum_{n=1}^{\infty} \left[\frac{1}{\Gamma_n} \int_0^L x f(x) J_0(\lambda_n x) dx \right] J_0(\lambda_n x), \quad 0 < x < L.$$

Comparing (14.78) and (14.81), we see that if the coefficients A_n in (14.78) are given by

(14.82)
$$A_n = \frac{1}{\Gamma_n} \int_0^L x f(x) J_0(\lambda_n x) dx, \quad (n = 1, 2, 3, \ldots),$$

then the requirement (14.78) will be formally satisfied. We note that the constants Γ_n in (14.82) are given by (14.79). That is,

$$\Gamma_n = \int_0^L x[J_0(\lambda_n x)]^2 dx, \quad (n = 1, 2, 3, \ldots).$$

This integral can be evaluated in terms of values of the Bessel function of the first kind of order one, J_1. Indeed, it can be shown that

$$\int_0^L x[J_0(\lambda_n x)]^2 dx = \frac{L^2}{2}[J_1(\lambda_n L)]^2, \quad (n = 1, 2, 3, \ldots),$$

and thus

$$\Gamma_n = \frac{L^2}{2}[J_1(\lambda_n L)]^2, \quad (n = 1, 2, 3, \ldots).$$

Thus the coefficients A_n in (14.78) are given by

$$A_n = \frac{2}{L^2[J_1(\lambda_n L)]^2} \int_0^L x f(x) J_0(\lambda_n x) dx, \quad (n = 1, 2, 3, \ldots).$$

Finally, then, we obtain the formal solution of the problem consisting of the partial differential equation (14.60) and the conditions (14.61), (14.62), and (14.63). This formal solution is

$$u(x,t) = \sum_{n=1}^{\infty} A_n J_0(\lambda_n x) e^{-\lambda_n^2 t},$$

where

$$A_n = \frac{2}{L^2[J_1(\lambda_n L)]^2} \int_0^L x f(x) J_0(\lambda_n x) dx, \quad (n = 1, 2, 3, \ldots),$$

the λ_n, $(n = 1, 2, 3, \ldots)$, are the positive roots of the equation $J_0(\lambda L) = 0$, and J_0 and J_1 denote the Bessel Functions of the first kind of orders zero and one, respectively.

Remarks and Observations. At the risk of being unduly repetitious, but with the good intentions of promoting a cautious attitude, we emphasize that the results which we have obtained are strictly formal results. We *assumed* "appropriate convergence" of the series in (14.77), and we have said nothing concerning the convergence of the Bessel Function Expansion which we obtained for the function f. In order to relieve our consciences concerning the latter point, we state that there do exist classes of functions f such that the expansion (14.78), in which the coefficients A_n are given by (14.83), is valid on the interval $0 < x < L$. The study of these classes is definitely beyond the scope of this book, and we refer the reader to more advanced works for a discussion of this and other pertinent problems of convergence.

Finally, we point out that the problem which we have considered here gives some indication of the types of difficulties which may be encountered if the method of separation of variables is applied to a problem in which the partial differential equation has variable coefficients. The variable coefficient $(1/x)$ in the partial differential equation (14.60) led to the variable coefficient $(1/x)$ in the ordinary differential equation (14.66) which resulted from the separation of the variables. A similar situation occurs in other problems in which the partial differential equation has variable coefficients. In such problems, one or more of the ordinary differential equations which result from the separation process will also contain variable coefficients. Obtaining the general solutions of these ordinary differential equations can then be a formidable task in its own right. But even if these general solutions can be obtained, they may involve functions which will lead to further difficulties when one attempts to apply certain of the supplementary conditions. This sort of difficulty occurred in the problem of this section when we tried to apply the initial condition (14.62). We were forced to consider the problem of expanding the function f in a series of Bessel Functions, valid on the interval $0 < x < L$. A similar situation often occurs in other problems which involve a partial differential equation with variable coefficients. In such problems one is faced with the task of expanding a prescribed function f in a series of nonelementary orthonormal functions $\{\phi_n\}$, valid on a certain interval. The set of orthonormal functions $\{\phi_n\}$ might happen to be one of the many such sets which have been carefully studied, or it might turn out to be a set about which little is known. In any case, additional difficulties may occur which will necessitate further study and possibly some research.

Exercises

Use the method of separation of variables to find a formal solution $y(x,t)$ of each of the problems stated in Exercises 1 through 4.

1. $\dfrac{\partial^2 y}{\partial x^2} = \dfrac{\partial^2 y}{\partial t^2}$,

   $y(0,t) = 0, 0 \leq t < \infty$,

   $y(\pi,t) = 0, 0 \leq t < \infty$,

   $y(x,0) = \sin 2x, 0 \leq x \leq \pi$,

   $\dfrac{\partial y(x,0)}{\partial t} = 0, 0 \leq x \leq \pi$.

2. $\dfrac{\partial^2 y}{\partial x^2} = \dfrac{\partial^2 y}{\partial t^2}$,

   $y(0,t) = 0, 0 \leq t < \infty$,

   $y(10,t) = 0, 0 \leq t < \infty$,

   $y(x,0) = 2\sin^3 x, 0 \leq x \leq 10$,

   $\dfrac{\partial y(x,0)}{\partial t} = 0, 0 \leq x \leq 10$.

3. $4\dfrac{\partial^2 y}{\partial x^2} = \dfrac{\partial^2 y}{\partial t^2}$,

   $y(0,t) = 0, 0 \leq t < \infty$,

   $y(3,t) = 0, 0 \leq t < \infty$,

   $y(x,t) = \begin{cases} x, 0 \leq x \leq 1, \\ 1, 1 \leq x \leq 2, \\ 3 - x, 2 \leq x \leq 3. \end{cases}$

   $\dfrac{\partial y(x,0)}{\partial t} = 0, 0 \leq x \leq 3$

4. $4\dfrac{\partial^2 y}{\partial x^2} = 9\dfrac{\partial^2 y}{\partial t^2}$,

   $y(0,t) = 0, 0 \leq t < \infty$,

   $y(\pi,t) = 0, 0 \leq t < \infty$,

$$y(x,0) = \sin^2 x, \ 0 \le x \le \pi,$$

$$\frac{\partial y(x,0)}{\partial t} = \sin x, \ 0 \le x \le \pi.$$

5. Apply the method of separation of variables to obtain a formal solution $u(x,t)$ of the problem which consists of the Heat Equation

$$\frac{\partial^2 u}{\partial x^2} = \frac{\partial u}{\partial t},$$

the boundary conditions

$$u(0,t) = 0, \ t > 0,$$

$$u(L,t) = 0, \ t > 0,$$

and the initial condition

$$u(x,0) = f(x), \ 0 \le x \le L,$$

where $L > 0$, and f is a specified function of x, $0 \le x \le L$.

6. Use the method of separation of variables to find a formal solution $u(x,y)$ of the problem which consists of the partial differential equation

$$\frac{\partial^2 u}{\partial x^2} - \frac{\partial u}{\partial y} = -Ae^{-\alpha x},$$

where $A \ge 0$ and $\alpha > 0$, and the conditions

$$u(0,y) = 0, \quad y > 0,$$

$$u(L,y) = 0, \quad y > 0,$$

$$u(x,0) = f(x), \ 0 < x < L.$$

[*Hint.* Let $u(x,y) = v(x,y) + \psi(x)$, where ψ is such that v satisfies the "homogeneous" equation

$$\frac{\partial^2 v}{\partial x^2} - \frac{\partial v}{\partial y} = 0$$

and the homogeneous boundary conditions

$$v(0,y) = 0, \ v(L,y) = 0.]$$

7. Use the method of separation of variables to find a formal solution $u(x,y)$ of the problem which consists of Laplace's Equation

$$\frac{\partial^2 u}{\partial x^2} + \frac{\partial^2 u}{\partial y^2} = 0$$

and the boundary conditions

$$u(0,y) = 0, \ 0 \le y \le \pi,$$

$$u(\pi,y) = 0, \ 0 \le y \le \pi,$$

$$u(x,\pi) = 0, \ 0 \le x \le \pi,$$

$$u(x,0) = f(x), \ 0 \le x \le \pi,$$

where f is a specified function of x, $0 \leq x \leq \pi$.

8. Use the method of separation of variables to obtain a formal solution $u(r,\theta)$ of the problem which consists of the equation

$$\frac{\partial^2 u}{\partial r^2} + \frac{1}{r}\frac{\partial u}{\partial r} + \frac{1}{r^2}\frac{\partial^2 u}{\partial \theta^2} = 0,$$

the periodicity condition

$$u(r,\theta) = u(r,\theta + 2\pi),\ 0 \leq r \leq L,\ \text{for all values of } \theta,$$

and the boundary conditions

$u(0,\theta) = \alpha$, where α is finite,
$u(L,\theta) = f(\theta)$, where f is a prescribed function of θ, for all values of θ.

14.3   Canonical Forms of Second-Order Linear Equations with Constant Coefficients

A. Canonical Forms

In this section we restrict our attention to second order linear partial differential equations of the form

(14.84)
$$A\frac{\partial^2 u}{\partial x^2} + B\frac{\partial^2 u}{\partial x \partial y} + C\frac{\partial^2 u}{\partial y^2} + D\frac{\partial u}{\partial x} + E\frac{\partial u}{\partial y} + Fu = 0,$$

in which the coefficients A, B, C, D, E, and F are real *constants*. This equation is a special case of the more general equation (14.6) in which these coefficients are functions of x and y. In Section 14.1 we classified such equations according to the sign of $B^2 - 4AC$. Using this classification the equation (14.84) is said to be

(i)   *hyperbolic* if $B^2 - 4AC > 0$,
(ii)   *parabolic* if $B^2 - 4AC = 0$,
(iii) *elliptic* if $B^2 - 4AC < 0$.

We shall now show that in each of these three cases the equation (14.84) can be reduced to a more simple form by a suitable change of the independent variables. The simpler forms which result in this way are called *canonical forms* of Equation (14.84). We therefore introduce new independent variables ξ,η by means of the transformation

(14.85)
$$\xi = \xi(x,y), \quad \eta = \eta(x,y).$$

We now compute derivatives of u, regarding ξ and η as intermediate variables, so that $u = u(\xi,\eta)$, where ξ and η are given by (14.85). We first find

(14.86)
$$\frac{\partial u}{\partial x} = \frac{\partial u}{\partial \xi}\frac{\partial \xi}{\partial x} + \frac{\partial u}{\partial \eta}\frac{\partial \eta}{\partial x}$$

and

(14.87)
$$\frac{\partial u}{\partial y} = \frac{\partial u}{\partial \xi}\frac{\partial \xi}{\partial y} + \frac{\partial u}{\partial \eta}\frac{\partial \eta}{\partial y}.$$

Using (14.86), we next determine $\dfrac{\partial^2 u}{\partial x^2}$.

We find

$$(14.88) \quad \frac{\partial^2 u}{\partial x^2} = \frac{\partial}{\partial x}\left(\frac{\partial u}{\partial x}\right) = \frac{\partial u}{\partial \xi}\frac{\partial}{\partial x}\left(\frac{\partial \xi}{\partial x}\right) + \frac{\partial \xi}{\partial x}\frac{\partial}{\partial x}\left(\frac{\partial u}{\partial \xi}\right) + \frac{\partial u}{\partial \eta}\frac{\partial}{\partial x}\left(\frac{\partial \eta}{\partial x}\right) + \frac{\partial \eta}{\partial x}\frac{\partial}{\partial x}\left(\frac{\partial u}{\partial \eta}\right).$$

Since $\xi = \xi(x,y)$ and $\eta = \eta(x,y)$,

$$\frac{\partial}{\partial x}\left(\frac{\partial \xi}{\partial x}\right) \text{ is simply } \frac{\partial^2 \xi}{\partial x^2}$$

and

$$\frac{\partial}{\partial x}\left(\frac{\partial \eta}{\partial x}\right) \text{ is simply } \frac{\partial^2 \eta}{\partial x^2}.$$

However, in computing $\frac{\partial}{\partial x}\left(\frac{\partial u}{\partial \xi}\right)$ and $\frac{\partial}{\partial x}\left(\frac{\partial u}{\partial \eta}\right)$, the situation is somewhat more complicated and we must be careful to remember what is involved. We are regarding u as a function of ξ and η, where ξ and η are themselves functions of x and y. That is, $u = u(\xi,\eta)$, where $\xi = \xi(x,y)$ and $\eta = \eta(x,y)$. Thus $\frac{\partial u}{\partial \xi}$ and $\frac{\partial u}{\partial \eta}$ are regarded as functions of ξ and η, where ξ and η are themselves functions of x and y. That is, $\frac{\partial u}{\partial \xi} = u_1(\xi,\eta)$ and $\frac{\partial u}{\partial \eta} = u_2(\xi,\eta)$, where in each case $\xi = \xi(x,y)$ and $\eta = \eta(x,y)$. With this in mind, we compute $\frac{\partial}{\partial x}\left(\frac{\partial u}{\partial \xi}\right)$. We have

$$\frac{\partial}{\partial x}\left(\frac{\partial u}{\partial \xi}\right) = \frac{\partial}{\partial x}[u_1(\xi,\eta)] = \frac{\partial u_1}{\partial \xi}\frac{\partial \xi}{\partial x} + \frac{\partial u_1}{\partial \eta}\frac{\partial \eta}{\partial x},$$

and since $u_1 = \frac{\partial u}{\partial \xi}$, we thus find

$$\frac{\partial}{\partial x}\left(\frac{\partial u}{\partial \xi}\right) = \frac{\partial^2 u}{\partial \xi^2}\frac{\partial \xi}{\partial x} + \frac{\partial^2 u}{\partial \eta \partial \xi}\frac{\partial \eta}{\partial x}.$$

In like manner, we obtain

$$\frac{\partial}{\partial x}\left(\frac{\partial u}{\partial \eta}\right) = \frac{\partial^2 u}{\partial \xi \partial \eta}\frac{\partial \xi}{\partial x} + \frac{\partial^2 u}{\partial \eta^2}\frac{\partial \eta}{\partial x}.$$

Substituting these results into (14.88), we thus obtain

$$\frac{\partial^2 u}{\partial x^2} = \frac{\partial u}{\partial \xi}\frac{\partial^2 \xi}{\partial x^2} + \frac{\partial \xi}{\partial x}\left(\frac{\partial^2 u}{\partial \xi^2}\frac{\partial \xi}{\partial x} + \frac{\partial^2 u}{\partial \eta \partial \xi}\frac{\partial \eta}{\partial x}\right) + \frac{\partial u}{\partial \eta}\frac{\partial^2 \eta}{\partial x^2} + \frac{\partial \eta}{\partial x}\left(\frac{\partial^2 u}{\partial \xi \partial \eta}\frac{\partial \xi}{\partial x} + \frac{\partial^2 u}{\partial \eta^2}\frac{\partial \eta}{\partial x}\right).$$

Assuming $u(\xi,\eta)$ has continuous second derivatives with respect to ξ and η, the so-called cross derivatives are equal [see Widder, Reference (56), page 52], and we have

$$(14.89) \quad \frac{\partial^2 u}{\partial x^2} = \frac{\partial^2 u}{\partial \xi^2}\left(\frac{\partial \xi}{\partial x}\right)^2 + 2\frac{\partial^2 u}{\partial \xi \partial \eta}\frac{\partial \xi}{\partial x}\frac{\partial \eta}{\partial x} + \frac{\partial^2 u}{\partial \eta^2}\left(\frac{\partial \eta}{\partial x}\right)^2 + \frac{\partial u}{\partial \xi}\frac{\partial^2 \xi}{\partial x^2} + \frac{\partial u}{\partial \eta}\frac{\partial^2 \eta}{\partial x^2}.$$

In like manner, we find

$$(14.90) \quad \frac{\partial^2 u}{\partial x \partial y} = \frac{\partial^2 u}{\partial \xi^2}\frac{\partial \xi}{\partial x}\frac{\partial \xi}{\partial y} + \frac{\partial^2 u}{\partial \xi \partial \eta}\left[\frac{\partial \xi}{\partial x}\frac{\partial \eta}{\partial y} + \frac{\partial \xi}{\partial y}\frac{\partial \eta}{\partial x}\right] + \frac{\partial^2 u}{\partial \eta^2}\frac{\partial \eta}{\partial x}\frac{\partial \eta}{\partial y} + \frac{\partial u}{\partial \xi}\frac{\partial^2 \xi}{\partial x \partial y} + \frac{\partial u}{\partial \eta}\frac{\partial^2 \eta}{\partial x \partial y}$$

and

(14.91) $$\frac{\partial^2 u}{\partial y^2} = \frac{\partial^2 u}{\partial \xi^2}\left(\frac{\partial \xi}{\partial y}\right)^2 + 2\frac{\partial^2 u}{\partial \xi \partial \eta}\frac{\partial \xi}{\partial y}\frac{\partial \eta}{\partial y} + \frac{\partial^2 u}{\partial \eta^2}\left(\frac{\partial \eta}{\partial y}\right)^2 + \frac{\partial u}{\partial \xi}\frac{\partial^2 \xi}{\partial y^2} + \frac{\partial u}{\partial \eta}\frac{\partial^2 \eta}{\partial y^2}.$$

We now substitute (14.86), (14.87), (14.89), (14.90), and (14.91) into the partial differential equation (14.84), to obtain

$$A\left[\frac{\partial^2 u}{\partial \xi^2}\left(\frac{\partial \xi}{\partial x}\right)^2 + 2\frac{\partial^2 u}{\partial \xi \partial \eta}\frac{\partial \xi}{\partial x}\frac{\partial \eta}{\partial x} + \frac{\partial^2 u}{\partial \eta^2}\left(\frac{\partial \eta}{\partial x}\right)^2 + \frac{\partial u}{\partial \xi}\frac{\partial^2 \xi}{\partial x^2} + \frac{\partial u}{\partial \eta}\frac{\partial^2 \eta}{\partial x^2}\right]$$

$$+ B\left[\frac{\partial^2 u}{\partial \xi^2}\frac{\partial \xi}{\partial x}\frac{\partial \xi}{\partial y} + \frac{\partial^2 u}{\partial \xi \partial \eta}\left(\frac{\partial \xi}{\partial x}\frac{\partial \eta}{\partial y} + \frac{\partial \xi}{\partial y}\frac{\partial \eta}{\partial x}\right) + \frac{\partial^2 u}{\partial \eta^2}\frac{\partial \eta}{\partial x}\frac{\partial \eta}{\partial y} + \frac{\partial u}{\partial \xi}\frac{\partial^2 \xi}{\partial x \partial y} + \frac{\partial u}{\partial \eta}\frac{\partial^2 \eta}{\partial x \partial y}\right]$$

$$+ C\left[\frac{\partial^2 u}{\partial \xi^2}\left(\frac{\partial \xi}{\partial y}\right)^2 + 2\frac{\partial^2 u}{\partial \xi \partial \eta}\frac{\partial \xi}{\partial y}\frac{\partial \eta}{\partial y} + \frac{\partial^2 u}{\partial \eta^2}\left(\frac{\partial \eta}{\partial y}\right)^2 + \frac{\partial u}{\partial \xi}\frac{\partial^2 \xi}{\partial y^2} + \frac{\partial u}{\partial \eta}\frac{\partial^2 \eta}{\partial y^2}\right]$$

$$+ D\left[\frac{\partial u}{\partial \xi}\frac{\partial \xi}{\partial x} + \frac{\partial u}{\partial \eta}\frac{\partial \eta}{\partial x}\right] + E\left[\frac{\partial u}{\partial \xi}\frac{\partial \xi}{\partial y} + \frac{\partial u}{\partial \eta}\frac{\partial \eta}{\partial y}\right] + Fu = 0.$$

Rearranging terms, this becomes

$$\left[A\left(\frac{\partial \xi}{\partial x}\right)^2 + B\frac{\partial \xi}{\partial x}\frac{\partial \xi}{\partial y} + C\left(\frac{\partial \xi}{\partial y}\right)^2\right]\frac{\partial^2 u}{\partial \xi^2} + \left[2A\frac{\partial \xi}{\partial x}\frac{\partial \eta}{\partial x} + B\left(\frac{\partial \xi}{\partial x}\frac{\partial \eta}{\partial y} + \frac{\partial \xi}{\partial y}\frac{\partial \eta}{\partial x}\right) + 2C\frac{\partial \xi}{\partial y}\frac{\partial \eta}{\partial y}\right]\frac{\partial^2 u}{\partial \xi \partial \eta}$$

$$+ \left[A\left(\frac{\partial \eta}{\partial x}\right)^2 + B\frac{\partial \eta}{\partial x}\frac{\partial \eta}{\partial y} + C\left(\frac{\partial \eta}{\partial y}\right)^2\right]\frac{\partial^2 u}{\partial \eta^2} + \left[A\frac{\partial^2 \xi}{\partial x^2} + B\frac{\partial^2 \xi}{\partial x \partial y} + C\frac{\partial^2 \xi}{\partial y^2} + D\frac{\partial \xi}{\partial x} + E\frac{\partial \xi}{\partial y}\right]\frac{\partial u}{\partial \xi}$$

$$+ \left[A\frac{\partial^2 \eta}{\partial x^2} + B\frac{\partial^2 \eta}{\partial x \partial y} + C\frac{\partial^2 \eta}{\partial y^2} + D\frac{\partial \eta}{\partial x} + E\frac{\partial \eta}{\partial y}\right]\frac{\partial u}{\partial \eta} + Fu = 0.$$

Thus using the transformation (14.85) the equation (14.84) is reduced to the form

(14.92) $$A_1\frac{\partial^2 u}{\partial \xi^2} + B_1\frac{\partial^2 u}{\partial \xi \partial \eta} + C_1\frac{\partial^2 u}{\partial \eta^2} + D_1\frac{\partial u}{\partial \xi} + E_1\frac{\partial u}{\partial \eta} + F_1 u = 0,$$

where

$$A_1 = A\left(\frac{\partial \xi}{\partial x}\right)^2 + B\frac{\partial \xi}{\partial x}\frac{\partial \xi}{\partial y} + C\left(\frac{\partial \xi}{\partial y}\right)^2,$$

$$B_1 = 2A\frac{\partial \xi}{\partial x}\frac{\partial \eta}{\partial x} + B\left(\frac{\partial \xi}{\partial x}\frac{\partial \eta}{\partial y} + \frac{\partial \xi}{\partial y}\frac{\partial \eta}{\partial x}\right) + 2C\frac{\partial \xi}{\partial y}\frac{\partial \eta}{\partial y},$$

$$C_1 = A\left(\frac{\partial \eta}{\partial x}\right)^2 + B\frac{\partial \eta}{\partial x}\frac{\partial \eta}{\partial y} + C\left(\frac{\partial \eta}{\partial y}\right)^2,$$

$$D_1 = A\frac{\partial^2 \xi}{\partial x^2} + B\frac{\partial^2 \xi}{\partial x \partial y} + C\frac{\partial^2 \xi}{\partial y^2} + D\frac{\partial \xi}{\partial x} + E\frac{\partial \xi}{\partial y},$$

$$E_1 = A\frac{\partial^2 \eta}{\partial x^2} + B\frac{\partial^2 \eta}{\partial x \partial y} + C\frac{\partial^2 \eta}{\partial y^2} + D\frac{\partial \eta}{\partial x} + E\frac{\partial \eta}{\partial y},$$

and $F_1 = F$.

We now show that the new equation (14.92) can be simplified by a suitable choice of $\xi(x,y)$ and $\eta(x,y)$ in the transformation (14.85). The choice of these functions ξ and η and the form of the resulting simplified equation (the canonical form) depend upon whether the original partial differential equation (14.84) is hyperbolic, parabolic, or elliptic.

B. *The Hyperbolic Equation*

Concerning the canonical form in the hyperbolic case, we state and prove the following theorem.

THEOREM 14.3.

Hypothesis. Consider the second-order linear partial differential equation

$$(14.84) \qquad A\frac{\partial^2 u}{\partial x^2} + B\frac{\partial^2 u}{\partial x \partial y} + C\frac{\partial^2 u}{\partial y^2} + D\frac{\partial u}{\partial x} + E\frac{\partial u}{\partial y} + Fu = 0,$$

where the coefficients A, B, C, D, E, and F are real constants and $B^2 - 4AC > 0$ so that the equation is hyperbolic.

Conclusion. There exists a transformation

$$(14.85) \qquad \xi = \xi(x,y), \quad \eta = \eta(x,y)$$

of the independent variables in (14.84) so that the transformed equation in the independent variables (ξ,η) may be written in the canonical form

$$(14.94) \qquad \frac{\partial^2 u}{\partial \xi \partial \eta} = d\frac{\partial u}{\partial \xi} + e\frac{\partial u}{\partial \eta} + fu,$$

where d, e, and f are real constants.

If $A \neq 0$, such a transformation is given by

$$(14.95) \qquad \begin{aligned} \xi &= \lambda_1 x + y \\ \eta &= \lambda_2 x + y \end{aligned}$$

where λ_1 and λ_2 are the roots of the quadratic equation

$$(14.96) \qquad A\lambda^2 + B\lambda + C = 0.$$

If $A = 0$, $B \neq 0$, $C \neq 0$, such a transformation is given by

$$(14.97) \qquad \begin{aligned} \xi &= x \\ \eta &= x - \frac{B}{C}y. \end{aligned}$$

If $A = 0$, $B \neq 0$, $C = 0$, such a transformation is merely the identity transformation

$$(14.98) \qquad \begin{aligned} \xi &= x \\ \eta &= y. \end{aligned}$$

Proof. We shall first show that the transformations given by (14.95), (14.97), and (14.98) actually do reduce Equation (14.84) so that it may be written in the form (14.94) in the three respective cases described in the conclusion. We shall then observe that these three cases cover all possibilities for the hyperbolic equation, thereby completing the proof.

We have seen that a transformation of the form (14.85) reduces Equation (14.84) to the form (14.92), where the coefficients are given by (14.93). In the case $A \neq 0$, we apply the special case of (14.85) given by

$$\begin{aligned} \xi &= \lambda_1 x + y \\ \eta &= \lambda_2 x + y, \end{aligned}$$
(14.95)

where λ_1 and λ_2 are the roots of the quadratic equation

(14.96)
$$A\lambda^2 + B\lambda + C = 0.$$

Then the coefficients in the transformed equation (14.92) are given by (14.93), where $\xi(x,y)$ and $\eta(x,y)$ are given by (14.95). Evaluating these coefficients in this case we find that

$$\begin{aligned} A_1 &= A\lambda_1^2 + B\lambda_1 + C, \\ B_1 &= 2A\lambda_1\lambda_2 + B(\lambda_1 + \lambda_2) + 2C \\ &= 2A\left(\frac{C}{A}\right) + B\left(-\frac{B}{A}\right) + 2C = \frac{B^2 - 4AC}{-A}, \\ C_1 &= A\lambda_2^2 + B\lambda_2 + C, \\ D_1 &= D\lambda_1 + E, \\ E_1 &= D\lambda_2 + E, \quad \text{and} \quad F_1 = F. \end{aligned}$$

Since λ_1 and λ_2 satisfy the quadratic equation (14.96), we see that $A_1 = 0$ and $C_1 = 0$. Therefore in this case the transformed equation (14.92) is

(14.99)
$$\left(\frac{B^2 - 4AC}{-A}\right)\frac{\partial^2 u}{\partial\xi\partial\eta} + (D\lambda_1 + E)\frac{\partial u}{\partial\xi} + (D\lambda_2 + E)\frac{\partial u}{\partial\eta} + Fu = 0.$$

Since $B^2 = 4AC > 0$ [Equation (14.84) is hyperbolic], the roots λ_1 and λ_2 of (14.96) are real and distinct. Therefore the coefficients in (14.99) are all real. Furthermore, the leading coefficient $(B^2 - 4AC)/(-A)$ is unequal to zero. Therefore we may write the transformed equation (14.99) in the form

$$\frac{\partial^2 u}{\partial\xi\partial\eta} = d\frac{\partial u}{\partial\xi} + e\frac{\partial u}{\partial\eta} + fu,$$

where the coefficients

$$d = \frac{A(D\lambda_1 + E)}{B^2 - 4AC}, \quad e = \frac{A(D\lambda_2 + E)}{B^2 - 4AC}, \quad f = \frac{AF}{B^2 - 4AC}$$

are all real. This is the canonical form (14.94).

Now consider the case in which $A = 0$, $B \neq 0$, $C \neq 0$, and apply the special case of (14.85) given by

$$\begin{aligned} \xi &= x \\ \eta &= x - \frac{B}{C}y. \end{aligned}$$
(14.97)

In this case the coefficients in the transformed equation (14.92) are given by (14.93), where $\xi(x,y)$ and $\eta(x,y)$ are given by (14.97). Evaluating these coefficients (recall $A = 0$ here), we find that

$$A_1 = 0,$$

$$B_1 = -\frac{B^2}{C} \neq 0$$

$$C_1 = B\left(-\frac{B}{C}\right) + C\left(-\frac{B}{C}\right)^2 = 0,$$

$$D_1 = D, \quad E_1 = D - \frac{EB}{C}, \quad \text{and} \quad F_1 = F.$$

Therefore in this case the transformed equation is

$$\left(-\frac{B^2}{C}\right)\frac{\partial^2 u}{\partial\xi\partial\eta} + D\frac{\partial u}{\partial\xi} + \left(\frac{DC - EB}{C}\right)\frac{\partial u}{\partial\eta} + Fu = 0.$$

Since $(-B^2)/C \neq 0$, we may write this in the form

$$\frac{\partial^2 u}{\partial\xi\partial\eta} = d\frac{\partial u}{\partial\xi} + e\frac{\partial u}{\partial\eta} + fu,$$

where the coefficients

$$d = \frac{CD}{B^2}, \quad e = \frac{DC - EB}{B^2}, \quad f = \frac{CF}{B^2}$$

are all real. This is again the canonical form (14.94).

Finally, consider the case in which $A = 0$, $B \neq 0$, $C = 0$. In this case the equation (14.84) is simply

$$B\frac{\partial^2 u}{\partial x\partial y} + D\frac{\partial u}{\partial x} + E\frac{\partial u}{\partial y} + Fu = 0,$$

and the identity transformation (14.98) reduces it to

$$B\frac{\partial^2 u}{\partial\xi\partial\eta} + D\frac{\partial u}{\partial\xi} + E\frac{\partial u}{\partial\eta} + Fu = 0.$$

Since $B \neq 0$, we may write this in the form

$$\frac{\partial^2 u}{\partial\xi\partial\eta} = d\frac{\partial u}{\partial\xi} + e\frac{\partial u}{\partial\eta} + fu,$$

where

$$d = -\frac{D}{B}, \quad e = -\frac{E}{B}, \quad f = -\frac{F}{B}.$$

This is again the canonical form (14.94). In effect, in this special case ($A = 0$, $B \neq 0$, $C = 0$) the equation (14.84) may be put in the canonical form (14.94) simply by transposing the appropriate terms and dividing by B.

We now observe that the three special cases considered exhaust all possibilities for the hyperbolic equation (14.84). We first note that either $A = 0$ or $A \neq 0$. All cases in which $A \neq 0$ are covered by the first of the three special cases which we have considered. Turning to the cases in which $A = 0$, it would appear that the following four distinct possibilities deserve consideration: (a) $B \neq 0$, $C \neq 0$; (b) $B \neq 0$, $C = 0$; (c) $B = 0$,

$C \neq 0$; and (*d*) $B = 0$, $C = 0$. We note that (a) and (b) are covered by the second and third of the three special cases which we have considered. Concerning (c) and (d), in both cases $B^2 - 4AC = 0$, contrary to hypothesis. In particular, if (c) holds, Equation (14.84) is parabolic (not hyperbolic); and if (d) holds, Equation (14.84) is of the first order.

We thus observe that the three special cases considered cover all possibilities for the hyperbolic equation (14.84). Thus there always exists a transformation (14.85) which transforms the hyperbolic equation (14.84) into one which may be written in the canonical form (14.94).   Q.E.D.

Example 14.6.   Consider the equation

(14.100)
$$\frac{\partial^2 u}{\partial x^2} + 4\frac{\partial^2 u}{\partial x \partial y} - 5\frac{\partial^2 u}{\partial y^2} + 6\frac{\partial u}{\partial x} + 3\frac{\partial u}{\partial y} - 9u = 0.$$

We first observe that $B^2 - 4AC = 36 > 0$ and so Equation (14.100) is hyperbolic. Since $A \neq 0$, we consider the transformation

(14.95)
$$\xi = \lambda_1 x + y$$
$$\eta = \lambda_2 x + y,$$

where λ_1 and λ_2 are the roots of the quadratic equation $\lambda^2 + 4\lambda - 5 = 0$. We find that $\lambda_1 = 1$ and $\lambda_2 = -5$, and so the transformation (14.95) is

(14.101)
$$\xi = x + y$$
$$\eta = -5x + y.$$

Applying (14.101) to Equation (14.100), we see that this Equation transforms into

$$-36\frac{\partial^2 u}{\partial \xi \partial \eta} + 9\frac{\partial u}{\partial \xi} - 27\frac{\partial u}{\partial \eta} - 9u = 0.$$

Dividing by -36 and transposing terms, we obtain the canonical form

$$\frac{\partial^2 u}{\partial \xi \partial \eta} = \frac{1}{4}\frac{\partial u}{\partial \xi} - \frac{3}{4}\frac{\partial u}{\partial \eta} - \frac{1}{4}u.$$

C. The Parabolic Equation

We now investigate canonical form in the parabolic case and obtain the following theorem.

THEOREM 14.4.

Hypothesis.   Consider the second-order linear partial differential equation

(14.84)
$$A\frac{\partial^2 u}{\partial x^2} + B\frac{\partial^2 u}{\partial x \partial y} + C\frac{\partial^2 u}{\partial y^2} + D\frac{\partial u}{\partial x} + E\frac{\partial u}{\partial y} + Fu = 0,$$

where the coefficients A, B, C, D, E, and F are real constants and $B^2 - 4AC = 0$ so that the equation is parabolic.

Conclusion. There exists a transformation

(14.85) $$\xi = \xi(x,y), \qquad \eta = \eta(x,y)$$

of the independent variables in (14.84) so that the transformed equation in the independent variables (ξ,η) may be written in the canonical form

(14.102) $$\frac{\partial^2 u}{\partial \eta^2} = d\frac{\partial u}{\partial \xi} + e\frac{\partial u}{\partial \eta} + fu,$$

where d, e, and f are real constants.

If $A \neq 0$ and $C \neq 0$, such a transformation is given by

(14.103) $$\begin{aligned} \xi &= \lambda x + y \\ \eta &= y, \end{aligned}$$

where λ is the repeated real root of the quadratic equation

(14.104) $$A\lambda^2 + B\lambda + C = 0.$$

If $A \neq 0$ and $C = 0$, such a transformation is given by

(14.105) $$\begin{aligned} \xi &= y \\ \eta &= x. \end{aligned}$$

If $A = 0$ and $C \neq 0$, such a transformation is merely the identity transformation

(14.106) $$\begin{aligned} \xi &= x \\ \eta &= y. \end{aligned}$$

Proof. We shall proceed in a manner similar to that by which we proved Theorem 14.3.

If $A \neq 0$ and $C \neq 0$, we apply the transformation (14.103) to obtain the transformed equation (14.92) with coefficients (14.93), where in this case $\xi(x,y)$ and $\eta(x,y)$ are given by (14.103). Evaluating these coefficients we find that

$$A_1 = A\lambda^2 + B\lambda + C,$$
$$B_1 = B\lambda + 2C,$$
$$C_1 = C,$$
$$D_1 = D\lambda + E, \quad E_1 = E, \quad \text{and} \quad F_1 = F.$$

Since λ satisfies the quadratic equation (14.104), we see at once that $A_1 = 0$. Also, since $B^2 - 4AC = 0$, $\lambda = -B/2A$ and so

$$B_1 = -\frac{B^2}{2A} + 2C = \frac{4AC - B^2}{2A} = 0.$$

Thus in the present case the transformed equation (14.92) is

(14.107) $$C\frac{\partial^2 u}{\partial \eta^2} + (D\lambda + E)\frac{\partial u}{\partial \xi} + E\frac{\partial u}{\partial \eta} + Fu = 0.$$

Since λ is real, all coefficients in (14.107) are real; and since $C \neq 0$, we may write equation (14.107) in the form

$$\frac{\partial^2 u}{\partial \eta^2} = d\frac{\partial u}{\partial \xi} + e\frac{\partial u}{\partial \eta} + fu,$$

where the coefficients

$$d = -\frac{D\lambda + E}{C}, \quad e = -\frac{E}{C}, \quad f = -\frac{F}{C}$$

are all real. This is the canonical form (14.102).

   If $A \neq 0$ and $C = 0$, we apply the transformation (14.105) to obtain the transformed equation (14.92) with coefficients (14.93), where in this case $\xi(x,y)$ and $\eta(x,y)$ are given by (14.105). Evaluating these coefficients, we obtain

$$A_1 = C = 0,$$

$$B_1 = B = 0 \quad \text{(since } B^2 - 4AC = 0 \quad \text{and} \quad C = 0),$$

$$C_1 = A \neq 0,$$

$$D_1 = E, \quad E_1 = D, \quad \text{and} \quad F_1 = F.$$

   Thus in the case under consideration the transformed equation (14.92) is

$$A\frac{\partial^2 u}{\partial \eta^2} + E\frac{\partial u}{\partial \xi} + D\frac{\partial u}{\partial \eta} + Fu = 0.$$

Since $A \neq 0$, we may write this in the form

$$\frac{\partial^2 u}{\partial \eta^2} = d\frac{\partial u}{\partial \xi} + e\frac{\partial u}{\partial \eta} + fu,$$

where the coefficients $d = -E/A$, $e = -D/A$, and $f = -F/A$ are all real. This is again the canonical form (14.102).

   Finally, consider the case in which $A = 0$ and $C \neq 0$. Since $B^2 - 4AC = 0$, we must also have $B = 0$. Therefore in this case the equation (14.84) is simply

$$C\frac{\partial^2 u}{\partial y^2} + D\frac{\partial u}{\partial x} + E\frac{\partial u}{\partial y} + Fu = 0,$$

and the identity transformation (14.106) reduces it to

$$C\frac{\partial^2 u}{\partial \eta^2} + D\frac{\partial u}{\partial \xi} + E\frac{\partial u}{\partial \eta} + Fu = 0.$$

Since $C \neq 0$, we may write this in the form

$$\frac{\partial^2 u}{\partial \eta^2} = d\frac{\partial u}{\partial \xi} + e\frac{\partial u}{\partial \eta} + fu,$$

where $d = -D/C, e = -E/C, f = -F/C.$
This is again the canonical form (14.102). We thus see that in this special case ($A = 0$, $B = 0$, $C \neq 0$) the equation (14.84) may be put in the canonical form (14.102) simply by transposing the appropriate terms and dividing by C.

   Finally, we observe that the three special cases considered exhaust all possibilities for the parabolic equation (14.84). For, either $A = 0$ or $A \neq 0$. If $A \neq 0$, either $C \neq 0$ or $C = 0$.

These two possibilities are, respectively, the first and second special cases considered, and so all cases in which $A \neq 0$ are thus covered. If $A = 0$, either $C \neq 0$ or $C = 0$. The first of these two possibilities is the third special case considered. Finally, consider the situation in which $A = 0$ and $C = 0$. Since $B^2 - 4AC = 0$, we must also have $B = 0$ and so equation (14.84) reduces to a first order equation.

Therefore there always exists a transformation (14.85) which transforms the parabolic equation (14.84) into one which may be written in the canonical form (14.102).   *Q.E.D.*

Example 14.7.   Consider the equation

$$(14.108) \qquad \frac{\partial^2 u}{\partial x^2} - 6\frac{\partial^2 u}{\partial x \partial y} + 9\frac{\partial^2 u}{\partial y^2} + 2\frac{\partial u}{\partial x} + 3\frac{\partial u}{\partial y} - u = 0$$

We observe that $B^2 - 4AC = 0$, and so Equation (14.108) is parabolic. Since $A \neq 0$ and $C \neq 0$, we consider the transformation

$$(14.103) \qquad \begin{aligned} \xi &= \lambda x + y \\ \eta &= y, \end{aligned}$$

where λ is the repeated real root of the quadratic equation $\lambda^2 - 6\lambda + 9 = 0$. We find that $\lambda = 3$, and so the transformation (14.103) is

$$(14.109) \qquad \begin{aligned} \xi &= 3x + y \\ \eta &= y. \end{aligned}$$

Applying (14.109) to Equation (14.108), we see that this equation transforms into

$$9\frac{\partial^2 u}{\partial \eta^2} + 9\frac{\partial u}{\partial \xi} + 3\frac{\partial u}{\partial \eta} - u = 0.$$

Dividing by 9 and transposing terms, we obtain the canonical form

$$\frac{\partial^2 u}{\partial \eta^2} = -\frac{\partial u}{\partial \xi} - \frac{1}{3}\frac{\partial u}{\partial \eta} + \frac{1}{9}u.$$

D. The Elliptic Equation

Finally, we prove the following theorem concerning the canonical form in the elliptic case.

THEOREM 14.5.

Hypothesis.   Consider the second-order linear partial differential equation

$$(14.84) \qquad A\frac{\partial^2 u}{\partial x^2} + B\frac{\partial^2 u}{\partial x \partial y} + C\frac{\partial^2 u}{\partial y^2} + D\frac{\partial u}{\partial x} + E\frac{\partial u}{\partial y} + Fu = 0,$$

where the coefficients A, B, C, D, E, and F are real constants and $B^2 - 4AC < 0$ so that the equation is elliptic.

Conclusion.   There exists a transformation

$$(14.85) \qquad \xi = \xi(x,y), \quad \eta = \eta(x,y)$$

of the independent variables in (14.84) so that the transformed equation in the independent variables (ξ, η) may be written in the canonical form

(14.110)
$$\frac{\partial^2 u}{\partial \xi^2} + \frac{\partial^2 u}{\partial \eta^2} = d\frac{\partial u}{\partial \xi} + e\frac{\partial u}{\partial \eta} + fu,$$

where d, e, and f are real constants.

Such a transformation is given by

(14.111)
$$\xi = ax + y$$
$$\eta = bx,$$

where $a \pm bi$ (a and b real, $b \neq 0$) are the conjugate complex roots of the quadratic equation

(14.112)
$$A\lambda^2 + B\lambda + C = 0$$

Proof. Since $B^2 - 4AC < 0$, we can not have $A = 0$ in the elliptic case. Thus the equation (14.112) is a full-fledged quadratic equation with two roots. The condition $B^2 - 4AC < 0$ further shows that these two roots must indeed be conjugate complex.

We apply the transformation (14.111) to obtain the transformed equation (14.92) with coefficients (14.93), where in this case $\xi(x,y)$ and $\eta(x,y)$ are given by (14.111). Evaluating these coefficients we find that

$$A_1 = Aa^2 + Ba + C,$$
$$B_1 = 2Aab + Bb = b(2Aa + B)$$
$$C_1 = Ab^2 \neq 0 \quad (\text{since } A \neq 0, b \neq 0)$$
$$D_1 = Da + E, \quad E_1 = Db, \quad \text{and} \quad F_1 = F.$$

Since $a + bi$ satisfies the quadratic equation (14.112), we have

$$A(a + bi)^2 + B(a + bi) + C = 0$$

or

$$[A(a^2 - b^2) + Ba + C] + [b(2Aa + B)]i = 0.$$

Therefore

$$A(a^2 - b^2) + Ba + C = 0$$

and

$$b(2Aa + B) = 0.$$

Thus

$$A_1 = Aa^2 + Ba + C = Ab^2$$

and

$$B_1 = 0.$$

Hence the transformed equation (14.92) is

(14.113)
$$Ab^2\left(\frac{\partial^2 u}{\partial \xi^2} + \frac{\partial^2 u}{\partial \eta^2}\right) + (Da + E)\frac{\partial u}{\partial \xi} + Db\frac{\partial u}{\partial \eta} + Fu = 0.$$

Since a and b are real, all coefficients in (14.113) are real; and since $Ab^2 \neq 0$, we may write Equation (14.113) in the form

$$\frac{\partial^2 u}{\partial \xi^2} + \frac{\partial^2 u}{\partial \eta^2} = d\frac{\partial u}{\partial \xi} + e\frac{\partial u}{\partial \eta} + fu,$$

where the coefficients

$$d = -\frac{Da + E}{Ab^2}, \quad e = -\frac{D}{Ab}, \quad = -\frac{F}{Ab^2}$$

are all real. This is the canonical form (14.110).   *Q.E.D.*

Example 14.8.   Consider the equation

(14.114) $$\frac{\partial^2 u}{\partial x^2} + 2\frac{\partial^2 u}{\partial x \partial y} + 5\frac{\partial^2 u}{\partial y^2} + \frac{\partial u}{\partial x} - 2\frac{\partial u}{\partial y} - 3u = 0.$$

We observe that $B^2 - 4AC = -16 < 0$ and so Equation (14.114) is elliptic. We consider the transformation

(14.111) $$\xi = ax + y,$$
                     $$\eta = bx,$$

where $a \pm bi$ are the conjugate complex roots of the quadratic equation $\lambda^2 + 2\lambda + 5 = 0$. We find that these roots are $-1 \pm 2i$, and so the transformation (14.111) is

(14.115) $$\xi = -x + y,$$
                     $$\eta = 2x.$$

Applying (14.115) to Equation (14.114), we see that this equation transforms into

$$4\frac{\partial^2 u}{\partial \xi^2} + 4\frac{\partial^2 u}{\partial \eta^2} - 3\frac{\partial u}{\partial \xi} + 2\frac{\partial u}{\partial \eta} - 3u = 0.$$

Dividing by 4 and transposing terms, we obtain the canonical form

$$\frac{\partial^2 u}{\partial \xi^2} + \frac{\partial^2 u}{\partial \eta^2} = \frac{3}{4}\frac{\partial u}{\partial \xi} - \frac{1}{2}\frac{\partial u}{\partial \eta} + \frac{3}{4}u.$$

E.   Summary

Summarizing, we list in the following table the canonical forms which we have obtained for the second-order linear partial differential equation

(14.84) $$A\frac{\partial^2 u}{\partial x^2} + B\frac{\partial^2 u}{\partial x \partial y} + C\frac{\partial^2 u}{\partial y^2} + D\frac{\partial u}{\partial x} + E\frac{\partial u}{\partial y} + Fu = 0,$$

where A, B, C, D, E, and F are real constants.

Table 14.1

Type of the Equation (14.84)	Canonical Form (where d, e, and f are real constants)
Hyperbolic: $B^2 - 4AC > 0$	$\dfrac{\partial^2 u}{\partial \xi \partial \eta} = d\dfrac{\partial u}{\partial \xi} + e\dfrac{\partial u}{\partial \eta} + fu$
Parabolic: $B^2 - 4AC = 0$	$\dfrac{\partial^2 u}{\partial \eta^2} = d\dfrac{\partial u}{\partial \xi} + e\dfrac{\partial u}{\partial \eta} + fu$
Elliptic: $B^2 - 4AC < 0$	$\dfrac{\partial^2 u}{\partial \xi^2} + \dfrac{\partial^2 u}{\partial \eta^2} = d\dfrac{\partial u}{\partial \xi} + e\dfrac{\partial u}{\partial \eta} + fu$

Exercises

Transform each of the partial differential equations in Exercises 1 through 10 into canonical form.

1. $\dfrac{\partial^2 u}{\partial x^2} - 5\dfrac{\partial^2 u}{\partial x \partial y} + 6\dfrac{\partial^2 u}{\partial y^2} = 0.$

2. $\dfrac{\partial^2 u}{\partial x^2} - 4\dfrac{\partial^2 u}{\partial x \partial y} + 4\dfrac{\partial^2 u}{\partial y^2} = 0.$

3. $\dfrac{\partial^2 u}{\partial x^2} - 2\dfrac{\partial^2 u}{\partial x \partial y} - 8\dfrac{\partial^2 u}{\partial y^2} + 9\dfrac{\partial u}{\partial x} = 0.$

4. $2\dfrac{\partial^2 u}{\partial x^2} + 3\dfrac{\partial^2 u}{\partial x \partial y} - 9\dfrac{\partial^2 u}{\partial y^2} + 4\dfrac{\partial u}{\partial x} = 0.$

5. $\dfrac{\partial^2 u}{\partial x^2} - 4\dfrac{\partial^2 u}{\partial x \partial y} + 13\dfrac{\partial^2 u}{\partial y^2} - 9\dfrac{\partial u}{\partial y} = 0.$

6. $\dfrac{\partial^2 u}{\partial x^2} + 2\dfrac{\partial^2 u}{\partial x \partial y} + \dfrac{\partial^2 u}{\partial y^2} + 3\dfrac{\partial u}{\partial x} + 9u = 0.$

7. $6\dfrac{\partial^2 u}{\partial x \partial y} + 3\dfrac{\partial^2 u}{\partial y^2} + 2\dfrac{\partial u}{\partial x} = 0.$

8. $\dfrac{\partial^2 u}{\partial x^2} + 4\dfrac{\partial^2 u}{\partial x \partial y} + 3\dfrac{\partial u}{\partial x} + 5\dfrac{\partial u}{\partial y} = 0.$

9. $2\dfrac{\partial^2 u}{\partial x^2} - 2\dfrac{\partial^2 u}{\partial x \partial y} + 5\dfrac{\partial^2 u}{\partial y^2} + u = 0.$

10. $\dfrac{\partial^2 u}{\partial x^2} - 5\dfrac{\partial^2 u}{\partial x \partial y} + 5\dfrac{\partial u}{\partial x} - \dfrac{\partial u}{\partial y} + 3u = 0.$

11. Show that the transformation

$$\begin{cases} \xi = y - \dfrac{x^2}{2} \\[2mm] \eta = x \end{cases}$$

reduces the equation

$$\frac{\partial^2 u}{\partial x^2} + 2x\frac{\partial^2 u}{\partial x \partial y} + x^2\frac{\partial^2 u}{\partial y^2} = 0$$

to

$$\frac{\partial^2 u}{\partial \eta^2} = \frac{\partial u}{\partial \xi}.$$

12. Consider the equation

(A)
$$\frac{\partial^2 u}{\partial x^2} + (2x + 3)\frac{\partial^2 u}{\partial x \partial y} + 6x\frac{\partial^2 u}{\partial y^2} = 0.$$

(a) Show that for $x = 3/2$, Equation (A) reduces to a parabolic equation, and reduce this parabolic equation to canonical form.

(b) Show that for $x \neq 3/2$, the transformation

$$\begin{cases} \xi = y - 3x \\ \eta = y - x^2 \end{cases}$$

reduces equation (A) to

$$\frac{\partial^2 u}{\partial \xi \partial \eta} = \frac{2\dfrac{\partial u}{\partial \eta}}{4(\eta - \xi) - 9}.$$

14.4   An Initial-Value Problem; Characteristics

A. An Initial Value Problem

We shall now consider an initial-value problem for the second-order linear partial differential equation

(14.84)
$$A\frac{\partial^2 u}{\partial x^2} + B\frac{\partial^2 u}{\partial x \partial y} + C\frac{\partial^2 u}{\partial y^2} + D\frac{\partial u}{\partial x} + E\frac{\partial u}{\partial y} + Fu = 0,$$

where A, B, C, D, E, and F are real constants. In Chapters 4 and 11 we considered an initial-value problem for linear *ordinary* differential equations. Let us begin by recalling this problem for the second-order homogeneous linear ordinary differential equation with constant coefficients,

(14.116)
$$a\frac{d^2 y}{dx^2} + b\frac{dy}{dx} + cy = 0.$$

The problem is to find a solution f of (14.116) such that $f(x_0) = c_0$ and $f'(x_0) = c_1$, where x_0 is some definite real number and c_0 and c_1 are arbitrary real constants. Interpreting this geometrically, the problem is to find a solution curve $y = f(x)$ of (14.116) which passes through the point (x_0, c_0) and whose tangent line has the slope c_1 at this point.

Let us now attempt to formulate an analogous initial value problem for the *partial* differential equation (14.84). In doing this we shall let ourselves be guided by the geometric interpretation of the initial-value problem for the ordinary differential equation

(14.116). In this problem we must find a solution of Equation (14.116) which satisfies certain supplementary conditions (the initial conditions). A solution of Equation (14.116) is a function f of the one real variable x, and this defines a curve $y = f(x)$ (a solution curve) in the x,y plane. In the analogous problem for the partial differential equation (14.84), we shall also seek a solution which satisfies certain supplementary conditions. But a solution of Equation (14.84) is a function ϕ of the two real variables x and y, and this defines a surface $u = \phi(x,y)$ (a solution surface) in three dimensional x,y,u space. Geometrically speaking, then, for the partial differential equation (14.84) we must find a particular solution surface $u = \phi(x,y)$ in x,y,u space. Now in the initial value problem for the ordinary differential equation (14.116), there are two supplementary requirements which the solution curve $y = f(x)$ in the x,y plane must satisfy. First, the solution curve $y = f(x)$ must pass through a prescribed point (x_0,c_0) in the x,y plane; and, second, this solution curve must be such that its tangent line has a prescribed slope c_1 at this point. What sort of analogous requirements might be imposed in an initial value problem for the partial differential equation (14.84)? Instead of prescribing a point in the x,y plane through which the solution curve must pass, we would prescribe a curve in x,y,u space through which the solution surface must pass. Instead of prescribing a slope for the tangent line to the solution curve at the prescribed point, we would prescribe a normal direction for the tangent plane to the solution surface along the prescribed curve. We thus formulate an initial-value problem for the partial differential equation (14.84) in the following geometric language.

We seek a solution surface $u = \phi(x,y)$ of the partial differential equation (14.84) which (a) passes through a prescribed curve Γ (the initial curve) in x,y,u space, and (b) is such that its tangent plane has a prescribed normal direction at all points of the initial curve Γ.

Let us now proceed to formulate this initial-value problem analytically. To do so, let us assume that the prescribed curve Γ has the parametric representation

$$x = x(t), \qquad y = y(t), \qquad u = u(t)$$

for all t on some real interval I. Now let $t_0 \in I$ and consider the corresponding point on Γ. This point has coordinates (x_0,y_0,u_0), where $x_0 = x(t_0)$, $y_0 = y(t_0)$, $u_0 = u(t_0)$. If the solution surface $u = \phi(x,y)$ is to pass through Γ at (x_0,y_0,u_0), then we must have $u_0 = \phi(x_0,y_0)$ or, equivalently, $u(t_0) = \phi[x(t_0),y(t_0)]$. Therefore the requirement that the solution surface $u = \phi(x,y)$ pass through the entire curve Γ is expressed by the condition

(14.117) $$u(t) = \phi[x(t), y(t)]$$

for all $t \in I$.

We now consider the requirement that the tangent plane to the solution surface $u = \phi(x,y)$ have a prescribed normal direction at all points of Γ. Let us assume that this prescribed normal direction is given by $[p(t),q(t), -1]$ for all $t \in I$. Recalling that the nomal direction to the tangent plane to $u = \phi(x,y)$ is given by

$$[\phi_x(x,y), \quad \phi_y(x,y), \; -1], \dagger$$

†Here and throughout the remainder of the chapter it is convenient to employ subscript notation for the various partial derivatives of ϕ. Thus we denote

$$\frac{\partial \phi}{\partial x} \text{ by } \phi_x, \frac{\partial \phi}{\partial y} \text{ by } \phi_y, \frac{\partial^2 \phi}{\partial x^2} \text{ by } \phi_{xx},$$

$$\frac{\partial^2 \phi}{\partial y \partial x} \text{ by } \phi_{xy}, \text{ and } \frac{\partial^2 \phi}{\partial y^2} \text{ by } \phi_{yy}.$$

we see that the requirement under consideration is expressed by the conditions that

$$p(t) = \phi_x[x(t),y(t)],$$

(14.118)

$$q(t) = \phi_y[x(t),y(t)],$$

for all $t \in I$.

We have thus far said nothing concerning the nature of the functions x,y,u which define Γ or the functions p,q which prescribe the normal direction. Let us assume that each of these five functions is analytic for all $t \in I$. We must now observe that the functions p and q cannot be chosen arbitrarily. For, from (14.117) we must have

$$\frac{du(t)}{dt} = \phi_x[x(t),y(t)]\frac{dx(t)}{dt} + \phi_y[x(t),y(t)]\frac{dy(t)}{dt}$$

for all $t \in I$; and since (14.118) must hold for all $t \in I$, this reduces to

(14.119)
$$\frac{du(t)}{dt} = p(t)\frac{dx(t)}{dt} + q(t)\frac{dy(t)}{dt}$$

for all $t \in I$. Thus the functions p and q are not arbitrary; rather they must satisfy the problem identity (14.119).

In our attempt to formulate the initial-value problem analytically, we have thus introduced a set of five functions defined by $\{x(t),y(t),u(t),p(t),q(t)\}$, where (i) $x = x(t)$, $y = y(t)$, $u = u(t)$ is the analytic representation of a prescribed curve Γ in x,y,u space, (ii) $[p(t),q(t), -1]$ is the analytic representation of a prescribed normal direction along Γ, and (iii) these five functions satisfy the identity (14.119). Such a set of five functions is called a *strip*, and the identity (14.119) is called the *strip condition*.

We may now state the initial-value problem in the following way.

Initial-Value Problem. Consider the second-order linear partial differential equation

(14.84)
$$A\frac{\partial^2 u}{\partial x^2} + B\frac{\partial^2 u}{\partial x \partial y} + C\frac{\partial^2 u}{\partial y^2} + D\frac{\partial u}{\partial x} + E\frac{\partial u}{\partial y} + Fu = 0,$$

where A, B, C, D, E, and F are real constants. Let $x(t),y(t),u(t),p(t)$, and $q(t)$ denote five real functions, each of which is analytic for all t on a real interval I. Further, let these five functions be such that the condition

(14.119)
$$\frac{du(t)}{dt} = p(t)\frac{dx(t)}{dt} + q(t)\frac{dy(t)}{dt}$$

holds for all $t \in I$. Let R be a region of the x,y plane such that $[x(t),y(t)] \in R$ for all $t \in I$.

We seek a solution $\phi(x,y)$ for the partial differential equation (14.84), defined for all $(x,y) \in R$, such that

(14.117)
$$\phi[x(t),y(t)] = u(t),$$

and

$$\phi_x[x(t),y(t)] = p(t),$$
(14.118)
$$\phi_y[x(t),y(t)] = q(t),$$

for all $t \in I$.

Example 14.9. Consider the partial differential equation

(14.120)
$$\frac{\partial^2 u}{\partial x^2} + \frac{\partial^2 u}{\partial x \partial y} - 2\frac{\partial^2 u}{\partial y^2} = 0$$

and the five real functions defined by

(14.121) $\quad x(t) = t, \quad y(t) = t^2, \quad u(t) = t^4 + 2t^2, \quad p(t) = 4t, \quad q(t) = 2t^2$

for all real t. We observe that these five functions satisfy the strip condition (14.119); indeed we have

$$4t^3 + 4t = (4t)(1) + (2t^2)(2t)$$

for all real t. We may therefore interpret the set of five functions defined by (14.121) as a strip and state the following initial-value problem.

We seek a solution $\phi(x,y)$ of the partial differential equation (14.120), defined for all (x,y), such that

$$\phi(t,t^2) = t^4 + 2t^2,$$
(14.122)
$$\phi_x(t,t^2) = 4t$$
$$\phi_y(t,t^2) = 2t^2$$

for all real t.

Geometrically, we seek a solution surface $u = \phi(x,y)$ of the partial differential equation (14.120) which (a) passes through the space curve Γ defined by

$$x = t, \quad y = t^2, \quad u = t^4 + 2t^2$$

for all real t, and (b) is such that its tangent plane has the normal direction $(4t, 2t^2, -1)$ at all points of Γ.

We now observe that a solution of this problem is the function ϕ defined by

$$\phi(x,y) = 2x^2 + y^2$$

for all (x,y). In the first place, this function ϕ satisfies the partial differential equation (14.120). For we find that

$\phi_{xx}(x,y) = 4, \quad \phi_{yx}(x,y) = 0, \quad$ and $\quad \phi_{yy}(x,y) = 2$, so that

$$\phi_{xx}(x,y) + \phi_{yx}(x,y) - 2\phi_{yy}(x,y) = 0$$

for all (x,y). In the second place, the conditions (14.122) are satisfied. Clearly $\phi(t,t^2) = 2t^2 + t^4$ for all real t. From $\phi_x(x,y) = 4x$, we see that $\phi_x(t,t^2) = 4t$ for all real t; and from $\phi_y(x,y) = 2y$, we see that $\phi_y(t,t^2) = 2t^2$ for all real t.

We shall now examine the initial-value problem from a slightly different viewpoint, again employing useful geometric terminology in our discussion. Suppose, as before, that the curve Γ through which the solution surface $u = \phi(x,y)$ must pass is defined by

$$(14.123) \qquad x = x(t), \quad y = y(t), \quad u = u(t)$$

for all t on some real interval I. Then the projection of Γ on the x,y plane is the curve Γ_0 defined by

$$(14.124) \qquad x = x(t), \quad y = y(t)$$

for all $t \in I$. Employing this curve Γ_0, we may express the initial-value problem in the following form.

We seek a solution $\phi(x,y)$ of the partial differential equation (14.84) such that ϕ, ϕ_x, and ϕ_y assume prescribed values given by $u(t), p(t)$, and $q(t)$, respectively, for each $t \in I$, or, in other words, at each point of Γ_0 [where we assume that the five functions given by $x(t)$, $y(t), u(t), p(t)$, and $q(t)$ satisfy the strip condition (14.119)].

We shall find that this interpretation of the initial value problem will be useful in the discussion which follows.

B. Characteristics

Continuing our discussion of the initial value problem, let us now assume that the problem has a unique solution $\phi(x,y)$ defined on a region R (of the x,y plane) which includes the curve Γ_0. Let us also assume that at each point of Γ_0 the solution $\phi(x,y)$ has a power series expansion which is valid in some circle about this point. Now let $t_0 \in I$ and let $x_0 = x(t_0), y_0 = y(t_0)$, so that (x_0, y_0) is a point of Γ_0. Then for all (x,y) in some circle K about (x_0, y_0) we have the valid power series expansion

$$
\begin{aligned}
(14.125) \qquad \phi(x,y) = {} & \phi(x_0,y_0) + [\phi_x(x_0,y_0)(x - x_0) + \phi_y(x_0,y_0)(y - y_0)] \\
& + \frac{1}{2!} [\phi_{xx}(x_0,y_0)(x - x_0)^2 + 2\phi_{xy}(x_0,y_0)(x - x_0)(y - y_0) \\
& + \phi_{yy}(x_0,y_0)(y - y_0)^2] + \cdots.
\end{aligned}
$$

The solution $\phi(x,y)$ will be determined in the circle K if we can determine the coefficients

$$\phi(x_0,y_0), \quad \phi_x(x_0,y_0), \quad \phi_y(x_0,y_0), \quad \phi_{xx}(x_0,y_0), \ldots$$

in the expansion (14.125).

Now we already know the first three of these coefficients. For the initial-value problem requires that ϕ, ϕ_x, and ϕ_y assume prescribed values given by $u(t), p(t)$, and $q(t)$, respectively, at each point of Γ_0. Therefore at the point (x_0, y_0) at which $t = t_0$, we have

$$\phi(x_0,y_0) = u(t_0),$$

$$\phi_x(x_0,y_0) = p(t_0),$$

and

$$\phi_y(x_0,y_0) = q(t_0).$$

Let us now attempt to calculate the next three coefficients in (14.125). That is, let us see if we can determine

$$(14.126) \qquad \phi_{xx}(x_0,y_0), \quad \phi_{xy}(x_0,y_0), \quad \phi_{yy}(x_0,y_0).$$

To do this, we need to know conditions which these numbers must satisfy. One such condition is readily available: it can be obtained at once from the partial differential differential equation (14.84)! For, since $\phi(x,y)$ is a solution of (14.84) in the region R, we have

$$A\phi_{xx}(x,y) + B\phi_{xy}(x,y) + C\phi_{yy}(x,y) = -D\phi_x(x,y) - E\phi_y(x,y) - F\phi(x,y)$$

for all $(x,y) \in R$. Thus, since $(x_0,y_0) \in R$, we have the condition

(14.127) $\quad A\phi_{xx}(x_0,y_0) + B\phi_{xy}(x_0,y_0) + C\phi_{yy}(x_0,y_0)$

$$= -D\phi_x(x_0,y_0) - E\phi_y(x_0,y_0) - F\phi(x_0,y_0).$$

Now along the curve Γ_0 we know that

$$\phi_x[x(t),y(t)] = p(t)$$

and

$$\phi_y[x(t),y(t)] = q(t).$$

Differentiating these identities with respect to t, we find that along the curve Γ_0 we have

$$\phi_{xx}[x(t),y(t)]\frac{dx}{dt} + \phi_{xy}[x(t),y(t)]\frac{dy}{dt} = \frac{dp}{dt}$$

$$\phi_{xy}[x(t),y(t)]\frac{dx}{dt} + \phi_{yy}[x(t),y(t)]\frac{dy}{dt} = \frac{dq}{dt}.$$

Since (x_0,y_0) is a point of Γ_0, we thus obtain the two additional conditions

(14.128) $$x'(t_0)\phi_{xx}(x_0,y_0) + y'(t_0)\phi_{xy}(x_0,y_0) = p'(t_0)$$

and

(14.129) $$x'(t_0)\phi_{xy}(x_0,y_0) + y'(t_0)\phi_{yy}(x_0,y_0) = q'(t_0),$$

where $x'(t_0),y'(t_0),p'(t_0)$, and $q'(t_0)$ denote the values of $\dfrac{dx}{dt}, \dfrac{dy}{dt}, \dfrac{dp}{dt}$, and $\dfrac{dq}{dt}$, respectively, at $t = t_0$.

Let us examine more closely the three conditions (14.127), (14.128), and (14.129). They are actually a system of three linear algebraic equations in the three unknown numbers (14.126); all other quantities involved are known numbers! A necessary and sufficient condition that this system have a unique solution is that the determinant of coefficients be unequal to zero (see Chapter 11, Theorem C). Therefore in order to have a unique solution for the three coefficients (14.126), we must have

$$\Delta(t_0) = \begin{vmatrix} A & B & C \\ x'(t_0) & y'(t_0) & 0 \\ 0 & x'(t_0) & y'(t_0) \end{vmatrix} \neq 0.$$

Conversely, if $\Delta(t_0) \neq 0$, we can determine the three coefficients (14.126) from the linear system consisting of Equations (14.127), (14.128), and (14.129).

We have assumed that the solution $\phi(x,y)$ has a power series expansion of the form

(14.125) at *each* point of the curve Γ_0. Thus if the determinant

$$\Delta(t) = \begin{vmatrix} A & B & C \\ \dfrac{dx}{dt} & \dfrac{dy}{dt} & 0 \\ 0 & \dfrac{dx}{dt} & \dfrac{dy}{dt} \end{vmatrix} \neq 0$$

at all points of Γ_0, we can determine the values of ϕ_{xx}, ϕ_{xy}, and ϕ_{yy} all along Γ_0. We can then attempt to find the values of the higher derivatives of $\phi(x,y)$ along Γ_0, employing a procedure similar to that by which we found the values of the three second derivatives. One can show that if $\Delta(t) \neq 0$ at all points of Γ_0, then the values of these higher derivatives can be determined all along Γ_0. In this manner we find the coefficients in the series expansion of $\phi(x,y)$ along Γ_0.

It can be shown that if $\Delta(t) \neq 0$ at all points of Γ_0, then there exists a unique solution of the initial value problem. On the other hand, if $\Delta(t) = 0$ at all points of Γ_0, then there is either no solution or infinitely many solutions.

Let us now consider a curve Γ_0 at all points of which

$$\Delta(t) = \begin{vmatrix} A & B & C \\ \dfrac{dx}{dt} & \dfrac{dy}{dt} & 0 \\ 0 & \dfrac{dx}{dt} & \dfrac{dy}{dt} \end{vmatrix} = 0.$$

Expanding this determinant, we thus see that

$$A\left(\frac{dy}{dt}\right)^2 - B\frac{dx}{dt}\frac{dy}{dt} + C\left(\frac{dx}{dt}\right)^2 = 0$$

at all points of Γ_0. Therefore Γ_0 must be a curve having an equation $\zeta(x,y) = c_0$ which satisfies

$$(14.130) \qquad\qquad A dy^2 - B dx dy + C dx^2 = 0.$$

We thus investigate the solutions of equation (14.130). We shall divide this discussion into the following three subcases: (a) $A \neq 0$; (b) $A = 0$, $C \neq 0$; and (c) $A = 0$, $C = 0$.

Subcase (a): $A \neq 0$. In this case it follows from (14.130) that the curve Γ_0 is defined by $y = \phi(x)$, where $\phi(x)$ satisfies the ordinary differential equation

$$A\left(\frac{dy}{dx}\right)^2 - B\frac{dy}{dx} + C = 0.$$

From this equation we see that

$$\frac{dy}{dx} = \frac{B + \sqrt{B^2 - 4AC}}{2A} \quad \text{or} \quad \frac{dy}{dx} = \frac{B - \sqrt{B^2 - 4AC}}{2A}$$

Thus if $A \neq 0$ the curve Γ_0 must be a member of one of the families of straight lines defined by

$$y = \left[\frac{B + \sqrt{B^2 - 4AC}}{2A}\right]x + c_1 \quad \text{or} \quad y = \left[\frac{B - \sqrt{B^2 - 4AC}}{2A}\right]x + c_2,$$

where c_1 and c_2 are arbitrary constants.

Subcase (b): $A = 0$, $C \neq 0$. In this case it follows from (14.130) that Γ_0 is defined by $x = \theta(y)$, where $\theta(y)$ satisfies the ordinary differential equation

$$C\left(\frac{dx}{dy}\right)^2 - B\frac{dx}{dy} = 0.$$

From this equation we see that

$$\frac{dx}{dy} = \frac{B}{C} \quad \text{or} \quad \frac{dx}{dy} = 0.$$

Thus if $A = 0$ and $C \neq 0$, the curve Γ_0 must be a member of one of the families of straight lines defined by

(14.132) $$x = \frac{B}{C}y + c_1 \quad \text{or} \quad x = c_2,$$

where c_1 and c_2 are arbitrary constants.

Subcase (c): $A = 0$, $C = 0$. In this case it follows at once from (14.130) that the curve Γ_0 must be a member of one of the families of straight lines defined by

(14.133) $$y = c_1 \quad \text{or} \quad x = c_2,$$

where c_1 and c_2 are arbitrary constants.

Thus if Γ_0 is a curve at all points of which $\Delta(t) = 0$, then Γ_0 must be one of the straight lines defined by (14.131), (14.132), or (14.133). Any such curve Γ_0 in the x,y plane along which $\Delta(t) = 0$ is called a *characteristic* (or *characteristic base curve*) of the partial differential equation (14.84). In other words, a characteristic of (14.84) is any curve Γ_0 in the x,y plane having an equation $\zeta(x,y) = c_0$ which satisfies

(14.130) $$Ady^2 - Bdxdy + Cdx^2 = 0.$$

We have shown that the characteristics of the partial differential equation (14.84) are straight lines. Specifically, if $A \neq 0$, they are the straight lines defined by (14.131); if $A = 0$ and $C \neq 0$, they are those defined by (14.132); and if $A = 0$ and $C = 0$, they are given by (14.133).

Let us consider the connection between the characteristics of the partial differential equation (14.84) and the initial-value problem associated with this equation. Recall that in this problem we seek a solution $\phi(x,y)$ of (14.84) such that ϕ, ϕ_x, and ϕ_y assume prescribed values given by $u(t), p(t)$, and $q(t)$, respectively, at each point of a curve Γ_0 (in the x,y plane) defined by $x = x(t)$, $y = y(t)$ for all t on some real interval I.

Further recall that if

$$\Delta(t) = \begin{vmatrix} A & B & C \\ \dfrac{dx}{dt} & \dfrac{dy}{dt} & 0 \\ 0 & \dfrac{dx}{dt} & \dfrac{dy}{dt} \end{vmatrix}$$

is unequal to zero at all points of Γ_0, then this initial value problem has a unique solution; but if $\Delta(t) = 0$ at all points of Γ_0, then there is either no solution or infinitely many solutions. Now we have defined a characteristic of (14.84) as a curve in the x,y plane along which $\Delta(t) = 0$. Thus we may say that if the curve Γ_0 is nowhere tangent to a characteristic, then the initial-value problem has a unique solution; but if Γ_0 is a characteristic, then the problem has either no solution or infinitely many solutions.

We now examine the characteristics of Equation (14.84) in the hyperbolic, parabolic and elliptic cases. We shall find it convenient to consider once again the three subcases (a) $A \neq 0$, (b) $A = 0$, $C \neq 0$, and (c) $A = 0$, $C = 0$.

Subcase (a): $A \neq 0$. In this case the characteristics of (14.84) are the families of straight lines defined by (14.131). If the equation (14.84) is hyperbolic, then $B^2 - 4AC > 0$ and (14.131) defines two distinct families of real straight lines. If (14.84) is parabolic, then $B^2 - 4AC = 0$, the two families of straight lines coincide, and (14.131) defines only one family of real straight lines. If (14.84) is elliptic, then $B^2 - 4AC < 0$, the lines defined by (14.131) are not real, and there are no real characteristics.

Subcase (b): $A = 0$. $C \neq 0$. In this case the characteristics are defined by (14.132). Since $A = 0$, $B^2 - 4AC = B^2 \geq 0$ and so the elliptic case can not occur. In order for Equation (14.84) to be hyperbolic, we must have $B \neq 0$ and then (14.132) defines two distinct families of real straight lines. In the parabolic case, we must have $B = 0$ and then the two families coincide, so that (14.132) defines only one family of real straight lines.

Subcase (c): $A = 0$, $C = 0$. In this case we must have $B \neq 0$ in order for Equation (14.84) to be of the second order. But then $B^2 - 4AC = B^2 > 0$, and so Equation (14.84) must be hyperbolic. The characteristics are given by (14.133) and hence are two distinct families of real straight lines.

Let us summarize what we have thus found concerning the nature of the characteristics of Equation (14.84). If Equation (14.84) is hyperbolic, then the characteristics consist of two distinct families of real straight lines. If Equation (14.84) is parabolic, then the characteristics consist of a single family of real straight lines. If Equation (14.84) is elliptic, then there are no real characteristics.

We observe the significance of these results as they relate to the initial value problem associated with Equation (14.84). Recall that if the curve Γ_0 is nowhere tangent to a characteristic, then the initial value problem has a unique solution. In the elliptic case there are no real characteristics and so this requirement concerning Γ_0 is automatically satisfied. Thus if Equation (14.84) is elliptic, the associated initial-value problem has a unique solution. In the hyperbolic and parabolic cases real characteristics exist; they are certain straight lines. Thus if Equation (14.84) is hyperbolic or parabolic, the associated initial-value problem has a unique solution if the curve Γ_0 is nowhere tangent to one of the straight lines which is a characteristic.

Example 14.10.   Find the characteristics of the equation

(14.120)
$$\frac{\partial^2 u}{\partial x^2} + \frac{\partial^2 u}{\partial x \partial y} - 2\frac{\partial^2 u}{\partial y^2} = 0.$$

We first note that $A = 1$, $B = 1$, $C = -2$, and $B^2 - 4AC = 9 > 0$. Therefore equation (14.120) is hyperbolic and so that characteristics consist of two distinct families of real straight lines. Let us proceed to find them. We have observed that they satisfy the equation

(14.130)
$$A dy^2 - B dx dy + C dx^2 = 0.$$

For the equation (14.120) the equation (14.130) reduces to

$$dy^2 - dx dy - 2 dx^2 = 0,$$

and so the characteristics of Equation (14.120) are the solutions of

$$\left(\frac{dy}{dx}\right)^2 - \frac{dy}{dx} - 2 = 0.$$

From this we see that

$$\frac{dy}{dx} = 2 \quad \text{or} \quad \frac{dy}{dx} = -1.$$

Thus the characteristics of Equation (14.120) are the straight lines of the two real families defined by

(14.134)
$$y = 2x + c_1 \quad \text{and} \quad y = -x + c_2,$$

where c_1 and c_2 are arbitrary constants (see Figure 14.3).

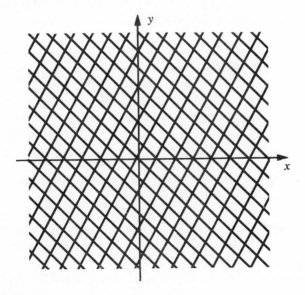

Figure 14.3

In Example 14.9 we considered an initial value problem associated with equation (14.120). We sought a solution $\phi(x,y)$ of Equation (14.120), defined for all (x,y), such that

(14.122)
$$\phi(t,t^2) = t^4 + 2t^2$$
$$\phi_x(t,t^2) = 4t$$
$$\phi_y(t,t^2) = 2t^2$$

for all real t. The curve Γ_0 defined for all real t by $x = t$, $y = t^2$ is tangent to a characteristic (14.134) of Equation (14.120) only at $t = 1$ and $t = -\frac{1}{2}$. Thus on any interval $a \le t \le b$ *not* including either of these two values, we are assured that this initial-value problem has a unique solution. Recall that in Example 14.9 we observed that a solution valid for all (x,y) is the function ϕ defined by $\phi(x,y) = 2x^2 + y^2$.

In Section 14.3 we proved that the equation (14.84) can always be transformed into an equation having a so-called canonical form. This reduction involved a transformation

(14.85)
$$\xi = \xi(x,y), \quad \eta = \eta(x,y)$$

of the independent variables in (14.84). In Theorems 14.3, 14.4, and 14.5 we listed specific transformations of this form which led to the desired reduction in the hyperbolic, parabolic, and elliptic cases, respectively. The resulting canonical forms were given by (14.94), (14.102), and (14.110) in these three respective cases. The specific transformations listed for the various cases are directly related to the characteristics of the equation (14.84). We shall not attempt to determine the exact nature of this relation in all cases; rather we shall restrict our investigation to the case in which Equation (14.84) is hyperbolic and $A \ne 0$.

Theorem 14.3 states that if Equation (14.84) is hyperbolic and $A \ne 0$, then a specific transformation which leads to the desired canonical form is given by

(14.95)
$$\xi = \lambda_1 x + y$$
$$\eta = \lambda_2 x + y,$$

where λ_1 and λ_2 are the roots of the quadratic equation

(14.96)
$$A\lambda^2 + B\lambda + C = 0.$$

More explicitly, this transformation may be written

(14.135)
$$\xi = \left[\frac{-B - \sqrt{B^2 - 4AC}}{2A} \right] x + y,$$
$$\eta = \left[\frac{-B + \sqrt{B^2 - 4AC}}{2A} \right] x + y.$$

Turning to the characteristics of Equation (14.84) in the case under consideration, we note that they are the two distinct families of straight lines defined by

(14.131) $\quad y = \left[\dfrac{B + \sqrt{B^2 - 4AC}}{2A} \right] x + c_1 \quad$ and $\quad y = \left[\dfrac{B - \sqrt{B^2 - 4AC}}{2A} \right] x + c_2,$

where c_1 and c_2 are arbitrary constants. Comparison of (14.135) and (14.131) clearly indicates the relation between the canonical form-producing transformation and the characteristics in this case. For here the transformation is given by $\xi = \xi(x,y)$, $\eta = \eta(x,y)$, where $\xi(x,y) = c_1$, $\eta(x,y) = c_2$ are the two families of characteristics of Equation (14.84).

Example 14.11.   Let us again consider the equation

(14.120)
$$\frac{\partial^2 u}{\partial x^2} + \frac{\partial^2 u}{\partial x \partial y} - 2\frac{\partial^2 u}{\partial y^2} = 0.$$

Since Equation (14.120) is hyperbolic and $A \neq 0$, a canonical form-producing transformation is given by $\xi = \xi(x,y)$, $\eta = \eta(x,y)$, where $\xi(x,y) = c_1$, $\eta(x,y) = c_2$ are the two families of characteristics of Equation (14.120). In Example 14.10 we found that the characteristics of Equation (14.120) are the straight lines defined by (14.134). Therefore the two families of characteristics are given by

$$y - 2x = c_1 \quad \text{and} \quad y + x = c_2,$$

and a canonical form-producing transformation of Equation (14.120) is given by

(14.136)
$$\xi = y - 2x$$
$$\eta = y + x.$$

Applying (14.136) to Equation (14.120), we see that this equation transforms into

(14.137)
$$-7\frac{\partial^2 u}{\partial \xi \partial \eta} = 0 \quad \text{and hence into} \quad \frac{\partial^2 u}{\partial \xi \partial \eta} = 0,$$

which is the canonical form in the hyperbolic case. We observe that the particular characteristics $y = 2x$ and $y = -x$ transform into the coordinate axes $\xi = 0$ and $\eta = 0$, respectively, in the ξ, η plane.

We note that we may obtain a solution of Equation (14.137) involving two arbitrary functions merely by integrating first with respect to ξ and then with respect to η. We thus obtain the solution

$$u = f(\xi) + g(\eta),$$

where f and g are arbitrary functions of their respective arguments. Using (14.136) to return to the original independent variables x and y, we obtain the solution

$$u = f(y - 2x) + g(y + x)$$

of Equation (14.120) involving the two arbitrary functions f and g. We point out that this solution could be obtained directly by the prodedure outlined in Section 14.1.

Exercises

1. Consider the partial differential equation

(A)
$$\frac{\partial^2 u}{\partial x \partial y} = 0$$

and the five real functions defined for all real t by

$$x(t) = t, \quad y(t) = 3 - t, \quad u(t) = t,$$

$$p(t) = t, \quad q(t) = t - 1.$$

(a) Show that these five functions satisfy the strip condition (14.119). Then consider the initial value problem in which one seeks a solution $\phi(x,y)$ of partial differential equation (A), defined for all (x,y), such that

$$\phi(t, 3 - t) = t,$$

$$\phi_x(t, 3 - t) = t,$$

$$\phi_y(t, 3 - t) = t - 1$$

for all real t. Interpret this problem geometrically.

(b) Show that the function ϕ defined for all (x,y) by

$$\phi(x,y) = \frac{x^2}{2} - \frac{y^2}{2} + 2y - \frac{3}{2}$$

is a solution of the initial-value problem considered in part (a).

2. Consider the partial differential equation

(B)
$$\frac{\partial^2 u}{\partial x^2} - \frac{\partial^2 u}{\partial y^2} = 0$$

and the five real functions defined for all real t by

$$x(t) = t, \qquad y(t) = 0, \quad u(t) = t^4 + t^2,$$

$$p(t) = 4t^3 + 2t, \quad q(t) = 4t.$$

(a) Show that these five functions satisfy the strip condition (14.119). Then consider the initial value problem in which one seeks a solution $\phi(x,y)$ of partial differential equation (B), defined for all (x,y), such that

$$\phi(t,0) = t^4 + t^2,$$

$$\phi_x(t,0) = 4t^3 + 2t,$$

$$\phi_y(t,0) = 4t$$

for all real t. Interpret this problem geometrically.

(b) Show that the function ϕ defined for all (x,y) by

$$\phi(x,y) = x^4 + 6x^2y^2 + y^4 + x^2 + y^2 + 4xy$$

is a solution of the initial-value problem considered in part (a).

For each of the partial differential equations in Exercises 3 through 6, determine whether or not real characteristics exist. For those equations for which families of real characteristics exist, find these families and sketch several members of each family.

3. $\dfrac{\partial^2 u}{\partial x^2} - 2\dfrac{\partial^2 u}{\partial x \partial y} - 8\dfrac{\partial^2 u}{\partial y^2} = 0.$

4. $\dfrac{\partial^2 u}{\partial x^2} + 4\dfrac{\partial^2 u}{\partial x \partial y} + 4\dfrac{\partial^2 u}{\partial y^2} = 0.$

5. $2\dfrac{\partial^2 u}{\partial x^2} - 2\dfrac{\partial^2 u}{\partial x \partial y} + 5\dfrac{\partial^2 u}{\partial y^2} = 0.$

6. $2\dfrac{\partial^2 u}{\partial x^2} + 7\dfrac{\partial^2 u}{\partial x \partial y} + 6\dfrac{\partial^2 u}{\partial y^2} = 0.$

SUGGESTED READING

I. Basic Methods and Applications:

Churchill (10)
Ford (17)
Hildebrand (22)
Martin and Reissner (38)

Miller (40)
Rainville (45)
Sokolnikoff and Redheffer (49)
Wylie (57)

II. Basic Theory and Methods:

Greenspan (19)

III. Advanced Theory:

Courant and Hilbert (14)
Epstein (16)
John (27)
Lax (34)

Petrovsky (44)
Sneddon (48)
Tamarkin and Feller (53)
Webster (55)

G

Special Fourth - Class Rate - Books

Postmaster: *This parcel may be opened for postal inspection if necessary.*

From GINN AND COMPANY • *Publishers*

6900 EAST 30th STREET, INDIANAPOLIS, INDIANA 46218

RETURN REQUESTED

TO

PROF D H BUCKLEY
MATH DEPT JR COLLEGE
POLK JUNIOR COLLEGE
999 AVENUE H NE
WINTER HAVEN FLA 3388

OFFICE	STATE	AGENT	CT
06	66	10	

VIA

DATE 12/02/68

ANSWERS
TO ODD-NUMBERED EXERCISES

Chapter 1

1. Ordinary; first; linear.
3. Partial; second; linear.
5. Ordinary; fourth; nonlinear.
7. Ordinary; second; linear.
9. Ordinary; sixth; nonlinear.

SECTION 1.3

1. No; one of the supplementary conditions is not satisfied.
3. (a) $y = 3e^{4x} + 2e^{-3x}$; (b) $y = -2e^{-3x}$.
5. $y = 2x - 3x^2 + x^3$.
7. Yes.

Chapter 2

SECTION 2.1

1. $3x^2 + 4xy + y^2 = c$.
3. $x + x^2y + 2y^2 = c$.
5. $3x^2y + 2y^2x - 5x - 6y = c$.
7. $y\tan x + \sec x + y^2 = c$.
9. $s^2 - s = ct$.
11. $x^2y - 3x + 2y^2 = 7$.
13. $-3y + 2x + y^2 = 2xy$.
15. (a) $A = 3/2$; $2x^3 + 9x^2y + 12y^2 = c$.
    (b) $A = -2$; $2x^2 - 2y^2 - x = cxy^2$.
17. (b) x^2; (c) $x^4 + x^3y^2 = c$.
19. $4 \arctan\dfrac{x}{y} + (x^2 + y^2)^2 = c$.

SECTION 2.2

1. $(x^2 + 1)^2y = c$.
3. $r^2 + s = c(1 - r^2s)$.

5. $r\sin^2\theta = c$.

7. $(x + 1)^6(y^2 + 1) = c(x + 2)^4$.

9. $y^2 + xy = cx^3$.

11. $\sin\dfrac{y}{x} = cx$.

13. $(x^2 + y^2)^{3/2} = x^3 \ln cx^3$.

15. $x + 4 = (y + 2)^2 e^{-(y+1)}$.

17. $16(x + 3)(x + 2)^2 = 9(y^2 + 4)^2$.

19. $(2x + y)^2 = 12(y - x)$.

SECTION 2.3

1. $y = x^3 + cx^{-3}$.

3. $x = 1 + ce^{1/t}$.

5. $3(x^2 + x)y = x^3 - 3x + c$.

7. $y = x^{-1}(1 + ce^{-x})$.

9. $r = (\theta + c)\cos\theta$.

11. $2(1 + \sin x)y = x + \sin x \cos x + c$.

13. $x^3 y^3(2x^3 + c) = 1$.

15. $x^2 = 2 + ct^{-1}e^{-t}$.

17. $3y = 1 + 5e^{-x^3}$.

19. $2r = \sin 2\theta + \sqrt{2} \cos \theta$.

21. $x^2 y^4 = x^4 + 15$.

23. (a) $y = \dfrac{ke^{-\lambda x}}{b - a\lambda} + ce^{-bx/a}$ if $\lambda \neq b/a$;

$y = \dfrac{kxe^{-bx/a}}{a} + ce^{-bx/a}$ if $\lambda = b/a$.

25. $y = 5 + e^{-x}, 0 \leq x < 10$; $y = 1 + (4e^{10} + 1)e^{-x}, x \geq 10$.

29. (b) $y = \sin x - \cos x + \sin 2x - 2\cos 2x + ce^{-x}$.

31. (b) $y^2 + 2y = 1 + ce^{-x^2}$.

SECTION 2.4

1. $4x^5 y + 4x^4 y^2 + x^4 = c$.

3. $xy^2 e^x + ye^x = c$.

5. $5x^2 + 4xy + y^2 + 2x + 2y = c$.

7. $\ln[c(x^2 + y^2 - 2x + 2y + 2)] + 4 \arctan\left(\dfrac{y + 1}{x - 1}\right) = 0$.

9. $\ln\left[\dfrac{3x^2 - 6x + y^2 + 6y + 12}{4}\right] + \dfrac{2}{\sqrt{3}}\arctan\left[\dfrac{y + 3}{\sqrt{3}\,(x - 1)}\right] = \dfrac{\pi}{3\sqrt{3}}$.

Chapter 3

SECTION 3.1

1. $x^2 + 3y^2 = k^2$.

3. $x^2 + y^2 - \ln y^2 = k$.

5. $x = y - 1 + ke^{-y}$.

7. $x^2 y + y^3 = k$.

9. $y^2 = 2x - 1 + ke^{-2x}$.

11. $x^2 + y^2 = ky$.

13. $n = 3$.

SECTION 3.2

1. (a) $v = 8(1 - e^{-4t})$, $x = 2(4t - 1 + e^{-4t})$.

   (b) 8 ft/sec, 38 feet.

3. Rises 55.08 feet, or 61.08 feet above ground.

5. (a) 10.36 ft/sec; (b) 13.19 ft/sec.

7. $v = \dfrac{(60{,}000\sqrt{5} + 12{,}500) + (60{,}000\sqrt{5} - 12{,}500)e^{0.256\sqrt{5}t}}{(1200 + 50\sqrt{5}) + (50\sqrt{5} - 1200)e^{0.256\sqrt{5}t}}$.

9. $v = \dfrac{\sqrt{5}(1 - e^{-8\sqrt{5}t})}{1 + e^{-8\sqrt{5}t}}$.

11. 16.18 feet.

13. (a) 10.96 ft/sec; (b) 20.46 ft/sec.

15. 4.03 ft/sec.

SECTION 3.3

1. (a) 59.05%; (b) 2631 years.

3. (a) $50\sqrt{2}$ grams; (b) 12.5 grams; (c) 10.29 hours.

5. 40,833.

7. (a) 112.31 lbs; (b) 17.33 minutes.

9. (a) 318.53 lbs; (b) 2.74 minutes.

11. (a) 0.072%; (b) 1.39 minutes.

13. (a) 63.33° F.; (b) 13.55 minutes.

15. 7.14 grams.

Chapter 4

SECTION 4.1

5. (c) $y = \dfrac{x^2}{4} + 8x^{-2}$.

9. $y = c_1 e^{2x} + c_2(x + 1)$.

SECTION 4.2

1. $y = c_1 e^{2x} + c_2 e^{3x}$.

3. $y = c_1 e^{x/2} + c_2 e^{5x/2}$.

5. $y = c_1 e^x + c_2 e^{-x} + c_3 e^{3x}$.

7. $y = (c_1 + c_2 x)e^{4x}$.

9. $y = e^{2x}(c_1 \sin 3x + c_2 \cos 3x)$.

11. $y = c_1 \sin 3x + c_2 \cos 3x$.

13. $y = (c_1 + c_2 x)e^x + c_3 e^{3x}$.

15. $y = (c_1 + c_2 x + c_3 x^2)e^{2x}$.

17. $y = c_1 e^x + c_2 \sin x + c_3 \cos x$.

19. $y = c_1 + c_2 x + c_3 x^2 + (c_4 + c_5 x)e^x$.

21. $y = c_1 e^{2x} + c_2 e^{3x} + e^{-x}(c_3 \sin x + c_4 \cos x)$.

23. $y = e^{\frac{\sqrt{2}\,x}{2}}\left(c_1\sin\frac{\sqrt{2}\,x}{2} + c_2\cos\frac{\sqrt{2}\,x}{2}\right) + e^{-\frac{\sqrt{2}\,x}{2}}\left(c_3\sin\frac{\sqrt{2}\,x}{2} + c_4\cos\frac{\sqrt{2}\,x}{2}\right).$

25. $y = 2e^{4x} + e^{-3x}.$

27. $y = e^{2x}\sin 5x.$

29. $y = e^x - 2e^{2x} + e^{3x}.$

SECTION 4.3

1. $y = c_1 e^x + c_2 e^{2x} + 2x^2 + 6x + 7.$

3. $y = e^{-x}(c_1\sin 2x + c_2\cos 2x) + 2\sin 2x - \cos 2x.$

5. $y = e^{-x}(c_1\sin\sqrt{3}x + c_2\cos\sqrt{3}x) + \dfrac{\sin 4x}{26} - \dfrac{3\cos 4x}{52}.$

7. $y = c_1 e^x + e^{-x}(c_2\sin 2x + c_3\cos 2x) - \dfrac{9\sin 2x}{17} + \dfrac{2\cos 2x}{17} - 2x^2 - \dfrac{9x}{5} - \dfrac{82}{25}.$

9. $y = c_1 e^{2x} + c_2 e^{-3x} + 2xe^{2x} - 3e^{3x} + x + 2.$

11. $y = c_1 + c_2\sin x + c_3\cos x + \dfrac{2x^3}{3} - 4x - 2x\sin x.$

13. $y = c_1 e^x + c_2 e^{2x} + c_3 e^{3x} + \dfrac{x^2 e^x}{4} + \dfrac{3xe^x}{4} + 4xe^{2x} + e^{4x}.$

15. $y = c_1\sin 2x + c_2\cos 2x + 3x^2 - \dfrac{3}{2} - 2x^2\sin 2x - x\cos 2x.$

17. $y = c_1 + c_2 x + c_3 e^x + c_4 e^{-3x} - \dfrac{x^4}{2} - \dfrac{4x^3}{3} - \dfrac{19}{6}x^2 + 2x^2 e^x - 9xe^x + \dfrac{e^{3x}}{27}.$

19. $y = \dfrac{1}{29}\left[e^{-2x}\left(-\dfrac{2\sin 3x}{3} + 37\cos 3x\right) + 9\sin 2x - 8\cos 2x\right].$

21. $y = \dfrac{7e^{-x}}{20} - \dfrac{31e^{2x}}{40} + \dfrac{3xe^x}{4} + \dfrac{5e^x}{4} - \dfrac{\sin x}{10}.$

23. $y_p = Ae^{3x} + Be^{-3x} + Ce^{3x}\sin 3x + De^{3x}\cos 3x.$

25. $y_p = Ax^4 e^{2x} + Bx^3 e^{2x} + Cx^2 e^{3x} + Dxe^{3x} + Ee^{3x}.$

27. $y_p = Ax^3\sin 2x + Bx^3\cos 2x + Cx^2\sin 2x + Dx^2\cos 2x + Ex\sin 2x + Fx\cos 2x$
$\qquad + Gx^5 e^{2x} + Hx^4 e^{2x} + Ix^3 e^{2x} + Jx^2 e^{2x} + Kxe^{2x}.$

29. $y_p = A + Bx\sin 2x + Cx\cos 2x + Dxe^x + Exe^{-x}$
$\quad$ or $y_p = Ax\sin^2 x + Bx\cos^2 x + Cx\sin x\cos x + Dx\sinh x + Ex\cosh x.$

SECTION 4.4

1. $y = c_1\sin x + c_2\cos x + (\sin x)[\ln|\csc x - \cot x|].$

3. $y = c_1\sin x + c_2\cos x + (\cos x)[\ln|\cos x|] + x\sin x.$

5. $y = c_1\sin 2x + c_2\cos 2x + \dfrac{\sin 2x}{4}[\ln|\sec 2x + \tan 2x|] - \dfrac{1}{4}.$

7. $y = c_1 e^x + c_2 xe^x - \dfrac{5x^3 e^x}{36} + \dfrac{x^3 e^x\ln x}{6}.$

9. $y = c_1 e^x + c_2 xe^x + \dfrac{e^x\sin^{-1}x}{4} + \dfrac{x^2 e^x\sin^{-1}x}{2} + \dfrac{3xe^x\sqrt{1 - x^2}}{4}.$

11. $y = c_1 e^{-x} + c_2 e^{-2x} + (e^{-x} + e^{-2x})[\ln(1 + e^x)].$

13. $y = c_1\sin x + c_2\cos x + (\sin x)[\ln(1 + \sin x)] - x\cos x - \dfrac{\cos^2 x}{1 + \sin x}.$

15. $y = c_1 x + c_2(x + 1)^{-1} + x^2 - \dfrac{(2x^3 + 3x^2)(x + 1)^{-1}}{6}.$

SECTION 4.5

1. $y = c_1 x + c_2 x^3$.
3. $y = c_1 |x|^{1/2} + c_2 |x|^{3/2}$.
5. $y = c_1 \sin(\ln x^2) + c_2 \cos(\ln x^2)$.
7. $y = c_1 x + c_2 x^2 + c_3 x^3$.
9. $y = (c_1 + c_2 \ln|x|)x^3 + c_3 x^{-2}$.
11. $y = c_1 x^2 + c_2 x^4 - 2x^3$.
13. $y = c_1 \sin(\ln x^2) + c_2 \cos(\ln x^2) + \dfrac{x \ln x^2}{5} - \dfrac{4x}{25}$.
15. $y = (c_1 + c_2 \ln|x|)x + c_3 x^2 + \dfrac{x^3}{4}$.
17. $y = -2x^2 + x^3$.
19. $y = \dfrac{1}{6}\left(\dfrac{x^{-2}}{2} + \dfrac{x^3}{3} - \ln x + \dfrac{1}{6}\right)$.
21. $y = c_1(2x - 3) + c_2(2x - 3)^3$.

Chapter 5

SECTION 5.2

1. $x = \dfrac{\cos 16t}{6}$; 1/6 (ft), $\pi/8$ (sec), $8/\pi$ oscillations/sec.

3. (a) $x = \dfrac{\sin 8t}{4}$; (b) 1/4 (ft), $\pi/4$ (sec), $4/\pi$ oscillations/sec;

  (c) $t = \dfrac{\pi}{48} + \dfrac{n\pi}{4}$ $(n = 0,1,2,\ldots)$; (d) $t = \dfrac{5\pi}{48} + \dfrac{n\pi}{4}$ $(n = 0,1,2,\ldots)$.

5. (a) $x = -\dfrac{\sin 10t}{5} + \dfrac{\cos 10t}{3}$; (b) $\dfrac{\sqrt{34}}{15}$ (ft); $\pi/5$ (sec); $5/\pi$ oscillations/sec;

  (c) 0.103 (sec); -3.888 ft/sec.
7. 18 lbs.

SECTION 5.3

1. (a) $\dfrac{1}{4}\dfrac{d^2x}{dt^2} + 2\dfrac{dx}{dt} + 20x = 0$, $x(0) = 1/2$, $x'(0) = 0$;

  (b) $x = e^{-4t}\left(\dfrac{\sin 8t}{4} + \dfrac{\cos 8t}{2}\right)$.

  (c) $x = \dfrac{\sqrt{5}}{4}e^{-4t}\cos(8t - \phi)$, where $\phi \approx 0.46$;

  (d) $\pi/4$ (sec).
3. $x = \left(6t + \dfrac{3}{4}\right)e^{-8t}$.

5. (a) $x = e^{-8t}\left(\dfrac{\sin 16t}{3} + \dfrac{2\cos 16t}{3}\right)$; $x = \dfrac{\sqrt{5}}{3}e^{-8t}\cos(16t - \phi)$, where $\phi \approx 0.46$;

  (b) $\pi/8$ (sec.); π; (c) 0.127.
7. (a) $x = \left(\dfrac{1}{4} + 2t\right)e^{-8t}$;

  (b) $x = e^{-4t}\left(\dfrac{\sqrt{3}}{12}\sin 4\sqrt{3}\,t + \dfrac{1}{4}\cos 4\sqrt{3}\,t\right)$.

(c) $x = \left(\dfrac{3 + 2\sqrt{3}}{24}\right)e^{(-16+8\sqrt{3})t} + \left(\dfrac{3 - 2\sqrt{3}}{24}\right)e^{(-16-8\sqrt{3})t}.$

9. (a) 64; (b) $8\sqrt{3}.$

SECTION 5.4

1. $x = \dfrac{\cos 12t - \cos 20t}{4}.$

3. $x = -2te^{-8t} + \dfrac{\sin 8t}{4}.$

5. $x = e^{-8t}\left(\dfrac{\sqrt{2}}{2}\sin 4\sqrt{2}\,t + \cos 4\sqrt{2}\,t\right) + \sin 4t - \cos 4t.$

7. $x = e^{-2t}\left(-\dfrac{3\sin 4t}{2} - 2\cos 4t\right) + \sin 2t + 2\cos 2t,\ 0 \le t \le \pi;$

   $x = (e^{2\pi} - 1)e^{-2t}\left(\dfrac{3\sin 4t}{2} + 2\cos 4t\right),\ t > \pi.$

9. (a) $x = \cos 7t - \cos 8t.$

SECTION 5.5

1. (a) $\dfrac{2\sqrt{2}}{\pi};\ \ x = \dfrac{e^{-4t}(-\sqrt{3}\sin 4\sqrt{3}t - \cos 4\sqrt{3}t)}{18} + \dfrac{\sqrt{2}\sin 4\sqrt{2}t + \cos 4\sqrt{2}t}{18};$

   (b) 8; $x = \dfrac{t\sin 8t}{3}.$

3. (b) $2/\pi;\ \ 3\sqrt{5}/4;$ (c) $\sqrt{22}/2\pi;\ \ 15\sqrt{23}/23.$

SECTION 5.6

1. $i = 4(1 - e^{-50t}).$

3. $q = \dfrac{1 - e^{-500t}}{50};\ \ i = 10e^{-500t}.$

5. $i = e^{-80t}(-4.588\sin 60t + 1.247\cos 60t) - 1.247\cos 200t + 1.331\sin 200t.$

7. $q = e^{-\frac{Rt}{2L}}\left[\dfrac{Q_0\sqrt{c}R}{\sqrt{4L - R^2c}}\sin\left(\dfrac{\sqrt{4L - R^2c}}{2\sqrt{c}\,L}t\right) + Q_0\cos\left(\dfrac{\sqrt{4L - R^2c}}{2\sqrt{c}\,L}t\right)\right],$

   $i = -\dfrac{2Q_0}{\sqrt{4Lc - R^2c^2}}e^{-\frac{Rt}{2L}}\sin\left(\dfrac{\sqrt{4L - R^2c}}{2\sqrt{c}\,L}t\right).$

Chapter 6

SECTION 6.1

1. $y = c_0\left[1 + \displaystyle\sum_{n=1}^{\infty} \dfrac{(-1)^n x^{2n}}{[2\cdot 4\cdot 6\cdots(2n)]}\right] + c_1\left[x + \displaystyle\sum_{n=1}^{\infty} \dfrac{(-1)^n x^{2n+1}}{[3\cdot 5\cdot 7\cdots(2n+1)]}\right].$

3. $y = c_0\left(1 - \dfrac{x^2}{2} - \dfrac{x^4}{24} + \cdots\right) + c_1\left(x - \dfrac{x^3}{3} - \dfrac{x^5}{30} + \cdots\right).$

5. $y = c_0\left(1 - x^2 - \dfrac{x^3}{2} + \dfrac{x^4}{3} + \dfrac{11x^5}{40} + \cdots\right) + c_1\left(x - \dfrac{x^3}{2} - \dfrac{x^4}{4} + \dfrac{x^5}{8} + \cdots\right).$

7. $y = c_0\left(1 - \dfrac{x^3}{6} + \dfrac{3x^5}{40} + \cdots\right) + c_1\left(x - \dfrac{x^3}{6} - \dfrac{x^4}{12} + \dfrac{3x^5}{40} + \cdots\right).$

9. $y = c_0\left(1 + \dfrac{x^3}{6} + \dfrac{x^6}{18} + \cdots\right) + c_1\left(x + \dfrac{x^4}{6} + \dfrac{17x^7}{252} + \cdots\right).$

11. $y = 1 + \displaystyle\sum_{n=1}^{\infty} \dfrac{x^{2n}}{[2\cdot4\cdot6\cdots(2n)]} = \sum_{n=0}^{\infty} \dfrac{x^{2n}}{2^n n!}$

13. $y = 2 + 3x - \dfrac{7x^3}{6} - \dfrac{x^4}{2} + \dfrac{21x^5}{40} + \cdots.$

15. $y = c_0\left[1 - \dfrac{(x-1)^2}{2} + \dfrac{(x-1)^3}{2} - \dfrac{5(x-1)^4}{12} + \dfrac{(x-1)^5}{3} + \cdots\right]$
$+ c_1\left[(x-1) - \dfrac{(x-1)^2}{2} + \dfrac{(x-1)^3}{6} - \dfrac{(x-1)^5}{12} + \cdots\right].$

17. $y = 2 + 4(x-1) - 4(x-1)^2 + \dfrac{4(x-1)^3}{3} - \dfrac{(x-1)^4}{3} + \dfrac{2(x-1)^5}{15} + \cdots.$

SECTION 6.2

1. $x = 0$ and $x = 3$ are regular singular points.

3. $x = 1$ is a regular singular point; $x = 0$ is an irregular singular point.

5. $y = C_1 x\left(1 - \dfrac{x^2}{14} + \dfrac{x^4}{616} - \cdots\right) + C_2 x^{-1/2}\left(1 - \dfrac{x^2}{2} + \dfrac{x^4}{40} - \cdots\right).$

7. $y = C_1 x^{4/3}\left(1 - \dfrac{3x^2}{16} + \dfrac{9x^4}{896} - \cdots\right) + C_2 x^{2/3}\left(1 - \dfrac{3x^2}{8} + \dfrac{9x^4}{320} - \cdots\right).$

9. $y = C_1 x^{1/3}\left(1 - \dfrac{3x^2}{16} + \dfrac{9x^4}{896} - \cdots\right) + C_2 x^{-1/3}\left(1 - \dfrac{3x^2}{8} + \dfrac{9x^4}{320} - \cdots\right).$

11. $y = C_1\left(1 + x + \dfrac{3x^2}{10} + \cdots\right) + C_2 x^{1/3}\left(1 + \dfrac{7x}{12} + \dfrac{5x^2}{36} + \cdots\right).$

13. $y = C_1 x^{1/2}\left(1 - \dfrac{x^2}{6} + \dfrac{x^4}{120} - \cdots\right) + C_2 x^{-1/2}\left(1 - \dfrac{x^2}{2} + \dfrac{x^4}{24} - \cdots\right).$

15. $y = C_1\left[1 + \displaystyle\sum_{n=1}^{\infty} \dfrac{x^{2n}}{2^n n!}\right] + C_2 x^3\left[1 + \sum_{n=1}^{\infty} \dfrac{x^{2n}}{[5\cdot7\cdot9\cdots(2n+3)]}\right]$
$= C_1\left(1 + \dfrac{x^2}{2} + \dfrac{x^4}{8} + \cdots\right) + C_2 x^3\left(1 + \dfrac{x^2}{5} + \dfrac{x^4}{35} + \cdots\right).$

17. $y = C_1\left(1 - x + \dfrac{x^2}{2} - \dfrac{x^3}{6} + \cdots\right) + C_2 x^{-1}\left(1 + \dfrac{3x^2}{2} - \dfrac{x^3}{3} + \cdots\right)$
$= Ce^{-x} + C_2 x^{-1}e^x$, where $C = C_1 - C_2$.

19. $y = C_1 x\left[1 + 2\displaystyle\sum_{n=1}^{\infty} \dfrac{(-1)^n x^n}{n!(n+2)!}\right]$
$+ C_2\left[x^{-1}\left(-\dfrac{1}{2} - \dfrac{x}{2} + \dfrac{29x^2}{144} + \cdots\right) + \dfrac{1}{4}y_1(x)\ln|x|\right]$, where $y_1(x)$ denotes the
solution of which C_1 is the coefficient.

21. $y = C_1 x^4\left(1 - \dfrac{x^2}{2} + \dfrac{x^4}{10} - \cdots\right)$
$+ C_2\left[x^{-2}\left(-\dfrac{1}{6} - \dfrac{x^2}{6} - \dfrac{x^4}{6} + \cdots\right) + \dfrac{2}{9}y_1(x)\ln|x|\right]$, where $y_1(x)$ denotes the
solution of which C_1 is the coefficient.

23. $y = C_1\left[1 + \sum\limits_{n=1}^{\infty} \dfrac{(-1)^n 2^n x^n}{(n!)^2}\right]$

$\quad + C_2\left[4x - 3x^2 + \dfrac{22x^3}{7} + \cdots + y_1(x)\ln|x|\right]$, where $y_1(x)$ denotes the solution of which C_1 is the coefficient.

25. $y = C_1 x\left[1 + \sum\limits_{n=1}^{\infty} \dfrac{(-1)^n x^{2n}}{[2\cdot 4\cdot 6 \cdots (2n)]^2}\right]$

$\quad + C_2\left[\dfrac{x^3}{4} - \dfrac{3x^5}{128} + \dfrac{11x^7}{13824} + \cdots + y_1(x)\ln|x|\right]$, where $y_1(x)$ denotes the solution of which C_1 is the coefficient.

SECTION 6.3

3. $y = \dfrac{c_1\sin x + c_2\cos x}{\sqrt{x}}$.

Chapter 7

SECTION 7.1

1. (c) $x = 2e^{5t} - e^{-t}$, $y = e^{5t} + e^{-t}$.

SECTION 7.2

1. $x = c_1 e^t + c_2 e^{3t}$, $y = 2c_1 e^t + c_2 e^{3t}$.
3. $x = 2c_1 e^{4t} + c_2 e^{-t}$, $y = 3c_1 e^{4t} - c_2 e^{-t}$.
5. $x = c_1 e^t + c_2 e^{5t}$, $y = -2c_1 e^t + 2c_2 e^{5t}$.
7. $x = 2c_1 e^t + c_2 e^{-t}$, $y = c_1 e^t + c_2 e^{-t}$.
9. $x = c_1 e^{4t} + c_2 e^{-2t}$, $y = c_1 e^{4t} - c_2 e^{-2t}$.
11. $x = c_1 e^t + c_2 t e^t$, $y = 2c_1 e^t + c_2(2t - 1)e^t$.
13. $x = -2c_1 e^{3t} + c_2(2t + 1)e^{3t}$, $y = c_1 e^{3t} - c_2 t e^{3t}$.
15. $x = 2e^t(-c_1\sin 2t + c_2\cos 2t)$, $y = e^t(c_1\cos 2t + c_2\sin 2t)$.
17. $x = e^t(c_1\cos 3t + c_2\sin 3t)$, $y = e^t(c_1\sin 3t - c_2\cos 3t)$.
19. $x = 2e^{3t}(c_1\cos 3t + c_2\sin 3t)$, $y = e^{3t}[c_1(\cos 3t + 3\sin 3t) + c_2(\sin 3t - 3\cos 3t)]$.
21. $x = e^{3t}(c_1\cos 2t + c_2\sin 2t)$, $y = e^{3t}(c_1\sin 2t - c_2\cos 2t)$.
25. $x = 3c_1 t^4 + c_2 t^{-1}$, $y = 2c_1 t^4 - c_2 t^{-1}$.
27. $x = c_1 e^t + c_2 e^{2t} + c_3 e^{-3t}$, $y = c_1 e^t + 2c_2 e^{2t} + 7c_3 e^{-3t}$,
$\quad z = c_1 e^t + c_2 e^{2t} + 11c_3 e^{-3t}$.
29. $x = c_1 e^{2t} + c_2 e^{3t} + c_3 e^{-2t}$, $y = -c_2 e^{3t} - c_3 e^{-2t}$, $z = -c_1 e^{2t} - c_2 e^{3t} + 4c_3 e^{-2t}$.

SECTION 7.3

1. $x = ce^{-2t}$, $y = -\dfrac{2}{3}ce^{-2t} + \dfrac{1}{3}e^{4t} - \dfrac{1}{3}e^t$.

3. $x = ce^{-3t} + \dfrac{e^t}{4}$, $y = -\dfrac{2ce^{-3t}}{3} + \dfrac{e^{3t}}{3} - \dfrac{e^t}{2}$.

5. $x = c_1\sin t + c_2\cos t$, $y = -\left(\dfrac{3c_1 + c_2}{2}\right)\sin t + \left(\dfrac{c_1 - 3c_2}{2}\right)\cos t + \dfrac{e^t}{2} - \dfrac{e^{-t}}{2}$.

7. $x = c_1 e^{\sqrt{6}t} + c_2 e^{-\sqrt{6}t} + t - \dfrac{1}{6}$, $y = \dfrac{\sqrt{6}\, c_1 e^{\sqrt{6}t}}{6} - \dfrac{\sqrt{6}\, c_2 e^{-\sqrt{6}t}}{6} - \dfrac{t}{6} + \dfrac{1}{6} - \dfrac{e^{3t}}{3}$.

9. $x = c_1 e^t - \dfrac{\sin t}{2}$, $y = -\dfrac{c_1 e^t}{3} + \dfrac{\sin t}{2}$.

11. $x = c_1 e^{4t} + c_2 e^{-2t} - t + 1$, $y = -c_1 e^{4t} + c_2 e^{-2t} + t$.

13. $x = c_1 + c_2 e^{-2t} + 2t^2 + t$, $y = (1 - c_1) - 3c_2 e^{-2t} - t^2 - 3t$.

15. $x = (c_1 + c_2 t)e^{-2t} + te^t$, $y = \left(\dfrac{2c_2 - 4c_1}{3} - c_2 t \right)e^{-2t} - \dfrac{2e^t}{3}$. $\left(\dfrac{1}{3} - c_1 \right) e^t - \dfrac{c_2}{3} e^{-2t} + te^t$

17. $x = c_1 e^{3t} + \dfrac{t}{3} - \dfrac{2}{9}$, $y = c_2 e^t - \dfrac{5c_1 e^{3t}}{2} - \dfrac{t}{3} - \dfrac{4}{9}$.

19. $x = c_1 + c_2 t + c_3 e^t + c_4 e^{-t} - \dfrac{t^2}{2}$, $y = (c_1 - c_2 + 1) + (c_2 + 1)t + c_4 e^{-t} - \dfrac{t^2}{2}$.

21. $x = c_1 + c_2 e^t + c_3 e^{-3t} - \dfrac{t^2}{6} - \dfrac{14t}{9}$,

$y = \left(3c_1 + \dfrac{17}{9} \right) + c_2 e^t - 3c_3 e^{-3t} - \dfrac{t^2}{2} - \dfrac{4t}{3}$.

SECTION 7.4

1. $x_1 = 2\cos t - \cos 2t$, $x_2 = 4\cos t + \cos 2t$.

3. $i_1 = -\dfrac{10e^{-1000t}}{3} - \dfrac{5e^{-4000t}}{3} + 5$,

$i_2 = -\dfrac{10e^{-1000t}}{3} + \dfrac{5e^{-4000t}}{6} + \dfrac{5}{2}$.

Chapter 8

SECTION 8.2

1. $y = 1 + x + 2 \displaystyle\sum_{n=2}^{\infty} \dfrac{x^n}{n!} = -x - 1 + 2e^x$.

3. $y = 2 + x + 2x^2 + \dfrac{4x^3}{3} + \dfrac{9x^4}{4} + \cdots$.

5. $y = \dfrac{x^2}{2} + \dfrac{x^3}{6} + \dfrac{x^4}{24} - \dfrac{x^5}{60} + \cdots$.

7. $y = x + x^2 + \dfrac{x^3}{6} - \dfrac{x^4}{12} + \cdots$.

9. $y = 1 + 2(x - 1) + \dfrac{7(x - 1)^2}{2} + \dfrac{14(x - 1)^3}{3} + \dfrac{73(x - 1)^4}{12} + \cdots$.

11. $y = \pi + \dfrac{(x - 1)^2}{2} + \dfrac{(x - 1)^5}{40} + \cdots$.

SECTION 8.3

1. $\phi_1(x) = 1 + \dfrac{x^2}{2}$, $\phi_2(x) = 1 + \dfrac{x^2}{2} + \dfrac{x^4}{8}$, $\phi_3(x) = 1 + \dfrac{x^2}{2} + \dfrac{x^4}{8} + \dfrac{x^6}{48}$.

3. $\phi_1(x) = \dfrac{x^2}{2}$, $\phi_2(x) = \dfrac{x^2}{2} + \dfrac{x^5}{20}$, $\phi_3(x) = \dfrac{x^2}{2} + \dfrac{x^5}{20} + \dfrac{x^8}{160} + \dfrac{x^{11}}{4400}$.

5. $\phi_1(x) = e^x - 1$, $\phi_2(x) = \dfrac{e^{2x}}{2} - e^x + x + \dfrac{1}{2}$,

$$\phi_3(x) = \frac{e^{4x}}{16} - \frac{e^{3x}}{3} + \frac{xe^{2x}}{2} + \frac{e^{2x}}{2} - 2xe^x + 2e^x + \frac{x^3}{3} + \frac{x^2}{2} + \frac{x}{4} - \frac{107}{48}.$$

7. $\phi_1(x) = x^2$, $\phi_2(x) = x^2 + \dfrac{x^7}{7}$, $\phi_3(x) = x^2 + \dfrac{x^7}{7} + \dfrac{x^{12}}{28} + \dfrac{x^{17}}{833} + \dfrac{x^{22}}{7546}$.

SECTION 8.4B

1. (a) 0.800, 0.650, 0.540, 0.462; (b) 0.812, 0.670, 0.564, 0.488;
   (c) 0.823, 0.688, 0.586, 0.512.

SECTION 8.4C

1. (a) 1.239, 1.564, 1.995; (b) 1.238, 1.562, 1.991; (c) 1.237, 1.561, 1.989.
3. 1.112, 1.255, 1.445.

SECTION 8.4D

1. (a) 1.2374, 1.5606, 1.9886; (b) 1.2374, 1.5606, 1.9887.
3. 1.1115, 1.2531, 1.4398.

SECTION 8.4E

1. 2.5447.

Chapter 9

SECTION 9.1

1. (a) $\dfrac{2}{s^3}$; (b) $\dfrac{b}{s^2 - b^2}$.

3. $\mathcal{L}\{\sin^3 at\} = \dfrac{6a^3}{(s^2 + a^2)(s^2 + 9a^2)}$, $\mathcal{L}\{\sin^2 at \cos at\} = \dfrac{2a^2 s}{(s^2 + a^2)(s^2 + 9a^2)}$.

5. $\dfrac{24}{s^5}$.

7. (a) $-\dfrac{e^{-\frac{\pi s}{2}}}{s^2 + 1}$; (b) $\dfrac{e^{-2s}(2s + 1)}{s^2}$.

9. $\dfrac{2\sin 3t}{3}$.

11. $\dfrac{5}{6}t^3 e^{2t}$.

13. $e^{-2t}\cos\sqrt{3}t$.

15. $\dfrac{1}{3} - \dfrac{e^{-t}}{2} + \dfrac{e^{-3t}}{6}$.

17. $\dfrac{4t\sin 2t + 3\sin 2t - 6t\cos 2t}{16}$.

SECTION 9.2

1. $Y = \dfrac{3e^t + e^{3t}}{2}$.

3. $Y = e^{2t}$.
5. $Y = 2e^{2t} - 3e^{-t} - e^{-t}\sin 3t + e^{-t}\cos 3t$.
7. $Y = (3 - 4t)e^t + \sin t - 3\cos t$.

9. $Y = -2e^t + e^{2t} + 1, 0 < t < 4$;
   $Y = 2(e^{-4} - 1)e^t + (1 - e^{-8})e^{2t}, t > 4$.

11. $X = -\dfrac{e^t}{2} + \dfrac{e^{-t}}{2} + 2e^{2t}, Y = \dfrac{e^t}{2} + \dfrac{e^{-t}}{2} - e^{2t}$.

Chapter 10

SECTION 10.2

1. (a) There exists a solution ϕ on some interval $|x - x_0| \leq h$ about $x = x_0$.
   (b) There exists a *unique* solution on $|x - x_0| \leq h$.

3. (a) $|x| \leq \dfrac{1}{2}$; $y = \tan x, |x| < \dfrac{\pi}{2}$.

   (b) $|x| \leq \dfrac{1}{2e}$; $y = -\dfrac{\ln(1 - 2x)}{2}, -\infty < x < \dfrac{1}{2}$.

Chapter 11

SECTION 11.1

1. (a) Yes.

   (b) $\dfrac{dy_1}{dx} = y_2, \dfrac{dy_2}{dx} = y_3, \dfrac{dy_3}{dx} = x^2 + y_1 y_2 + y_3^2$.

3. Theorem 11.4.

SECTION 11.2

1. (a) $f_1(x) = \dfrac{e^x}{2} - \dfrac{\sin x}{2} + \dfrac{\cos x}{2}, f_2(x) = \sin x, f_3(x) = \dfrac{e^x}{2} - \dfrac{\sin x}{2} - \dfrac{\cos x}{2}$.
   (b) $8f_1(x) + 7f_2(x) + 2f_3(x)$.

9. $\dfrac{d^2u}{dx^2} - u = 0$; $u = e^x, u = e^{-x}$; $y = e^{-\frac{x^2-x}{2}}, y = e^{-\frac{x^2+3x}{2}}$.

SECTION 11.3

3. (a) $y = x^3$; (b) $y = c_1 x^3 + c_2 x e^x$.

SECTION 11.5

1. (a) $x^2 \dfrac{d^2y}{dx^2} + x \dfrac{dy}{dx} + 2y = 0$.

   (b) $(2x + 1)\dfrac{d^2y}{dx^2} + (4 - x^3)\dfrac{dy}{dx} + (1 - 3x^2)y = 0$.

   (c) $-x^3 \dfrac{d^3y}{dx^3} - 8x^2 \dfrac{d^2y}{dx^2} - 15x \dfrac{dy}{dx} - 4y = 0$.

   (d) $\dfrac{d^4y}{dx^4} - x \dfrac{d^3y}{dx^3} + (x^2 - 3)\dfrac{d^2y}{dx^2} + (4x - x^3)\dfrac{dy}{dx} + (x^3 - 3x^2 + 2)y = 0$.

3. $y = c_1 x^{-4} + c_2 x^{-4} e^{-x^2}$.

5. (a) $\dfrac{d}{dx}\left[x \dfrac{dy}{dx}\right] + \dfrac{1}{x}y = 0$.   (b) $\dfrac{d}{dx}\left[(x^2 + 1)\dfrac{dy}{dx}\right] + \dfrac{3}{x^2}y = 0$.

   (c) $\dfrac{d}{dx}\left[\cos x \dfrac{dy}{dx}\right] + (\cos x)y = 0$.   (d) $\dfrac{d}{dx}\left[\dfrac{dy}{dx}\right] + \dfrac{g(x)}{f(x)}y = 0$.

Chapter 12

SECTION 12.1

1. $\lambda = 4n^2$, $(n = 1,2,3, \cdots)$; $y = c_n\sin2nx$, $(n = 1,2,3, \cdots)$.

3. $\lambda = \left(\dfrac{n\pi}{L}\right)^2$, $(n = 1,2,3, \cdots)$; $y = c_n\sin\dfrac{n\pi x}{L}$, $(n = 1,2,3, \cdots)$.

5. $\lambda = \alpha_n^2$, where $\alpha_n(n = 1,2,3, \cdots)$ are the positive roots of the equation $\alpha = \tan\pi\alpha$;
   $y = c_n\sin\alpha_n x$, $(n = 1,2,3, \cdots)$.

7. $\lambda = n^2$, $(n = 1,2,3, \cdots)$; $y = c_n\sin(n\ln|x|)$, $(n = 1,2,3, \cdots)$.

9. $\lambda = 16n^2$, $(n = 1,2,3, \cdots)$; $y = c_n\sin(4n\arctan x)$, $(n = 1,2,3, \cdots)$.

SECTION 12.3

3. $\dfrac{2}{\pi}\displaystyle\sum_{n=1}^{\infty}\dfrac{1 - (-1)^n}{n}\sin(n\ln|x|) = \dfrac{4}{\pi}\displaystyle\sum_{n=1}^{\infty}\dfrac{\sin[(2n-1)\ln|x|]}{2n-1}.$

SECTION 12.4B

1. $2\displaystyle\sum_{n=1}^{\infty}\dfrac{(-1)^{n+1}\sin nx}{n} = 2\left[\sin x - \dfrac{\sin2x}{2} + \dfrac{\sin3x}{3} - \cdots\right].$

3. $\dfrac{4}{\pi}\displaystyle\sum_{n=1}^{\infty}\left(\dfrac{1 - \cos n\pi}{n}\right)\sin nx = \dfrac{8}{\pi}\displaystyle\sum_{n=1}^{\infty}\dfrac{\sin(2n-1)x}{2n-1}.$

5. $\dfrac{\pi^2}{6} + \displaystyle\sum_{n=1}^{\infty}\left\{\left[\dfrac{2(-1)^n}{n^2}\right]\cos nx + \dfrac{1}{\pi}\left[\left(\dfrac{2}{n^3} - \dfrac{\pi^2}{n}\right)(-1)^n - \dfrac{2}{n^3}\right]\sin nx\right\}$

$= \dfrac{\pi^2}{6} + \left[-2\cos x + \left(\pi - \dfrac{4}{\pi}\right)\sin x\right] + \left[\dfrac{\cos2x}{2} - \dfrac{\pi\sin2x}{2}\right]$

$+ \left[-\dfrac{2\cos3x}{9} + \dfrac{1}{3}\left(\pi - \dfrac{4}{9\pi}\right)\sin3x\right]$

$+ \left[\dfrac{\cos4x}{8} - \dfrac{\pi\sin4x}{4}\right] + \cdots.$

7. $\dfrac{2}{\pi}\displaystyle\sum_{n=1}^{\infty}\left[\left(\dfrac{2}{n^3} - \dfrac{\pi^2}{n}\right)(-1)^n - \dfrac{2}{n^3}\right]\sin nx.$

9. $3 + \dfrac{12}{\pi^2}\displaystyle\sum_{n=1}^{\infty}\left[\dfrac{(-1)^n - 1}{n^2}\right]\cos\dfrac{n\pi x}{6} = 3 - \dfrac{24}{\pi^2}\displaystyle\sum_{n=1}^{\infty}\dfrac{1}{(2n-1)^2}\cos\dfrac{(2n-1)\pi x}{6}.$

11. $\dfrac{1}{2} + \dfrac{1}{\pi}\displaystyle\sum_{n=1}^{\infty}\left[\dfrac{1 - (-1)^n}{n}\right]\sin\dfrac{n\pi x}{3} = \dfrac{1}{2} + \dfrac{2}{\pi}\displaystyle\sum_{n=1}^{\infty}\dfrac{1}{2n-1}\sin\dfrac{(2n-1)\pi x}{3}.$

13. $\dfrac{L}{2} + \dfrac{L}{\pi}\displaystyle\sum_{n=1}^{\infty}\left[\dfrac{1 - (-1)^n}{n}\right]\sin\dfrac{n\pi x}{L} = \dfrac{L}{2} + \dfrac{2L}{\pi}\displaystyle\sum_{n=1}^{\infty}\dfrac{1}{2n-1}\sin\dfrac{(2n-1)\pi x}{L}.$

15. $b + \dfrac{2aL}{\pi}\displaystyle\sum_{n=1}^{\infty}\dfrac{(-1)^{n+1}}{n}\sin\dfrac{n\pi x}{L}.$

SECTION 12.4C

1. (a) $\dfrac{2}{\pi} \displaystyle\sum_{n=1}^{\infty} \left[\dfrac{1-(-1)^n}{n}\right] \sin nx = \dfrac{4}{\pi} \displaystyle\sum_{n=1}^{\infty} \dfrac{\sin(2n-1)x}{2n-1}$; (b) 1.

3. (a) $\dfrac{4}{\pi} \displaystyle\sum_{n=1}^{\infty} \dfrac{\cos(n\pi/2) - \cos n\pi}{n} \sin nx.$

   (b) $1 - \dfrac{4}{\pi} \displaystyle\sum_{n=1}^{\infty} \dfrac{\sin(n\pi/2)}{n} \cos nx = 1 + \dfrac{4}{\pi} \displaystyle\sum_{n=1}^{\infty} \dfrac{(-1)^n}{2n-1} \cos(2n-1)x.$

5. (a) $\sin x.$ (b) $\dfrac{2}{\pi} - \dfrac{4}{\pi} \displaystyle\sum_{n=1}^{\infty} \dfrac{\cos 2nx}{4n^2 - 1}.$

7. (a) $\dfrac{4L}{\pi} \displaystyle\sum_{n=1}^{\infty} \left[\dfrac{1-(-1)^n}{n}\right] \sin \dfrac{n\pi x}{L} = \dfrac{8L}{\pi} \displaystyle\sum_{n=1}^{\infty} \dfrac{1}{2n-1} \sin \dfrac{(2n-1)\pi x}{L}.$

   (b) $2L.$

9. (a) $\dfrac{2L^2}{\pi} \displaystyle\sum_{n=1}^{\infty} \dfrac{\cos(n\pi/2) - \cos n\pi}{n} \sin \dfrac{n\pi x}{L}.$

   (b) $\dfrac{L^2}{2} - \dfrac{2L^2}{\pi} \displaystyle\sum_{n=1}^{\infty} \dfrac{\sin(n\pi/2)}{n} \cos \dfrac{n\pi x}{L} = \dfrac{L^2}{2} + \dfrac{2L^2}{\pi} \displaystyle\sum_{n=1}^{\infty} \dfrac{(-1)^n}{2n-1} \cos \dfrac{(2n-1)\pi x}{L}.$

11. (a) $\dfrac{4L^2}{\pi^3} \displaystyle\sum_{n=1}^{\infty} \left[\dfrac{1-(-1)^n}{n^3}\right] \sin \dfrac{n\pi x}{L} = \dfrac{8L^2}{\pi^3} \displaystyle\sum_{n=1}^{\infty} \dfrac{1}{(2n-1)^3} \sin \dfrac{(2n-1)\pi x}{L}.$

   (b) $\dfrac{L^2}{6} - \dfrac{2L^2}{\pi^2} \displaystyle\sum_{n=1}^{\infty} \left[\dfrac{1+(-1)^n}{n^2}\right] \cos \dfrac{n\pi x}{L} = \dfrac{L^2}{6} - \dfrac{L^2}{\pi^2} \displaystyle\sum_{n=1}^{\infty} \dfrac{1}{n^2} \cos \dfrac{2n\pi x}{L}.$

SECTION 12.4D

1. At $x = 0$, series converges to $1/2$; at $x = \pi/2$, to $(3\pi + 2)/4$; and at $x = \pi$, to π.

Chapter 13

SECTION 13.1

1. (i) (0,0), (1,1); (ii) $\dfrac{dy}{dx} = \dfrac{x^2 - y}{x - y^2}$; (iii) $x^3 - 3xy + y^3 = c.$

3. (a) $x = e^t$, $y = 3e^t + te^t$; (b) $x = e^{t-3}$, $y = te^{t-3}$;
   (c) The equation of the common path is $y = x(\ln|x| + 3)$;
   (d) The family of paths is $y = x(\ln|x| + c).$

SECTION 13.2

1. Saddle point, unstable.
3. Saddle point, unstable.
5. Center, stable.

7. Node, unstable.
9. (a) Saddle point;　(b) $x = c_1e^{2t} + c_2e^{-2t}$, $y = c_1e^{2t} - 3c_2e^{-2t}$;
　　(c) The general solution is $3x^2 - 2xy - y^2 = c$.

SECTION 13.3

1. Node, unstable.
3. Saddle point, unstable.
5. Saddle point, unstable.
7. (a) Saddle point;　(b) $y^2 = 2(x + e^{-x} + c)$;　(d) $x^2 - y^2 = c$.
9. (a) Critical points are $(-1,0)$, $(0,0)$, $(1,0)$, $(2,0)$, and $(3,0)$;
　　(d) $(0,0)$ and $(2,0)$ are centers; the other three are saddle points.
11. (a) Critical points are $(-1,0)$, $(0,0)$, $(1,0)$, and $(2,0)$.
　　(d) $(0,0)$ is a center; $(-1,0)$ and $(2,0)$ are saddle points;
　　　$(1,0)$ is a type of critical point called a "cusp."
13. (b) center at $(0,0)$, saddle point at $(6,0)$.
　　(c) center at $(1,0)$, saddle point at $(5,0)$.
　　(d) center at $(2,0)$, saddle point at $(4,0)$.
　　(e) $(3,0)$ is the critical point; it is called a "cusp."

SECTION 13.4

1. (a) $\dfrac{dr}{dt} = r(4 - r^2)$, $\dfrac{d\theta}{dt} = 4$.

　　(c) $x = \dfrac{2\cos(4t - t_0)}{\sqrt{1 + ce^{-8t}}}$, $y = \dfrac{2\sin(4t - t_0)}{\sqrt{1 + ce^{-8t}}}$;
　　　$x = 2\cos(4t - t_0)$, $y = 2\sin(4t - t_0)$.
3. Equation has periodic solutions.
5. Equation has no nontrivial periodic solutions.
7. Equation has no nontrivial periodic solutions.

SECTION 13.5

1. $x = a_0\sin\left\{\left[\dfrac{5\mu a_0^4 + 16\omega^2}{16\omega}\right]t + \phi_0\right\}.$

3. $x = \dfrac{2a_0}{\sqrt{3a_0^2\mu\omega^2t + 4}}\sin\left[\omega t + \dfrac{\ln(3a_0^2\mu\omega^2t + 4)}{2\omega^3} + \phi_0\right].$

5. $x = a_0e^{-\frac{\mu t}{2}}\sin\left[\omega t - \dfrac{3a_0^2e^{-\mu t}}{8\omega} + \phi_0\right].$

Chapter 14

SECTION 14.1

1. $u = f(y + x) + g(y + 6x)$; hyperbolic.
3. $u = f(y - 3x) + xg(y - 3x)$; parabolic.
5. $u = f(y + ix) + g(y - ix)$; elliptic.
7. $u = f(y) + g(y + 2x)$; hyperbolic.
9. $u = f\left(y - \dfrac{x}{2}\right) + g\left(y + \dfrac{3x}{4}\right)$; hyperbolic.
11. (b) Hyperbolic at all (x,y) such that $y < x^2/4$.

SECTION 14.2

1. $y(x,t) = \sin 2x \cos 2t$.

3. $y(x,t) = \sum_{n=1}^{\infty} b_n \sin\frac{n\pi x}{3}\cos\frac{2n\pi t}{3}$, where

$b_n = \dfrac{12}{n^2\pi^2}\sin\dfrac{n\pi}{2}\cos\dfrac{n\pi}{6}$, $(n = 1,2,3, \cdots)$

$= 6\sqrt{3}/n^2\pi^2$, $(n = 1,7,13, \cdots)$; $-6\sqrt{3}/n^2\pi^2$, $(n = 5,11,17, \cdots)$;
0, (n even or $n = 3,9,15, \cdots$).

5. $u(x,t) = \sum_{n=1}^{\infty} c_n \sin\frac{n\pi x}{L}e^{-\frac{n^2\pi^2 t}{L^2}}$, where

$c_n = \dfrac{2}{L}\displaystyle\int_0^L f(x)\sin\dfrac{n\pi x}{L}dx$, $(n = 1,2,3, \cdots)$.

7. $u(x,y) = \sum_{n=1}^{\infty} a_n \sin nx \, \sinh n(y - \pi)$, where

$a_n = -\dfrac{2}{\pi\sinh n\pi}\displaystyle\int_0^\pi f(x)\sin nx\,dx$, $(n = 1,2,3, \cdots)$.

SECTION 14.3

1. $\dfrac{\partial^2 u}{\partial\xi\partial\eta} = 0$.

3. $\dfrac{\partial^2 u}{\partial\xi\partial\eta} = \dfrac{\partial u}{\partial\xi} - \dfrac{1}{2}\dfrac{\partial u}{\partial\eta}$.

5. $\dfrac{\partial^2 u}{\partial\xi^2} + \dfrac{\partial^2 u}{\partial\eta^2} = \dfrac{\partial u}{\partial\xi}$.

7. $\dfrac{\partial^2 u}{\partial\xi\partial\eta} = \dfrac{1}{6}\left(\dfrac{\partial u}{\partial\xi} + \dfrac{\partial u}{\partial\eta}\right)$.

9. $\dfrac{\partial^2 u}{\partial\xi^2} + \dfrac{\partial^2 u}{\partial\eta^2} = -\dfrac{2}{9}u$.

SECTION 14.4

3. $y = 2x + c_1$, $y = -4x + c_2$.
5. No real characteristics exist.

BIBLIOGRAPHY

1. AGNEW, R. P., *Differential Equations*, McGraw-Hill, New York, 1960.

2. ANDRONOW, A. A., and CHAIKIN, C. E., *Theory of Oscillations*, Princeton University Press, Princeton, New Jersey, 1949.

3. APOSTOL, T. M., *Mathematical Analysis*, Addison-Wesley, Reading, Mass., 1957.

4. BELLMAN, R., *Stability Theory of Differential Equations*, McGraw-Hill, New York, 1954.

5. BIEBERBACH, L., *Einfuhrung in die Theorie der Differentialgleichungen im Reellen Gebiet*, Springer-Verlag, Berlin, 1956.

6. BIRKHOFF, G., and ROTA, G., *Ordinary Differential Equations*, Ginn and Company, Boston, 1962.

7. BRAND, L., *Advanced Calculus*, John Wiley & Sons, Inc., New York, 1955.

8. BURKHILL, J. C., *The Theory of Ordinary Differential Equations*, Oliver and Boyd, Edinburgh, 1956.

9. CESARI, L., *Asymptotic Behavior and Stability Problems in Ordinary Differential Equations*, Springer-Verlag, Berlin, 1959.

10. CHURCHILL, R. V., *Fourier Series and Boundary Value Problems*, McGraw-Hill, New York, 1941.

11. CHURCHILL, R. V., *Operational Mathematics*, McGraw-Hill, New York, 1958.

12. CODDINGTON, E. A., *An Introduction to Ordinary Differential Equations*, Prentice-Hall, Englewood Cliffs, N.J., 1961.

13. CODDINGTON, E. A., and LEVINSON, N., *Theory of Ordinary Differential Equations*, McGraw-Hill, New York, 1955.

14. COURANT, R., and HILBERT, D., *Methods of Mathematical Physics, Vol. II, Partial Differential Equations*, by Courant, Interscience, New York, 1962.

15. CUNNINGHAM, W. J., *Introduction To Nonlinear Analysis*, McGraw-Hill, New York, 1958.

16. EPSTEIN, B., *Partial Differential Equations*, McGraw-Hill, New York, 1962.

17. FORD, L. R., *Differential Equations*, McGraw-Hill, New York, 1955.

18. FRIEDRICHS, K. O., *Advanced Ordinary Differential Equations*, lecture notes, New York University, 1948–1949.

19. GREENSPAN, D., *Introduction to Partial Differential Equations*, McGraw-Hill, New York, 1961.

20. GREENSPAN, D., *Theory and Solution of Ordinary Differential Equations*, The Macmillan Co., New York, 1960.

21. HOLL, D., MAPLE, C., and VINOGRADE, B., *Introduction To The Laplace Transform*, Appleton-Century-Crofts, Inc., New York, 1959.

22. HILDEBRAND, F. B., *Advanced Calculus for Applications*, Prentice-Hall, Englewood Cliffs, N.J., 1962.

23. HILDEBRAND, F. B., *Introduction To Numerical Analysis*, McGraw-Hill, New York, 1956.

24. HOCHSTADT, H., *Special Functions of Mathematical Physics*, Holt, Rinehart, and Winston, New York, 1961.

25. HUREWICZ, W., *Lectures on Ordinary Differential Equations*, John Wiley & Sons, Inc., New York, 1958.

26. INCE, E. L., *Ordinary Differential Equations*, Dover Publications, Inc., New York, 1956.

27. JOHN, F., *Partial Differential Equations*, lecture notes, New York University, 1952–1953.

28. KAMKE, E., *Differentialgleichungen: Losungsmethoden und Losungen*, Akademische Verlagsgellschaft, Leipzig, 1943.

29. KAMKE, E., *Differentialgleichungen reeler Funktionen*, Akademische Verlagsgellschaft, Leipzig, 1930.

30. KAPLAN, W., *Ordinary Differential Equations*, Addison-Wesley, Reading, Mass., 1958.

31. KRYLOFF, N., and BOGOLIUBOFF, N., *Introduction To Nonlinear Mechanics*, Princeton University Press, Princeton, N.J., 1943.

32. KU, Y. H., *Analysis and Control of Nonlinear Systems*, Ronald Press, New York, 1958.

33. LAWDEN, D. F., *Mathematics of Engineering Systems*, John Wiley & Sons, Inc., New York, 1954.

34. LAX, P. D., *Partial Differential Equations*, lecture notes, New York University, 1949–1950.

35. LEFSCHETZ, S., *Differential Equations, Geometric Theory*, Interscience, New York, 1957.

36. LEIGHTON, W., *An Introduction To The Theory of Differential Equations*, McGraw-Hill, New York, 1952.

37. LEVY, H., and BAGGOTT, E. A., *Numerical Solutions of Differential Equations*, Dover Publications, Inc., New York, 1950.

38. MARTIN, W. T., and REISSNER, E., *Elementary Differential Equations*, Addison-Wesley, Reading, Mass., 1961.

39. MCLACHLAN, N. W., *Ordinary Non-linear Differential Equations*, Oxford University Press, New York, 1955.

40. MILLER, K. S., *Partial Differential Equations In Engineering Problems*, Prentice-Hall, Englewood Cliffs, N.J., 1959.

41. MILNE, W. E., *Numerical Solution of Differential Equations*, John Wiley and Sons, Inc., New York, 1953.

42. MINORSKY, N., *Introduction To Nonlinear Mechanics*, J. W. Edwards, Ann Arbor, Michigan, 1947.

43. NEMYTSKII, V., and STEPANOV, V., *Qualitative Theory of Differential Equations*, Princeton University Press, Princeton, N.J., 1959.

44. PETROVSKY, I. G., *Lectures On Partial Differential Equations*, Interscience, New York, 1954.

45. RAINVILLE, E. D., *Elementary Differential Equations*, The Macmillan Co., New York, 1958.

46. RUDIN, W., *Principles Of Mathematical Analysis*, McGraw-Hill, New York, 1953.

47. SCARBOROUGH, J. B., *Numerical Mathematical Analysis*, The Johns Hopkins Press, Baltimore, 1950.

48. SNEDDON, I. N., *Elements of Partial Differential Equations*, McGraw-Hill, New York, 1957.

49. SOKOLNIKOFF, I. S., and REDHEFFER, R. M., *Mathematics of Physics and Modern Engineering*, McGraw-Hill, New York, 1958.

50. SPIEGEL, M. R., *Applied Differential Equations*, Prentice-Hall, Englewood Cliffs, N.J., 1958.

51. STOKER, J. J., *Nonlinear Vibrations*, Interscience, New York, 1950.

52. STRUBLE, R. A., *Nonlinear Differential Equations*, McGraw-Hill, New York, 1962.

53. TAMARKIN, J. D., and FELLER, W., *Partial Differential Equations*, lecture notes, Brown University, 1941.

54. TRICOMI, F. G., *Differential Equations*, Hafner Publishing Co., New York, 1961.

55. WEBSTER, A. G., *Partial Differential Equations of Mathematical Physics*, Hafner Publishing Co., New York, 1950.

56. WIDDER, D. V., *Advanced Calculus*, Prentice-Hall, Englewood Cliffs, N.J., 1960.

57. WYLIE, C. R., JR., *Advanced Engineering Mathematics*, McGraw-Hill, New York, 1960.

58. YOSIDA, K., *Lectures on Differential and Integral Equations*, Interscience, New York, 1960.

INDEX

Printed in United States of America.

EFGHIJK 0987